Theory and Practice of Robots and Manipulators

Proceedings of RoManSy '84:
The Fifth CISM-IFToMM Symposium

Theory and Practice of Robots and Manipulators

Proceedings of RoManSy '84:
The Fifth CISM–IFToMM Symposium

Edited by
A Morecki, G Bianchi and K Kędzior

Sponsored by the CISM-Centre International des Sciences Mécaniques IFToMM-International Federation for the Theory of Machines and Mechanisms in association with the IVth Technical Division of the Polish Academy of Sciences

Co-sponsored by the Institute for Aircraft Engineering and Applied Mechanics, Technical University of Warsaw

The MIT Press
Cambridge, Massachusetts

First published 1985 by Kogan Page Ltd,
120 Pentonville Road, London N1 9JN
and Hermes Publishing, 51 rue Rennequin,
75017 Paris, France

Copyright © 1985 RoManSy and contributors

First MIT Press edition, 1985

All rights reserved. No part of this book may be
reproduced in any form or by any means, electronic
or mechanical, including photocopying, recording,
or by any information storage and retrieval system,
without permission in writing from the publisher.

Library of Congress Cataloging in Publication Data
RoManSy (5th : 1984 : Udine, Italy)
   Theory and practice of robots and manipulators.

   Includes bibliographical references.
   1. Robotics—Congresses. 2. Manipulators
(Mechanism)—Congresses.   I. Morecki, Adam.
II. Bianchi, G. (Giovanni), 1924-
III. Kedzior, K. IV. Title. V. Series.
TJ210.3.R66 1984   629.8'92   85-4320
ISBN 0-262-13208-7

Printed in Great Britain

Contents

Preface 11
Editorial Note... 13

Part 1 Opening Lecture   15
Biomechanical Aspects in Robotics............................ 17
A Morecki and K Kędzior

Part 2 Mechanics   23
Coordinate Transformations and Inverse kinematics for
Industrial Robots 25
*M S Konstantinov, P Y Genova, V B Zamanov,
S P Patarinski and D N Nenchev*
Industrial Robots with Recuperation of Mechanical Energy...... 31
K V Frolov, A I Korendiasev, B L Salamandra and L I Tyves
On the Optimal Selection and Placement of Manipulators 39
V Scheinman and B Roth
On the Geometry of Orthogonal and Reciprocal Screws 47
H Lipkin and J Duffy
Trajectory Planning for Redundant Manipulators in the
Presence of Obstacles.. 57
M Kirćanski and M Vukobratović
Implementation of Highly Efficient Analytical Robot
Models on Microcomputers 65
M Vukobratović and N Kirćanski
Computer-aided Generation of Multibody-system Equations 73
R Schwertassek and R E Roberson
Equations of Motion and Equations of Stress for Robots and
Manipulators: An Application of the NEWEUL Formalism 79
E J Kreuzer and W O Schiehlen
Modelling of Artificial Manipulators and Computer
Simulation of their Dynamics 87
T Kawase, H Nakano and R Magoshi
Dynamics of Robots and Manipulators Involving Closed
Loops.. 97
T R Kane and H Faessler

Part 3 Control of Motion — 107

Non-adaptive Dynamic Control for Manipulation Robots:
Invited Survey Paper 109
M Vukobratović and D Stokić

Robot Motion Control in Multi-operation assembly 123
D E Okhotsimsky and S S Kamynin

Some Considerations on Feedback Strategy for Assembly
Robots 127
J-P Merlet

Optimal Dynamic Trajectories for Robotic Manipulators...... 133
S Dubowsky and Z Shiller

Approximative Models in Dynamic Control of Robotic
Systems 145
M Vukobratović and D Stokić

Keyboard Playing by an Anthropomorphic Robot:
Fingers and Arm Model and its Control System of WAM-7R ... 153
S Sugano, J Nakagawa, Y Tanaka and I Kato

Control of Two Co-ordinated Robots by Using an Only-
kinematic Model 163
P Dauchez, A Fournier and R Zapata

A Method for Time-optimal Control of Dynamically
Constrained Manipulators 169
P Kiriazov and P Marinov

Bracing Strategy for Robot Operation 179
W J Book, S Le and V Sangveraphunsiri

Robot Control and Computer Languages 187
R P Paul and V Hayward

Robust Control for Industrial Robots 195
H Bremer and A Truckenbrodt

Controlling a Six-degrees-of-freedom Welding Robot along
a Randomly Oriented Seam with Reduced Sensor
Information 205
A Micaelli and J M Détriché

Principles and Algorithms for Industrial Robots Remote
Automatic Control 215
V S Kuleshov, Yu V Poduraev and V N Shvedov

Part 4 Man-Intelligent Machine Systems — 221

Manual Control Communication in Space Teleoperation 223
A K Bejczy and K Corker

Sensory-based Control for Robots and Teleoperators 233
B Espiau and G Andre

Tele-existence (I): Design and Evaluation of a Visual
Display with Sensation of Presence 245
S Tachi, K Tanie, K Komoriya and M Kaneko

New Approach to Robotic Visual Processing 255
B Macukow

Representing Three-dimensional Shape 261
M Brady and A Yuille
An Electropneumatic Actuation System for the Utah/MIT
Dextrous Hand.. 271
*S C Jacobsen, D F Knutti, K B Biggers, E K Iversen and
J E Wood*
Sensor-aided and/or Computer-aided Bilateral Teleoperator
System (SCATS)... 281
J Vertut, R Fournier, B Espiau and G Andre

Part 5 Synthesis and Design 293
Mechanical and Geometric Design of the Adaptive
Suspension Vehicle 295
K J Waldron, S Song, S Wang and V J Vohnout
Geometrical and Kinematical Qualitative Characteristics
for Functional Capacities of Manipulation Systems 307
L Lilov and B Bekjarov
Manipulation Devices Based on High-class Mechanisms................. 313
U A Djoldasbekov, L I Slutskii and J J Baigunchekov
Synthesis and Design of Mechanical Hands for Robots
with Application of Computer-aided Design 321
A Rovetta
A New Design Method of Servo-actuators Based on the
Shape Memory Effect... 339
S Hirose, K Ikuta and Y Umetani
Coverage Optimization of Articulated Manipulators.................. 351
G Fraize, J Vertut and R Hugon

Part 6 Biomechanics of Motion: Locomotion 363
Study of Propelling Agents Construction Features of
Orthogonal Walking Robots by Using Plane Mechanisms............... 365
V S Balbarov, A Bessonov and N V Umnov
A Hierarchically Structured System for Computer Control
of a Hexapod Walking Machine 375
R B McGhee, D F Orin, D R Pugh and M R Patterson
Realization of Plane Walking by the Biped Walking
Robot WL-10R.. 383
A Takanishi, G Naito, M Ishida and I Kato
Hexapod Walking Robots with Artificial Intelligence
Capabilities 395
J J Kessis, J P Rambaut, J Penné, R Wood and N Mattar
Legged Locomotion Machine Based on the Consideration
of Degrees of Freedom....................................... 403
*M Kaneko, M Abe, S Tachi, S Nishizawa, K Tanie and
K Komoriya*
Trotting and Bounding in a Planar Two-legged Model................ 411
K N Murphy and M H Raibert

Part 7 Application and Performance Evaluation 421
Determination of Important Design Parameters for
Industrial Robots from the Application Point of View:
Survey Paper 423
R D Schraft and M C Wanner
Automatic Assembly by Reference Searching and Position
Adjustment before Insertion 431
F Artigue and C François

Participants 439

Organizing and Programme Committee

Chairman:
Prof. G Bianchi
 CISM, Piazza Garibaldi 18, 33100 Udine (Italy)

Vice Chairman:
Prof. A Morecki
 Warsaw Technical University, Al Niepodległości 222 r 206, 00-663 Warsaw (Poland)

Members:
Prof. A P Bessonov
 Academy of Sciences of the USSR, Griboedova Street 4, Moscow-Centre 101000 (USSR)
Prof. I Kato
 Waseda University, Faculty of Science and Engineering, Ookubo, Shiniuku-ku, Tokyo 160 (Japan)
Prof. A E Kobrynskii
 Academy of Sciences of the USSR, Griboedova Street 4, Moscow-Centre 101000 (USSR)
Prof. M S Konstantinov
 Central Laboratory for Manipulators and Robots, Higher Institute of Mechanical and Electrical Engineering, 1156 Sofia, Darvenitza, PO Box 97 (Bulgaria)
Prof. H Rankers
 Bedrijfsmechanisatie, Landbergstraat 3, 2628(E) Delft, (The Netherlands)
Prof. B Roth
 Stanford University, Department of Mechanical Engineering, Stanford, CA 94305 (USA)
Dr R D Schraft
 Fraunhofer Institute for Production and Automation, University of Stuttgart, PO Box 951, Stuttgart (Federal Republic of Germany)
Dr J Vertut
 Commissariat à l'Energie Atomique, BP no. 2, 91190 Gif-sur-Yvette (France)
Prof. J Volmer
 Technische Hochschule, DDR-9010 Karl-Marx-Stadt, PSF 964 (German Democratic Republic)
Prof. M Vukobratović
 Institute 'Mihailo Pupin', Volgina 15, PO Box 906 (Yugoslavia)

Scientific Secretary:
Dr K Kędzior
 Warsaw Technical University, Al Niepodległości 222 r 206, 00-663 Warsaw (Poland)

Secretary:
Dr A Bertozzi
 CISM, Piazza Garibaldi 18, 33100 Udine (Italy)

Preface

The RO MAN SY Symposia have played an important role in the development of the theory and, to a lesser extent, the practice of manipulators, walking machines and robots.

Based on past experience of previous symposia, which have been held over the last 10 years, the problem arose as to what to do in the future. In other words, in what direction should further symposia be organized?

A panel discussion called 'Role of RO MAN SY Symposia' was held on 29 June 1984 during the final plenary session at CISM, Udine, Italy. The Members of the Organizing Committee, Professors Konstantinov, Morecki, Roth, Vukobratović and Vertut, and other participants were asked to give their opinions on the following important questions:

- should we organize future symposia?
- if we continue, which form should we choose?: small (60-70 participants, 35-40 invited papers); big (100-150 participants, 60-80 papers)
- what kind of topics should be included?: the more theoretical-oriented; more practical-oriented; both (what proportion?)
- how frequently should RO MAN SY Symposia be organized?: every other year; every third year
- what is working well and what should be maintained?
- what is not working well and what should be changed to increase the impact of the symposia?

I would like to underline that most of the participants agree that we should continue to hold our symposia every other year, but to limit their small form, with invited papers at high theoretical level only in mechanics, control of motion, synthesis and design, manipulation and locomotion and application and performance evaluation of manipulators and robots.

To improve the value of the symposia it is necessary to select for presentation only those papers which represent good new theoretical contributions and relate to the above-mentioned topics.

The survey papers, panel discussion and discussion following presentations should play an important role in future symposia.

I hope that this volume, which contains a set of papers presented during the latest symposium, will be welcomed by all those scientists who belong to the robotic family.

Professor A Morecki
Chairman of the CISM-IFToMM Technical Committee
for Robots and Manipulators
Warsaw, September 1984

Editorial Note

This volume contains the papers accepted for the Fifth Symposium on Theory and Practice of Robots and Manipulators 'RO MAN SY '84' held in Udine, Italy, 26-29 June 1984.

'RO MAN SY '84' was attended by 65 participants from 14 countries (as listed) who were selected experts in the field of robotics.

The symposium programme included:

- Opening and closing sessions attended by CISM and IFToMM officials
- General lecture given by Professor A Morecki, Chairman of the CISM-IFToMM Technical Committee for Robots and Manipulators
- Working sessions (mechanics, control of motion, synthesis and design, biomechanics of motion-locomotion, man-intelligent machine systems, application and performance evaluation)
- Panel discussion 'Role of RO MAN SY Symposia' organized by Professor A Morecki
- Two film sessions.

The papers in this book are in the same sequence as the sessions mentioned above. All linguistic and terminology corrections have been kept to a minimum.

The proceedings of the previous four symposia are available in the final form. The proceedings of the 'RO MAN SY '73' (5-8 September 1973, Udine, Italy) may be obtained from Springer-Verlag, Vienna. Those of 'RO MAN SY '76' (14-17 September 1976, Jadwisin, Poland) and 'RO MAN SY '78' (12-15 September 1978, Udine, Italy) may be purchased from Elsevier Scientific Publishing Co. (Amsterdam) or PWN-Polish Scientific Publishers (Warsaw) Proceedings of the 'RO MAN SY '81' (8-12 September 1981, Zaborow, Poland) may be obtained from PWN (Warsaw).

The next symposium 'RO MAN SY '86' will be held in Poland in early September 1986.

A Morecki, G Bianchi and K Kędzior

Part 1
Opening Lecture

Biomechanical Aspects in Robotics

A Morecki and K Kędzior

Technical University of Warsaw, Warsaw, Poland

Introduction

Biomechanics is an area common to mechanics, biology, medicine, sport and even environmental studies, but is particularly difficult to define. The same conclusion can be applied to robotics itself, as well.

The above-mentioned disciplines have grown up in a multidisciplinary way and in recent years have developed into an important area of scientific investigations that has many practical applications.

Let us assume two descriptive definitions concerning biomechanics and robotics: (1) 'Biomechanics is a study of movement and mechanisms of motion with special emphasis on human beings' (Vol A, p4); 'A robot is essentially a computer with arms, legs and sensors' (p107);[1] robotics is a branch of science and technology which concerns all problems of robot design, mechanics, control and sensing and applications.

Based on these definitions, the present paper will present some ideas concerning the biomechanical aspects which are used and applied in the theory and practice of manipulators and robots.

The left part of Figure 1 shows the generally accepted topics in modern biomechanics recognized by a representative forum of specialists who belong to the International Society of Biomechanics (ISB) and the right part of Figure 1 shows the topics accepted by the members of CISM-IFToMM Technical Committee for Robots and Manipulators.

The hatched area shows the commonly shared reactions which take place in all the topics (except for biomechanics of sport). Of course, the common area is not the quantitative measure of these relations; its aim is just to illustrate their interpenetration.

We shall outline only two examples of the interpenetration on the biomechanics-robotics line. To describe the manipulative and locomotive movement both in the technical system and in the whole man or his extremities, approximate models and mathematical descriptions with the Lagrange or Euler-Savari equations are used. While synthesizing rehabilitation manipulators one should take into consideration the appropriate interfaces on the manipulator-operator contact in the range of mechanics (range of movement, geometrical parameters of the manipulator).

We should like to underline the fact that, in all biomechanics-robotics relations, we do not mean just copying the features of living organisms, especially man, but only making use of certain properties of living organisms (structure, function, control, organs of sense) while attempting synthesis and design especially, but not only, for the so-called anthropomorphic manipulators and/or robots.

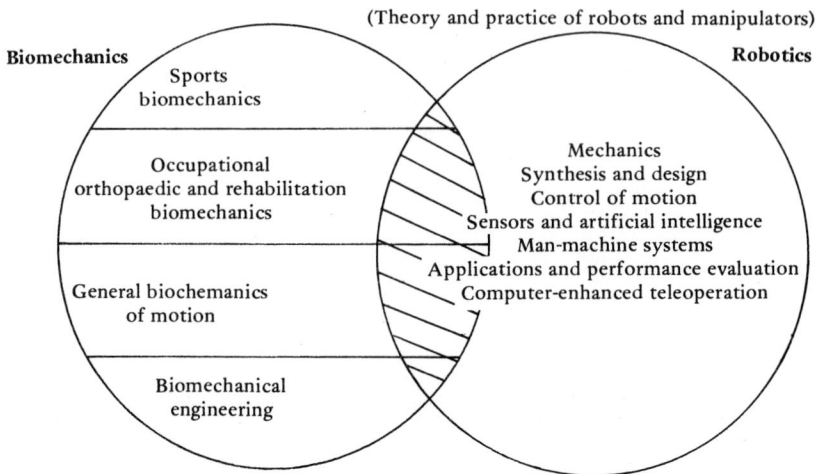

Figure 1 Accepted biomechanics and robotics topics and interpenetration

We should also like to underline the connection between biomechanics and robotics and other related sciences such as bionics and biomechanisms, biomedical and rehabilitation engineering, as well as with other interdisciplinary branches of science on the borderline with technology, biology and medicine.

Biomechanics of motion in previous 'RO MAN SY' Symposia

Analysis of previous 'RO MAN SY' Symposia with respect to the biomechanical aspects

Table 1 shows the contribution of problems contained in various subfields of biomechanics with regard to theory and practice of robotics. It is shown against the background of the recent output of 'RO MAN SY' Symposia held in 1973, 1976, 1978, 1981 and 1984.

By taking into consideration the topic 'Biomechanics of motion', the biomechanical aspects as represented by the number of papers presented in the years 1973, 1976, 1978 and 1981 were 14; but together with the 'man-machine' topic, they were 28, that is 14 per cent of the total number of papers.

Columns I, II and III show another analysis of the participation of biomechanics to the problems of the 'RO MAN SY' Symposia. Three groups (and in each group, two or three subgroups) have been singled out; they are: (1) human and animal motion and man-machine systems (subgroups 1, 2 and 3), 13 papers; (2) anthropomorphic manipulators and robots (subgroups 1 and 2), 26 papers; (3) prosthetic and orthotic manipulators, pedipulators and exoskeletons (subgroups 1, 2 and 3), 19 papers.

On the basis of this analysis we see that different biomechanical aspects were presented in 83 papers out of a total number of 227, that is about 36 per cent. Elements of biomechanics were also present in 3 of 20 accepted but not presented papers (they were published in *MMT*). So the total number of papers was 247; the proportion of biomechanical aspects about 35 per cent.

Biomechanical Aspects in Robotics   19

RO MAN SY Symposium	Total no of published papers	No of papers in the section		No of papers related to							
		Biomechanics of motion	Man-machine systems	I Biomechanics of human and animal motion			II Anthropomorphic robots and manipulators		III Prosthetic and orthotic devices		
				Human motion	Animal and insect motion	Control of motion	Anthropomorphic and master-slave devices	Man-machine systems	Manipulators	Pedipulators	Exoskeletons
'73	42	6		2	2	2	5				3
'76	48	3	7	1		1	1	3	4	1	1
'78 (MMT, 16 (1))	34 11	4	4			2	2	2	4	2	3
'81 (MMT, 18 (4))	38 9		2	2			2	1	2	1	
'84	45	0	7	1			5	3	1		
Totals	207+20=227	13	20	6	2 13	5	15+2=17 23+3=26	8+1=9	11	4 19	4

Table 1 Contribution of problems in biomechanics subfields in theory and practice of robotics

Of course, each systematization, as well as the one presented by the authors (Table 1), is conventional, but it proves the statistical significance of biomechanical problems in robotics.

General conclusions concerning methods, modelling, methodology and applications

While analysing methods and models presented in papers which had some biomechanical aspects, it is noteworthy that those authors whose knowledge is of a mechanical nature make use mainly of models and mathematical descriptions adopted from theoretical and general mechanics and from the theory of machines; they make use of them to construct models of manipulators of the upper-limb type or pedipulators of the lower-limb type, or of multilegged walking machines.

Those authors who are electronics and computer science oriented are concerned with theory and practice of automatic control, technical visual systems and methods of identification. In these cases, apart from the initial phase of analysis of the biological objects from the point of view of the technical systems, many authors, while continuing their analysis and synthesis, neglect the influence of these 'initial conditions' and their further studies are purely technical only. It leads to abuse of the word 'anthropomorphic', as neither the similarity of the shape nor the function is preserved in a technical object.

The only excuse that may be given for this procedure is the complication in such living organisms as, for example, in insects or vertebrates, which makes the designers of walking machines and manipulators, as well as of pedipulators, use great simplifications.

One should not forget the use of simplifications which, in some extreme cases, cause them to 'throw out the baby with the bath water'.

We would like to emphasize here the value of computer methods of simulation in the process of design, the methods which make it easier to investigate millions of possibilities, for example, while making the analysis of the structure of muscle drives. What is more, such methods make it possible to choose the optimum solution with the assumed criteria, such as energetic, minimum time or accuracy of positioning.

Place of biomechanics in future symposia

Based on present knowledge, it seems possible that the following areas of biomechanical investigations will be pointed out (with respect to making use of their results in robotics): studies of dynamics of upper and lower limbs in insects, the vertebrates and man in manipulating and locomotion processes; studies of structure, dynamics and co-operation of muscle drives; investigation into the criteria of control from the point of view of choosing the optimal control system.

Such studies should be conducted by interdisciplinary groups of engineers, biologists and physicians, by means of both experiment and theoretical investigation. Continuous widening of methods and research instruments is desirable. Such investigations should involve use of more advanced dynamic models of man or his parts, needed in synthesis and design of androidal robots and manipulators with a high degree of anthropomorphy of function, action and behaviour.

The making use of real machines of this kind, which will then be bionic or cybernetic machines, would represent the beginning of a new stage not only in the man-machine systems, but also, as I Kato suggests, in man-machine society. It is difficult at present to estimate the scale and range of application of such machines. Unmanned factories are only one example of the factory man-robotic society. Robotized medical and rehabilitation engineering seems to be another example of effect-influence-action.

Conclusions

This paper indicates the attempts made in the evaluation of the role of biomechanics in the development of robotics, as covered in the 'RO MAN SY' Symposia. Some examples show the influence of investigations made on the borderline between technology and biology, the influence on the possible development of machines of a new type, or systems, and, in future, mixed man-robotic societies.

One should realize the limitations of robots, as did M W Thring[1] at each level of development of robotics; 'A robot is an artefact, designed and made by men and I believe that man will never be able to build into his artefacts certain abilities which he himself possesses as a result of the biological processes by which he is formed.'

Thring also formulated two basic postulates. The first one corresponds closely to the second law of thermodynamics stated in the form that all systems run down to a 'heat death'. 'Postulate 1. A robot can never do any task more sophisticated than it has been instructed by a human to do, eg it can sort things into categories that have been given to it but it cannot by itself decide to create a new category ... Postulate 2. No robot or computer can ever be built by humans which will have true human emotions or feelings.'

Based on those two postulates let us be optimistic and hope that in possible competition the human being will still be the master.

References

[1] Proceedings of the First CISM-IFToMM Symposium on Theory and Practice of Robots and Manipulators, Udine, Italy, 5-8 September 1973, Vol II. Springer-Verlag, Vienna (1974)
[2] Proceedings of the Second CISM-IFToMM Symposium on Theory and Practice of Robots and Manipulators, Warsaw, Poland, 14-17 September 1976. Polish Scientific Publishers, Warsaw/Elsevier Scientific Publishing Co, Amsterdam (1977)
[3] Proceedings of the Third CISM-IFToMM Symposium on Theory and Practice of Robots and Manipulators, Udine, Italy, 12-15 September 1978. Polish Scientific Publishers, Warsaw/Elsevier Scientific Publishing Co, Amsterdam (1980)
[4] Proceedings of the Fourth CISM-IFToMM Symposium on Theory and Practice of Robots and Manipulators, Zaborow, Poland, 8-12 September 1981. Polish Scientific Publishers, Warsaw (1983)
[5] Morecki, A (ed) *Biomechanics of Motion* CISM Courses and Lectures No 263, Udine, Italy, 18-22 September 1978. Springer-Verlag, Vienna (1980)
[6] Preprints of the Summer School *Biomechanics in Robotics*, Bulgarian Academy of Sciences, Sofia, 1-10 October 1982
[7] Morecki, A, Fidelus, K, Kedzior, K & Wit, A (eds) (1981) *Biomechanics* VII. A, B, Proceedings of the Seventh International Congress of Biomechanics, Warsaw, Poland, 18-21 September 1979. Polish Scientific Publishers, Warsaw/University Park Press, Baltimore

[8] Morecki, A (1976) *Manipulatory Bioniczne* (Bionic Manipulators). Polish Scientific Publishers, Warsaw (in Polish)
[9] Morecki, A, Ekiel, J & Fidelus, K (1983) *Cybernetic Systems of Limb Movements in Man, Animals and Robots.* Ellis Horwood Publishing, Chichester
[10] *Control Aspects of Prosthetics and Orthotics.* Proceedings of the IFAC Symposium, Ohio, USA, 7-9 May 1982. Pergamon Press, Oxford (1983)
[11] von Muldan, H H (1975) *Mensh und Robots.* Verlag Herder
[12] Roth, B (1981) *What Robots Can and Cannot Do.* First Seminar on Industrial Robots. Robots. Institute for Precision Mechanics, Warsaw, Poland

Part 2
Mechanics

Coordinate Transformations and Inverse Kinematics for Industrial Robots

M S Konstantinov*[†], P Y Genova*, V B Zamanov*, S P Patarinski[†] and D N Nenchev*

*Central Laboratory for Manipulators and Robots, Higher Institute of Mechanical and Electrical Engineering, 1156 Sofia, and [†]Department of Robots, Institute of Mechanics and Biomechanics, Bulgarian Academy of Sciences, 1113 Sofia, Bulgaria

> **Summary:** An equivalent 3C kinematic structure is proposed by using the concept of instantaneous helicoidal motion for the general case, $mR - nP$ ($m + n \geq 6; m, n \geq 0$), robot. The direct and inverse transformations $2R \leftrightharpoons C$ are considered and a method is developed for the solution of the inverse kinematics for industrial robots. The method is a rate-type one in its nature and solves the problem at two stages: (i) desired motion distribution among the generalized co-ordinates of the equivalent 3C robot and (ii) splitting up these co-ordinates among the respective R joints of the actual robot.

Introduction

The inverse kinematics problem for industrial robots (IR) is of substantial interest in relation to the application of IR as technological devices. The basic result in this field, 'the resolved motion rate control' concept is due to D Whitney,[1,2] and some new ideas have been recently originated by M Renaud[3] and Luh et al.[4,5] and further developed.[6,7] The review of these and other results suggests that an efficient computational approach to the inverse kinematics problem should (explicitly, as far as possible) be based on structural considerations.

In this paper we propose an equivalent 3C kinematic structure for the general case, $mR - nP$ ($m + n \geq 6; m, n \geq 0$), robot using the concept of instantaneous helicoidal motion.[8] The direct and inverse transformations between $2R$ or RP or PR joints and a C joint are discussed and a new, two-stage method is developed for the solution of the inverse kinematics for IR. The method is a rate-type one and is believed to give deeper understanding of IR kinematics and certain computational advantages.

Geometry and kinematics of the 3C robot

Instantaneous helicoidal motion (IHM) is a conception used for modelling velocity distribution in a solid body, being free to move in three-dimensional Cartesian space by means of collinear angular and linear velocities vectors; that is, the classical conception of a kinematic screw. An interesting particular problem is to formulate relative motion screws that represent the IR joint motions in an equivalent manner. In the case of three relative motions defined among three moving bodies it can be shown that the three IHMs in question are simultaneously perpendicular to one straight line, their transversal. The disposition of the three axes w.r.t. a chosen reference and the transversal is determined by kinematic parameters, the relative angular velocity and pitch of the kinematic screw. From a structural point of view an IHM can be thought of as of C joints.

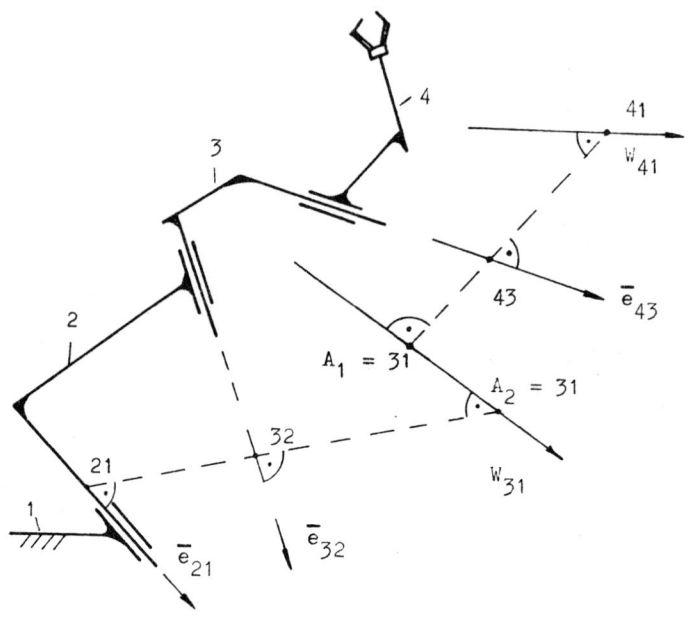

Figure 1 3C robot

A 3C robot, Figure 1, is capable of performing an arbitrary prescribed target function (positional, velocity, etc.), associated with the desired motion of the end effector. At every instant the target function itself can be represented by means of an instantaneous helicoidal axis (IHA) $\bar{W}_{41}$, expressing the kinematic state of the end effector at velocity level. The required number of relative IHA in the 'joints' of the 3C robot and the task is four, while the grand total of relative IHA is six, as follows:

$$\begin{array}{ccc} 12 & 13 & 14 \\ & 23 & 24 \\ & & 34 \end{array}$$

For a prescribed IHM $\bar{W}_{41} = [\bar{w}_{41}^T \mid \bar{v}_{41}^T]^T$ of the end effector, defined by the fourth C joint, and known $\bar{e}_{21}$, $\bar{e}_{32}$, $\bar{e}_{43}$ axes, the generalized co-ordinates vector $\bar{V} = [w_{12}\ w_{23}\ w_{34}\ v_{12}\ v_{23}\ v_{34}]^T$, where $w_{i,i+1}$, $v_{i,i+1}$, $i = 1, 2$ are the relative angular and linear velocities for the first three C joints, can be determined in a unique way. The relation between the $\bar{W}_{41}$ and $\bar{V}$ vectors is given by

$$\bar{W}_{41} = J \cdot \bar{V},$$

where J is the respective Jacobian matrix.

It can be easily shown that in the non-orthogonal basis $\bar{e}_{21}, \bar{e}_{32}, \bar{e}_{43}$ the J matrix has the block form

$$J = \left[\begin{array}{c|c} I_3 & O_{3,3} \\ \hline X & I_3 \end{array} \right]$$

where I_3 is the unit 3×3 matrix, $O_{3,3}$ is the null 3×3 matrix and X is a 3×3 matrix with elements dependent on the choice of the co-ordinate origin.

The block triangular form with unit matrices on the main diagonal of the Jacobian matrix greatly simplifies the inverse kinematic solution (i.e. the $\bar{V}$ vector determination), because its inverse is

$$J^{-1} = \left[\begin{array}{c|c} I_3 & O_{3,3} \\ \hline -X & I_3 \end{array} \right]$$

As can be seen below this result is not uninteresting regardless of the fact that 3C robots have not found wide practical application.

Consider a 6R robot that, together with the prescribed continuous strategy for its end effector motion, constitutes a closed instantaneous $6R - C$ structure. At velocity level this structure can be kinematically reduced to the conditionally closed homogeneous w.r.t. the type of the joints 4C spatial mechanism. The reduction can be performed solving a kinematic problem for three IHA defined by three indices.

Two arbitrary R kinematic joints axes of the actual robot structure can be chosen as prescribed IHA with zero screw pitches. Without loss of generality these can be two consequent axes $R_{s,s-1}$ and $R_{s,s+1}$, assumed to be completely kinematically defined w.r.t. position and velocity. This naturally means that the transversal $s, s-1+s+1, s$ is known following Denavit–Hartenberg's methodology (and see Figure 2)[9].

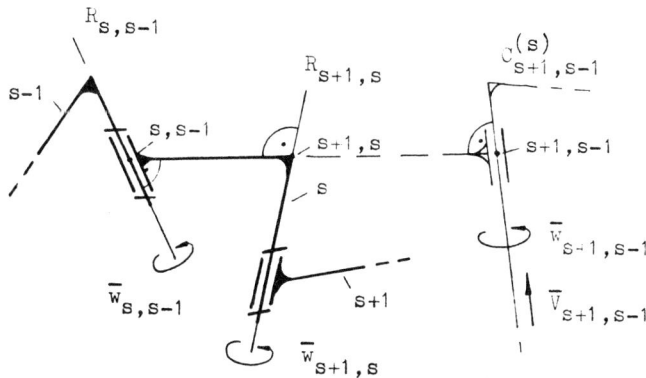

Figure 2 $2R \leftrightharpoons C$ transformation

The distance $l_{s,s+1}^{(s-1)}$ between the points $s, s-1$ and $s+1, s-1$ is defined by

$$l_{s,s+1}^{(s-1)} = l_{s-1,s+1}^{(s)} \frac{w_{s+1,s}^2 - w_{s,s-1} w_{s+1,s} \cos \alpha_{s+1,s}^{s,s-1}}{w_{s+1,s-1}^2}$$

The spatial orientation of the equivalent C kinematic joint coincides with the relative angular velocity

$$\bar{w}_{s+1,s-1} = \bar{w}_{s,s-1} - \bar{w}_{s+1,s}$$

Its module is determined by

$$w_{s+1,s-1}^2 = w_{s,s-1}^2 + w_{s+1,s}^2 - 2 w_{s,s-1} w_{s+1,s} \cos \alpha_{s+1,s}^{s,s-1}$$

and the angle between the $s+1, s$ and $s+1, s-1$ axes is

$$\alpha_{s+1,s}^{s+1,s-1} = \arccos(\bar{w}_{s+1,s} \bar{w}_{s+1,s-1})$$

Following the described algorithm, three equivalent C joints can be introduced for the considered $6R$ structure. The complete topology of these three axes is implicitly contained in the following scheme:

$$\begin{array}{cccccc}
(12) & 13 & 14 & 15 & 16 & \boxed{17} \\
(23) & 24 & 25 & 26 & 27 \\
& (34) & 35 & 36 & 37 \\
& & (45) & 46 & 47 \\
& & & (56) & 57 \\
& & & & (67)
\end{array}$$

where the encircled numbers denote robot R joints and the axis of the C joint, associated with the task, is enclosed by a square.

Three equivalent C joints

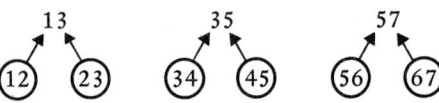

can be directly defined solely on the basis of the actual robot structure, and additional two ones

can be found by using a hybrid approach with the target C joint 17.

The existence of P joints in the actual robot structure does not imply any significant changes in the considerations carried out in this paragraph, and will not be discussed in detail.

Inverse kinematics

Starting with known initial robot configuration and joint velocities, the solution of the inverse kinematics problem for IR effectively proceeds through two stages: (1) determination of the equivalent $4C$ kinematic model and calculation of the relative angular and linear velocities, the components of the generalized velocities vector $\bar{V}$, that can be easily performed as shown above by using the target C joint; (2) calculation of the actual robot joint velocities by using the $\bar{V}$ vector, just determined.

The calculation of joint co-ordinates can be performed in the usual way by numerical integration.

Conclusions

The main idea behind the method presented in this paper is to split the solution of the inverse kinematics problem into two stages introducing an intermediate equivalent $3C$ kinematic structure considered together with an additional 'target' C joint. The original problem is solved with respect to the generalized velocities of the $3C$ structure first and then the latter are properly distributed among the respective joints of the actual robot.

References

[1] Whitney D L (1969) Resolved motion rate control of manipulators and human prosthesis. *IEEE Trans. Man-mach. Syst.*, **MMS-10**(2), 47–53
[2] Whitney D L (1972) The mathematics of coordinated control of prosthetic arms and manipulators. *J. Dynam. Syst., Meas. Control, Ser. G*, 303–309
[3] Renaud M (1980) Contribution a la modelisation a la commande dynamique des robots manipulateurs. PhD Thesis, Toulouse
[4] Luh J Y S et al. (1980) Resolved acceleration control of mechanical manipulators. *IEEE Trans. Automatic Control*, **AC-25**(3)
[5] Luh J Y S et al. (1980) On line computational scheme for mechanical manipulators. *Trans. ASME, Ser. G*, June
[6] Konstantinov M S et al. (1982) *A Contribution to the Inverse Kinematic Problem for Industrial Robots.* Proc. 12th ISIR, Paris, June
[7] Konstantinov M S et al. (1983) *A New Approach to the Solution of the Inverse Kinematic Problem for Industrial Robots.* Proc. 6th W. Congr., New Delhi, India, December *TMM*, 970–973
[8] Konstantinov M S and Markov M D (1980) Discrete position method in kinematics and control of spatial linkages. *Mech. Mach. Theory*, 5(1), 47–60
[9] Denavit J and Hartenberg R (1955) A kinematic notation for lower pair mechanisms based on matrices. *Trans. ASME, J. Appl. Mech.*, June

Industrial Robots with Recuperation of Mechanical Energy

K V Frolov, A I Korendiasev, B L Salamandra and L I Tyves

Institute for the Study of Machines, USSR Academy of Sciences, Moscow, USSR

Summary: In traditional drives of cycle robotic systems the main engine power is consumed by the system acceleration and is diffused in dampers and stops. There is another way of drive organization based on the use of vibratory system properties. In such systems, the energy consumed by the inertial mass acceleration is not lost in the system (is not transformed into heat), but is transformed from kinetic into potential energy. Moreover, much more than in traditional systems quick-action may be achieved, and drive power may be greatly reduced. To transfer robotic systems into the class of vibratory systems, the robot structure must possess minimum damping properties and must contain elastic elements, mechanical energy accumulators and controllable stops-locators.

The following problems have been solved in this work: choice of motor; synthesis of kinematic transmissions ensuring the system working capacity in the preset range of speeds and displacements; synthesis of multiposition systems with mechanical energy accumulators.

The proposed drive structure (Figure 1) includes a potential energy accumulator in the form of an elastic element (1) with stiffness and controllable stops-locators (2). In the mean position of the movable mass (3) between the stops-locators, the spring (1) is in a free state and its force $C\varphi = 0$. In the initial position the system is cocked and tightened to the stop-locator by the force $C\varphi_A$.

After the command to perform the motion, the locator magnet retracts the stop, and the mass m under the action of the spring force $C\varphi_A$ begins the acceleration, transforming the potential energy of the elastic element into the kinetic energy of the mass m. After passing the mean position ($\varphi = 0$), the mass m begins decelerating due to the transition of the mass m kinematic energy, back into the spring potential energy. If there were no friction in the system, the mass m would certainly reach the symmetrically placed second locator, and its speed in this position would be equal to zero. The presence of friction in the system makes necessary the installation of the drive (4), which restores the energy spent on these losses.

The quick-action of the system depends on its own dynamic properties of an organized mechanical oscillatory circuit and theoretically, with known system delay mr^2, it is always possible to select the spring stiffness C in such a way as to ensure the desired quick-action. In the range of the linear model of the quick-action growth limit there are no such systems. In constructing such systems, it is extremely important to co-ordinate the characteristics of the mechanical vibratory system with the drive properties, i.e. with the parameters of the engine dynamic characteristic and the reductor gear ratio.

The technique of drive parameter selection is based on the division of the general equation of motion into two. The first equation describes the conservative

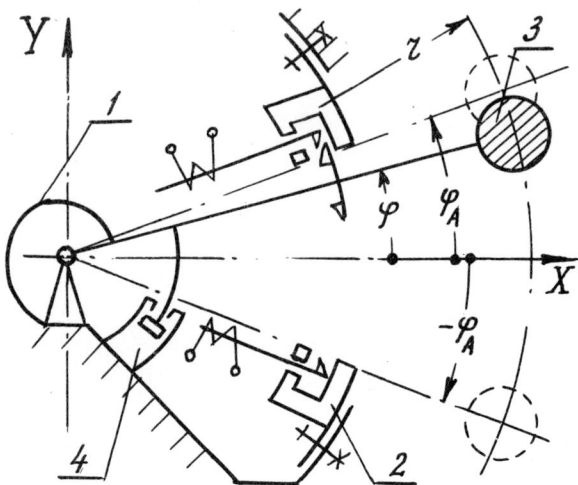

Figure 1 Proposed drive structure

vibratory system (without taking into account the energy for losses in the system and its recuperation) and defines the desired motion of the mechanical system; the second equation formalizes the processes connected with energy loss and its recuperation on the desired motion. The desired law of motion is substituted into the second equation and on its basis the engine parameters and the reductor gear ratio are defined. Then on the basis of obtained values of the engine and reductor parameters there is synthesized the elastic element characteristic, which ensures the realization of the desired law of motion of the conservative system.

The full equation of motion when using an electric DC motor and reductor, after bringing all the inertial components to the axis of rotation of the driven link, has the following form:

$$(mR^2 + J_{ab}i^2)\ddot{\varphi} + M_{TP}\sin\dot{\varphi} + C\varphi = M_{ab}i$$

$$M_{ab} = M_n \sin\dot{\varphi} - K_1\dot{\varphi}i - M_{XX}\sin\dot{\varphi}$$

where J_{ab} = inertia moment of the engine rotor, $M_n = \Phi K_m V_я / R_я$ = engine starting torque, $K_1 = K_e K_m \Phi^2 / R_я$ = viscous friction factor, M_{XX} = engine idling moment, Φ = excitation flow, $V_я$ and $R_я$ = voltage and resistance of the armature circuit, K_e and K_M = proportionality constants which characterize, respectively, the engine structure and the permeance of the magnetic circuit.

We suppose that at any moment the resistance force $M_{TP}\sin\dot{\varphi}$ is equal to the force $M_{ab}i$ generated by the engine, i.e.

$$M_{TP}\sin\dot{\varphi} - iM_n\sin\dot{\varphi} + K_1\dot{\varphi}i^2 + iM_{XX}\sin\dot{\varphi} = 0 \qquad (1)$$

By taking into account that the amount of energy pumped into the system is very small compared to the energy circulating in the system with an accumulator for finding the sought parameters M_n, K_1 and i, it is possible, with a sufficient degree of exactness, instead of the condition of force equality (1), to use the condition of the equality of their works in the preset motion interval with the amplitude φ_A. In this case the law of motion of the initial conservative system is not broken. Assuming that this law must be fulfilled, for example, harmonic ($\varphi = \varphi_A \cos \omega t$, where $0 < t < T$) the condition of the equality of works from forces (1) will have the following form

$$\tfrac{1}{4} K_1 \varphi_A \omega \pi i^2 + M_{XX} i + M_{TP} = M_n i \qquad (2)$$

The condition (2) is represented graphically in Figure 2. The loss curve in the system [the left part of equation (2)], depending on i, has the form of a parabola **1**, cutting off on the $[A/\varphi_A]_\pm$ axis a segment equal to M_{TP}. The right part (2) characterizes the useful work of the engine and is represented by the straight line **2**. If the straight line **2** does not cross the parabola **1** [there is no solution of equation (2)], the losses in the system are higher than the contribution A_+ of energy into the system, and it is impossible to ensure the working capacity of the system.

At the intersection of the parabola with the straight line, the whole area of the i-values is divided into three zones. At $i > i_{\max}$ (zone I) and $i < i_{\min}$ (zone III)

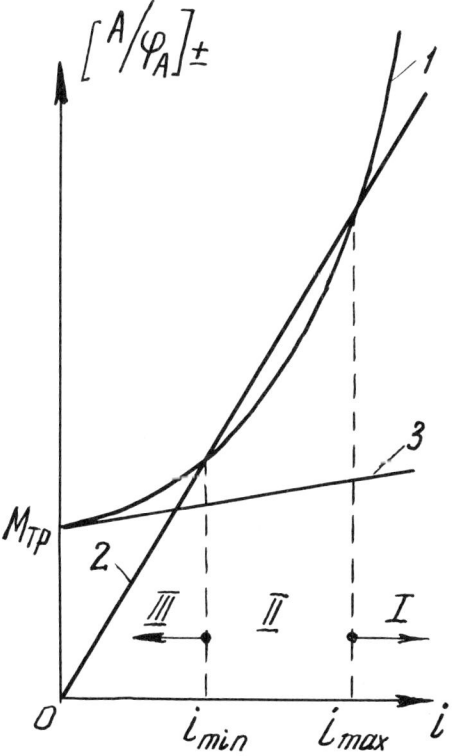

Figure 2 Graphic representation of $\tfrac{1}{4} K_1 \phi_A \omega \pi i^2 + M_{XX} i + M_{TP} = M_n i$

the system will be unable to function due to the above-mentioned cause. Only in zone II, at $i_{max} > i > i_{min}$, the contribution A_+ of energy is higher than the losses A_-, and the system will always be able to work. In this case it is expedient to choose the i-value near to i_{min}.

Then the following advantages will be achieved: (1) at smaller i, the contribution A_+ and the losses A_- of energy will be less than at i near to i_{max}, i.e. the efficiency of the system will increase; (2) since the point with i_{min} is nearer to the basis of the parabola, the sensitivity of the system to the motion parameters φ_A and T in this point will be smaller than at i_{max}.

This means that with adjustment of the system to different amplitudes φ_A, the system with different loads influencing the quick-action T, the overcompensation on the energy contribution will be rather small. The same is valid for engine parameters K_1, M_{xx} and M_n, and their fluctuations in the process of system exploitation do not impair its working capacity.

The change of coefficients in equation (2) deforms the parabola 1, either compressing it to the $[A/\varphi_A]_\pm$ axis or drawing it nearer to the straight line 3.

The necessity of an obligatory intersection of the straight line 2 and the parabola 1 demands the calculation of parameters on the basis of an extreme case, when the parabola is extremely compressed. This means that the choice of the gear ratio i must be made with the orientation in the case when the frequency ω and the angle φ_A of the link rotation are maximum. It must be noted that maximum ω corresponds to the idling of the system (without load). These considerations allow selection of the engine and the reductor for the system with one degree of freedom, for two points in the space. For serving for more than two points, it is proposed to use a differential gear drive.[1]

The model of the differential gear drive is shown in Figure 3. Here the mass m,

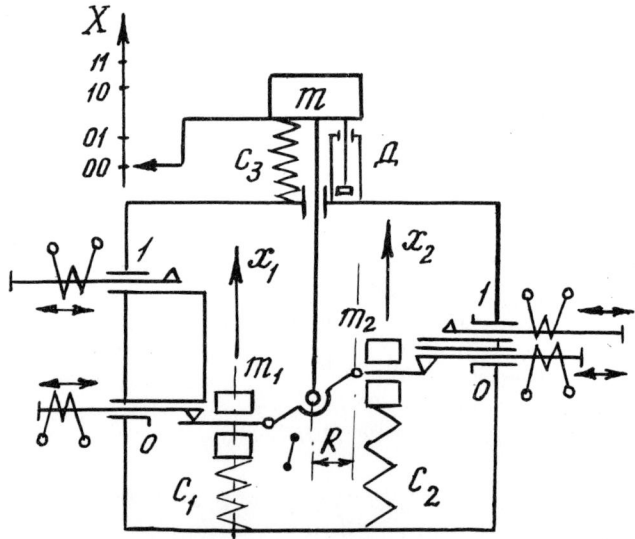

Figure 3 Model of the differential gear drive

actuated by spring elasticity C_3, may be displaced under the action of two accumulators with springs C_1 and C_2 and the engine II, which pumps energy into the system. Each accumulator is equipped with two controlled stops. Accumulators using transmitters with masses m_1 and m_2 are connected to the mass m in a differential scheme, by means of a rocker with an arm R and moment of inertia J (the rocker arm is reduced to the mass m). Depending on the state of accumulators, the mass m can occupy one out of four possible positions defined by a binary two-bit code $\delta_1 \delta_2$. The displacement S_m of the mass m is defined on the basis of the relation

$$S_m = \tfrac{1}{2}(\delta_1 S_1 + \delta_2 S_2)$$

where S_1 and S_2 are the displacements of masses m_1 and m_2 of the accumulators; δ_1 and δ_2 assume the values 0 or 1.

Thus, in the range of the displacement of mass m, there are four fixed positions. However, the dynamic features of the differential scheme do not allow an arbitrary transition from one position to another. This is connected with the fact that the considered model possesses two degrees of freedom (its state is described by the co-ordinates of masses m_1 and m_2) with mutual dynamic influence between partial systems.

Having introduced the co-ordinates x_1 and x_2 of the masses m_1 and m_2, we can put down the expression for the kinetic energy T_* and the potential energy U of the model

$$T_* = A_1 \dot{x}_1^2 + 2H \dot{x}_1 \dot{x}_2 + A_2 \dot{x}_2^2; \quad U = a_1 x_1^2 + 2b x_1 x_2 + a_2 x_2^2$$

Here the values of the coefficients are $A_j = \dfrac{1}{2} m_j + \dfrac{1}{8} m + \dfrac{1}{8R^2} J$, $j = 1, 2$, $a_j = \dfrac{1}{2} C_j + \dfrac{1}{8} C_3$, $H = \dfrac{1}{8} m - \dfrac{1}{8R^2} J$, $b = \dfrac{1}{8} C_3$. Then the differential equation of the model motion will have the following form

$$A_1 \ddot{x}_1 + H \ddot{x}_2 + a_1 x_1 + b x_2 = 0$$
$$H \ddot{x}_1 + A_2 \ddot{x}_2 + b x_1 + a_2 x_2 = 0 \qquad (3)$$

The alternative insertion of the accumulators always changes the position of the mass and causes its coming to a corresponding fixed position, since in this case the system degenerates into a system with one degree of freedom for which $T_* = A_j \dot{x}_j^2$, $U = a_j x_j^2$ is then valid.

When mass m is substantially greater than masses m_1, m_2 and J/R^2, the considered system also becomes a system with one degree of freedom in which accumulators work in quasistatic conditions. In this case, neglecting the masses m_1, m_2 and J/R^2, we obtain the equation of motion (3) in the following form

$$C_1 x_1 - C_2 x_2 = 0$$
$$\tfrac{1}{2} m (\ddot{x}_1 + \ddot{x}_2) + C_1 x_1 + C_2 x_2 = 0$$

The first equation is an algebraic equation connecting displacements and stiffnesses in the accumulators. Using it we can reduce the second equation to the following form

$$m\frac{(\ddot{x}_1+\ddot{x}_2)}{2}+\frac{2C_1C_2(x_1+x_2)}{C_1+C_2}$$

Thus the predominance of mass m produces a system with one degree of freedom in which, because of the condition $C_1 x_1 = C_2 x_2$, either simultaneous displacement of both accumulators from conditions 00 to 11 and back, or separated in time, insertion of accumulators is permitted. It means that the transition of mass m from the state 01 into 10 and back is possible in two steps: 01 00 10 or 01 11 10. All the other transitions are performed in one step.

The possibility of simultaneous action of two accumulators is achieved either due to full dynamic isolation of the system according to the degrees of freedom or due to its work on two natural modes of oscillation. In the latter case the system is adjusted in such a way that at simultaneous insertion of both accumulators it performs oscillation in one of its natural modes.

Full dynamic isolation of the system in the condition of absence of mutual 'pumping' of energy from one accumulator into another is equivalent to reducing the system (3) to two independent equations, the first of which would contain only the co-ordinate x_1 and its derivatives, and the second $-x_2$ and its derivatives. This requirement is realized superimposing some restrictions on the coefficients A_j, a_j, H, b of the system (3) by means of selecting the model parameters. Let us consider two important-for-practice variants.

1. As seen from equation (3), it is possible to use the condition $H = b = 0$ for the dynamic isolation of the system. In the model parameters this means $C_3 = 0$, $m = J/R^2$. Thus, if we remove the spring and select the rocker inertia moment properly, we shall make simultaneous independent (in any direction) work of accumulators possible. In this case there are no restrictions for the selection of springs C_1 and C_2, displacement S_j of accumulators and arbitrary transition from one position of the mass m into another is possible.

2. The same result may be obtained, if proportionality of coefficients is provided:

$$\frac{a_1}{A_1}=\frac{a_2}{A_2}=\frac{b}{H} \qquad (4)$$

Then the system (3) is reduced to two independent equations[2]

$$(A_1A_2-H^2)\ddot{x}_1+(a_1A_2-Hb)x_1=0$$
$$(A_1A_2-H^2)\ddot{x}_2+(a_2A_1-Hb)x_2=0$$

The proportionality (4) can be provided by means of different sets of parameters. One of them may be, for example, $C_1 = C_2$, $m_1 = m_2$ and $C_3 = 2C_1(m-J/R^2)/(2m_1+J/R^2)$.

Both variants show the possibility of full dynamic isolation of the system which, as a result, may be arbitrarily transferred into any of the four fixed positions. In this case the accumulators do not affect each other and any of them may be inserted at any moment independently of the other accumulator position or state (whether it is in motion or at rest).

The described principles of dynamic system isolation were used as a basis for practical development of an industrial robot with 3 DOF. On the constructed model with an arm having general mass 2.5 kg and with electric motor capacity 6 W each, there were obtained the mean velocities: for the first DOF, 6 rad/s; for the second DOF, 11 rad/s; for the third DOF, 20 rad/s. By comparing traditional structures of cyclic robots, the discussed solutions allow to increase the quick-action by three to four times, simultaneously decreasing the engine capacity by six times.

References

[1] Korendiasev A I, Salamandra B L and Tyves L I (1981) Particularities of designing functional diagrams of automatic manipulators (in Russian). *Stanki i instrument* (2), 9–13
[2] Mandelstam L I (1972) Lectures on vibration theory (in Russian). *Nauka Pol*.

On the Optimal Selection and Placement of Manipulators

V Scheinman and B Roth*

Advanced Systems, Automatix Incorporated, Billerica, MA 01821, and *Department of Mechanical Engineering, Stanford University, Stanford, CA 94305, USA

Summary: This paper deals with the determination of manipulator proportions which minimize the time for motions starting from and ending in a rest state. These results also aid the layout of a manipulator workstation. The effects of physical constraints such as joint torques, overall length and joint travel limits are considered.

Introduction

Industrial robots are now more than just a research laboratory curiosity. Many companies throughout the world are building, marketing and installing them in significant numbers. They are offered in a large variety of configurations, sizes and performance ranges. Selection of the manipulator for the task at hand typically consists of either estimating whether the working range of the manipulator is sufficient or trying it out in mock-up form at the manufacturer's applications centre. Job-cycle times are estimated from basic performance data such as maximum joint angular velocity and linear travel speed.

Most industrial applications are cycle-time critical, as system pay-off is a strong function of the rate of doing useful work. For many assembly operations that use fast tools, or require simple end-point robot motion, manipulator gross motion time is a significant portion of the total cycle time.

Once the manipulator is purchased, actual installation typically involves locating the manipulator and its workpieces in convenient locations. The task is tried, and motion optimization, to reduce cycle times, is performed by manually reprogramming each individual motion, or slightly relocating or reorienting workstations until performance is satisfactory.

Background

Others have looked at this type of optimal-motion problem in an attempt to compute shortest time motion between given end points[1] or along a given path.[2] All have had to constrain their solution and the scope of their results, as is also the case in the present work. In this paper we show that by using some principles of optimization the selection of manipulator size and geometry and the layout of the workplace can be performed in an organized and rigorous manner. This yields a more optimum installation on the first try. Although laborious, the calculations reveal several interesting results which can be used as guidelines for less critical installations, requiring only approximate optimal selection and layout.

Modelling and assumptions

In our work the manipulator is modelled as a rigid kinematic serial link chain. In this paper, the specific manipulator configuration considered is a two-link planar linkage with two revolute joints. Each link is considered to have a mass and each joint is given a fixed torque magnitude. From principles of mass and inertia equivalence,[3] distributed masses are lumped into equivalent point masses located such that the equivalent link inertia remains the same. In the case of planar mechanisms the equivalent masses may be considered to be point masses located at the joints of the mechanism.

Each joint is considered to have a specific level of torque capability. This is equivalent to having a torque motor at each joint with a fixed peak torque independent of joint speed or angular velocity. In an extension of this work a profiled torque is considered in which a fixed peak torque is used over a given range of velocities and, above this velocity, the peak torque linearly ramps down to zero at some larger velocity. All applied torques are considered to be uniformly bidirectional, meaning that the joint motor can exert the same torque in either direction, as necessary. It should be noted that with the increasing interest and popularity of AC drive motors (also referred to as brushless DC motors), high-impedance current-mode switching-power amplifiers and low reduction ratio or direct joint drives, the potential velocity range of manipulator joints is high. Thus the assumption of constant peak torque is not unrealistic.

A further idealization initially made is to eliminate friction and gravity effects. For the well-known SCARA (Selective Compliance Assembly Robot Arm) class of manipulators (Figure 1) gravity acts only on the Z motion and as such can be treated independently. For high-performance manipulators, having acceleration capability in excess of 1g (peak accelerations of 4-10gs are realizable today), gravity effects on performance are relatively diminished. Joint related friction comes from several sources. For ball or roller-bearing mounted revolute joints, joint friction is generally small. Most of the friction comes from electromagnetic hysteresis drag, cogging torques, brush drag and bearing seal and grease friction in the drive motor and gear train (if used). For the purposes of this analysis, all friction is lumped into the motor torque parameter, and is seen only as a peak joint torque which is less than the theoretical frictionless joint torque.

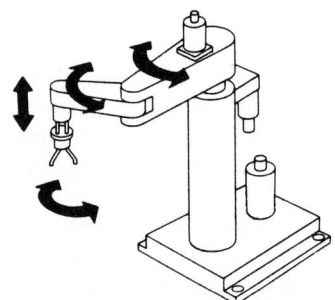

Figure 1 SCARA robot configuration

Optimal control theory was applied to a manipulator system, for which the inputs are joint torques (which are a function of time) and the desired output is an endpoint displacement motion. In optimal-control theory terms, the system model is the manipulator, with initial conditions. The control objective is to drive the system to the end conditions such that the performance index is minimized. This performance index is time of travel.

The equations of motion indicate that for a planar two degree of freedom manipulator (Figure 2) this is a fourth-order non-linear two-point boundary value problem. A numerical solution is indicated. From optimal control and dynamics theory certain initial assumptions may be made: (1) admissible control is bang-bang; (2) each joint control has a maximum of two switch points; (3) total + torque time equals the total − torque time for the first joint if the end conditions represent stationary states.

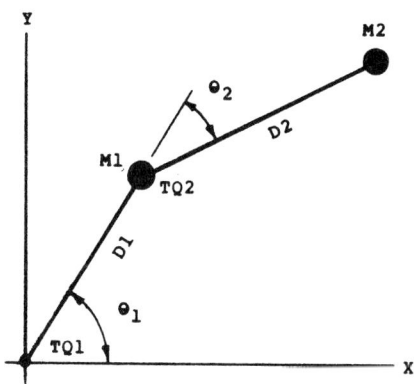

Figure 2 Kinematic configuration and notation

The first assumption is an extension of linear optimal-control theory and, although not a law, it appears to be a reasonable simplifying assumption with high probability of correctness for this problem.

The second assumption also comes from linear optimization theory. This assumption is considered to be reasonable as experience with other similar problems indicates a good probability that the optimal solution will have at most two switch times for each torque. It is also a vitally needed restriction if the solution space is to be restricted to a manageable size, although this is not a justification for its validity.

The third simplifying consideration, which comes from conservation of angular momentum considerations, restricts the motion to be from rest state to rest state, but still allows handling of a wide range of point to point motions. Without this assumption, the calculation of switch times is more complicated, as end-point angular momentum is not zero.

Solution approach

We begin the solution of our problem by choosing a two-link manipulator with given joint torques, link lengths and masses, and a starting location and state (generally at rest). Rather than try to integrate the equations of motion until some time when satisfactory end conditions may be reached and attempt to minimize this time, we integrate over a fixed time interval and adjust switching times during this interval to maximize motion distance. This is carried out with the aid of a standard differential equation solver (by using the Kutta-Merson numerical approach). The first joint switch times are selected according to the simplifying assumptions listed above. A trial set of second joint switch times is also chosen.

The equations are integrated and one of the joint number 2 switch times is adjusted, based on the computer velocity at the end of the integration time, so that after several iterations the final velocity of both joints is close to zero. The magnitude of the distance travelled is recorded and another set of first or second joint switch times is selected. This process is repeated for a set of first and second joint switch times representing a uniform subset of all combinations of first and second joint switch times for the given manipulator and initial conditions. The set of computed end points represents the locus of possible end states for the selected configuration in the chosen fixed time interval (Figure 3). Another mirror-image set (not shown) of end states representing the other configuration complements the plotted end states to provide a symmetric pattern of the entire set.

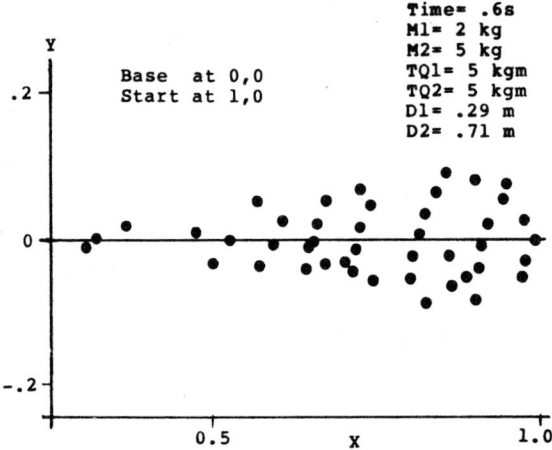

Figure 3 Set of end states

For a manipulator with fixed physical parameters, the end points located along the envelope of the set of end states generally represent the time optimal motion for the manipulator for the given initial and end conditions (points). The end point located the greatest distance from the starting point represents the time optimal motion as well as the best end location as defined by our objective function (the greatest distance in a given time period).

This certainly helps in a physical layout, as it suggests the best place to locate the work given a starting position, but further optimization can be done. Ideally, it would be desirable to be able to choose an optimal starting point as well as an end point. This is done, rather laboriously, by picking a set of starting points and finding the optimum end point for each starting point for each total motion time.

Results

The results of these calculations are indicated in Figure 4. They show that one of the best end points is at full extension of the manipulator. It is noteworthy that due to symmetry for the type of manipulator chosen, and lack of gravity or friction, the starting and end points are interchangeable. This requires the reversal of switching times. The locations of these points are only relative to each other and independent of the angle of the first joint. They are also configuration independent in this kinematically and dynamically symmetric case which has two configurations for each end-point position. Reversed-switch time signs are required for the alternative configuration.

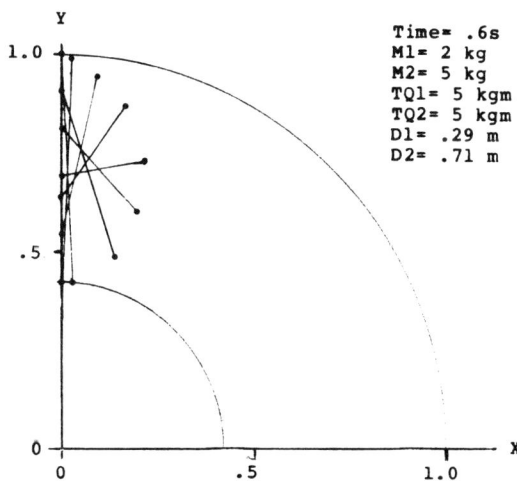

Figure 4 Travel vs start location

Based on our optimization criteria, this part of the study indicates that the shortest overall link-length manipulator for the task is the best suited, and that radial- rather than circumferential-type motions are more optimal.

In a modularly designed manipulator it is practical to choose link lengths according to specific task needs. This is, of course, provided that a value can be put on the need in the form of the best link lengths for the application. Other modular elements such as joint torque (drive motor, transmission and power amplifier selection) can also be tailored to the application, but this is more costly and difficult.

We executed such an optimization by using a first-order gradient method to determine the optimum ratio of link lengths. The overall manipulator length was held constant. The results indicate that although equal link lengths give the greatest accessible area[4] (the inner radius of the access annulus is zero), they are not necessarily the optimum lengths to use. With respect to selection of individual link lengths, the plot in Figure 5 shows how this affects the travel distance for a fixed starting point and time interval.

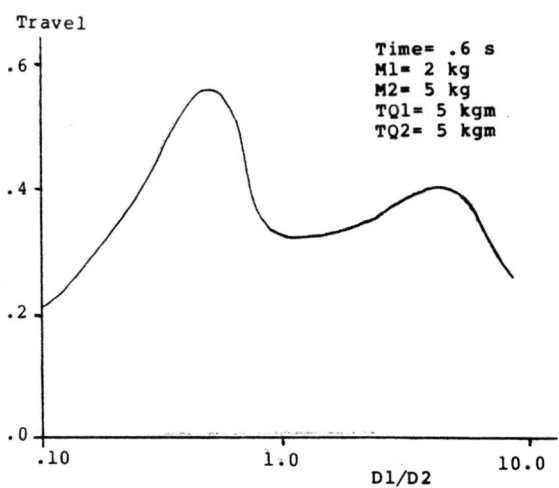

Figure 5 Travel vs link-length ratio

The computations indicate that when optimum link-length ratios are used, large joint travel range appears to be required. This may be a real physical constraint to application of this optimization study. It is interesting to note that for the few cases evaluated the joint number 2 travel is about 180°, indicating that the best link lengths may be those which allow the manipulator to move between the enclosing circles of its access annulus. Although not investigated, where joint travel limits exist, alternatives may include the use of joint travel limit stops as torquers to assist in the required motion. Several possibilities are elastic, inelastic or locking stops.

Observations

For the class of two-link planar manipulators with the motion and performance objectives studied, and from the limited set of cases evaluated, several specific observations may be made: (1) Manipulators with optimal link lengths move farthest in a given time interval when the initial and final end points are located near the same radial through the base pivot. (2) For typical physical configurations, shorter inner-link lengths and longer outer-link lengths are suggested. This is contrary to most SCARA configurations. (3) One of the motion end points should be at or near the maximum extension of the manipulator, suggesting the use of the shortest overall length manipulator.

In general, it has been shown that for the specific class of manipulators studied, it is possible to select a manipulator size, and geometry best suited to a given motion requirement. It is also possible to set up the initial and final motion points such that the motion time is minimized. The numerical calculations are tedious but, once done, the resulting guidelines can be applied to more easily partially optimized similar systems and installations.

Financial support of the System Development Foundation and the National Science Foundation is acknowledged. The LOTS computer facility at Stanford University was used for the computations.

References

[1] Kahn, M E (1970) The near-minimum time control of open-loop articulated kinematic chains. PhD Dissertation, Stanford University
[2] Bobrow, J E, Dubowsky, S & Gibson, J S (1983) *On the Optimal Control of Robotic Manipulators with Actuator Constraints*. Proc. Am. Control Conf., pp782-787, San Francisco June 1983
[3] Wiederrich, J L & Roth, B (1976) *Momentum Balancing of Four-bar Linkages*. ASME Paper No 76-DET-28, 15 June 1976
[4] Gupta, K C & Roth, B (1982) Design considerations for manipulator workspace. *Trans. ASME J. Mech. Design*, 104, 704-711

On the Geometry of Orthogonal and Reciprocal Screws

H Lipkin and J Duffy

University of Florida, Center For Intelligent Machines and Robotics, Gainesville, FL 32611, USA

Summary: Screw theory is an elegant method for describing the equilibrium and instantaneous motion of rigid bodies and is widely applied to the analysis of robot manipulators. The objective here is to advance the theory of screws by establishing fundamental geometric principles for orthogonal and reciprocal screws. Dualistic and reciprocal properties are delineated by considering two distinct but equivalent spaces whose fundamental elements are points and planes respectively. In projective and elliptic space, homogeneous Plücker co-ordinates are used to derive various relations for lines which are extended to screws by linear principles. In this way it is shown that the one-to-one relation between orthogonal and reciprocal screws is a transformation of elliptic polars. Euclidean space is developed and the formulation of alternative kinematic models is discussed. The results are illustrated by using the example of inserting a peg in a hole.

Background

Briefly, the analytical representation of points, planes and lines is available in many texts on projective and non-Euclidean geometry.[1-5] A thorough treatment of screws and reciprocal screws is given elsewhere.[6,7] Orthogonal screws have only recently been introduced.[8,9] Also recently, constrained motion has been modelled by using natural and artificial constraints.[10] These constraints can be elegantly expressed in terms of orthogonal and reciprocal screw systems.

Dual and reciprocal transformations

The dualistic properties of space can be developed by following Klein[4] who considered two distinct yet identical spaces. Here the discussion will be restricted to the three-dimensional projective space S_3, although the principles can be extended to S_n. In the first space the point is chosen as the fundamental element; a line is the join of two points; a plane is the join of three points. In the second space a plane (which is the dual of the point) is chosen as the fundamental element; a line is said to be the meet (intersection) of two planes; a point is the meet of three planes.

A transformation is defined as a one-to-one and on to mapping; a collineation is a transformation of a single space on to itself and maps each element (point, line, plane) on to a corresponding (point, line, plane); a correlation is a transformation between two spaces and maps each element (point, line, plane) in the first space on to its dual element (plane, line, point) in the second space. Two spaces in correlation play complementary roles which Klein describes as 'dual in the narrower sense'. When the two spaces coincide and the correlation is symmetrical, it makes no difference whether an element is considered to belong to one space or the other;

in this context the roles of the spaces are said to be 'reciprocal'. The concept of distinct yet coincident spaces is especially important because it permits a distinction to be made between collineations and correlations of lines which are self-dual elements. For example, a line can be used to specify the action of a force; dually, a line can be used to represent an axis of instantaneous rotation, and a correlation thus relates two physically different concepts. On the other hand, a collineation relates the same physical phenomenon. In general, self-dual elements such as the line occur in spaces of odd dimension (S_{2n+1}, $n = 0, 1, \ldots$).

Two distinct representations of S_3 are determined by choosing homogeneous co-ordinates for each of the fundamental elements, the point and plane, by assigning to each an ordered quadruple which is unique to a non-zero scalar multiple. This is accomplished by first establishing respective tetrahedra of reference.[1] Each system of co-ordinates describes a vector space of rank four, V_4. When the two spaces and tetrahedra are coincident the two systems of co-ordinates are said to be *contragradient*. (In tensor analysis the two systems of co-ordinates are distinguished by labelling them with subscripts and superscripts; this convention, however, will not be used here.)

Plücker line co-ordinates

By using the Grassmann determinant principle,[4] the four homogeneous co-ordinates of both the point and the plane can be elegantly used to assign six homogenous co-ordinates to the line in S_3 which are elements in a vector space of rank six, V_6. These are the so-called Plücker line co-ordinates.[11]

A line in S_3 is the joint of two points x, y or dually the meet of two planes U, V (see Figure 1). Introduction of the homogeneous point co-ordinates x, y and

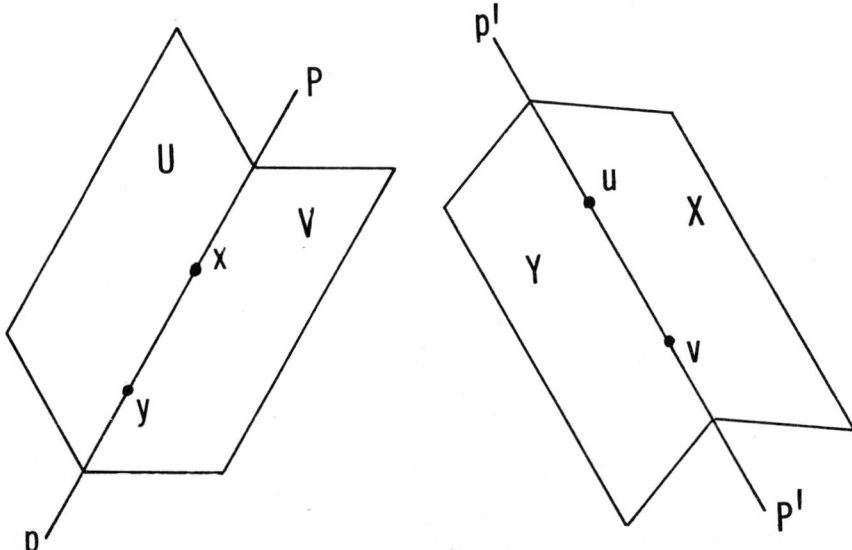

Figure 1 Plücker line co-ordinates: line in S_3 is join of two points x, y or dually meet of two planes U, V

plane co-ordinates U, V and use of Grassmann's principle yields two distinct sets of homogeneous line co-ordinates which are determined by the 2×2 determinants of

$$\begin{bmatrix} x_0 & x_1 & x_2 & x_3 \\ y_0 & y_1 & y_2 & y_3 \end{bmatrix} \quad (1) \qquad \begin{bmatrix} U_0 & U_1 & U_2 & U_3 \\ V_0 & V_1 & V_2 & V_3 \end{bmatrix} \quad (2)$$

taken in the order 01, 02, 03, 23, 31, 12 and,

$$p = (p_{01}\ p_{02}\ p_{03}\ p_{23}\ p_{31}\ p_{12})^t \quad (3) \qquad p_{ij} = x_i y_j - y_i x_j \quad (4)$$

$$P = (P_{01}\ P_{02}\ P_{03}\ P_{23}\ P_{31}\ P_{12})^t \quad (5) \qquad P_{ij} = U_i V_j - V_i U_j \quad (6)$$

The 6×1 arrays p and P are respectively the radial (or ray) and axial Plücker line co-ordinates.

The relation between radial and axial co-ordinates can be derived from the incidence of the two points with the two planes,

$$U^t x = 0 \quad (7) \qquad U^t y = 0 \quad (8) \qquad V^t x = 0 \quad (9) \qquad V^t y = 0 \quad (10)$$

The following four relations can be deduced from (7)–(10)

$$[P]x = 0 \quad (11) \qquad [P]y = 0 \quad (12) \qquad [p]U = 0 \quad (13) \qquad [p]V = 0 \quad (14)$$

For example, $U \cdot (9) - V \cdot (7)$ yields (11). The matrices $[p]$ and $[P]$ are skew-symmetric and their elements are defined by (4) and (6). Each of the four rows in $[P]$ represents the co-ordinates of a plane which passes through the line and a vertex of the tetrahedron of reference. Analogously, each of the four rows in $[p]$ represents the co-ordinates of the points of intersection of the line with the faces of the reference tetrahedron. Equating the determinants of $[p]$ and $[P]$ to zero yields two important identities

$$p_{01} p_{23} + p_{02} p_{31} + p_{03} p_{12} = 0 \quad (15) \qquad P_{01} P_{23} + P_{02} P_{31} + P_{03} P_{12} = 0 \quad (16)$$

A single matrix equation relating radial and axial co-ordinates can be obtained by combining either (11),(12) or (13),(14) which yields,

$$[P][p] = [0] \quad (17)$$

Expansion of the left side of (17) and use of the twelve off-diagonal terms yields the following relations between radial and axial co-ordinates,

$$\frac{P_{01}}{P_{23}} = \frac{P_{02}}{P_{31}} = \frac{P_{03}}{P_{12}} = \frac{P_{23}}{P_{01}} = \frac{P_{31}}{P_{02}} = \frac{P_{12}}{P_{03}} = \mu \quad (18)$$

which can be expressed in the alternative matrix forms (19),(20)

$$P = \Delta p \quad (19) \qquad p = \Delta P \quad (20) \qquad \Delta = \begin{bmatrix} \cdot & I_3 \\ I_3 & \cdot \end{bmatrix} \quad (21) \qquad \Delta \Delta = I_6 \quad (22)$$

and where I_n is the $n \times n$ identity matrix. Only the ratios of homogeneous co-ordinates have meaning and it is proper to include the non-zero factor of proportionality μ in (19),(20). However, for the concepts developed here there is no loss in generality by absorbing μ into the homogeneous co-ordinates themselves, i.e. by making the substitution $\mu = 1$.

The condition that two lines p, q (P, Q) meet may be expressed in the alternative bilinear forms

$$P^t \Delta q = 0 \quad (23) \qquad P^t \Delta Q = 0 \quad (24) \qquad p^t Q = 0 \quad (25) \qquad P^t q = 0 \quad (26)$$

Equation (23) can be deduced by considering the pairs of points x, y and s, t which lie on p and q respectively. When the lines intersect all four points are coplanar and the determinant $|xyst|$ vanishes. The Laplacian expansion on the first two columns of this determinant yields the left side of (23). Further, (24)–(26) are readily deduced from (23), (19), (20). Finally, as a line always meets itself then

$$p^t \Delta p = 0 \quad (27) \qquad P^t \Delta P = 0 \quad (28) \qquad p^t P = 0 \quad (29)$$

which are alternative expressions for the identities (15), (16).

Elliptic polars

Cayley[12] was the first to show that metrical geometries can be developed from projective geometry by establishing a second-order form which he called the Absolute. In S_3 the Absolute can be defined by the point locus together with the plane envelope of a quadric surface. It is possible to develop metrical geometries such as Elliptic, Parabolic (Euclidean) and Hyperbolic by an appropriate choice of the Absolute. Here it is convenient to derive metrical geometry in S_3 by establishing a polarity together with its adjoint. A polarity is defined as a symmetrical correlation which can be represented by a symmetric 4×4 matrix. This is equivalent to Cayley's development since there is a one-to-one relation between polarities and quadric surfaces.

Elements of basic elliptic geometry are now developed and will be subsequently utilized to distinguish between the concepts of orthogonal and reciprocal screws. By a suitable choice of the reference tetrahedron, the elliptic polarity and its adjoint are both represented by the identity matrix and

$$X = I_4 x \quad (30) \qquad\qquad x = I_4 X \quad (31)$$

The plane X is said to be the *elliptic polar* of x and the point x is said to be the *elliptic pole* of X. Two points (planes) are said to be *conjugate* when each is incident with the other's polar (pole) and

$$x^t I_4 y = 0 \quad (32) \qquad\qquad X^t I_4 Y = 0 \quad (33)$$

The Absolute is defined by the locus and envelope of self-conjugate points and planes,

$$x^t I_4 x = 0 \quad (34) \qquad\qquad X^t I_4 X = 0 \quad (35)$$

which represent a virtual (imaginary) quadric.

In Figure 1 the join of points x,y is the line p and the meet of their polar planes X,Y defines the polar line P'. (Analogously the join of u,v determines p' and the meet of U,V determines P.) Since the polarity (30), (31) is the identity matrix the co-ordinates x,y and X,Y are identical; further, since the radial and axial line co-ordinates (3), (5) are formed in the same order, the polarity between a line and its polar can be represented by,

$$P' = I_6 p \quad (36) \qquad p' = I_6 P \quad (37) \qquad P' = \Delta P \quad (38) \qquad p' = \Delta p \quad (39)$$

where (38), (39) are obtained by substituting (19), (20) in (36), (37).

Two lines p,q (P,Q) are said to be conjugate when each meets the other's polar and from (25), (26) and (36), (37), the condition that a pair of lines be conjugate is

$$p^t I_6 q = 0 \quad (40) \qquad\qquad P^t I_6 Q = 0 \quad (41)$$

Finally, a line which is self-conjugate has imaginary co-ordinates since from (40), (41)

$$p^t I_6 p = 0 \quad (42) \qquad\qquad P^t I_6 P = 0 \quad (43)$$

Screws

A linear combination of lines $a \ldots c$ $(A \ldots C)$,

$$p = \alpha a + \ldots + \gamma c \quad (44) \qquad\qquad P = \alpha A + \ldots + \gamma C \quad (45)$$

where $\alpha \ldots \gamma$ are scalar multipliers, is defined as a screw since the two identities for lines (15), (16) will in general not be satisfied. The 6×1 arrays p and P now represent the radial and axial homogeneous co-ordinates of a screw. Because (44), (45) are linear relations many of the results previously established for lines may now be reinterpreted and extended to screws: (a) the transformations between radial and axial screw co-ordinates are given by (19), (20); (b) screws which satisfy (23)–(26) are said to be reciprocal; (c) there are no real self-reciprocal screws (27)–(29) (except lines); (a') the transformation between a screw and its elliptic polar screw is given by (36)–(39); (b') screws which satisfy (40), (41) are elliptic conjugates and are said to be orthogonal; (c') there are no real self-orthogonal screws (42), (43).

The meaning of the term *orthogonal* may be explained by considering a screw to be the general element in V_6. Identifying in V_6 two disjoint subspaces of dimension n and $6 - n$ with respective representatives p and q, then the condition for orthogonality is

$$p^t q = 0 \quad (46) \qquad\qquad P^t Q = 0 \quad (47)$$

which is identical with the condition that p and q are elliptic conjugates (40), (41). Further, there is a one-to-one correspondence between orthogonal and reciprocal screws which is given by the polar relations (36)–(39), such that when p is orthogonal to q then its elliptic polar P' is reciprocal to q. This can be demonstrated by using (46), (36) and the reciprocity condition (26),

$$q^t p = q^t P' = 0 \quad (48)$$

Euclidean space

Cayley's development of Euclidean geometry is based on a degenerate form of the Absolute.[12] Here it is preferred to follow the systematic development of Klein[4] by commencing with a non-degenerate polarity and then treating Euclidean geometry as a limiting case,

$$X = \begin{bmatrix} 1 & \cdot & \cdot & \cdot \\ \cdot & \epsilon & \cdot & \cdot \\ \cdot & \cdot & \epsilon & \cdot \\ \cdot & \cdot & \cdot & \epsilon \end{bmatrix} x \quad (49) \qquad x = \begin{bmatrix} \epsilon & \cdot & \cdot & \cdot \\ \cdot & 1 & \cdot & \cdot \\ \cdot & \cdot & 1 & \cdot \\ \cdot & \cdot & \cdot & 1 \end{bmatrix} X \quad (50)$$

where in the limit $\epsilon \to 0$ and $x_0 = 0$, $(X_0\ 0\ 0\ 0)^t$ respectively denote the equation and the co-ordinates of the plane at infinity. From the polarity (49), the polar of any finite point is the plane at infinity; the polar of any point on the plane at infinity is indeterminate $(0\ 0\ 0\ 0)^t$. From the adjoint polarity (50), the pole of any plane other than the plane at infinity lies on the plane at infinity; the pole of the plane at infinity is indeterminate $(0\ 0\ 0\ 0)^t$. The quadric forms of the Absolute are determined by the locus of self-conjugate points and the envelope of self-conjugate planes

$$x_0^2 + \epsilon(x_1^2 + x_2^2 + x_3^2) = 0 \quad (51) \qquad \epsilon X_0^2 + X_1^2 + X_2^2 + X_3^2 = 0 \quad (52)$$

In the limit $\epsilon \to 0$, the locus and envelope represent respectively the plane at infinity taken twice and the imaginary circle at infinity which together form the Euclidean Absolute.[3]

The transformation of a line $p(P)$ to its Euclidean polar line P'' (p'') may be expressed in the alternative forms

$$P'' = \begin{bmatrix} I_3 & \cdot \\ \cdot & \epsilon I_3 \end{bmatrix} p \quad (53) \qquad p'' = \begin{bmatrix} \epsilon I_3 & \cdot \\ \cdot & I_3 \end{bmatrix} P \quad (54)$$

$$p'' = \begin{bmatrix} \cdot & \epsilon I_3 \\ I_3 & \cdot \end{bmatrix} p \quad (55) \qquad P'' = \begin{bmatrix} \cdot & I_3 \\ \epsilon I_3 & \cdot \end{bmatrix} P \quad (56)$$

Equation (53) is obtained from (49) and (5), (6) and by dividing the result throughout by the common factor ϵ before passing the limit; (54) is obtained directly from (50) and (3), (4); and (55), (56) are obtained from (53), (54) and (19), (20). It follows from the polar relations between points and planes that the polar of any line which does not lie on the plane at infinity is, in fact, a line on the plane at infinity; the polar of a line on the plane at infinity is indeterminate $(0\ 0\ 0\ 0\ 0\ 0)^t$. Therefore the polar of the polar of a line vanishes; this is exactly equivalent to the double application of Clifford's polar operator ω, $(\omega^2 = 0)$ to a line (rotor).[13] It is interesting to note in elliptic space, double application of Clifford's polar operator $(\omega^2 = 1)$ transforms a line back to itself. Analogously, in hyperbolic space the polar operator has the property $\omega^2 = -1$.[14]

Because of the linear relations between screws and lines (44), (45) the preceding results deduced for lines can be extended analogously to screws; specifically

(53)–(56) demonstrate that the polar of a screw is a line on the plane at infinity and, further, Clifford's polar operators are equally applicable to screws (motors).

A screw can be expressed by the linear combination of a unique line and its polar[13] and in Euclidean space.

$$p = \alpha s + \beta s'' \quad (57) \qquad P = \alpha S + \beta S'' \quad (58) \qquad h = \beta/\alpha \quad (59)$$

where $s(S)$ is the line of the screw axis and the ratio h is defined as the pitch of the screw. Hence a screw as defined by Ball[6] is a line together with an associated pitch. When $\beta = 0$ then $h = 0$ and the screw is a line; when $\alpha = 0$, then $h = \infty$ and the screw is a line at infinity.

Clifford's motor representation of a screw $p + \omega p_0$ ($P + \omega P_0$) where $\omega^2 = 0$ is now expressed without the operator ω in the form

$$p = [\underline{p}; \underline{p}_0] \quad (60) \qquad\qquad P = [\underline{P}_0; \underline{P}] \quad (61)$$

where an underline is used to denote a 3×1 vector and where the left and right sides are 6×1 arrays. In this way Plücker's co-ordinates are conveniently expressed by a pair of vectors.

Reciprocal and orthogonal screw systems in Euclidean space

It is well established[6] that a general system of forces and couples acting on a rigid body can be reduced to a wrench acting on a screw and that the general instantaneous motion of a rigid body is equivalent to a twist on a screw. It is useful to introduce the concept of two distinct yet coincident spaces $S_5(V_6)$ in the study of the statics and instantaneous kinematics of a rigid body, one space composed of wrenches and the other composed of twists. For convenience, the tetrahedron of reference is aligned with the usual Cartesian co-ordinate system. Following Plücker's convention for wrenches and twists,[11] a wrench (twist) will be expressed as a screw in radial (axial) co-ordinates. It follows that a wrench (twist) can be expressed by

$$f = [\underline{f}; \underline{m}_0] \quad (62) \qquad\qquad \Omega = [\underline{V}_0; \underline{\Omega}] \quad (63)$$

where $\underline{f}, \underline{m}_0$ are the resultant force and moment about the origin of a system of forces and couples. Analogously, $\underline{\Omega}, \underline{V}_0$ are the angular velocity and rectilinear velocity of a point on the rigid body which is coincident with the origin.

A wrench and a twist are said to be reciprocal when they satisfy (25) and,

$$f^t \Omega = \underline{f} \cdot \underline{V}_0 + \underline{\Omega} \cdot \underline{m}_0 = 0 \quad (64)$$

Therefore when f is reciprocal to Ω there is no instantaneous virtual power[7] and the body is in static equilibrium. It is important to note that the property of reciprocity is invariant with a change of co-ordinate system and is a relation between elements of the two distinct spaces.

This is in direct contrast to the non-invariant condition that a pair of wrenches f_1, f_2 (twists Ω_1, Ω_2) are orthogonal which will be designated as a relation between elements of the same space and

$$f_1^t f_2 = \underline{f}_1 \cdot \underline{f}_2 + \underline{m}_{01} \cdot \underline{m}_{02} = 0 \quad (65) \qquad \Omega_1^t \Omega_2 = \underline{\Omega}_1 \cdot \underline{\Omega}_2 + \underline{V}_{01} \cdot \underline{V}_{02} = 0 \quad (66)$$

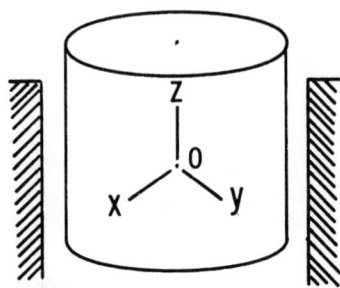

Figure 2 Motion of a peg in a hole

Consider now the motion of a peg in a hole (Figure 2). The motion of the peg is a linear combination of the translational velocity $[\underline{V}_{oz};\underline{0}]$ and the rotational velocity $[\underline{0};\underline{\Omega}_z]$ which together span what will be called the 'twists of freedom', T_2. The unavailable motion of the peg is a linear combination of the four motions $[\underline{V}_{ox};\underline{0}]$, $[\underline{0};\underline{\Omega}_x]$, $[\underline{V}_{oy};\underline{0}]$, $[\underline{0};\underline{\Omega}_y]$ which span what will be called the 'twists of non-freedom', T_4, and which is the orthogonal complement of T_2. Analogously, the reaction wrenches acting on the pin $[\underline{f}_x;\underline{0}]$, $[\underline{0};\underline{m}_{ox}]$, $[\underline{f}_y;\underline{0}]$, $[\underline{0};\underline{m}_{oy}]$ form a base for the 'wrenches of freedom', W_4, and the base for the wrenches of 'non-freedom' W_2 are the wrenches $[\underline{f}_z;\underline{0}]$, $[\underline{0};\underline{m}_{oz}]$. Clearly the wrenches of freedom W_4 are reciprocal to the twists of freedom T_2 (any wrench in the subspace W_4 cannot produce a twist in T_2).

The various screw systems associated with the motion and constraint of a rigid body can be represented by Figure 3 which is constructed for a body with n

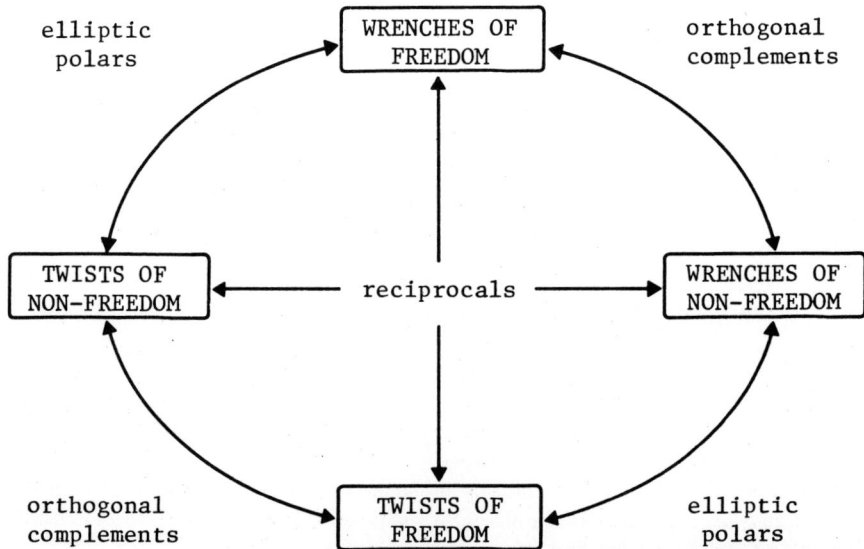

Figure 3 Screw systems associated with motion and constraint of a rigid body

degrees-of-freedom of motion ($0 \leq n \leq 6$), and the following important results can be deduced: (a) twists of freedom (twists of non-freedom) and wrenches of freedom (wrenches of non-freedom) are mutually reciprocal and together their bases span a six space; (b) twists of freedom (wrenches of freedom) and twists of non-freedom (wrenches of non-freedom) are orthogonal complements; (c) twists of non-freedom (wrenches of non-freedom) and wrenches of freedom (twists of freedom) are elliptic polars.

Result (a) is especially important in the operation of a robot manipulator where it is necessary to simultaneously control the motion of a rigid body and the forces acting on it. The six degrees-of-freedom of a manipulator are naturally partitioned in two controllable disjoint subspaces, one composed of wrench freedoms and the other composed of twist freedoms and together the subspaces span a (mixed) V_6. An alternative partition into uncontrollable subspaces is given by the wrenches and twists of non-freedom. The two partitions in V_6 are described[10] respectively as artificial and natural constraints.

The authors gratefully acknowledge the financial support of the National Science Foundation (Grant no. MEA83-24725) and of Westinghouse Research and Development Center (Pittsburg, PA, USA). The authors also acknowledge Professor K H Hunt, Monash University, for his discussions on orthogonal and reciprocal screw systems.

References

[1] Veblen O and Young J W (1910/1917) *Projective Geometry* Blaisdell Publishing Co., New York (published vol I 1938 vol II 1946)
[2] Busemann H and Kelly P J (1953) *Projective Geometry and Projective Metrics* Academic Press, New York
[3] Sommerville D M Y (1934) *Analytical Geometry of Three Dimensions* Cambridge University Press, Cambridge (published 1947)
[4] Klein F (1939) *Geometry* Dover Publications, New York
[5] Coxeter H S M (1942) *Non-Euclidean Geometry* University of Toronto Press, Toronto (published 1956)
[6] Ball R S (1900) *A Treatise on the Theory of Screws* Cambridge University Press, Cambridge
[7] Hunt K H (1978) *Kinematic Geometry of Mechanisms* Oxford University Press, Oxford
[8] Sugimoto K, Duffy J and Hunt K H (1982) Applications of linear algebra to screw systems. *Mech. Mach. Theory*, **17**(2)
[9] Lipkin H and Duffy J *Analysis of Industrial Robots Via the Theory of Screws* Proc. 12th Int. Sym. Indus. Robots, Paris, 1982
[10] Mason M T (1981) Compliance and force control for computer controlled manipulators. *IEEE Trans. Systems, Man and Cybernetics*, **SMC-11** (6), June
[11] Plücker J (1866) Fundamental views regarding mechanics. *Philos. Trans. R. Soc. Lond.*
[12] Cayley A (1859) A sixth memoir upon quantics. In *Phil. Trans. R. Soc. Lond.*
[13] Clifford W K (1873) Preliminary sketch of biquaternions. *Mathematical Papers* Chelsea Publishing Co., New York (published 1968)
[14] Yaglom I M (1968) *Complex Numbers in Geometry* Academic Press, New York

Trajectory Planning for Redundant Manipulators in the Presence of Obstacles

M Kirćanski and M Vukobratović

Institute 'Mihailo Pupin', 11000 Beograd, Yugoslavia

Summary: The class of problems involving motion synthesis for redundant manipulators in the environment with obstacles will be discussed. An algorithm for calculating collision-free trajectory in the space of joint co-ordinates, given an end-effector trajectory in the space of external co-ordinates, is proposed. The algorithm is based on the use of performance indices in the space of joint co-ordinates and external co-ordinates which prevent any of the manipulator links from entering a forbidden zone around the obstacle. The algorithm is completely automatized, i.e. provides motion synthesis for arbitrary structures of redundant manipulators, different trajectories and obstacles. The algorithm is illustrated by an example of a five-degree-of-freedom manipulator moving along a trajectory specified by three Cartesian co-ordinates.

Introduction

The solution to the class of problems that involve manipulator motion synthesis in the environment with obstacles is essential to the automatic planning of manipulator transfer movements. This includes suboptimal or optimal trajectory synthesis with respect to some performance index, obstacle modelling, handling sensor information concerning obstacles, searching for the algorithms providing obstacle avoidance, etc. In this paper we shall treat the latter problem.

Trajectory planning in the environment in the presence of obstacles has already been considered in the literature.[1-3] The conditions to be satisfied by the increment of joint co-ordinates, so that the obstacle is avoided, have been derived.[1] An attempt to solve this problem, by introducing potential functions around obstacles, has been proposed.[2] However, because of the complexity of specifying such functions which produce forces that act on the gripper, this method is of modest practical importance. The most complete and effective method for optimizing manipulator configuration in the presence of obstacles by using linear programming has been proposed.[3]

In the present paper, obstacle avoidance is achieved by employing modified performance criteria for inverse kinematic problem solution for redundant manipulators. The utility of two performance indices is discussed. The first one is formed in the space of joint co-ordinates and the second in the space of external co-ordinates. Motion synthesis according to these criteria ensures that the critical point on the manipulator does not reach the obstacle during manipulation task execution.

Problem statement

Let us consider an arbitrary manipulator in the form of an open kinematic chain with n degreees of freedom (DOF). The corresponding joint co-ordinates vector $q = [q_1 \cdots q_n]^T$ belongs to the configuration space $Q = \{q : q_i \leq q \leq \bar{q}_i, i = 1,\ldots,n\}$, where $q_i, \bar{q}_i$ denote the minimal and maximal values of the ith joint co-ordinate, defined by constructional constraints of the mechanism. Each point in the manipulator work space may be specified by a vector $x = [x\ y\ z]^T \epsilon R^3$, where x, y, z are Cartesian co-ordinates with respect to a reference co-ordinate from $0xyz$.

Let us designate by M the set of the points in the work space which are occupied by the manipulator itself. This set is uniquely defined by the manipulator configuration, i.e. by the vector of joint co-ordinates q.

Let us assume that in the manipulator environment there exists an immobile convex body representing an obstacle. The set of the points in the work space occupied by the obstacle will be denoted by C. We shall assume that the manipulation task is given and specified by a time schedule $x_e(t)$, $t \epsilon [0, T]$ of the external co-ordinates vector in the task execution time T.

We shall consider a general case, when $x_e = [x_{e1} \ldots x_{em}]^T \epsilon X_e R^m$, $m < n$. The first three components of the external co-ordinates vector are usually adopted to be Cartesian co-ordinates of the end-effector, while the remaining $(m - 3)$ components specify, completely or partially, the gripper orientation. Since the number of degrees of freedom n is greater than the number of external co-ordinates m, the time history of the joint co-ordinates $q(t)$ which corresponds to the required spatial track $x_e(t)$ is not uniquely defined.

The problem is to determine such a trajectory $q(t)$ in the configuration space that motion along the given trajectory $x_e(t)$ can be provided and collisions avoided. The manipulator will avoid a convex obstacle C, if the following condition is satisfied

$$d(M,C) \geq d_{\min} \qquad (1)$$

where

$$d(M,C) = \min_{x \epsilon M} d(x,C) \qquad (2)$$

represents the minimal distance between the manipulator and the obstacle, and $d_{\min}$ is a given minimal value of this distance.

Here

$$d(x,C) = \min_{y \epsilon C} \|x - y\| \qquad (3)$$

denotes the distance between the point x and the obstacle C. $\|x\|$ is a given norm in the space R^n (in this paper the Euclidean norm is adopted).

The above-mentioned problem involves the solution of the inverse kinematic problem. Since we are concerned with redundant manipulators which move in the environment filled with obstacles, the solution of this problem is ambiguous. To obtain a unique solution an additional condition should be introduced, such as minimization of a performance index, e.g. energy or the criterion of minimal norm of the joint velocities vector. Two algorithms which yield the solution of the above-mentioned task are proposed in this paper.

Configuration space performance index

The position and orientation of manipulator gripper are uniquely defined by the manipulator configuration, i.e. by the joint co-ordinates vector q. This relation is described by the kinematic model $x_e(t) = f_e[q(t)]$, where $f_e: R^n \to R^m$ is a continuous differentiable vector function. To solve the inverse kinematic problem, in the scope of the above-mentioned task, we shall consider the linearized kinematic model

$$\dot{x}_e = J(q)\dot{q} \qquad (4)$$

where $J = \partial f_e/\partial q \in R^{m \times n}$ is the Jacobian matrix and $\dot{x}_e$ and $\dot{q}$ are vectors of external and joint co-ordinates velocities. Given a vector $\dot{x}_e$, there exists an unlimited number of solutions to equation (4) if the Jacobian matrix is a full-rank matrix, or if rank $J = \text{rank}[J \vdots \dot{x}_e] < m$. If rank $J \neq \text{rank}[J \vdots \dot{x}_e]$ holds, there exists no solution to system (4).

From the unlimited set of solutions to system (4), one should select those which satisfy condition (1) and, if possible, minimize the performance index. When the manipulator is put far away from the obstacle, i.e. when $d(M,C) \geq d_{\max}$ holds, where $d_{\max}$ is a given positive constant ($d_{\max} > d_{\min} > 0$), the solution to the inverse kinematic problem can be obtained in a classical manner, by minimizing the quadratic criterion

$$\Omega(\dot{q}) = \tfrac{1}{2}\dot{q}^T M \dot{q} \qquad (5)$$

the matrix $M \in R^{n \times n}$ is usually set to be a unit matrix, or a matrix of kinetic energy.[4] Dynamic performance indices, involving the total energy consumption of actuators, can also be introduced.[5] The optimal solution of system (5) which minimizes (6) is given by

$$\dot{q} = G\dot{x}_e, \quad G = M^{-1}J^T(JM^{-1}J^T)^{-1} \qquad (6)$$

where G is the generalized inverse matrix.

Let us now consider the case when some manipulator link approaches the obstacle. Let us denote by x_c the point on the manipulator which belongs to the lth link and which is the closest one to the obstacle.

In the zone where

$$d_{\max} > d(x_c, C) > d_{\min} \qquad (7)$$

we shall modify the matrix M of performance index (5), so that

$$M(q) = \text{diag}(m_i), \qquad i = 1, \ldots, n \qquad (8)$$

$$m_i = \begin{cases} \dfrac{d_{\max} - d_{\min}}{d(x_c, C) - d_{\min}}, & i = 1, \ldots, l \\ 1 & i = l+1, \ldots, n \end{cases} \qquad (9)$$

This performance index 'penalizes' more the motion of those DOF which influence the motion of the point x_c on the lth link. Thus the first l DOF are braked while preventing the point x_c from approaching the obstacle. If the remaining $(n - l)$ DOF are not sufficient enough to ensure the execution of the imposed task, a certain modification of the task is required. The use of index (5), (8), (9), is rather attractive because of its inherent simplicity.

Performance index in the space of external co-ordinates

In this section, a modification of criterion (5) is proposed, so that actually the minimization of the velocity of the point x_c is performed. We shall consider

$$\Omega(\dot{q}) = \tfrac{1}{2}\dot{q}^T M \dot{q} = \tfrac{1}{2}[\dot{q}^{LT} \dot{q}^{UT}] \begin{bmatrix} M^L & 0_{1,n-1} \\ \hline 0_{n-1,1} & 1_{n-1} \end{bmatrix} \begin{bmatrix} \dot{q}^L \\ \dot{q}^U \end{bmatrix} \qquad (10)$$

where $\dot{q}^L = [\dot{q}_1 \ldots \dot{q}_l]^T$, $\dot{q}^U = [\dot{q}_{l+1} \ldots \dot{q}_n]^T$, l is the number of the link closest to the obstacle, 1_{n-1} a unit matrix of the order $(n-l) \times (n-l)$, $M^L \epsilon R^{l \times l}$ a submatrix of the performance criterion.

Index (10) can be presented as

$$\Omega(\dot{q}) = \Omega_1(\dot{q}^L) + \Omega_2(\dot{q}^U) \qquad (11)$$

$$\Omega_1(\dot{q}^L) = \tfrac{1}{2}\dot{q}^{LT} M^L \dot{q}^L, \quad \Omega_2(\dot{q}^U) = \tfrac{1}{2}\dot{q}^{UT} 1_{n-l} \dot{q}^U \qquad (12)$$

If it is to prevent the motion of the critical point x_c, the first part of the criterion becomes

$$\Omega_1(\dot{q}^L) = \tfrac{1}{2}\dot{x}_c^T M_c \dot{x}_c \qquad (13)$$

where $\dot{x}_c = [\dot{x}\ \dot{y}\ \dot{z}]^T \epsilon R^3$, $M_c \epsilon R^{3 \times 3}$ is the matrix of the performance index in the space of external co-ordinates.

Form (13) can be transformed into form (12) if the relation $\dot{x}_c = J_c \dot{q}^L$ is introduced into (13), where J_c is the Jacobian for the point x_c. Then the matrix M^L becomes

$$M^L = J_c^T M_c J_c \qquad (14)$$

The matrix M_c can be selected in different ways. Here, we suggest the following form

$$M_c = \mathrm{diag}(m_{cj}) \qquad (15)$$

$$m_{cj} = \begin{cases} \dfrac{d_{max} - d_{min}}{d_j - d_{min}}, & d_{min} < d_j < d_{max} \\ 1, & d_j > d_{max} \end{cases}, \quad j = 1, 2, 3$$

where d_j, $j = 1, 2, 3$ denote components of the distance vector between the point x_c and the point on the obstacle which is the nearest one to the manipulator. Accordingly, the motion of the first l DOF is optimized so as to ensure that the point x_c does not approach the obstacle, especially in the direction of the co-ordinate (x, y or z) which is closest to the value d_{min}. The motion of the remaining $(n-l)$ DOF is governed by the standard criterion of the minimal norm of the joint velocities vector.

However, it may also happen that if the obstacle is close to some of the final links in the kinematic chain, the required task cannot be realized by stopping the critical point x_c, although this would eventually be possible if the point x_c moved. Hence, a generalization of the performance index $\Omega_1(\dot{q}^L)$ (13) is proposed

$$\Omega_1(\dot{q}^L) = \tfrac{1}{2}(\dot{x}_c - v)^T M_c(\dot{x}_c - v) \tag{16}$$

where $v \in R^3$ is a given velocity vector of the point x_c, chosen in such a way that the point moves away from the obstacle.

However, index (16) cannot be reduced to form (12), but to the form

$$\Omega_1(\dot{q}^L) = \tfrac{1}{2}\dot{q}^{LT} M^L \dot{q}^L + M_1^{LT} \dot{q}^L \tag{17}$$

$$M_1^L = -(v^T M_c J_c)^T \tag{18}$$

and M^L is still given by (14). The constant term $\tfrac{1}{2} v^T M_c v$ from the index (16) is not taken into account as it has no influence on the optimal solution. The total performance index $\Omega(q)$ now becomes

$$\Omega(q) = \tfrac{1}{2}\dot{q}^T M \dot{q} + M_1^T \dot{q} \tag{19}$$

where the matrix M is given by (10), and $M_1 = [M_1^{LT} \mid 0 \cdots 0]^T \in R^n$. The solution to system (4), which is optimal with respect to (19), is now given by

$$\dot{q} = G\dot{x}_e + (GJ - 1_n)M^{-1}M_1 \tag{20}$$

where G is given by (6). Evidently, a more complex criterion requires a greater computational complexity. The problem of how to select the velocity v so as to move the manipulator away from the obstacle, without preventing task execution, is very complex and will not be considered here. In case it is not possible to determine a collision-free motion, a modification of the desired end-effector trajectory is necessary.

At the end, it should be noted that we are actually concerned with suboptimal trajectory synthesis, as the synthesis is performed in parts, on integration intervals Δt.

Numerical examples

The algorithm presented in **Configuration space performance index** section is illustrated by an example of a trajectory for a manipulator with 5 rotational DOF (Figure 1). The first DOF corresponds to a rotation about a vertical axis, while the remaining ones have horizontal joint axes.

The manipulation task to be performed is a straight-line motion $x_e(t)$ of the manipulator tip between the initial and final points x_e^O and x_e^F described by three Cartesian co-ordinates, $x_e^O = [0.91 - 0.57]^T[m]$, $x_e^F = [0.05 - 0.5]^T[m]$.

The initial configuration of the manipulator is presented by dotted lines in Figures 1 and 2. If the motion synthesis in the absence of obstacles is performed by applying the minimum norm of velocity vector, one obtains the manipulator configuration in the final point presented by broken lines in these figures. On the contrary, if the synthesis is performed while taking into account the presence of obstacles in Figures 1 and 2 by using the algorithm presented in the above-

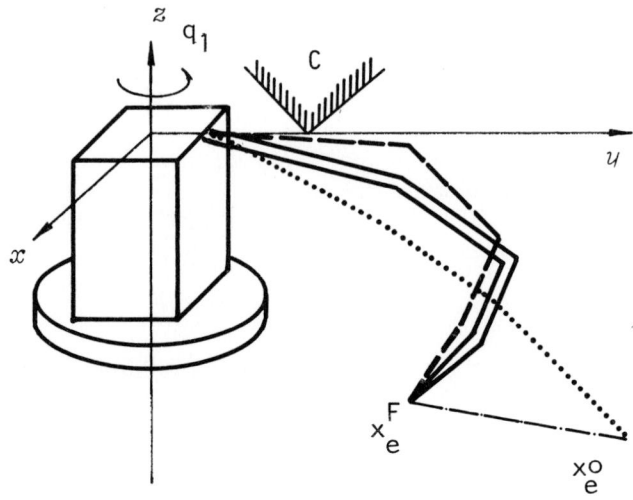

Figure 1 Redundant manipulator motion

mentioned section, the motion of the links is modified, so that the second and the third link stay away from the obstacles.

The obtained configurations in the final point are presented by solid lines in these figures. It is evident that in these cases it was feasible to synthesize a collision-free motion along the prescribed tip trajectory, i.e. that the imposed conditions were satisfied. A dynamic analysis, however, shows that the total energy consumption of the actuators is increased due to the increased accelerations of some links. Therefore, the motion synthesis should also include a test as to whether the required task is realizable in the given time interval, i.e. whether the constraints on maximal actuator input signals are satisfied. If the obstacle is sufficiently near the final link so that the manipulation task cannot be realized, one should modify the manipulator task, taking the deviation from the desired trajectory as the criterion and providing a collision-free motion. This complex problem will be the subject of further investigation.

References

[1] Kobrinski A A and Kobrinski A E (1975) Manipulation system trajectory synthesis in the environment with obstacles. *Comm. Acad. Sci. USSR*, **T224**(6)
[2] Khatib O and Le Maitre J F *Dynamic Control of Manipulators Operating in a Complex Environment.* Proc. 3rd Int. CISM-IFToMM Symp., Udine, September 1978, pp 267–282
[3] Generozov V L *Manipulator Trajectory Planning in the Environment with Obstacles.* Proc. 1st Soviet-Yugoslav Symp. on Ind. Robotics, Moscow, February 1983
[4] Renaud M (1975) Contribution a l'etude de la modélisation et de la commande des systemes mécaniques articulés. PhD Thesis, Toulouse
[5] Vukobratović M and Kirćanski M (1984) A dynamic approach to nominal trajectory synthesis for redundant manipulators. *IEEE Trans. Systems, Man and Cybernetics*, January–February

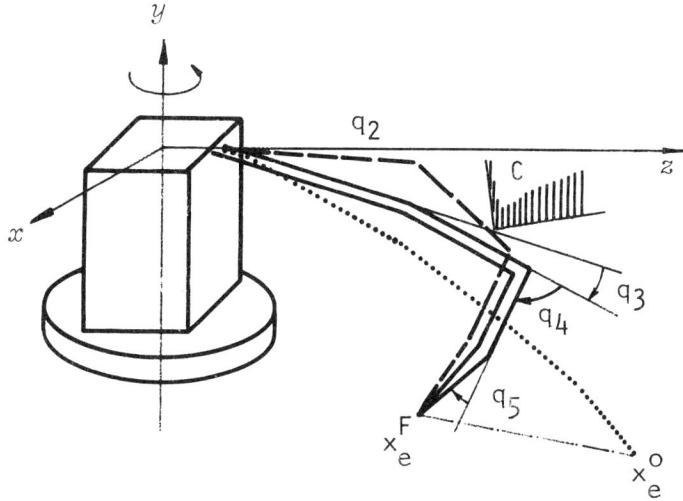

Figure 2 Redundant manipulator motion

Implementation of Highly Efficient Analytical Robot Models on Microcomputers

M Vukobratović and N Kirćanski

Institute 'Mihailo Pupin', 11000 Beograd, Yugoslavia

Summary: The paper considers a program package for non-linear, linearized and sensitivity model generation for manipulation robots. An input/output communication module, dynamic equations' module, time optimization module and the module for microcomputer language real-time model generation are considered. The program package is illustrated by using the example of an arthropoidal robot.

Introduction

The control of complex, multivariable, non-linear mechanical systems, and the implementation of different control schemes, require the use of computers differing in complexity, from large systems employed in control synthesis and simulation to microcomputers used at the implementation level. One of the central programs, essential to industrial robots control synthesis, is real-time dynamic model generation. This assumes the use of a single microcomputer or several microcomputers in a multiprocessing operation.

The existing methods for robot modelling (e.g. methods based on Newton–Euler equations, Lagrange formulations, etc.[1-3]) are, however, burdened by a large number of numerical operations and cannot be implemented in real time. The time required for model calculation is several 10 times longer than the maximal time acceptable for on-line application. This is mostly due to the: mathematical model complexity; fact that the methods are usually directly mapped into high-level language programs; model generality producing inherent numerical redundancy; fact that the methods are recursive which hinders their implementation by parallel processing.

In the present paper a program system is presented that eliminates these drawbacks to a great extent. Instead of a direct numeric model calculation made according to some classical methods, a concept of symbolic model generation is adopted. It can be shown[4,5] that the compact analytical model obtained employs up to two orders of magnitude fewer numerical operations (multiplications and additions) than the previously developed methods.

In the second program module the linearized symbolic model[6], and/or sensitivity model are formed. The linearized dynamic models are important for the application of linear control theory,[7] and the sensitivity models for the examining control robustness and in the adaptive control synthesis.

In the third program module, the optimization of the obtained symbolic forms intended to minimize the number of numerical operations, is performed. The result is an 'optimal graph' that defines the sequence of operations in dynamic model calculation. Afterwards, the corresponding program code in a law-level language (e.g. assembler) or a high-level language (e.g. ALGOL, FORTRAN, etc.) is automatically generated.

The program obtained is then transferred into a compiled microcomputer development system, which is in the end transferred into the memory of the executive microcomputer. An example illustrating the generation of the real-time program code, which corresponds to INTEL 8086 processor with the arithmetic coprocessor and LSI-11, is presented in the paper.

Basic modules of the program package

Input—output module

Within the input—output module the communication with the user is realized by an interactive communication language. The following primary parameters should be imposed by the user: number of the degrees of freedom of the mechanism; geometrical parameters; dynamic parameters; parameters and position/orientation of a payload.

The output module provides: error messages for incorrectly supplied parameters; a graphical representation of the robot kinematic chain; the results of all modelling and optimization phases; model output file, i.e. the source program which contains model equations of the mechanical manipulator.

The interactive part of the input—output module supplies: a graphical representation of any desired analytical expression; model simplification with graphical evaluation; model-type selection (non-linear dynamic model, linearized model or sensitivity model); choice of programming language of model output file.

Module for the development of manipulators mathematical models in numerical—symbolic forms

This module represents the essential part of the program system. The purpose of this module is to perform the generation of the analytical model of any single arm open-chain mechanism. The basic principles used in module design are explained in the text to follow.

Mathematical model

Mechanical systems that can be modelled by open kinematic chains are usually described by a series of non-linear dynamic equations. The equations can be presented in matrix form

$$P = H(q,\theta)\ddot{q} + \dot{q}^T C(q,\theta)\dot{q} + g(q,\theta) \tag{1}$$

where $P \epsilon R^n$ represents the vector of driving torques or forces in sliding joints, $q = q(t)$:

$R \rightarrow R^n$ is the vector of joint co-ordinates, $H(q,\theta)$:
$R^n \chi \theta \rightarrow R^{n \times n}$ is the inertial matrix of the system, $C(q,\theta)$:
$R^n \times \theta \rightarrow R^{n \times n \times n}$ is the matrix involving the centrifugal and Coriolis effects, $g(q,\theta)$:
$R^n \times \theta \rightarrow R^n$ is the vector which takes into account gravitational forces, θ is the parameter vector and n is the number of degrees of freedom of the manipulator.

Starting from any of the well-known methods for manipulator models building, e.g. Lagrangian or Newton–Euler's methods,[1-3] one can derive the closed-form terms of the matrices in (1).[5,6] As the derivation may be rather tedious and subject to error, we shall present only the final results:

$$H_{ik} = \sum_{j=\max(i,k)}^{n} [m_j \underline{\rho}_{ji} \cdot \underline{\rho}_{jk} + \sum_{\mu=1}^{3} \eta^i_{j\mu} \eta^k_{j\mu} J_{j\mu} \bar{\xi}_i \bar{\xi}_k] \quad (2)$$

$$C^i_{kl} = \sum_{j=\max(i,k)}^{n} \{m_j \underline{\rho}_{ji} \cdot (\underline{e}_l \times \underline{\rho}_{jk})$$
$$(k \geqslant l)$$

$$+ \frac{1}{2} \sum_{\mu=1}^{3} [\eta^i_{j\mu} \epsilon_{lk} + \eta^k_{j\mu} \epsilon_{il} + \eta^l_{j\mu} \epsilon_{ik}] \cdot q_{j\mu} J_{j\mu} \bar{\xi}_k \} \bar{\xi}_l \quad (3)$$

$$g_i = - \sum_{j=i}^{n} m_j \underline{\rho}_{ji} \cdot \underline{G} \quad (4)$$

where $\underline{e}_i$ is the unit vector of the ith joint axis;
$\underline{\rho}_{ij} = (\underline{e}_i \times \underline{r}_{ij}) \bar{\xi}_j + \underline{e}_j \xi_j$ where $\underline{r}_{ij}$ is the centre of mass vector for the ith link with respect to the jth joint centre, $\xi_j = 0$ if b the jth joint is rotational and $\xi_j = 1$ if it is n sliding one, $\bar{\xi}_j = 1 - \xi_j$;
$\eta^i_{j\mu} = \underline{e}_i \cdot q_{j\mu}$ with $q_{j\mu}$ being the unit vector of the μth axis of the co-ordinate frame attached to ith link; $\epsilon_{ij} = \underline{e}_i \times e_j$;
m_i is the mass of the ith link; J_{i1}, J_{i2} and J_{i3} are the moments of inertia about the principal axes of the ith link; $\underline{G}$ is the gravity acceleration vector.

Numerical–symbolic approach to system modelling
Determination of the functional dependence of any variable (e.g. $\underline{e}_i$, r_{ij}, etc.) in (2)–(4) on joint co-ordinates, for a given parameter vector θ, impose a non-numerical approach to system modelling. It means that the variables should be treated as functions of joint co-ordinates and the parameters as numerical constants. It has been shown[3] that in linkage mechanical systems any variable $a^l_j \in R$, $j \in N = \{1, \ldots, n\}$ (l is usually 1 for a scalar and 3 for a vector variable) can be presented in the form

$$a_j = \sum_k a_{jk} (\cos q_1)^{c_1} \cdots (\cos q_n)^{c_n} (\sin q_1)^{s_1} \cdots (\sin q_n)^{s_n} q_1^{k_1} \cdots q_n^{k_n} \quad (5)$$

where q_i, $i \in N$ is the ith component of the co-ordinate vector q, the exponents $c_i, s_i, k_i \in \{0, 1, 2\}$ depend on k, i.e. $c_i = c_i(k)$, $s_i = s_i(k)$, $k_i = k_i(k)$; $a_{jk} \in R^1$, $k \in K$ where K is the set of indices $\{1, \ldots, k_m\}$ with k_m being related to the observed variable a_j.

Obviously, the system variable a_j can be presented by a vector $A_j = [a_{j1} \cdots a_{jk_m}]^T \in R^{k_m \times 1}$ and the matrix of exponents

$$E_j = \begin{bmatrix} c_1(1) & \cdots & c_n(1) & s_1(1) & \cdots & s_n(1) & k_1(1) & \cdots & k_n(1) \\ \vdots & & \vdots & \vdots & & \vdots & \vdots & & \vdots \\ c_1(k_m) & \cdots & c_n(k_m) & s_1(k_m) & \cdots & s_n(k_m) & k_1(k_m) & \cdots & k_n(k_m) \end{bmatrix} \quad (6)$$

with the dimension $k_m \times 3n$.

In such a way the variable a_j can be described by the ordered set (A_j, E_j). This set will be denoted symbolically by A and called 'a structural matrix' of a_j.

On the other hand, the sum (5) represented by the structural matrix A can be regarded as a polynomial.

$$a_j = \sum_k a_{jk} x_1^{k_1} \cdots x_{3n}^{k_{3n}} \qquad (7)$$

where $x_i = \cos q_i$, $x_{n+i} = \sin q_i$, $x_{2n+i} = q_i$, $i \in N$.

The variables $x_j = x_j(t): R \to R$ are dependent due to the trigonometric identities $x_i^2 + x_{n+i}^2 = 1$. The polynomial (7) is very suitable for considering the algebraic relations that appear in the modelling of linkage mechanical systems.

If we look at these expressions which define the terms of model matrices (2)–(4), we can see that the following algebraic computations should be developed for structural matrices: dot product $A \cdot B$, cross-product $A \times B$, addition $A + B$ and multiplication by a polynomial argument $x_i A$.

While the polynomials (7) are used these operations can be derived easily and implemented on a digital computer. For example, the cross-product $\underline{a}_j \times \underline{b}_j$ is of the form

$$A_j \times B_j = \sum_K \sum_M (\underline{a}_{jk} \underline{b}_{jm}) x_1^{k_1 + m_1} \cdots x_{3n}^{k_{3n} + m_{3n}} \qquad (8)$$

or

$$(A_j, E_{A_j}) \times (B_j, E_{B_j}) = (A_j \times B_j, E_{A_j} + E_{B_j}) \qquad (9)$$

The form (8) is potentially redundant because of the dependence of variables x_i and x_{n+i}, $i \in N$. By taking into account the relations $x_i^2 + x_{n+i}^2 = 1$, the form (7) may be simplified. The procedure for simplification can be systematically performed by a computer program. Such a program is developed and applied after any algebraic operation. Following the relations of the closed-form model (4)–(6), one can calculate the structural matrices for all the terms of the dynamic model matrices $H(q, \theta)$, $C(q, \theta)$ and $g(q, \theta)$ for a given set of parameters Θ. The obtained structural matrices are obviously constant ones for a given manipulator.

The calculation of numerical values for the elements of model matrices is now quite simple due to the equivalence of the structural matrices and the corresponding polynomials (7). Nevertheless, the problem becomes more serious when we state the question of a minimal number of floating-point multiplications and additions/subtractions required for calculating polynomials (7). This leads to the problem of optimal factorization of multivariable polynomials.

Program module for computing optimization and model output file generation

The optimization of calculations of polynomials can be reduced to the analysis of distributions of exponents in corresponding structural matrices. In any optimization step the greatest exponent present in the maximal number of rows in the exponent matrix should be determined. Thereafter, the factorization of polynomials and memorization of sequences of operations (floating-point multiplications and additions subtractions) should be performed. These sequences can be presented by graphs in which branches correspond to additions and nodes to multiplications. By using the obtained graphs this program module generates the

Implementation of Analytical Robot Models 69

sets of instructions which realize, in a desired program language, the calculation of model equations for the desired manipulator. Such output files are intended for real-time applications. Thus they are usually referred to as 'real-time model output files'.

Numerical example

Consider the three-degree-of-freedom arthropoidal mechanical manipulator shown in Figure 1. The parameters of the manipulator are given by numerical values in

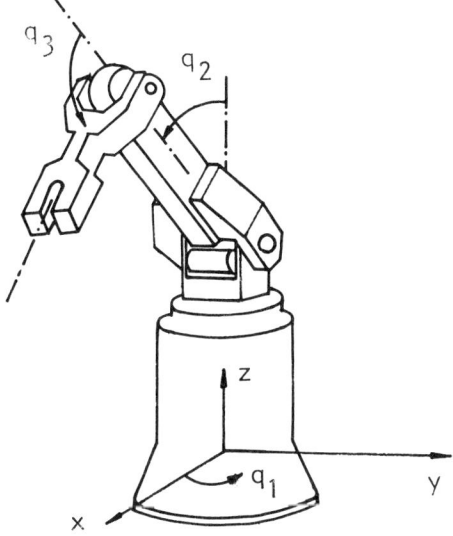

Figure 1 Arthropoidal robot (local frames coincide with xyz for $q_1 = q_2 = q_3 = 0$)

Table 1. The output of the second module of the program system represents the structural matrices of the dynamic model. For example, for $(H_{11}, E_{H_{11}})$ we obtain

$$H_{11} = \begin{bmatrix} 4.57 \\ 112.98 \\ 26.80 \\ 26.80 \\ 2.68 \\ 5.36 \\ 2.68 \end{bmatrix} \quad E_{H_{11}} = \begin{bmatrix} 0\ 0\ 0 & 0\ 0\ 0 & 0\ 0\ 0 \\ 0\ 0\ 0 & 0\ 2\ 0 & 0\ 0\ 0 \\ 0\ 0\ 1 & 0\ 2\ 0 & 0\ 0\ 0 \\ 0\ 1\ 0 & 0\ 1\ 1 & 0\ 0\ 0 \\ 0\ 0\ 2 & 0\ 2\ 0 & 0\ 0\ 0 \\ 0\ 1\ 1 & 0\ 1\ 1 & 0\ 0\ 0 \\ 0\ 2\ 0 & 0\ 0\ 2 & 0\ 0\ 0 \end{bmatrix}$$

The output of the third program module represents the optimal sequence of calculations. The corresponding real-time output model file is obtained in FORTRAN as

P3 = X2*0.26800E+01
P2 = X3*0.53600E+01
P1 = X3*0.26800E+01
Q3 = X2*P3
Q2 = X2*(P2+0.26800E+02)
Q1 = X3*(P1+0.26800E+02)
P3 = X6*Q3
P2 = X6*Q2
P1 = X5*(Q1+0.11298E+03)
Q2 = X6*P3
H(1,1) = Q1+Q2+0.45700E+01

where $X2 = x_2 = \cos q_2$, $X3 = x_3 = \cos q_3$, $X5 = x_5 = \sin q_2$, $X6 = x_6 = \sin q_3$. Note that the program presented here is only a small part of the complete output file, which contains the calculations for all terms of dynamic model matrices (1)–(4).

Table 1 Masses (kg) and inertias (kgm^2) of robot links

i	m_i	J_{i1}	J_{i2}	J_{i3}
1	–	–	–	4.57
2	152	–	21.74	–
3	67	–	1.22	–

The number of floating-point multiplications n_{mul} and additions/subtractions n_{add} can be obtained by simple enumeration in the output file. These data are given in Table 2, as well as the corresponding computing times necessary for dynamic model matrices calculation on a minicomputer and two 16-bit microcomputers. We can see that the results obtained are very attractive for real-time applications.

Table 2 Number of operations and computing times for arthropoidal robot (L, cosines/sines calculated by using system libraries; C, cosines/sines •calculated from tables by using linear interpolations)

cos/sin	n_{mul}	n_{add}		t (ms)		
				PDP 11/70	PDP 11/03	INTEL 86/87
4	49	23	L	1.1	54	6.3
			C	0.5	11	4.5

References

[1] Uicker J J (1967) Dynamic force analysis of spatial linkages. *Trans. ASME, J. Appl. Mech.*, June, 418–424
[2] Hollerbach J M (1980) A recursive formulation of Lagrangian manipulator dynamics. *IEEE Trans. Systems, Man and Cybernetics* **10**(11), 730–736
[3] Vukobratović M and Potkonjak V (1982) *Dynamics of Manipulation Robots*. Springer-Verlag, Heidelberg

[4] Vukobratović M and Kirćanski N *A Method for Computer-aided Construction of Analytical Models of Robotic Manipulators*. 1st IEEE Conf. on Robotics, Atlanta, 1984
[5] Vukobratović M and Kirćanski N (1984) Computer assisted generation of robot dynamics models in analytical form. *Acta Applicandae Mathematica, Int. J. Applying Mathematics Mathematical Applications*, 2(2)
[6] Vukobratović M and Kirćanski N (1981) Computer-oriented method for linearization of dynamic models of active spatial mechanisms. *J. Mech. Mach. Theory*, 16(2)
[7] Vukobratović M and Kirćanski N (1983) Decoupled control of robots via asymptotic regulators. *IEEE Trans. Automatic Control*, **AC-28** (10), October

Computer-aided Generation of Multibody-system Equations

R Schwertassek and R E Roberson

Deutsche Forschungs- und Versuchsanstalt für Luft- und Raumfahrt, Oberpfaffenhofen, Obb, Federal Republic of Germany, and University of California San Diego, La Jolla, California, USA

Summary: The structure of a general-purpose computer code for the generation and integration of the equations of motion of multibody systems is given. The code is based on the state space equations for arbitrary, i.e. large motions of systems with tree configuration and with closed loops given previously. The computer program solves the inverse problem of robot dynamics. The usage of the equations of motion for the solution of the direct problem of robot dynamics is discussed as well.

Introduction

One of the main fields of application of multibody-system dynamics appears when investigating manipulators and robots.[1] In this field of application one has two main problems called the *direct* and the *inverse problem* as described (chapter 1.1)[1]. Moreover, the topology of the multibody model of a robot may change from tree configuration to a closed-loop system during the motion. Because of this variable structure of the models and because of the complexity of the system equations one can study the system dynamics efficiently only, if the equations of motion are separated and evaluated by digital computers. As demonstrated[1] there exists a variety of automatic methods for the generation and solution of the system equations. The development of one of these approaches based on the work of Roberson and Wittenburg has been described.[2] The essential features of a computer code, called MULTIBODY, for the solution of the inverse problem for systems with tree configuration have been published.[3,4] The state space equations for systems with closed loops in a computer-oriented form have also been given.[2] In the present paper the structure of a general-purpose computer code for the simulation of the large motions of multibody systems based on the equations developed[2] will be discussed. In addition we demonstrate how the equations given[2] may be used to treat the direct problem of robot dynamics. In many applications one needs only the linearized equations of motion. These have been derived (R Schwertassek and R E Roberson, unpublished work) from the non-linear equations[2] by matrix linearization techniques.[5]

Structure of a general-purpose multibody program

The kinematical and dynamical equations of motion of a purely mechanical multibody system have the form [2.39] (numbers in brackets and separated by a point refer to the equations in ref [2]) with the position- and velocity-variables y_I and

y_{II} and with the right-hand sides Y_I and Y_{II} developed.[2] As robots are active mechanisms one must adjoin the equations for the controller dynamics

$$\dot{y}_{III} = Y_{III}(y_I, y_{II}, y_{III}, t) \tag{1}$$

where the y_{III} are the control state variables. Equation (1) is coupled with equation [2.39] as the generalized applied interaction forces λ^s (see equation [2.60]) in the joints $s\epsilon\Sigma$ of the system depend not only on the relative motion across the joint s but also on the control variables y_{III} in the case of active mechanisms. The λ^s are submatrices of the partitioned matrices λ_A and λ_C (equations [2.64] and [3.14a]) appearing on the right-hand sides Y_{II} of the dynamical equations as given by equations [2.66] and [3.34].

The computer code to be discussed here generates the right-hand sides Y_I and Y_{II}, given the data representing the mechanical properties of the system. Provision is made in the code for an easy introduction of the right-hand sides Y_{III} resulting from the control laws used in a specific manipulator to be simulated. As shown (section 4)[2], one can divide the input data representing the mechanical properties of a multibody system into five groups. These are as follows:

Parameters of the system topology. They are the functions $f = ab(s)$ and $t = an(s)$ (defined in ref [2], section 2, step 2).

Parameters of the motion of the reference frame. These are ϵ (defined in ref [2], section 2, step 1) and functions of the time describing the motions of $0°$ and $\underline{e}°$.

Parameters associated with the individual bodies of the system. These are the: co-ordinates c^{is}, $i\epsilon Y$, $s\epsilon\Sigma$ of the attachment point vectors; masses m^i, inertia matrices I^i and co-ordinates h^i of internal angular momentum vectors; external actions L^i, F^i on the bodies $i\epsilon Y$. The m^i have been assumed to be constant[2] but the I^i, h^i and c^{is} may be variable. The L^i and F^i are variable as well of course.

Parameters of the interconnections between the bodies. These are the: mode vectors $\varphi_i^s, i = 1, 2, \ldots nf^s$ and $\bar{\varphi}_j^s, j = 1, 2, \ldots nc^s$ representing the free and the constrained modes of motion across the interconnections; kinematical excitations $\kappa_k^s(t)$, $k = 1, 2, \ldots nck^s$; relations $B^s = B^s(p^s, t)$ and $z^s = z^s(p^s, t)$ representing the position variables B^s and z^s in terms of a minimum set of position variables p^s and the time t; functions $\lambda^s = \lambda^s(p^s, g^s, y_{III})$ for the generalized applied forces across the interconnections. The mode vectors φ^s and $\bar{\varphi}^s$ may be constant or they may depend on the state.

Initial values of the state variables y_I, y_{II} and y_{III} at an initial time t_0.

The structure of a program generating and integrating the equations of motion of the multibody system, i.e. the matrices Y_I, Y_{II} and Y_{III}, is represented in Figure 1.

There are two preprocessors SGRAPH and PARAMS and a simulation program SIMULA. The preprocessors transform the input data from a form in which they may be specified conveniently by a user into forms required for an efficient simulation. In particular, SGRAPH accepts as input data the functions $ab(s)$ and $an(s)$ and generates index lists required for a fast calculation of products with the graph-associated matrices S, T and U.

The preprocessor PARAMS accepts as input data all the constant parameters of the groups II–IV and transforms them into representations required in the

Generation of Multibody-system Equations 75

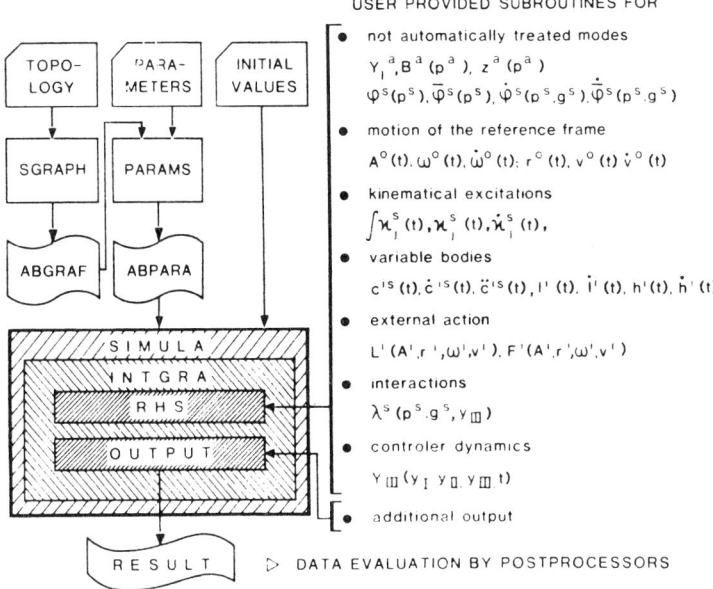

Figure 1 Structure of a general-purpose multibody program

simulation program SIMULA; the latter program is the main part of the entire package. Its input data are the outputs of SGRAPH and PARAMS and the initial values. It calls one of the various routines for numerical integration denoted in the diagram by the general name INTGRA.

The routine INTGRA, in turn, calls a subroutine RHS for the generation of the right-hand sides of the equations of motion for a given time and a given state. The routine RHS is the heart of the simulation program and will be discussed shortly.

A second subroutine of INTGRA is OUTPUT, which stores the time history of the state variables into the file RESULT. The subroutine OUTPUT is built in such a way that a user can introduce easily statements for storing additional quantities he needs for the evaluation of the motions of his specific system. The data available in RESULT may be used for further investigations, e.g. for the determination of the generalized constraint forces $\bar{\lambda}_A$ and $\bar{\lambda}_C$ resulting from the motion of the system by evaluating equations [2.67b], [3.36] and [3.15b].

The right-hand sides $Y_I = [Y_I^a]$ of the kinematical equations [2.39a] are generated in RHS first and then the right-hand sides Y_{II} of the dynamical equations as given by equation [3.34], The derivation of the elements of matrices Y_{III} and χ

have been described in refs [3] and [4]. These details must not be repeated. We summarize those steps globally and do mention explicitly only the additional steps required for the treatment of closed-loop systems thus demonstrating where they must be introduced into the sequence of computations known.[4] One proceeds as follows: (1) As in ref [4] one generates the motion of the reference frame, the kinematical excitations $\mu^s(t)$, the matrices B^a and z^a representing relative motions and A^{io} and A^1 for the absolute orientation of bodies. Moreover, one establishes the co-ordinates ζ^{ia} of the modified attachment point vectors and the mode vectors φ^a and $\bar{\varphi}^a$. (2) As suggested by the consistency conditions (equations [3.6] and [3.8]) one generates B^c and z^c and the modified-loop connection vectors ζ^{ic} (see equation [2.15]). (3) The matrices W^{ac}, as given by equations [2.33] and [2.34], the mode vectors φ^c, $\bar{\varphi}^c$ and the dual vectors ψ^c, $\bar{\psi}^c$ for the chords (equations [2.55] and [2.58]) are generated next. Then one evaluates equations [3.13] and [3.3] to obtain the matrices W_I, $W_{II},\bar{W}_I$ and $\bar{W}_{II}$. (4) After generating $Z(t)$ (equation [3.16b]) one obtains the matrices Φ, Θ and g_A as suggested by equations [3.16a] and [3.19]. (5) At this point all the additional computations on the kinematics of closed-loop systems (steps 2–4) have been performed and one can proceed as in ref [4] to generate the right-hand sides Y_I of the kinematical equations. Turning to the dynamics one generates, again as in ref [4], the matrices Ω^a, V^a and ω^i as well as J_I, χ and λ_A. With these matrices one obtains Y_{II} for systems with tree configuration as given by equation [2.66]. To develop Y_{II} for systems with closed loops one proceeds further on as follows: (6) Generate the velocities g_C via equation [3.15c] which are required for the evaluation of the laws for the λ_C. (7) Generate the derivatives $\dot{W}^{ac}$, as given by equations [3.29] and [3.30], the derivatives $\dot{\varphi}^c$, $\dot{\bar{\varphi}}^c$ and $\dot{\psi}^c$, $\dot{\bar{\psi}}^c$ of any variable mode vectors and dual vectors, and finally the derivatives $\dot{W}_{II}$ and $\dot{\bar{W}}_{II}$ (equations [3.28] and [3.32]). (8) Generate $\dot{Z}$ (equation [3.31]) and the particular solution Δ of equation [3.23]. (9) Evaluate the force laws across the chords to obtain λ_C and complete Y_{II} for closed-loop systems as given by equation [3.34].

By establishing the above sequence of computations all the functions collected in the right part of the diagram have been considered to be given. They are introduced into the computer code as described[4] for the code MULTIBODY via user-provided subroutines. Dummy subroutines for the generation of the desired functions are available. They are activated by the user when introducing the statements required for the generation of the specific functions for the multibody model under investigation. When dealing with specific areas of application, e.g. with robot dynamics, specific forms of these functions appear in a large variety of models again and again. Examples are external forces due to gravity or specific control laws. For these cases it is helpful to develop a library of subroutines available to all of the users.

Direct problem

A short comment may be helpful on the solution of the direct problem of robot dynamics, by applying the equations developed.[2] In the case of a system with tree configuration one obtains from equation [2.61b]

$$\lambda_A = J_I \dot{g}_A - \chi \tag{2}$$

These are N_{FA} equations for the determination of the N_{FA} driving forces and torques λ_A in the joints, given the motion of the system. In the case of a closed-loop system one obtains from equation [3.15a]

$$\lambda_A = J_I \dot{g}_A - \chi - W_I \lambda_C - W_{II} \bar{\lambda}_C \tag{3}$$

Again we have N_{FA} equations for the N_{FA} unknowns λ_A but on the right side of equation (3) there appear in addition the N_{FA}-generalized applied forces λ_C and the N_{CC}-generalized constraint forces $\bar{\lambda}_C$ across the chords.

We select the chords of the system graph such that they represent those interconnections in the system model, across which the motions of any robot terminal bodies are restricted because of executing some manipulation task. Then the λ_C, i.e. the applied forces on the terminal bodies due to the manipulation task, are known.

The force laws can be formulated easily in terms of the variables g^c, B^c and z^c representing the motion across the chords. These variables in turn are obtained from the known robot motion as described by the variables g^a, B^a and z^a, by using the consistency conditions given in equations [3.6], [3.8] and [3.15c]. Thus the only terms still unknown in equation (3) are the N_{CC}-generalized constraint forces $\bar{\lambda}_C$. They must be defined to obtain a problem specified completely. They may be zero or non-zero depending on the specific problem under consideration.

When using a manipulator to insert a cylinder into a hole, for example, one will control the λ_A in such a way that the $\bar{\lambda}_C$ are zero, i.e. that the manipulator hand does not press the cylinder against the walls of the hole during the insertion process. On the other side, when the manipulator is required to perform a grinding process, one must choose some of the elements of $\bar{\lambda}_C$ to have specific non-zero values, as the λ_A must be controlled such that the manipulator hand presses the object against the grinding wheel with a specific desired and known force. In any case, all of the matrices on the right side of equation (3) are known, and the driving forces and torques λ_A can be got for a closed-loop system too.

It should be kept in mind that we have assumed that the robot motion is known in terms of the variables g^a, B^a and z^a representing the motions across the joints. Usually, these motions are not available, but rather the functional motion of the manipulator, i.e. the motion of the manipulator hand required to execute a specific manipulation task. Thus one has to determine the former variables from the functional motion first. As shown[1] this problem can be considered to be solved, at least in most of the practically important cases.

References

[1] Vukobratović M and Potkonjak V (1982) *Dynamics of Manipulation Robots*. Springer-Verlag, Berlin
[2] Schwertassek R and Roberson R E (1985) A state space dynamical representation for multibody mechanical systems. Part I: Systems with tree configuration; Part II: Systems with closed loops. *Acta Mechanica*, in press
[3] Roberson R E *A Multibody Eulerian Dynamic Simulation as a Design Tool for Attitude Dynamics and Control*. Proc. AOCS Conf., Nordwijk, October 1977, pp 209–220
[4] Schwertassek R (1978) Der Roberson/Wittenburg-Formalismus und das Programmsystem MULTIBODY zur Rechnersimulation von Mehrkörpersystemen. DFVLR-FB-78-08, *DFVLR Wiss. Bericht., Köln* (In English; The Roberson/Wittenburg formalism and the package MULTIBODY for computer simulations of multibody systems *ESA-TT-557*, November 1979)
[5] Roberson R E and Likins P W (1969) A linearization tool for use with matrix formalisms of rotational dynamics. *Ing.-Arch.*, 37, 388–392

Equations of Motion and Equations of Stress for Robots and Manipulators: An Application of the NEWEUL Formalism

E J Kreuzer and W O Schiehlen

Institute of Mechanics, University of Stuttgart, 7000 Stuttgart 80, Federal Republic of Germany

> Summary: This paper presents a method for analysing the dynamics of robots and manipulators and the stress distribution in their arms. The kinematics and dynamics of robots are obtained by using the symbolic formalism NEWEUL. The resulting equations describe the motion, provide symbolical expressions for actuator forces and torques and allow the computation of joint forces. The inertia forces of robot arms are originally distributed forces that have to be considered in the stress analysis of the links, especially in high speed motion.

Introduction

Robots and manipulators are complicated mechanical systems with highly non-linear dynamic behaviour. It is often sufficient to model robots by rigid massless elements for the investigation of the non-linear kinematics of the arm configuration. As higher performance in terms of speed and accuracy is pursued, the complicated dynamics become more important. However, forming dynamical models or robots with paper and pencil is very time-consuming and produces unlimited possibilities of errors. To transfer this tedious task to the computer and to generate the equations of motion automatically a number of formalisms have been developed.[1-4] Additionally, the system operation should be close to the strength limits of the material to avoid an overdesign of the system. Therefore, for economic design of advanced robots, it is also important to know the stress distribution within each link of the system. In general, a link is loaded by applied and reaction forces and torques, all of which contribute to the magnitude and direction of stress. Therefore, not only the applied forces but also the reaction forces due to the kinematical constraints in the joints, are required for the proper design of a robot.

In this paper the formulation NEWEUL for the generation of symbolic equations of motion is described and it will be shown how the computation of reaction forces can be also implemented in a very systematic way. Then, all forces and torques appearing in the free-body diagram of each link of the robot are known. The distributed mass of rigid bodies results especially in high-speed motion in distributed inertia forces in the links which have to be considered in the stress analysis. The equations of stress resulting from all of these loads can be implemented in a computer program to make the application of the method more useful for practical design. The approach will be restricted to robots themselves with links to be considered as straight beams.

Dynamics of robots and manipulators

Various methods are available to formulate dynamic equations of robots and manipulators, such as the Lagrangian, the Newton–Euler, the recursive Lagrangian and the recursive Newton–Euler formulations. However, the recursive equations destroy the 'structure' of the dynamic model, which is useful for easy controller design. This paper describes a Newton–Euler formulation for the generation of symbolic equations of motion by using D'Alembert's principle. An extensive description of the method may be found elsewhere.[5,6] Therefore, only some fundamentals essential for robot and manipulator applications will be given here.

A multibody system representing a robot consists of rigid bodies, springs without inertia, dampers and actuators. The rigid bodies are interconnected by ideal joints.

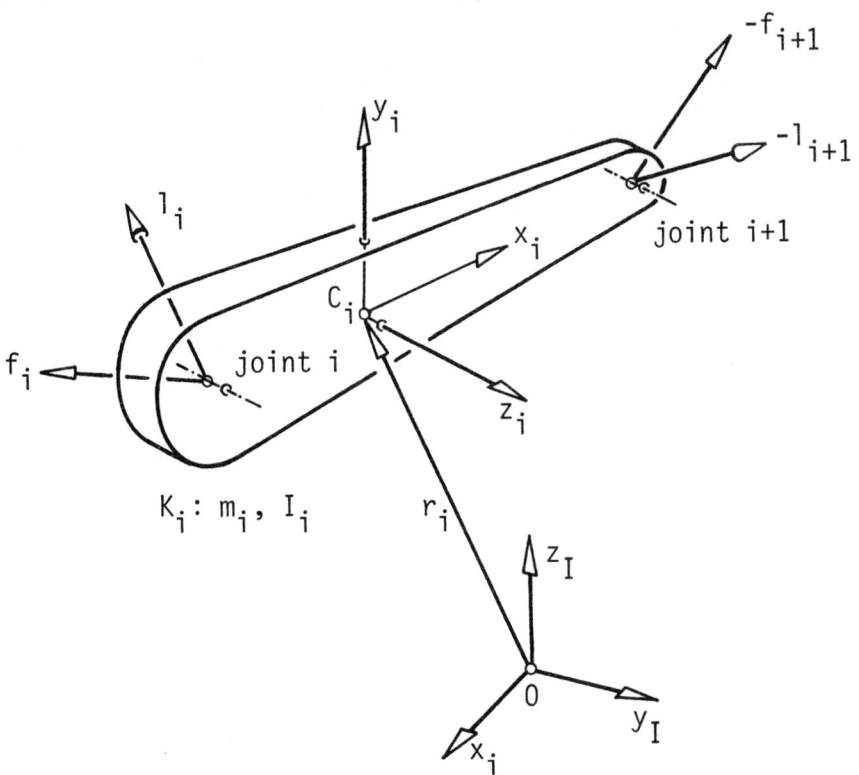

Figure 1 Description of link i

A robot model of p rigid links K_i, $i = 1(1)p$, is considered. The mass of link i is m_i, its centre of mass is C_i and its inertia tensor with respect to C_i is denoted by I_i. A body-fixed frame is associated with each link (Figure 1). The joints constrain the motion of the links. For q holonomic constraints the robot has

$$f = 6p - q \tag{1}$$

degrees of freedom. Then, the position of the system can be uniquely described by f generalized co-ordinates summarized in the position vector y. Therefore, the position of each link relative to an inertial frame is completely specified by the 3×1-translation vector of its centre of mass

$$r_i = r_i(y,t), \quad i = 1(1)p \qquad (2)$$

and the 3×3-rotation matrix

$$S_i = S_i(y,t), \quad i = 1(1)p \qquad (3)$$

of the body-fixed frame with respect to the inertial frame.

The application of linear and angular momentum principle based on the free-body diagram of each link result in Newton's equations

$$m_i \dot{v}_i = f_i^a + f_i^r, \quad i = 1(1)p \qquad (4)$$

and Euler's equations

$$I_i \dot{\omega}_i + \tilde{\omega}_i I_i \omega_i = 1_i^a + 1_i^r, \quad i = 1(1)p \qquad (5)$$

with respect to the centres of mass and put down in the inertial frame. The external forces and torques in (4) and (5) are composed of applied forces f_i^a and torques 1_i^a due to springs, dampers, actuators and weight and of reaction forces f_i^r and torques 1_i^r due to joints.

The summary of equations (4) and (5) leads to the global Newton–Euler equations

$$\bar{M}\ddot{y} + \bar{k} = \bar{q}^a + \bar{q}^r \qquad (6)$$

The equations of motion are obtained from (6) by D'Alembert's principle resulting in the non-linear vector differential equation

$$M(y)\ddot{y} + k(y,\dot{y}) = q(y,\dot{y},t) \qquad (7)$$

Here M is a symmetric and positive definite $f \times f$-inertia matrix, and k and q are $f \times 1$-vectors of centrifugal and generalized applied forces. Equation (7) describes the dynamics of the robot in terms of the minimal number of differential equations. These equations may also be derived by using a purely Lagrangian approach; however, this approach is less efficient than a computational point of view.

The inverse problem of robot dynamics, namely to find the appropriate drive forces or torques for a desired motion, is often solved by using recursive methods. But it is also possible to determine driving forces and torques analytically from equation (7) by decomposing the vector of the generalized applied forces:

$$q^d = M(y)\ddot{y}(t) + k(y,\dot{y}) - q^w(y,\dot{y}) \qquad (8)$$

The vector q^w describes the generalized applied forces due to weight, springs and dampers.

NEWEUL program

The presented method is the basis for the computer program NEWEUL for the generation of symbolic equations of motion.[7] The program is written in FORTRAN by using a special coding scheme allowing non-numerical symbolical computation and analytical differentiation. It has proved its high reliability for many technical applications.

To set up the equations of motion the program requires the following input data: position vector y; translation vector $r_i(y,t)$; rotation matrix $S_i(y,t)$; mass m_i; inertia tensor I_i or $_iI_i$; applied forces f_i^a and torques 1_i^a.

All these data can be obtained easily from the real system. The transformation of the inertia tensor $_iI_i$ from body-fixed frame into the inertial frame can be performed by the computer as well as the calculation of the applied forces and torques. An interactive dialogue system facilitates greatly the entry of all the input data. The resulting equations of motion are given symbolically in FORTRAN code as a printed listing or as a file ready for the numerical integration of the equations or as a basis for the calculation of driving forces and torques. By substituting symbols by numbers with NEWEUL symbolic equations highly efficient numerical simulation is possible.

Reaction forces and torques

In the equation of motion (7) the reaction forces and torques are completely eliminated but they are necessary for the stress analysis. The generalized constraint force approach is used to describe the reaction forces and torques acting on each link. Then, the $6p \times 1$-vector $\bar{q}^r$ depends linearly on the $q \times 1$-vector g of generalized constraint forces, distributed to the p links by a $6p \times q$-distribution matrix $\bar{Q}$ according to

$$\bar{q}^r = \bar{Q}(y,t)g \qquad (9)$$

The distribution matrix $\bar{Q}$ may be found from the implicit form of the constraint equations or by geometrical considerations. Introducing (9) into (6) a uniquely solvable system of linear algebraic equations for the constraint forces is obtained:

$$N(y)g + \hat{q}(y,\dot{y},t) = \hat{k}(y,\dot{y}) \qquad (10)$$

Here N is a symmetric positive definite $q \times q$-reaction matrix and $\hat{q}$ and $\hat{k}$ are $q \times 1$-vectors of the applied and centrifugal force components.

Equation (10) is characterized by the minimal number of equations. The reaction forces and torques introduced in the present paper have nothing to do with the indirect problem of robot dynamics. The reaction forces and torques in the joints are perpendicular to the motion, and knowledge of them is necessary for the analysis of friction phenomena.

Equations of stress

The stress distribution in a robot arm depends on the applied and reaction forces/torques in the joints as well as the forces and torques due to the distributed inertia properties. The load resulting from the high-speed motions of the robot may be an order of magnitude higher than the nominal load. Therefore, it cannot be neglected in the stress analysis. However, it is assumed that the elastic deformation of the robot arm is small compared with the nominal motion, and structural vibrations are neglected. For the formulation of the equations of stress for each link a second

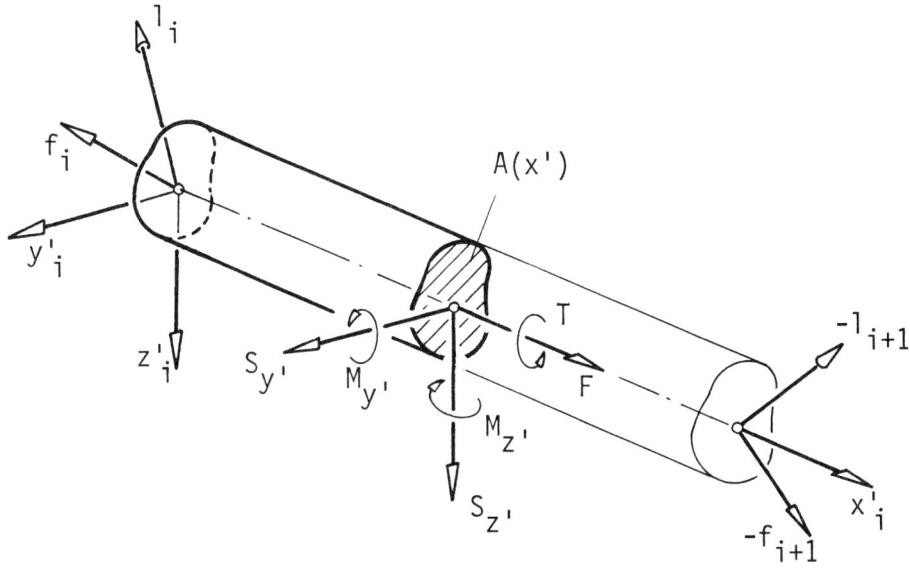

Figure 2 Forces and moments acting in link i

body-fixed reference frame is defined with its origin at the joint i between link $i-1$ and i and the x_i'-axis representing the elastic axis (Figure 2). The load distribution along the elastic axis can be found by repeated application of the free-body principle. Each link is then modelled by two rigid bodies and an artificial, completely rigid, constraint perpendicular to the elastic axis x_i'. If the position of the artificial constraint is introduced as a function of the co-ordinate x_i', the continuous load distribution in the link is obtained. Simultaneously, the number of bodies and the number of constraints increase by $6p$, but the number of degrees of freedom remains unchanged:

$$f = (6p + 6p) - (q + 6p) \tag{11}$$

Therefore, the dynamics are still described by (7) and the constraint forces are found from (10), but the matrix N and the vectors g, $\hat{q}$, and $\hat{k}$ now depend on the co-ordinate x_i', too, and the dimension has changed from q to $q + 6p$. Furthermore, the number of Newton–Euler equations (6) is doubled, where all the inertia and weight properties are also functions of the co-ordinate x_i'. The generalized constraint forces and torques acting in a cross-section of link i are defined as shown in Figure 2, each co-ordinate of which contributes an element to the vector g.

On the assumption that the principle of superposition applies one obtains the general state of stress by combining the individual states due to the elementary modes of loading. If $M_{y'}(x')$ and $M_{z'}(x')$ denote the bending moments, $J_{y'y'}(x')$, $J_{z'z'}(x')$ and $J_{z'y'}(x')$ are the second moments of area and the mixed second moment of area of the cross-section relative to the elastic axis, respectively, then the total bending stress is described by

$$\sigma_b(x') = \frac{(M_{y'}J_{z'y'} - M_{z'}J_{y'y'})y' + (M_{y'}J_{z'z'} - M_{z'}J_{z'y'})z'}{J_{z'z'}J_{y'y'} - J_{y'z'}^2} \quad (12)$$

Furthermore, with the normal force $F(x')$ and the area $A(x')$, the normal stress is given by

$$\sigma_n(x') = \frac{F}{A} \quad (13)$$

The average shear stress due to the shear forces $S_{y'}(x'), S_{z'}(x')$ is approximately given by

$$\tau_s(x') = \frac{\sqrt{S_{y'}^2 + S_{z'}^2}}{A} \quad (14)$$

From the twisting torque $T(x')$ results the average shear stress

$$\tau_t(x') = \frac{T\rho}{J_p} \quad (15)$$

where $J_p(x')$ is the polar second moment of area relative to the elastic axis and $\rho(x')$ the average distance from the elastic axis.

Applying the maximum distortion–energy theory the general stress distribution results in

$$\sigma_g(x') = \sqrt{(\sigma_b + \sigma_n)^2 + 3(\tau_s + \tau_t)^2} \leq \sigma_e \quad (16)$$

where σ_e denotes the elastic strength and therefore the margin of safety.

Conclusion

In this paper a method has been presented for a combined analysis of the dynamics of robots and manipulators and the stress distribution in robot links modelled as rigid bodies. The method presented may provide a useful tool for the design of lightweight high-speed robots and manipulators more productive than currently available systems.

References

[1] Vukobratović M and Potkonjak V (1982) *Dynamics of Manipulation Robots*. Springer-Verlag, Berlin
[2] Luh J Y S, Walker M W and Paul R P C (1980) On-line computational scheme for mechanical manipulators. *J. Dyn. Syst., Measurement, Control*, **102**, 69–76
[3] Hollerbach J M (1980) A recursive Lagrangian formulation of manipulator dynamics and a comparative study of dynamics formulation complexity. *IEEE Trans., Systems, Man and Cybernetics*, **10**, 730–736
[4] Kreuzer E J (1979) *Dynamical Analysis of Mechanism Using Symbolical Equation Manipulation*. Proc. of the Fifth World Congress on Theory of Machines and Mechanisms, Vol 1, pp 599–602

[5] Kreuzer E (1979) Symbolische Berechnung der Bewegungsgleichungen von Mehrkörpersystemen. VDI-Verl., Fortschr.-Ber. VDI-Z, Reihe 11, Düsseldorf, Nr. 32
[6] Schiehlen W O (1984) *Computer Generation of Equations of Motion*. Proc. of the Advanced Study Inst. on Computer-Aided Analysis and Optimization of Mechanical System Dynamics. Springer-Verlag, Berlin
[7] Kreuzer E, Schmoll K-P and Schramm D (1983) Programmpaket NEWEUL '83. Inst. B für Mechanik, AN-7, University of Stuttgart

Modelling of Artificial Manipulators and Computer Simulation of their Dynamics

T Kawase, H Nakano and R Magoshi

Department of Mechanical Engineering, Waseda University, Tokyo 160, Japan

Summary: While designing any manipulators it is indispensable (1) to determine the optimum co-ordination scheme for the manipulator to perform the prescribed operations under some kinematical constraints and (2) to predict a dynamical behaviour of the system under various control inputs and disturbances. In this paper we propose a modelling method of manipulator dynamics using the bond graph and the diakoptical method. The former enables us to envisage how the system components are interconnected and using the latter one we can systematize the process of derivation of the motion equations. They are employed to overcome the difficulties in modelling which chiefly come from the increase of the degrees of freedom according to the increase of the number of the rigid bodies involved. A large number of equations being thus systematically derived have strong non-linearities. So, for the efficient numerical integration, the complete set of the equations is tabulated and the resultant non-linear differential–algebraic equations are integrated by using the BDF method. Some simulated responses of the system having six degrees of freedom are presented. The above tabulated equations include a sparce matrix having the sparcity of about 3–4 per cent and hence it is suggested that we can further save the computation time fully utilizing the sparcity.

Fundamental symbolic tools to be used

Fundamental tools of the bond graph to be used are listed in Table 1. The power bond ⟶ represents the bond through which dynamical energy is transmitted toward the direction indicated by the half arrow and whose dynamical states are represented by force (torque) and velocity (angular velocity). The principal tool of the BG is the non-energic multiport which describes how the system components

Table 1   Symbols of the bond graph

Symbols	Meanings
SE ⟶	External force source
SF ⟶	External velocity source
$\mathcal{J}$ ⟶	Moment of inertia
m ⟶	Mass
⟶ 1 ⟵	1-junction
⟶ CTF ⟵	CTF
⟶ MTF ⟵	MTF
⟶ EJS ⟵	EJS

are interconnected; it is a so-called workless constraint in mechanics. Let us denote the generalized co-ordinate and its conjugate force by $\bar{q}$ and $\bar{R}$ respectively. Then the non-energicness is described as

$$\langle \dot{\bar{q}}, \bar{R} \rangle = 0 \quad \text{for every time } t \tag{1}$$

where $\langle , \rangle$ indicates the scalar product of vectors, $(\bar{})$ the column vector and $(\dot{})$ the time derivative. In this paper, we shall use the four categories of non-energic multiports.

(1) *1-Junction*. The 1-junction represents the equilibrium condition of forces and torques, which is equivalent to D'Alembert's principle.

(2) *Controlled transformer (CTF)*. The controlled transformer is the symbolic representation of the invertible co-ordinate transformation, not necessarily integrable (quasi-co-ordinate), described below including the parameter $\bar{\sigma}$,

$$\underline{\bar{C}}(\bar{q};\bar{\sigma})d\bar{q} = d\bar{\pi} \quad \text{or} \quad \underline{\bar{C}}(\bar{q};\bar{\sigma})\dot{\bar{q}} = \dot{\bar{\pi}} \tag{2}$$

where $\bar{\pi}$ indicates the new co-ordinate and $(\bar{})$ the matrix. Here, in this case, the non-energicness means the invariant property of the scalar function $\langle \dot{\bar{q}}, \bar{R} \rangle = -\langle \dot{\bar{\pi}}, \bar{\Pi} \rangle$, where $\bar{\Pi}$ indicates the force along the new co-ordinate $\bar{\pi}$. By the above power identity, we easily achieve the relation between the forces $\bar{R} = -\underline{\bar{C}}(\bar{q};\bar{\sigma})^T \bar{\Pi}$.

(3) *Modulated transformer (MTF)*. Any non-energic n-port whose characteristic is defined by the relation between velocities described below

$$d\bar{q}_2 = \underline{\bar{C}}(\bar{q}_1)d\bar{q}_1 \quad \text{or} \quad \dot{\bar{q}}_2 = \underline{\bar{C}}(\bar{q}_1)\dot{\bar{q}}_1 \tag{3}$$

is called a *modulated transformer*. Thus we have $\bar{R}_1 = -\underline{\bar{C}}(\bar{q}_1)^T \bar{R}_2$, where $\bar{R}_1, \bar{R}_2$ indicate the conjugate forces to $\dot{\bar{q}}_1$ and $\dot{\bar{q}}_2$ respectively. The ideal mechanical joints and kinematic constraints fall into this category.

(4) *Eulerian junction structure*.[2] Any free body when its motion is observed along the local frame whose origin is fixed to the mass centre and whose axes coincide with the principal axes is subjected to the coupling forces which satisfy the non-energicness. Such an element is then modelled as a non-energic three-port called an *Eulerian junction structure*.

So far it has been presumed that we have defined the reference frames to observe the body motion. The following preference is made for (1) the inertial frame for the translational motion of the mass centre and (2) the local frame for the rotational motion, whose origin is fixed to the mass centre and whose axes coincide with the principal axes of the body.

Modelling of manipulator

Let us consider the manipulator shown schematically in Figure 1, which has six degrees of freedom. The system is considered to be composed of the fundamental pairs each of which has a pair of an ideal mechanical joint and a rigid body. Hence we first give the model of the pair shown in Figure 2. At the joints, the system is driven by velocity sources and hence the velocity is the input to the system. Thus

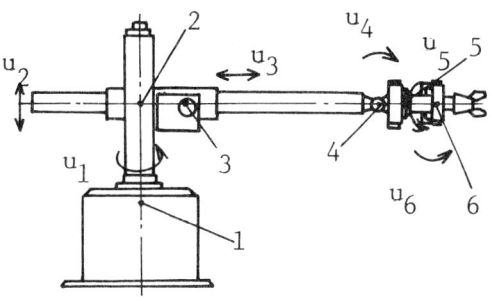

	Joint	Mass (kg)	θ (rad)	r_0 (m)	r_1 (m)	I_1 (kgm)	I_2 (kgm)	I_3 (kgm)
1	$RJ1$	15	$\pi/2$	0.16	0.25	0.81	0.06	0.81
2	$TJ1$	4.2	$\pi/2$	0.15	0.1	0.3	0.04	0.31
3	$TJ2$	6.3	$\pi/2$	0.45	0.1	0.4	0.05	0.4
4	$RJ'2$	1.3		0.06	0.1	0.1	0.003	0.007
5	$RJ1$	2.1	$\pi/2$	0.06	0.06	0.0	0.006	0.01
6	$RJ2$	1.6		0.06	0.06	0.0	0.003	0.007

Figure 1 Manipulator

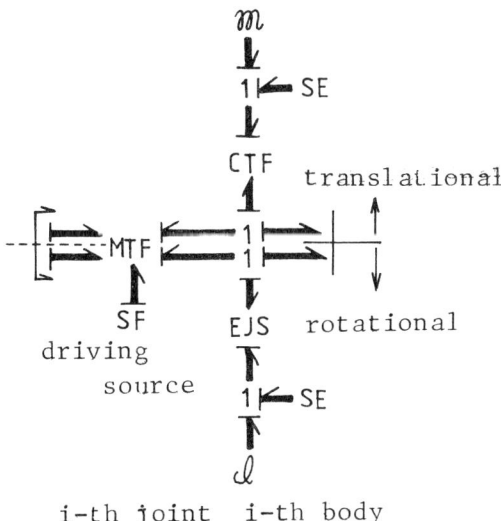

Figure 2 Fundamental pair

the driving force is the output variable. Next we define the dynamical variables: $\dot{\pi}$ and Π indicate the mutually conjugate velocity and force variables respectively. The superscripts ( )° and ( )* denote that the corresponding variables are respectively the left-hand and right-hand variables of the MTF representing the ith joint. The variables without any superscript represent those in the inertial frame for the translational motion and those in the local frame defined previously for the rotational motion. Thus we have the following kinematical or dynamical relations for the ith pair.

MTF of the ith joint.

$$\begin{bmatrix} \dot{\pi}^* \\ \Pi \\ \bar{R} \end{bmatrix} = \begin{bmatrix} \underline{0} & \underline{\bar{C}}(\bar{u}) & \underline{\bar{c}} \\ -\underline{\bar{C}}(\bar{u})^T & \underline{0} & \\ -\underline{\bar{c}}^T & & \end{bmatrix} \begin{bmatrix} \Pi^* \\ \dot{\pi} \\ \dot{u} \end{bmatrix} \qquad (4)$$

where ( )^T indicates the matrix transposition, $\dot{u}$ the driving velocity of the joint and $\bar{R}$ the required driving force. In the above, the matrices $\underline{\bar{C}}(\bar{u}), \underline{\bar{c}}$ representing the transformation of the velocities are determined by the kinematical relations of the joints as illustrated in Table 2 (*TJ*1).

Table 2 MTF model of the joint

Joint		Coefficient matrices
ith joint	Symbol DOF 1	$\underline{\bar{C}} = \begin{bmatrix} 1 & 0 & 0 & 0 & -r_1 c\theta & -(u+r_0+r_1 s\theta) \\ 0 & s\theta & -c\theta & -(u+r_0)c\theta & 0 & 0 \\ 0 & c\theta & s\theta & (u+r_0)s\theta & 0 & 0 \\ & & & +r_1 & & \\ 0 & 0 & 0 & 1 & 0 & 0 \\ 0 & 0 & 0 & 0 & s\theta & -c\theta \\ 0 & 0 & 0 & 0 & c\theta & s\theta \end{bmatrix}$ $\underline{\bar{c}} = \begin{bmatrix} 0 & s\theta & c\theta & 0 & 0 & 0 \end{bmatrix}^T$

CTF of the co-ordinate transformation. The co-ordinate transformation from the inertial frame to the local one is modelled as a CTF described below:

$$\begin{bmatrix} \dot{\pi}_{tr} \\ \Pi^*_{tr} \end{bmatrix} = \begin{bmatrix} \underline{0} & \underline{\bar{A}} \\ -\underline{\bar{A}}^T & \underline{0} \end{bmatrix} \begin{bmatrix} \Pi_{tr} \\ \dot{\pi}^*_{tr} \end{bmatrix} \qquad (5)$$

where the matrix $\underline{\bar{A}}$ is determined solely by the kinematical conditions for the body-fixed frames and the suffix 'tr' indicates translational motion.

1-Junction for the torque and force. By applying D'Alembert's principle to the 1-junction shown in Figure 2, we get the following relation.

$$\begin{bmatrix} \dot{\bar{\pi}} \\ \dot{\bar{\pi}}^c \\ \bar{\Pi}^* \end{bmatrix} = \left[\begin{array}{c|cc} \bar{0} & \bar{I} \\ \hline \bar{I} & \bar{I} & \bar{0} \end{array} \right] \begin{bmatrix} \bar{\Pi} \\ \bar{\Pi}^c \\ \dot{\bar{\pi}}^* \end{bmatrix} \tag{6}$$

where $\bar{I}$ and $\bar{0}$ denote the $n \times n$ unit matrix and $n \times m$ zero matrix. In the above n and m are used in the generic sense.

Now we write the equations of motion of the ith body. This may be easily done by inspecting the bond graph together with the relations so far obtained.

Thus we have the following Hamiltonian form of equations.

$$\frac{d}{dt}\bar{\pi} = \left[\frac{\partial H}{\partial \bar{p}}\right]^T = \bar{\Gamma}\bar{p}, \quad \bar{\Gamma} = [\text{diag}(m,m,m,I_1,I_2,I_3)]^{-1} \tag{7}$$

$$\frac{d}{dt}\bar{p} = -\left[\frac{\partial H}{\partial \bar{\pi}}\right]^T - \bar{f} + \bar{\Pi}^c + \bar{V} = \bar{U} - \bar{f} + \bar{\Pi}^c + \bar{V} \tag{8}$$

where H is the Hamiltonian, $\bar{p}$ the generalized momentum defined as $\bar{p} = (\partial L/\partial \dot{\bar{\pi}})^T$ by using the Lagrangian $L = L(\bar{q},\bar{\pi};t)$ and $\bar{f}, \bar{V}, \bar{\Pi}^c$ indicate the coupling force, external force and the interacting force with the $(i+1)$th body. In the above, coupling force $\bar{f}$ comes from the non-holonomic co-ordinate transformation and it is represented as $\bar{f} = \bar{S}\bar{p}$ where the coefficient matrix $\bar{S}$ is given below:

$$\bar{S} = \left[\begin{array}{c|c} \bar{0} & \bar{0} \\ \hline \bar{0} & \begin{array}{ccc} 0 & 0 & \alpha p_5 \\ 0 & 0 & \beta p_4 \\ -\alpha p_5 & -\beta p_4 & 0 \end{array} \end{array} \right] \quad \begin{array}{l} \alpha = 1/I_3 - 1/I_2 \\ \beta = 1/I_1 - 1/I_3 \end{array} \tag{9}$$

By using the above relations, we finally get the complete set of dynamical equations of the ith body and they are tabulated below.[3]

$$\bar{\pi}^* - \bar{C}(\bar{u})\dot{\bar{\pi}} - \bar{c}\int \dot{\bar{u}}dt = \bar{0} \qquad \text{joint constraint}$$

$$\dot{\bar{\pi}} - \bar{B}\dot{\bar{\pi}}^* = \bar{0} \qquad \text{co-ordinate transformation}$$

$$\dot{\bar{\pi}} - \dot{\bar{\pi}}^c = \bar{0} \qquad \text{1-junction}$$

$$\begin{bmatrix} \bar{\Pi}^\circ \\ \bar{R} \end{bmatrix} - \begin{bmatrix} \bar{C}(\bar{u})^T \\ \bar{c}^T \end{bmatrix} [-\bar{B}^T(\dot{\bar{p}} + \bar{U} + \bar{V} + \bar{S}\bar{p}) - \bar{\Pi}^c] = \bar{0} \quad \text{equation of motion}$$

$$\int \dot{\bar{u}}dt - \bar{u} = \bar{0} \qquad \text{kinematic relation} \tag{10}$$

where $\bar{B} = \begin{bmatrix} \bar{A} & 0 \\ 0 & \bar{I} \end{bmatrix}$

Thus complete dynamic equations for the ith body are put into the form

$$\bar{G}(\bar{x}, \dot{\bar{x}}; t) = \bar{0} \qquad (11)$$

where the variable $\bar{x}$ is defined below:

$$\bar{x}^T = [\dot{\bar{\pi}}^{\circ T} \dot{\bar{u}}^T \bar{\Pi}^{\circ T} \bar{R}^T \dot{\bar{\pi}}^{*T} \dot{\bar{\pi}}^T \bar{p}^T \dot{\bar{\pi}}^{cT} \bar{\Pi}^{cT}].$$

Setting up such equations for each body, we finally have the complete set of equations to be required. These equations are further combined by the following relations representing the continuation of the forces and velocities between the ith and $(i+1)$th bodies.

$$\dot{\bar{\pi}}_i^* - \dot{\bar{\pi}}_{i+1}^{\circ} = \bar{0} \quad \text{and} \quad \bar{\Pi}_i^c - \bar{\Pi}_{i+1}^{\circ} = \bar{0} \qquad (12)$$

Numerical simulation

Let us note that (equation 10) we have three sets of input and output variables besides $\bar{U}$ and $\bar{V}$: input variables $\dot{\bar{u}}(t)$, $\dot{\bar{\pi}}^{\circ}$ and $\bar{\Pi}^c$; output variables $\bar{R}$, $\bar{\Pi}^{\circ}$ and $\dot{\bar{\pi}}^c$. For the overall system, the ultimate inputs are

$$\dot{\bar{u}}_i(t)\ (i=1,\ldots,k),\ \dot{\bar{\pi}}^* = \lim_{i \to 0} \dot{\bar{\pi}}_i^*,\ \bar{\Pi}^c = \lim_{i \to k} \bar{\Pi}^c \qquad (13)$$

where k is the number of the joints.

These functions are usually predetermined in the design phase. There is a variety of problems concerning the numerical simulation.

The notables are as follows. (P1) Estimation of the driving forces (torques) at the joints under the prescribed motion of the manipulator hand. If the velocity is given as a function of time at the hand, then the required inputs $\dot{\bar{u}}_i(t)$ are determined by using the pseudo-inverse. In this case, the dynamical behaviour of each body is completely determined, and hence the simulation serves only to estimate the required driving forces and torques at the joints; (P2) Prediction of the dynamical behaviour of the system under arbitrary inputs $\dot{\bar{u}}_i(t)$ and disturbances, say in the torque (force) supplied by the driving actuators, or in external force (torque) exerted on each body.

In the following studies, we show some simulation results within the scope of the problem 2(P2) mentioned above: (1) the responses of the manipulator under the prescribed driving velocity inputs; (2) estimation of fluctuating torques and forces under the disturbances in the external force (torque) exerted on some parts of the system.

Equation 11 is usually stiff and, for numerical integration, we use the predictor–corrector method employing the BDF method.[4]

First, let us discretize the variable $\bar{x}$ and time t. Suppose we are given the states $\bar{x}_k = \bar{x}(t_k)$ $(k=0,\ldots,n)$ then we use the backward differences to estimate $\dot{\bar{x}}_{n+1}$ by

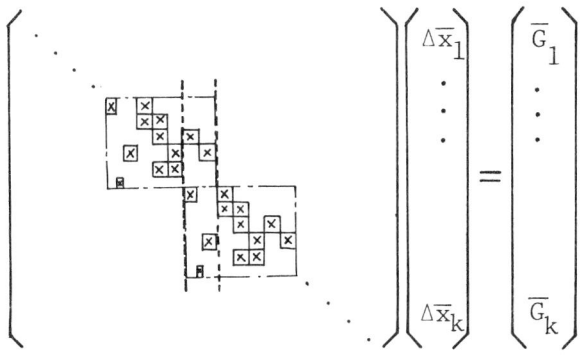

Figure 3 Sparce matrix

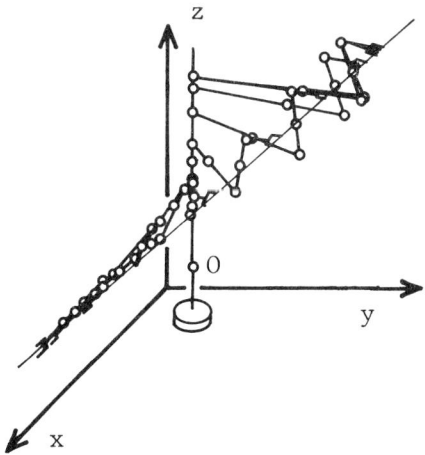

Figure 4 Locus of the manipulator

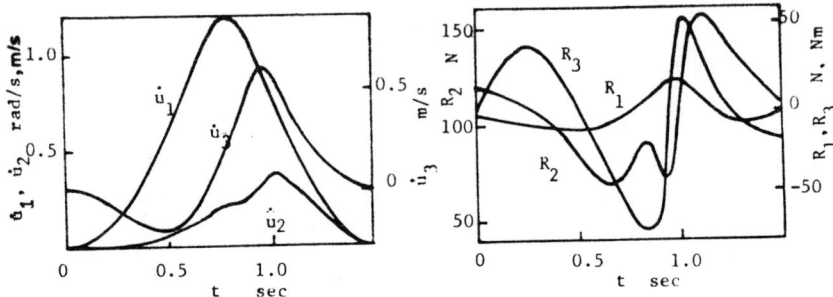

Figure 5 Driving velocity inputs and required force (torque)

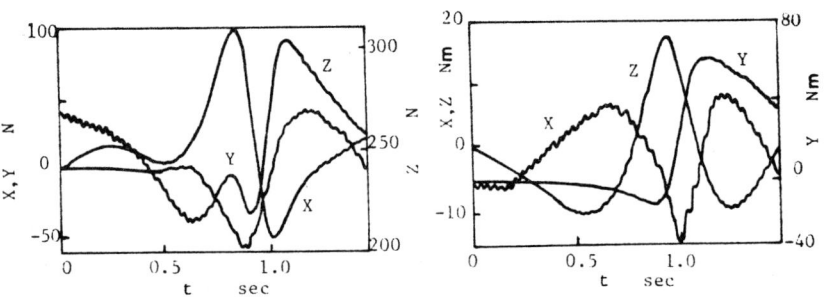

Figure 6 Responses to the disturbances (0th body).

Disturbances: $\bar{d}_{tr}^T = [2.72\sin(104.7t), 0, 0]$

$\bar{d}_{rot}^T = [0, 0, 0.16\sin(104.7t)]$

$$\dot{\bar{x}}_{n+1} = -(1/h) \sum_{i=0}^{k} \alpha_i \bar{x}_{n+1-i} \tag{14}$$

where $h = t_{n+1} - t_n$ and α_i are the coefficients. Putting the above expression into the discretized original equation $\bar{G}(\bar{x}, \dot{\bar{x}}, t) = \bar{0}$, we get the non-linear algebraic equations for $\bar{x}_{n+1}$. Thus we can get the $\bar{x}_{n+1}$ while using the Newton–Rapson method. The $(p + 1)$th corrector is thus given as

$$\left[\frac{\partial \bar{G}}{\partial \bar{x}} (\bar{x}_{n+1}^p, t_{n+1}) \right]^T \Delta \bar{x}_{n+1}^{p+1} = -\bar{G}(\bar{x}_{n+1}^p, t_{n+1}) \text{ (see Figure 3)} \tag{15}$$

Figure 5 shows the simulated responses under the prescribed velocity inputs at the joints (also see the locus of the manipulator in Figure 4). Figure 6 shows the estimated torque (force) fluctuations under the disturbances existing in the force and torque exerted on the fifth body. Estimated execution time in the above simulation is about 60 s for $h/T = 0.03$, where T is the time duration in which the complete cycle of the operation is accomplished.

The matrix $[\partial G/\partial \bar{x}]^T$ for our system has 192 rows and columns and also has the sparcity of about 3–4 per cent. This suggests to us that by utilizing the above sparcity we can further save the computation time.

Conclusions

We have proposed a modelling method using the bond graph and the diakoptical method and some simulation results obtained using the proposed method are presented. It is evident that the method serves to derive the required dynamical equations systematically and possibly symbolically for machine computation. It is also suggested that, although at present it takes too much time for on-line computation, we can further save the computation time by fully utilizing the sparcity of the involved matrix.

References

[1] Lur'e L (1968) *Mechanique Analytique* Masson et Cie, Paris
[2] Karnopp D C (1969) *J. Franklin Inst.*, **288**(3), 175
[3] Brayton R K et al. (1972) *Proc. IEEE*, **60**, 98–108, 137
[4] Gear C W (1968) Rep. 221, University of Illinois
[5] Greville T N E (1960) *SIAM Review*, **2**(1), 15

Dynamics of Robots and Manipulators Involving Closed Loops

T R Kane and H Faessler

Division of Applied Mechanics, Stanford University, Stanford, CA 94305, USA, and Institut für Mechanik, Swiss Federal Institute of Technology ETH-Zentrum, 8092 Zürich, Switzerland

Summary: The two formalisms most frequently employed to generate dynamical equations for robots and manipulators, namely classical Lagrange and Newton–Euler equations, become ineffective tools when applied to complex devices containing elements that form closed loops. It is the purpose of this paper to present a method based on Kane's dynamical equations which leads straightforwardly to an efficient formulation of the dynamical equations governing complex structures with closed kinematic loops. To this end, the general procedure is outlined step by step, and each step is illustrated in connection with an example.

Introduction

Figure 1 contains response curves for a manipulator of the kind depicted in Figure 2. It is the purpose of this paper to show how such curves can be generated efficiently. Despite the extensive literature dealing with the dynamics of manipulators (for extensive lists of references see, e.g. refs [1], [2]), almost nothing that has appeared to date is directly applicable to structures involving closed kinematic loops. This is mainly due to the fact that the two most widely used methodologies, namely the

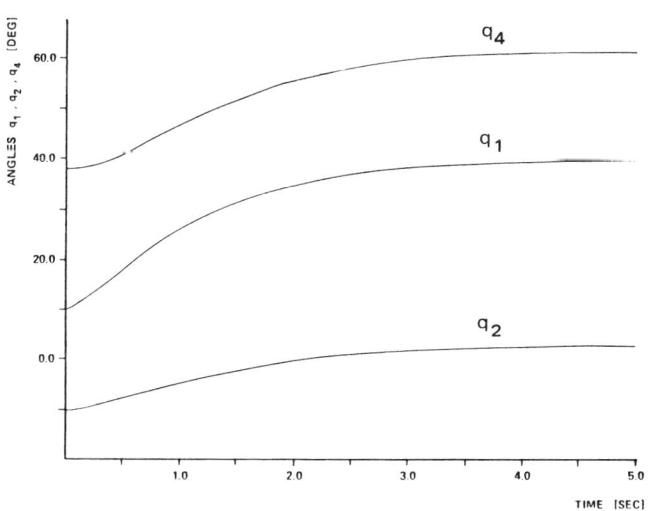

Figure 1 Manipulator response curves

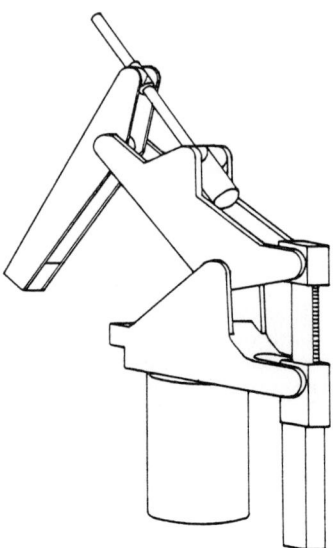

Figure 2 Manipulator

Lagrange approach and the Newton–Euler method, both suffer from serious deficiencies when applied to complicated structures with closed kinematic loops. It is to be made evident in the sequel that Kane's dynamical equations for nonholonomic systems[3] furnish a convenient tool to solve such problems. As will be shown, the method leads directly to easily programmable, computationally efficient, algorithms both for the problem of 'inverse dynamics' and for simulations of motions.

Since the fundamental concepts underlying Kane's dynamical equations are not yet readily available in the robotics literature (a paper entitled 'Use of Kane's dynamical equations in robotics' will soon appear in *Int. J. Robotics Res.*), the writers are faced with the problem of presenting an analysis of a complicated structure within the confines of a short paper, konwing that the reader is probably unfamiliar with some of the basic ideas. Therefore, we here report the highlights of our analysis, hoping thus to motivate the reader to consult HPFs thesis,[4] where the analysis is set forth in complete detail.

Analysis

Figure is a schematic representation of a three-degrees-of-freedom manipulator involving two closed kinematical loops. This device consists of seven bodies, designated $A, \ldots, G$, and a point mass situated at H. Body A can be rotated in a Newtonian reference frame N about a vertical axis fixed both in N and A. A supports body B and body C, and D is supported both by B and by C. C and D represent a linear actuator, D performing purely translational motions relative to C.

Dynamics of Robots Involving Closed Loops 99

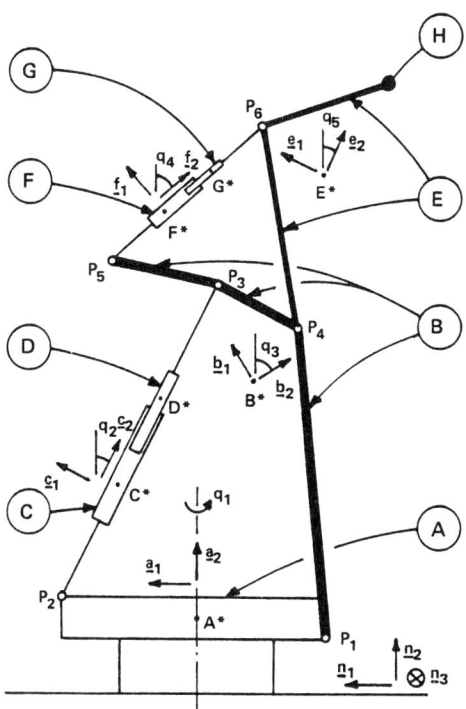

Figure 3 Three-degrees-of-freedom manipulator with two closed kinematical loops

Such motions cause B to rotate relative to A about a horizontal axis fixed in A and B passing through point P_1, and relative to D about a horizontal axis fixed in B and D and passing through point P_3. In addition, motion of D relative to C causes C to rotate relative to A about a horizontal axis fixed in A and C and passing through point P_2. B supports E and F and G is carried by E and F.

Purely translational motions of G relative to F cause E to rotate relative to B about an axis fixed in E and B, and passing through point P_4, and relative to G about an axis fixed in E and G and passing through point P_6. At the same time F rotates relative to B about an axis fixed in F and B and passing through point P_5. The axes passing through $P_1, \ldots, P_6$ all are parallel to each other.

Six dextral sets of mutually perpendicular unit vectors $\underline{n}_i, \underline{a}_i, \underline{b}_i, \underline{c}_i, \underline{e}_i, \underline{f}_i$ ($i = 1, 2, 3$) are introduced as follows: $\underline{n}_1, \underline{n}_2, \underline{n}_3$ are fixed in N with $\underline{n}_1$ and $\underline{n}_3$ horizontal and $\underline{n}_2$ pointing vertically upward; $\underline{a}_1, \underline{a}_2, \underline{a}_3$ are fixed in A with $\underline{a}_2$ parallel to $\underline{n}_2$ and $\underline{a}_3$ parallel to the axis passing through P_1; $\underline{b}_1, \underline{b}_2, \underline{b}_3$ are parallel to central principal axes of B with $\underline{b}_3 = \underline{a}_3$; $\underline{c}_1, \underline{c}_2, \underline{c}_3$ are parallel to central principal axes of C with $\underline{c}_3 = \underline{a}_3$ and $\underline{c}_2$ parallel to the direction of relative translation of D and C; $\underline{e}_1, \underline{e}_2, \underline{e}_3$ are parallel to central principal axes of E with $\underline{e}_3 = \underline{a}_3$; $\underline{f}_1, \underline{f}_2, \underline{f}_3$ are parallel to central principal axes of F with $\underline{f}_3 = \underline{a}_3$ and $\underline{f}_2$ parallel to the direction of relative translation of G and F. Position vectors from mass centres B^*, C^*, etc., to points of interest can be expressed as, for example,

$$\overrightarrow{B^*P_1} = L_3\underline{b}_1 + L_4\underline{b}_2 \quad \overrightarrow{B^*P_4} = L_5\underline{b}_1 + L_6\underline{b}_2 \quad \overrightarrow{B^*P_3} = L_7\underline{b}_1 + L_8\underline{b}_2$$

$$\overrightarrow{B^*P_5} = L_9\underline{b}_1 + L_{10}\underline{b}_2$$

$$\overrightarrow{C^*P_2} = L_{11}\underline{c}_2 \quad \overrightarrow{C^*D^*} = q_{10}\underline{c}_2 \quad \overrightarrow{F^*P_5} = L_{19}\underline{f}_2 \qquad (1)$$

$$\overrightarrow{F^*G^*} = q_{11}\underline{f}_2$$

To characterize the configuration of the system, we introduce co-ordinates $q_1, \ldots, q_{11}$, where q_1 measures the angle between $\underline{n}_1$ and $\underline{a}_1$, q_2 between $\underline{a}_2$ and $\underline{c}_2$, q_3 between $\underline{a}_2$ and $\underline{b}_2$, q_4 between $\underline{a}_2$ and $\underline{f}_2$, q_5 between $\underline{a}_2$ and $\underline{e}_2$, q_6 between $\underline{b}_2$ and $\underline{c}_2$, q_7 between $\underline{b}_2$ and $\underline{e}_2$, q_8 between $\underline{b}_2$ and $\underline{f}_2$ and q_9 between $\underline{e}_2$ and $\underline{f}_2$; q_{10} and q_{11} were defined in equations (1). These definitions lead to the following relations:

$$q_6 = q_2 - q_3 \quad q_7 = q_5 - q_3 \quad q_8 = q_4 - q_3 \quad q_9 = q_4 - q_5 \qquad (2)$$

Since the system has only three degrees of freedom, it is possible to specify the configuration by assigning values to three of $q_1, \ldots, q_{11}$ and to express the remaining eight in terms of these three. Regarding q_1, q_{10} and q_{11} as independent, one can express $q_2, \ldots, q_9$ in terms of q_1, q_{10}, q_{11} by taking equations (2) into account and writing 'loop' equations that lead to geometrical constraint equations reported previously.[4]

Now we introduce a process that is central to the method at hand, namely the process of defining quantities $Z_1, \ldots, Z_{228}$ which save much writing and assure the efficiency of the final computer code. The rule for introducing these quantities is that each time we encounter a mathematical expression, involving previously defined quantities later not needed explicitly in this expression, we define a Z_x as the expression in question. For example, $Z_{34}, \ldots, Z_{85}$ are displayed in Figure 4, where $s_i \triangleq \sin q_i$, $c_i \triangleq \cos q_i$, $i = 1, \ldots, 9$.

Next we introduce generalized speeds $u_1, \ldots, u_{34}$, quantities intimately associated with the motion of the system, rather than with its configuration; that is we write

$$\underline{v}^{A^*} = 0 \quad \underline{\omega}^A = u_1\underline{a}_2 \quad \underline{\omega}^B = u_2\underline{b}_1 + u_3\underline{b}_2 + u_4\underline{b}_3 \quad \underline{v}^{B^*} = u_5\underline{b}_1 + u_6\underline{b}_2 + u_7\underline{b}_3$$

$$\underline{\omega}^C = u_8\underline{c}_1 + u_9\underline{c}_2 + u_{10}\underline{c}_3 \quad \underline{v}^{C^*} = u_{11}\underline{c}_1 + u_{12}\underline{c}_2 + u_{13}\underline{c}_3 \quad \underline{\omega}^D = \underline{\omega}^C$$

$$\underline{v}^{D^*} = u_{14}\underline{c}_1 + u_{15}\underline{c}_2 + u_{16}\underline{c}_3 \quad \underline{\omega}^E = u_{17}\underline{e}_1 + u_{18}\underline{e}_2 + u_{19}\underline{e}_3 \quad \underline{v}^{E^*} = u_{20}\underline{e}_1 + u_{21}\underline{e}_2 + u_{22}\underline{e}_3$$

$$\underline{\omega}^F = u_{23}\underline{f}_1 + u_{24}\underline{f}_2 + u_{25}\underline{f}_3 \quad \underline{v}^{F^*} = u_{26}\underline{f}_1 + u_{27}\underline{f}_2 + u_{28}\underline{f}_3 \quad \underline{\omega}^G = \underline{\omega}^F \qquad (3)$$

$$\underline{v}^{G^*} = u_{29}\underline{f}_1 + u_{30}\underline{f}_2 + u_{31}\underline{f}_3 \quad \underline{v}^H = u_{32}\underline{e}_1 + u_{33}\underline{e}_2 + u_{34}\underline{e}_3$$

Dynamics of Robots Involving Closed Loops   101

where $\underline{\omega}^B$ is the angular velocity of B in N, $\underline{v}^{B*}$ is the velocity of B^* in N, and so forth. In other words, the generalized speeds are measure numbers of velocity vectors of mass centres or of angular velocities of rigid bodies. Three of the generalized speeds, namely u_1, u_{10} and u_{25}, are now designated as independent, and the rest are expressed in terms of these three, which leads to kinematical constraint equations.

For example, we write

$$\underline{\omega}^B = \underline{\omega}^A + {}^A\underline{\omega}^B = u_1\underline{a}_2 + u_4\underline{b}_3 \Rightarrow u_2 = s_3 u_1, \quad u_3 = c_3 u_1 \quad (4)$$

$$\underline{\omega}^C = \underline{\omega}^A + {}^A\underline{\omega}^C = u_1\underline{a}_2 + u_{10}\underline{c}_3 \Rightarrow u_8 = s_2 u_1, \quad u_9 = c_2 u_1 \quad (5)$$

where ${}^A\underline{\omega}^B$ and ${}^A\underline{\omega}^C$ are the angular velocities of B in A and C in A, respectively, and

$$\underline{v}^{P_1} = \underline{\omega}^A \times \overrightarrow{A^*P_1} = \underline{v}^{B*} + \underline{\omega}^B \times \overrightarrow{B^*P_1} \qquad \underline{v}^{P_2} = \underline{\omega}^A \times \overrightarrow{A^*P_2} = \underline{v}^{C*} + \underline{\omega}^C \times \overrightarrow{C^*P_2}$$

$$\underline{v}^{P_3} = \underline{v}^{B*} + \underline{\omega}^B \times \overrightarrow{B^*P_3} = \underline{v}^{D*} + \underline{\omega}^D \times \overrightarrow{D^*P_3} \qquad \underline{v}^{D*} = \underline{v}^{C*} + \underline{\omega}^C \times \overrightarrow{C^*D^*} + {}^C\underline{v}^{D*} \quad (6)$$

which leads us to

$$u_4 = Z_{44} u_{10} \quad u_5 = Z_{45} u_{10} \quad u_6 = Z_{46} u_{10} \quad u_7 = Z_{35} u_1 \quad u_{11} = L_{11} u_{10}$$
$$u_{12} = 0 \quad u_{13} = Z_{37} u_1 \quad u_{14} = Z_{42} u_{10} \quad u_{15} = Z_{47} u_{10} \quad u_{16} = Z_{41} u_1 \quad (7)$$

Note that only u_1, u_{10} and u_{25} are kept in evidence explicitly. Applying the same procedure to the upper loop and to point H leads to analogous expressions for $u_{17}, \ldots, u_{24}, u_{26}, \ldots, u_{31}$ in terms of u_1, u_{10}, u_{25}. By using the kinematic constraint equations together with equations (3) allows one to write

$$\underline{\omega}^B = \tilde{\underline{\omega}}_1^B u_1 + \tilde{\underline{\omega}}_{10}^B u_{10} + \tilde{\underline{\omega}}_{25}^B u_{25} \quad (8)$$

$$\underline{v}^B = \tilde{\underline{v}}_1^{B*} u_1 + \tilde{\underline{v}}_{10}^{B*} u_{10} + \tilde{\underline{v}}_{25}^{B*} u_{25} \quad (9)$$

These equations constitute definitions of $\tilde{\underline{\omega}}_r^B$ and $\tilde{\underline{v}}_r^{B*}$ as the coefficients of u_r ($r = 1, 10, 25$) in equation (8) and (9) respectively. The quantities $\tilde{\underline{\omega}}_r^B$ and $\tilde{\underline{v}}_r^{B*}$ play central roles in the construction of Kane's dynamical equations. For example, equations (3), (4) and (8) permit one to identify $\tilde{\underline{\omega}}_1^B$ as

$$\tilde{\underline{\omega}}_1^B = s_3 \underline{b}_1 + c_3 \underline{b}_2 \qquad \tilde{\underline{\omega}}_{10}^B = Z_{44} \underline{b}_3 \qquad \tilde{\underline{\omega}}_{25}^B = 0 \quad (10)$$

while equations (3), (7) and (9) show that

$$\tilde{\underline{v}}_1^{B*} = Z_{35} \underline{b}_3 \qquad \tilde{\underline{v}}_{10}^{B*} = Z_{45} \underline{b}_1 + Z_{46} \underline{b}_2 \qquad \tilde{\underline{v}}_{25}^{B*} = 0 \quad (11)$$

Similarly, expressions for $\tilde{\underline{\omega}}_r^A, \tilde{\underline{v}}_r^{A*}, \tilde{\underline{\omega}}_r^C, \tilde{\underline{v}}_r^{C*}, \tilde{\underline{\omega}}_r^D, \tilde{\underline{v}}_r^{D*}, \tilde{\underline{\omega}}_r^E, \tilde{\underline{v}}_r^{E*}, \tilde{\underline{\omega}}_r^F, \tilde{\underline{v}}_r^{F*}, \tilde{\underline{\omega}}_r^G, \tilde{\underline{v}}_r^{G*}, \tilde{\underline{v}}_r^H$ ($r = 1, 10, 25$) can be formed by inspecting equations (3) and the kinematical constraint equations. The quantities $\tilde{\underline{\omega}}_r^B$ and $\tilde{\underline{v}}_r^{B*}$ are called, respectively, the nonholonomic partial angular velocity of B and the non-holonomic partial velocity of B^*.[4]

In addition to partial angular velocities and partial velocities, we need the accelerations of $B^*, \ldots, G^*, H$ in N expressed in forms bringing $\dot{u}_1, \ldots, \dot{u}_{34}$ into evidence explicitly. For example, use of equations (3) allows one to form the acceleration of B^* in N as

$$Z_{34} = L_4 s_3 - L_3 c_3 \qquad Z_{35} = -L_1 - Z_{34} \qquad Z_{36} = L_{11} s_2$$

$$Z_{37} = -L_2 - Z_{36} \qquad Z_{38} = Z_{35} + s_3 L_8 - c_3 L_7 \qquad Z_{39} = -c_6 Z_4 - s_6 Z_3$$

$$Z_{40} = s_6 Z_4 - c_6 Z_3 \qquad Z_{41} = Z_{38} - s_2 L_{12} \qquad Z_{42} = L_{11} - q_{10} \qquad Z_{43} = Z_{42} - L_{12}$$

$$Z_{44} = Z_{43}/Z_{39} \qquad Z_{45} = L_4 Z_{44} \qquad Z_{46} = -L_3 Z_{44} \qquad Z_{47} = Z_{40} Z_{44}$$

$$Z_{48} = Z_{45} - L_6 Z_{44} \qquad Z_{49} = Z_{46} + L_5 Z_{44} \qquad Z_{50} = Z_{35} + s_3 L_6 - c_3 L_5$$

$$Z_{51} = c_7 Z_{48} + s_7 Z_{49} \qquad Z_{52} = -s_7 Z_{48} + c_7 Z_{49} \qquad Z_{53} = s_5 L_{14} - c_5 L_{13}$$

$$Z_{54} = Z_{50} - Z_{53} \qquad Z_{55} = Z_{45} - L_{10} Z_{44} \qquad Z_{56} = Z_{46} + L_9 Z_{44}$$

$$Z_{57} = Z_{35} + s_3 L_{10} - c_3 L_9 \qquad Z_{58} = c_8 Z_{55} + s_8 Z_{56} \qquad Z_{59} = -s_8 Z_{55} + c_8 Z_{56}$$

$$Z_{60} = Z_{57} - L_{10} s_4 \qquad Z_{61} = Z_{54} + s_5 L_{16} - c_5 L_{15} \qquad Z_{62} = c_9 Z_{51} + s_9 Z_{52}$$

$$Z_{63} = -c_9 Z_{20} - s_9 Z_{19} \qquad Z_{64} = -s_9 Z_{51} + c_9 Z_{52} \qquad Z_{65} = s_9 Z_{20} - c_9 Z_{19}$$

$$Z_{66} = Z_{61} - L_{20} s_4 \qquad Z_{67} = L_{19} - q_{11} \qquad Z_{68} = Z_{58} - Z_{62} \qquad Z_{69} = Z_{67} - L_{20}$$

$$Z_{70} = Z_{68}/Z_{63} \qquad Z_{71} = Z_{69}/Z_{63} \qquad Z_{72} = Z_{51} + L_{14} Z_{70} \qquad Z_{73} = L_{14} Z_{71}$$

$$Z_{74} = Z_{52} - L_{13} Z_{70} \qquad Z_{75} = -L_{13} Z_{71} \qquad Z_{76} = Z_{64} + Z_{65} Z_{70} \qquad Z_{77} = Z_{65} Z_{71}$$

$$Z_{78} = Z_{72} - L_{18} Z_{70} \qquad Z_{79} = Z_{73} - L_{18} Z_{71} \qquad Z_{80} = Z_{74} + L_{17} Z_{70}$$

$$Z_{81} = Z_{75} + L_{17} Z_{71} \qquad Z_{82} = Z_{64} + s_5 L_{18} - c_5 L_{17} \qquad Z_{83} = u_3 u_7 - u_4 u_6$$

$$Z_{84} = u_4 u_5 - u_2 u_7 \qquad Z_{85} = u_2 u_6 - u_3 u_5$$

Figure 4 Non-holonomic accelerations of $B^*, \ldots, G^*, H$ in N

$$\underline{a}^{B^*} = \frac{{}^B d \underline{v}^{B^*}}{dt} + \underline{\omega}^B \times \underline{v}^{B^*} = (\dot{u}_5 + Z_{83})\underline{b}_1 + (\dot{u}_6 + Z_{84})\underline{b}_2 + (\dot{u}_7 + Z_{85})\underline{b}_3 \qquad (12)$$

where Z_{83}, Z_{84}, Z_{85} are given in Figure 4.

Expressions for the accelerations, $\underline{a}^{C^*}, \underline{a}^{D^*}, \underline{a}^{E^*}, \underline{a}^{F^*}, \underline{a}^{G^*}, \underline{a}^{H}$ are constructed with equal ease. These expressions involve quantities $Z_{86}, \ldots, Z_{103}$ (see ref. 4). The next step is the formulation of inertia torques. For a rigid body R with moments of inertia R_1, R_2, R_3 about central principal axes respectively parallel to unit vectors $\underline{r}_1, \underline{r}_2, \underline{r}_3$, and with an angular velocity $\underline{\omega}^R$ in N, where $\underline{\omega}^R = \omega_1 \underline{r}_1 + \omega_2 \underline{r}_2 + \omega_3 \underline{r}_3$, the inertia torque $\underline{T}_R^*$ is given by

$$\underline{T}_R^* = [-\dot{\omega}_1 R_1 + \omega_2 \omega_3 (R_2 - R_3)]\underline{r}_1 + [-\dot{\omega}_2 R_2 + \omega_3 \omega_1 (R_3 - R_1)]\underline{r}_2$$
$$+ [-\dot{\omega}_3 R_3 + \omega_1 \omega_2 (R_1 - R_2)] \underline{r}_3 \qquad (13)$$

Again keeping $\dot{u}_1, \ldots, \dot{u}_{34}$ in explicit evidence, one can write, for example, with the aid of equations (3)

$$\underline{T}_B^* = (-\dot{u}_2 B_1 + Z_{104})\underline{b}_1 + (-\dot{u}_3 B_2 + Z_{105})\underline{b}_2 + (-\dot{u}_4 B_3 + Z_{106})\underline{b}_3 \tag{14}$$

where

$$Z_{104} = u_3 u_4 (B_2 - B_3) \quad Z_{105} = u_4 u_2 (B_3 - B_1) \quad Z_{106} = u_2 u_3 (B_1 - B_2)$$

The derivation of inertia torque expressions is analogous for A, C, D, E, F and G.

The analysis performed so far provides the ingredients needed for the construction of expressions for generalized inertia forces $\widetilde{K}_r^*$. The contribution $(\widetilde{K}_r^*)_R$ of a rigid body R to $\widetilde{K}_r^*$ can be shown to be given by (p.123)[3]

$$(\widetilde{K}_r^*)_R = \widetilde{\underline{\omega}}_r^R \cdot \underline{T}_R^* + \widetilde{\underline{v}}_r^{R*} \cdot \underline{F}_R^* \tag{15}$$

where, for our system, $r = 1, 10, 25$. $\underline{F}_R^*$ is the inertia force defined as

$$\underline{F}_R^* \triangleq -m_R \underline{a}^{R*} \tag{16}$$

and m_R is the mass of R while $\underline{a}^{R*}$ is the acceleration of R^* in N. The total generalized inertia force $\widetilde{K}_r^*$ for the system at hand is then given by

$$\widetilde{K}_r^* = (\widetilde{K}_r^*)_A + (\widetilde{K}_r^*)_B + (\widetilde{K}_r^*)_C + (\widetilde{K}_r^*)_D + (\widetilde{K}_r^*)_E + (\widetilde{K}_r^*)_F + (\widetilde{K}_r^*)_G + (\widetilde{K}_r^*)_H$$

$$= \widetilde{\underline{\omega}}_r^A \cdot \underline{T}_A^* - m_A \widetilde{\underline{v}}_r^{A*} \cdot \underline{a}^{A*} + \widetilde{\underline{\omega}}_r^B \cdot \underline{T}_B^* - m_B \widetilde{\underline{v}}_r^{B*} \cdot \underline{a}^{B*} + \widetilde{\underline{\omega}}_r^C \cdot \underline{T}_C^* - m_C \widetilde{\underline{v}}_r^{C*} \cdot \underline{a}^{C*}$$

$$+ \widetilde{\underline{\omega}}_r^D \cdot \underline{T}_D^* - m_D \widetilde{\underline{v}}_r^{D*} \cdot \underline{a}^{D*} + \widetilde{\underline{\omega}}_r^E \cdot \underline{T}_E^* - m_E \widetilde{\underline{v}}_r^{E*} \cdot \underline{a}^{E*} + \widetilde{\underline{\omega}}_r^F \cdot \underline{T}_F^*$$

$$- m_F \widetilde{\underline{v}}_r^{F*} \cdot \underline{a}^{F*} + \widetilde{\underline{\omega}}_r^G \cdot \underline{T}_G^* - m_G \widetilde{\underline{v}}_r^{G*} \cdot \underline{a}^{G*} - m_H \widetilde{\underline{v}}_r^H \cdot \underline{a}^H \quad (r = 1, 10, 25) \tag{17}$$

Since the dot multiplications in equation (17) only involve quantities that have been evaluated in corresponding components, building the generalized inertia forces $\widetilde{K}_1^*, \widetilde{K}_{10}^*, \widetilde{K}_{25}^*$ is a straightforward assembly task. For example, to find $\widetilde{K}_1^*$ we refer to equations (10), (11), (12), (14) and (17) for the contribution of body B to $\widetilde{K}_1^*$, and to the corresponding equations for bodies A, C, D, E, F, G and point H. This leads directly to

$$\widetilde{K}_1^* = -\dot{u}_1 A_2 + s_3(-\dot{u}_2 B_1 + Z_{104}) + c_3(-\dot{u}_3 B_2 + Z_{105}) - m_B Z_{35}(\dot{u}_7 + Z_{85})$$

$$+ s_2(-\dot{u}_8 C_1 + Z_{110}) + c_2(-\dot{u}_9 C_2 + Z_{111}) - m_C Z_{37}(\dot{u}_{13} + Z_{88})$$

$$+ s_2(-\dot{u}_8 D_1 + Z_{113}) + c_2(-\dot{u}_9 D_2 + Z_{114}) - m_D Z_{41} - m_D Z_{47}(\dot{u}_{16} + Z_{91})$$

$$+ s_5(-\dot{u}_{17} E_1 + Z_{116}) + c_5(-\dot{u}_{18} E_2 + Z_{117}) - m_E Z_{54}(\dot{u}_{22} + Z_{94})$$

$$+ s_4(-\dot{u}_{23} F_1 + Z_{122}) + c_4(-\dot{u}_{24} F_2 + Z_{123}) - m_F Z_{60}(\dot{u}_{28} + Z_{97})$$

$$+ s_4(-\dot{u}_{23} G_1 + Z_{125}) + c_4(-\dot{u}_{24} G_2 + Z_{126}) - m_G Z_{66}(\dot{u}_{31} + Z_{100})$$

$$- m_H Z_{82}(\dot{u}_{34} + Z_{103})$$

$$= -A_2 \dot{u}_1 - Z_{128} \dot{u}_2 - Z_{129} \dot{u}_3 - Z_{130} \dot{u}_7 - Z_{131} \dot{u}_8 - Z_{132} \dot{u}_9 - Z_{133} \dot{u}_{13}$$

$$- Z_{134} \dot{u}_{16} - Z_{135} \dot{u}_{17} - Z_{136} \dot{u}_{18} - Z_{137} \dot{u}_{22} - Z_{138} \dot{u}_{23} - Z_{139} \dot{u}_{24}$$

$$- Z_{140} \dot{u}_{28} - Z_{141} \dot{u}_{31} - Z_{142} \dot{u}_{34} + Z_{143} \tag{18}$$

So far, the generalized inertia forces still involve $\dot{u}_1, \ldots, \dot{u}_{34}$. The next step is to write $\dot{u}_2, \ldots, \dot{u}_9, \dot{u}_{11}, \ldots, \dot{u}_{24}, \dot{u}_{26}, \ldots, \dot{u}_{34}$ in terms of $\dot{u}_1, \dot{u}_{10}, \dot{u}_{25}$, the time derivatives of the three independent generalized speeds. The resulting expressions involve time derivatives of $Z_{34}, \ldots, Z_{82}$ and of the co-ordinates $q_1, \ldots, q_{11}$, which must be expressed in terms of already defined quantities. For q_r ($r = 1, \ldots, 11$) this leads to the following kinematical differential equations:

$$\dot{q}_1 = u_1 \quad \dot{q}_2 = u_{10} \quad \dot{q}_3 = u_4 \quad \dot{q}_4 = u_{25} \quad \dot{q}_5 = u_{19} \quad \dot{q}_6 = u_{10} - u_4 = Z_{171}$$

$$\dot{q}_7 = u_{19} - u_4 = Z_{172} \qquad \dot{q}_8 = u_{25} - u_4 = Z_{173} \qquad \dot{q}_9 = u_{25} - u_{19} = Z_{174}$$

$$\dot{q}_{10} = u_{15} \qquad \dot{q}_{11} = \dot{u}_{30} - u_{27} = Z_{175} \tag{19}$$

To obtain the desired relations for $\dot{Z}_{34}, \ldots, \dot{Z}_{82}$, we start with $\dot{Z}_{34}$ after defining $c_{1i} \triangleq \dot{c}_i = -s_i \dot{q}_i$ and $\dot{s}_{1i} \triangleq \dot{s}_i = c_i \dot{q}_i$ ($i = 1, \ldots, 9$), and work our way up to $\dot{Z}_{82}$ as follows:

$$\dot{Z}_{34} = Z_{176} = L_4 s_{13} - L_3 c_{13} \quad \dot{Z}_{35} = -Z_{176} \quad \dot{Z}_{36} = Z_{177} = L_{11} s_{12} \quad \dot{Z}_{37} = -Z_{177}$$

$$\dot{Z}_{38} = Z_{178} = -Z_{176} + s_{13} L_8 - c_{13} L_7 \quad \ldots \quad \dot{Z}_{41} = Z_{181} = Z_{178} - s_{12} L_{12} \quad \ldots$$

$$\dot{Z}_{82} = Z_{219} = Z_{192} + s_{15} L_{18} - c_{15} L_{17} \tag{20}$$

To bring the generalized inertia forces $\tilde{K}_r^*$ ($r = 1, 10, 25$) into final form, all that remains to be done is to differentiate first equations (7) and their analogues for $u_{17}, \ldots, u_{24}, u_{26}, \ldots, u_{31}$, which, for example, gives together with (20)

$$\ldots \quad \dot{u}_7 = Z_{35} \dot{u}_1 - Z_{176} u_1 \quad \ldots \quad \dot{u}_{13} = Z_{37} \dot{u}_1 - Z_{177} u_1 \quad \ldots$$

$$\dot{u}_{16} = Z_{41} \dot{u}_1 - Z_{181} u_1 \quad \ldots \tag{21}$$

Thereafter, we substitute into the previously formed expressions for $\tilde{K}_1^*$ [see equation (18)], $\tilde{K}_{10}^*$, $\tilde{K}_{25}^*$. For $\tilde{K}_1^*$ this yields

$$\tilde{K}_1^* = -A_2 u_1 - Z_{128}(s_3 \dot{u}_1 + s_{13} u_1) - Z_{129}(c_3 \dot{u}_1 + c_{13} u_1) - Z_{130}(Z_{35} \dot{u}_1 - Z_{176} u_1)$$

$$- Z_{131}(s_2 \dot{u}_1 + s_{12} u_1) - Z_{132}(c_2 \dot{u}_1 + c_{12} u_1) - Z_{133}(Z_{37} \dot{u}_1 - Z_{177} u_1)$$

$$- Z_{134}(Z_{41} \dot{u}_1 + Z_{181} u_1) - Z_{135}(s_5 \dot{u}_1 + s_{15} u_1) - Z_{136}(c_5 \dot{u}_1 + c_{15} u_1)$$

$$- Z_{137}(Z_{54} \dot{u}_1 + Z_{192} u_1) - Z_{138}(s_4 \dot{u}_1 + s_{14} u_1) - Z_{139}(c_4 \dot{u}_1 + c_{14} u_1)$$

$$- Z_{140}(Z_{60} \dot{u}_1 + Z_{198} u_1) - Z_{141}(Z_{66} \dot{u}_1 + Z_{204} u_1) - Z_{142}(Z_{82} \dot{u}_1 + Z_{219} u_1) + Z_{143}$$

$$= -x_{11} \dot{u}_1 + Z_{220} \tag{22}$$

For $\tilde{K}_{10}^*$, $\tilde{K}_{25}^*$ the final form is

$$\tilde{K}_{10}^* = -x_{22} \dot{u}_{10} - x_{23} \dot{u}_{25} + Z_{221} \qquad \tilde{K}_{25}^* = -x_{32} \dot{u}_{10} - x_{33} \dot{u}_{25} + Z_{222} \tag{23}$$

In addition to generalized inertia forces, Kane's dynamical equations involve generalized active forces. For a set of contact and/or body forces acting on a rigid body R and equivalent to a couple of torque $\underline{T}_R$ together with a force $\underline{R}$ applied at

Dynamics of Robots Involving Closed Loops   105

point Q of R, the contribution $(\widetilde{K}_r)_R$ of this set of forces to the rth generalized active force $\widetilde{K}_r$ is given by (p.81)[3]

$$(\widetilde{K}_r)_R = \widetilde{\omega}_r^R \cdot \underline{T}_R + \widetilde{\underline{v}}_r^Q \cdot \underline{R} \tag{24}$$

where ω_r^R and v_r^Q are, respectively, the rth partial angular velocity of R in N and the rth partial velocity of Q in N.

For our system there are two kinds of forces that contribute to generalized active forces, namely contact forces exerted to rotate A in N and to translate D relative to C and G relative to F, and gravitational forces exerted by the earth on $A, \ldots, H$.

All other forces, sometimes called *non-working forces*, make no contributions to generalized active forces. It can be shown[4] that for our system the total rth generalized active force $\widetilde{K}_r$ thus can be written as

$$\widetilde{K}_r = \widetilde{\omega}_r^A \cdot \underline{T}^{N/A} + (\widetilde{\underline{v}}_r^{D^*} - \widetilde{\underline{v}}_r^{C^*}) \cdot \underline{R}^{C/D} + (\widetilde{\underline{v}}_r^{G^*} - \widetilde{\underline{v}}_r^{F^*}) \cdot \underline{R}^{F/G} + \widetilde{\underline{v}}_r^{A^*} \cdot \underline{G}_A + \widetilde{\underline{v}}_r^{B^*} \cdot \underline{G}_B$$
$$+ \widetilde{\underline{v}}_r^{C^*} \cdot \underline{G}_C + \widetilde{\underline{v}}_r^{D^*} \cdot \underline{G}_D + \widetilde{\underline{v}}_r^{E^*} \cdot \underline{G}_E + \widetilde{\underline{v}}_r^{F^*} \cdot \underline{G}_F + \widetilde{\underline{v}}_r^{G^*} \cdot \underline{G}_G + \widetilde{\underline{v}}_r^H \cdot \underline{G}_H \tag{25}$$

where $\underline{T}^{N/A}$ is the torque of the set of contact forces exerted by N on A if this set is replaced with a couple together with a force at A^* and $\underline{R}^{C/D}$, $\underline{R}^{F/G}$ are, respectively, the resultant of D^* of the set of contact forces exerted by C on D and the resultant at G^* of the set of contact forces exerted by F on G. $\underline{G}_A, \ldots, \underline{G}_H$ denote the gravitational forces exerted by the earth on $A, \ldots, H$ respectively.

Once these gravitational forces have been written in components along the bodies' principal axes, e.g. $\underline{G}_B = -m_B g(s_3 \underline{b}_1 + c_3 \underline{b}_2)$, writing $\widetilde{K}_r$ in terms of defined scalar quantities is a simple assembly task involving equations (10), (11) and their analogues and equation (25). The final expressions turn out to be

$$\widetilde{K}_1 = \tau \qquad \widetilde{K}_{10} = Z_{47}\sigma_1 + Z_{223}\sigma_2 + Z_{224} \qquad \widetilde{K}_{25} = Z_{77}\sigma_2 + Z_{225} \tag{26}$$

where τ, σ_1, σ_2 are defined as follows:

$$\tau \triangleq \underline{T}^{N/A} \cdot \underline{a}_2 \qquad \sigma_1 = \underline{R}^{C/D} \cdot \underline{c}_2 \qquad \sigma_2 = \underline{R}^{F/G} \cdot \underline{f}_2 \tag{27}$$

To arrive at the dynamical equations governing a system of the type shown in Figures 2 and 3, all that remains to be done is to substitute from equations (22), (23) and (26) into Kane's dynamical equations (p.177)[3]

$$\widetilde{K}_r^* + \widetilde{K}_r = 0 \qquad (r = 1, 10, 25) \tag{28}$$

Thus one obtains

$$x_{11}\dot{u}_1 = Z_{220} + \tau \qquad x_{22}\dot{u}_{10} + x_{23}\dot{u}_{25} = Z_{221} + Z_{47}\sigma_1 + Z_{223}\sigma_2 + Z_{224}$$
$$x_{23}\dot{u}_{10} + x_{33}\dot{u}_{25} = Z_{222} + Z_{77}\sigma_2 + Z_{225} \tag{29}$$

Equations (29) participate pre-eminently in the solution of two classes of problems.

The first of these, sometimes called the *problem of inverse dynamics*, consists of finding τ, σ_1 and σ_2 when the time dependence of q_1, q_{10}, q_{11} is given explicitly. The algorithm leading to a solution of this problem is reported in detail.[4]

The second class of problems involves the rapid simulation of motions of the structure under consideration. Here, one must first specify τ, σ_1 and σ_2 as explicit functions of $q_1, \ldots, q_{11}, u_1, \ldots, u_{34}, Z_1, \ldots, Z_{225}$ and/or t. In many cases, this is equivalent to formulating a feedback-control law. Also, initial values must be assigned to q_1, q_{10}, q_{11} and u_1, u_{10}, u_{25}. For the purpose of determining any of $q_1, \ldots, q_{11}$ as functions of t for $t > 0$, one then performs a simultaneous numerical integration of the three kinematical differential equations involving $\dot{q}_1, \dot{q}_{10}, \dot{q}_{11}$, equations (19), and the three dynamical equations, equation (28). Aside from producing results of interest in their own right, a simulation program can furnish valuable tests of the validity of the underlying equations, and thus of torque and force calculations based on these equations. This is the case whenever one can construct an expression for one or more quantities known to remain constant throughout a motion of the system. It is shown[4] that for the system at hand expressions for several such quantities can be constructed.

Conclusions

A procedure leading to the dynamical equations for manipulators involving closed loops has been presented. Quantities $Z_1, \ldots, Z_{225}$ were introduced with the dual purpose of saving the analyst a great deal of writing and producing an easily programmable, computationally efficient, form of the equations. The use of Kane's equations frees one from the burden of either introducing and subsequently eliminating undetermined multipliers, as with the Lagrange approach, or bringing into evidence and then eliminating non-working constraint forces and torques, as with the Newton–Euler method. The CPU-time needed for the evaluation of τ, σ_1 and σ_2 was measured on a DEC 2050 computer. It amounts to 6.8 ms, which should allow a sampling frequency sufficiently high for on-line control applications.[4] Finally, it should be pointed out that for open-loop systems exactly the same procedure applies, except that one does not have to deal with geometrical constraints, since the number of co-ordinates is then equal to the number of degrees of freedom.

References

[1] Brady, Hollerbach, Johnson, Lozano-Perez and Mason (1982) *Robot Motion* MIT Press, Massachusetts
[2] Huston R L and Kelly F A New approaches in robot dynamics and control, *Computers in Engineering*, vol 2, Proc. Second Int. Computer Engineering Conf., San Diego, 1982
[3] Kane T R (1968) *Dynamics* Holt, Rinehart and Winston,
[4] Faessler H P (1983) Dynamics of manipulators with closed kinematic loops, Engineer's thesis, Stanford University, California

Part 3
Control of Motion

Non-adaptive Dynamic Control for Manipulation Robots: Invited Survey Paper

M Vukobratović and D Stokić

Institute 'Mihailo Pupin', 11000 Beograd, Yugoslavia

Introduction

This paper is a brief survey of non-adaptive dynamic control of manipulation robots. We shall concentrate mainly on the problems of control synthesis of executive control level, but as in some approaches tactical and executive control level are indistinguishable, we have to mention also some problems concerning trajectories planning and their generation.

Under dynamic control of manipulation robots we assume such control laws that take into account dynamic effects of the robotic systems while performing various trajectories. Thus, various kinematic approaches that are based exclusively on kinematic models of the robots, are not included in this survey. We also restrict ourselves to non-adaptive control of robots, i.e. to control schemes which do not include adaptation to robot parameter variation. However, we shall consider robots with variable parameters and discuss robustness of various control laws to parameter variations (variation of payload parameters).

Problems with dynamic control of robotic systems

The problems that are connected with dynamic control of manipulation robots have been discussed already.[1] Here we shall mention some of them.

Let us consider the robotic system S consisting of the mechanical part of the system S^M and actuators S^i. The system has n degrees of freedom each powered by one actuator S^i. The model of the actuator is given by linear time-invariant system

$$S^i: \dot{x}^i = A^i x^i + b^i u^i + f^i P_i, \qquad \forall i \epsilon I = \left\{i: i = 1, 2, \ldots, n\right\} \qquad (1)$$

where $x^i \epsilon R^{n_i}$ is the vector of state co-ordinates of S^i, n_i is the order of the model S^i, $A^i \epsilon R^{n_i \times n_i}$ is the system matrix, $b^i \epsilon R^{n_i}$ is the input distribution vector, $f^i \epsilon R^{n_i}$ is the load distribution vector, $u^i \epsilon R^1$ is the input to actuator S^i, P_i is the driving torque (load) acting on the ith DOF (actuator). The model of the mechanical part of the system is given in a general form[2]

$$S^M: P = H(q, \theta) \ddot{q} + h(q, \dot{q}, \theta) \qquad (2)$$

where $q(t) \epsilon R^n$ is the vector of internal mechanism co-ordinates, $\theta \epsilon R^{n_p}$ is the vector of mechanism parameters, $P(t) \epsilon R^n$ the vector of driving torques (forces); $H(q, \theta)$ is a full-rank positive definite inertial matrix-valued function, $h(q, \dot{q}, \theta)$ is a vector function due to gravity, centrifugal and Coriolis effects. It is also assumed that in each x^i two state co-ordinates coincide with q^i and $\dot{q}^i$. Thus, the state vector of the overall system S is given by $x = (x^{1T}, \ldots, x^{nT})^T$, the order of the system S is

$N = \sum_{i=1}^{n} n_i$. The following control task is imposed. The nominal trajectory of the state co-ordinates of the system S is given $x^o(t) = [x^{o1T}(t), x^{o2T}(t), \ldots, x^{onT}(t)]^T$, $\forall t \epsilon T$, $T = \{t: t\epsilon(0,\tau)\}$, τ = given time period. The control should be synthesized ensuring practical stability of the system around the nominal trajectory, so that $\forall x(0) \epsilon X^I$ and $\forall \theta \epsilon \Theta$ implies $x[t, x(0)] \epsilon X^t(t)$, $\forall t \epsilon T$, where $X^I C R^N$ is given finite region of allowable initial conditions and $X^t(t) C R^N$, $\forall t \epsilon T$, is given finite region of allowable system states at arbitrary moment $t \epsilon T$. Here, it is assumed that $x^o(0) \epsilon X^I$ and $x^o(t) \epsilon X^t(t)$, $\forall t \epsilon T$. Here, Θ denotes the set of allowable values of parameters, $\Theta \epsilon R^{n_p}$.

The main problem with control of robotic systems is 'To what extent is it necessary to include dynamic terms in the control law?' Namely, the mathematical model of the robotic mechanism S^M (2) in the general case is a very complex non-linear system of differential equations. The problem of on-line computation of robot's dynamic model is very difficult; here, we shall not discuss various methods for obtaining on-line computation of the dynamic model. It is noteworthy that a study[3] exists on the computational efficiency and comparison of various methods for computing the input torques P by (2). This study was based on a survey of numerical solution techniques made by Hollerbach.[4] However, the analytical models of robot dynamics, that have been proposed by Vukobratović and Kirćanski,[5] lead so far to the fastest computation of robot dynamic models. Unfortunately, even here computation of driving torques is too complex (for some types of robot structures) to be computed by temporary 16-bit microprocessors. Numerous attempts have been made to use simplified models of robot dynamics in which some terms have been neglected to simplify on-line computation of control. We shall mention some of them while discussing various control laws. Usually centrifugal and Coriolis terms in (2) have been neglected as these terms are insignificant while the robot approaches its goal position and orientation (since the joint velocities are low during that time). However, if we attempt to ensure precise tracking of fast trajectories, these velocity-dependent terms have to be compensated for too. To implement on-line computation of dynamic model of the robot we have to use a complex multiprocessor system. Thus trade-off between the complexity of control equipment and the performance of the robot has to be made; the more complex the law we use, the more complex is the controller hardware, but the performance of the robot would be better.

Thus, for various types of robots and robotic tasks it should be carefully considered as to which terms in the dynamic model might be neglected. This is the reason why a software package for computer-aided synthesis of dynamic control of manipulation robot has been developed.[1,6,7] Using this package, the designer of the robot can determine the simplest control law which is compatible with the robot dynamics and control task. We shall present this approach at the end of the survey.

In the text following we shall briefly present some solutions to the above-mentioned problems of dynamic control of robotic systems. We have tried to choose the most representative contributions to the dynamic control synthesis. For clarity of presentation we have divided all the approaches into six sections.

Optimal control synthesis

One of the dilemmas arising in control of robotic systems is whether or not we should minimize some criteria in control synthesis. To synthesize the control which would satisfy the given control task and minimize some adopted criteria is a very complex problem, for many reasons; some of these are listed following: (a) complexity of the highly non-linear model of robotic system (2); (b) choice of criterion is often conditional and heuristic; (c) constraints imposed by the control task [through region $X^t(t)$] are usually severe; (d) parameters of the robot are unknown and variable which make the optimization procedure very difficult. However, a few attempts to minimize some criteria in the control synthesis have been made.

Kahn and Roth[8] have considered the time-optimal control problem: given the robotic system with the initial state $x(0)$ and the terminal constraint $x^0(t_s)$, find the control $u(t)$ which transfers the state of the system from $x(0)$ to $x^0(t_s)$ in the minimum time. It can be shown that the analytical solution to this problem cannot be found even for a particular manipulation robot with three revolute joints which has been considered by Kahn and Roth.[8]

Owing to the non-linearity of the model, only a numerical solution is obtainable which yields the optimal control only as a function of time, and does not account for any unexpected disturbances which may act on the robot or parameter variations. In addition, the computations must be repeated for each new set of initial or terminal conditions. To obtain feedback control an approximation to optimal control has been proposed.[8]

Suboptimal control is obtained by linearizing the mathematical model of the robot around the terminal point and the decoupling of the model is performed by neglecting coupling. Thus, the robot model decouples into n double integrator systems for which analytical solution to the above-stated optimization problem is well-known.

It has been shown that, for a particular robot, suboptimal control results in response times and trajectories which are reasonably close to the optimal solutions. However, for more complex manipulation robots and longer distance between the terminal points this solution might be too suboptimal. On the other hand, the suboptimal control for this problem is bang-bang, which is hardly acceptable for robots due to overload of actuators.

A similar approach has been proposed by Young,[9] but instead of time-optimal control, he adopted criteria with respect to the robot's accelerations

$$J = \int_0^T \tfrac{1}{2}(\ddot{q}^T M \ddot{q})\, dt \qquad (3)$$

where $M \in R^{n \times n}$ is a positive definite matrix. Again the robotic system is considered as a set of n double integrator plants. Optimal trajectories $q^{io}(t)$ which drive the double integrators from a given initial state $x^{io}(0)$ to a desired state $x^{io}(\tau)$ are well known.

From (2) the driving torques that would drive the system along the desired trajectories are computed. Obviously, these result in open-loop control and this control requires on-line computation of the complete dynamic model of the robot. The control obtained is far from being optimal for a complete non-linear model of the robot. On the other hand, since the control is an explicit function of time, it is not robust to parameter variations.

Optimal regulator

The approaches described above were intended for positional control of robots.

The problem of tracking some prescribed path in work space is more complex, so approaches by optimal synthesis can hardly accommodate this problem.

An alternative approach is to compute nominal trajectory $x^0(t)$ by using a kinematic model of the robot and then to ensure tracking of this trajectory taking into account the dynamic model of the robot.

Combination of the models of actuators S^i (1) and the model of the mechanism S^M (2) gives the model of the robot in the centralized form

$$\dot{x} = A_D(x, \theta) + B_D(x, \theta) u(t) \qquad (4)$$

where A_D is $N \times 1$ vector function of the robot state x and parameter θ, B_D is $N \times n$ input distribution matrix which is also a function of x and θ. Let us assume that nominal (programmed) control $u^0(t)$ exists that satisfies

$$\dot{x}^0(t) = A_A[x^0(t), \theta^0] + B_D[x^0(t), \theta^0] u^0(t) \qquad (5)$$

where θ^0 denotes some nominal value of parameter. Now let us consider the model of deviation from nominal trajectory in the form

$$\Delta \dot{x} = \bar{A}^0(\Delta x, \theta, t) + \bar{B}^0(\Delta x, \theta, t) \Delta u \qquad (6)$$

where $\Delta x(t) = x(t) - x^0(t)$, $\Delta u(t) = u(t) - u^0(t)$ and $\bar{A}^0$ and $\bar{B}^0$ are the appropriate $N \times 1$ vector and $N \times n$ matrix respectively.

Now, if we want to synthesize control which should stabilize the model of deviation (6) [i.e. to ensure tracking of desired trajectory $x^0(t)$], we might again try to minimize some criteria. The most commonly applied criterion is the standard quadratic one. If we try to minimize such a criterion using the non-linear model of the robot (6) we shall encounter numerous problems. The common approach in solving this problem is to consider some approximate model. The linearized model of the robot around nominal trajectory leads to a well-known solution of optimal linear regulator.

Popov and co-authors[10] were the first to synthesize an optimal linear regulator for robotic manipulators. They have developed a numerical procedure for linearization of model (6) on a digital computer. The linearized model is obtained in the form

$$\Delta \dot{x} = \tilde{A}^0(\theta^0, t) \Delta x + \tilde{B}^0(\theta^0, t) \Delta u \qquad (7)$$

where $\tilde{A}^0$ and $\tilde{B}^0$ are $N \times N$ and $N \times n$ matrices respectively. It is well known that the optimal control-minimizing standard quadratic criterion

$$J = \int_0^T (\Delta x^T Q \Delta x + \Delta u^T R \Delta u) dt \qquad (8)$$

where $Q \epsilon R^{N \times N}$ is a positive semidefinite matrix and $\underline{R} \epsilon R^{n \times n}$ is a positive definite matrix, is given by:

$$\Delta u(t) = -\underline{R}^{-1} \tilde{B}^{0T}(\theta^0, t) K(\theta^0, t) \Delta x(t) = D(\theta^0, t) \Delta x(t) \qquad (9)$$

where $K \epsilon R^{N \times N}$ is a positive definite symmetrical matrix, which is the solution of the differential matrix equation of the Riccati type.

Obviously, control (9) requires time-varying gains in the feedback loops. The implementation of such a control is very difficult and it demands a large memory capacity of the control computer to store time-variable gains. To simplify implementation of the control law, a linear time-invariant model of deviation from nominal trajectory is obtained by 'time-averaging' the model (7) and involving criteria in which $\tau \to \infty$.

It is well known that the control is now obtained in the form

$$u(t) = -\underline{R}^{-1}\widetilde{\overline{B}}^{0T}(\theta^0)K(\theta^0)\Delta x(t) = D(\theta^0)\Delta x(t) \qquad (10)$$

where $K \in R^{N \times N}$ is the solution of the algebraic matrix equation of the Riccati type and $\widetilde{\overline{B}}^{0T}$ is $N \times n$ input distribution matrix of the time-invariant linearized model of the robot.

Three main problems arise concerning the optimal regulator (10): (a) it is evident that a linear regulator requires a complex control structure with many feedback loops ($N \times n$); (b) the linear regulator guarantees stability only of the linearized model of the robot (as robot models are usually highly non-linear it is very questionable whether such a linear control can accommodate a real non-linear model of the robot); (c) the linear regulator is not robust enough to withstand parameter variations.

Popov et al.[11] attempted to compensate for non-linearities of the real robot models and to make the control law more adequate for non-linear models of robots. For the sake of this, they observed the model of the robot (6) in the form

$$\Delta \dot{x} = \widetilde{\overline{A}}^0 \Delta x + f(\Delta x, \theta) + \widetilde{\overline{B}}^0 \Delta u \qquad (11)$$

where f is $N \times 1$ vector defined by $f = \overline{A}^0(\Delta x, \theta) - \widetilde{\overline{A}}^0(\theta)\Delta x$ and $\widetilde{\overline{A}}^0$ is the $N \times N$ matrix of the time-invariant linearized model of the robot. [We have assumed linearization around terminal point $x^0(\tau)$.] The control minimizing (8), for $\tau \to \infty$, with constraint given by (11), is taken in the form

$$\Delta u(t) = \Delta u_{\text{lin}}(t) + \Delta u_{\text{non}}(t) = -\underline{R}^{-1}\widetilde{\overline{B}}^{0T}K\Delta x$$
$$- \underline{R}^{-1}\widetilde{\overline{B}}^{0T}(\widetilde{\overline{A}}^0 - K\widetilde{\overline{B}}^0\underline{R}^{-1}\widetilde{\overline{B}}^{0T})^{-1} \cdot K \cdot f(\Delta x, \theta) \qquad (12)$$

Obviously, this control law differs from the classical optimal regulator due to the addition of the non-linear part Δu_{non} which has a role to compensate for non-linear effects of the robot model. However, the main problem with this control lies in its complexity. In addition to the complex control structure of optimal linear-regulator, control (12) it requires on-line computation of the non-linear term $f(\Delta x, \theta)$. This means that the complete model of the robot dynamics has to be computed on-line. On the other hand, the robustness of such a control scheme to parameter variations is questionable.

A similar idea to compensate for the non-linear effects of robot model by direct on-line computation of the model has been also used by several other authors. For example, Takegaki and Arimoto[12] have applied positional control in the form (actuator models are not taken into account)

$$u(t) = G[q^0(\tau)] - K_1[q(t) - q^0(\tau)] - K_2\dot{q}(t) \qquad (13)$$

where $G[q^0(\tau)]$ is $n \times 1$ vector of gravitational forces (moments) in the desired position $q^0(\tau)$, $k_1 \in R^{n \times n}$ is matrix of positional feedback gains, $K_2 \in R^{n \times n}$ is matrix of damping gains. It has been shown that (13) is optimal with respect to some criteria. In such a case only gravitational forces in the terminal point are to be computed on-line but this is only positional terminal control. Tracking of trajectory demands computation of more complex terms in the model of the robot. However, it has been shown[12] that this control law allows the avoidance of the inverse of Jacobian matrix, i.e. computation of internal co-ordinates of the desired position $q^0(\tau)$ can be avoided. Namely, if the desired position (trajectory) is imposed in external (hand) co-ordinates $s^0(\tilde{t})$ (which is often the case), we have to compute internal (joint) co-ordinates $q^0(\tau)$ using inverse of Jacobian matrix $J[q(t)]$. However, this problem might be very complex in some cases (if the order of external co-ordinates is less than the order n of internal co-ordinates). It has been shown[12] that instead of (13) we can use the control:

$$\Delta u = G[s(\tau)] - J^T \left\{ K_1[s(t) - s^0(\tau)] + K_2 \dot{s}(t) \right\} \tag{14}$$

where $s(t) \epsilon R^m$ is the $m \times 1$ vector of external (hand) co-ordinates of the robot and $J \epsilon R^{m \times n}$ is the Jacobian matrix. Thus, in (14) we have to compute only $J[q(t)]$ and not its inverse, which is by far an easier problem. However, this control scheme with constants K_1 and K_2 can hardly be acceptable for trajectory tracking and when parameter variations have to be taken into account.

The attempts presented above to synthesize control on the executive level by minimization of some criteria show that, due to high non-linearity of the robot model, optimal control is hardly acceptable for robotic systems.

'Inverse-problem' technique

Due to the above-mentioned problems connected with the optimal approach to control synthesis most researchers have attempted to synthesize dynamic control of the robots by some suboptimal approaches. They tried to include the directly mathematical model of robot dynamics in the control scheme to achieve good tracking of given trajectory.

Paul[13] has investigated the 'inverse-problem' technique, which was called the 'computed torque' technique by Bejczy.[14] A similar approach has been taken up by Pavlov and Timofeyev.[15] Their approaches include on-line computation of the complete model of robot's dynamics, i.e. the computation of driving torques by (2) with measured values of internal co-ordinates q and velocities $\dot{q}$ of the robot and computed values of desired internal accelerations $\ddot{q}^0(t)$. It has been shown[15] that the robot is asymptotically stable around nominal trajectory $q^0(t)$ if the driving torques are computed as

$$P(t) = H(q, \theta) \cdot [\ddot{q}^0(t) + K_1 q(t) - q^0(t)] + K_2 [\dot{q}(t) - \dot{q}^0(t)] + h(q, \dot{q}, \theta) \tag{15}$$

where K_1, K_2 are matrices of position and velocity feedback gains which must be chosen in such a way that the solution of the equation

$$\ddot{e} = K_1 e + K_2 \dot{e} \tag{16}$$

is asymptotically stable ($e \epsilon R^n$). However, only driving torques are computed in (15); also, the models of actuators (1) should be included in the control scheme.

Obviously, in this scheme compensation is provided for time-varying gravitational, centrifugal and Coriolis forces: the feedback gains are adjusted according to the changes in inertia matrix $H(q, \theta)$; an acceleration feedforward term is also included to compensate for changes along nominal trajectory.

The main problem with this approach is that in (15) computation of the complete dynamic model of the robot is required. This was the reason why some authors tried to apply approximate models of robot dynamics. They have omitted the off-diagonal moment of the inertia term in matrix $H(q, \theta)$, as well as centrifugal and Coriolis terms in $h(q, \dot{q}, \theta)$.

By this the computation is considerably simplified but it is still time consuming for some robotic structures. On the other hand, it is questionable whether by these simplifications the efficiency of control is lost or not. Paul[13] has found that, in his experiments with the Stanford manipulator, the contribution from Coriolis and centrifugal terms is relatively insignificant. However, this is true at low speeds of the robot. Further reduction of computation time has been made by Bejczy.[14] He has investigated a specific manipulator and found approximations to the diagonal terms in matrix H and in gravity terms. These approximations lead to a tremendous reduction of computing time, but they are valid for a specific manipulator only and for relatively slow motion conditions. Paul[13] also suggested that some terms in (2) could be precalculated and stored and thus reduce time necessary for on-line calculation. Raibert and Horn[16] have used a partial table look-up approach to simplify the computation. Rather than compute for the coefficients in (15) each time they are needed, their approach is to look them up in a pre-defined multi-dimensional memory organized by the positional variables $q(t)$. The disadvantage of this approach is the need for a large memory.

Besides the problem regarding on-line computation of the dynamic model of the robot, there are also several other problems concerning the 'inverse-problem' technique. The robustness of this control with respect to parameter variation has not been precisely analysed. The problem of choice of gains in (15) also is critical. If full matrices K_1 and K_2 are chosen in (15) the control structure becomes complex and thus it suffers from all the disadvantages that were mentioned concerning the centralized linear regulator. Obviously, gain matrices in the diagonal form can be chosen. However, the problem with such a choice lies in its suboptimality regarding energy consumption. Saridis and Lee[17] have proposed the method for suboptimal choice of gains; the choice is made by taking into account the complete non-linear model of the robot. However, the method results in choice of full matrices K_1 and K_2.

In our opinion the main problem with all the above-mentioned control schemes lies in their centralized approach to control problems; i.e. the robot is considered as a single plant which makes the implementation and maintenance of such control schemes very difficult and impractical.

Force feedback in controlling robots

The main problem with dynamic control of robots is not to avoid on-line computation of complex terms in the robot model but to compensate for robot dynamics. The force feedback offers such a possibility. There are several aspects in which force feedback can be used with robotic systems. We shall briefly mention some of them.

The forces (torques) acting on the robot joints can be directly measured. Thus, by introducing feedback from these forces we can compensate for dynamics of the robot and decouple the robotic manipulator into a set of subsystems. Force feedback allows easy compensation for the complete dynamics of the robot. This attractive idea was recognized and elaborated by Vukobratović and Stokić and co-workers.[1,18,19] This idea has been exploited recently also by several authors. Hewit and Burdess[20] introduced force transducers in the robot joints, but they also introduced accelerometers to provide information on acceleration $\ddot{q}(t)$ of robots. They computed on-line the inertia matrix H. Thus, their control scheme was relatively complex [although the computation is less than in (15)] and it was not analysed as to whether all the implemented equipment was necessary to achieve good tracking of nominal trajectory. Several attempts were made to include force feedback in servocontrol of joints. Wu and Paul[21] experimented with a single-joint manipulator with force sensor in the joint and with all the hardware of the analog type. Luh et al.[22] experimented with the Stanford manipulator; the first two joints fabricated to include torque sensors. They analysed each joint separately. However, the stability of the complete robot was not analysed in their paper.

All above-mentioned attempts concern the use of force sensors directly in the joints to compensate for dynamics of the robot. However, many attempts were made to measure forces in the wrist of the manipulator. A force-sensing wrist was suggested by Nevins and Whitney.[23] Paul and Shimano[24] developed a control scheme with sensing wrist so that load forces with respect to the axis of the wrist co-ordinates could be measured on-line. Force controllers employing sensing wrist were implemented by Raibert and Craig.[25] All these attempts were mostly concerned with the use of the force feedback for assembly task with manipulation robots, as one of the most difficult control tasks in robotics.

The force feedback also offers a possibility of avoiding the inverse of the Jacobian matrix when the desired trajectory is imposed in external co-ordinates. Vukobratović and Stokić[1,26] proposed a dynamic control scheme for the so-called 'drink-test' task. Popov et al.[27] also discussed the implementation of force feedback for solving various robotic tasks and to avoid the inverse of Jacobian matrix.

Wu and Paul[28] proposed position control of the manipulator in external co-ordinates which they called *resolved-motion force control*. This control scheme adapts the force convergence concept to control the hand forces and position of the robot instead of classical joint control. In this scheme computation of the inverse of Jacobian matrix and calculation of complicated dynamics of the manipulator are replaced by an iterative stochastic method (force convergent control) which also might be time consuming.

Thus, we have listed several control schemes that include force feedback. It is obvious that force feedback offers a good opportunity to simplify control computation and to compensate for the influence of robot dynamics and external forces that might act on the robot (e.g. in the assembling process). However, there are several drawbacks to the implementation of force feedback. The price of the precise force transducers is not negligible and there are some technical problems regarding the noise appearing at the force sensors. Thus the trade-off between the complexity and price of the control computer and the price of the sensor system has to be studied carefully.

Decoupled control

In many control schemes the aim is to decouple the robotic system into a set of decoupled subsystems of lower order which can be controlled separately. Since in most cases the trajectory given in external co-ordinates is resolved into compatible internal co-ordinates trajectories, we usually want to use these internal trajectories as inputs for servos which drive individual joints. Thus, we usually want to control each joint separately.

A few attempts to decouple the robot's dynamics have been made. Yuan[29] tried to decouple dynamically the manipulation system by linear control. He considered a linearized model of the robot in which Coriolis, centrifugal and gravity forces were neglected. Actually, he considered the model of the mechanical part of the robot in the form

$$H[q^0(t), \theta^0] \Delta \ddot{q} = \Delta P \quad (17)$$

The models of actuators (1) were also taken into account. In (17) coupling among joints of the robot are given by off-diagonal elements of the inertia matrix $H[q^0(t), \theta^0]$. Thus, the model (17) can be decoupled by linear control which compensates for these cross-inertia terms in (17). Then, for each decoupled joint (together with its actuator), local servos can be introduced. However, this scheme suffers from many disadvantages. Since the model (17) is very approximate, this control cannot compensate for many dynamic effects. The simplicity of the linear control is a consequence of the very hard approximation of the robot model. If the complete non-linear model were taken, the decoupled control would be much more complex.

Roessler[30] applied non-linear hierarchical control to decouple the robot model. He 'divided' the control vector into two terms which correspond to two control levels. On the level of local subsystems local controllers are synthesized as usual to stabilize local decoupled subsystems (joints with their corresponding actuators). The 'second part' of the control vector is aimed to decouple the robotic manipulator into a set of local subsystems. This part of the control includes on-line computation of the driving torques P_{acc} to (2). Practically, this control is similar to the 'inverse-problem' technique described previously, i.e. the 'inverse-problem' technique also might be regarded as decoupled control since this control also compensates for the effects of dynamics of the robot and decouples the robot into a set of separate subsystems corresponding to joints. However, all problems concerning the implementation of the 'inverse-problem' technique are also encountered with the non-linear hierarchical control of Roessler. It should be mentioned that this control scheme has a similarity with the approach of Vukobratović and Stokić[1] which will be presented in *Decentralized control*.

Non-linear decoupling control of the robot has been also proposed by Freund.[31] Starting from a very general control strategy for decoupling of non-linear systems, he attempts to decouple completely the non-linear model of robot dynamics in hand (external) co-ordinates. However, such a control would be extremely complex and very hard to implement. Thus when dealing with a particular robot the author simplifies the control by neglecting acceleration in the coupling and he decouples the robot in internal (joint) co-ordinates. In essence, this approach also reduces to the 'inverse-problem' technique. The crucial problem of the robot stability if such a simplified controller is applied has not been considered by Freund.[31]

As we have already mentioned previously, force feedback also can be used to decouple dynamics of the robotic system, and can thus also be regarded as decoupled control of robots.

Decentralized control

Decoupled control presented in the previous section is intended to decouple the robotic system into a set of independent subsystems which can be stabilized by local servos. Thus, we arrive at the most simple and most commonly used control in practice-decentralized control. In this approach to control synthesis the robot is, at once, regarded as a set of decoupled subsystems, each corresponding to the separate joint and coupling among them is neglected. Starting from the model of the robot (1), (2), the robot is considered as a set of local decoupled actuators

$$S^i: \dot{x}^i = A^i x^i + b^i u^i, \quad i = 1, 2, \ldots, n \tag{18}$$

in which the coupling term $f^i P_i$ is neglected. For each subsystem (18) local control is synthesized to stabilize the free (decoupled) subsystem. Local control is usually taken into the linear form

$$\Delta u^i_{\text{loc}} = -K_i^T [x^i(t) - x^{io}(t)] \tag{19}$$

where $K_i \epsilon R^{n_i}$ is vector of local feedback gains. In many applications it has been assumed that local control (1) can stabilize the whole robotic system. This most commonly used approach is effective for the positioning of the manipulator and the tracking of relatively slow trajectory. However, if fast trajectory has to be tracked precisely, this approach is unacceptable. Medvedov et al.[32] have analysed overall system behaviour when only local controllers (19) are implemented. They linearized the robot model (7) around nominal trajectory and analysed the stability of the linearized model with local controllers in frequency domain. The validity of this analysis is limited by the validity domain of the linearized model (7).

Paul[33] has presented several servosystem schemes in which compensation for some dynamic effects of the robot is introduced (but only on the servosystem level). He presented compensation for the influence of gravitational forces and Coulomb friction, the velocity and acceleration changes along the trajectory, etc. However, all these improvements were made at the local level, and thus the effects of them might be very limited (not analysed by Paul[33]).

Arimoto and Miyazari[34] have proved that a PID local controller can be used effectively for the positional control of manipulation robots. They proved the global asymptotic stability of the robot around target point under the condition of a PID local feedback-control scheme. However, they did not consider the ability of the control to ensure tracking of nominal trajectory. Following the results presented,[23] they modified their PID feedback scheme to suit the case when the target point is described in external (hand) co-ordinates (cf. ref [14]). The asymptotic stability of such a PID sensory-feedback scheme is also proved.[34]

The efficiency of the decentralized control (19) to stabilize the robotic system and to ensure tracking of the nominal trajectory has been studied by Vukobratović and Stokić.[1,35,36] We have elaborated on a procedure for the asymptotic stability analysis of the non-linear model of the robot if local control (19) together with nominal programmed control, $u^0(t)$, is applied. We have proposed control in the form

$$u^i(t) = u^{io}(t) + \Delta u^i_{loc}(t) \tag{20}$$

The nominal control has to be computed off-line for a prescribed trajectory, $x^0(t)$, so as to satisfy (5) and it must be stored in the computer memory. Nominal control $u^0(t)$ is aimed at feed-forward compensation for velocity and acceleration changes along nominal trajectories and compensation for coupling at the nominal level. However, implementation of off-line computed nominal control using a centralized model of the robot is restricted to some obvious cases when a nominal trajectory can be prescribed. Some other drawbacks of such a solution (large memory demands, sensitivity to parameter variations, etc.) limit the applicability of this control scheme. It should be mentioned that nominal control (but without additional local controllers) also has been proposed by Waters.[37]

To avoid disadvantages of nominal control $u^0(t)$ synthesized on centralized model, we have also proposed a complete decentralized control in the form

$$u^i(t) = u^{io}_{loc}(t) + \Delta u^i_{loc}(t) \tag{21}$$

where local nominal control $u^{io}_{loc}(t)$ is computed to satisfy local (decoupled) models of subsystems

$$\dot{x}^{io}(t) = A^i x^{io} + b^i u^{io}_{loc}(t) \tag{22}$$

We have considered practical stability of the global robotic system if decentralized control (21) is applied;[38] and have analysed,[39] for the first time, the stability of the non-linear model with variable parameters and we have determined the validation of decentralized control (21), i.e. we have developed a procedure by which we can determine the allowable variation of parameter θ which can be withstood by the local controllers (21). We have shown[1,39] that it is always possible to stabilize the robot around nominal trajectory by sufficiently high local feedback gains K^i (19) (and for some sufficiently small variation of parameters). However, such a high gain solution suffers from numerous drawbacks the main one being that noise (vibrations of the robot due to its elasticity and influence of environments, etc.) is also amplified (since the frequency bandwidth of the robot is increased by high gains). So, Vukobratović and Stokić and co-workers[2,35,36,39] have proposed an introduction of additional global control the aim of which is to compensate for the destabilizing influence of the robot's dynamics which has not been taken into account on the subsystem level. Thus our control law is now given by

$$u^i(t) = u^{io}_{loc}(t) + \Delta u^i_{loc}(t) + \Delta u^i_G(t) \tag{23}$$

where Δu^i_G is global control in the ith joint which is computed as

$$\Delta u^i_G(t) = -K^{Gi} \cdot \tilde{P}_i(x, \theta) \tag{24}$$

where K^{Gi} is global gain and $\tilde{P}_i$ is function of coupling (i.e. driving torques).

Various forms of global control have been discussed,[2] depending on how $\tilde{P}_i$ is obtained. $\tilde{P}_i$ might be the measured force (torque) acting into ith joint (see **Force Feedback in controlling robots**) or it may be on-line computed driving torque according to the mathematical model of the robot dynamics (2). Obviously, various approximative dynamic models of the robot also might be applied (see '**Inverse-problem' technique**).

At this point, this approach to control synthesis 'converges' with 'inverse-problem' technique and also to non-linear decoupled control of Roessler[30] (since the role of global control (24) is to compensate for the influence of the robot's dynamics on the ith joint and, thus, to decouple the ith subsystem from the rest of the control). Thus, all disadvantages of the 'inverse-problem' technique that were listed previously, are encountered with this approach too.

However, there is a large difference between this approach and those presented in **Inverse-problem technique** and **Decoupled control**. Both approaches consider the robot as a whole and try to stabilize it by a centralized control. The decentralized approach allows 'piece-by-piece' control synthesis and enables the introduction of only those global feedback loops which are necessary to compensate for the undesirable influence of the robot's dynamics. It should be mentioned that global control allows compensation for the destabilizing influence of coupling, while the other control scheme automatically compensates for the complete influence of dynamics.

A software package for computer-aided synthesis of dynamic control of robotic system which is based on the control law given by (23) has been developed.[6,7] The package enables the user to determine the simplest control law which can accommodate the user's particular control task and his specific robot. The package is based on the above-mentioned procedure for the analysis of the robot's behaviour using decentralized and global control.

Other approaches

We have briefly discussed some of the most characteristic approaches of dynamic control of manipulation robots. We have started with the most complex (optimal control) and arrived at the most simple (decentralized-joint servocontrol). The considered approaches are, in our opinion, the most characteristic and the most representative (but not necessarily the most successful). Besides the considered approaches there were many other attempts for dynamic control of robots which also should be mentioned; Albus[40] attempted to control manipulators by control signals directly memorized in the computer memory and Young[41] attempted to synthesize the control for manipulators using the theory of variable structure systems, etc. There are also a few papers dealing with the problem of flexibility of the manipulator. Book *et al.*[42] have considered a simple two-beam two-joint manipulator with distributed flexibility. A more general case has been described by Truckenbrodt[43] where a manipulator with rigid and flexible elements is properly modelled.

References

[1] Vukobratović M and Stokić D (1982) *Control of Manipulation Robots: Theory and Application*, Monograph. Springer-Verlag, Berlin

[2] Vukobratović M and Potkonjak (1982) *Dynamics of Manipulation Robots: Theory and Application*, Monograph. Springer-Verlag, Berlin

[3] Cvetković V and Vukobratović (1982) Computer-oriented algorithm of variable complexity for mathematical modelling of active spatial mechanisms for application in robotics. *IEEE Trans. Systems, Man and Cybernetics*, **SMC-12**

[4] Hollerbach M J (1980) A recursive Lagrangian formulation of manipulator dynamics and a cooperative study of dynamics formulation complexity. *IEEE Trans. Systems, Man and Cybernetics*, **SMC-10**, 730–736

[5] Vukobratović M and Kirćanski N (1984) Computer-assisted generation of robot dynamic models in analytical form. *Int. J Applying Mathematics Mathematical Applications*, (2)

[6] Vukobratović M, Stokić D and Kirćanski M *A Procedure for Interactive Dynamic Control Synthesis of Manipulators* Proc. IV CISM-IFToMM Symposium on Theory and Practice of Robots and Manipulators, pp. 77–89. Zaborow, Poland, September, 1981

[7] Vukobratović M and Stokić D (1982) A procedure for interactive dynamic control synthesis of manipulators. *IEEE Trans. Systems, Man and Cybernetics*, **SMC-12** (4)

[8] Kahn M E and Roth B (1971) The near minimum time control of open loop articulated kinematic chains. *Trans. ASME, Dynam. Syst., Meas. Control*, September, 164–172

[9] Young D K K *Control and Optimization of Robot Arm Trajectories* Proc. IEEE Milwaukee Symp. on Automatic Computation and Control, pp. 175–178, April 1976

[10] Popov E P, Vereschagin A F, Ivkin A M, Leskov A S and Medvedov V S *Synthesis of Control System of Robots Using Dynamic Models of Manipulation Mechanisms* Proc. VI IFAC Symp. on Autom. Contr. in Space, Erevan, USSR, 1974

[11] Popov E P, Vereschagin A F and Filaretov V F (1976) Synthesis of quasioptimal nonlinear feedback control system of manipulator (in Russian). *Teknich. Kibernet.*, (6) 91–101

[12] Takegaki M and Arimoto S (1981) A new feedback method for dynamic control of manipulators. *Trans. ASME, J. Dynam. Syst., Meas. Control*, **102**, 113–125

[13] Paul R C *Modeling, Trajectory Calculation and Serving of a Computer Controlled Arm A I* Memo 177, Stanford Artificial Intelligence Laboratory, Stanford University, California, September, 1972 (also in Russian, Nauka, Moscow, 1976)

[14] Bejczy K A (1974) *Robot Arm Dynamics and Control* Technical Memorandum 33-669, Jet Propulsion Laboratory, February

[15] Pavlov A V and Timofeyev A V (1976) Calculation and stabilization of programmed motion of a moving robot-manipulator (in Russian). *Teknich. Kibernet.*, (6) 91–101

[16] Raibert H M and Horn B H P (1978) Manipulator control using the configuration space method. *Indust. Robot*, **5** (20), 69–73

[17] Saridis M G and Lee G C -S (1979) An approximation theory of optimal control for trainable manipulators. *IEEE Trans. Systems, Man and Cybernetics*, **SMC-9** (3), March

[18] Vukobratović M, Stokić D and Hristić D *A New Control Concept of Anthropomorphic Manipulators* Proc. Second Conf. of Remotely Manned Systems, Los Angeles, June

[19] Vukobratović M, Hristić D and Stokić D *Algorithmic Control of Anthropomorphic Manipulators* Proc. V Int. Symp. on Industrial Robots, Chicago, Illinois, September

[20] Hewit R J and Burdess S J (1981) Fast dynamic decoupled control for robotics, using active force control. *J. Mech. Mach. Theory*, **16** (5), 535–542

[21] Wu H C and Paul P R *Manipulator Compliance Based on Joint Torque Control* Proc. 19th IEEE Conf. Decision Control, Alboquerque, NM, vol. 1, pp. 88–94, December 1980

[22] Luh Y S J, Fisher D W and Paul C P R (1983) Joint torque control by a direct feedback for industrial robots. *IEEE Trans. Automatic Control*, **AC-28** (2), February

[23] Nevins L J and Whitney E D *The Force Vector Assembler Concept* Proc. I Int. Conf. on Robots Manipulator Systems, Udine, Italy, September, 1973

[24] Paul P C R and Shimano E B *Compliance and Control* Proc. of Joint Automatic Control, San Francisco, CA, pp. 694–699

[25] Raibert H M and Craig J J (1981) Hybrid position/force control of manipulators. *Trans. ASME, J. Dyn. Syst., Measurement, Control*, Trans. of the ASME, **103** (2), 126–133

[26] Vukobratović M and Stokić D (1982) Dynamic control of manipulators via load-feedback. *J. Mech. Mach. Theory*, **17** (2), 107–118

[27] Popov E P, Vereschagin F A and Zenkevich S L (1978) Manipulation robots: dynamics and algorithms (in Russian). *Scientific Fundamentals of Robotics Series* (Nauka, Moscow)

[28] Wu H C and Paul P R (1982) Resolved motion force control of robot manipulator. *IEEE Trans. Systems, Man and Cybernetics*, **SMC-12** (3), May/June

[29] Yuan S-C J *Dynamic Decoupling of a Remote Manipulator System* Proc. JACC, pp. 1702–1707, San Francisco, 1977

[30] Roessler J *A Decentralized Hierarchical Control Concept for Large-scale Systems* Proc. II IFAC Symp. on Large-scale Systems, pp. 171–179, Toulouse, 1980
[31] Freund E (1982) Fast nonlinear control with arbitrary pole-placement for industrial robots and manipulators. *Int. J. Robotic Res.*, 1(1), 65–78
[32] Medvedov B S, Leskov G A and Juschenko S A (1978) *Control Systems of Manipulation Robots* (in Russian) Nauka, Moscow
[33] Paul P R (1981) *Robot Manipulators: Mathematics, Programming and Control* MIT Press, Cambridge
[34] Arimoto S and Miyazari F *Stability and Robustness of PID Feedback Control for Robot Manipulators and Sensory Capability* First Int. Symp. of Robotic Research, Bretton-Woods, New Hampshire, 1983
[35] Vukobratović M and Stokić D (1981) One engineering concept of dynamic control of manipulators. *Trans. ASME, J. Dyn. Syst., Measurement Control.* (Special Issue, papers on Control of Robotic Devices), **102**, June
[36] Vukobratović M and Stokić D (1983) Is dynamic control needed in robotic systems and, if so, to what extent? *Int. J. Robotics Res.*, **2** (2)
[37] Waters R (1979) *Mechanical Arm Control* Memo AIM-549, Mass. Inst. of Tech., Artif. Intel. Lab., October
[38] Stokić D and Vukobratović M (1984) Practical stabilization of robotic systems by decentralized control. *Automatica*, **20** (3), 353–358
[39] Vukobratović M, Stokić D and Kirćanski N *Non-Adaptive and Adaptive Control of Manipulation Robots* Series: Scientific Foundations of Robotics, No. 5, Springer-Verlag, Berlin, in press
[40] Albus S J (1975) A new approach to manipulator control: the cerebellar model articulation controller (CMAC). *Trans. ASME, J. Dyn. Syst., Measurement, Control*, September, 220–227
[41] Young K K D (1978) Controller design for a manipulator using theory of variable-structure systems. *IEEE Trans. Systems, Man and Cybernetics*, **SMC-8**
[42] Book J W, Maizza-Meto O and Whitney D E (1975) Feedback control of two beam, two joint systems with distributed flexibility. *Trans. ASME, J. Dyn. Syst. Measurement, Control*, **97**, 424–431
[43] Truckenbrodt A *Modelling and Control of Flexible Manipulator Structure* Preprints of IV CISM-IFToMM Symposium on Theory and Practice of Robots and Manipulators, pp. 110–120, Warsaw, 1981

Robot Motion Control in Multi-operation Assembly

D E Okhotsimsky and S S Kamynin

Keldysh Institute of Applied Mathematics, USSR Academy of Sciences, Moscow, USSR

Summary: This paper describes an approach to the problem of industrial assembly automation using manipulating robots. An experimental automatic assembly system developed at the Keldysh Institute of Applied Mathematics of the USSR Academy of Sciences is generally described, the main principles used to construct the algorithms for automatic assembly implementation are considered and the results of experiments on the assembly of industrial products are given. The main purpose of the experiments with the automatic assembly system was to demonstrate the feasibility of complex multi-operation assembly using versatile manipulators controlled by a minicomputer and equipped with the simplest sensors, tools and devices.

Assembly robot

A laboratory breadboard model of the assembly robot was used as a technical basis for the research. It included two electromechanical 2 kg load-carrying capacity manipulators UEM-2 that were developed at the Bauman's Institute. Each manipulator had six degrees of freedom (plus the seventh one of the gripper) and was connected to the M-6000 minicomputer. The indications of the potentiometric sensors of the manipulator link positions were inputted to the computer via a 10-bit A/D converter. The computer was included in the manipulator motor control loop and used to vary the motor control parameters with a frequency of about 30 Hz. A special robot control interface was employed to convert digital signals of the computer into pulse-duration outputs to control the manipulator motors.

The manipulator grippers were changeable. There were both non-sensitized grippers and ones equipped with the simple sensors providing force sensing. In particular, spring-loaded fingers with sensors of linear shifts were used.

The robot may be connected to a technical vision device. The latter was developed in two versions. One of them was based on a photoresistant matrix. The other modification was developed by the Institute of Information Transfer Problems of the USSR Academy of Sciences on the basis of a standard Electronica L-50 TV camera.

The UEM-2 manipulators operate with a modest positioning accuracy. The accuracy that may be achieved by versatile manipulators often seems to be lower than that needed for mating the assembled parts. So, in any case, methods of adaptive control should be developed while applying force feedback, search motions and other means to manage assembly operations successfully.

Software

The automatic assembly system software is comprised of a number of modules to provide the robot control in a basic operating mode (automatic assembly mode) as well as to allow preliminary planning of the robot operation by a programmer-operator. The latter plans the assembly at three levels: (1) it composes an assembly plan where a sequence of assembly operations to be fulfilled is specified and the response to faulty executed operations is provided; (2) it composes a plan of each operation where a sequence of manipulator motions necessary to fulfil an operation is specified and where the conditions, under which the transfer from one motion to another is possible, are described (besides, the operation plan indicates a response to faulty executed motions); (3) it composes programs of motions listed in the operation plans.

An alphabet-digital Videoton-340 display was used as an operator terminal. The motions may be specified also by 'choreographic' programming, ie by the sequential placing of the manipulators (by hand or with the aid of a special console) at the positions through which they must pass.

In accordance with the above conditions the following software modules were developed: (1) module for assigning and editing the assembly plan; (2) module for assigning and editing the assembly operation plans; (3) module for assigning and editing the condition plans; (4) module for assigning and editing the motion contours; (5) module for assigning and editing the servosystem coefficients; (6) module for the automatic assembly control.

Modules 1 - 5 operate at the assembly planning stage. A programmer-operator can refer to them in any order convenient to him/her. The planning must result in the assembly plan, the operation plans, the condition plans and the motion contours. It is of no importance in what order these data are prepared, so the operator may carry out programming in a 'bottom-up' or 'top-down' mode, or in any other way.

Module 6 executes the automatic assembly control and comprises two processes. The first one, basic, is a part of the servosystem operation. It starts using a timer's interruptions of frequency about 30 Hz. During this process the sensor indications are scanned and the commands to servomotors are produced and transmitted to provide the given programmed motion. The second process is a background one. It uses a residual of the time cycle. It includes inspection of the assembly plan and operation plans, necessary preparations and start of a current motion in the main process as well as testing of the conditions of transfer from one motion to another.

Thus the automatic assembly arrives at a situation where the assembly robot performs sequential motions required for the assembly. Transfer from one motion to another is performed in accordance with the assembly plan and operation plans. Simultaneously, with the start of each motion, testing of the condition assigned to the given motion begins. By involving the simplest sensing devices, a robot control system analyses the current situation and, while executing given conditions, organizes completion of a given motion and transfer to another one.

Experiments

In experiments with the assembly automatic system the assembly of units was performed. In particular, the assembly of an oil-gearing pump was implemented.

The pump consisted of the following parts: a base, a cover, two gears, a gasket, four bolts, four nuts, four spring rings; all in all 17 parts. The clearance between the gear axle and the walls of a hole in the base was about 30 μm. The pump assembly was performed by two manipulators whose simultaneous motions were co-ordinated. An electropower nutdriver was used as a tool to screw nuts on the bolts. The total assembly time was about 4 min 17 s.

Since an accuracy in positioning the manipulators used for the automatic assembly was in the range of 3 - 5 mm, the assembly could be performed only due to interaction between mated surfaces of parts and their utilization as stops and guides. The compliance of grippers was also used.

From the above it follows that an important problem to be solved by the robot sensors is to detect the touching of the stops. Simple sensors can do it. Note that touching of the stop may also be detected by the position sensor indicating the manipulator's interlink angles. If indications of the sensor do not change in time, though the control signals are being sent to the respective motor, the situation may be interpreted as contact with the stop. Thus the robot equipped only with position sensors proves to be sufficiently sensitized and capable of using adaptive behaviour and developed control logic.

The automatic assembly system was also used for the assembly of a case of the motor. In this experiment the assembled parts were a base, a cover, a gasket and 10 screws.

As the cover was rather heavy and bulky it was mounted on the base with the aid of both manipulators. An electrical screwdriver was used as a tool for setting screws. The total assembly time was about 4 min 30 s.

The idea was to manage the above experiments with a minimum of tools and devices. Adaptive behaviour of the robot in assembling the pump and the motor case was based on indications of the potentiometric sensors of the manipulator link positions without the use of the force-moment sensors or any technical vision system.

Inspection vision

Along with the development of the motion—control algorithms, work had been under way to construct algorithms for visual information processing. The main attention was paid to an inspection vision system designed for checking the correctness of performing the operations during assembly.

The inspection vision concept is based on good organization of the scene observed by a TV camera. Correctly assembled parts occupy the assigned positions in the field of vision of the inspection system. Thus the system must make image fragments conform to stored standard fragments corresponding to the correct assembly process.

In terms of the automatic performance of the assembly the inspection vision system executes the testing of a certain condition and, depending on test results, assembly plan branching takes place (ie the transfer to some or other motion of the manipulator). Standard fragments corresponding to correct assembly are prepared in the planning stage by means of showing the respective objects to the inspection vision system.

Since the inspection vision system solves a comparatively simple problem concerning the conformity of elements of small image fragments, the visual-data-processing algorithms obtained are compact and fast. Regular conformity under varying illumination or slight shifts of images was implemented.

The experiments performed showed that the use of small image fragments (20 x 20 elements) with a large number of half-tone levels allows a reliable solution to problems such as testing the correctness of gear insertion into the base of the oil pump, putting the gasket on guiding pins, checking the presence of a nut in a feeder, etc, to be obtained.

Some Considerations on Feedback Strategy for Assembly Robots

J-P Merlet

INRIA Domaine de Voluceau-Rocquencourt, BP 105, 78153 Le Chesnay, Cédex, France

Summary: Wedging or jamming risks, security, surface qualities justify force control in assembly tasks. The number of measurements that are necessary to calculate contact forces in the most general case has been considered in this paper. In the first part the planer case is discussed and as an example there is treated briefly the insertion of a given flexible circular peg in a fixed stiff part. We show that in this case on certain assumptions the measurement of the applied force and moments at the wrist of the robot may be sufficient to find an insertion strategy. In the second part the spatial case is considered and it is shown that to measure all the unknowns which are necessary to calculate the contact forces is difficult. As an example the insertion of a square stiff peg into a stiff part has been studied. In the last part some information for insertion-strategy including force control is given.

Introduction

Part-mating with robots needs sensory feedback in most cases; there are many reasons justifying force control: jamming risks, surface qualities of the surfaces to be assembled, security. For these reasons contact forces must be calculated on the assumption that the inertial forces are neglected due to the low speed of operation. In this study we consider the number of contact points between the parts to be assembled (forces on contact line or surface may be reduced to a resultant force applied at a point).

Planar case

In this section we consider the case where a planar study is sufficient. Let n be the number of contact points. The $2n$ component of the contact forces are the unknowns. Since we cannot measure them directly we need to develop some relations between these components. Equilibrium requirements give us three linear equations but introduce other unknowns: three components of the force-vector acting on the peg, $3n$ co-ordinates of the contact points and n orientations for the surface of contact (so that we can calculate tangential and normal forces). Thus the total number of the unknowns is $5n + 3$. Let m' be the outer equilibrium requirements, we must have

$$m + m' \geq 5n \qquad (1)$$

We will consider now how we may obtain supplementary relations.

Coulomb's law

Sliding conditions yield at least one equation. In fact if the sliding condition gives us p equalities and q inequalities we have

$$p + q = n \quad (2) \qquad\qquad p \geq 1 \quad (3)$$

But there will be $2n - 1$ sliding cases to consider.

Material resistance laws

These laws give one relation between the two co-ordinates of each contact point and r for the slope wherever it is defined ($r \leq n$).

For the same reasons we have for the hole $n + s$ relations ($s \leq n$) but we need two co-ordinates to obtain this relation in the same frame. We have also $r + s = n$. Hence we have $2n + r + s - 2$ i.e. $3n - 2$ relations.

Number of measurements

According to (1), (3) we obtain therefore

$$m' \geq 2n + 1 \quad (4)$$

Example

We shall briefly study the case of the insertion of a flexible circular peg in a fixed stiff part. The whole study is reported in reference 1. In this case $n = 2$ (Figure 1), $r = 1$, $s = 1$. Thus according to (4) $m' \geq 5$. The unknowns are $Fx_1, Fx_2, M_I, T_1, N_1, T_2, N_2, \gamma, \theta, x_{1B}, x_{2B}, x_{1A},$ and x_{2A}; we suppose we can measure $Fx_1, Fx_2, M_I, x_I, z_I$, where x_I, z_I, are the co-ordinates of the point I in the absolute frame. We shall consider now the sliding conditions. According to (2), (3) there will be $2n - 1 = 3$ cases.

A, B are sliding

Equilibrium requirements and sliding conditions give five linear equations with four unknowns. Thus we get a non-jamming condition (the determinant of the system must not be zero) and one sliding condition. The remaining unknowns are $\theta, \gamma, x_{1B}, x_{2B}, x_{1A}, x_{2A}$.

We have

$$\gamma = \frac{-\dfrac{M_I}{Fx_1} k \sin k x_{1B} + \dfrac{Fx_2}{Fx_1}(1 - \cos k x_{1B})}{1 + \dfrac{krM_I}{Fx_1} \cos k x_{1B} + \dfrac{Fx_2}{Fx_1} kr \sin k x_{1B}} \quad (5)$$

where

$$k^2 = \frac{Fx_1}{EI_3}$$

(E is Young's modulus and I_3 the quadratic moment).

At the stage of one contact point (B) we can determine the co-ordinates of $B(x_B, z_B)$ if we suppose we know the initial inclination of the peg. Assuming that B does

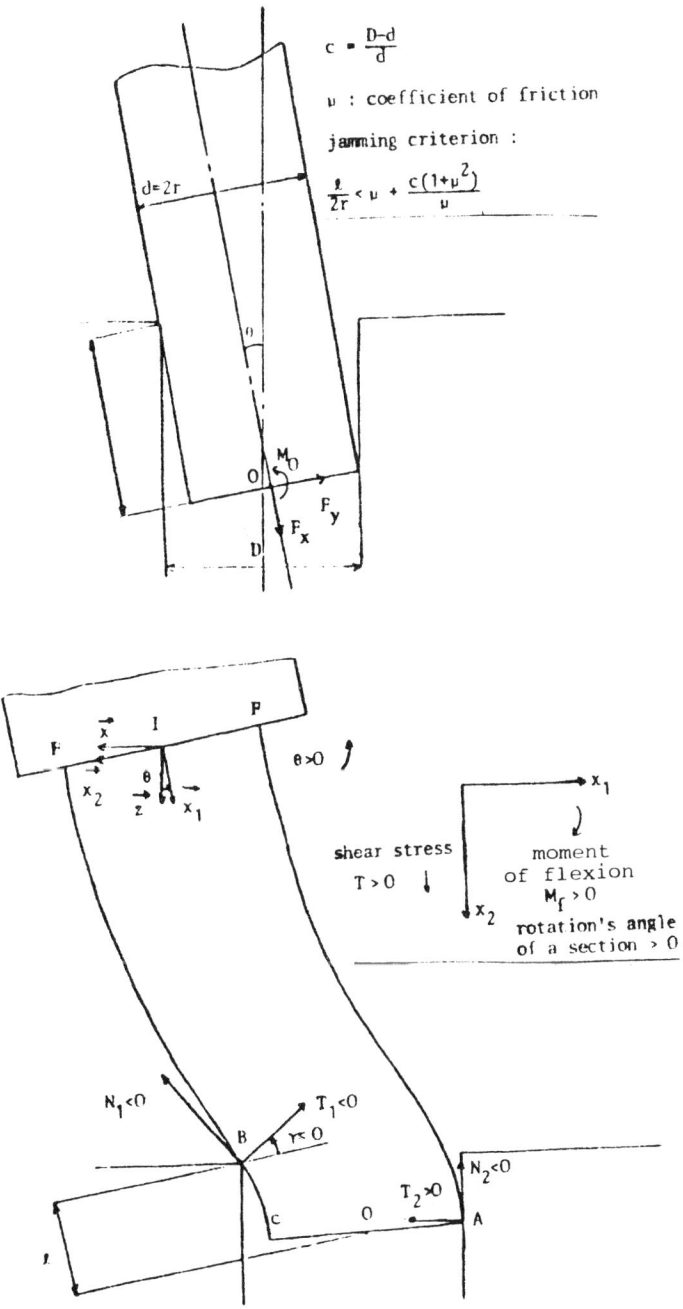

Figure 1 Insertion of a flexible circular peg in a fixed stiff part, $n = 2$

not change during intersection we have

$$\theta = \frac{X_1 - X_B + r - \dfrac{M_I}{Fx_1}(1 - \cos kx_{1B}) + \dfrac{Fx_2}{Fx_1}(x_{1B} - \dfrac{\sin kx_{1B}}{k})}{x_{1B}} \qquad (6)$$

where r = peg radius.

If we can calculate x_{1A} and x_{1B} the material resistance laws give us x_{2A} and x_{2B}. For example we have

$$x_{2B} = r - \frac{M_I}{Fx_1}(1 - \cos kx_{1B}) + \frac{Fx_2}{Fx_1}(x_{1B} - \frac{\sin kx_{1B}}{k}) \qquad (7)$$

we have also

$$Z_B = Z_I + x_{2B}\theta + x_{1B} \qquad (8)$$

Using (6), (7), (8) we shall see that x_{1B} is the solution of an equation like (9)

$$x_{1B}^2 + ax_{1B} + b\cos kx_{1B}\, c\sin kx_{1B} + d\sin^2 kx_{1B} + e = 0 \qquad (9)$$

A sliding or B sliding

The reasoning is the same as for A, B, sliding but the sliding condition to be verified an inequality arises.

Spatial case

We shall consider now two kinds of parts to be assembled: stiff or flexible parts.

Assembly of stiff parts

The unknowns are the $3n$ components of the forces. Equilibrium requirements yield six linear equations but they add the following unknowns: three co-ordinates for the contact points, six components of the force-vector acting on the peg and three angles which are used to write the equilibrium requirements in the same frame. Thus

$$m + m' \geqslant 6n + 3 \qquad (10)$$

If we have the three co-ordinates of a point of the peg (hole) in the hole (peg) frame we shall calculate the $3n$ co-ordinates of the contact points.

Finally, if we introduce Coulomb's law we obtain:

$$m' \geqslant 3n + 5 \qquad (11)$$

Assembly of flexible parts

Here we have $9n + 6$ unknowns: $3n$ for the forces, $3n$ co-ordinates of the contact points, $3n$ orientations and six for the force-vector; thus

$$m + m' \geqslant 9n \qquad (12)$$

The physical laws may give us $6n$ unknowns ($3n$ co-ordinates, $3n$ orientations)

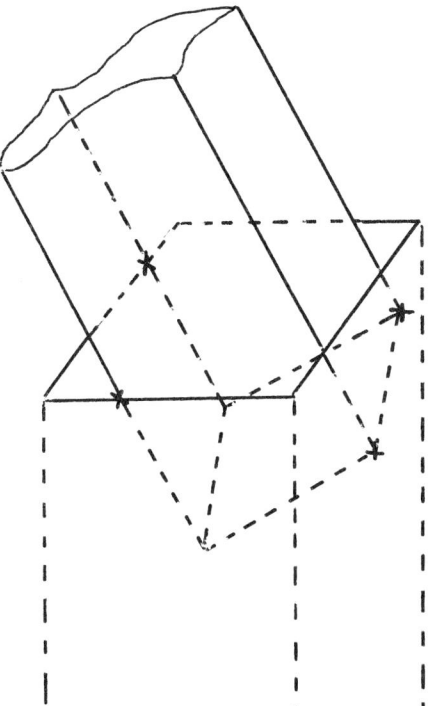

Figure 2 Assembly of square stiff peg, maximum of four contact points

but we introduce three co-ordinates and three limit-conditions for the slopes of the peg.

The use of Coulomb's law yields

$$m' \geq 3n + 5 \qquad (13)$$

Example

For a square stiff peg the maximum of contact points should be four (Figure 2).

Assuming that we know x_I, y_I, z_I the co-ordinates of point I in the x, y, z frame and ψ, θ, ϕ the Euler's angles, we can calculate the 12 co-ordinates of the contact points. The 12 components of the forces and $x_I, y_I, z_I, \psi, \theta, \phi$ i.e. 18 unknowns $(3n + 6)$, remain the unknowns. The use of force sensor and Coulomb's law allows us to measure 11 quantities, although this seems to be quite difficult.

Other feedback strategies

Some other ways have been proposed to realize part-mating. The first one is passive compliance where the deformations of a mechanism, due to the contact-forces, permit the position of the peg[2-5] to be corrected. All these methods are fast and use low-cost devices but they are applicable only for particular tasks.

A most general way is use of active compliance where the measured force-vector is used to generate the displacements of the peg[6,7] The active compliance method seems to be quite more universal than the passive one. But there is a lack of velocity and the algorithms for insertion are difficult to carry out.[8]

Other methods that use both active and passive compliance have also been developed.[9,10] For the future we are looking for the rigidity matrix concept; such a matrix is used to predict force evolution according to the displacements of the robot's wrist. Learning may give us this matrix for all sorts of parts and the command may be elaborated quite systematically with such a model. Another way is to elaborate a cost function with a term for each constraint. A non-linear minimization method is then used to reach the goal in a constraint space.

Conclusion

We have shown that the study of the insertion mechanism is difficult. Some other methods have been proposed but the command laws are not systematically elaborated at the present time. We are trying now to elaborate such a method.

References

[1] Merlet J-P *A Control Law for the Insertion of a Flexible, Cylindrical Peg using a Robot* ROVISEC 3, Washington, DC, November 1983
[2] MacCallion, Johnson, Phamm (1979) A Compliant Device for Inserting a Peg in a Hole *Industrial Robot*, June, 81-87
[3] Whitney, Nevins *What is the Remote Center Compliance (RCC) and what Can it Do?* 9th ISIR, Washington, DC, 13-15 March, 1979, pp. 135-147
[4] Simunovic *Part-mating Theory for Robot Assembly* 9th ISIR, Washington, DC, 13-15 March, 1979, pp. 183-193
[5] Rebman *Compliance for Robotic Assembly using Elastomeric Technology* 9th ISIR, Washington, DC, 13-15 March, 1979, pp. 153-166
[6] Van Brussel, Simons *Automatic Assembly by Active Force-feedback Accommodation* 8th ISIR, Stuttgart, 30 May – 1 June, 1978, pp 181-193
[7] Kasai, Takeyasu, Muraoka *Trainable Assembly System with an Active Sensory Table Possessing 6 Axes* 11th ISIR, Tokyo, 7-9 October, 1981, pp. 393-404
[8] Goto, Takeyasu, Inoyama (1980) Control Algorithm for Precision Insert Operation Robot. *IEEE Trans. Systems, Man and Cybernetics*, SMC-10 (1), 19-25, 1980.
[9] Goto, Inoyama *Precise Insert Operation by Tactile Controlled Robot HI-T-HAND Expert 2* 4th ISIR, Tokyo, Japan, 19-21 November, 1974, pp. 209-218
[10] Stepourjine, Lhote *Terminal d'Insertion Automatique pour Robot d'Assemblage 3ème* Journée Scientifiques et Techniques de la Production Automatisée, Toulouse, 3-5 June, 1981, pp. 31-1-31-14

Optimal Dynamic Trajectories for Robotic Manipulators

S Dubowsky and Z Shiller

Department of Mechanical Engineering, Massachusetts Institute of Technology, Cambridge, MA 02139, USA

Summary: Higher manipulator speeds are essential to achieve increased productivity, but are limited by the manipulator's dynamic and actuator capabilities. This paper presents a control algorithm which determines the manner in which a six-degree-of-freedom manipulator should move along a specified path in three-dimensional space to complete its motion in minimum time without violating actuator constraints, thus greatly increasing its speed. The algorithm is computationally efficient and does not require the extensive iterative calculations optimal control laws normally demand. Applications are presented and results that show significant reductions in time over current planning methods for typical manipulators to perform complex manoeuvres. Also shown is how the method is used to improve the design of manipulators and their work stations for better performance.

Introduction

Manipulator productivity is often limited by speed. Too fast, and the dynamics of manipulator motion causes its actuators to become saturated and the manipulator to leave its desired path. Consequently, most industrial manipulators are programmed so that their speed is constrained to a constant maximum value at its end effector after a constant initial acceleration and stop with the same constant deceleration. The values of maximum constant velocity, acceleration and deceleration selected to prevent the actuators' limitations from being exceeded at any point on the path demonstrably require a significantly longer time for a given task to be performed than that required by optimal control.[1]

The highly coupled non-linear characteristic of manipulators' dynamics makes conventional optimal-control theory difficult to apply. Linear optimal-control theory has been applied to a linearized manipulator model subjected to constant actuator constraints with a free path.[2] A method to find the minimum energy path for a specified time has been developed also.[3] However, these methods are computationally very complex and do not yield the minimum time motion in cases where it is desired to constrain the manipulator's motion to a specified path, as in many industrial applications. A method has been proposed with constant maximum velocity, acceleration and deceleration to minimise the travelling time on a path composed of straight lines connected by circular curves.[4,5] As stated above, such constant-motion parameters require more time for execution. Another method developed finds the time needed to perform a given motion with a given velocity profile along the path.[6] Although this profile is scaled to insure that the actuators constraints are not violated, it is not intended to find the time optimal-velocity profile.

A recently developed algorithm has proved to be rigorously optimal for the minimum time control of a manipulator travelling on a specified path subjected to actuator constraints.[1] It uses a full non-linear dynamic manipulator model and the actuators' constraints may be arbitrary functions of the system state. It is computationally efficient since it does not require the usual extensive multi-parameter iteration common in optimal control. To date this algorithm's practicality has been demonstrated only for manipulators with three-degrees-of-freedom.

This paper extends the algorithm to a six-degree-of-freedom manipulator and shows the method practical and capable of being run on a mini-computer in a relatively short time. The technique is shown able to evaluate and modify the design of robotic manipulators, their trajectory for given tasks and the design of their work spaces to reduce the time required to do a given task to achieve greater levels of productivity.

Time optimal control

This algorithm yields the actuators' torques/forces for a manipulator to move along a specified path P (see Figure 1) in minimum time. The actuator effort for the ith joint, T_i, is subject to the constraint of the form

$$T_{i\min}(\theta_i, \dot{\theta}_i) \leqslant T_i \leqslant T_{i\max}(\theta_i, \dot{\theta}_i) \tag{1}$$

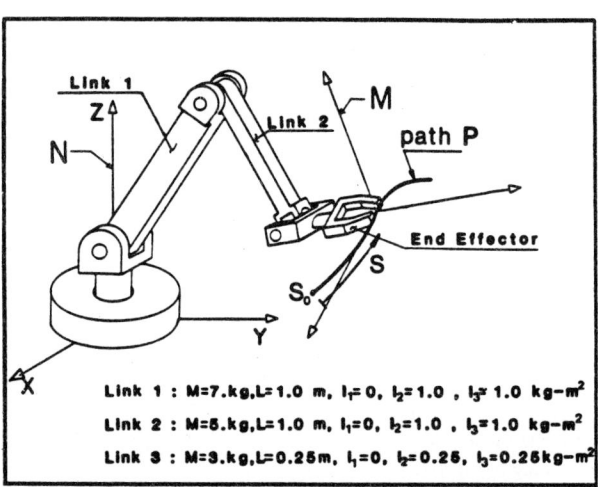

Figure 1   Six-degrees-of-freedom robotic manipulator

where θ_i and $\dot{\theta}_i$ are the joint displacements and velocities respectively.

The path of an end-effector fixed frame, M, is specified by the vector $\underline{X} = (x, y, z, \phi_1, \phi_2, \phi_3)^T$, composed of the position and orientation of M with respect to the N frame. $\underline{X}$ is assumed to be a known function of S, the distance along the path, P (see Figure 1). Ref. [1] shows that the total time needed to move along the path is minimal if $\ddot{S}$ is equal to either the maximum or minimum permissible values of

Optimal Dynamic Trajectories for Manipulators 135

acceleration, $\ddot{S}_a$ or $\ddot{S}_d$, along the path. $\ddot{S}_a$ and $\ddot{S}_d$ are obtained by the transformation of the manipulator's equations of motion into functions of S, $\dot{S}$ and $\ddot{S}^1$ in the form

$$\underline{m}(\underline{\theta})\ddot{S} + \underline{b}(\underline{\theta})\dot{S}^2 + \underline{g}(\underline{\theta}) = \underline{T} \qquad (2)$$

Where $\underline{m}$, $\underline{b}$, $\underline{g}$ and $\underline{T}$ are vectors defined in detail.[7] It is assumed that $\underline{\theta}$, the vector of joint variables, can be obtained either explicitly or numerically as a function of S.

Given S, $\dot{S}$ and T_i, each of the six scalar equations represented by the vector equation (2) will yield a different value of $\ddot{S}$, given by

$$\ddot{S}_i = \frac{T_i - b_i \dot{S}_i^2 - g_i}{m_i} \qquad i = 1,\ldots,6 \qquad (3)$$

Substituting either the maximum or minumum values of T_i from equation (1) into (3) gives the maximum and minimum values for $\ddot{S}_i$. Figure 2 shows that the range

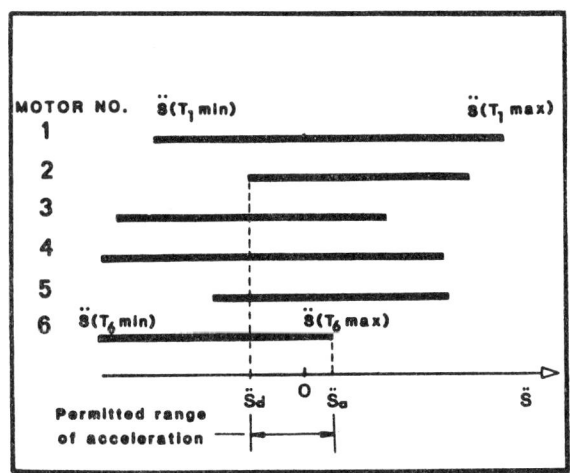

Figure 2 Permissible acceleration at S and $\dot{S}$

of permissible $\ddot{S}$, at any S and $\dot{S}$, is bounded by the combined limits on the $\ddot{S}_i$s imposed by each of the actuators. As expressed below

$$\ddot{S}_d(S,\dot{S}) \leqslant \ddot{S} \leqslant \ddot{S}_a(S,\dot{S}) \qquad (4)$$

$$\ddot{S}_a = \min_i \left(\frac{T_{i\min} - b_i \dot{S}^2 - g_i}{m_i}\right) \qquad (5)$$

$$\ddot{S}_d = \max_i \left(\frac{T_{i\man} - b_i \dot{S}^2 - g_i}{m_i}\right) \qquad (6)$$

assuming $m_i > 0$.

At every point on the path there is a maximum velocity, $\dot{S}_m$, at which $\ddot{S}_a = \ddot{S}_d$. If this velocity is exceeded, the actuators are incapable of keeping the end effector on its path. The locus of these points as a function of S is the velocity limit curve, $\dot{S}_m(S)$, shown in Figure 3.

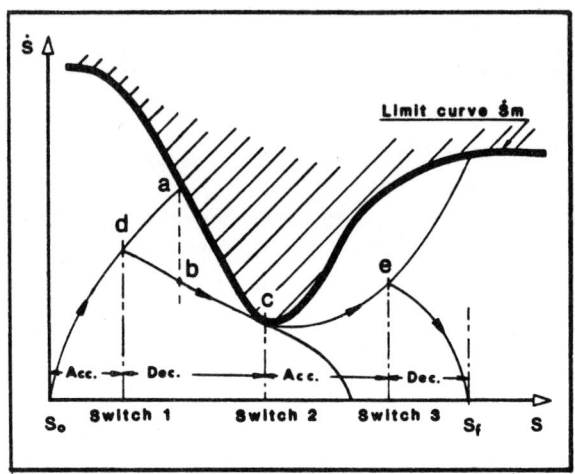

Figure 3 Construction of optimal trajectory in the phase plane

The minimum time motion is achieved when, at every point on the path, $\ddot{S}$ is equal to either $\ddot{S}_a(S,\dot{S})$ or $\ddot{S}_d(S,\dot{S})$. This reduces the minimum time-control problem to finding the switching points from maximum to minimum acceleration and vice versa, such that $\dot{S}(S)$ is maximum, but remains less than $\dot{S}_m(S)$.

The switching points are obtained from the following algorithm, with reference to Figure 3: (1) integrate $\ddot{S} = \ddot{S}_a(S,\dot{S})$ forward in time, with the initial conditions S_0, $\dot{S}_0$, until the trajectory intersects the $\dot{S}_m$ curve at some point a; (2) at point a, reduce the velocity along the dotted path until b, where $\ddot{S} = \ddot{S}_d(S,\dot{S})$ can be integrated forward until it coincides with $\dot{S}_m$ at some single point c, a point of tangency for continuous $\dot{S}_m$ curves; (3) from b, integrate $\ddot{S} = \ddot{S}_d(S,\dot{S})$ backward in time to yield the first switching point, d, from acceleration to deceleration; (4) point c is a switching point from deceleration to acceleration from c, integrate $\ddot{S} = \ddot{S}_a(S,\dot{S})$ forward in time until either the final position, S_f, is reached or the trajectory again intersects the $\dot{S}_m$ curve and, if the $\dot{S}_m$ curve is intersected, repeat the process starting with step 2 at this intersection point; (5) from S_f, integrate $\ddot{S} = \ddot{S}_d(S,\dot{S})$ backward in time to find the final switching point at e.

This algorithm has been implemented in a program called OPTARM (Optimal Time Control of Articulated Robotic Manipulators). It is written for six-degrees-of-freedom manipulators for which inverse kinematic solutions exist. Its output includes such important information for the designer as actuator torques and power. OPTARM requires less than 1 min of computation time on a small minicomputer such as the PDP 11/44.

Optimal Dynamic Trajectories for Manipulators 137

Examples and results

This algorithm can be used to greatly improve manipulator performance, manipulator designs and the design of their work stations, as shown following.

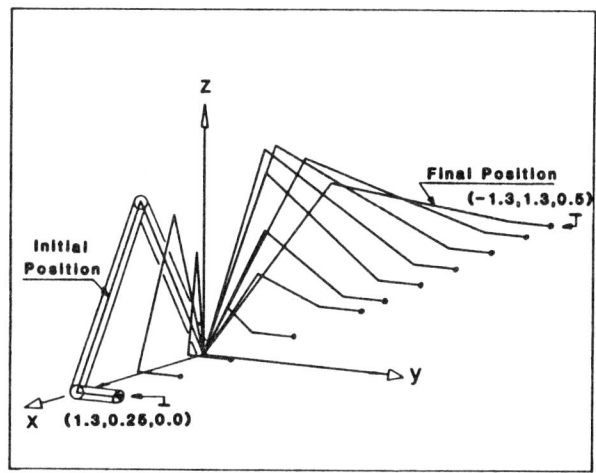

Figure 4 Three-dimensional view of path no. 1

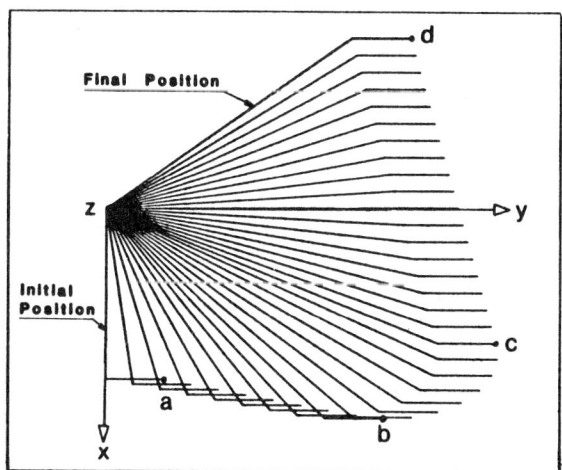

Figure 5 Top view of path no. 1

Figures 4–6 show a typical move of a 6 DOF manipulator, where it moves its end effector along a straight line from a to b, around a circular curve to c, and then moves along a straight path coming to rest at d. The end effector remains parallel to the y axis during the move. OPTARM determined the minimum time motion

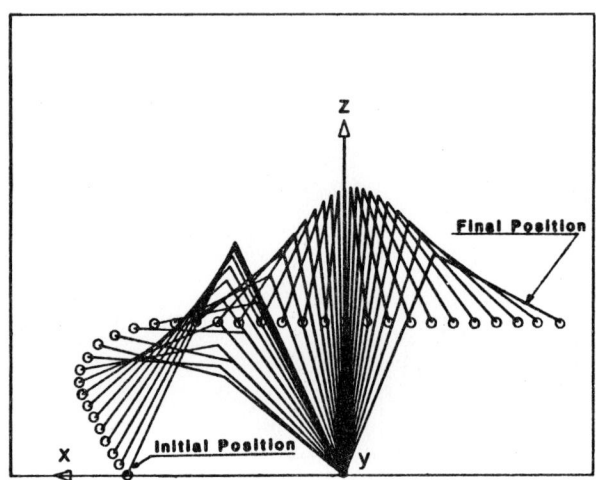

Figure 6 Side view of path no. 1

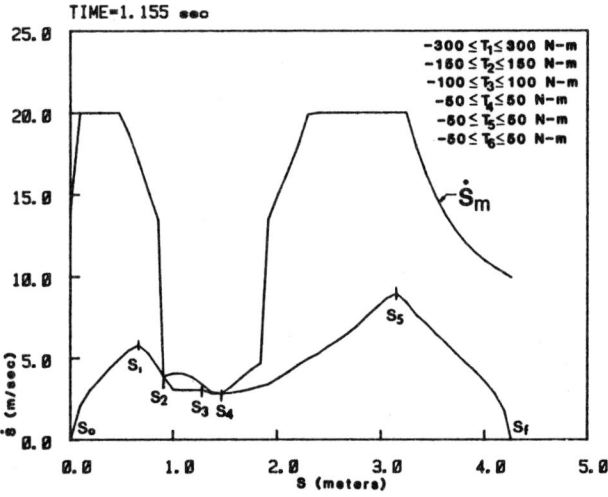

Figure 7 Phase plane trajectory for path no. 1 and switching points S_i

for this path. See Figure 7 for the phase plane trajectory of the optimal motion obtained by OPTARM. The actuators' constraints chosen were constants, but this is not a limitation of the method or OPTARM. Five switches are shown in the acceleration profile; the time required for the motion is 1.155 s. The use of a conventional control with the maximum possible constant velocity and acceleration required 1.66 s, 43 per cent longer.

Figures 8–11 show further system-performance improvements while still meeting the task requirements. First the radius of the curved section of the path from b to

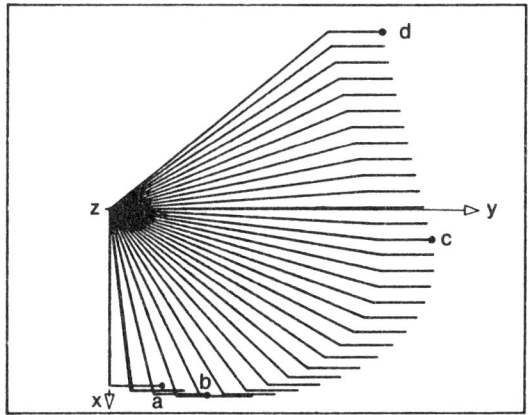

Figure 8 Top view of path no. 2

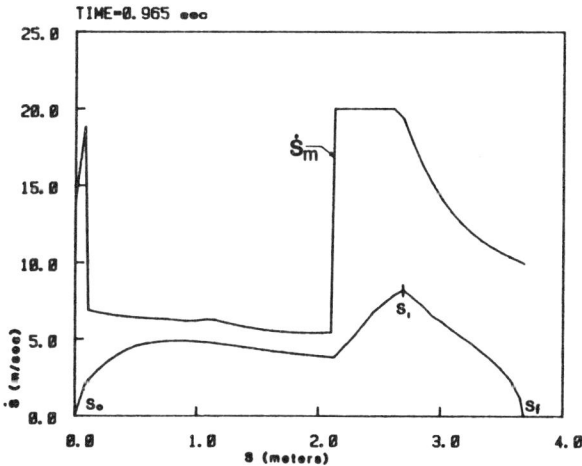

Figure 9 Phase plane trajectory for path no. 2

c is increased from 0.5 to 1.0m while keeping the end points the same. Figure 9 shows a time reduction for this improved move to 0.965 from 1.155 s, a saving of 16 per cent. Also, this manoeuvre shows one switching point, and does not approach the limit curve, indicating that the system is overdesigned for this task. Figure 10 shows the first three actuator torques for this motion. Although at each instant one of these motors (or one of the other three, not shown) is at its limit as required for the trajectory to be optimal, motor 3 never reaches its limits. If this path was a design extreme for this system, then reducing the torque capabilities,

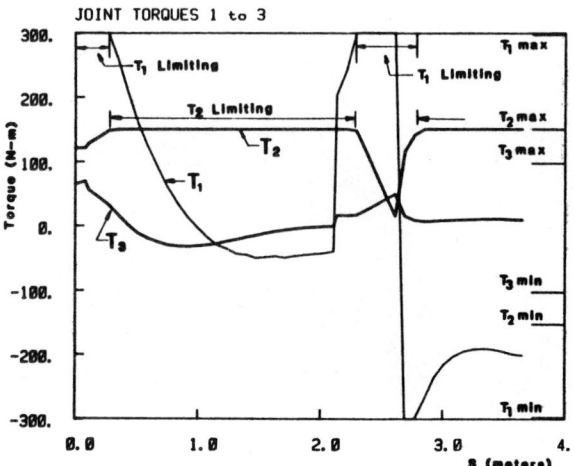

Figure 10 Actuator torques as a function of S

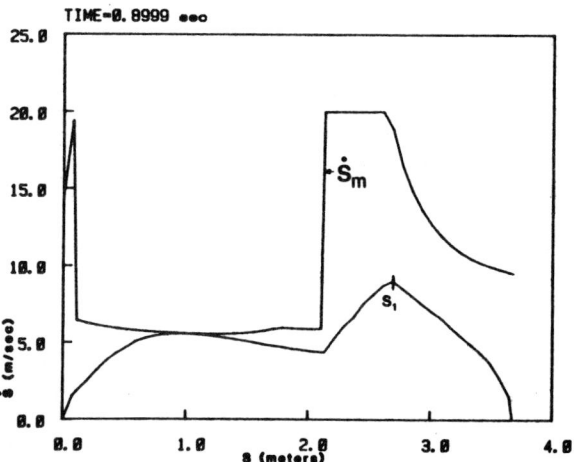

Figure 11 Phase plane trajectory for path no. 2 with a reduced actuator 3

and hence the cost and weight, of motor 3 should be considered.

Figure 11 shows an optimal trajectory as a result of reducing the torque capability and weight of actuator 3 by half. The time with the smaller motor actually decreases from 0.965 to 0.899 s, nearly one-half the time of the original system with conventional control. This improvement is due to the reduced motor weight which presents a lower load to the other actuators.

The algorithm can be used also to improve the layout of the workspace. Figure 12 shows a case in which the final position of the end effector at d is turned 90°

Optimal Dynamic Trajectories for Manipulators 141

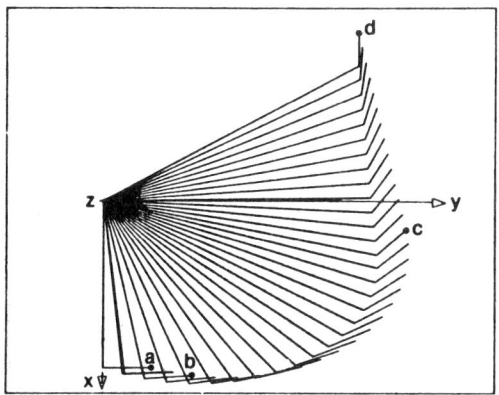

Figure 12 Top view of path no. 3

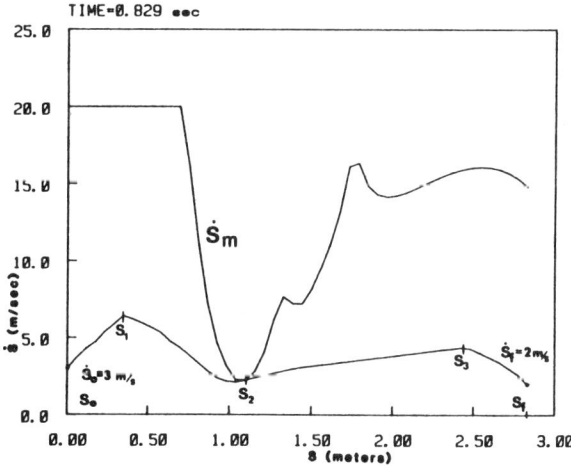

Figure 13 Phase plane trajectory for path no. 4 (a straight line path)

to the prior cases. This may be done if the station at d is rotated $90°$. This results in the reduction of the movement time from nearly 0.9 to 0.85 s, due to the decrease in the inertia seen by the other joints during this motion.

Figure 13 shows an even more dramatic performance improvment resulting from changes in the workspace. Here a simple straight-line motion of the end-effector tip in three-dimensional space from (1.3, 0.0, 0.0) to (−1.3, 1.0, 0.5) with an initial velocity of 3 m/s and a final velocity of 2 m/s has an optimal time of 0.829 s as shown. By keeping the path the same, but moving either the base

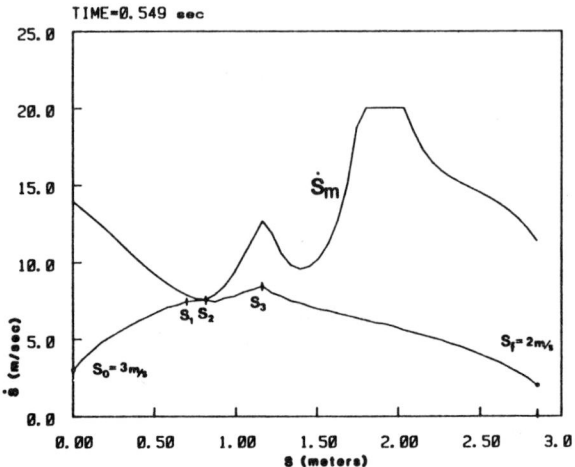

Figure 14 Phase plane trajectory for path no. 5 (improved straight line path)

manipulator toward the work stations from (0.0, 0.0, 0.0) to (0.0, 0.25, 0.0) or the work stations toward the manipulator base, results in a very different limit curve (see Figure 14) where the time is reduced significantly by 34 per cent to 0.549 s. This case also demonstrates that the initial or final velocities need not be zero. This feature is useful when the manipulator must interact with devices like moving conveyors.

Conclusions

This paper shows the practicality of time optimal control of six-degree-of-freedom manipulators moving with prescribed motion and with actuator constraints. Such optimal motion is shown the significantly faster than conventional control strategies currently in use and can lead to greater system productivity. The method is also useful for improving the designs of manipulators and their work stations.

References

[1] Bobrow J E, Dubowsky S and Gibson J S *On the Optimal Control of Robotic Manipulators with Actuator Constraints* Proc. of the Am. Control Conf., June 1983, San Francisco, California
[2] Kahn M E and Roth B (1971) The near minimum-time control of open-loop articulated kinematic chains. *ASME Trans., J. Dyn. Syst. Meas. Control*, **93** (3), 164–171
[3] Burgevin K J M (1983) Optimal Open-Loop Control of Industrial Robots, MSc Thesis, MIT, Cambridge, Massachusetts
[4] Luh J Y S and Lin C S (1981) Optimum path planning for mechanical manipulators *ASME Trans., J. Dyn. Syst., Meas. Control*, **102** (2) 142–151

[5] Luh J Y S and Walker M W *Minimum-time Along the Path for a Mechanical Arm* Proc. of the IEEE Conf. on Decision and Control, December, 1977, New Orleans, Los Angeles, pp 755-759
[6] Hollerbach J M *Dynamic Scaling of Manipulator Trajectories* Proc. of the American Control Conf., June, 1983, San Francisco, California
[7] Shiller Z (1984) Time optimal control of robotic manipulators, MSc Thesis, MIT, Cambridge, Massachusetts

Approximative Models in Dynamic Control of Robotic Systems

M Vukobratović and D Stokić

Institute 'Mihailo Pupin', 11000 Beograd, Yugoslavia

Summary: Various approximative models of robot dynamics may be used at various levels in hierarchical control of robotic systems. It is clear that the choice of the models determines robot capabilities for accomplishing various tasks as well as the equipment to be employed to implement the chosen control law. In this paper we consider various approximative models and control laws at the lowest control level, the executive level. In practice robots are controlled by local servomechanisms which are synthesized by using a decoupled model of the robot. However, if fast movements are to be realized and if coupling among the degrees of freedom of the robot is strong, it is necessary to take care of the dynamics of the complete robot. Thus it is necessary to implement the model of dynamics of the robot to ensure sufficiently accurate realizations of the movements prescribed by higher control levels. We have developed a software package allowing the most appropriate control law to be selected for an arbitrary manipulation robot. Microprocessor implementation of various control laws for a particular manipulation robot is also presented in the paper.

Introduction

Various levels in hierarchical control of robotic systems may use various approximative models of robot dynamics. The strategic level (which divides the imposed operation into elementary movements) deals with very global knowledge of dynamic system capabilities. This level usually does not employ precise dynamic models of robots.[1] There is also the tactical level (which performs the distribution of an elementary movement into the motions of each degree of freedom of the robot). It is common to use a kinematic model of the robot only,[2] but various approximative (or precise) dynamic models may also be used.[3] The executive level (which executes the imposed motion of each degree of freedom) may be realized in different modes. In the present paper, because of the lack of space, we shall concentrate on various control laws and approximative dynamic models of the robot implemented at the executive control level only.

First, we shall briefly present the synthesis of various control laws using different approximative models of the robot. Then we shall describe our software package for computer-aided synthesis of control for manipulation robots. Finally, we shall present microprocessor implementation of the various synthesized control laws using our package for a particular manipulation robot.

Control synthesis by using various approximative models

Let us suppose that at the tactical control level is calculated the desired trajectories of all internal angles (displacements) of the robot $q^°(t)$, $\forall t \epsilon T$, where q is $n \times 1$ vector of internal angles, n is the number of degrees of freedom of the particular robot, $T = [t: t\epsilon(0,\tau)]$, τ is the duration of the desired motion. The executive control level has to ensure tracking of the desired trajectories $q^°(t)$.

The model of the robot using actuators (DC motors of hydraulic actuators) can be given in the form[4]

$$\dot{x}^i = A^i x^i + b^i N(u^i) + f^i P_i(x), \qquad i = 1, 2, \ldots, n \qquad (1)$$

where x^i is $n_i \times 1$ vector of actuator state co-ordinates, A^i is $n_i \times n_i$ matrix, b^i, f^i are $n_i \times 1$ vectors, n_i is the order of the ith actuator model, u^i is the scalar input to the ith actuator, $N(u^i)$ is the non-linearity saturation type of the amplitude, $P_i(x)$ is the load acting on the ith DOF which is a function of all state co-ordinates of the robot $x = (x^{1T}, x^{2T}, \ldots, x^{nT})T$.

If DC motors are used as actuators and if we choose the third-order models of actuators, then the state vector of the ith actuator is given by $x^i = (q^i, \dot{q}^i, i^i)T$, where i^i is the rotor current. If hydraulic actuators are implemented, then the ith actuator state vector is given by $x^i = (q^i, \dot{q}^i, p^i)T$, where p^i is the oil pressure in the cylinder.

Model (1) can be regarded as a complete precise model of the robotic system, if $P_i(x)$ includes all the components of mechanical forces acting on the ith DOF (inertia forces, gravity, centrifugal, Coriolis and friction forces).

To synthesize control that can accomplish the tracking of the desired nominal trajectory $q^°(t)$ we can use the complete model of the robot (1).[5,6] However, as it is well known,[4,7] the model of the mechanical part of the system may be very complex, i.e. $P_i(x)$ is a very complex function of the state co-ordinates x. Because of this, control synthesized by using a complete dynamic model (1) may require a relatively complex and powerful computer to achieve a sampling period compatible with robot dynamics.

In our previous papers[4,8,9] we have proposed one possible way to overcome this problem. We have proposed an off-line calculation of nominal control $u^°(t) = (u^{1°}, u^{2°}, \ldots, u^{n°})T$ which satisfies the complete model of the system[4]

$$\dot{x}^{i°} = A^i x^{i°} + b^i N(u^{i°}) + f^i P_i^°[x^°(t)], \qquad i = 1, 2, \ldots, n \qquad (2)$$

where $\dot{x}^{i°}(t)$ corresponds to the desired trajectory $q^°(t)$. The nominal programmed control $u^°(t)$ would lead the robot along the prescribed trajectory under ideal conditions, i.e. when no perturbation is acting on the robot and when $x(0) = x^°(0)$. However, the main drawbacks of such an approach are that nominal trajectory has to be known in advance, a large memory may be needed to memorize the nominal trajectory and control (if τ is long) and it is assumed that all the parameters of the robot are precisely known in advance, which is not always true.

To simplify control, we have to use some approximative model of the robot. The most common synthesis of robot control involves the use of the decentralized model of the robot, i.e. the model consisting of a set of actuator models where interconnections among actuators are neglected:

$$\dot{x}^i = A^i x^i + b^i N(u^i), \qquad i = 1, 2, \ldots, n \qquad (3)$$

In model (3) load $P_i(x)$ is neglected and each actuator is considered as a separate subsystem. For each subsystem (3) independent local control is synthesized so as to accomplish the tracking of the desired trajectory $q^°i(t)$ of the corresponding

DOF. Since (3) is a linear time-invariant model, the local controller can be synthesized in the form

$$u^i(t) = u_L^{i\circ}(t) - K^{iT}[x^i(t) - x^{i\circ}(t)], \qquad i = 1, 2, \ldots, n \qquad (4)$$

where $u^{i\circ}(t)$ is the local programmed control, satisfying

$$\dot{x}^{i\circ}(t) = A^i x^{i\circ}(t) + b^i N[u_L^{i\circ}(t)], \qquad i = 1, 2, \ldots, n \qquad (5)$$

and k^i is $n_i \times 1$ gain vector of the local regulator. The local programmed control $u_L^{i\circ}(t)$ can easily be computed on the basis of (5) since the local subsystems are of low orders.

Thus implementation of the local control (4) is simple and acceptable. However, the decentralized control (3) is a very poor approximation to the complete model (1) since all the interconnections among DOF of the robot are neglected. In most robots, coupling among DOF is very strong, or, in other words, dynamics of the mechanical part of the robot cannot be completely neglected. Actually, control (4) does not take robot dynamics into account. Such a control can be satisfactory only if a relatively slow trajectory has to be tracked. Even more, if precise tracking of $q^\circ(t)$ is not required, control is usually implemented in the form

$$u^{\circ i}(t) = -k^{iT}[x^i(t) - x^{i\circ}(t)], \qquad i = 1, 2, \ldots, n \qquad (6)$$

where local nominal programmed control is omitted. However, if we want to ensure precise tracking of a fast trajectory we have to take care of robot dynamics, i.e. we have to implement such a control that will include some dynamic effects of the robot mechanism.[4] This means that we have to use such a model of the robot which includes some most significant components of dynamic forces.

We have proposed to add global control, so that the complete control law is given by

$$u^i(t) = u_L^{i\circ}(t) - k^{iT}[x^i(t) - x^{i\circ}(t)] - k_i^G P_i^*(x), \qquad (7)$$

where k_i^G is the global gain and $P_i^*(x)$ is the value representing the acting on the ith DOF, i.e. P_i^* is some approximation of $P_i(x)$.

We have considered various approximative models of robot dynamics.[4] If the model of the robot dynamics is not too complex, we can exactly compute the load P_i, taking into account all the components of moments. Usually it is quite sufficient to calculate on-line only inertia and gravity forces (or, only gravity forces). It is also possible to measure driving torques P_i directly by introducing force transducers into joints; in that case we get complete information about robot dynamics with very simple additional computations, but force transducers increase the cost of the robot-control equipment.[4,8]

Obviously, local control (6) and global control can be combined with synthesized off-line nominal control $u^\circ(t)$ to improve tracking and robot performance. In Table 1 we present some combinations of various control laws. The robot model that has to be used with each particular control law is also shown in Table 1, together with the number of additions and multiplications that have to be made in each sampling period to compute the corresponding control. Note that the number of additions and multiplications for computing the model of mechanism depends on the specific manipulator configuration.

Table 1 Various control laws

No.	Control law	Model	No. of calculations Add	No. of calculations Mul	UMS-2 Add	UMS-2 Mul
1	Local regulators	Decentralized	$n \times (2n_i - 1)$	$n \times n_i$	15	10
2	Local nominal control + local regulator	Decentralized	$(1) + n \times (2n_i - 1)$	$(1) + 2n \times \times n_i$	30	30
3	Local nominal control + local regulator + global	Decentralized and approximate model of mechanism	$(2) + n +$ dynamic model	$(2) + n +$ dynamic model	33+	33+
		Complete model			9	12
		Inertia force			5	8
		Gravity force			1	—
4	Nominal (on-line) + local regulator	Complete control model	$n \times (4n_i - 1)$ + dynamic model	$n \times (3n_i + 1)$ + dynamic model	42	45
5	Nominal (off-line) + local regulator	Decentralized (on-line) Centralized (off-line)	$n \times 2n_i$	$n \times n_i$	20	10

Add = additions; Mul = multiplications

Computer-aided choice of approximate model

Obviously, our aim is to synthesize as simple a control law as possible and to minimize computation efforts to reduce the complexity and cost of the control equipment. On the other hand, the executive control level must satisfy the requirements imposed on the robot performance, i.e. it must ensure sufficiently precise tracking of the trajectories imposed by the higher control levels. Thus a trade-off between the complexity of control and robot performance has to be made.

To enable efficient and precise choice of the control law and appropriate approximative model of the robot we have developed a software package for computer-aided synthesis of control of industrial manipulators. This package allows control synthesis for non-redundant manipulators of arbitrary type.[10] To utilize the robot designer's experience, the package has been made interactive in nature. A very brief flowchart of the algorithm is presented in Figure 1.

The designer can easily combine various control forms with various approximative models of the robot. First, the data on the manipulator configuration and dynamic parameters together with the data on the chosen actuators are set. Then, the control task into external robot co-ordinates is imposed and the desired trajectories of the internal co-ordinates are computed. Afterwards, the algorithm synthesizes local controllers, by using the decentralized model of the robot (3) in accordance with its user's requirements.

The nominal programmed control is synthesized by using either the centralized complete model (1) or the decentralized model (5). Then the stability of the robot is tested by using either method for asymptotic stability analysis[4] or the method for practical system stability.[11] If all the requirements concerning the robot performance are not met by the nominal (centralized or local) and local control only, the user can introduce global control. First, he can choose the simplest global control which utilizes only gravitational and/or inertia forces of the robot, and try to stabilize the manipulator in a desired manner. The user can introduce

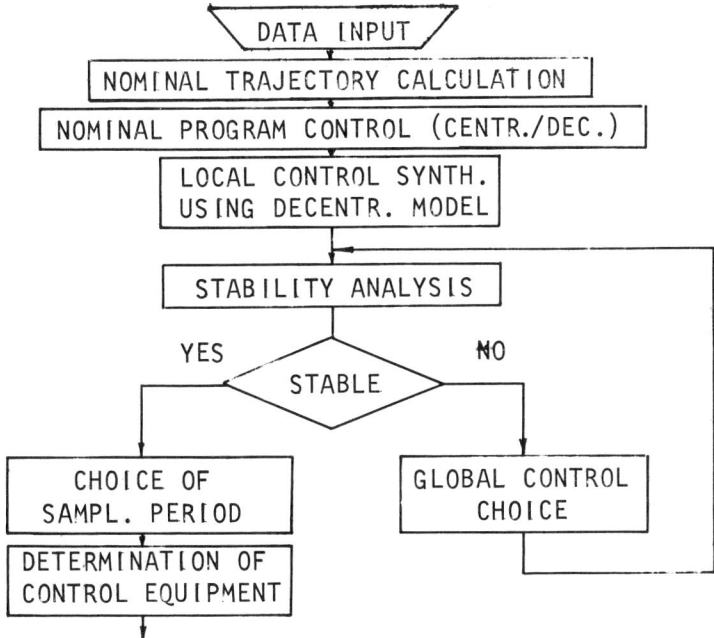

Figure 1 Flowchart of the algorithm for control synthesis

global feedback loops only in those DOF in which the influence of the coupling of the remaining part of the robot is significant. If the stability requirements are not met again, the user can introduce a more complex approximative model of the robot for global control. If the control requirements are very severe (precise tracking and fast trajectory) and coupling among DOF for the particular robot is very strong, the user has to introduce either on-line calculation of robot dynamics using complete model (1) or force feedback. Thus, this package permits the user to choose the simplest model of the robot by which all the requirements on the robot performance can be satisfied. In this way, the control equipment acceptable for the particular robot and the control task can be determined.

Control implementation: an example

Microprocessor implementation of control has been tested for a particular manipulation robot. We have implemented various control laws for manipulator UMS-2, presented in ref.[4]. The manipulator has $n=5$ DOF. Parameters of the mechanism and actuators have been given.[4] We have assumed that $n_i=2$, $x^i=(q^i, \dot{q}^i)T$, for $i=1, 2, \ldots, 5$, so that the order of the complete system is $N=n \times n_i=10$. The model of this robot is quite simple. The number of additions and multiplications required to be performed in each sampling period for various control laws is also given in Table 1. Note that the dynamic model includes the first three DOF only, since there is no

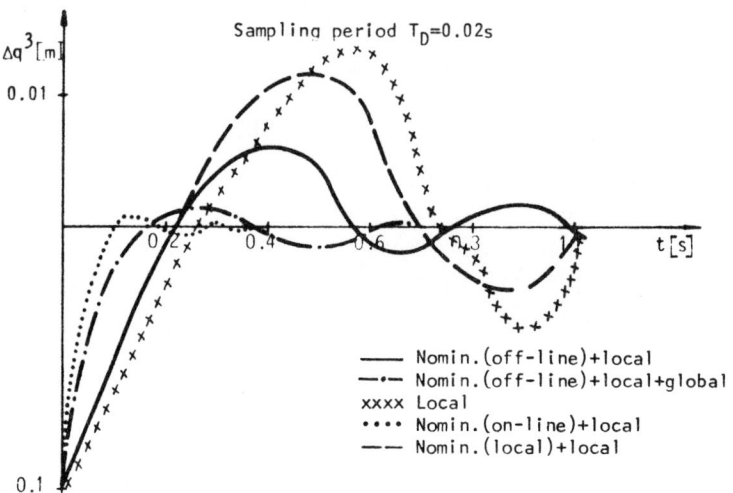

Figure 2 Trajectories tracking of UMS-2: discrete control

need to consider gripper dynamics.

Software package for control synthesis, described in the previous section, has been set on DIGITAL-computer PDP 11/70. By using this package the parameters of various control laws have been selected for the manipulator UMS-2. Synthesized control laws at the executive level have been implemented by microcomputer PDP 11/03. By using the software package we have determined the longest acceptable sampling period to 20 ms. The simplicity of the model of this particular robot allows all control laws to be realized by a single microprocessor. All the control laws, presented in Table 1, have been realized by discrete control loops only, i.e. no analog servomechanisms have been implemented. The same nominal trajectories $q^\circ(t)$, $\forall t \epsilon T$, (τ=1s), have been tracked by various control laws. The results of experimental trackings by various control laws are presented in Figure 2. All experiments have been performed under identical conditions: initial errors with respect to nominal initial states were $\Delta q^1(0) = -0.1$[rad], $\Delta q^3(0) = -0.01$[m], $\Delta q^2(0) = \Delta q^4(0) = 0$. Trackings for the third DOF are presented in the Figure. It is clear that the best tracking is achieved by the on-line computation of the complete dynamic model of the robot (case no. 4). Tracking by local nominal control, local regulators and global control (by using the complete dynamic model of the robot; case no. 4) is also very good. Tracking by off-line synthesized nominal control and local regulators (case no. 5) is also acceptable. However, tracking by local nominal control and local regulators (case no. 2) or by local regulators only (case no. 1) is poor. Evidently, the better the dynamic model used in control, the better the tracking is. On the other hand, more complex models require more

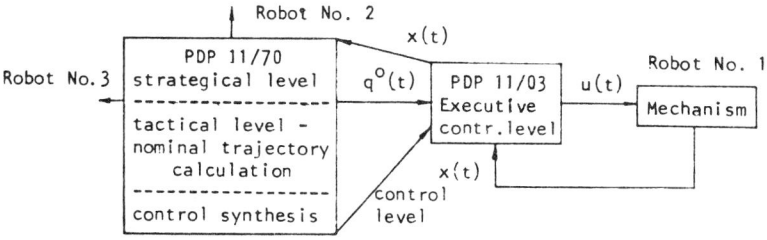

Figure 3 Block-scheme of the control

computations to be performed in each sampling period.

In this case, we were able to implement the computation of nominal control by a microprocessor. In a general case, this is impossible with robots of a more complex configuration. In addition, higher control levels cannot be implemented by a single microprocessor (even if we use faster microprocessors than PDP 11/03). Thus, in a general case we must either implement parallel processing by several microprocessors, or use one central minicomputer for a number of manipulators contributing to the same industrial process.

We have considered the second solution with the manipulator UMS-2. Higher control levels (tactical and strategic) have been implemented by computer PDP 11/70 and the executive level has been implemented by PDP 11/03, as described above. Computer PDP 11/70 can serve as the central unit for several manipulators and can synchronize their work on the strategic level. It also calculates the nominal trajectories of internal angles of the manipulator and sends them to PDP 11/03 to be realized. The central computer can also serve to calculate the off-line nominal programmed control and send it to the executive microprocessor connected to each robot. In Figure 3 we present the global control scheme with which we have realized the control of the manipulator UMS-2. The tactical control level (synthesis) of the nominal trajectories $q^u(t)$ has been realized while the kinematic model of the manipulator has been used. However, the executive control level utilizes the approximative dynamic model of the manipulator to optimize synchronization among manipulators. This problem will be treated in our future works.

References

[1] Medvedov B S, Leskov A G, Yuschenko A S (1978) Systems of manipulation robots control (in Russian) Series *Scientific Fundamentals of Robotics* ed. E P Popov, Nauka, Moscow

[2] Whitney D E (1969) Resolved motion rate control of manipulators and human prosthesis. *IEEE Trans. MMS*, 10 (2)

[3] Vukobratović M, Kirćanski M (1982) A method for optimal synthesis of manipulation robot trajectories. *J. Trans. ASME, J. Dyn. Syst., Meas. Control*, 104 (2)

[4] Vukobratović K M, Stokić M D (1982) *Control of Manipulation Robots: Theory and Application* Monograph, Springer-Verlag, Berlin
[5] Paul C R (1976) Modelling, trajectory calculation and servoing of a computer controlled arm (in Russian), Nauka, Moscow
[6] Timofeyev A V, Ekalo V J (1976) Stability and stabilization of programmed motion of robots-manipulators (in Russian) *Avtomatika Telemechanika*, (10) 148–156
[7] Cvetković V, Vukobratović M (1982) Computer-orientated algorithm modelling of active spatial mechanisms for application in robotics. *IEEE Trans. Systems, Man and Cybernetics*, SMC-12 (6)
[8] Vukobratović K M, Stokić M D (1980) Contribution to the decoupled control of large-scale mechanical systems. *Automatica*, January (1)
[9] Vukobratović K M, Stokić M D (1981) One engineering concept of dynamic control of manipulators *Trans. ASME, J. Dyn. Syst., Meas. Control*, 103 (2) 108–118
[10] Vukobratović M, Stokić D (1982) A procedure for interactive dynamic control synthesis of manipulators. *IEEE Trans. Systems, Man and Cybernetics*, September/October

Keyboard Playing by an Anthropomorphic Robot: Fingers and Arm Model and its Control System of WAM-7R

S Sugano, J Nakagawa, Y Tanaka and I Kato

Department of Mechanical Engineering, Waseda University, Tokyo 160, Japan

Summary: The purpose of this study is to improve dexterity, speed and 'intelligence' of robots by the development of an anthropomorphic robot playing keyboards. The basic necessary data for the design of this robot are obtained by analysis of human postures and motions of arms and fingers playing keyboards, by regarding them as a link mechanism. The robot with 14 degrees of freedom (DOF) for fingers, 7 DOF for the arm, totalling 21 DOF, has been developed based on these data. Fingers and the arm are made of CFRP and driven by DC motors. In terms of the control system, a computer system of hierarchical structure with three levels is constituted, modelling a human central-nervous-system structure, since this robot is an anthropomorphic multidegrees-of-freedom system. The optimum fingering and wrist positioning determination algorithm has been developed and it has been possible to determine the trajectories of fingers and an arm by inputting series of notes only. Evaluation of the above system has resulted in the realization of 10 Hz tapping and 1.5 m/s maximum wrist velocity and smooth playing has been made possible.

Introduction

It can be considered that, in the near future, robots will play important roles not only in secondary industry, in which they already fulfil active roles, but also in tertiary industry, ie service industry. The necessary functions for such advanced robots are dexterity, speed, flexible handling, 'intelligence', etc. It is more efficacious for robots to be anthropomorphic in order to activate multifunctions.

Among the functions shown above, dexterity and speed are concerned with information activities of human beings; keyboard playing, for which all 10 fingers are used equally, may be taken as an example.

This study began in 1981,[1] with the aim of improving dexterity, speed, 'intelligence', etc, of robots, with the capability to play tunes from an elementary piano textbook and application to more universal uses. In 1981 high-frequency response of a single-finger model was realized; in 1982 a five-finger model and an arm model were realized; in 1983 this model played tunes for beginners.

This paper describes the development of the keyboard-playing robot WAM-7R (Waseda Automatic Manipulator — 7R) with a focus on the five finger model and an arm model.

Configuration of five-fingers model

Specification

Since this robot is premised to be anthropomorphic, a hand is designed to have five fingers. In the development of the five-finger model, movable ranges and tapping rates of fingers necessary for manual operation of the keyboards are investigated in 'Beyer' textbook. Based on this investigation, degrees of freedom (DOF) and shape of the model are examined.

Degree of freedom

While human fingers consist of 4 DOF for each, fingers of this robot, excluding a thumb, are designed to have 3 DOF; 1 DOF for PIP joint and 2 DOF for MP joint, by ignoring DIP joint, the motions of which are found to be dependent on that of PIP joint.

The thumb is designed to have 2 DOF by ignoring DOF for posturing opposite to the other four fingers, because the thumb can be considered to be used only for playing the keyboards for this robot. As a result, DOF of fingers total 14. The thumb is designed to be located at a lower position than the other four fingers by considering the intersection with the index finger and/or the middle finger.

Tapping rate

The maximum playing speed in 'Beyer' textbook is *allegro* and its shortest musical note is a *semiquaver*. It is necessary for one finger to tap at 8.8 Hz frequency to meet the above condition. However, it is sufficient to realize 4.4 Hz of tapping rate because two out of five fingers are used for the actual playing.

Design of driving unit

The degrees of freedom in the fingers of this robot are 14. Hence, it is nearly impossible for actuators (DC servomotors), position and velocity sensors to be installed at the hand. Therefore, several sensors and actuators are installed in the body of the robot, and their power is transmitted through the reduction gears to the fingers by wire ropes and outer tubes (Figure 1).

The position sensors for flection and extension motion, and radial and ulnar flection motion of MP joint are installed at the hand. The velocity sensors of all the joints and the position sensors of PIP joint are installed in the body beside the motors.

When wire ropes are attached aligned with the arm from the body through the fingers, the tension of the wire ropes increases due to the variation of outer tube routes caused by arm motions. This results in the increase of frictional forces and greatly affects response of the fingers.

Spring elements are attached to the outer tubes to minimize this effect as illustrated in Figure 1. This mechanism can decrease frictional forces because the length of the outer tubes changes in accordance with the route variations and thus the tension of the wire ropes is reduced.

Five-finger model

A five finger model based on the above examination is developed. Its specification is shown in Table 1. Fingers are made of CFRP (carbon fibre reinforced plastics) to reduce loads on the arm. The model is controlled by software-servo using single-chip microcomputers. Its details will be discussed later. Figure 2 shows the response of the finger. A high-speed response was made possible and a 10 Hz frequency was realized in successive tapping motion. The efficacy of spring elements was also ascertained.

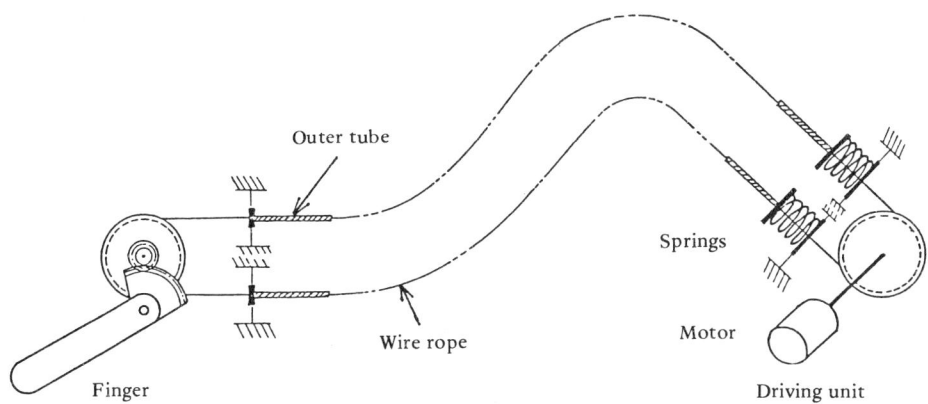

Figure 1 Finger-driving mechanism

Table 1 Five-finger model

Number of fingers	5
Degrees of freedom	Thumb MP 2 Other four fingers MP 2 Total 14 PIP 1
L x W x H (mm)	213 x 132 x 79
Wait (g)	350
Actuator	DC motor
Power transmission method	Wire rope and outer tube

Configuration of arm model

Specification

Design policy

The following three points are emphasized in the development of the arm model.

(1) Shape of the arm model. It is necessary for the arm to be nearly the same as that of a human one in size and shape, to meet the condition that it has to be anthropomorphic and that it has to be able to play ordinarily used electric organs.

(2) Motion rate of each joint. High-speed arm motion is required to play the keyboards.

(3) Positioning accuracy. Positional accuracy of each joint should be within a range of errors such that its precision enables the fingers to strike the black keys with certainty.

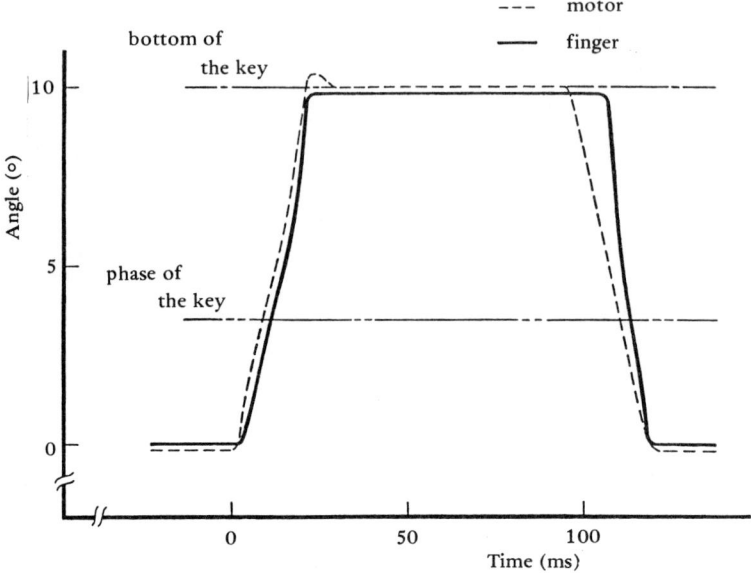

Figure 2 Response of the finger

In summary, the problem is to develop the arm model of almost the same size as that of human beings, and also the driving unit which realizes high speed and high accuracy.

Configuration of the degrees of freedom
In the design of an artificial arm for universal use more than 6 DOF are needed. This is because 6 DOF are required at minimum to determine position and orientation of the hand arbitrarily in the work space. The degrees of freedom of a human arm, however, are 7.

The seventh degree of freedom (the redundant one) makes it possible to vary the position of the elbow by keeping the position and orientation of the hand fixed. Thus, the arm of this robot is determined to be 7 DOF which are configured to be the same as those of human beings. The configuration of the degrees of freedom is depicted in Figure 3.

The configuration of these 7 DOF is determined with the consideration on velocity and torque of each joint, and on the movable range of the wrist which affects the possible posture of the arm, based on the analysis on postures and motions of the human arm in playing the keyboards as a link mechanism.

Actuators
According to the analysis stated in the previous section, the motion rate of the wrist necessary for playing the keyboard is found to be approximately 1 m/s.

The capability of the manipulator is dependent virtually on the selected actuators. Though introduction of new actuators such as direct-drive DC torque motors

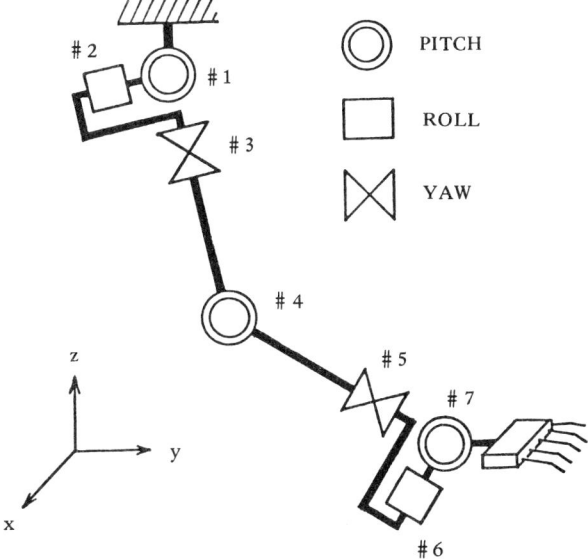

Figure 3 Degrees of arm model

and shape memory alloy has been tried in recent years, they are inappropriate for this robot from the point of view of size, power, etc. DC servomotors, the capacity of which has rapidly progressed, are thus adopted for this robot. Velocity and position sensors are installed.

Arm model

The specification of the arm model is shown in Table 2, its capacity in Table 3 and the complete view in Figure 4. The arm is made of CFRP, as are the fingers. The maximum wrist velocity is 1.5 m/s.

Synthesis of control system

Computer system

This robot has 21 DOF for one arm. It will have two arms and two legs (4 DOF for each) for pedalling, totalling 50 DOF. There is no precedent for the development of the robot system with so many DOF and synthesis of a computer system capable of efficient control of such miltidegrees emerges as a big problem.

The concept of the structure of the human central nervous system is introduced to constitute the computer system of this robot. The motions of the human arms are controlled by the central nervous system, which is hierarchically structured by the association area, the motor area and the spinal cord.

Table 2 Arm specification

Shape	Anthropomorphic
Degrees of freedom	7
Actuator	DC motor
Driving method	PWM
Sensors	Rotary encoder Tachogenerator
Movable range (°)	1 −30 − +90 2 −90 − +30 3 −90 − +90 4 −10 − +120 5 −120 − +60 6 −60 − +60 7 −60 − +60
Length (mm)	Elbow-shoulder 271 Wrist-elbow 272 Elbow-shoulder 271 Total 543
Total weight (kg)	14

Table 3 Capability of arm model

Joint no.	Max velocity (°/s)	Max acceleration (°/s^2)
1	145.8	4440
2	145.8	4440
3	208.0	7500
4	208.0	7500
5	211.2	17 045
6	150.0	15 000
7	270.0	40 000

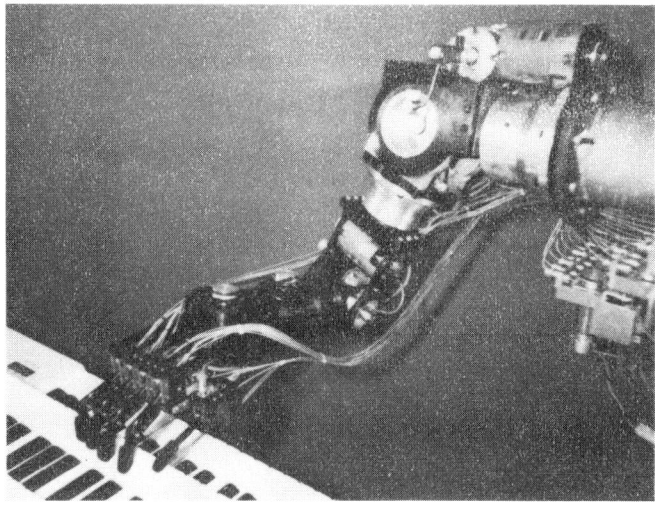

Figure 4 WAM-7R (frontal view)

The association area produces the plans of motions based on the information on outer environments and past experience, then outputs them to the motor area. The motor area converts the information to be sent to the spinal cord by co-ordinating the information on motions and it, furthermore, supervises and adjusts the function of the spinal cord. The spinal cord is connected with muscles and controls their various reflexes.

The computer system of this robot is also hierarchically structured at three levels, with reference to that of human beings (Figure 5).

System 8000 (CPU:Z-8001) with UNIX as OS is used for the upper level. Two 16-bit microprocessor Z-8002 (for right and left side of the body) are used for the middle level. The single-chip microcomputer Z-8094 is used for each degree (50 chips in total) for the lower level.

The upper level, system 8000, determines fingering and wrist positions according to the score data sent from the vision system, and it also plans trajectories of fingers, arms and legs. The middle level, Z-8002, sends the reference position to each degree according to the trajectory plan and realizes the co-ordination control by monitoring the condition of each degree when required. The lower level, Z-8094, processes the data interpolation and software servoing.

Algorithm for fingering

While playing the instruments, human beings judge the optimum finger and/or arm motion required from the scores. It is necessary for this robot, also, to possess the capability of producing the plans of finger and arm motions from the score information input; especially of great importance when playing the keyboards, how to correspond fingers to each note and where to locate the wrist. The algorithm used to solve this problem is described below.

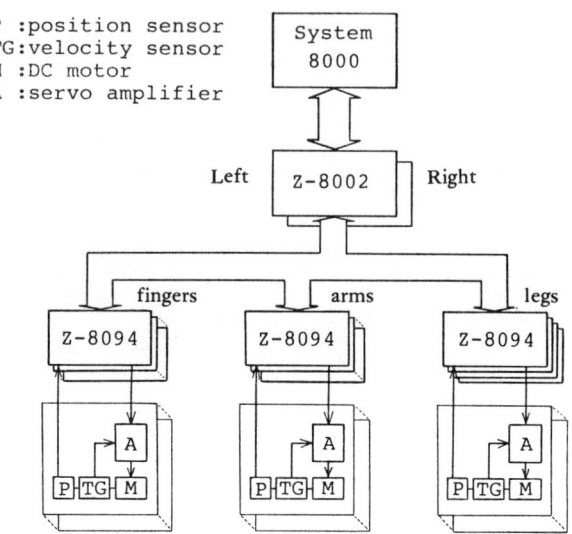

Figure 5 Computer system

The basic strategy is to determine such fingering that rapid arm motions are avoided as much as possible, since motions of robot arms have much more confinement than those of fingers. The movable ranges of fingers and wrists of the robot are the important data for the determination of fingering. The two following concepts are introduced in the determination of fingering.

The first concept is a 'block'. Series of notes strikable without changing position and orientation of the hand can be treated as a block, because the range movable by fingers only with position and orientation of the hand fixed has certain limits. Such blocks are determined by the hardware specification of fingers. When a certain part of the score is extracted and the chord composed of all the notes contained in that part is playable, then that part (block) is playable without moving the wrist. These blocks are obtained by retrieving the memories storing the precomputed results.

The second concept is an 'area', which is the musical interval translated from the movable range of fingers. This is the group of data which shows the ranges, when keeping one finger striking the key, where the other fingers are reachable on the keyboards. Special fingering patterns such as intersection of fingers are also categorized as areas. These areas are retrieved from the memories according to the given intervals and kind of finger.

The fingering determination procedure is, roughly speaking, to divide the score into several blocks. Hereafter, the nth block is called block (n).

There is the same number of methods to move from block (n) to block $(n+1)$ as that of notes contained in block (n), because you can move from any note in block (n). This moving point is called CP (changing point), the point to change the block. Among CPs in block (n), the optimum CP which enables the robot to play smoothly with the consideration of the co-ordination of fingers and wrist is selected by having a reference to area data. If more than one CP are selected, then the CP which makes the next block the longest is finally selected (Figure 6). When the appropriate CP cannot be found, the last note in block (n) becomes CP.

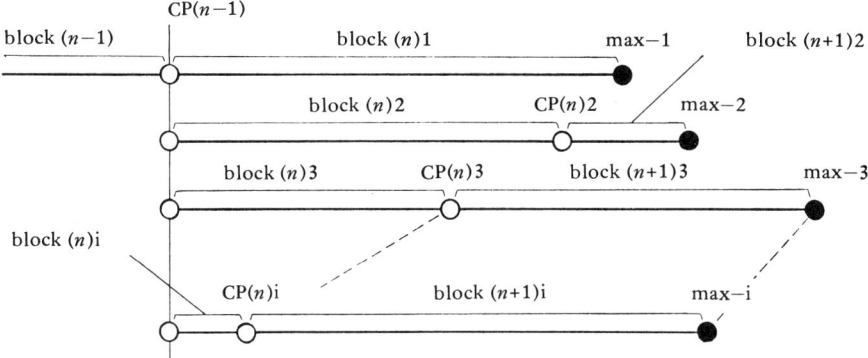

Figure 6 Fingering-determination method

In the above procedure the parts of the score where the frequency of CP appearance is high can be considered to be the parts containing the special series of notes which needs much computation time. Therefore, by storing such series of notes as patterns, these patterns can be referred to in determining fingering of other scores. This algorithm can judge if the given series of notes are special and store them automatically, which can be regarded as one kind of learning. These patterns are stored as functions concerned with time, compass and the rate of change of interval. Using this algorithm for fingering, it was made possible to process the proper fingering patterns of scores in elementary piano textbooks.

Conclusion

An anthropomorphic robot that can play keyboards with 21 DOF has been developed. Computer system capable of controlling multi-degrees of freedom has been developed. Software such as fingering-determination program, etc, has also been developed. As a result, this robot system has realized fluent performance of tunes in the 'Beyer' textbook on a keyboard instrument, by giving information on musical scores only.

Reference

[1] Sugano S *et al.* (1983) *Tajiyudo Ningengata Robot no Kaihatsu* (The development of an anthropomorphic robot). Proc. of Biomechanism Symp. (in Japanese)

Control of Two Co-ordinated Robots by Using an Only-kinematic Model

P Dauchez, A Fournier and R Zapata

Laboratoire d'Automatique et de Microélectronique de Montpellier, USTL, 34060 Montpellier, Cédex, France

Summary: Use of the Jacobian matrix of an industial robot is an easy way to express differential changes in position and orientation of the tool caused by differential changes in joint co-ordinates. In the case of two co-ordinated robots we use the same method to express the differential changes of a terminal device with respect to the other one caused by differential changes in joint co-ordinates of both robots, without any reference to the external world. In this way we create redundancy that can be used to avoid collisions between both arms or between the arms and the environment or to use the mechanism where one or several joints are locked. The method is applied to simulate and to control co-ordinated arms for moving heavy objects or for doing assemblies.

Introduction

In robotics there are two ways for manipulating large or heavy objects, either by using a very powerful robot or by using two co-ordinated robots.[1] The present paper describes a method of control for two robots carrying together the same object. The first problem is to avoid any constraint in the moved object and to control the kinematic loop made up of both robots and the carried object. The second one is to avoid any collision in the stage before grasping the object.[2] In this paper we develop some properties of the kinematic model and use them for controlling a closed kinematic chain. We develop different methods according to the stage of the task, before grasping the object by the two robots and after grasping it. According to the number of degrees of freedom with respect to the task it is better to choose a specific method rather than another one.

Some definitions and properties about the kinematic model

The kinematic model has been used already in robot control for 10 years.[3-5] Several properties of this model are very interesting, especially in assembly tasks and to control redundant mechanisms. Furthermore, kinematic control allows any criterion being a function of the state of the robots in its environment to be taken into account. In this section we present the only definitions and properties we need for controlling a closed chain.

Let $\underline{\Delta X}$ be the (6 × 1) vector of the elementary motions of a solid S-

$$\underline{\Delta X} = \begin{bmatrix} \underline{V}(P, S/Ro\,;Ro)\Delta t \\ \underline{\widehat{\ }}(S/Ro\,;Ro)\Delta t \end{bmatrix} \quad (1)$$

$\underline{V}(P, S/Ro\,;Ro)$ is the linear velocity of a point P of the solid element S with respect to a fixed reference frame Ro and expressed in this reference frame. $\triangleq (S/Ro; Ro)$ is the angular velocity of $\underline{S}$ with respect to the reference frame and expressed in this frame.

Let
$$\underline{\Delta Y} = [\Delta Y1, \ldots, \Delta Yn]^T \qquad (2)$$
be the $(n, 1)$ vector of the elementary variations of the n joint variables acting on $\underline{S}$. It is very well known that we can write

$$\underline{\Delta X} = H(\underline{Y}) \underline{\Delta Y} \qquad (3)$$

where $\underline{H}(\underline{Y})$ is a $(6, n)$ matrix the elements of which are functions of the joint variables vector Y. If S is the last solid element of the robot (either the tool or the grasping device) $\underline{\Delta X}$ represents the task vector expressed in the reference frame. In fact $\underline{\Delta X}$ is not really the controlled task; generally we do not need to control all the six degrees of freedom of the tool but only some of them.

Let $\underline{\Delta x}$ be the $(m, 1)$ controlled task vector. This vector has up to six independant elements, depending on the type of task, for example three components to put a point of the tool on a reference point or four or five components to put a line on another reference line. The controlled task vector is linearly dependant on the task vector x and we have

$$\underline{\Delta x} = R \underline{\Delta X} = RH \underline{\Delta Y} = J \underline{\Delta Y} \qquad (4)$$

where J is the Jacobian matrix of the system for the specific controlled task. If $\underline{J}^+$ denotes the pseudoinverse matrix of $\underline{J}$, it can be shown that

$$\underline{\Delta Y} = J^+ \underline{\Delta x} + (J^+ J - In)\underline{Z} \qquad (5)$$

where In is the $(n \times n)$ unit matrix and $\underline{Z}(\underline{Y}, \underline{X})$ is an arbitrary vector which can be used for increasing or decreasing a criterion.

Kinematic co-ordination of two robots doing the same task[1,6]

Let Rob 1 and Rob 2 be two robots and $R1$ and $R2$ two frames linked to the terminal device of each one (Figure 1). The co-ordination of both terminal devices consists in locating the frame $R2$ with respect to $R1$. In fact the reference frame Ro does not appear in this relative task, but the common way to solve this problem is to express each displacement of the frames $R2$ and $R1$ with respect to the reference frame Ro.

Let $n1$ and $n2$ be, respectively, the number of independant joints of the robots Rob 1 and Rob 2 and k the number of independant components of the relative controlled task vector.

To solve this geometric problem through the reference frame Ro it is necessary to have at least k independant joints for each robot and, secondly, to plan the absolute task in the common part of the workspace of each robot. Therefore, solving an absolute task in the place of a relative task is harder.

For example, let us assume that the two robots Rob 1 and Rob 2 have only one rotating joint and a common workspace (Figure 2). The relative controlled task consists in putting the terminal device $T1$ of Rob 1 on the terminal device $T2$ of Rob 2. Generally, there exist two different cases for the solution. To solve the

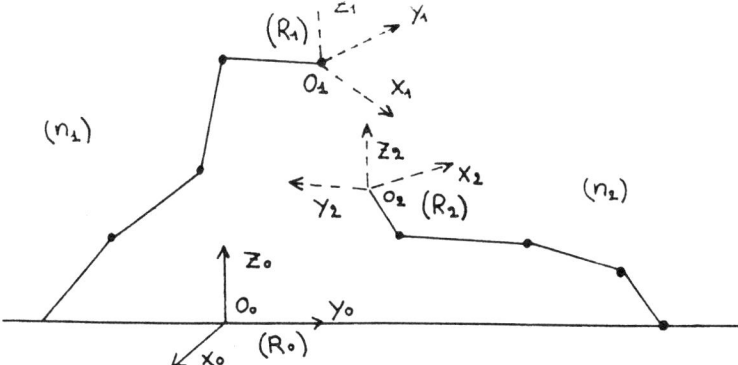

Figure 1 Differential task

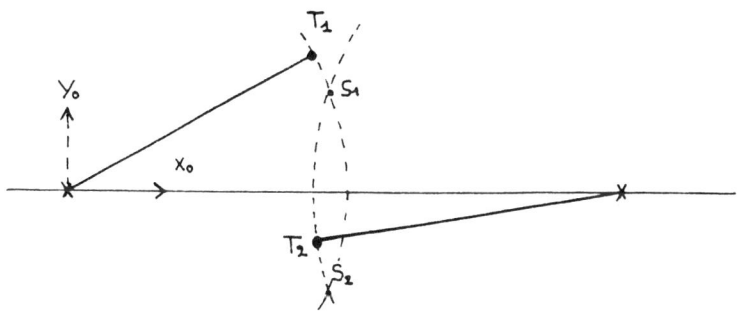

Figure 2 Two one-degree-of-freedom robots

relative task it is not necessary to know anything about the meeting point. On the other hand, to solve twice the absolute task it is necessary to compute the common points of the intersecting circles before the only absolute possible task is controlled.

Let us consider that both robots Rob 1 and Rob 2 constitute a single robot with $n1 + n2$ independant joints. The frame linked to the terminal device becomes only $R2$ and the reference frame becomes $R1$ in the place of Ro. By using hypotheses and notations of the second section the relative controlled task can be written as

$$\underline{\Delta x1} = J1(Y)\underline{\Delta Y} \qquad (6)$$

where the $(k,1)$ vector $\underline{\Delta x1}$ describes the relative task, the $(n1 + n2)$ vector, $\underline{Y}$ is the joint description vector of both robots and $J1(\underline{Y})$ is the Jacobian matrix of both robots for the relative task.

If the total number of independant joints $(n1 + n2)$ within their articular limits

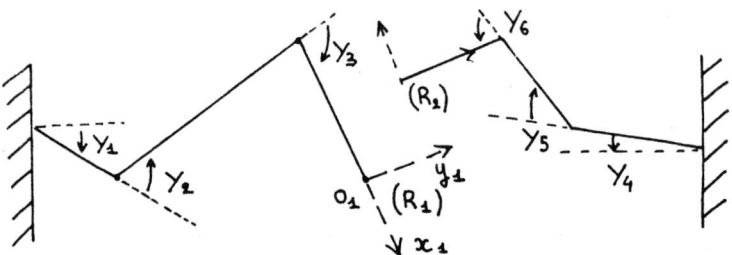

Figure 3 Co-operation of two planar robots

is equal or greater than the number of independent components of the relative controlled task, it is generally possible to achieve exactly this task.

Let us consider another example (Figure 3). Two planar robots Rob 1 and Rob 2 are used to carry the same object in their plane. For carrying out this task, It is necessary to put the end of the robot Rob 1 on the end of robot Rob 2 and to align their terminal link. Therefore, three independant components are necessary to describe the relative controlled task. The two robots have six independant joints altogether, the relative task is generally possible. If no joint is locked for any mechanical reason, then it is possible to set up three other linear conditions on the joints. However, it is very hazardous to choose these other linear equations. For instance, if we lock three of the six articulated joints we have to make sure that the relative task is still possible within the mechanical limits of the other three.

It is better to keep the smallest number of linear equations for describing the controlled relative task and to take into account an optimization criterion. The most useful criteria are used to keep the articular joint variables within their mechanical limits or to keep the robots far away from external obstacles known before achieving the task or conversely to bring the terminal devices closer to a target.

On the one hand, this previous method is very useful in the stage before grasping the object. When the object is grasped by two robots, both terminal devices and the carried object are joined together and any further relative displacement of these three objects is impossible. However, with this method it is unsure that the last condition still applies. If several joints reach their limits, then one risks breaking the part or losing it.

When the object is grasped, the relative controlled task vector should always be zero whatever the robots joints are. From the general solution (5) we can write

$$\underline{\Delta Y} = (J^+ J - I_n)\underline{Z} \qquad (7)$$

and the only way to achieve the task is then to control vector $\underline{Z}$.

Let vector $\underline{Z}$ be equal to $-\mathrm{grad}\,\phi(\underline{Y})$; computation by (7) makes $\phi(\underline{Y})$ decreasing. Let us assume that the current location of the object is represented by vector x and the location to be reached is represented by vector x_f in the reference frame.

Let D be the Euclidean length of the line from $\underline{x}(\underline{Y})$ to $\underline{x}_f$ (in R^m) (equation 4).

$$\underline{D} = \|\underline{x}_f - \underline{x}(\underline{Y})\|$$

Then, by assigning $\underline{Z}$ to $-\text{grad } \underline{D}(\underline{Y})$ makes the object closer to the target. If this target belongs to both workspaces of the robots then the carried object will reach it for the initial grasping condition.

As the solution $\underline{\Delta Y}$ from equation (7) belongs to the null space of the Jacobian matrix J it can be applied without any effect on the controlled relative task which remains to zero.

Conclusion

In this paper some aspects of the kinematic control of two co-ordinated robots are developed. We emphasize, too, the different ways to use the solutions expressed from the pseudoinverse matrix. From the same computation of the pseudoinverse matrix, it is possible to achieve two independant tasks or to control a relative task of the first robot with respect to the second one by taking into account additional conditions on the joint variables or in optimizing a criterion. Furthermore this method allows carrying of an object grasped by both terminal devices without any relative displacement of these grippers.

In future, use of several co-ordinated robots should become a very interesting way of carrying objects too heavy or too large for only one, consequently the methods developed in this paper should become very useful.

References

[1] Dauchez P (1983) Etude de la commande de deux robots manipulateurs lors de tâches coordonées. Thèse 3° cycle, USTL
[2] Zapata R (1983) Le problème de l'évitement des collosions lors de la commande des robots-manipulateurs. Thèse 3° cycle, USTL
[3] Boullion T L & Odell P L *Generalized Inverse Matrices* Wiley-Interscience
[4] Fournier A (1980) Génération des movements en robotique; applications des inverses généralisées et des pseudo-inverses. Thèse d'Etat, USTL
[5] Fournier A & Khalil W *Coordination and Reconfiguration of Mechanicals Redundant Systems* Proc. of Int. Conf. on Cybernetics and Society, Washington, DC, 19–21 September, 1977
[6] Fujii S & Kuruno S (1975) Coordinated computer control of a pair of manipulators. *Industrial Robot*, December

A Method for Time-optimal Control of Dynamically Constrained Manipulators

P Kiriazov and P Marinov

Bulgarian Academy of Sciences, Institute of Mechanics and Biomechanics, Academy G Bonchev str, bl 8, 1113 Sofia, Bulgaria

Summary: Limitation improved by the strains and vibrations of manipulators, in the case of higher operation speeds and heavier manipulation loads, is to be taken into consideration. The problem for time-optimal point-to-point control in the presence of dynamic constraints is the subject of this work. An algorithm for control synthesis of the correspondent two-point boundary value problem (TPBVP) is proposed. The minimization of the movement execution time is performed over the set of all so-obtained feasible solutions. The method is illustrated with respect to a manipulator with cylindrical co-ordinates under the constraint of the gripper's acceleration.

Introduction

It is well known that in the present status of technology, manipulators are used mainly as positioning devices. The path between motion end points is not specified and depends on the control algorithm and hardware. A control system must operate in such a way that the basic qualities of point-to-point manipulation may be achieved.

Designers aspire to optimize the mechanical structure of manipulators to reduce cost of materials and energy consumption. The minimization of manipulator's inertial characteristics may lead to considerable limitations on the dynamic motion in point-to-point operations. In the case of higher operational speeds and heavier manipulation loads, the reduction of strains and vibrations of that flexible mechanical system must be taken into consideration.[1-3] Besides, in fast simultaneous highly coupled joint motion controllability has to be ensured. Finally, existing geometrical and control saturation constraints have to be taken into account, as well.

So, one gets to the problem for time-optimal control of dynamically constrained manipulators in point-to-point operation, which is the subject of this work. The inclusion of dynamic constraints on the manipulator motion is an extension of previously published papers (also P Marinov and P Kiriazov, unpublished work).[4]

As application of the classical optimal control theory to this very complex problem is practically impossible, a direct method based on an algorithm for control synthesis of the correspondent two-point boundary value problem (TPBVP) is proposed.

The optimization procedure is performed over the set of all feasible solutions of the TPBVP, which are obtained by this algorithm.

Statement of the problem

In general, the mathematical model of the dynamical motion of the manipulator with n degrees of freedom, incorporating all relevant mechanical parameters, can be written as

$$M(q)\ddot{q} + N(q,\dot{q}) + V\dot{q} = R(t) \qquad (1)$$

where $q(t) \in R^n$ = vector of generalized (joint) co-ordinates, $M(q)$ = inertial matrix, $N(q,\dot{q})$ = vector of centrifugal, Coriolis and gravity forces, V = diagonal viscous friction matrix and $R(t) \in R^n$ = vector of input generalized forces. Denote by:

boundary conditions

$$q(t^\circ) = q^\circ, \qquad \dot{q}(t^\circ) = 0 - \text{initial state} \qquad (2)$$

$$q(t^f) = q^f, \qquad \dot{q}(t^f) = 0 - \text{final state} \qquad (3)$$

where $t^\circ = \min t_i^\circ$, $t^f = \max t_i^f$, $i = 1, \ldots, n$;

control constraints

$$|R_i(t)| \leq R_{i\max}, \quad i = 1, \ldots, n; \qquad (4)$$

dynamic constraints

$$|b_i| = |f_i(t,q,\dot{q})\ddot{q}_i + g_i(t,q,\dot{q})| \leq c_i, \quad i = 1, \ldots, n \qquad (5)$$

where f_i and g_i are some functions, $f_i > 0$.

To ensure satisfaction of the existing joint constraints for any point-to-point operation, the following condition with regard to the velocities will apply

$$\operatorname{sin}\dot{q}_i(t) = \operatorname{sin}(q_i^f - q_i^\circ) = \operatorname{sin}_i, \quad i = 1, \ldots, n \qquad (6)$$

By having an algorithm for control synthesis of the TPBVP (1÷3) under the constraints (4÷6), one can obtain a set of feasible solutions.

As the set is described by a number of parameters, then the suboptimal procedure consists in minimization of the operation time $T = t^f - t^\circ$, depending on these parameters. In this last step, the application of the well known steepest descent method[5] is easily performed.

In the following the problem is to elaborate a control synthesis algorithm, generating feasible solutions. The control laws will be derived in accordance with the relay principle, as a time-optimal control concept. To provide substantial reduction of T, sequential starting times t_i° ($i = 1, \ldots, n$) of joint motions are adopted. In the switching reversal from acceleration to deceleration, an appropriate time-lag for each actuator is involved to ensure at this stage good dynamical performance without jerks of the manipulator. The general appearance of the requested control functions and correspondent joint motions is shown in Figure 1.

Control synthesis algorithm

Let us take the equality sign in the dynamic constraints (5)

$$f_i(t,q,\dot{q})\ddot{q} + g_i(t,q,\dot{q}) = (\operatorname{sin}R_i)c_i, \quad i = 1, \ldots, n, \qquad (7)$$

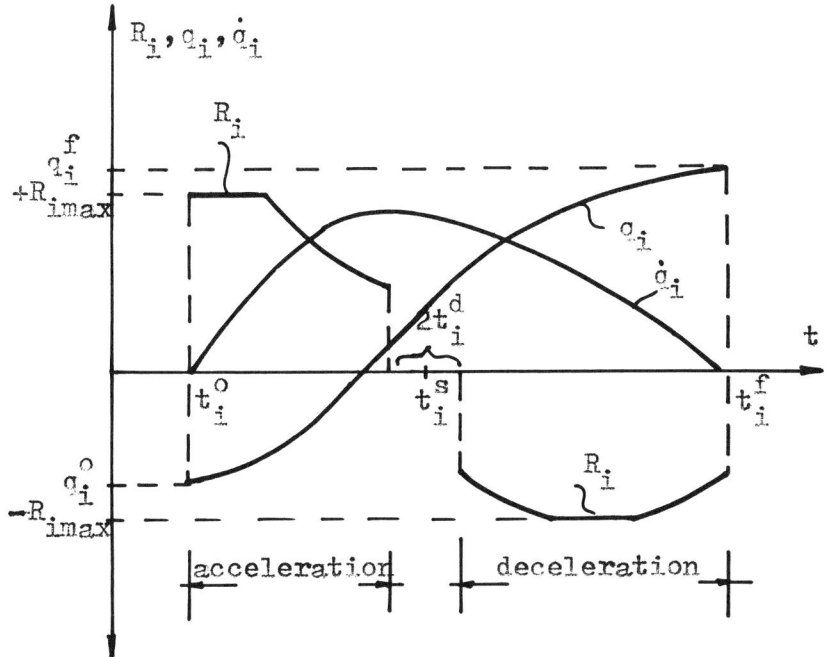

Figure 1 Control functions and correspondent joint motions

where

$$\sin R_i = \sin_i, \qquad t \in [t_i^o; t_i^s - t_i^d] \qquad (8)$$
$$\sin R_i = -\sin_i, \qquad t \in [t_i^s + t_i^d; t_i^f]$$

With given initial conditions (2), one can express in each time-step the acceleration $\ddot{q}_i$ from (7) and substitute in the equation of coupled motions (1) to obtain the values $R_i(t)$ needed to satisfy (7). In the case that some value $R_i(t)$ violates the correspondent control constraint (4), then its own extremal value will be taken in

$$R_i(t) = (\sin R_i) R_{i\max}, \qquad [R_i = 0, \ t \in (t_i^s - t_i^d; t_i^s + t_i^d)] \qquad (9)$$

Otherwise, the obtained value $R_i(t)$ will be left the same.

If the simultaneous joint motions are too much coupled, then dynamic constraints (5) may be substantially disturbed sometimes, despite the above proposed control laws. For this reason, during the whole manipulator motion, the satisfaction of (5) with accepted tolerances Δc_i needs to be verified

$$|h_i| \leq c_i + \Delta c_i \qquad (10)$$

In the off-line sense, that control synthesis algorithm for the TPBVP (1÷3) with the so-defined control laws and the observations of (6), (8) and (10), consists in performing several simulation test movements from the given initial state to a terminal state, converging to the required one. Each such movement means that the system of differential equations (1) with the initial values (2), given starting times t_i^o and some approximate switching times t_i^s, is integrated until satisfying the terminal condition $(3)_2$: $\dot{q}_i(t_i^f) = 0$. Each joint motion settles down after the moment t_i^f with some terminal value of the correspondent co-ordinate: $q_i(t_i^f) = F_i$. The n-dimensional vector F only depends on the vector t^s of the switching times t_i^s, $i = 1, \ldots, n$, if the values of all other parameters are fixed. So, to satisfy the final condition $(3)_1$, one has to solve the following shooting equation

$$F(t^s) = q^f \qquad (11)$$

Solving this equation by Newton's or bisection methods,[5] one obtains a feasible motion $q(t)$ with the correspondent control $R(t)$ and movement execution time T. The steepest descent method is applied to minimization of T as a function of initial times t_i^o, $i = 1, \ldots, n$.

Simulation example

The manipulator model with cylindrical co-ordinates (Figure 2) has been taken into consideration as a typical example for manipulators, performing point-to-point operations. The system of differential equations describes the two coupled joint motions (no friction involved):[4,6]

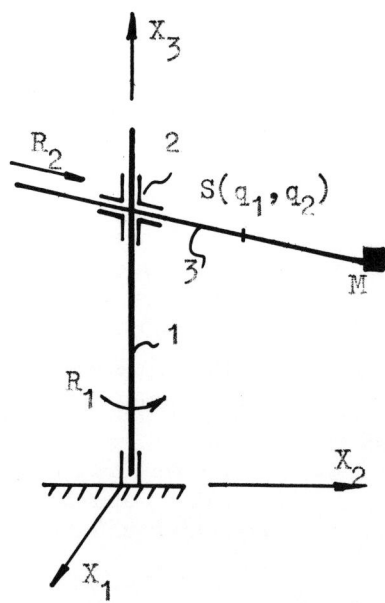

Figure 2 Manipulator model with cylindrical co-ordinates

$$\{[J_1 + J_2 + mq_2^2 + M(q_2 + a)^2]\dot{q}_1\}^{\cdot} = R_1(t) \quad (12)$$
$$(m + M)\ddot{q}_2 - [mq_2 + M(q_2 + a)]\dot{q}_1^2 = R_2(t)$$

where (q_1, q_2) = polar co-ordinates of the mass centre S of the link 3, M = total mass (mass of the gripper and tipmass), m = mass of the link 3, J_1 = total momentum of inertia of the links 1 and 2 with respect to X_3 axis, J_2 = momentum of inertia of the link 3 with respect to the axis that passes through the point S and is parallel to the X_3 axis and a = distance between the M mass centre and S.

As dynamical constraints, the following inequalities for the M mass acceleration are taken:

$$|b_1| = |\ddot{q}_1(q_2 + a) + 2\dot{q}_1\dot{q}_2| \leqslant c_1 \quad (13)$$
$$|b_2| = |\ddot{q}_2 - \dot{q}_1^2(q_2 + a)| \leqslant c_2$$

The numerical values of the model parameters have been applied:

$m = 97$ kg, $M = 50$ kg, $a = 1.1$ m, $J_1 + J_2 = 193$ kg m^2, $R_{1\max} = 600$ Nm, $R_{2\max} = 500$ N, $t^\circ = 0$ s, $q_1^\circ = 0$ rad, $q_2^\circ = 0$ m, $q_1^f = 2.0$ rad, $q_2^f = 1.0$ m, $2t_1^d = 2t_2^d = 0.05$ s, $c_2 = 3.6$ m/s^2, $\Delta c_1 = \Delta c_2 = 0.3$, $c_1 = 2.9$ rads^{-2}m^{-1}

Integration of the system of differential equations (12) has been carried out using a fourth-order Runge–Kutta method. The feasible solution for the initial times $t_1^\circ = t_2^\circ = t^\circ$ is presented in Figures 3 and 4. This solution ($T = 2.52$ s) is taken as an initial guess for the time minimization procedure that finds the optimal feasible solution ($T = 2.01$ s), shown in Figures 5 and 6.

Conclusions

A direct method for synthesis of time-suboptimal point-to-point control of manipulators in the presence of state and dynamical constraints, has been elaborated. This method is applicable when the dynamic constraints do not have to be satisfied during the whole manipulator motion, for example, only at the ends of the joint motions. If the identification is not sufficiently exact, then the algorithm of the proposed method can be performed on the manipulator itself for the final adjustment of the switching times (or control levels). Moreover, since the method requires minimum time computation efforts, on-line control using observation of the dynamical constraints may be performed in a direct self-learning process.

The method is useful for evaluation of the manipulators' dynamical performance and for the optimal design of their mechanical structure and control system hardware.

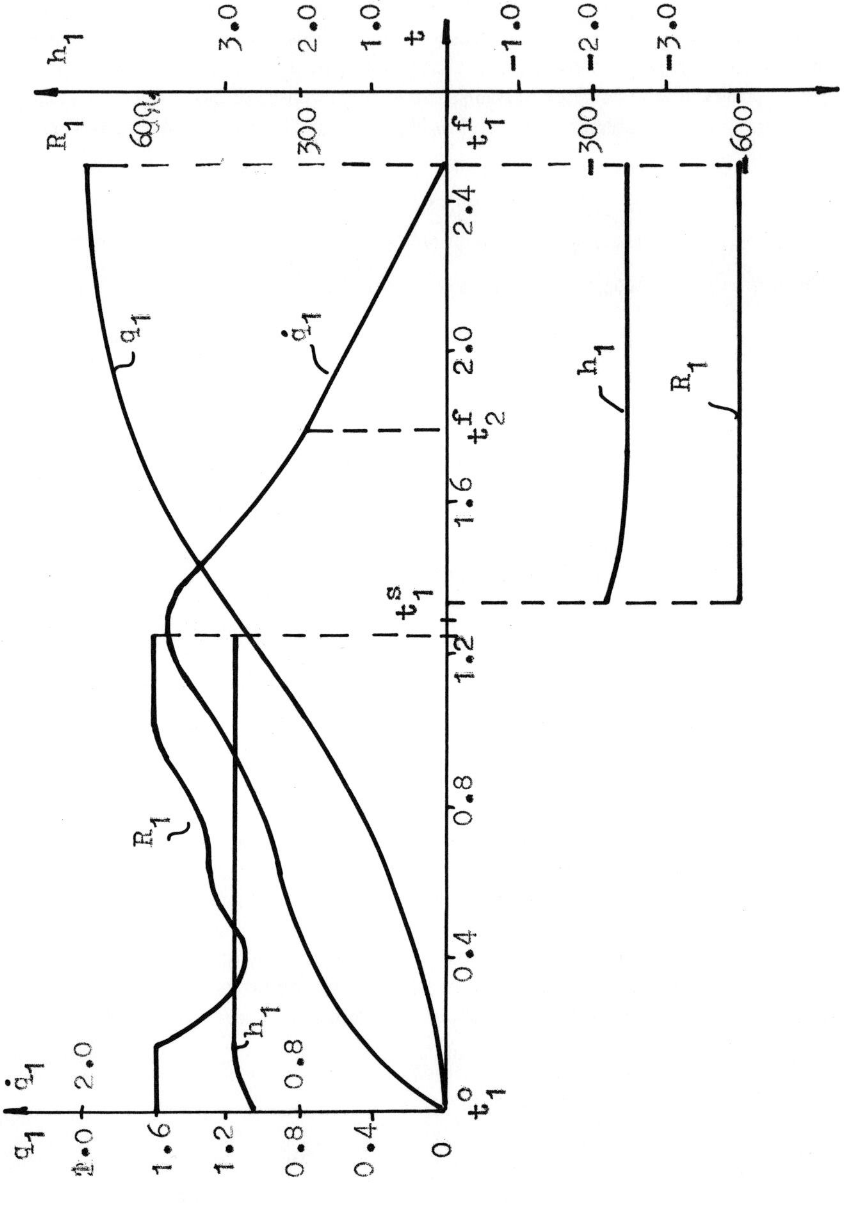

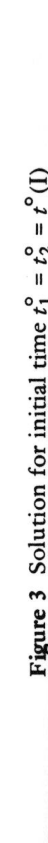

Figure 3 Solution for initial time $t_1^o = t_2^o = t^o(I)$

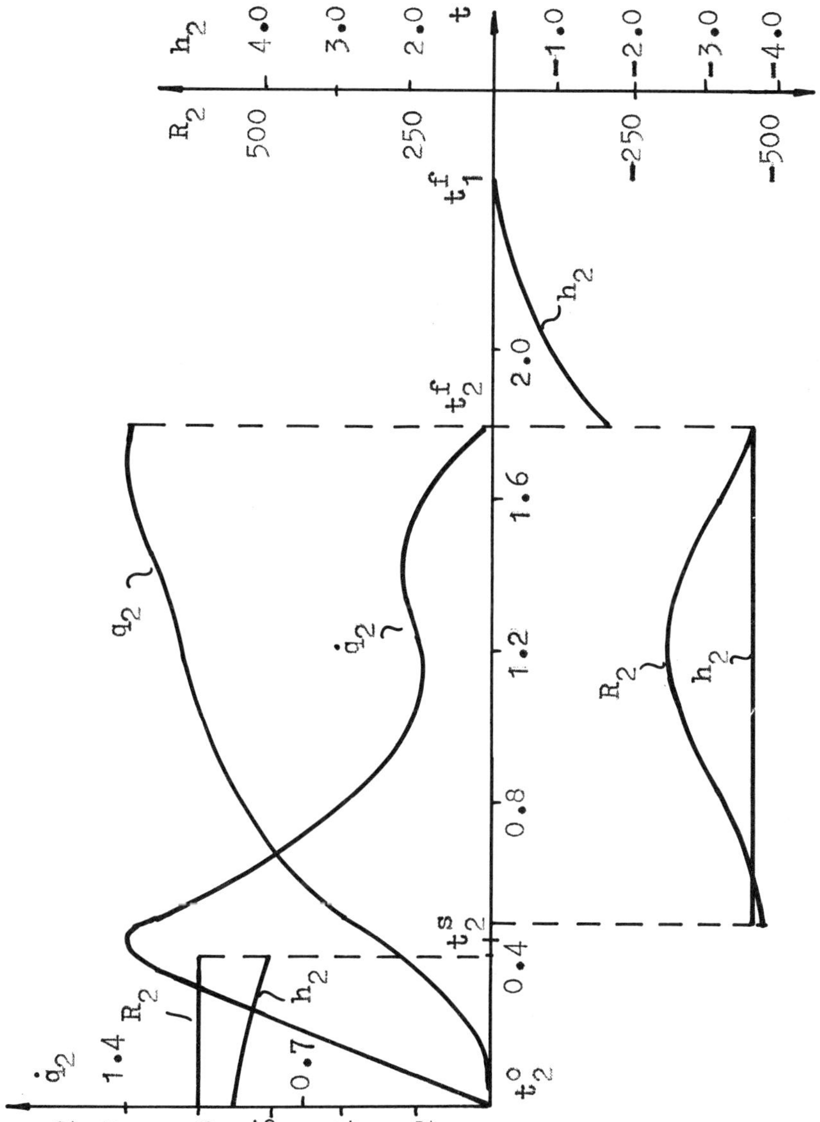

Time-optimal Control and Dynamic Constraints 175

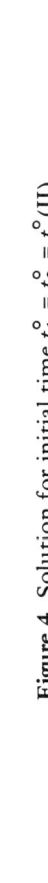

Figure 4 Solution for initial time $t_1^o = t_2^o = t^o(\text{II})$

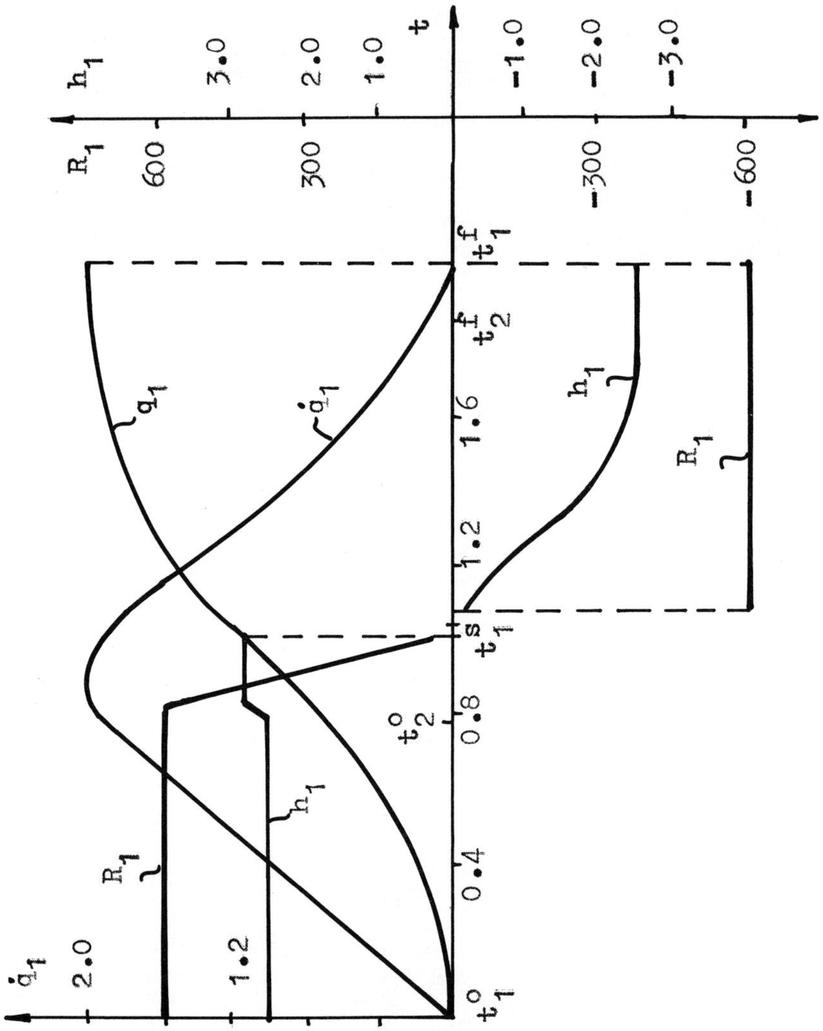

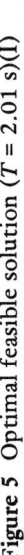

Figure 5 Optimal feasible solution ($T = 2.01$ s)(I)

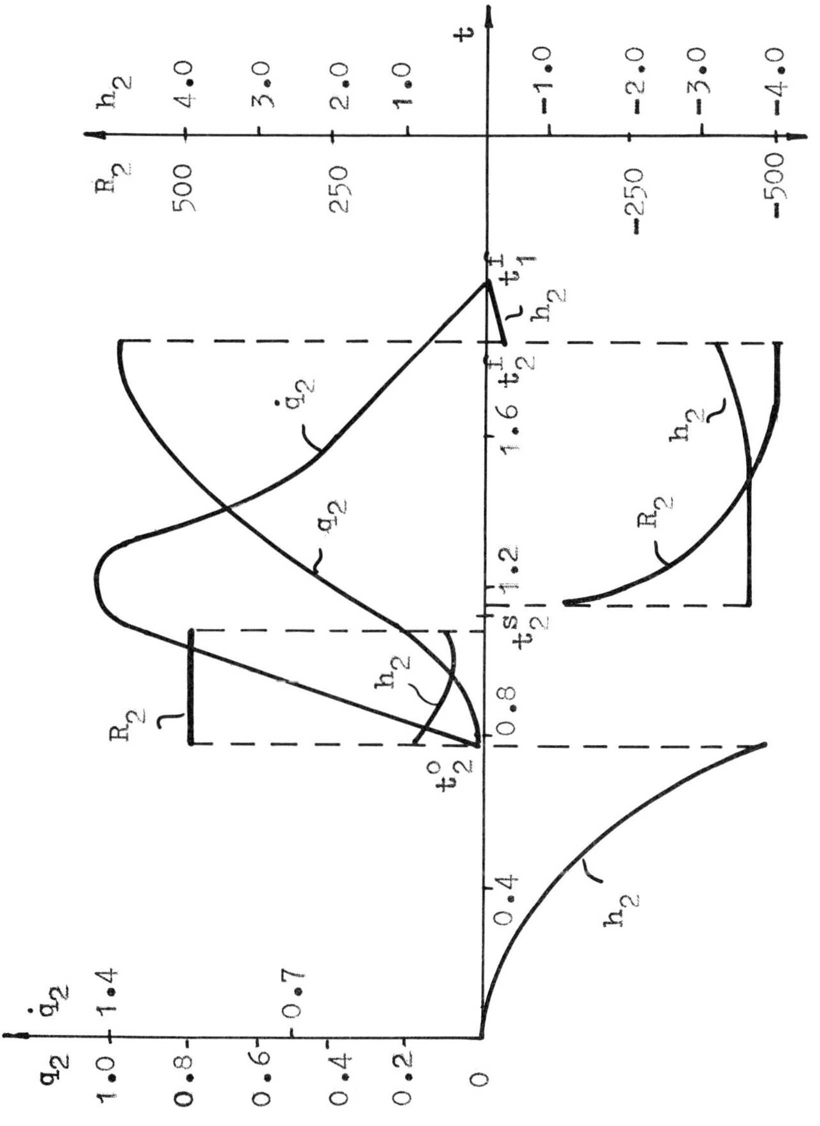

Figure 6 Optimal feasible solution ($T = 2.01$ s)(II)

References

[1] Vucobratović M, Potkonjak V and Hristić D (1981) *Contribution to the Computer-aided Design of Industrial Manipulators* Fourth CISM-IFToMM Symposium on Theory and Practice of Robots and Manipulators, September 8-12, 1981, Zaborów near Warsaw, Poland (preprints, pp 220-230)

[2] Truckenbrodt A (1980) *Dynamics and Control Methods for Moving Flexible Structures and their Application to Industrial Robots* Proc. of the Fifth Cong. on the Theory of Machines and Mechanisms, 1979, (published by *ASME, 345 E* 1, 831-834)

[3] Markus L (1981) *Optimal Control of Damping of Vibration in Robotic Manipulator* Fourth CISM-IFToMM Symposium on Theory and Practice of Robots and Manipulators, September 8-12, 1981, Zaborów near Warsaw, Poland (preprints, pp 67-75)

[4] Kiriazov P and Marinov P (1983) Control synthesis of manipulator dynamics in handling operations. *Theor. Appl. Mech., Publ. House Bulg. Acad. Sci.*, year 14th, no. 2

[5] Stoer J and Bulirsch R (1980) *Introduction to Numerical Analysis* chapters 5 and 7, Springer-Verlag, New York Heidelberg Berlin

[6] Heimann B, Loose H and Schuster G (1981) *Contribution to Optimal Control of an Industrial Robot* Fourth CISM-IFToMM Symposium on Theory and Practice of Robots and Manipulators, September 8-12, 1981, Zaborów near Warsaw, Poland (preprints, pp 211-219)

Bracing Strategy for Robot Operation

W J Book, S Le and V Sangveraphunsiri

School of Mechanical Engineering, Georgia Institute of Technology, Atlanta, GA 30332, USA

Summary: A new strategy of robot operation, the bracing strategy, is presented. Under this strategy an arm is moved into position, and then rigidized by bracing against either the workpiece or an auxiliary static structure. Subsequent precision motion does not involve the entire arm, but only degrees of freedom at the end of the arm. The advantage of this strategy is that it allows high-speed precision motion with a light-weight flexible arm. Light arms require smaller actuators and less energy, may be faster, and are safer and less expensive. Four means of clamping to the structure are considered: a simple normal force, mechanical clamping, vacuum attachment and magnetic attachment. Each means has restrictions and advantages. Arm control with the bracing strategy requires four modes: gross motion control, rendezvous with the bracing structure, control of gross actuators after bracing and control of fine-motion actuators distal to the bracing point.

Rationale for a bracing strategy

Ultimately, one must have fast motion to have the highest performance for a robot arm. Most robot tasks consist of gross-motion and fine-motion phases. Gross motion involves large movements with a relatively predictable destination enabling trajectory planning. These motions require a high force/inertia ratio for rapid completion. Fine motion involves smaller more precise movements which are less predictable. They could arise from sensory or joint-angle feedback in response to disturbances, statistical variation in dimensions or changes in the environment. To accomplish these motions quickly a high-bandwidth servo system is required. Such bandwidth typically requires rigidity in the actuated structure, hence additional structural mass. The traditional approach accomplishes both gross and fine motions with the same actuators and linkage. Thus the structural mass required for the fine-motion speed detracts from the gross-motion speed.

The research under way seeks to eliminate the conflict between gross- and fine-motion speed. The configurations studied effectively reduce the distance from the end point to a 'fixed' base during the fine-motion phase by 'bracing' it against a static structure or the workpiece itself. This approach is especially relevant to long arms with light payloads as documented by the author previously.[1] This is analogous to the strategy of human workers who steady their hand for precise work by bracing their arm against a workbench. It is also a variation of the strategy of extending the range of an arm by providing it with mobility. For mobile robots the strategy is typically to transport the arm to the vicinity of the workpiece, deactivate the mobility subsystem and activate the arm. Both cases are examples of allocation of the motion responsibilities to the most appropriate degrees of freedom. Similar approaches have been proposed by Moore & Hogan[2] and applied specifically to drilling.

The advantages and disadvantages of bracing compared with other strategies for the use of lightweight arms are being considered. Particular consideration is given to the mechanical design and joint-control consequences of employment of this strategy as opposed to conventional rigid-arm strategies. The increased control complexity, additional degrees of freedom and end-point location issues penalize the bracing strategy.

Alternative means of bracing

For a bracing mechanism design, the following parameters are evaluated for comparison purposes: holding force/unit weight, size, required working environment, power consumption, reliability, maintenance. In all cases the controllable force for clamping is applied normal to the surface of the bracing structure. Consequently, the coefficient of friction between the robot and structure is an important parameter.

Simple normal force

The most simple and least reliable means of bracing for robots is the one used extensively by humans. By simply applying a normal force to the bracing structure as shown in Figure 1, rigidization can be achieved. Unlike the other methods, a net

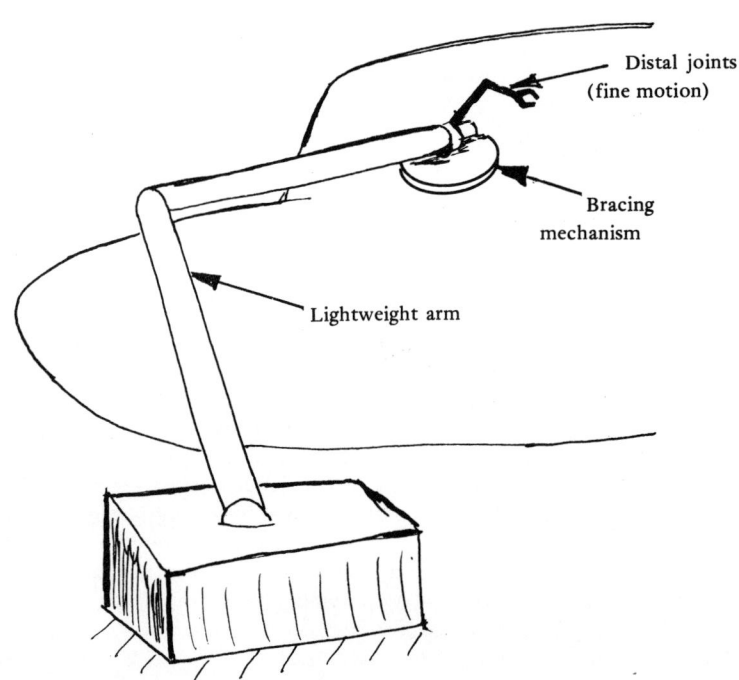

Figure 1 Bracing strategy

force is imparted to the bracing structure which may be unacceptable. Since the joint actuators would apply this force, a means of force control would be necessary in addition to position and/or velocity control. A continuous actuation would mean substantial energy consumption. Brakes or other means of locking the joints would circumvent this consumption. As observed in the human, an appropriate design can be effective and require low levels of actuation or rely totally on gravity. The mobile robot typically relies on gravity to achieve bracing. This method can also be used to supplement other bracing means. The only additional mechanical design consideration is to provide a durable high-friction surface for contact with the bracing surface.

Mechanical clamping device

This type of device requires edges, holes or other features of a bench or workpiece for attachment. The general design force/weight ratio is limited by the strain/stress relation of the material. Commercially available clamping devices achieve a force/weight ratio of up to 1000. This estimate does not include the weight of the actuating solenoid or hydraulic cylinder. The latter may dominate the total system weight and may reduce the ratio by one-half. Hydraulic, pneumatic or electromagnetic actuation devices may be employed. A hydraulic ram may be used directly as in Figure 2 with quite favourable size and weight advantages. Pneumatic and electromechanical actuation would likely require some type of mechanical linkage to provide mechanical advantage.

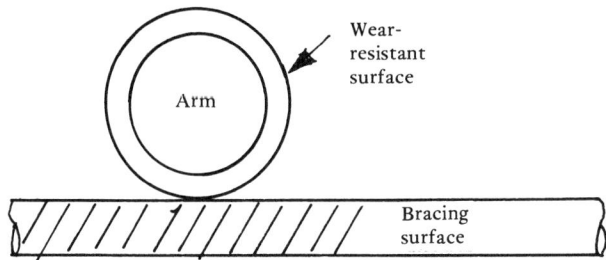

Figure 2 Simple normal force for bracing

The energy consumption of the hydraulic clamping device is proportional to the stroke and area of the piston. Additional energy is consumed by the valving. If hydraulic actuators are used in the joints of the arm, the additional cost of hydraulic clamping will be greatly reduced. Simple on-off control of the clamping actuator will produce fast clamping but with high impacts on the workpiece and high-pressure transients. A more complex control circuit will be necessary to produce fast clamping without these adverse effects.

One obvious limitation of mechanical clamping is that the point of clamping must be near an edge so that opposing forces can be applied. A practical limitation on the range of separation of the opposing surfaces (thickness) for fast bracing exists. Positioning of the arm to engage the clamping mechanism requires more complex manoeuvres in the gross motion.

Vacuum attachment

By providing suction to a cup with a pliable rubber-like material on its lip, a normal bracing force can be achieved as shown in Figure 3. Suction will provide a normal force to the bracing surface limited by the atmospheric pressure around the arm and the area to which a vacuum is applied. Consequently, it is appropriate only where fairly large smooth surfaces are available. The weight of such a system is derived from its mechanical structure and the vacuum fixtures such as connecting hoses and the cup. Thus, based on strength its force/weight ratio will be of the same order as the mechanical clamping devices. Because of the limit on negative pressure the force is proportional to area. The resulting large size may dictate that stiffness of the bracing point be increased by adding material to the cup. The energy consumption will depend on the strategy of controlling the air flow. Consequently the bulk and mass is expected to be larger than for mechanical clamping.

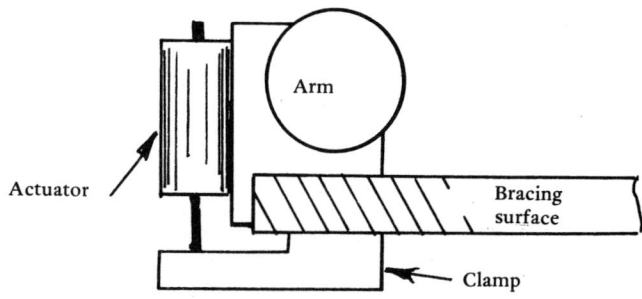

Figure 3 Mechanical clamping for bracing

Permanent magnets

Magnetic forces can be used to attach to ferrous clamping structures. Because of the constant current requirements for electromagnets, they have not been considered for providing the normal force directly. The permanent magnet is popular in temporary holding applications. A strong holding force is provided once good contact is established with the working surface. The force is strongly dependent on the gap between the magnet and the working surface. In general a permanent magnet circuit is designed with pole pieces to concentrate the flux density in the gap so as to increase the holding force as in Figure 4. With a rare earth magnet a force/weight ratio of about 200 can be achieved in a small volume (5 cm^3 for 900 N). For a given geometry, the magnetic holding force is proportional to K^2 where K is the scale factor of the geometry.

There are basically two methods for releasing a workpiece: flux diversion and depolarization. In flux diversion, an alternative return path is connected to the magnetic circuit to divert flux going through the workpiece, thereby releasing it from the magnet. This diversion may be actuated by a separate actuator or by the arm motion. In depolarization, a high impulse of unidirectional current is passed through the pole pieces to temporarily reverse the polarity of the poles and thus disrupt the flow path of the magnetic circuit and allow release. For a 2.5 cm diameter $SeCO_5$ rare earth magnet, a 10 ms pulse of 100 A current is required for depolarization. This is a substantial complication to the method but one that is being explored.

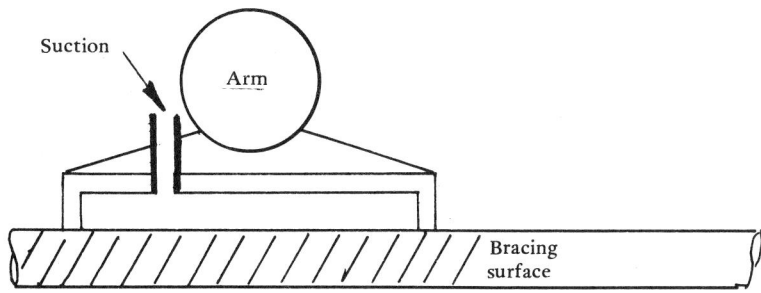

Figure 4 Vacuum attachment for bracing

Comparison of bracing means

All the candidate bracing means have advantages which could dominate in certain applications. Table 1 summarizes the characteristics which have been largely discussed above.

Table 1 Summary of clamping designs producing a holding force (normal) of 900 N

Characteristic	Magnet	Vacuum	Mechanical
Material	$SeCO_5$	Metal + rubber	Steel
Work environment	Surface ferrous	Surface smooth	Edge or hole
Size (cm)	3 x 2.5 x 1.3	(10 diameter)	$\leqslant 2.5$ diameter
Force/weight	200	500	500
Action (speed)	Good	Fair	Excellent
Energy consumption	Low	Moderate	Moderate
Maintenance	Low	Moderate	High
Reliability	Excellent	Good	Good
Other	Compact	Noisy bulky	Difficult rendezvous

Control issues in bracing

To implement the bracing strategy several control issues must be addressed: (1) gross motion control of a lightweight arm; (2) rendezvous of the bracing mechanism with the bracing structure; (3) control of the actuators between the base and the bracing point after bracing; (4) control of the actuators distal to the bracing point after bracing.

It should be clarified also that the ability to successfully perform the first two

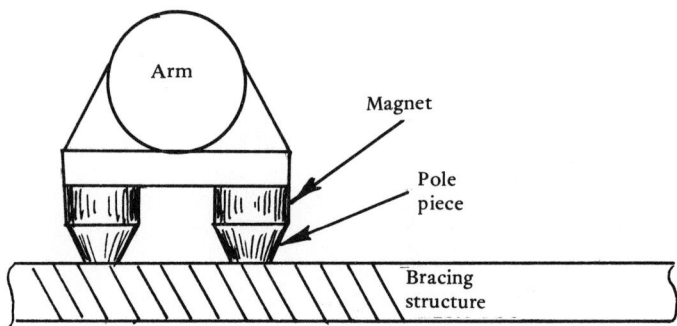

Figure 5 Magnetic bracing mechanism

tasks above does not constitute the ability to successfully manipulate with a flexible arm. The accuracy needed to rendezvous can be made less than required for the final manipulation task. Certainly, the speed of manipulation after bracing can be made higher. Perhaps most importantly, the effects of disturbances on the braced arm are not as troublesome as for the unbraced arm.

Issues one and two above are quite challenging and have been treated by Truckenbrot,[3] Book & Majette[1] and others. The two may be treated together, or separately, but separate treatment may allow for a robust treatment of errors and uncertainty in rendezvous while maintaining high-speed gross motions.

After bracing has begun the arm is no longer an open-loop kinematic chain and dynamics of the links between the base and the point of bracing are quite different than before bracing. If clamping prevents all translation and rotation the joints may move only by deforming the structure. If only some translations or rotations are restricted the arm has become a closed-loop mechanism. The remaining degrees envisioned for the actuators in this case and application of a downward force to enhance the clamping action will be helpful.

The control of distal joints after bracing contends with dynamics similar to conventional manipulation. The short links are essentially rigid. The exact position of the end effector may be poorly known based on the joint angles alone. A decreased emphasis on this source of information and increased reliance on direct measurements of the end point, either absolute or relative to the workpiece, is appropriate.

Ongoing work

Research is under way to construct alternative bracing mechanisms and simple lightweight arms and to devise control algorithms. This will allow practical evaluation of the bracing strategy.

This work is partially supported by the National Science Foundation of the USA, grant no MEA-8303539.

References

[1] Book W J & Majette M (1985) Controller design for flexible distributed parameter mechanical arms via combined state space and frequency domain techniques. Trans ASME, *J. Dynam. Syst, Meas. Control*, in press

[2] Moore S R & Hogan N (1983) Part referenced manipulation: a strategy applied to robotic drilling. In *Control of Manufacturing Processes and Robotic Systems* eds D Hardt & W J Book, American Society of Mechanical Engineers, New York, pp 183-191

[3] Truckenbrot A *Modelling and Control of Flexible Manipulator Structures* Proc. of the Symposium on the Theory of Robots and Manipulators, Saborow, Poland, September, 1981

Robot Control and Computer Languages

R P Paul and V Hayward

School of Electrical Engineering, Purdue University, West Lafayette, IN 47906, USA

Summary: From the earliest stages of their development, robot manipulators have been tied to computers by robot-control languages. These special languages have endeavoured to deal with the complexities of real-time control, multiple processes, the description of robot-manipulation tasks and the integration of sensors. In every case, these languages have been able to provide only partial solutions to the general problem. We propose a new solution to the problem by integrating the robot control into an existing high-level language. The robot manipulator is integrated in such a manner that conventional programming techniques can be used to solve the special requirements of manipulator control. We use the 'C' language and run the manipulator under the UNIX operating system. The robot manipulator is integrated into the language in the same manner as is input/output; that is, integration into the language is handled by a small set of functions included in a library. The robot program thus becomes a conventional 'C' program. The implementation language of the library is also written in 'C', which provides a 'user transparent' system, allowing complete freedom in the mode of controlling the manipulator.

Introduction

The earliest work in robotics was that of Ernst[1] who in 1960 interfaced a teleoperator 'slave' arm to a small digital computer. The 'arm', equipped with touch and force sensors, was able to search a workspace to locate a box and a number of blocks which were then placed into the box. The control algorithms for this task were programmed in a high-level computer language. The program for the task consisted of many conditional statements testing sensors and requesting small manipulator motions. It would be hard to imagine expressing such algorithms in any other than a high-level computer language. This trend continued into the sixties, with the manipulator embedded into such languages as LISP and FORTRAN. Not only were sensors integrated into the manipulator control but co-ordinate transformations between vision systems and the manipulator had also to be made. Once again, the data structures and control of a high-level language were used naturally.

At the same time that these developments were taking place, the industrial robot was developed. This device was directly programmed by moving the manipulator through a task and recording the task positions. While this appeared to be a much simpler approach to programming, it was in reality no more than the input of task positions. The industrial robot was in fact only a programmable positioning and orienting device, a very useful component in automation systems but, lacking all forms of task sensor input and task plan or model, it had no need for algorithms or for the languages in which they might be expressed. The program for an industrial robot was in fact hard wired and simply consisted of moving the manipulator from one position to the next through the taught sequence.

The use of high-level languages for robot manipulator control had a major drawback due to the lack of concurrency. A motion would be planned and then executed, but during execution no other processing could be performed. Any form of sensor interaction had to be included in the real-time program that moved the manipulator, a difficult task. A second difficulty was that the manipulator had to be brought to rest before a subequent motion could be planned. Although this did not appear to be a problem in the early development of robotics, it soon became apparent that the time lost due to the continual need to interrupt motion by bringing the manipulator to rest was a serious limitation. The solution found to the problem was to define the robot control task in terms of two concurrent processes. One process would run in real time to control the motion of the robot; the other process would run in background to compute the next motion so that it would be ready as soon as the current motion was completed. With such a system it was possible to move the robot through a number of path positions without needing to bring it to rest at any intermediate position. Sensor integration could also be performed in terms of additional concurrent processes. Unfortunately, none of the available operating systems supported this type of concurrent process.

Although no general solution to the operating-system problem was undertaken, a number of stand-alone robot-control systems were developed which provided for concurrency. Within these systems various feedback and control strategies were developed. But with the advent of these special-purpose systems the generality of the high-level languages was lost; gone were the data structures, input/output, control statements, subroutines, etc. Their lack was apparent as soon as the fundamental robot-control problems were solved and more ambitious tasks were undertaken. The special-purpose languages were then extended to include many of the features of high-level languages and while this seemed like a reasonable approach it necessitated that the user become familiar with a new language. These systems were also fairly inefficient computationally, lacking the many man years of development on which some of the more standard high-level languages are based. The implementation language in these new systems was different from the user language, making extension difficult or impossible.

The approach we take here is to identify the robot as an input/output device and to integrate it directly with an existing high-level language. Concurrency is provided within the operating system. An optimizing compiler is available for both the user and as implementation language. There are no special data types as the entire system is represented in terms of standard language features. We have included the manipulator into the 'C' programming language in the form of a library, RCCL — the Robot 'C' Control Library.

Overview

Manipulator-task description

The location of an object is described by its position and orientation with respect to some reference co-ordinate frame. In the following, the word 'location' will implicitly mean 'position and orientation'. Tasks are described in terms of locations to be reached in space to grasp, displace or exert forces on objects located in the robot workspace. Tasks are also described by the sequence and the type of motions necessary to carry out the work. Location descriptions require special data structures and sequential operations of a robot also require special primitives. Both can, however, be implemented with the tools provided by high-level languages, namely, data structures, functions and structured flow of control.

Structured location description

RCCL handles what is referred to as *structured location description*.[2] The basic construct is the homogeneous transformation which is a mathematical construct describing the location of co-ordinate frames. A homogeneous transformation can be interpreted either as the description of the location of a co-ordinate frame with respect to another or as a transformation performed on the first co-ordinate frame. Homogenous transformations are a very general tool.[3] However, in manipulation we will restrict them to orthogonal transformations, built in terms of a 3 x 3 rotation matrix constructed with three orthogonal vectors n, o and a, and a position vector p.

Relative locations of objects can be described with transformation products. For example, let *OBJ*, a transformation, describe the location of an object relative to a reference co-ordinate frame. Let *HOLE* represent the location of a hole with respect to the frame *OBJ*. The matrix product *OBJ HOLE*, which is also a homogeneous transformation, describes the location of the hole relative to the reference co-ordinate frame. One important property of orthogonal homogeneous transformations is that the inverse transformation can be obtained very simply.

One dedicated transformation *T6*, represents the location of the end of the manipulator with respect to the reference co-ordinate frame located at the base of the manipulator. A given manipulator location can be specified in base co-ordinates by writing

$$T6 = POS$$

However, such a description is usually insufficient. For instance, one might need to express that a tool is attached to the end of the manipulator which must reach the location *POS*. This is achieved by writing

$$T6\ TOOL = POS$$

A more complete description of a motion to a goal location might be written as

$$REF\ T6\ TOOL = CONV\ OBJ\ PG$$

Where *REF* is the location of the manipulator with respect to the reference co-ordinate frame; *T6* describes the location of the end of the manipulator with respect to the reference co-ordinate frame attached to the shoulder or to the base of the manipulator; *TOOL* expresses the location of a tool attached to the end of the manipulator; *CONV* represents a conveyor belt, defined as a co-ordinate frame moving with respect to the reference co-ordinate frame; *OBJ* is the location of the object to be grasped lying on the conveyor belt; *PG* is the required location of the tool, relative to *OBJ*, where the object is to be grasped.

Location equations are solved for *T6* to obtain the desired location of the end of the manipulator with respect to the reference co-ordinate frame

$$T6 = REF^{-1}\ CONV\ OBJ\ PG\ TOOL^{-1}$$

One RCCL system call directly constructs location equations in terms of dynamic data structures. The locations can be modified at the level of the move statement in terms of small translations and rotations described with respect to the tool frame.

This provides a convenient shorthand for specifying approach and deproach locations, or for specifying motions which purposely overshoot the described location when the manipulator is to perform guarded motions.[4]

Motion description

A task is made up of a number of path segments between successive locations. There are many ways to generate trajectories for a manipulator.[5,6] RCCL provides two types of motions. The first, called joint mode, consists of computing the set of joint values for each path segment end and generating all intermediate values by linear interpolation. The second type, which we will call Cartesian mode, requires the system to solve a modified location equation at each sample interval and to compute the corresponding joint co-ordinates. The location equation is internally modified in such a way that one frame, called the tool frame, moves along straight lines and rotates around a fixed axis. These motion types are discussed elsewhere.[3,7]

When the manipulator is to move while exerting forces or torques on objects, the manipulator must be controlled in such a way that forces and torques are controlled directly in place of locations. The manipulator is then said to be controlled in a comply mode. Several methods[8-11] are proposed for such control. RCCL implements a variation of Shimano's joint matching method.[12] RCCL provides for compliance specifications in the tool co-ordinate frame which is defined in the location equation. Compliance is specified in terms of forces along, and torques around, the principal axes of the tool frame. The manipulator loses one degree of freedom for each direction along or around which it is complying, in force or torque respectively. The trajectory is then constrained by the geometrical features of the objects in contact. A more complete discussion of this subject can be found in reference 13.

Sensor integration; updatable world representation

One of the main goals of RCCL is to facilitate the integration of sensors.[14] Sensors are used to modify the behaviour of the manipulator according to information acquired from the manipulator or from its environment. Sensor information can be classified in many different ways: according to the data type necessary to represent it, booleans, scalars, vectors, arrays, tensors, etc; by meaning, touch, limit, distance, location, temperature, vibration, force, etc; by the order of magnitude of the acquisition time, whether minutes, seconds, milliseconds or microseconds; by accuracy and so on. Considering this variety, the RCCL approach is deliberately to ignore, when possible, the type of information we may have to deal with but, on the other hand, to provide means for an efficient utilization of this information.

Modifying locations

End of segment locations can be modified according to information acquired at run time. This is achieved by changing the value of transformations within location equations. Transformations likely to be modified at run time must be declared as such (hold transforms). The system makes a copy of the transformation at the time the corresponding move request is issued and enters it in the motion queue. It is therefore possible to use the same transformation to describe a co-ordinate frame whose value is different from one path segment to another. Use of a copy of the transformation makes it possible to change the value at an arbitrary instant even if the corresponding location equation is currently being evaluated. A typical use of this kind of transformation is the description of an object location that is variable and obtained from sensor readings at discrete time intervals.

User interaction and slow sensors like computer vision require the use of hold transformations. Location data can be acquired ahead of time in a completely asynchronous manner.

Modifying trajectories

Fast sensors can provide for direct synchronous sensory feedback. This corresponds to the class of functionally defined transformations. In this case, a transformation is attached to a function that will be evaluated each sample time. The purpose of the function is to calculate the value of the transformation as a function of sensor readings. The location equation in the *Structured location description* section makes use of such a functionally defined transform to describe a location with respect to a conveyor belt. If the motion is performed in Cartesian mode, the tracking is perfectly accurate, since the location equation is evaluated at sample time intervals. When the motion is performed in joint mode, the system estimates the expected location at the end of the segment by linear extrapolation. If the functionally defined transform is computed as a function of time, we can obtain mathematically described motions (circles, ellipses, etc).

The transitions to or from path segments involving moving co-ordinate frames must deal with unpredictable velocity changes. Smooth transitions are obtained by adding a modifying third-order polynomial trajectory during the transition time. We have seen that the manipulator is stopped by repeating a move to the same location. When the location involves moving co-ordinate frames, the stop will be relative to those moving co-ordinate frames. If a stop in absolute co-ordinates is required, a move to a fixed location must be performed before specifying the stop. The system internally maintains a location equation which always reflects the current location of the manipulator. It is therefore possible to have the manipulator stop at an arbitrary instant at the location it currently occupies. Functionally described transformations can be used anywhere in a location equation. Trajectories can be modified with respect to any co-ordinate frame which provides unlimited applications.

Internal sensing

Internal information is acquired from the manipulator itself. Two particularly useful kinds of information are internally maintained in RCCL: location and force.

Location. For any motion terminated on a condition, the world model may have to be updated to account for the actual location where the manipulator stopped. The system is then asked to update a transformation in a location equation. The equation is solved for the requested transformation by using the actual value of $T6$ when the path segment ends. This new location information might be very useful in any subsequent motion related to this location. For example, consider the case of a manipulator picking up an object which it had previously placed on a surface whose height is only approximately known. The manipulator is able to retrieve the object immediately if the final location of the object has been updated.

Force. Joint torques are also obtained from the manipulator state. The complete determination of the forces and torques exerted on an object, based on the joint torques, leads to lengthy computations;[15] RCCL, however, provides a mechanism that compares the actual forces and torques against expected values. This information may be used to cause a path-segment termination when some specified limit is reached. The subsequent path segment will usually contain compliance specifications.

RCCL implementation

When a manipulator is under RCCL control, four processes are running concurrently. At the lower level, a servoprocess controls the location or the torque of each manipulator joint. The setpoint process, running at interrupt level, computes the Cartesian trajectories and determines the corresponding joint parameters. A real-time communication channel swaps information between the servoprocess and the setpoint process. The user process running under time sharing is the user program and makes the RCCL system calls. The setpoint process communicates with the user process via a motion-request queue containing all the necessary information.

Conclusion

The main goal of this project was to show that manipulator control could be developed in a more general context than within the framework of a stand-alone robot controller with its own language. The current RCCL implementation does not yet offer the convenience of dedicated robot controllers because it requires a large machine. However, as microprocessor-based computers become more powerful and can run operating systems like UNIX, the RCCL approach exhibits many advantages over conventional robot-controller designs. The conclusion we draw is that robot control can be viewed as an addition to an already existing, tested and standardized system, rather than the design from scratch of a system which provides only for robot control.

This material is based on work supported by the National Science Foundation under the grant no MEA-8119884. Any opinions, findings, conclusions or recommendations expressed in this publication are those of the authors and do not necessarily reflect the views of the National Science Foundation. This work is also supported by a grant from the CNRS project ARA (Automatique et Robotique Avancée), France. Richard Paul receives support as the Ransburg Professor of Robotics. Facilities to perform this research are provided by the Purdue University CIDMAC Project.

References

[1] Ernst H A A (1961) A computer operated mechanical hand. ScD Thesis, Massachusetts Institute of Technology, Massachusetts
[2] Paul R P *Manipulator Language* Workshop On The Research Needed to Advance The State Of Knowledge In Robotics, 15-17 April 1980 (organized by J Birk & R Kelley, supported by NSF)
[3] Paul R P (1981) *Robot Manipulators: Mathematics, Programming and Control* MIT Press, Massachusetts
[4] Will P M & Grossman D D (1975) An experimental system for computer controlled mechanical assembly. *IEEE Trans. Computers* **C-24 9**, 879-888
[5] Derby S (1983) Simulating motion elements of general-purpose robot arms. *Int. J. Robotic Res.* **2** (1)

[6] Castain R H & Paul R P (1982) Polynomial robotic trajectories: a new approach, TR-EE 82-37, December
[7] Hayward V & Paul R P *Robot Manipulator Control Using the C Language Under UNIX* IEEE Workshop on Languages for Automation, Chicago, November, 1983
[8] Inoue H (1974) *Force Feedback In Precise Assembly Tasks*, MIT Artificial Intelligence Laboratory, Memo 308, August
[9] Raiberg M H & Craig J J (1981) Hybrid position/force control of manipulators. *J. Energy Resources Technol.* **103**, June
[10] Salisbury J K. Active stiffness control of a manipulator. In *Cartesian Coordinates* 19th IEEE Conf. on Decision and Control, December 1980, Albuquerque, New Mexico (1983)
[11] Geschke C C (1983) A system for programming and controlling sensor-based robot manipulators. *IEEE Trans, Pattern Matching and Machine Intelligence,* **PAMI-5** (1).
[12] Shimano B E (1978) The kinematic design and force control of computer controlled manipulators, PhD Dissertation, Memo AIM-313, Stanford University, California
[13] Mason M T (1979) Compliance and force control for computer controlled manipulators, MIT TR-515, April
[14] Rosen C A & Nitzan D (1977) Use of sensors in programmable automation. *Computer Magazine*, December
[15] Paul R P Computational Requirements of Third Generation Manipulators

Robust Control for Industrial Robots

H Bremer and A Truckenbrodt*

Institute for Mechanics, Technical University Munich, Munich and *TC Technologie Consulting, Institute for Applied Research, Munich, Federal Republic of Germany

Summary: The control of industrial robots is a demanding problem as we have strongly non-linear multi-degree-of-freedom systems, disturbances like elasticity or parameters varying within a range of some 100 per cent (e.g. due to payload changes). The object of this paper is to design a control which is insensitive (robust) with respect to parameter variations or disturbances such as non-linear coupling and elasticity. This goal is achieved by following a proposition of LEITMANN, BREINL: a linear control (Riccati-regulator) designed for a nominal system is superposed by a non-linear control compensating the effects of the unknown parameters. The general theory is specified for SCARA-type robots, including such effects as elastic gears ('harmonic drives') and elastic arms. The control is completely decentralized, i.e. decoupled for the different axes. This is easy to realize and is therefore well suited for real-time computation. To show the efficiency of the proposed control concept, simulations for an exemplary manoeuvre are presented. If we increase the payload mass for 1000 per cent and reduce the gear elasticity for 10 per cent, a classical control would show intolerable overshoot and motion times. The robust control, however, is able to guarantee no overshoot and only small motion time prolongations.

Introduction

Industrial robots often change their parameters within a range of some 100 per cent, e.g. due to different payload ratios or manoeuvres. The control design for such systems, in general described by highly non-linear differential equations, will consequently be even more ambitious than is already in common for non-linear systems. The method of non-linear decoupling, for instance,[1] which enables one to use optimal control concepts for linear systems, requires the 'inverse system' which is, due to unknown parameters, unknown, too. Control algorithms based on a hierarchical concept,[2] will in general be problematic concerning the complete system co-ordination because of the uncertain parameter-dependant terms. Adaptive control, identifying the actual parameters during the manoeuvre,[3] may fail not only because of the requested computer time but also due to too large initial parameter errors. Most of these problems can be solved by using a robust control proposed.[4,5] It allows one to use optimal linear regulators for a nominal system (with averaged nominal parameters) superposed by an easy to realize non-linear control compensating all parameter- and coupling-induced disturbances of all robot axes; the co-ordination is implicitly carried out by the non-linear again decoupled part. The object of this paper is to describe the application of this robust control to industrial robots including certain effects like elasticity in drives or structural elements.

Robust control: general theory

The dynamics of multibody systems as robots are described by the state equations

$$\dot{x} = (A_0 + \Delta A)x + (B_0 + \Delta B)u \qquad (1)$$

where x contains all generalized co-ordinates and velocities A_0 and B_0 are state matrices and control input matrices, respectively, for nominal parameter values. The parameter variations are condensed within the terms ΔA, ΔB; these may include the unknown parameters as well as non-linear coupling terms of the plant. Whenever ΔA, ΔB are proportional to the nominal input matrix B_0

$$\Delta A = B_0 G \qquad \Delta B = B_0 H \qquad (2)$$

(A_0, B_0 — controllability supposed), and the control vector u is written as

$$u = u_L + u_N \qquad (3)$$

where u_L = linear, u_N = non-linear control, a robust control is possible,[4,5] i.e. stability and proximity to the nominal state are guaranteed for all parameter values within a (known) range.

Linear control u_L. The nominal system is optimized with respect to

$$J = \frac{1}{2} \int (x^T Q x + u_L^T R u_L)\, dt \to \min \qquad (4)$$

($Q = Q^T \geqslant 0$, $R = R^T > 0$), yielding the well known Riccati regulator

$$u_L = -Kx, \qquad K = R^{-1} B_0^T P \qquad (5)$$

with $P = P^T > 0$ from the Riccati equation

$$PA_0 + A_0^T P - PB_0 R^{-1} B_0^T P + Q = 0 \qquad (6)$$

This optimal nominal system defines the desired trajectories even when parameter variations arise. It must be noted that Riccati regulators react in general good naturedly to disturbances (e.g. as centrifugal or Coriolis forces).

Non-linear control u_N. In the second step the non-linear control compensating the parameter variations ΔA, ΔB is defined by

$$u_N = \begin{cases} \dfrac{u_L}{\|u_L\|} \rho(x), & \|u_L\| > \epsilon \\ \dfrac{u_L}{\epsilon} \rho(x), & \|u_L\| \leqslant \epsilon \end{cases} \qquad (7)$$

where $\epsilon \to 0$ is a positive constant (needed only for the realization of u_N) and

$$\rho(x) = (1 - \max_{\Delta B}\|H\|)^{-1} (\max_{\Delta A}\|Gx\| + \max_{\Delta B}\|HKx\|) \qquad (8)$$

is a 'control radius' mainly determined by the expected maximum parameter variations, $\max\|G\|$, $\max\|H\|$. With this control, stability and 'robustness', i.e. minimum deviations from the nominal path, are guaranteed.

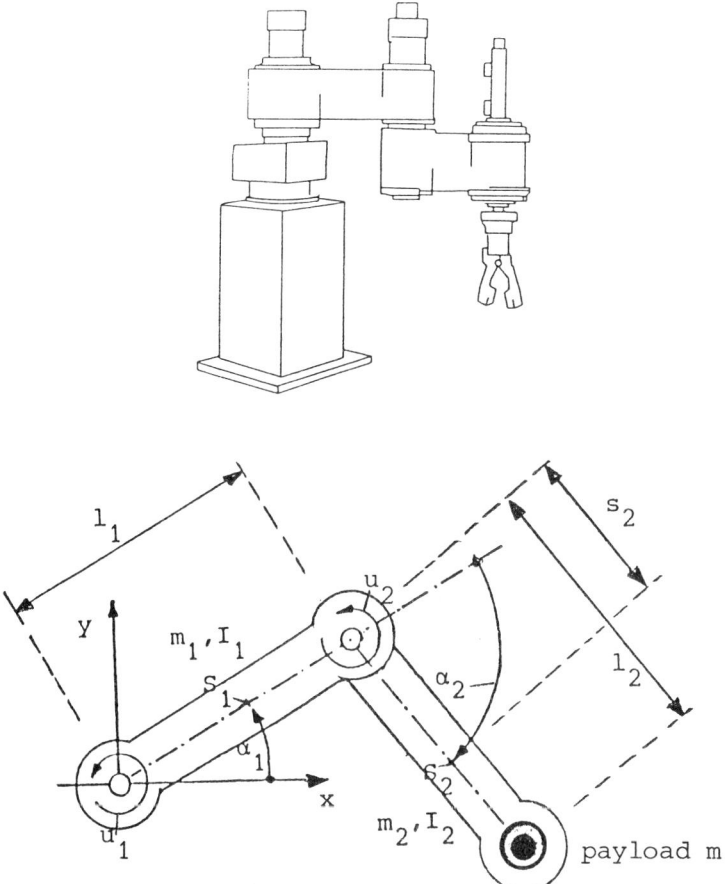

Figure 1 Robot system

Robust control of SCARA-type robots

To demonstrate the effectiveness of the proposed control concept, a SCARA-type robot is considered (Figure 1). In this configuration, the vertical motion of the gripper, including the actual payload, is decoupled from the in-plane motion of the two arms, which is treated in the following. The load is, for simplicity in this paper, modelled as point mass at the distance l_2 from the α_2 axis.

Equations of motion

With masses m_1, m_2 (m_2 = arm 2 + payload), moments of inertia I_1, I_2, centre of gravity co-ordinates s_1, s_2 and lengths l_1, l_2 the equations of motion read

$$\underbrace{\begin{bmatrix} I_1 + I_2 + m_2(s_2^2 + l_1^2) + m_1 s_1^2 + 2m_2 s_2 l_1 \cos\alpha_2 & I_2 + m_2 s_2^2 + m_2 s_2 l_1 \cos\alpha_2 \\ I_2 + m_2 s_2 l_1 \cos\alpha_2 + m_2 s_2^2 & I_2 + m_2 s_2^2 \end{bmatrix}}_{M(q)} \begin{bmatrix} \ddot{\alpha}_1 \\ \ddot{\alpha}_2 \end{bmatrix}_{\ddot{q}}$$

$$+ \underbrace{\begin{bmatrix} -m_2 s_2 l_1 \sin\alpha_2 (\dot{\alpha}_2^2 + 2\dot{\alpha}_1 \dot{\alpha}_2) \\ m_2 s_2 l_1 \sin\alpha_2 \dot{\alpha}_1^2 \end{bmatrix}}_{g(q,\dot{q})} = \underbrace{\begin{bmatrix} u_1 \\ u_2 \end{bmatrix}}_{u} \qquad (9)$$

Due to different payloads ($\rightarrow$ varying m_2, I_2) and positions α_2 of arm 2, strongly varying parameters exist in the mass matrix M. This is the main effect that the robust control should be designed for. The vector g describes coupling terms due to centrifugal and Coriolis forces.

According to the model under consideration, the torques u_1, u_2 have different interpretations.

Rigid arms, rigid gears
In this case, u_1 and u_2 are directly the torques applied by the actuators. Here, there are no uncertain parameters in the control input, $\Delta B = 0$.

Rigid arms, elastic gears
Usually, 'harmonic-drive' gears are used which have non-negligible elasticity, modelled by a linear massless spring with uncertain spring constant c (Figure 2). Here, we have

$$u_i = c_i \bar{u}_i = c_i(\alpha_i - \beta_i), \qquad i = 1, 2 \qquad (10)$$

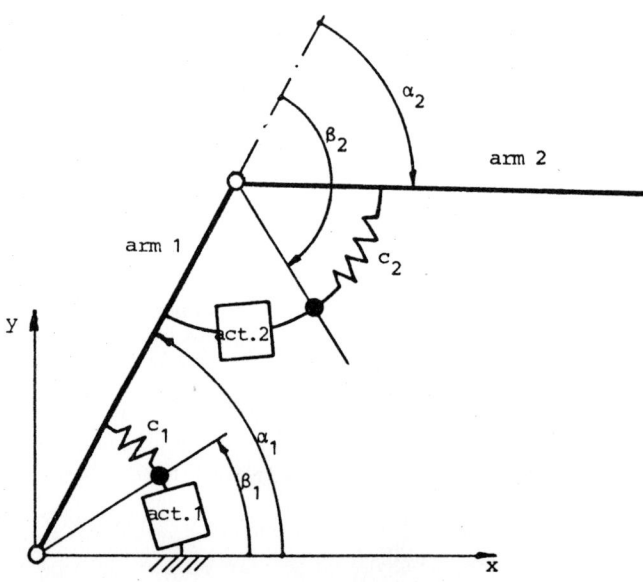

Figure 2 Model for elastic gears

The 'true' control for the arm is the spring elongation u_i, which means that we have parameter variations in the control input $\Delta B \neq 0$ as the spring constant is, in general, not exactly known.

Elastic arms, elastic gears

A suitable model for elastic structures is a 'hybrid multibody system' (cf.[6]). The model shown in Figure 2 is, however, able to include 'soft arms' if a resulting spring constant is taken by means of averaging the elasticity of at least for the first bending mode. Robust control of more elaborate elastic models is possible but would be beyond the scope of the present paper.

Parameter values, manoeuvre

In the following, one example of many different simulation runs is shown to demonstrate the efficiency of the control concept. The robot studied has the parameter values:

arms $l_1 = l_2 = 0.5$ m, $s_1 = s_{2_0} = 0.25$ m, $m_1 = m_{2_0} = 5$ kg,
            $I_1 = I_{2_0} = 0.105$ kg m^2

payload $m = m_o \ldots 10\, m_o$, $m_o = 1$ kg $\rightarrow m_2 = m_{2_0} + m$
                               $s_2 = (s_{2_0} m_{2_0} + l_2 m)/m_2$

spring $c_1 = c_2 = 0.9\, c_o \ldots 1.1\, c_o$, $c_o = 5.56\, 10^4$ Nm
                ($\hat{=}$ eigenfrequency 10 Hz)

torques $u_{1\max} = 200$ Nm, $u_{2\max} = 40$ Nm

For simplicity, only the model shown in Figure 2 (rigid arms, elastic gears) is treated as it includes the other models. The robot is executing a point-to-point manoeuvre from start point (0.9, 0) to the end point (−0.5, 0.5)(cf. Figure 3).

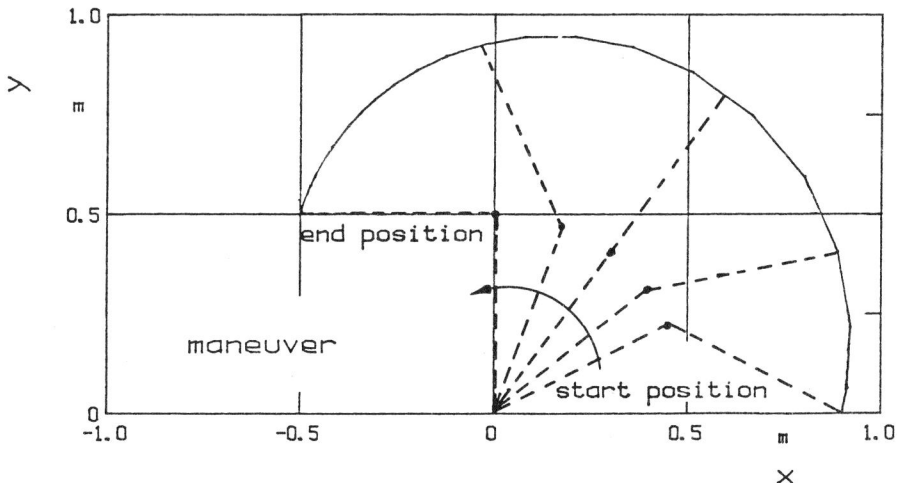

Figure 3 Manoeuvre

With the 'distances' from the end angles as generalized co-ordinates

$$x_i = \alpha_i - \alpha_{i\,\text{end}}, \quad i = 1, 2; \quad \alpha_{1\,\text{end}} = \alpha_{2\,\text{end}} = \pi/2 \tag{11}$$

the task is an unusual control task

$$x_i \to 0, \quad i = 1, 2 \tag{12}$$

Control-system design

The equations of motion (9) are rewritten as

$$\begin{aligned}(J_{1o} + \Delta J_1)\ddot{x}_1 + \dot{J}_1 \dot{x}_1 &= M_1(\dot{x}_2^2, \ddot{x}_2, x_2) + u_1 \\ (J_{2o} + \Delta J_2)\ddot{x}_2 + \dot{J}_2 \dot{x}_2 &= M_2(\dot{x}_2^2, \ddot{x}_1, x_2) + u_2\end{aligned} \tag{13}$$

where

$$J_{1o} = I_1 + I_2 + m_1 s_1^2 + m_{2o}(s_{2o}^2 + l_1^2) \qquad J_{2o} = I_2 + m_{2o} s_{2o}^2 \tag{14}$$

characterize the nominal system,

$$\begin{aligned}\Delta J_1 &= m(l_1^2 + l_2^2) + 2(m_{2o} + m)s_2 l_1 \cos(x_2 + \alpha_{2\,\text{end}}), \quad \Delta J_2 = m l_2^2 \\ \dot{J}_1 &= -2(m_{2o} + m)s_2 l_1 \sin(x_2 + \alpha_{2\,\text{end}})\dot{x}_2, \quad \dot{J}_2 = 0\end{aligned} \tag{15}$$

are the uncertain parameters (nominal and uncertain parameters for the linear design system) and

$$\begin{aligned}M_1 &= -J_K \ddot{x}_2 + (m_{2o} + m)s_2 l_1 \sin(x_2 + \alpha_{2\,\text{end}})\dot{x}_2^2, \\ M_2 &= -J_K \ddot{x}_1 - (m_{2o} + m)s_2 l_1 \sin(x_2 + \alpha_{2\,\text{end}})\dot{x}_1^2\end{aligned} \tag{16}$$

with $J_K = J_{2o} + \Delta J_2 + (m_{2o} + m)s_2 l_1 \cos(x_2 + \alpha_{2\,\text{end}})$

The non-linear terms coupling the axes. It has to be noted that 'artificial' linear systems were created by interpretating coupling terms as uncertain parameters. The state equations are easily calculated form (13).

Classical robot control (linear control)
A classical control, derived from NC-machine technology, has linear independent control loops for both axes:

$$\bar{u}_i = -k_{i1} x_i - k_{i2} \dot{x}_i, \quad i = 1, 2 \tag{17}$$

The control gains are computed to yield eigenvalues $\lambda_1 = -3.1/\text{s}$, $\lambda_2 = -10.1/\text{s}$ of both nominal arm systems. With these values, an ideal robot (with nominal parameters, no elasticity and no coupling between the axes) would exhibit the motion shown in Figure 3.

In reality, this regulator works satisfactorily only for nominal parameters (Figure 4). If we increase the payload, the overshoot and resulting manoeuvre times get untolerably high.

Robust control
Linear control. The linear control $\bar{u}_{iL}$

$$\bar{u}_{iL} = -k_{i1} x_i - k_{i2} \dot{x}_i, \quad i = 1, 2 \tag{18}$$

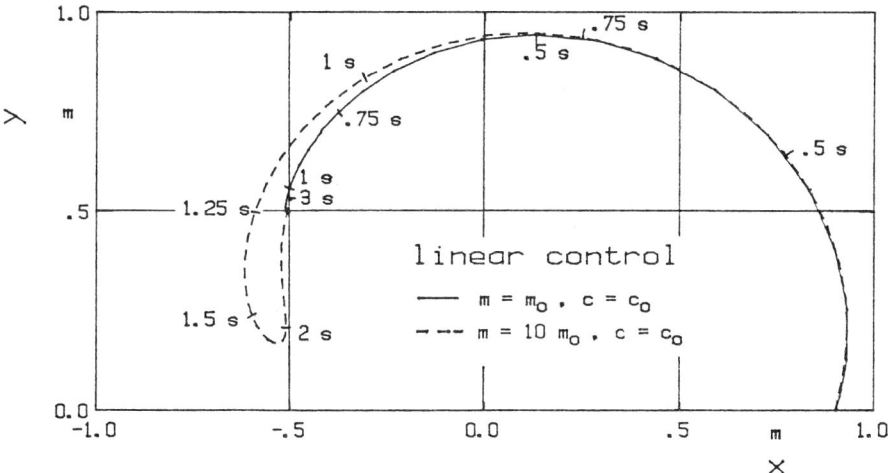

Figure 4 Classical control

for the nominal system is calculated by solving the Ricatti equation (6) (which is very easy as 1 DOF systems are dealt with, i.e. 2×2 matrices A_o). By a proper choice of Q, R all closed-loop pole configurations satisfying

$$\lambda_1 = -\delta_1 < 0, \quad \lambda_2 = -\delta_2 < 0 \text{ or } \lambda_{1,2} = -\delta \pm i\omega, \quad \delta > 0 \qquad (19)$$

are possible. This means that the Riccati design is, observing the restrictions (19), equivalent to a pole-assignment technique

$$k_{i1} = -\frac{\delta_1 \delta_2}{v_{io}^2}, \quad k_{i2} = -\frac{\delta_1 + \delta_2}{v_{io}^2},$$

$$v_{io}^2 = \frac{c_{io}}{J_{io}} \qquad (20)$$

or

$$k_{i1} = \frac{\delta^2 + \omega^2}{v_{io}^2}, \quad k_{i2} = -\frac{2\delta}{v_{io}^2}$$

To compare with the classical design, $\lambda_1 = -3.1/s$, $\lambda_2 = -10.1/s$ are chosen again.

Non-linear control. By (7), the non-linear control is given by

$$\bar{u}_{iN} = \text{sign}(\bar{u}_{iL}) \rho_i, \quad i = 1, 2 \qquad (21)$$

where evaluating (8) yields

$$\rho_i = \frac{1}{1 - |\Delta v_i^2/v_{io}^2|_{\max}} \left[\left| \frac{\dot{J}_i}{v_{io}^2 J_i} \right|_{\max} |\dot{x}_i| + \left| \frac{\Delta v_i^2}{v_{io}^2} \right|_{\max} |\bar{u}_{iL}| \right], \quad \Delta v_i^2 = \frac{c_i}{J_i} - \frac{c_{io}}{J_{io}} \qquad (22)$$

The non-linear control is easy (and fast!) to realize. It requires only the computation of $\text{sign}(\bar{u}_{iL})$, $|\dot{x}_i|$, $|\bar{u}_{iL}|$ and multiplication with the constant estimates of maximum parameter variations. The following figures are simulated by using $|\dot{J}/(v_{io}^2 J)|_{\max} = 0$ (!), $|\Delta v_1^2/v_{1o}^2|_{\max} = 0.84$, $|\Delta v_2^2/v_{2o}^2|_{\max} = 0.8$, resulting from the given parameter variations in the *Parameter values, manoeuvre* section. The block diagram of the control loop is shown in Figure 5.

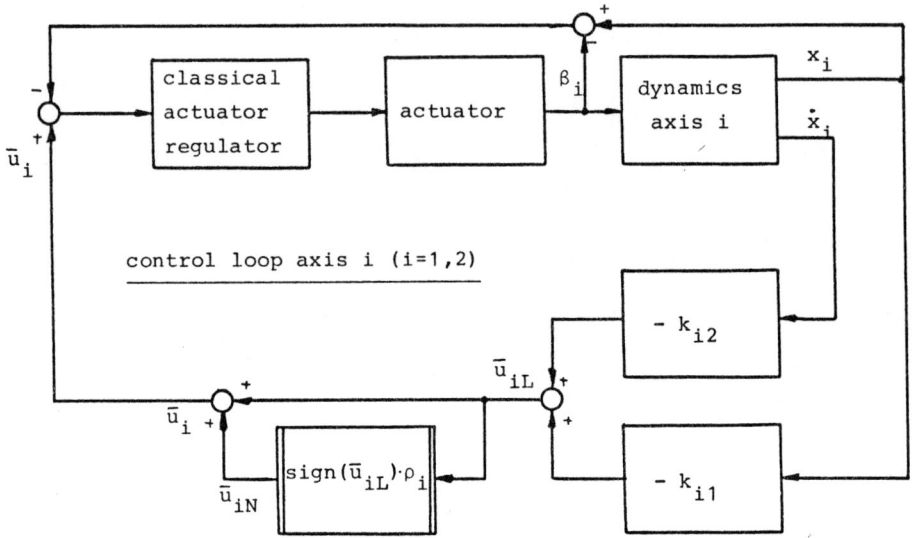

Figure 5 Control loop: block diagram

The quality of the robust design is demonstrated exemplarily by Figure 6. In spite of payload changes of 1000 per cent and spring-constant changes of 10 per cent (which is the most critical case due to extreme lowering of the eigenfrequency), there is no overshoot and very similar manoeuvre times. The path 'deformations' at the beginning result from the restricted torques (Figure 7).

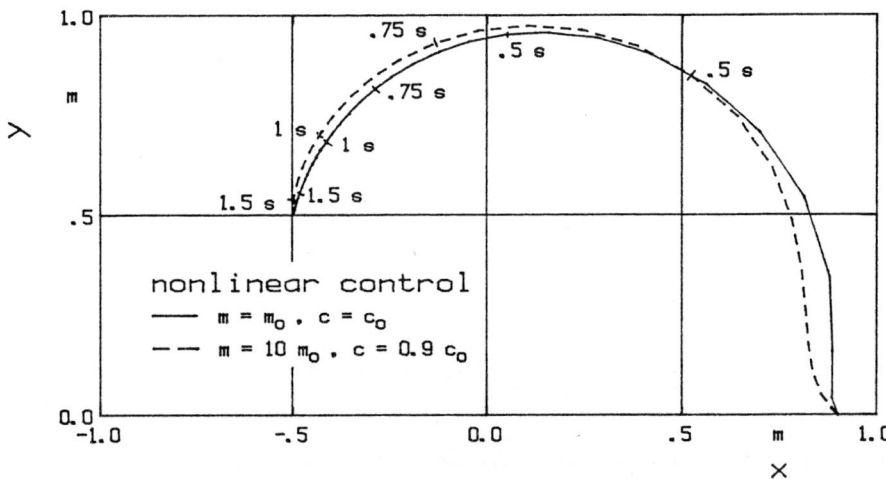

Figure 6 Robust control

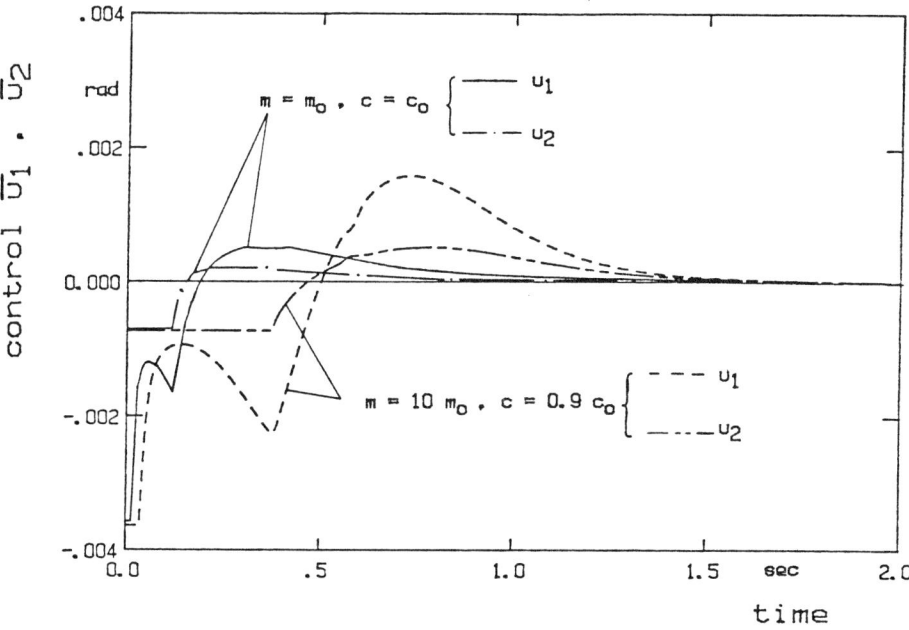

Figure 7 Robust control: control 'forces'

Conclusions

Following the non-linear robust control concept, a simple control could be designed which is able to compensate unknown parameter changes as well as non-linear effects of the plant. The regulator is easy to implement — essential with respect to real-time computation — and does not require crucial modifications of the classical control loops. The use of the robust control can show the way how to increase the efficiency of robot systems which is determined by low-energy consumption or better use of the installed power in addition to higher-action velocities.

References

[1] Patzelt W (1981) Regelung des nichtlinear gekoppelten mehrgrößensystems roboter. *Messen, Steuern, Regeln*, **4**, 42–57
[2] Rössler J (1981) Entwurf und Untersuchung einer hierarchischen 2-Ebenen-Rege-lung für Industrieroboter. *VDI-Fortschr. Bericht R. 8* Düsseldorf, no. 41
[3] Koivo P and Paul R P *Manipulator with Self Tuning Controller* Proc. Int. Conf. Cybernetics, Boston, 1980, pp 1085–1089
[4] Leitmann G (1979) Guaranteed asymptotic stability for some linear systems with bounded uncertainties. *Trans. ASME, J. Dynam. Syst., Meas. Control*, **101**, 212–216
[5] Breinl W and Leitmann G (1983) Zustandsrückführung für dynamische systeme mit parameterunsicherheiten. *Regelungstechnik*, **31**, 95–103
[6] Truckenbrodt A *Modelling and Control of Flexible Manipulator Structures* Proc. 4th Symp. Theory and Practice of Robots and Manipulators, Zaborow, Poland, 1981, pp 90–101

Controlling a Six-degrees-of-freedom Welding Robot along a Randomly Oriented Seam with Reduced Sensor Information

A Micaelli and J M Détriché

CEA, STEP LGR, 91190 Gif sur Yvette, France

Summary: Control of a six-degrees-of-freedom welding robot, along a randomly oriented seam usually requires five independent extra-informations, when the longitudinal position along the joint is known. By knowing the trajectory already followed by the torch, it is possible to forecast two of the five required data, so a sensor delivering only three independent informations will drive the robot.

Generalities

A joint in space can be defined by a succession of points and orientations, i.e. a succession of frames. Each frame is characterized by its origin which is a point J

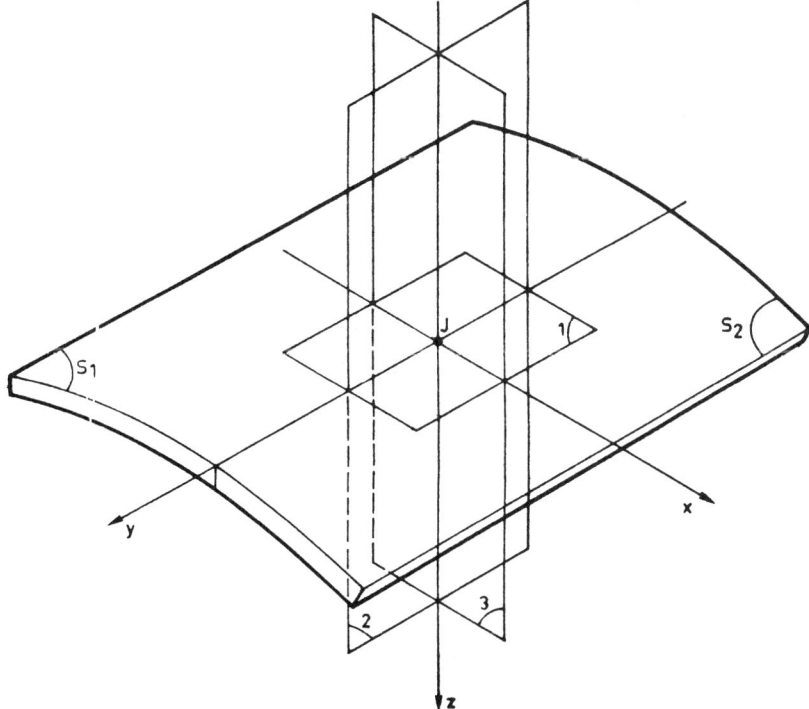

Figure 1 A joint in space. Planes: 1 = tangent; 2 = longitudinal; 3 = transverse

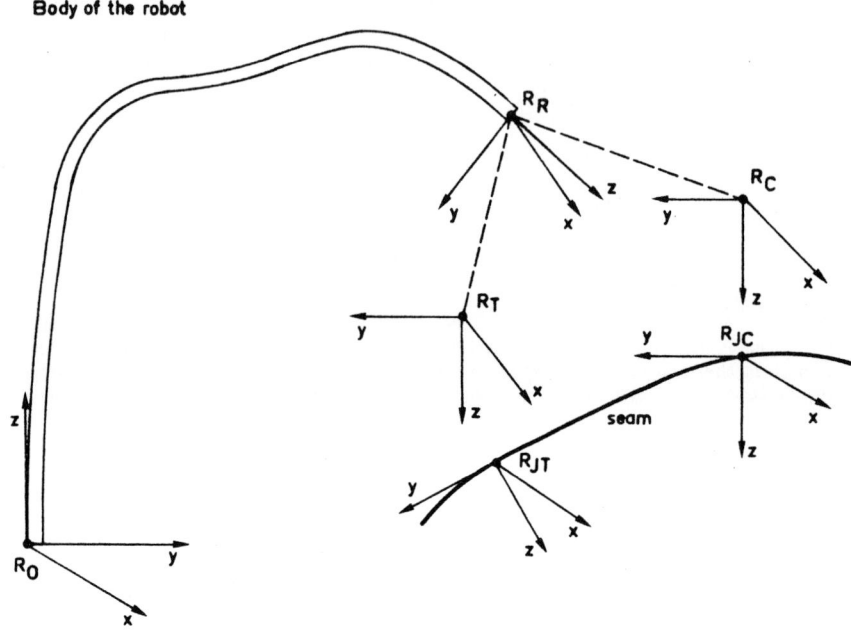

Figure 2 Different reference frames associated with subsystems of a robotized welding system

attached to the joint, and by three perpendicular axes, which are the intersections of the three planes locally tangential, transverse and longitudinal to the joint (Figure 1).

A robotized welding system can be divided into different subsystems: torch carrier (robot); welding torch; seam sensor.

The different reference frames associated with these subassemblies are the following (Figure 2): RO, absolute frame associated with the robot; RR, frame associated with the end of the robot; RC, frame associated with the seam sensor; RT, frame associated with the welding torch; RJC, frame associated with the point of the joint detected by the sensor; RJT, frame associated with the point of the joint at which the end of the welding torch electrode is located.

Presentation of the problem

The problem of automatic welding using a robot can be expressed as follows. Depending on the data concerning the location of a point JC of the joint, supplied by the sensor, it is necessary to determine the torch displacement so that the latter is situated on the same point, with a lag time due to the gap between the sensor and the torch (if the sensor is located before the torch). The sensor we used delivers only the position and the orientation of the joint in the detection plane. Thus it is necessary to reconstruct the whole frame from the succession of the different detected frames (Figure 3).

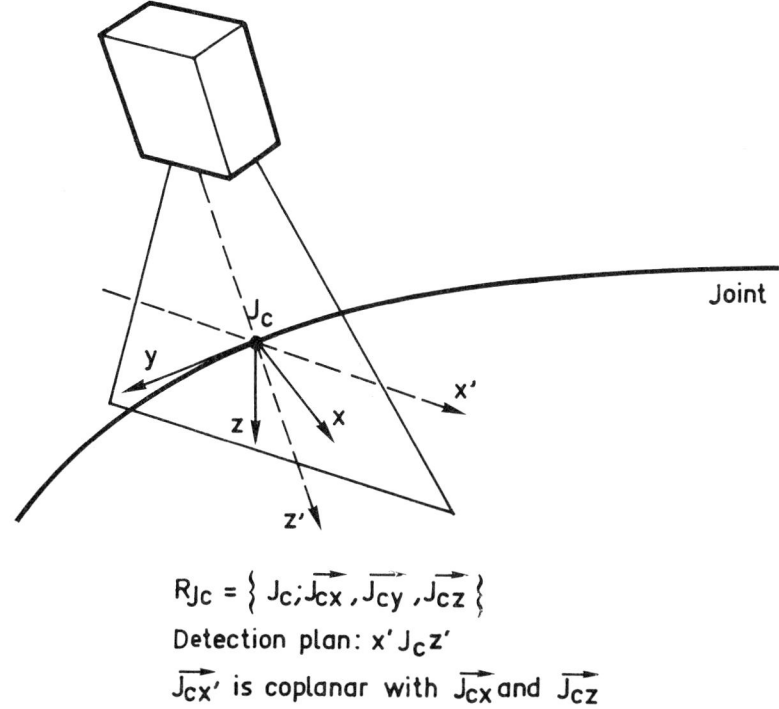

$R_{JC} = \{ J_C; \vec{J_{cx}}, \vec{J_{cy}}, \vec{J_{cz}} \}$
Detection plan: $x' J_c z'$
$\vec{J_{cx'}}$ is coplanar with $\vec{J_{cx}}$ and $\vec{J_{cz}}$

Figure 3 Reconstruction of whole frame from the succession of the different detected frames

At first, we will present a few methods for the estimation of the frame RJC attached to the joint, then we will detail two control modes for a six-degrees-of-freedom robot, to follow a joint in space.

We consider that the relation between: RT and RR is constant; RC and RR is constant.

Remark. The relation between the welding torch and the joint can be expressed as a relation between RT and RJT. This relation is defined by the execution mode of the welding process which determines also the torch speed along the joint, i.e. along $\vec{J_y}$ axis.

To simplify the presentation, we will consider that this relation is the identity. This assumption does not limit the generality of this presentation. The same remark can be made for the relation between the frames RC and RJC and the frame RR.

Estimation of the frame RJC

JC will be noted J in this paragraph. The sensor supplies the co-ordinates of the point J and the $\vec{J}x'$ vector, which is the intersection between the plane tangential to the joint and the detection plane (Figure 3).

To calculate the vectors of the RJ frame, we only need to know the vector $\vec{J}y$

$$\begin{cases} \vec{J}x = N[\vec{J}x' - (\vec{J}x' \cdot \vec{J}y)\vec{J}y] \\ \vec{J}z = \vec{J}x \wedge \vec{J}y \end{cases}$$

Let us assume that $N(\vec{u})$ normalizes the vector $\vec{u}$. The vector $\vec{J}y$ represents the tangential vector of the curve attached to the joint (succession of the points J). This vector will be very sensitive to the noise which affects acquisition of the point J.

Let us define the following:

$$J(k) = \text{point of the trajectory seen by the sensor}$$

$$\dot{j}(k) = \frac{d}{dp}[J(k)] \text{ if } p \text{ is the curvilinear abscissa}$$

$$\ddot{j}(k) = \frac{d^2}{dp^2}[J(k)]$$

$$P = \text{sampling step of the curve}$$

We must estimate $\dot{j}(k)$, knowing that $\vec{J}y(k) = -N[\dot{j}(k)]$ and propose the following methods:

Interpolation formula of STIRLING [4]

With three points, we obtain the following equation

$$\vec{J}y(k) = \frac{1}{2P}[3J(k) - 4J(k-1) + J(k-2)]$$

Polynomial interpolation formula [5]

We approximate a function defined by m points with a polynomial of degree n, using a quadratic criterion. For $m = 4$ and $n = 2$ we obtain the following formula

$$\hat{J}_y(k) = \frac{1}{20P}[21J(k) - 13J(k-1) - 17J(k-2) + 9J(k-3)]$$

KALMAN filtering [6]

The trajectory is unknown but we can suppose that its curvature variations are low and use the following model which is a development in TAYLOR series

$$\begin{bmatrix} J(k+1) \\ \dot{j}(k+1) \\ \ddot{j}(k+1) \end{bmatrix}_{/x,y,z} = \begin{bmatrix} 1 & P & \frac{P^2}{2} \\ 0 & 1 & P \\ 0 & 0 & 1 \end{bmatrix} \begin{bmatrix} J(k) \\ \dot{j}(k) \\ \ddot{j}(k) \end{bmatrix}_{/x,y,z} + \begin{bmatrix} \frac{P^2}{2} \\ P \\ 1 \end{bmatrix} \lambda(k)/x,y,z$$

where x,y,z means that we have a similar equation for each component.

If we suppose that $\lambda(k)$ is a centre pseudo-white noise with the covariance $\mathcal{L}(k)$. We can therefore write

$$J = \begin{bmatrix} J \\ \dot{J} \\ \ddot{J} \end{bmatrix}$$

$$\mathcal{F} = \begin{bmatrix} 1 & P & \frac{P^2}{2} \\ 0 & 1 & P \\ 0 & 0 & 1 \end{bmatrix}$$

$$\mu = \begin{bmatrix} \frac{P^2}{2} \\ P \\ 1 \end{bmatrix} \lambda$$

We can write the state equation

$$J(k+1) = \mathcal{F} J(k) + \mu(k) \qquad (1)$$

where $\mu(k)$ is centred pseudo-white noise with the covariance $\mathcal{M}_0(k)$ and

$$\mathcal{M}_0(k) = \begin{bmatrix} \frac{P^4}{4} & \frac{P^3}{2} & \frac{P^2}{2} \\ \frac{P^3}{2} & P^2 & P \\ \frac{P^2}{2} & P & 1 \end{bmatrix} \mathcal{L}(k)$$

If we suppose that the measure of J position is perturbed by centred pseudo-white noise $\nu(k)$, with the covariance $\mathcal{N}(k)$, we have the observation equation

$$z(k) = \mathcal{C} J(k) + \nu(k) \qquad (2)$$

with $\mathcal{C} = [1\ 0\ 0]$

Equations (1) and (2) are the description of a MARKHOV process to which we can apply a KALMAN filtering to allow us to obtain $\hat{J}_y(k)$.

Other methods: second-order linear filtering

If $\hat{J}$ is the estimated position of J

$$\hat{J}(k+1) = \alpha J(k+1) + (1-\alpha)[\hat{J}(k) - P\hat{J}_y(k)]$$

and

$$\hat{J}_y(k+1) = -N[\hat{J}(k+1) - \hat{J}(k)]$$

with $0 < \alpha < 1$

Control modes

To control such a system, we have the six-degrees-of-freedom of the robot; we describe two control modes, corresponding to two different uses of these degrees of freedom, which can assume the positioning of the sensor or of the pair torch–sensor, on the joint.

Sensor position and orientation servoing

In this mode, we control the displacements of the sensor, to place it on the joint. without considering the torch location, in relation to the joint.

Considering $\delta 3$, we can determine the whole frame RJC; so, if $\vec{\delta}$ is the translation vector, and $\vec{\omega}$ the rotation vector, that we have to apply to the sensor, i.e. to the frame RC, we can write

$$\vec{\delta} = -P * \vec{J_y}$$
$$\vec{\omega} = \mathcal{P}_z \, (\vec{C}_y \wedge \vec{J_y}) + (\vec{C}_z \wedge \vec{J_z})$$

with $\mathcal{P}_z$ = projection on $\vec{J_z}$ axis.

This mode supposes that the torch is near the sensor; if the joint curvature in the tangent plane and in the longitudinal plane can be approximated by a circular arc the torch positioning error will be given by

$$\epsilon = \frac{TC^2}{2R} \qquad \text{(Figure 4a)}$$

with R = radius of curvature and TC = distance between the torch and the sensor.

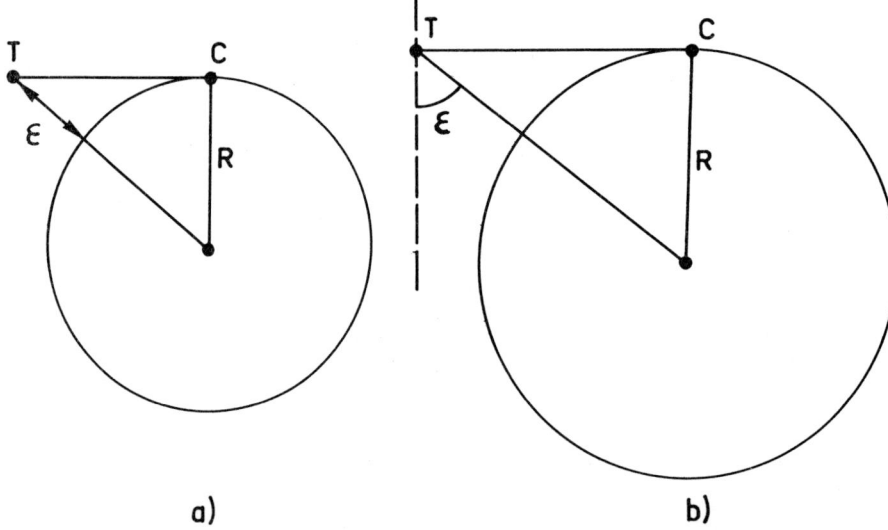

Figure 4 Joint curvature in tangent and longitudinal planes, approximated by a circular arc. **a** = torch positioning error; **b** = orientation error

Numerical application: if we want $\epsilon \leqslant 10^{-3}$ m with $TC = 3.1 \times 10^{-2}$ m, we must have $R \geqslant 4.5 \times 10^{-1}$ m.

The orientation error is given by

$$\epsilon = \operatorname{arctg} \frac{TC}{R} \simeq \frac{TC}{R} \qquad \text{(Figure 4b)}$$

Numerical application: if we want $\epsilon \leqslant 5°$, we must have $R \geqslant 3.5 \times 10^{-1}$ m.

One of the advantages of this mode is that it minimizes the coupling between the different information that the sensor delivers. For example, with the Foucault's current detector used, the position J seen by the sensor is all the more wrong since the error between the orientation of the sensor and the orientation of the joint in the longitudinal plane is important.

The inconvenience arising from the error of position and orientation of the torch is important. Thus this method will be used when the radius of curvature is big, when the required precision is small or when the sensor is very near to the torch. This is a case when the sensors are placed in the plane of the torch[7] and the sensors use the length of the electric arc.[8]

Servoing the sensor while the extremity of the torch stays on the joint

This mode permits us theoretically to nullify the positional error of the torch and to reduce the orientation error.

If $J(k)$ is the succession of the positions J and $T(l)$ the succession of the position T (the torch) we propose the following algorithm to servo the torch (see also (Figure 5):

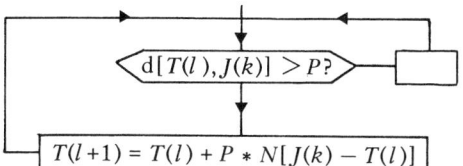

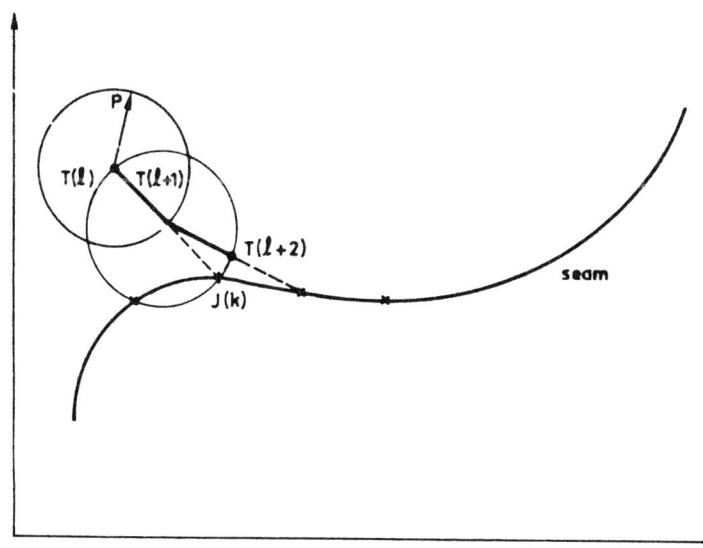

Figure 5 Algorithm to servo the torch

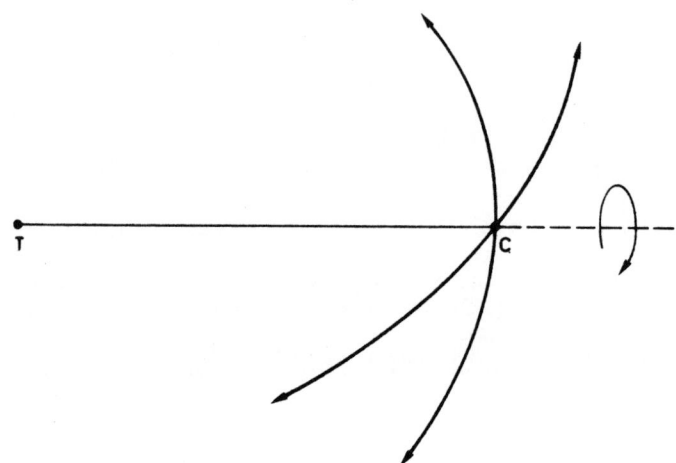

Figure 6 Servoing the sensor

For servoing the sensor (position and orientation in the sensor's plane) (Figure 6).

$$\vec{\omega} = \frac{1}{TC^2}(\vec{T}C \wedge \vec{T}J) + (\vec{C}_x \wedge \vec{J}_x)$$

where $\vec{\omega}$ is the rotation applied to the torch.

$\frac{1}{TC^2}(\vec{T}C \wedge \vec{T}J)$ is the position correction on the sphere of freedom of the sensor

$\vec{C}_x \wedge \vec{J}_x$ is the orientation correction in the transverse plane.

The orientation error of the torch is given by

$$\epsilon = \frac{TC}{2R} \qquad \text{(Figure 7)}$$

Numerical application: if we want $\epsilon \leq 5°$, then we must have $R \geq 1.75 \times 10^{-1}$ m.

Validation

Validation of these algorithms has been realized on a six-axes robot (SCEMI) controlled by an Intel 8086 system. We tested the following: (1) The mode of § 4.1 with the filter of § 3.4: The positional error was smaller than 0.5×10^{-3} m and the orientation error was smaller than $5°$ with a 10^{-1} m radius of curvature and $TC = 0$. (2) The mode of § 4.2: the positional error was smaller than 0.5×10^{-3} m and the orientation error was smaller than $5°$ with a 3×10^{-1} m radius of curvature and $TC \simeq 3 \times 10^{-2}$ m.

These very simple methods allow an on-line calculation with a 25 ms sampling period of the curve; this means that the sampling step is 0.6×10^{-3} m at a 2×10^{-2} m/s

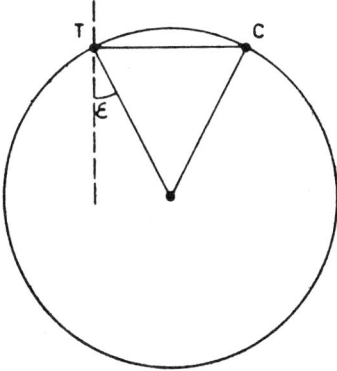

Figure 7 Orientation error of the torch

speed; so we can say that these results offer an improvement toward those which can be found in the literature.[9]

References

[1] Marchal, Détriché, Cornu *Self Adaptive Arc Welding by Means of Automatic Joint Following Systems* 4th Ro Man Sy, Varsovie, September 1981
[2] Sergatskii, Nazarenko, Lolotum E O *Welding Robot Guidance Systems* 12th ISIR, Tokyo, October, 1981. Paton Electric Welding Institute USSR
[3] Marchal, Fraize, Détriché, Cornu *Organe Terminal Adaptatif pour Robot de Soudage à l'Arc* 4th Int. Conf. on Welding Robots BRNO, February, 1982
[4] Donatien C (1959) *Éléments de Calculus d'Interpolation* Publications scientifiques et techniques du ministère de l'air (France)
[5] Eykhoff P (1974) *System Identification* University of Technology Eindhoven, The Netherlands, Wiley – Interscience,
[6] Amblard M (1983) *Etude Dynamique d'un Système de Télémanipulation Maître-esclave à Retour d'Effort Rapport de stage*, Centre d'Etudes Nucléaires de Saclay (France), STEP/LGR
[7] Takano, Ishizaka, Sejima, Enomoto, Araya, Kokura, Saito *Development and Actual Application of Arc Welding Robot with Sensor* IIW Document XII, K, pp 82–77, March, 1977. Hitachi Ltd, Ibaraki, Japan
[8] Cook G E *Position Sensing with an Electric Arc* 13th ISIR, Chicago, April, 1983. Vanderbilt University and CRC Welding Systems Inc.
[9] Ando S, Mikaye N Development of a new robot profile following method. Mechanical Engineering Research Laboratory, Hitachi Ltd, SO2 Kandatou-cho, Tsuchiura-Ohi, Ibaraki 300, Japan

Principles and Algorithms for Industrial Robots Remote Automatic Control

V S Kuleshov, Yu V Poduraev and V N Shvedov

Moscow Machine Tool Institute, Moscow, USSR

> **Summary:** This paper introduces an algorithm-type control system for industrial robots, based on the use of force-speed control algorithms. These algorithms provide for adaptive system properties in regard to the parameters of the operation performed and the object being manipulated both in robot teaching mode and in automatic performance of the programme.

In creating complex automated production systems one would often need robotic systems to perform infrequently occurring complex non-conventional operations in unspecified working-space conditions. The introduction of industrial robots with automatic control under such conditions is inseparable from the necessity to equip them with complex adaptation and sensor systems, which does not always prove economical. The use of remote-control manipulators may also prove of little benefit unless the simpler operations are automated.

The solution to the problem lies in a rational combination of remote- and automatic-control principles with a single microprocessor control and software system. To fit the robot out with remote- and automatic-control systems, leaving its mechanics intact, would mean enriching its functional capacities.

Remote-automatic control systems are preferable when programming robot performance from a movable operator's control panel when the programmer's presence in the working area is impossible, which is, for example, typical in the painting-booths. A reliable performance in either emergency or equipment-repair conditions harmful to human health also calls for fitting out the industrial robot with an additional remote-control unit.

An adaptive remote-automatic robot control system structure is given in Figure 1. It is meant for the following modes of operation: remote control in the manual mode of an operation with handle-type controls and the corresponding means of semi-automatic control; automatic adaptive control to perform conventional operations; automatic control with remote compensation when the operator can provide a remote-automatic control programme correction.

The analysis of typical technological operations showed that to make these models of operation effective one should build the remote-automatic control system on the basis of microcomputers as a double-action force–speed system for the remote control mode and as a point-to-point and a continuous path control system in case of the automatic industrial robot control.

Force–speed systems are a variety of remote semi-automatic control systems governing the manipulator gripper movements, a control signal for every degree of freedom being produced by a special calculator (microcomputer). Such systems provide the gripper-speed vector control in the transportation zone, which allows

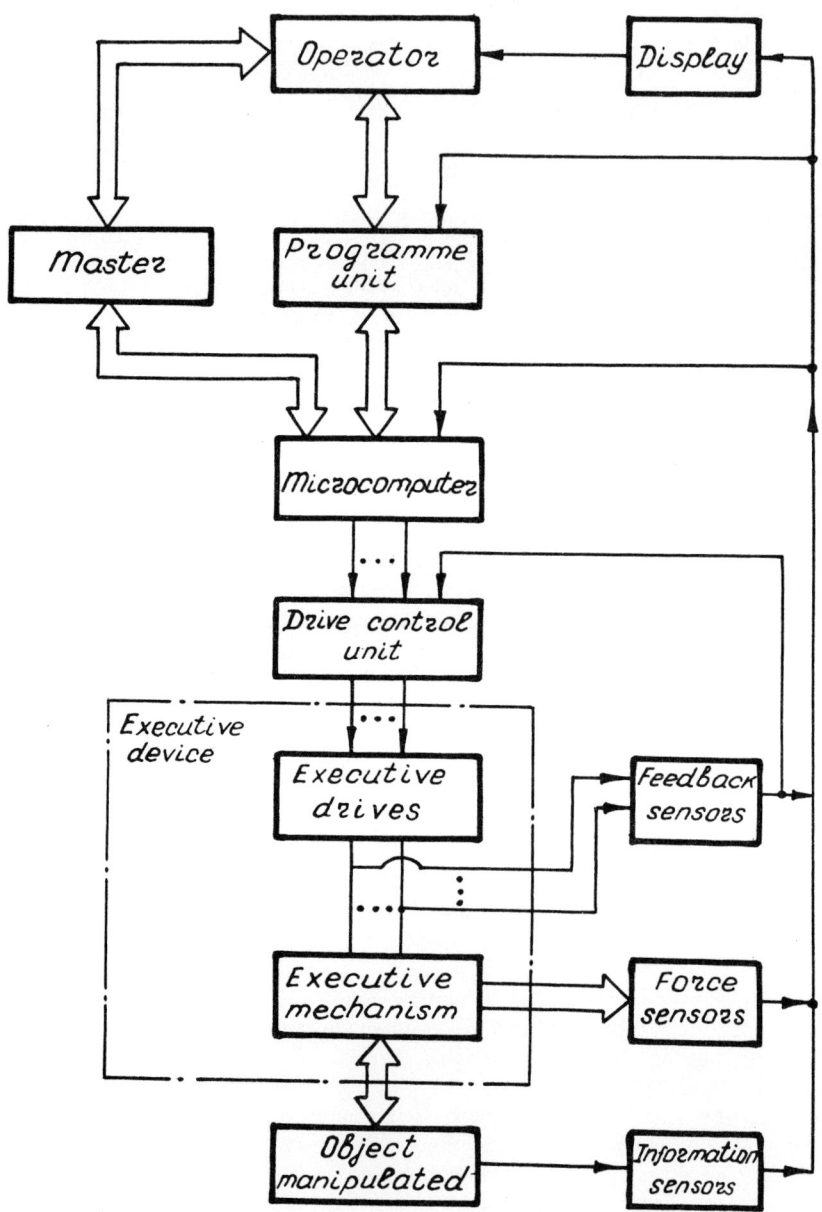

Figure 1 Adaptive remote-automatic robot control system

Principles and Algorithms for Industrial Robots 217

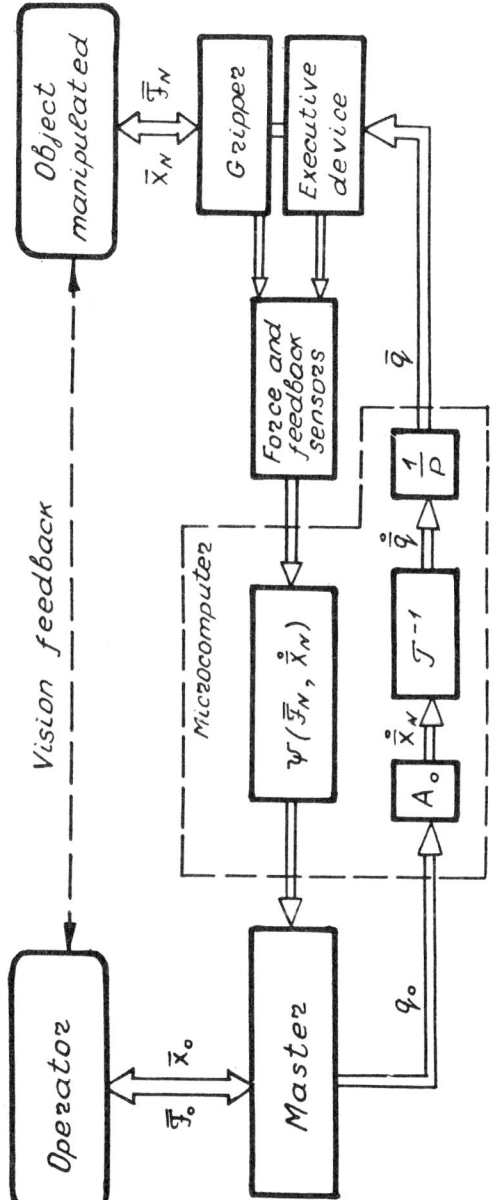

Figure 2 Block diagram of a double-action manipulator control system with force–speed control

considerable manipulator travel control with slight handle shifting and make it possible to achieve force feedback to the master in the operational area. This makes the operator aware of the load applied to the manipulator and helps achieve the desired performance accuracy by controlling the force value exerted on the performed work.

Force–speed control is usually achieved by switching to a different mode of operation either to the operator's command or automatically. The introduction of a single force–speed control algorithm for the mechanical system drive and the master drive can perceptibly simplify the operator's work.

In Figure 2 is shown a block diagram of a double-action manipulator control system with a force–speed control.

Symbolic designations in the diagram are as follows:

$\bar{F}_o, \bar{F}_N$ = general forces vectors acting on the master and the gripper correspondingly

$\bar{q}_o, \bar{q}$ = joint co-ordinate vectors of the control handle and the mechanical system

$\bar{X}_o, \bar{X}_N$ = deviation vectors of the master and the gripper handle

A_o = transformation matrix of the master

J^{-1} = Jacobian inverse matrix

$\frac{1}{P}$ = integrator module.

In general form the force–speed system work algorithm is given by the equations

$$\begin{cases} \dot{\bar{q}}_o = K_1 \cdot \bar{F}_o + K_2 \psi(\bar{F}_N, \dot{\bar{X}}_N), \\ \dot{\bar{q}} = A_o \cdot J^{-1} \cdot \dot{\bar{q}}_o \end{cases} \quad (1)$$

The force–speed algorithm of the effort reflection for the operator is defined by a non-linear function and a means of its realization.

If the operation performed requires simultaneous control of all the components of the general forces vector $\bar{F}_N$ developed by the gripper, it is necessary to realize the function ψ in the form of

$$\psi(\bar{F}_N, \dot{\bar{X}}_N) = K \cdot \bar{F}_N$$

In performing operations in the remote-control mode which require a direct force application, it is sufficient to provide the reflection of the purposeful effort for the operator. Under the term 'purposeful effort' we understand the projection of the general forces vector $\bar{F}_N$ on the tangent to the gripper travel trajectory. Bearing in mind that translational speed $\dot{\bar{X}}_N(t)$ of the gripper is always directed along this tangent, the function ψ may be given as

$$\psi(\bar{F}_N, \dot{\bar{X}}_N) = K_v \cdot |\bar{F}_N| \cdot \cos(\bar{F}_N \wedge \dot{\bar{X}}_N) \quad (2)$$

The given algorithm would come in useful in performing the following technological operations. (a) The calculation of the mass of an arbitrary load with its furthest travel in the horizontal plane (Figure 3a). When lifting a load $(a - b)$ we obtain $\psi = -K_v \cdot G$, i.e. the operator senses the load weight G with the proportion quotient K_v. In horizontal travel $(b - c)$ we obtain $\psi = 0$, the gripper speed being constant, which makes it possible to relieve the operator of the burden of the

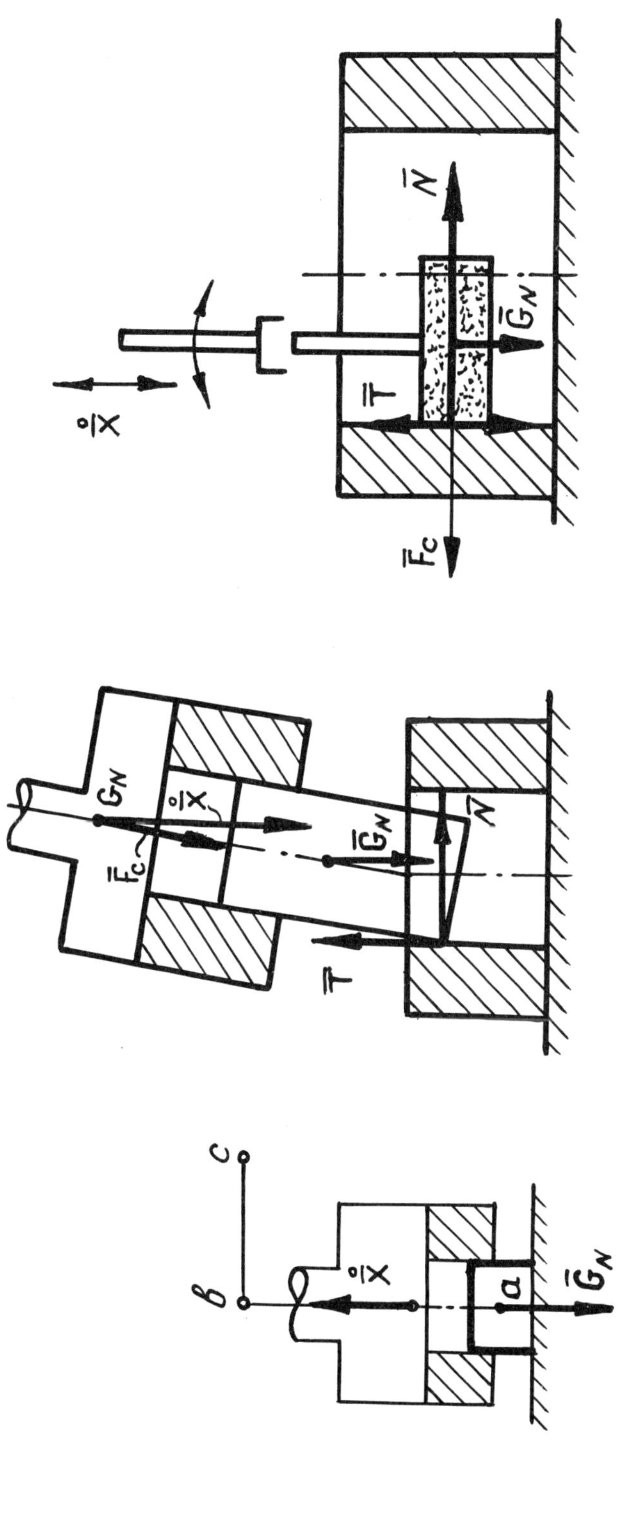

Principles and Algorithms for Industrial Robots 219

Figure 3 Algorithm used to perform: **a**, calculation of mass of load travelling in a horizontal plane; **b**, shaft bushing mating; **c**, grinding

unnecessary force data. Thus F algorithm compares favourably with the double-action system which uses algorithm (2). (b) Shaft bushing mating (Figure 3b). In this case we have

$$\bar{F}_N = \bar{G}_N + \bar{T} + \bar{N} \qquad (3)$$

where $\bar{T}$ is friction value between the components with the quotient μ and $\bar{N}$ is reaction value in the point of contact.

For robots with a system of static unloading $\bar{G}_N = 0$, in accordance with (3) we get

$$\psi = -K_v \cdot \mu \cdot N$$

In this way the operator senses the force value with the scale quotient K_v which makes it possible for him to regulate the effort developed by the manipulator and to assess whether or not there is a contact between the components (in this case $\psi = 0$). The latter information is indispensable for such operations as grinding (Figure 3c) when it is necessary to ensure a continuous contact between the grinding wheel and the workpiece.

Experiments in dynamic mode of operation with a human operator with remote-control performance of various operations have shown that robot motion control supplied by him prove reasonable from the point of view of energy consumption. To create such a mode of automatic control it is necessary to form control signals by means of the mechanical system drive with regard to the power developed by the gripper.

The use of such an algorithm in a teaching mode ensures efficient co-ordination between the dynamic characteristics of the human operator and the manipulator system. It should be noted that for a manipulator in static position, the force–speed system feedback equals zero. These force–speed algorithms may be used in automatic control as well as to correct the continuous path control module of the gripper speed. The use of the force–speed algorithms given allows us an approach to the problem of optimization with energy consumption reduction in view as a starting point.

The principles and algorithms given have been experimentally tried out with an electromechanical manipulation robot with remote-automatic control.

Part 4
Man-Intelligent Machine Systems

Manual Control Communication in Space Teleoperation

A K Bejczy and K Corker

Jet Propulsion Laboratory, California Institute of Technology, Pasadena, CA 91109, USA

Summary: Manual control in teleoperation with a multi-dimensional force-reflecting position-control device can be interpreted as a 'body language' two-way control communication between operator and remote manipulator. The kinematic and dynamic performance of the operator's arm and hand play a fundamental role in this control mode since the operator's manual actions are sending commands to and receiving information from the remote manipulator. An experimental investigation has been undertaken at JPL to study the effect of weightlessness on the operator's performance in force-reflecting position control of remote manipulators. A gravity compensation system has been developed to simulate the effect of weightlessness on the operator's arm. In the experiment a universal force-reflecting position hand controller was employed. This device is a backdrivable six-dimensional isotonic joystick which conforms to the range of motion of an operator seated at a console. In the light of possible disturbances of the human arm neuromotor control in a weightless condition, three types of control experiments were performed in a part-simulation of weightless conditions: (i) attainment of a learned final position, (ii) trajectory formation and stability in response to unit pulse disturbance and (iii) force tracking of planes and intersection of planes. The experiments confirmed the existence of disturbance of human manual-control performance caused by the weightless condition. The disturbance, however, can be compensated to a high degree because both elements of the coupled system (human arm and hand controller) are actively adjustable. The adjustments are operator dependent.

Introduction

Remotely operated manipulators (teleoperators) extend and augment the human manual working capabilities to perform non-repetitive and partly unpredictable mechanical tasks at places inaccessible to or undesirable for humans. The physical separation between human operator and remote manipulator presents major challenges to the development of control systems which connect the operator to the remote manipulator. In general, the control system should provide man-machine interfaces which enable the operator (i) to formulate and communicate control commands to the remote manipulator efficiently and (ii) to receive information on the kinematic and dynamic performance of the remote manipulator effectively.

The bilateral master-slave manipulator systems widely and successfully used in the nuclear industry provide an efficient and effective two-way control communication between operator and remote manipulator. The general idea and capability of the master-slave manipulator systems is that the master arm (i) automatically transforms the operator's six-dimensional hand motion into an equivalent six-dimensional motion of the slave hand and (ii) automatically transmits ('reflects') the acting forces from the slave arm back to the operator's hand. Thus, by using control-systems terminology, the master arm as a man-machine interface device performs feedforward and feedback motion and force transformation and transmission between the operator's hand and the remote manipulator's hand.

The kinematic and dynamic performance of the operator's arm and hand play a fundamental role in the overall bilateral master-slave manipulator control system. The operator's arm and hand are active control system elements since the transmission of control signals and the reception of feedback information occur simultaneously at the operator's arm and hand. Consequently, there are two critical man-machine interface elements in bilateral master-slave manipulator control systems. (i) The neuromotor characteristics of the human operator's arm and hand, including motion-control functions with proprioceptive sensitivity, and their stability and sensitivity to environmental disturbances. (ii) The control-system parameters of the master arm acting as a control and feedback transmission device in consonance with the human neuromotor parameters in motion control. In space teleoperator systems, basic environmental disturbances occur when the human operator is in weightless condition in a control station in earth orbit.

An experimental investigation has been initiated at JPL to study the effect of weightlessness on the operator's performance in bilateral master-slave manipulator control. The experimental system utilizes a universal or generalized six-dimensional force-reflecting hand controller in position-control mode as a 'master-arm'. This manual-control input device is universal in the sense that it is kinematically and dynamically dissimilar to the remote slave arm it controls. This is a radical departure from existing standard industry practices where the master arm is a one-to-one replica of the slave arm.

The specific purpose of the JPL study is to evaluate and quantify control system and human factors which critically affect the performance of generalized force-reflecting manual control in space teleoperation when the operator is in a weightless condition in earth orbit.

A brief discussion is presented in the section on **Manual control** interpreted as a 'body language' two-way control communication in force-reflecting position control in teleoperation. The next section contains a brief description of a gravity-compensation system developed for the laboratory experiments to simulate the effect of weightlessness on the operator's arm and hand in force-reflecting position control. Thereafter is a summary description of three control experiments with a brief analysis of the results. General conclusions are summarized last.

Manual control

Manual control in teleoperation by using a six-dimensional force-reflecting position-control device can be interpreted as a 'body language' two-way control communication between operator and remote manipulator. In general, the basic output from the operator in this mode of control is a goal-directed patterned motion of his arm and hand in three translational and three orientational co-ordinates of the operator's work space or task space, including also the first and second time derivatives (velocity and acceleration) along these co-ordinates. The kinematic pattern of manual motion can be rich enough to formulate and communicate complex motion commands to a remote manipulator in six work space or task space co-ordinates and their first and second time derivatives in the time continuum. The basic input to the operator in this mode of control is forces and torques along three orthogonal work or task space co-ordinates transmitted from the remote manipulator. The operator in his hand and arm has an integrated feeling of work or task space forces and torques acting at the remote manipulator as a consequence of his manual motion commands. Consequently, the operator's manual actions perform a two-way control communication in goal-directed 'body language' terms: they send control commands to and receive control information from the remote manipulator.

There are two critical man-machine interface elements in manual force-reflecting position control: (i) the master arm as a control command and control feedback transmission device and (ii) the neuromotor-control characteristics of human arm and hand motion.

Master arm

The standard industry practice (master arm in bilateral manipulator control as a one-to-one replica of the slave arm) can severely limit the application of bilateral (force-reflecting) manual control of remote manipulators. To avoid these limitations in the control experiments reported in this paper, a universal six-dimensional force-reflecting hand controller was utilized. This device exemplifies generalization of bilateral manual control of remote manipulators.

This hand controller is essentially a backdrivable six-dimensional isotonic joystick which has been designed to conform to the motion range of an operator seated at a console. Its hand grip is able to follow all the translational and orientational motions that the operator's hand can comfortably make within a 30cm cube work space. This device performs a dual function: (i) it reads the position and orientation of the operator's hand and (ii) it applies forces and torques to the operator's hand. This hand controller is general purpose in that it does not have any geometric or dynamic similarity to the slave arm it controls; it is not a replica of any slave arm, but it can be coupled to and used for the control of any slave arm through a computer.

The mechanical design of this universal hand controller is shown in Figure 1. It is a dynamically 'transparent' input/output device. This is accomplished by low-backlash, low-friction and low-effective inertia at the hand grip and by a self-balance system which renders the hand controller neutral with respect to gravity. Further reference on the mechanism and control system of this hand controller can be found[1-3] and preliminary control experiments with this device are described.[4]

Human neuromotor control

The importance of understanding human arm and hand neuromotor-control characteristics to develop design specifications for force-reflecting hand controllers cannot be overstated. Quantitatively, specified models of human arm and hand neuromotor-control characteristics are required for specifying human interaction in the design of teleoperator hand controllers.

A robust descriptive and prescriptive model of human-arm movement control has recently been the subject of intensive research efforts.[5,6] That model seeks to describe movement control in trajectory formation and positioning as a linear damped harmonic oscillator. Thus

$$I\ddot{\theta} + B\dot{\theta} + K\theta = N$$

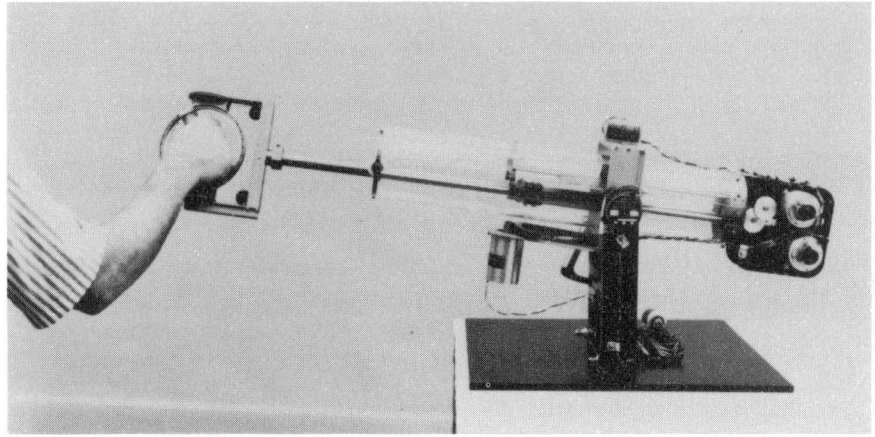

Figure 1 Mechanism of six-degrees-of-freedom force-reflecting hand controller

where I represents system inertia, B represents system viscosity, K represents system stiffness and N, the torque input to the system, is assumed to account for the non-linearities and non-stationary physiological characteristics of actual muscle control. Such models of the neuromotor system have proven to account for a number of characteristics of mammalian motor control including control in deafferented and environmentally perturbed conditions. We have extended the control model to account for system positioning in three-dimensional space[7] and have used the model as a basis for description of results in microgravity teleoperator control, reported here. Additionally, the contribution of the highly developed network of neural feedback that is sensitive to limb position, muscle tension and load, as well as visual and auditory information, must be considered in the design of a complete control system.

Gravity compensation of operator's arm

To provide an experimental platform for research characterizing the human controller's interaction with a bilateral-force-reflecting manipulator system in zero gravity, a gravity compensation system for the upper limb has been designed. The system will support the operator's upper arm and hand throughout the range of motion for control of the force-reflecting hand controller (FRHC).

The part-simulation technique provides an unrestricted view of the control-system displays and freely moving lateral and extensive movements through the use of low-friction bearings. The compensation system makes use of negator springs which have the characteristics of being low-inertia constant-tension springs which are adjustable: (a) to individual anthropometric requirements and (b) throughout the range of compensation from one gravity to zero gravity for the individual subject. The compensation system provides a constant force at the centre of mass of each limb segment that is equal to and opposite the gravity force acting on that limb. Determination of that force requirement was effected as follows. For a limb in an arbitrary position in a **1g** environment, Figure 2 illustrates the parameters of interest in limb compensation and provides a schematic of the suspension system, where

F_O = force of support of shoulder girdle
M_1, M_2, M_3 = mass of limb segments
T_1, T_2, T_3 = torque about shoulder, elbow and wrist
L_1, L_2, L_3 = length of limb segments
l_1, l_2, l_3 = length to centre of mass for each segment
$\theta_1, \theta_2, \theta_3$ = segment angle to gravity perpendicular

Force balance requires that

$$F_O = g\,(M_1 + M_2 + M_3)$$

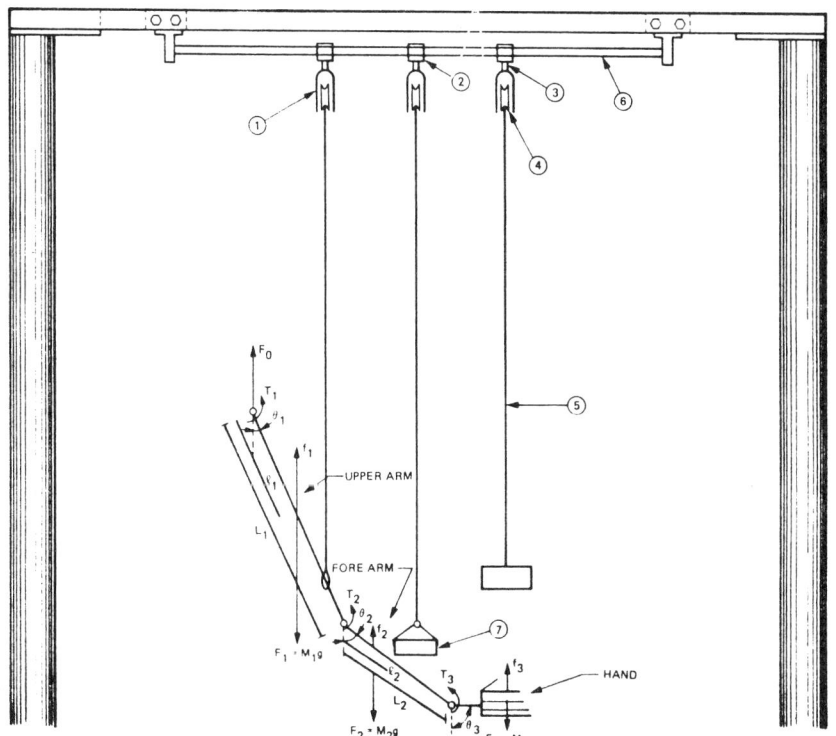

Figure 2 Limb-suspension schematic. 1, Low-friction turning-bearing support; 2, Low-friction linear bearing; 3, Swivel couple; 4, Adjustable radius take-up spool; 5, Negator spring band; 6, Stainless steel bearing rods; 7, Three-degrees-of-freedom limb-segment support

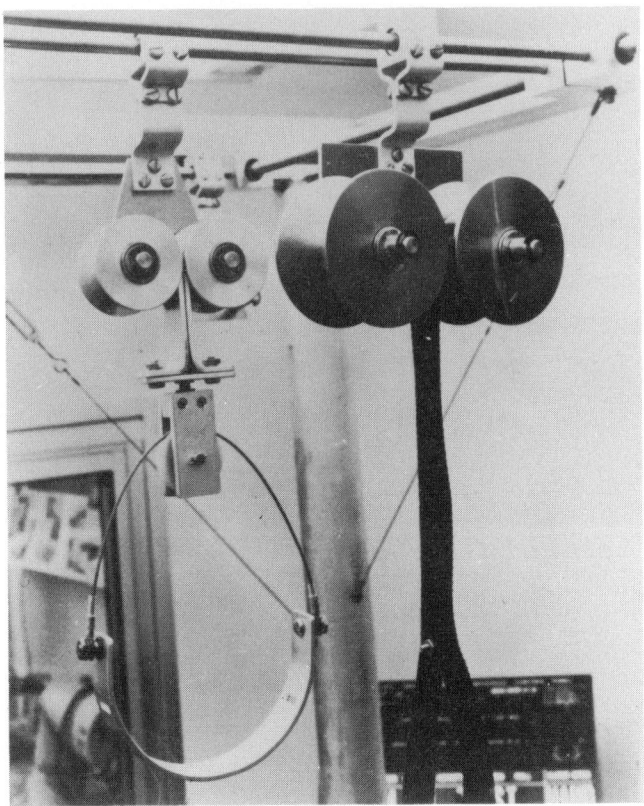
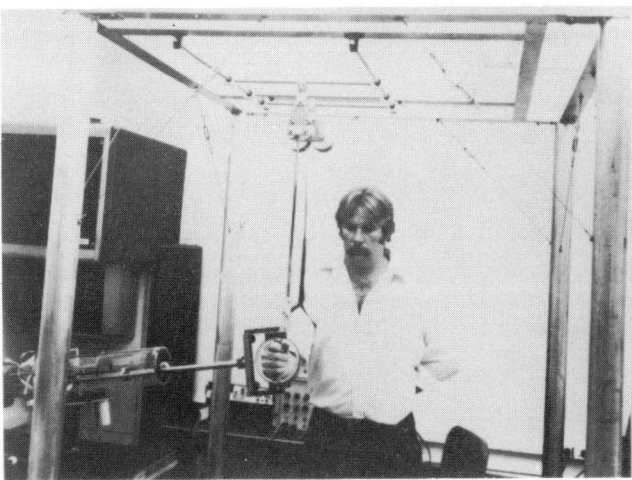

Figure 3 Gravity-compensation system and force-reflector hand controller (detail: negator springs, adjustable radii take-up spools, low-friction translation bearings)

In this design each limb segment will be supported at the centre of mass of each segment. Consequently, the compensation forces (f_1, f_2, f_3) can be calculated independent of the joint torques by assuming frictionless coupling at the joints. Figure 3 shows the compensation system in place in the laboratory with some detail.

Anthropometric measurement for each subject's body segments was performed to determine the weight and centre of mass of each limb segment. Mass was determined by using the procedure developed by Drillis & Contini[8] in which a body-build index has been determined. Centre of mass was approximated to statistical population parameters, and determined exactly for each subject by a force-balancing technique when the limb is suspended.

Human performance experiments

In the light of human arm neuromotor-control disturbances in a weightless condition, three types of control experiments have been performed with the universal force-reflecting hand controller in position-control mode. The three types of experiments were addressed to the study of: (1) the effects of microgravity on the attainment of a learned final controller position subject to changes in controller stiffness; (2) the effect on trajectory formation and stability in response to unit pulse disturbances, microgravity conditions and changes in controller damping; (3) the effects of microgravity on force-tracking performance by using computer-generated resistance planes in the control volume of the FRHC.

All experiments were performed in a within-subjects repeated-measures design under conditions of one gravity and gravity compensation. A brief summary of the experiments and the results are presented in Table 1.

Figure 4 presents representative data from trajectory formation and force-tracking tasks. We will refer to these data to illustrate conclusions drawn from our experiments. The interactive function of the human operator neuromotor viscosity and system-damping-gain value K_V is shown in Figure 4 (A-C). Figure 4A shows a gain in stability in a 5s trajectory as a function of increased damping. The subject initially shows a (2-5Hz) physiological tremor (left panel) that is effectively eliminated by increased K_{vN} (right panel); the response to disturbance (see arrow) is attenuated in the highly damped condition. In counterpoint, Figure 4B and C show data that illustrate a high initial neuromotor viscosity resulting in smooth motion (4B) which, with additional system damping, is moved to a region of instability (4C). Zero-gravity effects and damping compensation in force tracking are illustrated by the data in Figure 4D-F. Figure 4D shows a corner overshoot and response to disturbance (see arrow) in one gravity. Figure 4E shows similar effects in zero-gravity conditions characterized by two and three times higher amplitude responses. Figure 4F shows reduction of disturbance effect and stability compensation resultant from increased damping in zero-gravity conditions.

Complete data analysis and description of experiments are forthcoming in a JPL publication by the authors.

Conclusions

The simulated microgravity experiments allow several conclusions as follows.

Table 1 Summary of experiment

Experiment no.	Procedure	Conditions	Results
Experiment 1: Attainment of learned final position	(1) Within-subjects repeated measures (2) Target position proprioceptively defined and learned in one gravity (3) Gravity condition and controller stiffness varied as 'target' position sought	(1) One gravity vs zero gravity (2) High, medium, low controller stiffness (K_p) resistive or augmentative in relation to trajectory to target position	(1) Position inaccuracy in zero gravity (2) Final position accuracy affected by system stiffness (3) Stiffness balancing varying (K_p) can reduce zero gravity disturbance effect
Experiment 2: Trajectory formation and stability	(1) Within-subjects repeated measures (2) One gravity trajectory learned among target visual points (3) Gravity conditions and controller damping varied as trajectory is repeated with unit pulse disturbance at hand controller	(1) One gravity vs zero gravity (2) Fast vs slow trajectory (3) High, medium, low controller damping (K_v) (4) Random unit pulse disturbance on each axis (x, y, z) of motion	(1) Trajectory stability reduced in zero gravity (2) Neuromotor damping changes as a function of imposed trajectory velocity (3) Trajectory stability operator-dependent function of total system damping (4) Stability in response to disturbance: a, in zero gravity, b, with reduced system damp
Experiment 3: Force tracking in a geometrically constrained proprioceptively defined task	(1) Within-subjects repeated measures (2) One gravity force tracking with computer simulated planes of resistance in controller workspace (3) Gravity conditions and controller damping varied as force tracking performed with unit pulse disturbance at hand controller	(1) One gravity vs zero gravity (2) High, medium, low controller damping (K_v) (3) Random unit pulse disturbance on each axis (x, y, z)	(1) Force tracking accuracy reduced in zero gravity (2) Viscosity (damping) effect replicates (exp. 2) (3) Disturbance recovery: a, reduced in zero gravity; b, stability reduction replicates exp. 2; c, performance decrement can be compensated by system parameters

Manual Control in Space Teleoperation 231

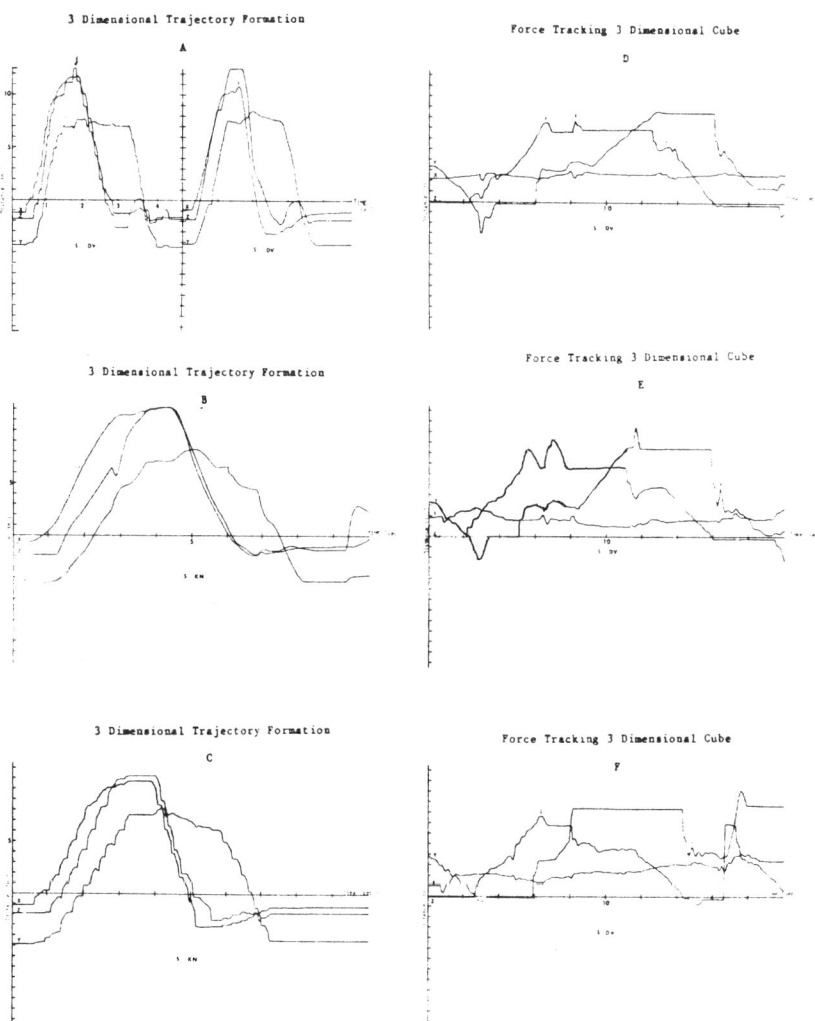

Figure 4 Three-dimensional (3D) trajectory formation;
A, 5s trajectory, **1g**, low damping, high damping; B, 10s trajectory, **1g**,
low damping: C, 10s trajectory, **1g**, high damping. Force-tracking 3D cube;
D, **1g**, low damping; E, **0g**, low damping
F, **0g**, high damping (1 inch = 2.54×10^{-2} m)

(1) There is a disturbance acting on the human operator in force-reflecting manual control of a remote manipulator caused by the weightless condition of the operator.
(2) This disturbance can be compensated to a high degree because both elements of the coupled system (human arm and hand controller) are actively adjustable.
(3) The adjustments are operator dependent.
(4) Addition of a multifunction hand grip to the hand controller requires careful design and experimental evaluation since the mechanical finger actions on the hand grip can evoke internal system disturbance in addition to the weightless condition disturbance.
(5) It is desirable that the operators learn manual force-reflecting control in the laboratory microgravity environment and, finally, the laboratory evaluation will be validated and extended in flight experiments.
(6) It is desirable to extend the microgravity experiments to six-dimensional force-reflecting control tasks in one-handed operations.
(7) It is desirable to perform experiments in two-handed operations under microgravity conditions.

This work has been carried out at the Jet Propulsion Laboratory, California Institute of Technology, under NASA Contract No. NAS7-918.

References

[1] Bejczy A K and Salisbury J K, Jr *Kinesthetic Coupling Between Operator and Remote Manipulator* Proc. of ASME Computer Technology Conf. Vol. 1, San Francisco, California 12-15 August 1980/Controlling remote manipulators through kinesthetic coupling. *Computers in Mechanical Engineering*, **1** (1), 48-60
[2] Handlykken M & Turner T *Control System Analysis and Synthesis for a Six-Degree-of-Freedom Universal Force-reflecting Hand Controller* Proc. of the 19th IEEE Conf. on Decision and Control, Albuquerque, New Mexico, 10-12 December, 1980
[3] Turner T L *Joint Co-ordination for Manipulator Tracking* Proc. of the 20th IEEE Conf. on Decision and Control, San Diego, California, 16-18 December, 1981
[4] Bejczy A K and Handlykken M *Generalization of Bilateral Force-reflecting Control of Manipulators* Proc. of RO MAN SY-81, Warsaw, Poland, 8-12 September, 1981
[5] Abend W, Bizzi E & Morasso P (1982) Human arm trajectory formation. *Brain*, **105**, 331-348
[6] Polit A & Bizzi E (1978) Processes controlling arm movements in monkeys. *Science*, **201** (4362) 1235-1237
[7] Corker K M (1984) Investigation of neuromotor control and sensory sampling in bilateral teleoperation. PhD Thesis, Department of Psychology, UCLA
[8] Drillis R & Contini R (1966) *Body Segment Parameters* Technical Report No. 1166.03. Office of Vocational Rehabilitation, New York University School of Engineering, New York

Sensory-based Control for Robots and Teleoperators

B Espiau and G Andre

IRISA, Laboratoire d'Automatique, Campus de Beaulieu, 35042 Rennes, France

Summary: This paper presents an overview of the problem of controlling a robot or a teleoperator using sensory information coming from the neighbourhood of the effector. After the principles of the local environment were recalled, and the IRISA 'sensory system' presented, the control problem was set in terms of elementary actions. Then the synthesis in a frame linked to the end effector was performed, as well in force as velocity; then, the dynamic-control problem was reset in a useful form, and the loop with respect to sensory information closed. The second part of the paper gives a way to apply this approach to teleoperation. A master—slave system was used, and the sensors provide an artificial force feedback information to the operator, or a velocity-control loop to the slave. Various modes of interaction with the operator were used. A videotape summarizes the main results obtained.

Introduction

The project developed at IRISA is concerned with the use of exteroceptive sensors, to allow the increase in adaptivity of manipulators related to their environment,[1] with application to robotics and, more specifically, to CAT (computer-aided teleoperation) (J Vertut, R Fournier, B Espiau and G Andre, unpublished work). In complement to classical sensory systems (global vision with camera, contact analysis with force sensors), the methods based on the perception of the local environment, without any physical contact, present several advantages, because it is often possible to consider that the actions and the evolution of an effector are time-and-space local phenomena, for which classical vision is inadequate. The proposed approach, based on the design of a multiproximity sensor system, integrated within the end effector, allows a real closed-loop control with respect to objects (obstacles or targets), either fixed or mobile ones.

IRISA proximity sensor system

The necessity of 'smart sensors' leads to design of a complete multisensor system composed of the following.

A set of various transducers. Our laboratory has developed a 'new generation' of infrared proximity sensors (with or without fibre optics). The optical heads are very small (less than 2 cm^3); three aperture half-angles may be selected (8, 25 or 60°). The response function of the distance is linearized; practical range is 40 cm in detection and 15 cm in distance estimation. The response time for a numerical measure, is about 50 μs. Ultrasonic sensors (range 20 cm–2 m) and inductive

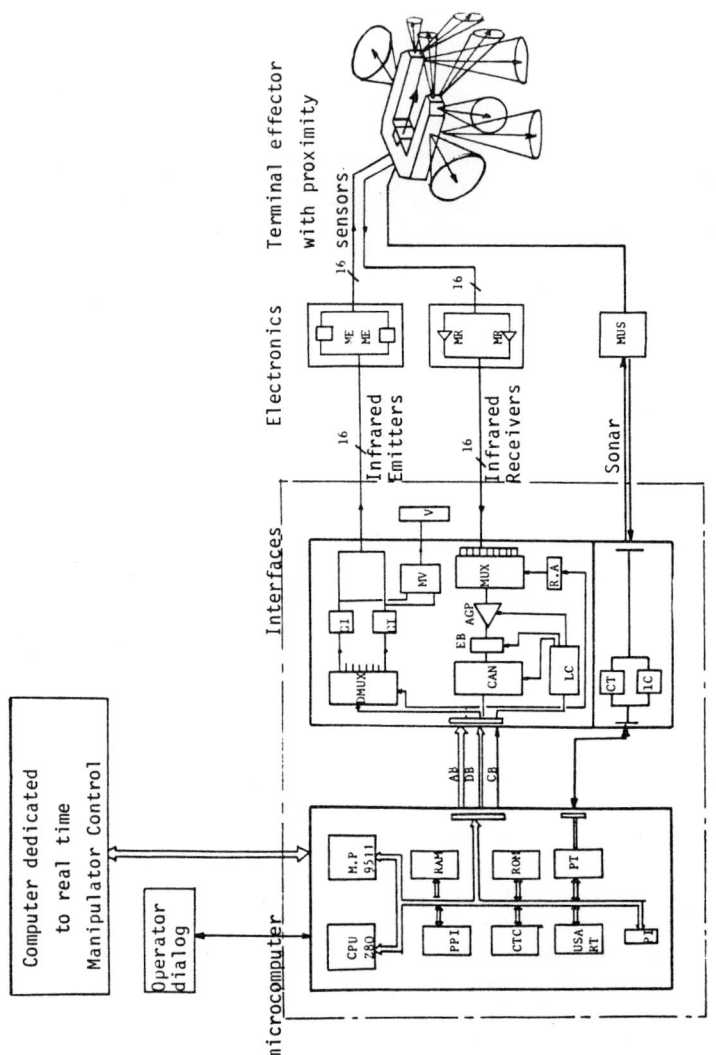

Figure 1 Structure of the proximity sensor (infrared and ultrasound) preprocessing system

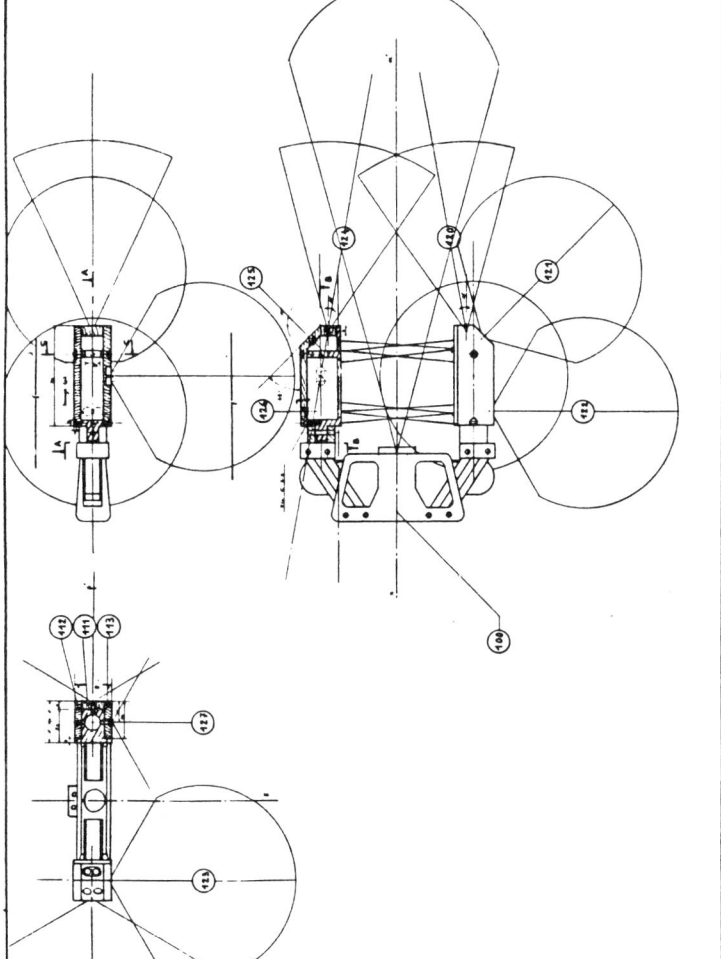

Figure 2 A bidigital sensate hand

sensors may also be used.

Fast electronics and AD interfaces for preprocessing.

A microcomputer. In a multiprocessor approach, dedicated to data handling (32 infrared sensors channels and two ultrasound sensors channels), signal processing and communication with the executive computer (Figure 1).

Several sensitive devices have been designed (with the assistance of a CAD simulation program), for example: a four-sensor matrix for surface following and a sensate hand for interactive manipulation (Figure 2).[2,3]

Elementary actions: primitives[4]

To build control loops based on sensory information, we define a frame R_n related to the end effector, which is supposed to be a rigid solid (S). Let C be a set of n_c given elementary sensors c_j (each providing a scalar measure y_j). An elementary action a_i ($i = 1, n_v$) is then the set $(\underline{x}_i, \underline{d}_i, s_i)$ with, in R_n:

$\underline{x}_i$ the origin of the action
$\underline{d}_i$ the basic direction of the action $\|\underline{d}_i\| = 1$ dim$(\underline{d}_i) = 3$
s_i a scalar multiplying coefficient of $\underline{d}_i$, depending on the measurements.
We thus define $\underline{v}_i = s_i \underline{d}_i$

Remark. The actions are defined here without particular physical attribution (force, torque, velocity, etc.). It is then possible to associate a subset C_k of C to sets A_k of actions such as the couples P_k: (C_k, A_k), $k = 1, \ldots, n_v$ are mutually independent and the C_k make a partition of C. In practical applications it is interesting to define P_k in such a way as they belong to given classes corresponding to well-defined basic functions. A primitive is then an element of a class, in which the elementary actions are clustered.

In the general case we may distinguish three kinds of primitives: (a) a simple primitive, if all the actions have the same significance (e.g. all the $\underline{V}_i$ are velocity translation vectors); (b) a mixed primitive, in the other case; (c) an external primitive, a set of actions not associated to a subset of sensors (e.g. nominal trajectory, contribution of a priori environment modelling, etc.).

As shown,[5] definition of the actions by primitives provides a connection with the kinematic description of contacts between bodies; a primitive realizes an artificial contact between S and the objects in the environment. Thus it is possible to describe a primitive by classical twist and wrench characteristics.

Sensory-based control

A complete control with sensory feedback includes three levels of computation: (1) synthesis of a vectorial summarized action in R_n; (2) expression of this action with the parameters describing the position and the orientation of R_n with respect to a fixed frame R_o (operational co-ordinates); (3) insertion in the servo control algorithms and closing of the loop. We present the main related problems.

Vectorial synthesis

We consider the case defined by the hypothesis: H_1, all elementary actions are translations (forces or Cartesian velocities); H_2, no constraints.

Force synthesis

In that case S is supposed to be submitted to a finite set of external point forces. We define:

a point O in R_n
antisymmetric matrix Δ_i corresponding to the vector product $X \vec{ox_i}$
elementary forces $\underline{f}_i = s_i \underline{d}_i$ (1)

Synthesis in O is thus given by the two vectors (Figure 3)

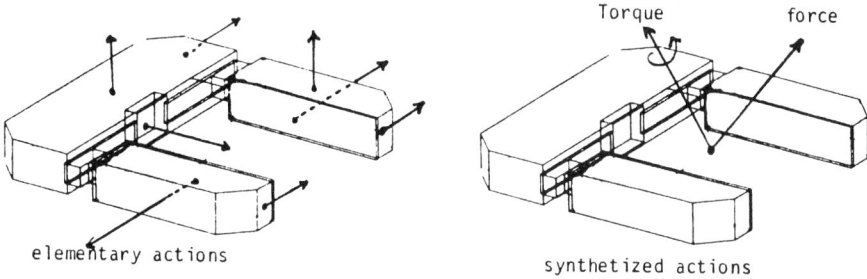

Figure 3 Synthesis of force elementary actions

$$\left| \begin{array}{l} \underline{\sigma} = \sum_{i=i}^{n_v} \underline{f}_i \quad \text{(force)} \quad (2) \\ \underline{\rho} = \sum_{i=i}^{n_v} \Delta_i \underline{f} \quad \text{(torque)} \quad (3) \end{array} \right.$$

We note $\underline{F}_e^o(.)$ the corresponding expression of $(\underline{\sigma}, \underline{\rho})$ in the operational space.

Velocity synthesis

In that case the elementary actions are the desired elementary velocity $\underline{V}_i$ of x_i points. This representation is useful for a finer trajectory control in R_o than in the previous case or when the robot or teleoperator is controlled in velocity.

Unfortunately, the velocity vector field V of a rigid solid (S) has the well known property.

$$\forall A, B \, \sigma(S): \underline{V}(A) = \underline{V}(B) + \underline{R} \, X \, \vec{BA} \quad (4)$$

$\underline{R}$ given. In the general case, of course, the v_is have no reason to satisfy (4) thus to belong to V. By (4) V may be defined by a couple $(\underline{s}, \underline{r})$, where $\underline{s}$ is the velocity of a given point O', and $\underline{r}$ rotation vector, both expressed in R_n. A way to realize synthesis is to find field V where $\underline{V}(x_i)$ is closed to $\underline{V}_i \; \forall i = 1, n_v$.

We define the quadratic cost function $= J = \sum_{i=i}^{n_v} \lambda_i \, \| \underline{V}_i - (\underline{s} + \Delta_i \underline{r}) \|^2$ (5)

where the parameters ($d_i i = 1, n_v; \Sigma \lambda_i = \lambda$) are a weighing set.

By minimizing (5) the following result is obtained:[5] by defining (S') as a new solid constituted by Dirac masses λ_i, rigidly linked, under the condition that the x_is are not on the same line, by choosing O' as the mass centre of (S'), and R_n as the central inertia frame of (S'), then the solution is given by the quasi kinetic components of (S'):

$$\hat{\underline{s}} = \sum_{i=i}^{n_v} \lambda_i \underline{V_i} \qquad (6)$$

$$\hat{\underline{r}} = D^{-1} \sum_{i=i}^{n_v} \lambda_i \Delta_i \underline{V_i} \qquad (7)$$

where D is a non-singular diagonal matrix.

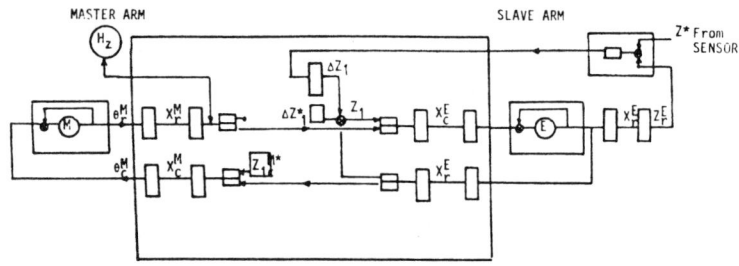

Figure 4 Teleoperator control: mixed mode

The important consequence of the previous results is that, by an adequate choice of O and R_n, it is possible to use very closed expressions for velocity and force synthesis (Figure 4), with $\underline{V}$ and $\underline{W}$ being the expressions of translation and rotation velocities in the used parameters for the operational space.

Remark. Previous cases are the simplest ones. It is not possible to present in the present paper all the other situations (constraints, mixed primitives, etc.). They are studied elsewhere.[5]

Insertion in the global control loops

Resetting the control problem
Modelling. It is well known that the dynamic model of a robot has the form[7]

$$A(\underline{q}) \, \underline{\ddot{q}} + \underline{B}(\underline{q}, \underline{\dot{q}}) = \underline{\tau} \qquad (8)$$

where $A(\underline{q})$ is the inertia matrix, $\underline{q}$ the joint co-ordinates and $\underline{B}(\underline{q}, \underline{\dot{q}})$ includes gravity, Coriolis and centrifugal forces, dry friction, damping; $\underline{q}$ is supposed to belong to an hypercube of R^6 defining a domain D_x by $\underline{X} = f(\underline{q})$.

A Jacobian matrix is defined by

$$J(\underline{q}) = \left[\frac{\delta f_i}{\delta q_i}(\underline{q}) \right] \qquad (9)$$

The singularities of J lie on a small finite set of points $\underline{q}$ or $\underline{X}$ called D_x^*. By assuming that $\underline{X} \in D_x' = D_x - (D_x \cap D_x^*)$, we may write an operational model in the form

$$M(\underline{x})\underline{\ddot{X}} + \underline{N}(\underline{X}, \underline{\dot{X}}) = \underline{F} \tag{10}$$

Control. The general form of the control law in D_x' is

$$\underline{F} = \hat{M}(\underline{x})\underline{U} + \underline{\hat{N}}(\underline{x}, \underline{\dot{x}}) \tag{11}$$

where $\hat{M}$ and $\underline{\hat{N}}$ are the user's choices made for M and N, and $\underline{U}$ tunes the behaviour of the servo loop with respect to the desired trajectory, called $\underline{X}_c(t), \underline{\dot{X}}_c(t)$.

For convenience, we introduce a so-called reference model

$$\underline{\ddot{X}}_r = \underline{U}_r \tag{12}$$

which is an ideal double integrator. The basic servo loop is then

$$\underline{U} = -\kappa_p \underline{e} - \kappa_v \underline{\dot{e}} + \underline{U}_r \tag{13}$$

with $\underline{e} = (\underline{X} - \underline{X}_r)$.

The theorem given[7] ensures a good behaviour of $\underline{e}$, by using non-linear gains κ_p and κ_v depending at each time on $\underline{X}, \underline{\dot{X}}, \underline{e}, \underline{\dot{e}}$ in a way given by the accuracy of the choice $(\hat{M}, \hat{N})$. If the dynamics of (12) and (13) are well chosen and compatible with the possibilities of the actuators, it is possible for the user to have only to control the system (12), provided that $\kappa_p(\cdot)$ ensures that $\underline{e}$ and $\underline{\dot{e}}$ are small. With this important result, the introduction of sensory-based feedback is easy. Note that the control of (13) may include some actuator characteristics like their limits.

Case of bilateral telemanipulators. Models (8) and (10) may be extended to telemanipulators. For a master–slave pair, we have two models. Control is classically obtained by setting $\underline{F}_i = \hat{M}_i(\underline{Y}_i)\underline{U}_i + \underline{\hat{N}}(\underline{Y}_i)$, $i = 1$ (master) or 2 (slave) and $\underline{Y}_i = \underline{q}_i$ or $\underline{X}_i$

with
$$\underline{U}_i = -\kappa_p^i(\underline{Y}_i - \underline{Y}_i^c) - \kappa_v^i(\underline{\dot{Y}}_i - \underline{\dot{Y}}_i^c) \tag{14}$$

$$\underline{Y}_1^c = \underline{Y}_2, \quad \underline{Y}_2^c = \underline{Y}_1 \tag{15}$$

and possibly $\underline{\dot{Y}}_1^c = \underline{\dot{Y}}_2$, $\underline{\dot{Y}}_2^c = \underline{\dot{Y}}_1$
the case $\underline{Y}_i = \underline{q}_i$, $\underline{\dot{Y}}_1^c = \underline{\dot{Y}}_2^c = 0$ gives the classical bilateral force reflecting M/S control.

Principles of introduction of sensory feedback

Force synthesis. *Robot control: In (10) $\underline{F}_e^o(\cdot)$ is added to $\underline{F}$; *M/S control: In (14) $\underline{F}_e^o(\cdot)$ may add an artificial position error, by writing $\underline{X}_2^c = \underline{X}_1 + \kappa_p^2 \hat{M}_2^{-1}(\underline{X}_2)\underline{F}_e^o$. The stiffness of the loop gives an artificial force feedback to the master operator, who feels a sensation of attraction and repulsion with respect to objects.

Velocity synthesis. By setting $\underline{\dot{X}}_c^T = (\underline{V}^T, \underline{W}^T)$, we directly constitute the required sensor-based control, acting on the reference model (12) for example by $\underline{U}_r = -L_v(\underline{\dot{X}}_r - \underline{\dot{X}}_c)$.

The dynamic behaviour of these loops (equilibrium points, stability) has been studied by J Vertut, R Fournier, B Espiau and G Andre (unpublished work).

Sensor-referenced control in CAT (Computer-aided teleoperation)

Smart sensors and computing capabilities enable the efficiency of the teleoperator system to be increased. In CAT context (i.e. an interactive, multifunctional and real-time computer-controlled system), several sensor-referenced modes of control are possible.

We note the following:
- M = Master
- E = slave
- c = input
- r = output
- DOF = degree of freedom
- ★ = programmed
- ~ = free
- − = blocked
- $\underline{\theta}$ = angular co-ordinates
- $\underline{X}$ = operational co-ordinates
- $\underline{Z}$ = function co-ordinates

The modes then are as follows.

Robot mode and master-slave decoupled mode

R. A sensor-referenced and computer-controlled mode is developed to increase the slave's autonomy. Here, proximity sensors allow automatic subtasks to be performed, in the form of a sensor-based compliance without contact. General equations (in position control) are

$$\begin{cases} \underline{Z}_c^E = \underline{Z}_r^E + \underline{\Delta Z} \\ \underline{X}_c^M = \underline{X}_r^{-M} \end{cases}$$

with $\underline{\Delta Z}$ an increment resulting from sensor-based and nominal action.

We can apply this fully automatic mode to many examples where adaptive position control is required, like automatic guiding and grasping, surface following, tracking of moving targets, etc

Unilateral master-slave mode

MSI 1. The simple manual mode where the slave is position controlled by the master (without force-reflecting control) leads to limited performances.

MSI 2. The second possibility of unilateral control allows the slave to execute predefined automatic functions (under programmed or sensor-referenced control) with passive copy on the master.

$$\begin{cases} \underline{Z}_c^E = \underline{Z}_r^E + \underline{\Delta Z} \\ \underline{X}_c^M = \underline{X}_r^E \end{cases}$$

This method is interesting when DOF sharing is used to create artificial constraints in the work space.[2]

Bilateral master–slave modes

MSII 1. Generalized bilateral force-reflecting control (with contact).
MSII 2. Interactive (shared or traded) human and computer control with programmed constraints and force feedback.
MSII 3. Idem, with sensor-referenced force feedback.

The sensor and computer manipulator control is developed in the framework of a supervisory control system. All these efficient CAT modes greatly increase performances and reduce the work tension of the operator. As mentioned by Bejczy[7] the human operator can act in parallel, or in series, with the computer in a semi-automatic context.

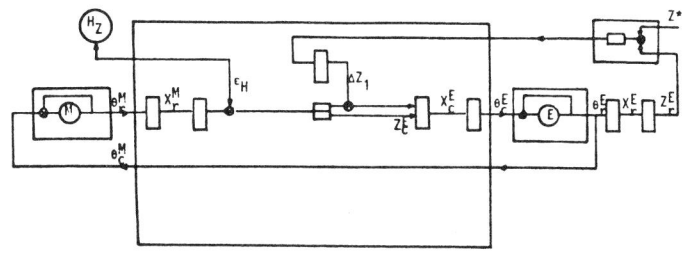

Figure 5 Teleoperator control: reflex mode

Mixed mode (Figure 5)

This mode implies that the operator is able to act in parallel with the computer. Furthermore DOF sharing is essential for a lot of tasks. The slave performs automatic functions which can be referenced to sensor data for Z_1 (dim n_1) (with or without passive feedback to the master). The other DOF Z_2 (dim n_2) are given to the operator in a standard bilateral force-reflecting mode.

$$\begin{cases} Z_{1c}^E = Z_{1r}^E + \Delta Z_1 & \Delta Z_1 \text{ sensor-based control} \\ Z_{2c}^E = Z_{2r}^M & Z_{2r}^M = H_z \\ Z_{1c}^M = Z_{1c}^{M\star} & Z_{1c}^{M\star} = \overline{Z}_{1c}^M \text{ or } \widetilde{Z}_{1c}^M \\ Z_{2c}^M = Z_{2r}^E & \end{cases}$$

For example, sensor-referenced control is used to correct range, pitch and yaw errors relative to a surface; translation is controlled by the operator.

Reflex mode (Figure 5)

The proposed (so-called reflex) mode realizes both classical force-reflecting feedback and a supplementary sensor-referenced force feedback. Real-time computer programs provide an efficient 'shared control' between man and computer in such a way that the operator can feel, in the master arm, artificial (sensor-based) forces,

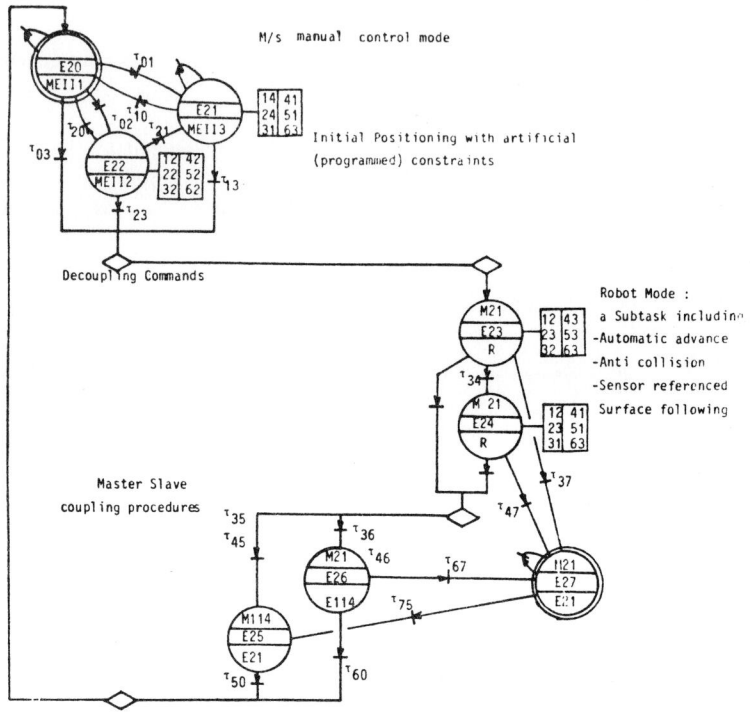

Figure 6 Action graph in computer-aided teleoperation (obstacle avoidance, surface following)

as if objects (in the slave's work space) were magnets. However, he keeps on-line the priority of actions. Different schemes have been studied. Figure 6 gives an example with a simple position feedback.

$$\begin{cases} \underline{Z}_c^E = \underline{Z}_r^M + \underline{\Delta Z} \\ \underline{X}_c^M = \underline{X}_r^E \quad \text{(position feedback)} \\ \text{or } \underline{F}_c^M = \underline{F}_r^E \quad \text{(force feedback)} \end{cases}$$

This kinesthetic coupling results in a very impressive 'remote touch' technique for obstacle avoidance, orientation of effectors, surface following (for inspection, etc.).

Experimental results and conclusions

The experiments, shown in a videotape, have been performed with the IRISA sensory system, implemented by using the CAT system on an experimental site (J Vertut, R Fournier, B Espiau and G Andre, unpublished work) composed of a master slave MA 23 telemanipulator and a minicomputer, SOLAR. The sampled rate is 100 Hz. Typical useful operations are: obstacle avoidance with proximity sensor-based feedback ($\simeq$ 1 to 3 daN); automatic tracking of a moving object (30 cm/s) and automatic grasping of a cylinder on a conveyor belt; automatic subtask, like tool grasping (in 4 s); surface tracking with 5 DOF controlled, with 20 cm/s velocity.

References

[1] Espiau B and Andre G *Using Proximity Sensors in Teleoperation* 4th Ro Man Sy, Warsaw, Poland, September, 1981
[2] Andre G (1983) Conception et modélisation de systèmes de perception proximétrique; application à la commande en téléopération. PhD, Université de Rennes, France
[3] Espiau B (1984) Optical reflectance sensors. *In Recent Advances in Robotics* John Wiley, New York
[4] Espiau B and Andre G *Utilisation d'Informations Proximétriques en Téléopération* Congrès AFCET, Journée Bilan ARA, Besançon, France, November, 1983
[5] Espiau B *Commande en Boucle Fermée de Robots Munis de Capteurs Extéroceptifs Terminaux* Internal Report, IRISA, Rennes, France, February, 1984
[6] Samson C *Robust Non-linear Control of Robotic Manipulators* IEEE Decision and Control Conf., San Antonio, Texas, December, 1983
[7] Bejczy A K *Sensor and Computer Aided Control of Manipulators in Space* Symposium MIDCON/79, Chicago, USA, 1979

Tele-existence (I): Design and Evaluation of a Visual Display with Sensation of Presence

S Tachi, K Tanie, K Komoriya and M Kaneko

Mechanical Engineering Laboratory, MITI Tsukuba Science City, Ibaraki, 305 Japan

Summary: The tele-existence system is a teleoperator system that enables a human operator at the controls to perform remote manipulation tasks dexterously with the feeling that s/he exists in the slave anthropomorphic robot in the remote environment. The Mechanical Engineering Laboratory has started an 8-year national project of advanced robotics to realize this tele-existence system. In this paper the project goal is described first. Next, the visual display system that measures the operator's head movement, controls the slave robot's vision system according to the movement, and displays the acquired two visual images to both the operator's eyes through head-mounted CRT displays, whose images in turn fuse to give the visual sensation (which is very natural), when designed and constructed. Evaluation of the system has been carried out by measuring the metric of binocular visual space of a human operator with or without the display device. The experiment reveals that the metric of the binocular visual space viewed with the naked eye can be reserved in tele-existence system by servoing the focal length of the display lenses and the angle of the convergence of the two CRTs appropriately.

Introduction

Remote operation plays an important role in such hostile environments as nuclear, high temperature and deep space. In spite of the efforts of many researchers a teleoperation system that is comparable to man's direct operation has not yet been developed. There are three problems to be solved for the realization of an ideal remote operation system: (1) to design an anthropomorphic slave manipulator with human dexterity; (2) to measure human movement thoroughly and establish the control scheme of a slave manipulator (design of a master system); (3) to present the human operator with sensory information of the slave robot's environment as naturally as possible.

Problems (1) and (2) have been studied as teleoperator systems.[1] However, problem (3), the problem of remote presence, has not been studied enough. A conventional three-dimensional display presents a very unnatural scene to the operator, entailing an awkward operation and exhaustion of the operator.[2]

An ideal teleoperation system should be such a system that at the remote-control site a human operator can perform remote manipulation tasks dexterously with the feeling that s/he exists in the slave anthropomorphic robot in the remote environment. We call this type of advanced robot teleoperator system with real-time sensation of remote presence a tele-existence system. A pioneering study for a realistic three-dimensional display was conducted by Sutherland[3] as a head-mounted three-dimensional display to demonstrate the 'kinetic depth effect', i.e. moving perspective images appear to be strikingly three-dimensional even without any stereo presentation. He used only line drawings generated by the computer and did not use the real scene.

At Kernforschungszentrum Karlsruhe GmbH,[4] DCAN and CEA,[5] MBA Co. (personal communication), University of California in Los Angeles (J Lyman, personal communication) and Naval Ocean Systems Center,[6] pioneering studies using real scene have been proposed and some experiments have been conducted.

The idea *per se* has shown promise, but much remains unsolved toward the realization of an ideal tele-existence system including general design procedures, evaluation methods and test and evaluation in specific work environments.

In this paper the National Tele-existence Project is outlined for the first time. Then the fundamental idea of the tele-existence visual-display method and design procedure is proposed. A method of evaluation of the visual display is proposed and typical results are shown.

Tele-existence

The Japanese Ministry of International Trade and Industry has just started its 8-year National Project dubbed JUPITER (JUvenescent PIoneering TEchnology for Robot) to research and develop advanced robot technology for the system that avoids the need for humans to work in potentially hazardous working environments.

The Mechanical Engineering Laboratory is in charge of the fundamental research for the realization of the tele-existence system.

The final version of the tele-existence system will consist of intelligent mobile robots, their supervisory subsystem, a remote-presence subsystem and a sensory augmentation subsystem, which allows an operator to use robot's ultrasonic, infrared and other, otherwise invisible, sensory information with the computer-graphics-generated pseudorealistic sensation of presence. In the remote-presence subsystem realistic visual, auditory, tactile, kinesthetic and vibratory displays must be realized. In this paper, however, only the visual display is discussed as the first step.

Then, how can we display a realistic scene to the operator? How can we maintain the relationship between an object and a robot's upper extremities (arms and hands) at the remote site?

Figure 1a shows the traditional concept of a three-dimensional display. All waves coming into a robot at the remote site are recorded at ideally infinite points on a closed surface enclosing the robot. These recorded waves are transmitted and played back in real time at the corresponding points on a surface enclosing an operator.

The above method of wave reconstruction has the following disadvantages: (1) it is difficult to create an adequate recording and playback system so as to enclose a robot or operator. This results in a small display, entailing lack of realistic feeling; (2) when an operator tries to handle an object, s/he sees both robot's upper extremities and her/his upper extremities; it is thus difficult to avoid the feeling of remoteness (in other words, the relation between the object and upper extremities cannot be preserved in this type of display).

Figure 1b shows a new type of display with robot technology. This is based on the principle that the world we see is reconstructed by the human brain using only two real-time images on the two retinas. What we can see are only two-dimensional pictures on the retinas changing in real time according to the movement of the eyeballs and the head. We reconstruct the world image in the brain and project back the reconstructed image to the real three-dimensional world.

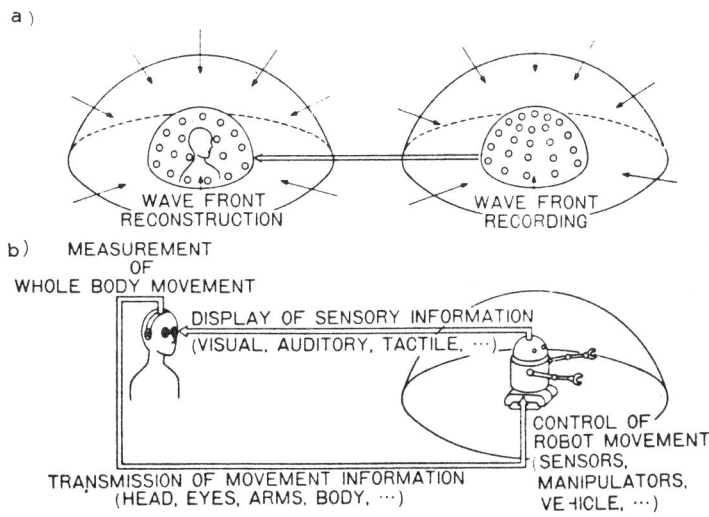

Figure 1 (a) Concept of wave-front reconstruction display and (b) tele-existence display

In a new type of robotic display: (a) human movements, including head and eyeballs, are precisely measured in real time; (b) robot sensors are constructed anthropomorphically in function and size; (c) movements of the robot sensors are controlled precisely to follow the human operator's movement; (d) pictures taken by the robot sensors are displayed directly to the human eyes in a manner to induce the feeling of presence.

Thus an operator sees the robot's upper extremities instead of her/his own at the position her/his upper extremities should be. The robot's upper extremities are controlled to track in real time precisely the same movement and force condition of the operator's and are seen through the visual display and felt by the tactile communication subsystem.

Visual-display design

Essential parameters for human perception of the monochromatic three-dimensional space are: (1) accommodation of the crystalline lens; (2) visual angle, i.e. retinal image size; (3) convergence of two eyes or disparity of two retinal images.

An ideal visual-display system should control all three parameters of display device in real time so that it would coincide with the parameters seen directly with the naked eyes. These conditions can be realized, as shown in Figure 2.

Suppose two posture-controlled TV cameras on board the robot in the remote

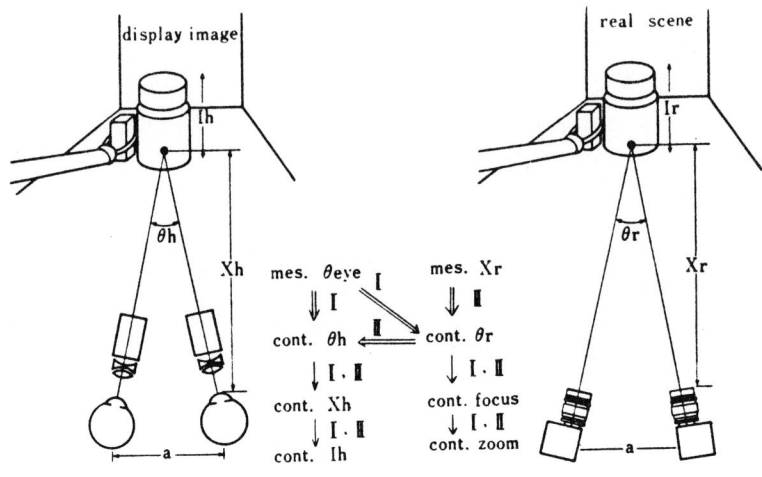

Figure 2 Ideal display method of tele-existence system

environment see the object at the distance of Xr. This distance is measured by the robot using the method of disparity[7] or ultrasonic measurement.[8] The foci of the two cameras are adjusted to the distance Xr. The two cameras are controlled so that the two lines of sight converge at the object location. The convergence angle θr and visual angles Vr (or object size Ir) for both the right and the left camera are calculated.

In the left-hand side of Figure 2, an ideal display method is proposed. The above parameters are considered in displaying the scenes taken by remote TV cameras as follows: two CRT displays with appropriate lens systems are placed immediately in front of an operator's eyes. Remote scenes taken by left and right cameras are displayed on left and right CRTs which, in turn, are focused by the lens systems on the corresponding left and right retinas respectively. The visual angle Vh at which each eye sees the object on the CRT display is controlled so that $Vh = Vr$. The location of a virtual image of the object picture on the CRT is controlled to be at the distance of $Xh = Xr$. The convergence angle of the two CRT displays is also servoed to $\theta h = \theta r$.

Thus each eye of the operator sees the same image that would be seen directly in the remote environment.

Among the three parameters of display, crystalline lens accommodation plays the least important role. If we accommodate to 1m, for instance, it covers the convergence range of 20cm to infinity. This fact leads to the simpler design method as shown in Figure 3. In the simpler design the location of virtual image is set at a fixed distance (e.g. $hL = hR = 2m$). However, visual angle (image size) and convergence angle are strictly controlled to coincide with the condition of which a direct observation can be made with naked eyes.

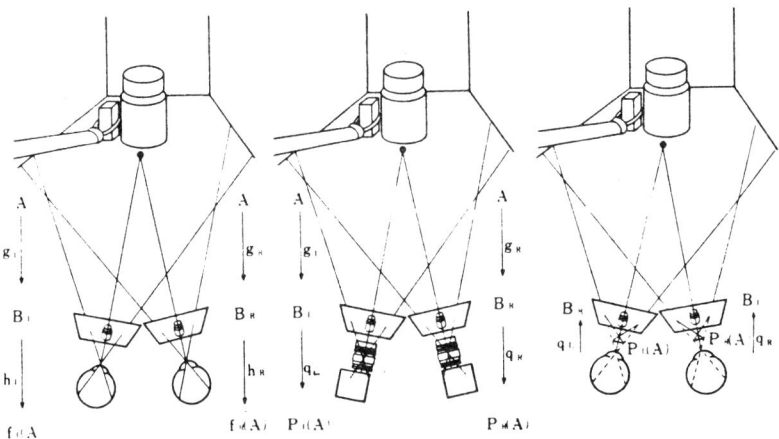

Figure 3 Simpler display method of tele-existence system

Such a condition can be realized easily by finding the transform qL from the plane BL to $PL(A)$ and the transform qR from the plane BR to $PR(A)$. Then by realizing the inverse transform qL^{-1} and qR^{-1} using the lens system of the display, we can easily get the appropriate virtual images at the planes BL and BR.

Experiments

Experimental Apparatus

Figure 4 shows the experimental-system diagram used for the evaluation of the design concept. Only one degree of freedom, i.e. the operator's right and left head turning, is measured by the goniometer in this experimental set-up.

The turntable, where two MOS (metal-oxide-semiconductor) TV cameras are mounted, is servoed after the goniometer measurement (Figure 5). Video signals from the cameras are displayed on CRT displays of the binocular display device which can be fixed with respect to the operator by the special cross-hairs (Figure 6).

The focal length of the object lens of the TV camera and that of the eye lens of the binocular display apparatus can be changed.

Evaluation Experiments

It is found that the so-called visual space has a uniquely determined non-Euclidean metric, or psychometric distance function, the numerical parameters of which depend on the individual observer.[9]

These parameters of visual space can be measured, for example, in a dark room with the observer's head and therefore approximately also the rotational centres

250 S Tachi et al.

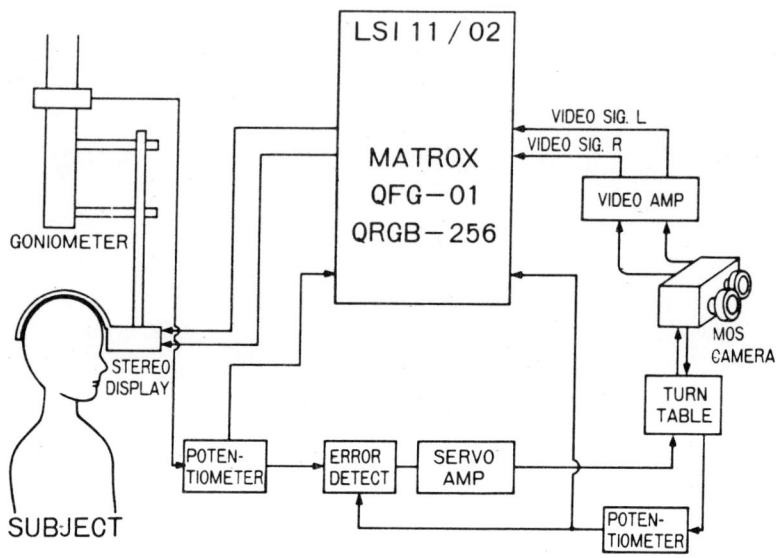

Figure 4 Schematic diagram of the experimental system

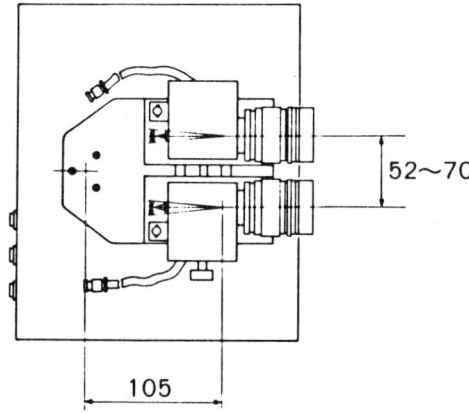

Figure 5 MOS TV cameras mounted on a turntable

of her/his eyes, fixed by means of a head rest[10] and precisely measuring the individual parameters of the Helmholtz horopter.[11]

Figure 7 shows an example of Helmholtz horopter. An observer, placed into the above described position, is given the task of arranging a number of light points (three iñ this case) so that they appear to lie on a horizontal straight line, symmetric

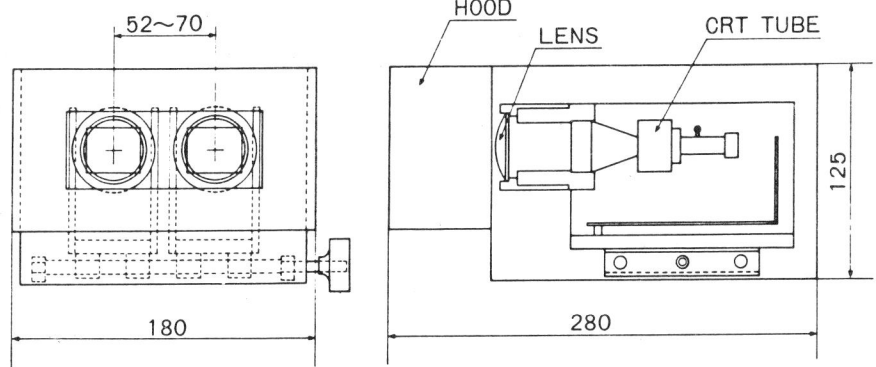

Figure 6 Binocular visual-display apparatus

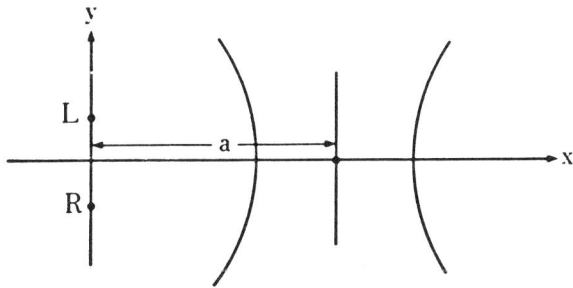

Figure 7 Helmholtz horopter curves for different fixations

to the median plane. It is found that the points are set consistently on certain physical curves which are, in general, not straight in the physical sense. The form of these so-called horopter curves depends on the distance x of the centre point. At a certain distance $x = a$ the horopter is practically straight. At nearer distances, $x < a$ the horopters are concave to the observer; at greater distances, $x > a$, they are convex. These horopter curves can be described as follows:[10,12]

$$\frac{\cosh[\sigma(\gamma+\mu)]}{\cosh[\sigma(\gamma_0+\mu)]} = \cos\varphi$$

where angle γ is the bipolar parallax, approximating to the convergence angle, and angle φ is the bipolar latitude in x-y space, γ is the co-ordinate of the intersection point of the horopter with x axis and σ and μ are individual parameters of the horopter. Angle γ and angle φ, in terms of Cartesian co-ordinates, can be expressed with sufficient accuracy as

$$\gamma = \frac{p\cos^2\varphi}{x}$$

$$\tan \varphi = y/x$$

where p is the interpupillary distance measured in centimeters.

In the design of the realistic binocular display of the tele-existence system, these individual parameters of the binocular visual space, i.e. σ and μ, were used. First, σ and μ of a subject operator under the condition that s/he sees directly with naked eyes were measured by the three-rod Helmholtz frontal-plane horopter experiment. Figure 8 shows an example of the results.

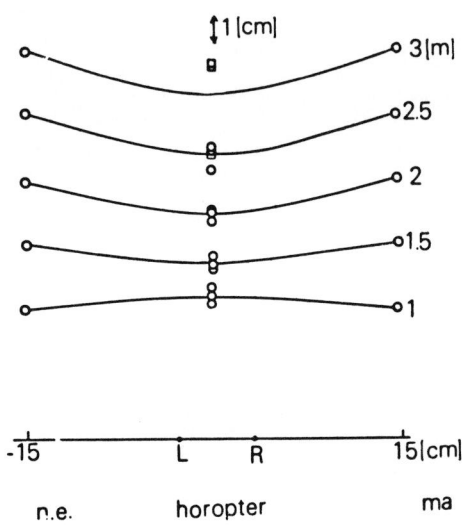

Figure 8 An example of the results for direct observation

Next the same experiments of the horopter were repeated under the condition of indirect observation with the tele-existence system for several values of object lens and eye lens focal lengths. Figure 9 shows an example of the experiments observed through tele-existence system. These experiments reveal that the optimal focal lengths are functions of the distance between the object and the TV cameras.

Figure 10 shows an example of the results for the distance of 2m. In this example, the condition that object lens focal length o = 13mm and eye lens focal length e = 50mm gives the best result in a sense that the parameters are almost the same.

This supports our design concept that the best display can be obtained by servoing not only the convergence but also the image size by controlling the focal length of the eye lens. A new test hardware with the ability to exercise such control is now being designed and experiments made on trial.

Conclusions

(1) The concept of tele-existence, advanced type of teleoperator with real-time

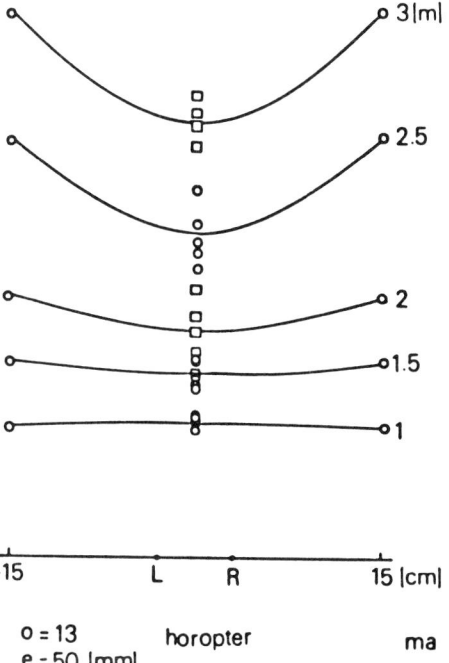

Figure 9 Indirect observation

sensation of presence by using robot technology, was proposed and evaluated.
(2) A design method of binocular display with sensation of presence was proposed.
(3) A binocular monochromatic display system with one degree of freedom of movement was made on trial according to the design procedure of (2).
(4) A psychophysical experimental method using the measure of visual space to evaluate the correspondence between directly observed visual space and visual space observed indirectly through the tele-existence system was proposed.
(5) Evaluation experiments were conducted by using the horopter measurement method as proposed in (4).
(6) The results showed a good correspondence between direct visual space and indirect visual space through tele-existence system, if the display conditions are appropriate.
(7) Further experiments are being planned with a new experimental system with binocular colour display with six degrees of freedom of movement.

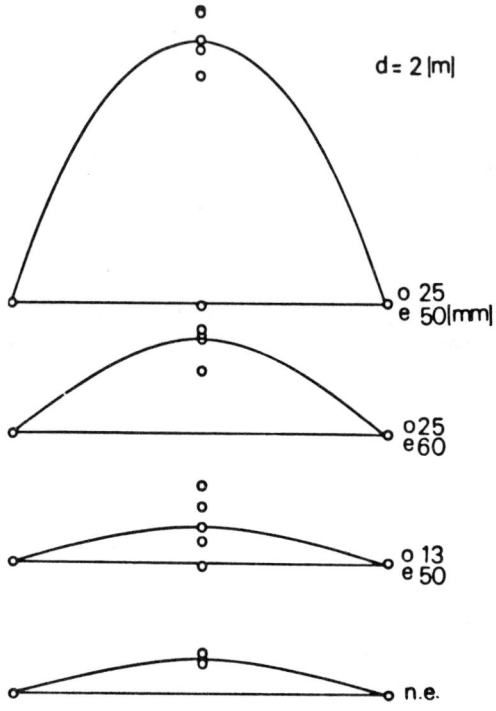

Figure 10 Horopter curves

References

[1] Johnsen E G & Corliss W R (1967) *Teleoperators and Human Augmentation* NASA SP 5047
[2] Orton A (1971) A system for stereo viewing. *Computer Journal*, **14** (2), 140-144
[3] Sutherland I E (1968) *A Head-mounted Three Dimensional Display* Fall Joint Computer Conf., 757-764
[4] Köhler G W (1978) *Status of Remote Systems Technology* Proc. 8th Int. Symp. on Industrial Robots, 805-828
[5] Charles J & Vertut J (1977) Cable controlled deep submergence teleoperator system. *J. Mech. Mach. Theory*, **12**, 481-492
[6] Hightower J D & Smith D C (1983) *Teleoperator Technology Development* 12th Meeting of UJNR/MFP, 43-47
[7] Julesz B (1971) *Foundations of Cyclopean Perception* University of Chicago Press, Chicago
[8] Tachi S et al (1981) *Guide Dog Robot — Feasibility Experiments with MELDOG MARK III* Proc. 11th Int. Symp. on Industrial Robots, 95-102
[9] Tachi S & Komoriya K (1982) The 3rd generation robot. *J. Soc. Instrument Control Eng.* **21**, 1140-1146
[10] Luneburg R K (1950) The metric of binocular visual space. *J. Opt. Soc. Am.* **40** (10), 627-642
[11] Helmholtz H V *Treatise on Psychological Optics* vol. 3, ed.
[12] Zajaczkowska A (1956) Experimental test of Luneburg's theory. Horopter and alley experiments. *J. Opt. Soc. Am.*, **46** (7), 514-527

New Approach to Robotic Visual Processing

B Macukow

Institute of Mathematics, Warsaw Technical University, 00-590 Warsaw, Poland

Summary: A new visual processing model based on multichannel neural organization selectively sensitive to a range of spatial frequencies is described. The Fourier transformation of the input signal multiplied by a transfer function of a special filter and then the inverse Fourier transformation gives at the output a planed cross- or auto-correlation signal which allows for the recognition of the object and its location. The computer and physical modelling of the system, and its application to robot visual systems are discussed.

Introduction

Visual systems have been studied for many years from neurophysiological and technical points of view. The optics of the eye, the nature of transformation of light into neural activity and the first few stages of neural processing are understood. However, what happens to visual information in the cortical areas inside the brain, is still unclear and dimly understood. For some years the theory that individual cells act as a feature detector was dominant. Since the first papers published by McCulloch & Pitts and Hubel & Weisel[1,2] and others, models with feature detectors responding selectively to the environment were widely investigated.[3,4] In recent years a new theory on operation of the visual system was introduced. Instead of the non-linear processing characteristics of a feature detector the idea of linear transformation with multiple spatial frequency channels is now under investigation. This theory assumes that the cortical cells in certain areas are selective to a limited range of spatial frequencies for a particular portion of the two-dimensional Fourier spectrum.

The ease with which the Fourier transform is performed by an optical system allows us to build a very simple and efficient recognition system. This idea can also solve the important problem of a shift-and-rotation invariance for pattern recognition systems. Such an optical or digital recognition system can be very useful in dealing with the problems of robot vision.

Classical model versus spatial frequency channels

The classical model of striate organization and the models of visual processing based on it have been questioned recently. There exists strong physiological evidence against a strictly hierarchical arrangement of cells in a striate cortex and the idea of fairly linear processing with multiple spatial frequency channels has been proposed.[5] According to this model, the visual system is composed of the

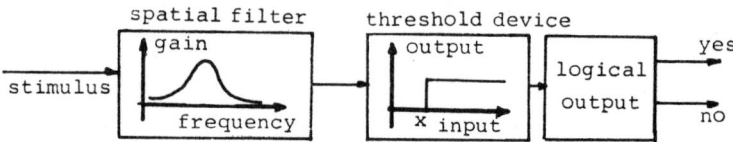

Figure 1 Block diagram of a single channel mode

neural channels each selectively sensitive to a different range of spatial frequencies. An idealized block diagram is shown in Figure 1. This model can be extended also to a multichannel one, each sensitive to another spatial frequency and with a common logical output. The signal will be detected if the threshold of any channel is exceeded. The model with noise representing the uncertainty of detection has been investigated by Sachs et al.[6] Experiments carried out by De Valois et al.[7] on cats and monkeys gave strong evidence in support of the above ideas. For example, they showed that the tested cortical cells were more selective for different spatial frequencies (of gratings) than for bars of different widths. The cells could easily detect the bar but in fact they could not show a decrease in sensitivity when the bar widths were varied. However, the cell is much more narrowly tuned for a grating of different spatial frequencies.

Physical and mathematical background of experiment

This approach, when the recognition system uses two-dimensional Fourier transformation of the object, transmission of its Fourier spectrum and then discrimination and recognition on the basis of the Fourier components (or retransformation and detection) is based on one of the most remarkable and useful properties of a converging lens, its inherent ability to perform two-dimensional (2D) Fourier transformation and to perform it digitally (FFT) with ease also. The method, based on Fourier transform of the input signal, seems to be very promising from the point of view of robot vision. The method of matched spatial filters (MSF) with its optical and digital representation should be especially useful. The physical and mathematical background of these two representations is now discussed.[8] Let us assume that we have a filter matched to the particular signal $s(x,y)$. The impulse response of the filter $h(x,y)$ is given by

$$h(x,y) = s^*(-x,-y)$$

where s^* is a function conjugate with s.
If the input signal is $g(x,y)$ and the filter is matched to $s(x,y)$, then the output is found to be

$$v(x,y) = \int_{-\infty}^{\infty}\int h(x-\xi, y-\eta) \cdot g(\xi,\eta) \, d\xi \, d\eta$$

$$= \int_{-\infty}^{\infty}\int g(\xi,\eta) \cdot s^*(\xi-x, \eta-y) \, d\xi \, d\eta$$

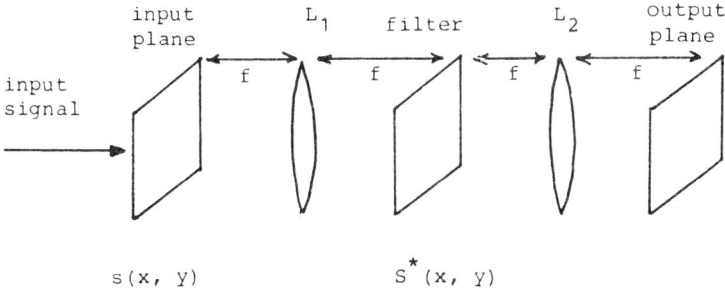

Figure 2 Optical interpretation of the matched filtering

which is a cross-correlation function of g and s. The optical interpretation of the matched filtering is shown[8] in Figure 2.

The filter, synthesized by means of a frequency-plane mask, matched to the input signal $s(x, y)$, should have an amplitude transmittance proportional to S^*, where

$$S^*(f_x, f_y) = F(s) = \int_{-\infty}^{\infty}\!\!\int s(x,y) \cdot \exp[-i2\pi(f_x \cdot x + f_y \cdot y)] \, dx \, dy$$

Assume that the signal s is presented at the input plane. Incident at the filter is a field distribution proportional to S and after the filter there is a field distribution proportional to SS^*. The lens L_2 realizes the inverse Fourier transform of a product SS^* which gives the autocorrelation function at the output plane (focal plane of lens L_2). This function is characterized by the high and narrow-shape maximum (peak). If the input s is shifted by a vector $[a, b]$, at the output plane the peak is also shifted by $[a, b]$. When the input signal is different from $s(x, y)$, at the output plane the cross-correlation function is obtained (without the maximum typical of autocorrelation).

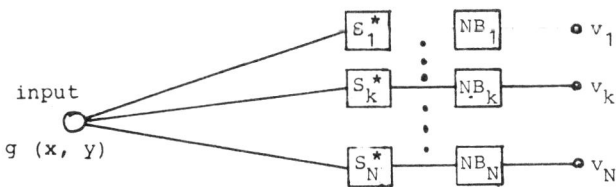

Figure 3 Block diagram of a multichannel recognition system.
NB = normalization block

If the processing system is composed of N channels each with a filter matched to a different object (with a different transfer function $S_1^*, S_2^*, \ldots, S_N^*$; as shown in Figure 3), the kth output will be the largest if at the input

$$g(x,y) = s_k(x,y)$$

is presented.

The optical recognition system yields recognition instantly and the conventional MSF system is a shift invariant which allows us to detect and locate the input pattern within an image. Since MSF works only with coherent light, laser light should be used. Special transducers, such as a liquid-crystal light valve which can convert the image of incoherent light image into that of coherent light, have been developed.

Digital pattern recognition with its flexibility and practical applicability should become an important method in robotics systems of recognition and control. However, this is a conventional correlation method and only the object (image) of the known orientation can be found. In many applications object location and orientation are unknown. Sometimes, even its size cannot be defined precisely.

Generally a recognition system is said to be a shift and rotation invariant if: (1) whenever the input image is shifted by a vector $[a, b]$, all the locations of recognized targets are also shifted by a vector $[a, b]$; (2) whenever the input image is rotated around some centre by an angle α, all the locations of recognized targets are also rotated around the corresponding centre by the same angle α.

Since the conventional MSF can detect only targets with the same orientation as the filter, a rotation of the filter relative to the input for sequential detection has been suggested. This operation that can be relatively simply carried out by the digital system is difficult in the optical one. The problem of multiple correlation with matched filters of different orientation can be reduced by sampling the input image and the standard pattern.[9]

The subsequent comparison with the different standard patterns allows the input object to be recognized and the location of the correlation peak gives information about its position.

Description of the model

Most experiments were performed for both the optical and digital system and each time the results were in agreement.

An ideal recognition system should detect the presence and both the location and orientation of the object in recognition. A general outline of the digital system is shown in Figure 4.[10] The first one is the correlation operation block which gives

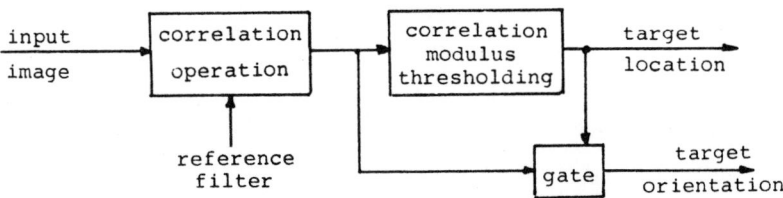

Figure 4 Digital system outline

the spatial function of the correlation between the input and filter reference. The modulus thresholding block finds the target location. Next the target orientation can be found. The input image is Fourier-transformed by a classical FFT subroutine. Fourier spectrum of the input is multiplied by the stored conjugate spectrum of the reference (matched filter). The inverse Fourier transform gives the whole spatial function of the correlation between the input and the reference. After thresholding the largest modules, the value indicates the object location.

The experimental optical recognition system was familiar to the one shown in Figure 2 with the standard Fourier transform system with a computer-generated hologram filter matched to one of the possible objects. Satisfactory results were obtained.

Conclusions

Very often industrial robots in their classical application work on the same task for a very long time. Once the computer-generated filter has been fabricated, the optical system in operation costs much less than when a computer in real time is used.

If the object to be recognized can be rotated by an unknown angle in its working area, the multiple use of different filters makes the recognition process much more difficult, and increases the time. Substitution of the optical system by the microprocessor system allows for the detection of the input pattern in a reasonable time (in co-operation with the microcomputer of 64B byte memory plus floppy discs it was less than 1 s).

Modelling and detection of complicated objects in a large area (2D-Fourier transform of at least 500 x 500 pixels) needs a big computer (e.g. IBM 360 or 370). It produces very good and immediate results, but low cost and real-time operation (independent of the external computer system) are lost.

References

[1] McCulloch W S and Pitts W (1943) A logical calculus of the ideas immanent in nervous activity *Bull. Math. Biophys.*, **5** 115-133
[2] Hubel D H and Wiesel T N (1962) Receptive fields, binocular interaction and functional architecture in the cat's visual cortex *J. Physiol.* (Lond.), **160**, 106-154
[3] Macukow B (1974) Analysis of the net composed of neuron-like elements and investigation of the edges influence *Control Cybernet.* **3**, 65-78
[4] Macukow B (1985) A neuronal model for pattern recognition and learning, in press
[5] Campbell E W and Robson J G (1968) Application of Fourier analysis to the visibility of gratings *J. Physiol.* (Lond.), **197** 551-566
[6] Sachs M B, Nachmias J and Robson J G (1971) Spatial-frequency channels in human vision *J. Opt. Soc. Am.*, **61/9**, 1176-1186
[7] De Valois K K, De Valois R L and Yund W E (1979) Responses of striate cortex cells to grating and checkerboard patterns *J. Physiol.* (Lond.), **291**, 483-505
[8] Goodman J W (1968) *Introduction to Fourier Optics* McGraw-Hill, San Francisco
[9] Hsu Y-N, Arsenault H H and Yang Y (1982) Digital multiple correlation for pattern recognition *Appl. Opt.*, **21**, 616-620
[10] Hsu Y-N (1983) Shift and rotation invariant pattern recognition. PhD Thesis, Laval University, Quebec, Canada

Representing Three-dimensional Shape

M Brady and A Yuille

MIT Artificial Intelligence Laboratory, 545 Technology Square, Cambridge, MA 02139, USA

Summary: Recent work aimed at generating rich representations of shape for three-dimensional objects is summarized. The curvature patch representation of three-dimensional shape is based on ideas of differential geometry.

Introduction

Manufacturing automation, including robotics, is deficient in a number of ways that prevent its full potential from being realized, especially in automating assembly. Sensory perception, whether of force, touch or vision, is particularly inadequate, and yet it is crucial for inspection, parts acquisition and compliant assembly. Underlying all applications of vision, in particular those to robotics, is the need for rich representations of two- and three-dimensional shape having local support.

Most current robotic vision systems are two-dimensional. Shape is represented in terms of global features such as the centre of area. Such features can be computed reasonably efficiently, and are reasonably insensitive to noise, but they fail to deal with occlusion, and are useful mainly for inspecting for gross defects (see ref. 1 for discussion). Brady & Asada[1] have introduced a representation of two-dimensional shape called smoothed local symmetries. It can make more detailed shape descriptions allowing more flexible recognition and inspection.

Much less work has been done to exploit three-dimensional vision for automation. The next section summarizes recent progress in three-dimensional vision. A key problem is to develop rich representations of three-dimensional shape analogous to smoothed local symmetries. This paper reports progress on that problem.

We propose a symbolic representation of visible surfaces based on curvature patches, which provide a local co-ordinate system for describing pieces of a surface, analogous to local symmetries for a two-dimensional shape. The essential idea is to locally determine tangent vectors that indicate directions in which the surface change, for example its curvature, is intrinsically important. Example directions include the principal curvature directions and the directions in which the normal curvature is zero. Smooth changes in curvature patch descriptions are computed, in a manner analogous to region growing, to determine the larger-scale structure of a surface, for example the fact that it is a surface of revolution, a developable or ruled surface, or a generalized cone. We demonstrate the computation of principal curvatures of example surfaces.

Background

Work in image understanding[2-4] has centred on the development of modules that compute three-dimensional depth or depth gradients. Such modules include: shape from stereo;[5-6] shape from shading[7] and photometric stereo; shape from contour (see the **Curvature patches** section); shape from motion.[8] Other work has concentrated on shape from texture.[9] In applying vision to robotics, direct range finding and structured light have been investigated as techniques for recovering depth.[10-14] Although the work referred to in this paragraph is currently largely experimental, it is clear that robust, efficient, practical three-dimensional vision systems will soon be available.

Several authors have suggested that the output of the 'shape from' processes listed above is a representation variously called the 2½-D sketch,[4] the needle map and Gaussian image[15] and intrinsic images.[16] It is supposed that this (or these) representation(s) make explicit information such as the local surface normal. There are several unresolved issues, including: the parameterization of the local surface normal; whether depth is made explicit or computed by integration; whether second-order quantities, such as the Hessian, the principal curvatures (or some combination of them) or the second fundamental form of the surface, are made explicit or computed by differentiation; how accurately information is recorded in the representation(s) and how susceptible it is to noise; how many separate representations are maintained. The last of these points bears on the issue of multiple scales of representation of surfaces, discussed by Tersopoulos.[17]

Of the names proposed for the representation of visible surfaces, 'intrinsic image' is particularly apt, since the representation, completed by interpolation, has a lack of structure similar to an image. Just as applications of two-dimensional vision depend on the development of rich descriptions, so will applications of three-dimensional vision. To this end we are developing a representation of visible surfaces called curvature patches.

First, we need to choose a suitable representation of a local piece of surface. Several definitions are possible, including formulations based on the familiar notion of neighbourhood of a metric or topological space. The local representation we propose blends ideas from three sources: (i) observations about human perception of surface curves; (ii) the definition of parameterized surface patch developed in computer-aided design; (iii) the work on surface interpolation discussed in the previous section.

Stevens[18] has discussed the perception of drawings, such as that shown in Figure 1, as three-dimensional surfaces. He suggests that people are mostly only capable of making qualitative judgements of surface shape, such as the sign of the Gaussian curvature. In general, it appears that surface contours are often interpreted either as lines of curvature, whether or not they are planar, or as asymptotes, lines along which the normal curvature is zero. It is also clear that we can make quantitative estimates of surface curvature, even in impoverished line drawings like those in Figure 1.

Ikeuchi et al.[19] and Brou[20] propose a representation of surface shape called the extended Gaussian image (EGI). The EGI suppresses spatial structure, in part because the Gaussian curvature is a divergence expression. One argument in support of such a representation, advanced by several authors, supposes that second-differential quantities such as the Gaussian curvature and the principal curvatures cannot be computed reliably. We will later provide evidence that they can.

Figure 1 Interpreting line drawings as surfaces

It requires two parameters, say u and v, to define a surface $r(u, v)$. Computer-aided design (CAD) has developed the idea of a surface patch formed by quantitizing the parameters u and v. Typically the values of $r(u_i, v_j)$, $r_v(u_i, v_j)$, $r_{uv}(u_i, v_j)$ and, sometimes, $r_{uu}(u_i, v_j)$ and $r_{vv}(u_i, v_j)$, are given at the patch corners (u_i, v_j). The surface is then interpolated by a suitable set of blending functions, such as the cubic blending functions of Ferguson, Coons, Forrest and Bezier.[21,22] Other work uses splines in tension and bicubic splines.

The representations of surfaces proposed for CAD are a compromise between numerical convenience and the desire to achieve perceptual 'fairing' of a surface. Although they have been of immense practical value in the design of ships, aeroplanes and automobiles, current CAD techniques are not completely satisfactory. Surfaces often have unaesthetic highlights or portions that appear flattened.

Generally, no restriction is placed on the choice of parameterization u and v of a surface in CAD. Typically, parameterizations are chosen for analytical convenience, or for convenience in design, as a network of points is defined in crosssections or by 'lofting'. We saw above, however, that the lines in drawings such as Figure 1 are not interpreted arbitrarily but, most often, as lines of curvature. Choice of the surface parameterization so that the webbings are the lines of curvature has some convenient consequences. First, since the lines of curvature are mutually perpendicular at a point, r_u, r_v, and the surface normal n, which is their normalized cross-product, form a local orthogonal co-ordinate frame. It is easy to show[23] that parametric curves are lines of curvature if and only if the first and second fundamental forms of the surface are diagonal. This is if and only if $r_u^T r_v = n^T r_{uv} = 0$. It follows that the principal curvatures are especially easy to compute, being $n^T r_{uu}/r_u^2$ and $n^T r_{vv}/r_v^2$.

In the case of tensor-product patches, for example Ferguson patches, where the parameterization is additionally chosen to correspond to the lines of curvature, the defining matrix

$$\begin{bmatrix} r(0,0) & r(0,1) & r_v(0,0) & r_v(0,1) \\ r(1,0) & r(1,1) & r_v(1,0) & r_v(1,1) \\ r_u(0,0) & r_u(0,1) & r_{uv}(0,0) & r_{uv}(0,1) \\ r_u(1,0) & r_u(1,1) & r_{uv}(1,0) & r_{uv}(1,1) \end{bmatrix}$$

is essentially lower triangular. This is also true if the blending functions are chosen to achieve specified cross-boundary second derivatives, and the matrix is 6 x 6. Ferguson's original formulation assumed that the cross-derivative r_{uv} was zero. Faux and Pratt (p.15)[22] observe that 'a notable application of this restricted type of patch is in the APT surface-fitting routine FMILL'. However, Forrest (Appendix 2)[21] claims that assuming the cross-derivative is zero at all webbing intersection points (u_i, v_j) produces the appearance of local flattening of the interpolated surface near patch corners. He notes that the effect is minimized when the webbings are coincident with lines of curvature.

We remarked earlier that the representations of surfaces proposed for CAD are a compromise between numerical convenience and the desire to achieve perceptual 'fairing' of a surface. In fact, this remark essentially applies to the choice of blending functions that define the interpolation of the surface from the information at the patch corners. A thin-plate theory of surface interpolation has been developed[17,24] to model human perception of surfaces. It is suggested that curvature patch surfaces are perceptually 'fairer' than bicubic splines and the other surfaces developed in CAD. Assuming that the claim is correct, it may be objected that the perceptual advantage has been bought at the cost of considerable computation. For von Neumann computers this is probably so. However, the algorithms implemented by Grimson[6] and Terzopoulos[17] are inherently well suited to being computed efficiently by arrays of microprocessors.

The idea of interpolating a surface by a minimization process has been hinted at, though not to my knowledge stated explicitly, in the CAD literature. Mehlum[25] observes that the non-linear splines he develops by a variational technique could 'serve as patch boundaries'. Nielson[26] observes that splines under tension can be characterized as functions that minimize an appropriate norm (cf. Terzopoulos[17] use of Sobolev norms) and he proposes an alternative called ν-splines. Finally, Pilcher[27] fits an elastic skin to the given points. The membrane typically only guarantees continuity, however, not smoothness.

We conclude that (i) human perception of line drawings suggests that curves are attributed significance in terms of the underlying surface, often being interpreted as principal lines of curvature; (ii) there are advantages to using such curves as the webbing in a CAD patch representation of a surface; (iii) Terzopoulos' work on surface interpolation has advantages over conventional techniques. In the next section, we develop a representation based on these observations.

Curvature patches

We begin by defining a set of local descriptors at all points on a surface. Then we determine tangent vectors that indicate directions in which the surface change, for example its curvature, is intrinsically important. More precisely, at each point of the surface, we define a set of intrinsic directions $\theta_i(x, y)$ and we compute a corresponding descriptor $\delta_i(x, y)$ for each of them. Currently, our set of intrinsic directions consists of the directions of principal curvature and the asymptotic directions (directions in which the normal curvature is zero). The corresponding descriptors $\delta_i(x, y)$ are the principal curvatures and, for the asymptotes, the geodesic curvature. We may find it necessary to incorporate additional intrinsically important directions in due course, though the principal curvatures and zero normal curvature directions suffice for a broad class of analytic surfaces that includes surfaces of revolution, ruled and developable surfaces, and generalized cones.

The directions and descriptors are local statements about the surface. Next, we attempt to determine the larger-scale structure of the surface by growing contours on the surface that either (i) correspond to small smooth changes in the descriptors δ_i in the directions θ_i, for example contours along which a descriptor is constant, or (ii) are constrained space curves, for example are planar. In general, some of the local descriptors will not propagate far, while others will, giving a (relatively) global description of the surface. Whereas local surface structure is thoroughly discussed in differential geometry, the (relatively) global structure we are computing is not.

Consider first a surface of revolution. Suppose that the axis is aligned with the z axis. The surface is formed by rotating the (one-parameter) curve $p(u)i + z(u)k$ about k. The surface is $r(u, \theta) = p(u)\cos\theta i + p(u)\sin\theta j + z(u)k$. The principal curvatures (see, for example, Millman & Parker[28]) are the meridians and the parallels, all of which are planar. In addition, the parallels are circular, so the curvature along any one of them is constant. The curvature along a parallel is $n^T \dot{r}/p(u)$, where $\dot{r} = (\cos\theta \sin\theta 0)^T$. The foreshortening of the expected curvature $p(u)$ exemplifies Meusnier's theorem.[23] On the other hand, the asymptotes on a surface of revolution are, in general, complex space curves and the geodesic curvature is a complex function of position along the asymptote.

As a second example, consider a ruled surface, such as the helicoid of a single blade ($\rho\cos\theta$, $\rho\sin\theta$, $k\theta$) (the surface of a uniformly twisted ribbon). The principal curvatures are functions of the parameterization (ρ, θ) and vary from point to point. The lines of curvature are complex space curves. The asymptotes correspond to the rulings and to the helices. Together these form an intuitively satisfying description of the helicoid.

It may be objected (see, for example, Stevens[18]) that the important point about the rulings is that they are geodesics. However, there are at once too many geodesics and, in many cases, too few. There are too many since there is a geodesic through every point on a surface in every direction. The geodesics on a cylinder, for example, are all the helices ($R\cos\theta$, $R\sin\theta$, $k\theta$), where R is the radius of the cylinder. On the other hand, only those meridians of a surface of revolution that are extrema of the surface width (skeletons, see below) are geodesics.

As a final example, we consider generalized cones. Marr[29] considered a restricted class of generalized cones that he called generalized cylinders, whose axis is a straight line. Based on considerations of volumetric representations, he suggested that a generalized cylinder is effectively represented by (i) those cross-sections, called skeletons, for which the expansion function attains an extreme value; (ii) the tracings, called flutings, for which the cross-section function attains an extreme value. (A tracing is the space curve formed by a point of the cross-section contour as the cross-section is drawn along the axis.) We have recently proved the following theorem: If the axis of a generalized cone is planar, and the eccentricity of the cone is zero, then (i) a cross-section is a line of curvature if either the generalized cone is a surface of revolution or the cross-section is a skeleton; (ii) a tracing is a line of curvature if the generalized cone is a tube surface (the expansion function is a constant) or the tracing is a fluting. It follows that the flutings and skeletons of a (planar axis) generalized cone are implied by both surface-based curvature patches and Marr's considerations of volumetric representations.

Figure 2 shows the representation at which we are aiming. The smooth surfaces s_1 and s_3 are planar, while s_2 is described symbolically by using the hierarchy of surface types suggested in differential geometry. The curves c_i are all circles in this case. More generally, they are space curves. One important fact about them is that they are the curves of intersection of a pair of surfaces. They are given additional descriptors only in special cases, such as when they are planar.

a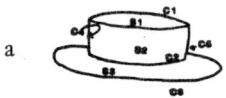

b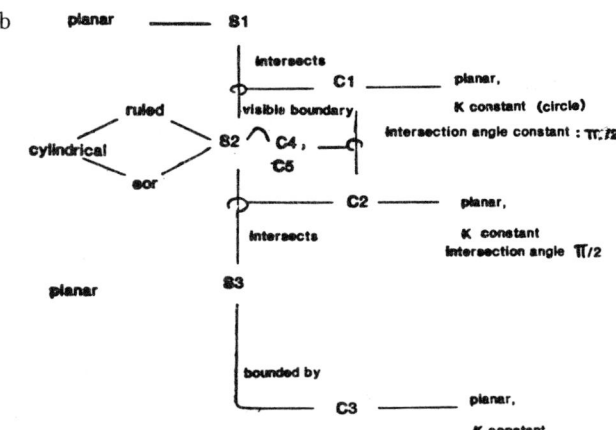

Figure 2 Representation at which we are aiming. a, (full) Intrinsic surface; b, the representation makes explicit important information about the smooth surfaces and about their curves of intersection

Brou[20] has recently built a two-laser single-camera scanning device that computes accurate depth information along 'stripes' on the surface. It is accurate to about 0.5mm. Brou's system computes a dense map: but occasionally points are missed, leaving holes in the surface. We use Terzopoulos' multigrid algorithm to compute full-depth maps at a variety of scales. Figure 3 shows the raw data obtained from Brou's system for a styrofoam cup. Figure 4 shows the multiple-scale versions of Figure 3 obtained by Terzopoulos' program. Figure 5 shows the directions of curvature computed for the styrofoam cup. Figure 6 shows the lines of curvature of a cylindrical pen, computed in the same way, and Figure 7 shows

Representing Three-dimensional Shape   267

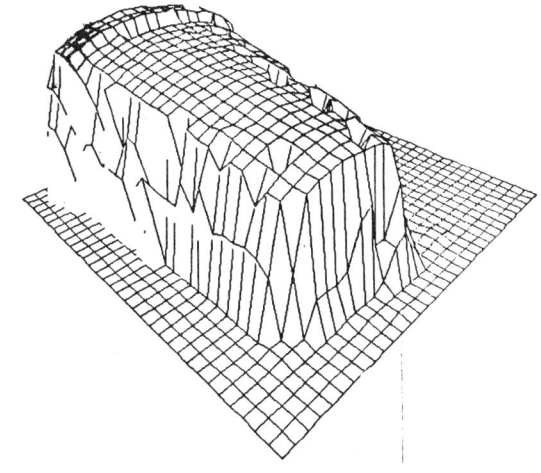

Figure 3 Raw depth data obtained from Brou's structured light system for a styrofoam cup

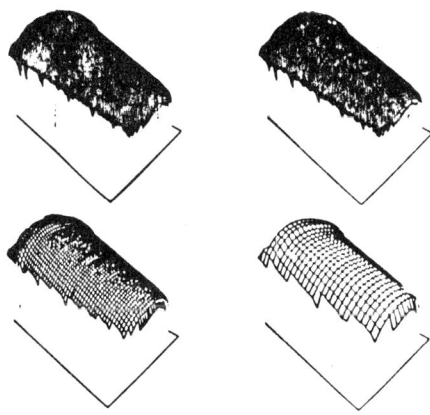

Figure 4 Multiple-scale representations of the styrofoam cup, the result of processing the data in Figure 3 by Terzopoulos' program

them for a light bulb. Finally, Figure 8 shows the regions of the light bulb for which the Gaussian curvature is positive and negative, demonstrating that the asymptotes can be computed.

We are currently experimenting with techniques such as relaxation for propagating the local descriptors to extract a tesselation of the surface along intrinsic

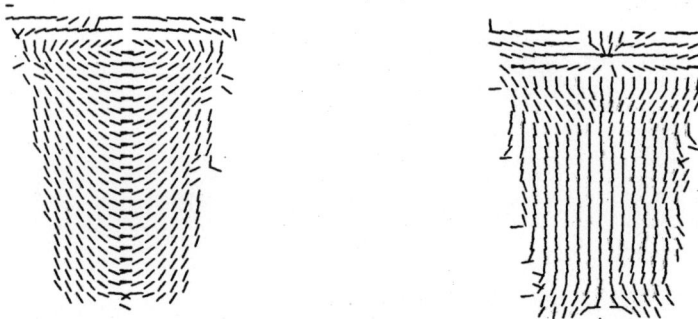

Figure 5 Lines of curvature computed for the next to coarsest representation shown in Figure 4

Figure 6 Lines of curvature found for a cylindrical pen

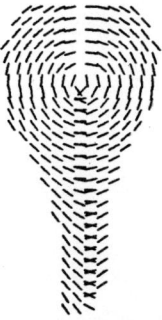

Figure 7 Lines of curvature found for a light bulb in the next to coarsest representation

Figure 8 Segmentation of the light-bulb surface according to the sign of the Gaussian curvature. Black indicates negative Gaussian curvature and white positive. This demonstrates that the asymptotes are computable, either directly or as zero crossings of the Gaussian curvature

contours. The principal application of the curvature patch representation is to recognize objects in a CAD database from surface layout, and to simultaneously compute the viewpoint. However, Agre is using the curvature patch representation to develop a program that learns how and where to grasp three-dimensional objects with a multifingered hand. Since we also have intensity data, we will be able to test Yuille's theorems about directional edge finders as well, which suggest that the principal curvatures are directly computable in an image.

This report describes research done at the Artificial Intelligence Laboratory of the Massachusetts Institute of Technology. Support for the laboratory's artificial intelligence research is provided in part by the Advanced Research Projects Agency of the Department of Defense under Office of Naval Research contract N00014-75-C-0643, the Office of Naval Research under contract number N0014-80-C-0505 and the System Development Foundation.

References

[1] Brady M & Asada (1983)
[2] Ballard D H & Brown C M (1982) *Computer Vision* Prentice-Hall,
[3] Brady M (1982) Computational approaches to image understanding *Computing Surveys*, **14**, 3-71
[4] Marr D (1982) *Vision* Freeman, San Francisco
[5] Baker H & Binford T O (1981) Depth from edge and intensity based stereo. *Int. J. Conf. Artif. Intell.*,
[6] Grimson W F I (1981) *From Images to Surfaces: a Computational Study of the Human Early Visual System* MIT Press, Cambridge
[7] Ikeuchi K & Horn B K P (1981) Numerical shape from shading and occluding boundaries *Artif. Intell.* **17**, 141-185
[8] Bruss & Horn B K P (1981)
[9] Vilnrotter F, Nevatia R & Price K E (1981) *Structural Analysis of Natural Textures* Proc. Image Understanding Workshop, ed. L S Baumann, pp. 61-68
[10] Agin G J (1980) Computer vision systems for industrial inspection and assembly. *Computer*, **13**, 11-1

[11] Holland S W, Rossol I & Ward M R (1979) CONSIGHT 1: a vision controlled robot system for transferring parts from belt conveyors. In *Computer Vision and Sensor Based Robots* eds G Dodd & I Rossol, Plenum Press, New York
[12] Bolles R C (1983)
[13] Faugeras O D et al. (1982) Towards a flexible vision system. In *Robot Vision* ed. A Pugh. IFS, UK
[14] Porter G & Mundy J (1982) *A Non-contact Profile Sensor System for Visual Inspections* IEEE Workshop on Ind. Appl. of Mach. Vis.
[15] Horn B K P (1982) Sequins and quills – representations for surface topography. In *Representation of 3-Dimensional Objects* ed R Bajcsy, Springer Verlag, Heidelberg
[16] Barrow & Tenenbaum (1978)
[17] Terzopoulos D (1983) Multi-level reconstruction of visual surfaces. In *Computer Graphics and Image Processing*.
[18] Stevens K A (1981) The visual interpretation of surface contours. In *Artif.Intelligence*, **17**, 47-75
[19] Ikeuchi K, Horn B K P (1984) Picking up an object from a pile of objects. First Int. Symp. on Robotics Research eds M Brady & P Richard, MIT Press, Cambridge
[20] Brou, P (1983) *Finding the Orientation of Objects in Vector Maps* MIT Press, Cambridge
[21] Forrest A R (1972) On Coons and other methods for the representation of curved surfaces. Comput. Gr. Im. Proc., **1**, 341-359
[22] Faux, I D & Pratt M J (1979) *Computational Geometry for Design and Manufacture* Ellis Horwood, Chichester
[23] Weatherburn C F (1927) *Differential Geometry of Three Dimensions*, Cambridge University Press, Cambridge, p. 72
[24] Brady M & Horn B K P (1983)
[25] Mehlum F (1974) Nonlinear splines. In *Computer Aided Geometric Design* eds Barnhill & Riesenfeld, p. 175
[26] Nielson G M (1974) Some piecewise polynomial alternatives to splines under tension. In *Computer Aided Geometric Design* eds   Barnhill & Riesenfeld,
[27] Pilcher D T (1974) Smooth parametric surfaces. In *Computer Aided Geometric Design* eds Barnhill & Riesenfeld
[28] Millman R S & Parker G D (1977) *Elements of Differential Geometry* Prentice-Hall, p. 86
[29] Marr D (1977) Analysis of occluding contour. *Proc. R. Soc. Lond. Biol. Sci.* **197**, 441-475

An Electropneumatic Actuation System for the Utah/MIT Dextrous Hand

S C Jacobsen, D F Knutti, K B Biggers, E K Iversen and J E Wood

Center for Biomedical Design, Department of Mechanical and Industrial Engineering, University of Utah, USA

Introduction

General comments

The Center for Biomedical Design at the University of Utah and the Artificial Intelligence Laboratory at the Massachusetts Institute of Technology are developing a tendon-operated multiple-degree-of-freedom (MDOF) robotic hand with multi-channel touch-sensing capability (see Figures 1 and 2).

The project includes a number of subdevelopment activities which are more generally described[1] and which are itemized as follows: (1) the definition of required control systems; (2) the design of hand and wrist structures; (3) the development of touch sensors and other monitoring transducers; (4) the development of high-strength polymeric tendons; (5) the design and construction of a high-performance electropneumatic actuator.

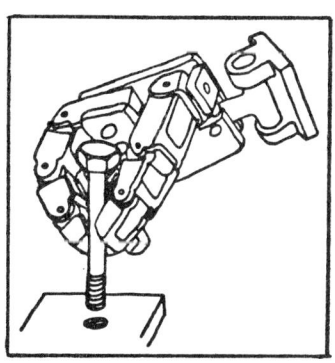

Figure 1 Dextrous hand

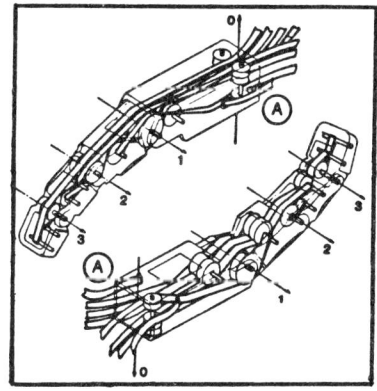

Figure 2 Tendon routing

The fifth area, actuator design, is critical to the project's success. In fact, actuator capabilities are probably the most important determinants of overall dextrous-hand (DH) performance. This paper reviews our actuator development project in the following sections: (1) introductory comments; (2) controlled pressure pneumatic valve; (3) complete one-joint actuator system; (4) conclusions.

General actuator requirements

The first DH will be approximately anthropomorphic in both geometry and size. The complete hand will include three each four-degree-of-freedom (4DOF) fingers, one 4DOF thumb and a 3DOF wrist for hand orientation.

Our general goal is to produce a hand which exhibits static and dynamic performance levels roughly equivalent to the natural human hand. To achieve this goal, the fingers must be capable of producing motions with frequency components up to 6 Hz. Since actuators are to be used in feedback configurations which can degrade system bandwidth and stability, the actuators are being designed to generate a flat response for small motions up to frequencies of approximately 30 Hz. To develop required finger-grasping forces the actuators are being designed to produce tendon tensions from 0 to 300 N with excursions of 3 cm.

Since 38 actuators are to be used they must be compact, somewhat energy conservative and lightweight. To ensure smooth well-controlled operation of the hand, a number of undesirable characteristics must be eliminated including backlash, striction and excessive intrinsic damping. Furthermore, it is our intention to produce an actuation system that exhibits extremely low mechanical output impedence (force-source behaviour). Important characteristics such as compliance and damping will be modulated via a smart controller using feedback information from various sensors.

Selection of actuator system

At the beginning of our project both electric and hydraulic systems were investigated but rejected. Pneumatic systems were eventually explored and finally selected as the most desirable approach, provided that certain problems associated with pneumatic systems could be solved. The pneumatic approach allows for the construction of a low-weight compact actuator which can generate required speeds and forces. In our case we are developing a valve which produces a specified pressure in response to its input electrical signal (see Figure 3). The pressure is then applied to a glass/graphite cylinder assembly which develops an output force with very low frictional effects. The actuator, operating within its bandwidth limits, produces

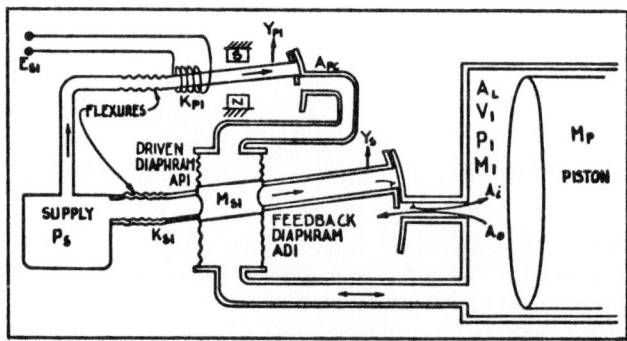

Figure 3 Valve schematic

a velocity-independent and position-independent force thus eliminating some of the undesirable effects of compressibility usually associated with pneumatic systems.

Control issues

When high-performance valve/cylinder combinations are operated as antagonist force sources, modulated via feedback to produce a position controller, the resulting system is highly oscillatory (Figure 4). Although space limitations preclude a detailed discussion of various control approaches which can adjust system behaviour, two brief comments can be made to clarify the problem. First, to achieve performance levels illustrated in later sections, it was necessary to use non-linear adaptive stiffness and damping terms modulated by a valve-dedicated controller. Secondly, to eventually maximize system performance, it will probably be necessary to use system-model based controllers for this class of systems which are further described.[2]

Controlled-pressure pneumatic valve

Version I configuration

The development of a viable pneumatic valve has been a challenging task (see Figures 3 and 4). Electropneumatic valves possess significant inherent non-linearities due to complex dynamic and fluid mechanical interactions and they require the

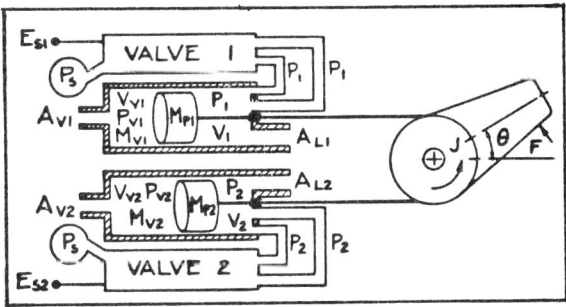

Figure 4 One-joint model

maintenance of close precision in both component fabrication and assembly. After design, construction and testing of a number of alternative basic configurations, the system shown in Figure 3 was produced. The valve includes two stages. The first stage is an electromagnetically deflected jet pipe which, in response to an input current, produces an output pressure to drive the second stage. The second stage is a higher-flow capacity deflection jet-pipe system which is positioned by antagonist diaphragms. The upper diaphragm is pressurized by the first-stage valve and the lower diaphragm is pressurized by the load being driven. The resulting behaviour of the entire valve is then as a pressure source which is modulated by the input current applied to the first stage of the valve.

Performance of valve driving a controlled slightly leaky volume

Performance of the valve can be investigated by using two fundamental experiments.

Fixed-volume test

The valve drives a fixed slightly leaky volume (Figure 5). Note that the valve must alternately fill and vent the gas from the chamber as the desired pressure is varied sinusoidally. The gain-phase plot shown by trace a in Figure 7 briefly illustrates the result of a sequence of actual tests.

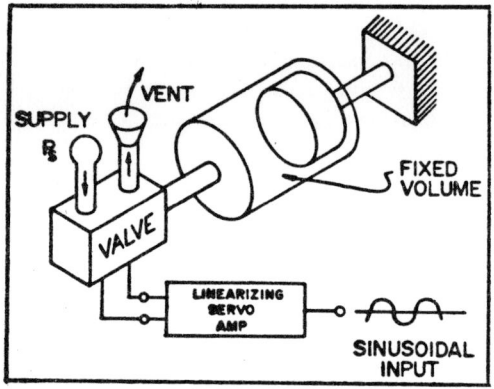

Figure 5 Fixed-volume set-up

Oscillating-volume test

The configuration for the oscillatory-load test is shown in Figure 6. At a given stroke-volume range and frequency the valve attempts to regulate pressure at a specified set point. As the frequency increases the valve becomes less capable of maintaining the pressure as shown by trace a of the gain/phase plot in Figure 8.

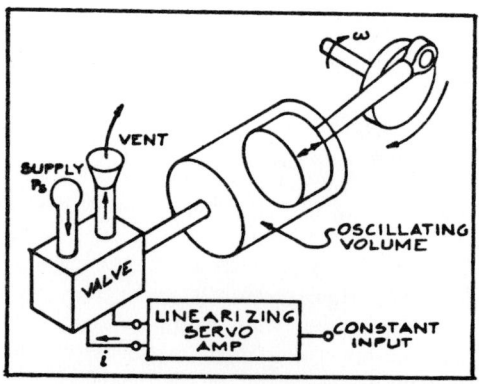

Figure 6 Oscillating-volume set-up

Version I valve model

A schematic of the lumped parameter non-linear model for version I valve is shown in Figure 3. By including all terms, the valve model was approximately eighth order. However, after a sequence of experiments the model was simplified to a fifth-order system.

The model for the preliminary stage is represented by two first-order lags. The first time constant modulates the response of the jet pipe to the input signal and the second time constant represents the charging of the primary diaphragm chamber ($\tau_1 = 0.004$ s) ($\tau_2 = 0.005$ s).

By neglecting the resistance of the feedback orifice, the second stage was represented by a third-order system. Because of the moderate pressures and temperatures involved, the following mass-continuity equations are applicable:[3]

$$M_1 = \frac{P_1 V_1}{RT} = \int (\dot{M}_{in} - \dot{M}_{out})\, dt$$

where, if $0.5 < \dfrac{P_1}{Ps} < 1$ $\quad \dot{M}_{in} = \dfrac{(K)(Ps)(A_i)}{\sqrt{T}}$ (2) $\sqrt{\dfrac{P_1}{Ps}\left(1 - \dfrac{P_1}{Ps}\right)}$

or if $\dfrac{P_1}{Ps} \leqslant 0.5$ $\quad \dot{M}_{in} = \dfrac{(K)(Ps)(A_i)}{\sqrt{T}}$

and, if $0.5 < \dfrac{Pa}{P_1} < 1$ $\quad \dot{M}_{out} = \dfrac{(K)(P_1)(A_o)}{\sqrt{T}}$ (2) $\sqrt{\dfrac{Pa}{P_1}\left(1 - \dfrac{Pa}{P_1}\right)}$

or if $\dfrac{Pa}{P_1} \leqslant 0.5$ $\quad \dot{M}_{out} = \dfrac{(K)(P_1)(A_o)}{\sqrt{T}}$

The areas A_i and A_o are a function of displacement of the secondary jet pipe Ys which is given by the following force balance equation

$$(A_d)[(P_{p_1}) - (P_{d_1})] = (M_{s_1})(\ddot{Y}s) + (B_1)(\dot{Y}s) + (K_s)(Ys)$$

Comparison between valve model and actual version I valve

The differences between the performance of the actual valve (trace a) and the Valve I model (trace b) in Figures 7 and 8 can be attributed primarily to simplifications made to the model to decrease computation time.

Version II valve design

Based on valve simulations with the version I valve model presented previously, several modifications to the version I valve were determined to be advantageous. These modifications include the following: (1) larger charging and venting areas in primary and secondary stages; (2) lighter diaphragm back plate; (3) linearization of primary stage output by modifying the shape of the charging and venting restrictions. The improvements in performance are shown in trace c of Figures 7 and 8.

276 S C Jacobsen *et al.*

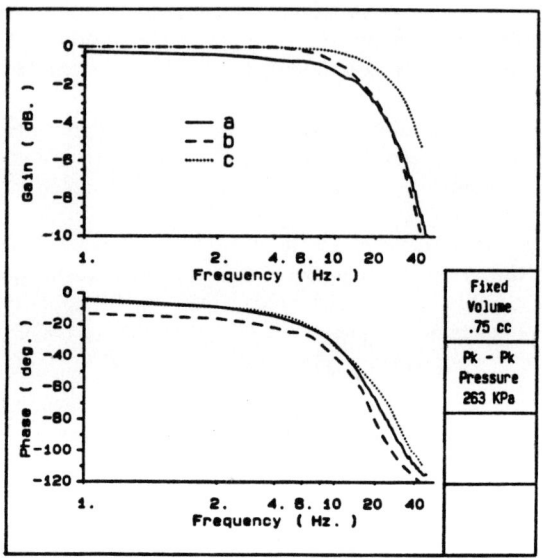

Figure 7 Gain phase plot of the actual system during a fixed volume test of actual valve (trace a), version I valve model (trace b) and version II valve model (trace c)

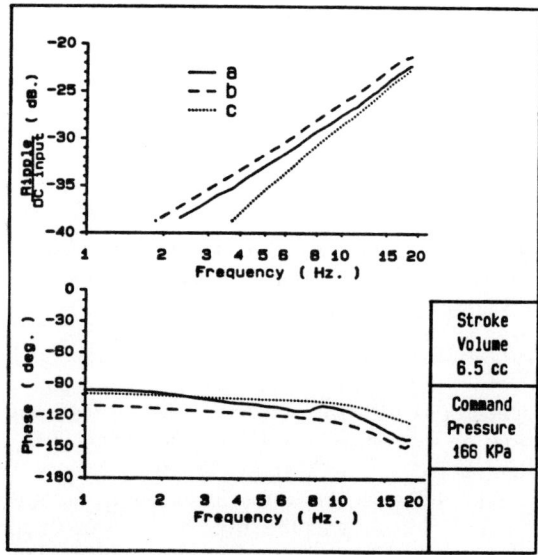

Figure 8 Gain phase plot of oscillating-volume test of actual valve (trace a), version I valve model (trace b) and version II model (trace c)

Complete one-joint actuation system

Performance of actual system

A prototype joint actuation system was constructed for evaluation of valves, cylinders and control schemes. Although space limitations do not permit extensive discussion of the actual machine, Figure 9 illustrates free motion of the system (with no touch forces present) in response to a step command in angular position. Note that the plot shows the system response utilizing the single-joint control equations discussed.[1]

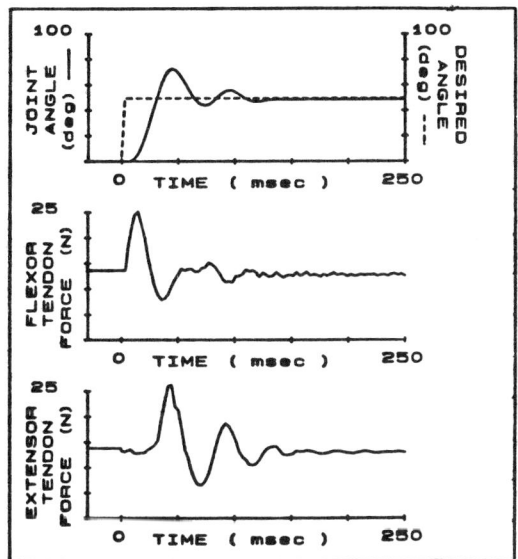

Figure 9 Response of actual one-joint actuation system with version I valve

Model of one-joint actuation system

The lumped parameter model of the complete one-joint actuation system is shown in Figure 4. Note that an explanation of parameters is listed in the Appendix.

In addition to the version I valve model equations shown previously for each of the two valves, the following equations were needed to simulate the one-joint actuation system.

Mass-continuity equations

Cylinder no. 1 Charging chamber $M_1 = \int (\dot{M}_{in} - \dot{M}_{out})\, dt = (P_1)(V_1)/(R)(T)$
Cylinder no. 1 Vent chamber $Mv_1 = \int (\dot{M}_{in} - \dot{M}_{out})\, dt = (Pv_1)(Vv_1)/(R)(T)$
Cylinder no. 2 Charging chamber $M_2 = \int (\dot{M}_{in} - \dot{M}_{out})\, dt = (P_2)(V_2)/(R)(T)$
Cylinder no. 2 Vent chamber $Mv_2 = \int (\dot{M}_{in} - \dot{M}_{out})\, dt = (Pv_2)(Vv_2)/(R)(T)$
where M_{in} and M_{out} are the mass-flow equations shown previously.[3]

Volume/piston-displacement equations

| $V_1 = V_{10} + (Ap)(X_1)$ | $V_2 = V_{20} + (Ap)(X_2)$ | cylinder no. 1 |
| $Vv_1 = Vv_{10} - (Ap)(X_1)$ | $Vv_2 = Vv_{20} - (Ap)(X_2)$ | cylinder no. 2 |

Dynamic-force and torque equations

$(Ap_1)(P_1 - Pv_1) = (Mp_1)(\ddot{X}_1) + (B_1)(\dot{X}_1) \pm F_{f1} + F_{t1}$ piston no. 1

$(Ap_2)(P_2 - Pv_2) = (Mp_2)(\ddot{X}_2) + (B_2)(\dot{X}_2) \pm F_{f2} + F_{t2}$ piston no. 2

$(r)\{[(\theta)(r) - X_1](K_{t1}) - [(\theta)(r) - X_2](K_{t2})\} = (J)(\ddot{\theta}) + (B_3)(\dot{\theta}) + T_f + T_L$ (joint)

By utilizing data relating to the cylinders and the version I valve models, the one-joint actuation system model was employed to predict the performance shown in Figure 10 (trace a).

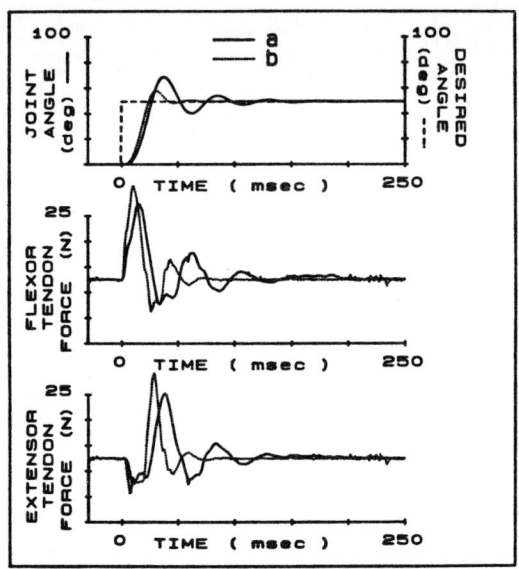

Figure 10 Simulated responses of one-joint actuation system with version I valve (trace a) and version II valve (trace b) (see Appendix; note)

Performance with version II valve

Trace b of Figure 10 shows operation of the model utilizing an initial optimized version II valve with cylinder parameters also slightly modified. Observe the improvement in rise time with the damping ratio remaining similar to the version I system. These data represent only a first attempt at valve optimization. Additional iterations should produce a higher-performance system.

Conclusions

A system of pneumatic components has been designed to produce a two-stage jet-pipe pneumatic valve which produces a specified pressure in response to valve input current. The dynamics of the version I system have been experimentally characterized via studies of the valve alone and also by experiments with the complete one-joint actuation system.

To proceed with the next stage of optimization, an analytic model of the entire system has been formulated and tested. Initial application of the model has indicated several valve modifications which would produce a version II system with superior performance characteristics. The model will also be used for further development of dedicated control systems capable of stabilizing an actuator configured for very rapid and high-strength operation.

References

[1] Jacobsen S C, Wood J E, Knutti D F and Biggers K B (1983) The Utah/MIT Dextrous hand: work in progress. *Int. J. Robotics Res.*, in press
[2] Cannon R H and Schmitz E (1983) *Precise Control of Flexible Manipulators*, report from Department of Aeronautics, Stanford University, California
[3] Andersen B W (1976) *The Analysis and Design of Pneumatic Systems* Robert E. Kreiger Publishing, New York

Appendix

Nomenclature

Ad	= area of diaphragm	Pa	= ambient pressure
Ai	= cylinder-charging area	Ps	= supply pressure
Ao	= cylinder-venting area	Pv_1	= pressure-vent chamber no. 1
Ap_1	= area of piston no. 1	Pv_2	= pressure-vent chamber no. 2
Ap_2	= area of piston no. 2	P_1	= pressure in cylinder no. 1
B_1	= viscous damping piston no. 1	P_2	= pressure in cylinder no. 2
B_2	= viscous damping piston no. 2	r	= radius of joint pulley
B_3	= viscous damping joint	R	= universal gas constant
Ff_1	= friction piston no. 1	T	= temperature
Ff_2	= friction piston no. 2	Tf	= friction at joint
Ft_1	= force in tendon no. 1	TL	= load at joint
Ft_2	= force in tendon no. 2	Vv_1	= volume-vent chamber no. 1
Jt_2	= joint moment of inertia	Vv_2	= volume-vent chamber no. 2
K	= gas constant	Vv_{10}	= initial volume-vent chamber no. 1
Ks	= spring constant of secondary jet pipe	Vv_{20}	= initial volume-vent chamber no. 2
Kt_1	= spring constant tendon no. 1	V_1	= volume in cylinder no. 1
Kt_2	= spring constant tendon no. 2	V_2	= volume in cylinder no. 2
M	= mass flow	V_{10}	= initial volume cylinder no. 1
Mp_1	= mass piston no. 1	V_{20}	= initial volume cylinder no. 2
Mp_2	= mass piston no. 2	X_1	= displace piston no. 1
Ms_1	= effective mass of diaphragm	X_2	= displace piston no. 2
Mv_1	= mass of air-vent chamber no. 1	Ys	= deflection secondary jet pipe
Mv_2	= mass of air-vent chamber no. 2	τ_1	= deflection time lag
M_1	= mass of air cylinder no. 1	τ_2	= charging time lag
M_2	= mass of air cylinder no. 2	θ	= angular displacement of joint

Note

For Figure 10, the non-linear damping coefficients (see ref. [1] for description of these coefficients) for trace c were changed to take advantage of the increased frequency response of the version II valve model.

Sensor-aided and/or Computer-aided Bilateral Teleoperator System (SCATS)

J Vertut, R Fournier, B Espiau* and G Andre*

CEA-DPT, BP 6, 92260 Fontenay aux Roses, and *IRISA, Campus de Beaulieu, 35042 Rennes, France

Introduction

Teleoperator in this paper is taken to mean remote manipulator(s) on a transporter, possibly on a vehicle with several TV cameras. The computer is introduced in the system to help the operator(s) and to enhance total efficiency. This enables the operator's task for generating all commands to be simplified (co-ordinating motions, changing co-ordinate frame, adapting slave mechanism to its environment and to the task, generating automatic subtasks, controlling the transporter, etc.), and an increase in his decision capability through enriched information feedback (kinesthetic, visual and others).

The computer also monitors the whole system; this provides plan generation and decision making capacity according to the operator(s) and system's respective ability to carry out the task. This ensures as well operating safety of the system itself (with a 'spy' failure detection system) and while executing the task (collision avoidance, force limitation, etc.). It results in shared control between the operator and the computer that must be without any conflict, either in time sharing or in parallel. This work on supervisory control is carried in the framework of the French Advanced Robotics and Automation project (ARA), an advanced teleoperation group.

Architecture of the computer-aided bilateral teleoperator system

As shown in Figure 1, the man-intelligent machine system that we propose comprises three subsystems: master subsystem in the control room with one or several operator(s), a slave subsystem which is the teleoperator itself, and a processing and control subsystem which processes all information and commands.[3] The master subsystem can also comprise press-button control boxes and/or master arms, including controls for vehicle, transporter, cameras, etc., and the various information feedback (vision, forces, etc.).

Figure 1 shows our proposed system architecture, especially designed to prevent conflict between the man and the intelligence level of the system. This representation considers three 'universes'; the master universe with the operator, master subsystem in central room, and the slave subsystem where the task is remotely executed. These universes have a physical significance. The operator physically interacts with the master subsystem and the slave physically modifies the environment into the slave universe. This physical man also senses kinesthetic feedback from the master subsystem and uses the other senses. The sensory man receives

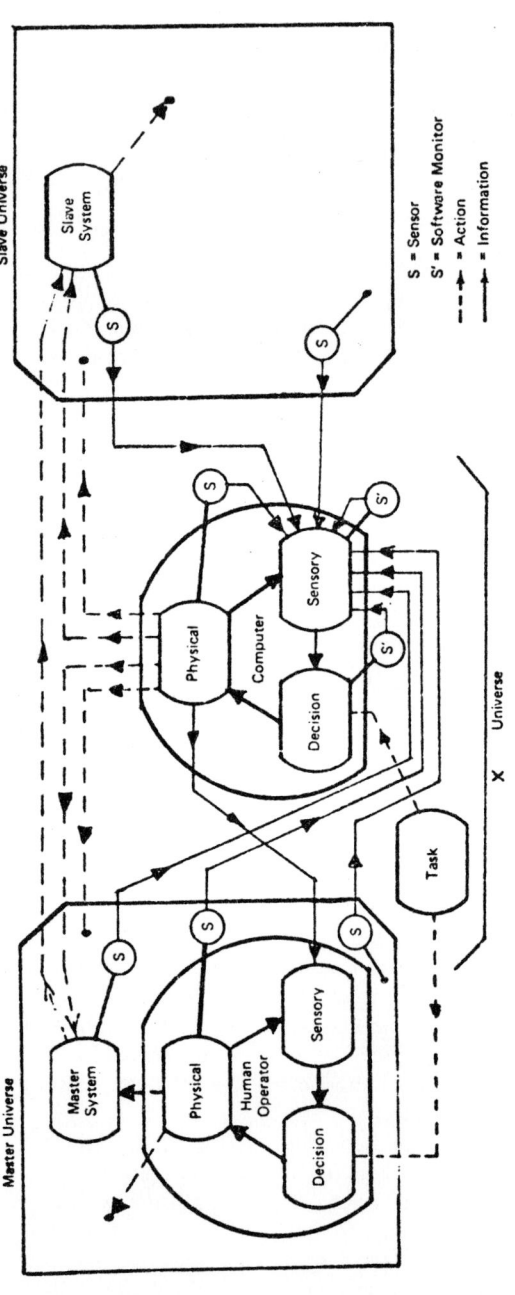

Figure 1 Computer-enhanced teleoperated system

in particular visual feedback for the slave universe and other displays. The man intelligence is also identified as planning and decision making. These three activities of the operator are linked together.

The intelligence level of the operator has a representation (a model) of the task which has no physical location. This model is represented in a mathematical universe X. For easy graphics, the functions of the computer have been located in the X universe, so far as their physical location has no connection to this architectural analysis. There are different sensors, some (S) with a physical existence, others (S') monitor the system by software.

If we consider the existing nuclear teleoperators, all actions and information flow go directly from master universe to slave and back. In the advanced system the computer is 'transparent' to the operator. If we consider only the X universe and slave universe, that system is an advanced robot (after man has completed its preparation).

This system can provide the operator with three kinds of assistance: display synthetic information, safety and substitution (time shared or parallel). In the case of tasks with possible description, the system is an advanced autonomous robot. The present paper deals only with the study and implementation of generalized bilateral control modes with master and slave arms difference (now the same architecture with different positions, soon with a completely different architecture), task DOF sharing with the computer prestored programmed sequences and sensor-aided kinesthetic (force) feedback.

Generalized bilateral force-reflecting position-control mode

This mode can be called generalized master slave, and our colleague A Bejczy used the term generalized bilateral force-reflecting control.[4] We prefer to add 'position' as far as both master and slave arms are controlled in position.

A force-reflecting rate-control mode with corresponding slave rate for master differential position can be included in bilateral force reflecting ... (for both position and rate modes we prefer kinesthetic bilateral-control modes).

Generalized position control

On the Saclay experimental site we use the MA 23 25 kg prototype manipulator[5] and 6 kg capacity standard master as shown in Figure 2, geometrically identical. We can obtain the following modes: *position indexing* to keep operator's hand in the best comfort zone; *scaling up and down* (to scale-down operator 'pumps' by decoupling master and recoupling sequence); reference *frame rotation*, to get the correct hand–eye orientation when TV camera is in a given position.

These indexing and homothetic displacements are processed in a Cartesian frame referred to slave and master arms and co-ordinate transformations are used in both subsystems, with

θm, θe master and slave joint co-ordinate

Xm, Xe Cartesian generalized co-ordinates (position and orientation) of a corresponding point of master and slave terminal

CCm, CCe master and slave co-ordinate transformation.

284 J Vertut et al.

This transformation is written as follows

$$\underline{\theta m} \longrightarrow \boxed{CCm} \xrightarrow{Xm} \boxed{Xe = A\,Xm + Xo} \xrightarrow{Xe} \boxed{CCe^{-1}} \underline{\theta e} \qquad (1)$$

Kinesthetic feedback

Position and force feedbacks are keys of feedback information to ensure remote manipulation performance (when this is impossible, indirect visual force information can be used with lower performance[6,7]).

The force and torque feedback can also be optimized according to the task: *force scaling* (up and down) to reduce fatigue or augment precision; *force indexing*, in particular weight suppression of the tool or of the object. This is a very efficient way of reducing fatigue, as far as constant forces are not of interest compared with relative variations.

On the MA 23 the force and torque vectors are measured from motor currents, by using the master and slave co-ordinate transformations, with

$C_{\theta m}, C_{\theta e}$ master and slave joint torque

Fm, Fe force and torque vector

$[Jm], [Je]$ Jacobian matrix

Figure 2 Generalized position control. 1,

we can write

$$\underline{C_{\theta e}} \longrightarrow \boxed{Je^{-T}} \xrightarrow{\underline{Fe}} \boxed{\underline{Fm} = B\,\underline{Fe} + \underline{Fo}} \xrightarrow{\underline{Fm}} \boxed{Jm^{T}} \longrightarrow \underline{C_{\theta m}}$$

The weight suppression is with Fo vertical. This constant force suppression applies also to any static effort on a tool like cutting or drilling.

Figure 2 shows a 5 kg lead brick 'balanced' in space but any other force is returned to the operator. In this mode the master force—torque feedback includes: *slave inertial forces* (slave inertia plus object mass) used by the operator for dynamic control; *interaction forces* with the environment (friction, impacts), used by the operator to execute the task; noise due to *arm friction*, *delay* due to servo and sampling, etc. This is extremely difficult to reduce and depends on the arm technology; the no-load arm inertia appears again here as a noise. [Dynamic control of the load and arm is nevertheless possible, but feeling of a light object as an inertia is last and the quick manipulation becomes slow. Again this point relies on arm technology. For this reason light objects must be handled with a light arm. (State of art of no-load inertia is half of payload in worst conditions.) Further work to improve this is in progress.]

Man computer sharing control

The implicit sharing is time sharing, by using programming as with industrial robots. Any practical application needing a reasonable extent of self-adaptativity where possible; that means the use of sensors, which will be discussed in the next section.[8]

We concentrated our efforts in parallel sharing between the operator and the control computer, by giving to it some degrees of freedom relative to the task and by leaving to the operator the most important one(s). In particular, we got sensible quality and time improvements on current tasks using control modes with the computer keeping the following geometrical constraints.

Effector tip in a fix point. In this case the master position is free, and bilateral orientation control is possible. This mode is useful to line up some effectors after having adjusted the tip position (initiating screwing, unscrewing, etc.).

Keep effector on a straight line. Then the operator controls this displacement, with additional rotation or not, depending on a second rotation constraint around that line ... (drilling holes, cords, long screwing, etc). This mode can be applied to any given arc as well.

Keep the effector parallel to a given plane. The operator can have two or three degrees of freedom (disc cutting, grinding, etc.) with remaining position and force feedback (see Figure 3).

These experiments impressed master—slave users for ease and safety of operation, due to suppression of the risk to brake drills or discs (these functions are combined with weight suppression). Teaching these functions to the computer requires provision of corresponding parameters in the task-related frame $\underline{Z}$. Operator

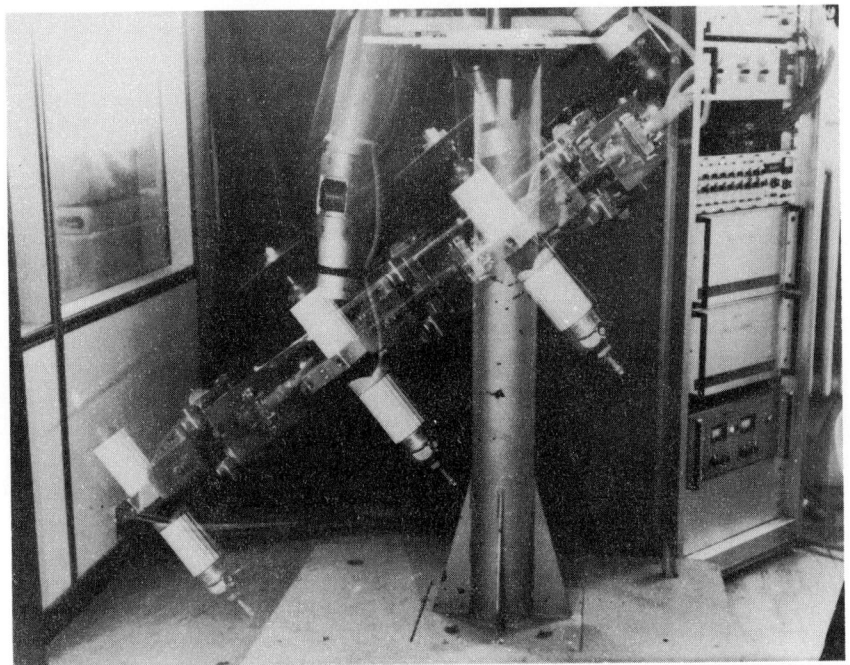

Figure 3 Effector parallel to given plane

command induces real-time definition of functional co-ordinate $\underline{Z}$, selection of those controlled by the master arm (free) and those locked. This is the teaching sequence, followed by execution sequences, selected successively by the operator along the state graph of a mode (sensors can also act in this, see the next section). The structure shown in Figure 4 is implemented on our bilateral servo manipulator.

In this system I is a real-time interpreter that generates commands or sequences of commands for the geometric constraint generator. It proposes to human operator H the menu of possible functions available at the moment phase of execution (teach, play, end), operator errors (syntax or scheduling of commands) and system errors (not executed, no sensor output).

The constraint generator comprises a nucleus N of elementary functions, having access to all variables (operational and functional) of the system and to sensors information. It generates the various position-control modes (relations between master and slave motions) and kinesthetic feedback (inverted relationship), realizes the teaching and keeps parameter memorization.

From the operator's view all this structure is absolutely visible. His communication is via press-buttons or voice control. After mode selection, parameters are given on line (plan, line, etc.) by direct teaching when positioning the effector and initiating 'play' by pressing a switch or by voice. Force feedback then gives a kinesthetic feeling of the constraint. On request the operator can 'release', move parameters and 'play' again. This appears to provide a new semi-kinesthetic language.

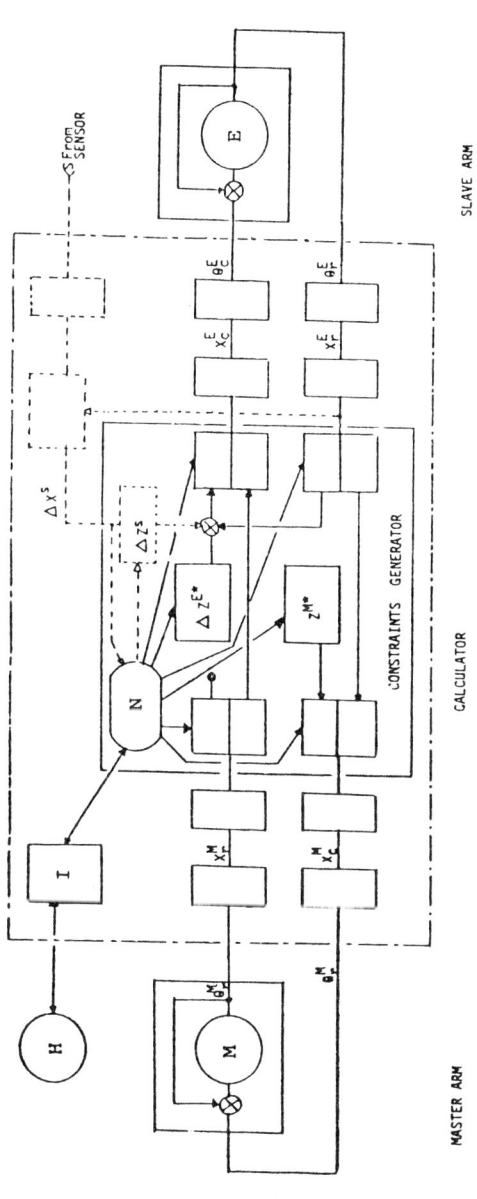

Figure 4 Parallel computer control of task-related degrees of freedom. M = master; E = slave; H = human operator; c = input; r = output; S = sensor; * programmed DOF θ = angular co-ordinates; X = operational co-ordinates; Z = function co-ordinates; I = real-time interpreter; N = constraint generator

Sensor-aided operation

The broken lines in Figure 4 show sensor information interfacing with the system. In our experiments sensors are infrared proximity sensors on the slave effector (and/or evidently force–torque sensors, see Figure 2).

As related[8] (in the same proceedings), the multiproximity sensors control subsystem generates either force–torque commands or rate commands (velocity and rotation) in the effector co-ordinate frame. Local sensors can be used in two different operating modes.

Mixed mode. In the functional co-ordinate frame, the slave command is servoed on the sensor's information for certain co-ordinates and under operator command for others; sensors are servoing the plane, line point, etc. that was only stored in the last modes of the previous section.

Reflex mode. In this mode a sensor-based error ΔZ^s is added to the master arm command. With the bilateral control system, this feeds back a force. Here, opposed to mixed mode there is not shared control, but the kinesthetic feedback helps the operator who is free for any action. Different applications of these modes have been implemented.

Remote touch of a surface

When a sensor is used to servo at a given distance or to avoid contact in the effector axis once an object is detected, the operator feels either an elastic force referring to the given distance, or repulsion with a fixed-distance force function (elastic potential or Newton potential), avoiding contact at any velocity (sensor range being larger than stopping distance at maximal speed). This enables one to remotely explore the environment in bad viewing conditions.

Catching and tracking mobile targets

This function is very important and appears as one unique feature of proximity sensor-based control, enabling a real three-dimensional (3D) closed-loop servoing in real time.

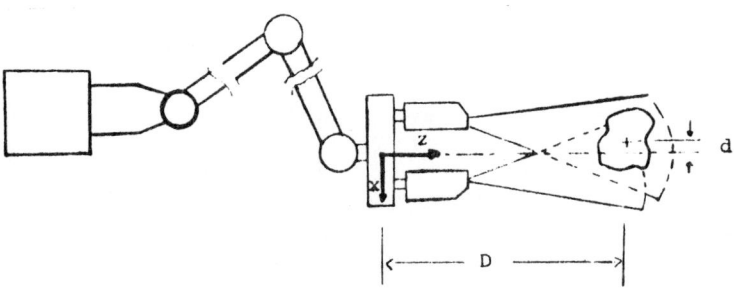

Figure 5 Dual sensor-tracking gripper

As shown in Figure 5, in the effector (gripper) detection plane we generate

$$\Delta x = f_1(S_1 - S_2) \qquad (2)$$

and

$$\Delta z = f_2(S_1 + S_2) \qquad (3)$$

In search phase the operator can get a proximetry 'catch' in reflex mode, then 'tracking' in the same mode, or automatically switch in mixed-mode tracking in the effector plane, when other DOF can be programmed (scanning) or under operator control.

Obstacle avoidance, plane contouring and 3D contouring

Here, after manual or automatic approach close to an object with large radius of curvature (but unknown shape) 2D or 3D surface contouring can be realized automatically.

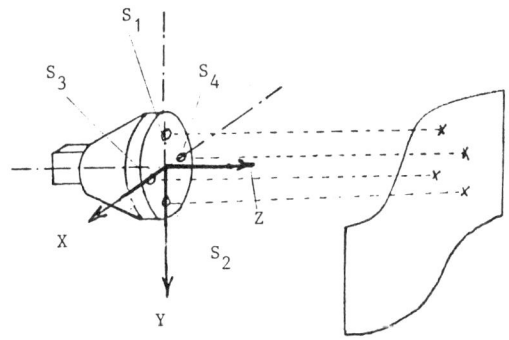

Figure 6 Sensor ring for tracking and/or contouring

As shown in Figure 6, the sensor-equipped ring (around any effector) will generate linear action

$$Tz = f_1(S_1 + S_2 + S_3 + S_4) \qquad (4)$$

and rotations

$$Rx = f_2(S_1 - S_2) \qquad (5)$$

and

$$Ry = f_3(S_3 - S_4) \qquad (6)$$

Use in bilateral mode

With

$$Z_C^E = Z^M \oplus Z^S \qquad (7)$$

Reflex mode. This will give

$$Z^M = (x, y, z, Rx, Ry, Rz) \quad (8)$$

and

$$\Delta Z^S = (\Delta z, \Delta Rx, \Delta Ry) \quad (9)$$

Mixed mode

$$Z^M = (x, y, Rz) \quad (10)$$

and

$$\Delta Z^S = (\Delta z, \Delta Rx, \Delta Ry) \quad (11)$$

So the operator can feel the third D easily and avoid mistakes in 2D scene vision.

Use in automatic mode

With

$$\underline{\Delta Z_C^E} = \Delta Z^* \oplus \underline{\Delta Z^S} \quad (12)$$

$$\Delta Z^* = (\Delta x, \Delta y, \Delta Rz) \quad (13)$$

and

$$\Delta Z^S = (\Delta z, \Delta Rx, \Delta Ry) \quad (14)$$

On MA 23 experiment, position and orientation performances are: catching (transient regimen) 800 ms; precision 1 cm in position, 1°4 angle; tracking velocity 20 cm per s and 10° per s.

Picking an object

Picking an object with our two-finger sensor-equipped gripper is carried out in five steps, either in bilateral reflex or mixed mode, or in automatic mode, as shown in Figure 7. Each step is a combination of functions described earlier, end of execution starts the next step. Additional obstacle-avoidance sensors around the gripper can play their role during these sequences to prevent touching the table and/or lateral obstacles.

Conclusion

This work is only part of the joint research between eight laboratories. The present paper deals only with operator assistance and/or substitution. Other work on sensory aids will be reported soon, with computer-generated pictures of task and slave arm. Important work concerned with system monitoring, operational safety and major issues are expected from automatic mode-switching by using system and real-time task and operator(s) analysis.

The increasing autonomy of the system will in the next few years keep the operator more and more to high-level decision making and the system will be able to control most operating levels such as co-ordination of transporter and vehicle to slave dextrous arms as well as the TV camera tracking (already achieved[9]).

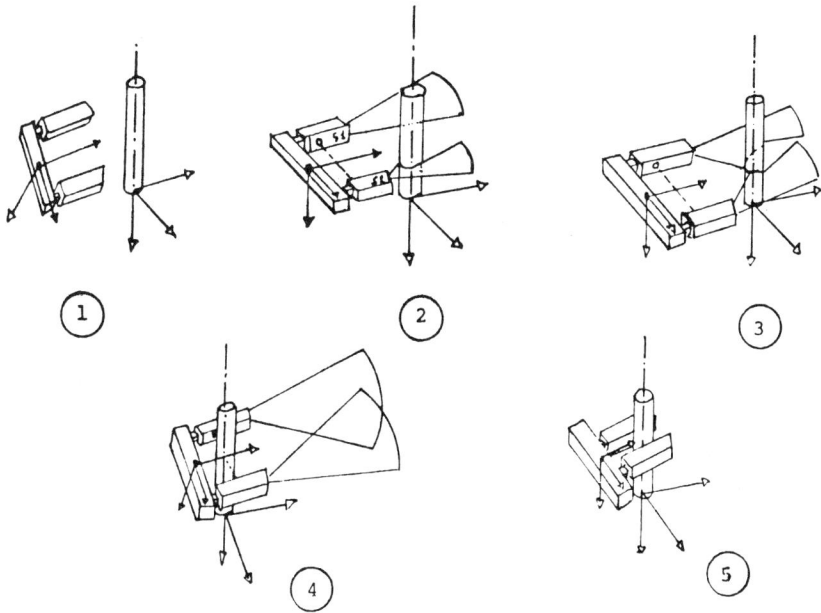

Figure 7 Multisensor gripper sequence. 1, approximate location (by operator or program); 2, positioning in perpendicular plane to object main axis; 3, centring; 4, forward up to stop when object is between fingers; 5, gripping

At the present time this research has led to the marketing of CAT 1 multiprocessor control system, in particular with the recent MA 23 M and next-generation MAE 200 slave arms. This introduces a new approach of mixed kinesthetic and modal man—teleoperator language, that has more general applications for teaching industrial robots

References

[1] Vertut J et al. (1983) *Human Factors Aspects of Computer Enhanced Teleoperation* Proc. 31st RSTD Conf. ANS, vol 1
[2] Vertut J et al. (1984) *Advances in a Computer Aided Bilateral System* Proc. 32nd RSTD Conf. ANS, vol 1
[3] Vertut J and Coiffet P (1984) *Téléopération* Hermes Publishing, Paris (in French) Kogan Page, London and Prentice-Hall, New Jersey (in English)
[4] Bejczy A and Dotson R S (1981) *Generalization of Bilateral Force Reflecting Control of Manipulators* 4th Romansy, p 242
[5] Vertut J et al. (1976) *Advances in the New MA 23 Force Reflecting Manipulator System* 2nd Ro Man Sy, p 307
[6] Bejczy A and Dotson R S *A Force Torque Sensing and Display System for Large Robots* Proc. IEEE, SE Conf., April, 1982

[7] Gaillard J P (1981) *The Persistance of a Visual Dominance Effect in a Telemanipulation Task. A Comparison Between Visual and Electrotactile Force Feedback* Proc. 17th Annual Conf. on Manual Control, p 127

[8] Espiau B and Andre G (1984) *Sensory-based Control for Robots and Teleoperators* 5th Romansy (see other references in this paper)

[9] Kuspriyanto P *et al*. Coordination caméra-télémanipulateur par microprocesseur, 6th IFToMM Congress, New Delhi, 1983

Part 5
Synthesis and Design

Mechanical and Geometric Design of the Adaptive Suspension Vehicle

K J Waldron, S M Song, S L Wang and J Vohnout

Department of Mechanical Engineering, Ohio State University, Columbus, OH 43210, USA

Summary: Some aspects of the mechanical and geometric design of the adaptive suspension vehicle are presented. In particular, there is an emphasis on aspects of the leg design and vehicle geometry, which affect the ability of the vehicle to operate on steep grades or to cross obstacles. A mechanism that maintains the attitude of the foot approximately parallel to the body is described. Geometric aspects of maintaining static stability on steep grades are discussed. Geometric and gait sequence aspects of crossing severe obstacles are also discussed.

Introduction

The adaptive supsension vehicle (ASV) will be a mobility system for use in very rough terrain. It uses a legged locomotion principle rather than wheels or tracks. The motivation for using a legged system is that about half of the earth's land surface is inaccessible to wheeled or tracked vehicles[1] but presents little problem to animals using legged locomotion. An artist's conception of the ASV is shown in Figure 1. Its principal characteristics and design goals are summarized in Table 1.

Figure 1   Artist's conception of the adaptive suspension vehicle

The machine will not be a robot since it will carry an operator. However, the operator's role is purely strategic, as in a conventional vehicle.

The ASV will have considerable on-board data processing power and sophisticated environmental sensing capability. This is needed to relieve the operator of the burden of co-ordinating the 18 actuated degrees of freedom in the system. In most operating conditions control of leg motion it is fully automatic. This type of operation was not feasible before the advent of powerful microcomputers,

Table 1 Principal characteristics and design goals of adaptive suspension vehicle (ASV)

Dimensions	5.0 m long, 2.1 m wide, 3.3 m high (average), 1.6 m track
Weight	260 kg
Payload	225 kg
Endurance	10 h
Speed	2.25 m/s cruise, 3.6 m/s dash
Grade climbing ability	>60%, 70% cross-slope

within the last few years. The ASV was the second, computer-co-ordinated fully self-contained walking vehicle when it entered testing in summer 1984. A smaller machine which differs in using a finite-state co-ordination system and which is limited by its mechanical configuration to relatively even terrain, has been tested recently.[2] Further details of the electronic and computational features of the system may be found in the companion paper.[3] The configuration of the sensing system, which is of great importance to operation of the machine, is described elsewhere.[4]

Configuration

As can be seen from Figure 1, the vehicle will have six legs arranged in a bilaterally symmetric pattern. The choice of six legs is a compromise between stability and complexity.[4,5] The leg geometry is shown schematically in Figure 2. It is a planar pantograph hinged to the body of the machine about an axis parallel to the longitudinal axis of the body. The reasons for choosing this configuration have been extensively discussed elsewhere.[4,6,7] Its proportions and the dimensions of its working volume are shown in Figure 3. The working-volume dimensions are basically fixed by the limits of motion of the actuating slides. These produce a rectangular generating curve. The rectangle is modified by a mechanical limit on knee-joint motion, which clips off a top corner, and by geometric limits of the mechanism which clip the bottom corners.

As is shown in Figure 1, the shank of the leg will be cranked. This is necessary to avoid contact of the shank with the ground during some obstacle-crossing manoeuvres. The leg will also be fitted with a passive hydraulic system which will maintain the sole of the foot approximately parallel to the body at all times. This

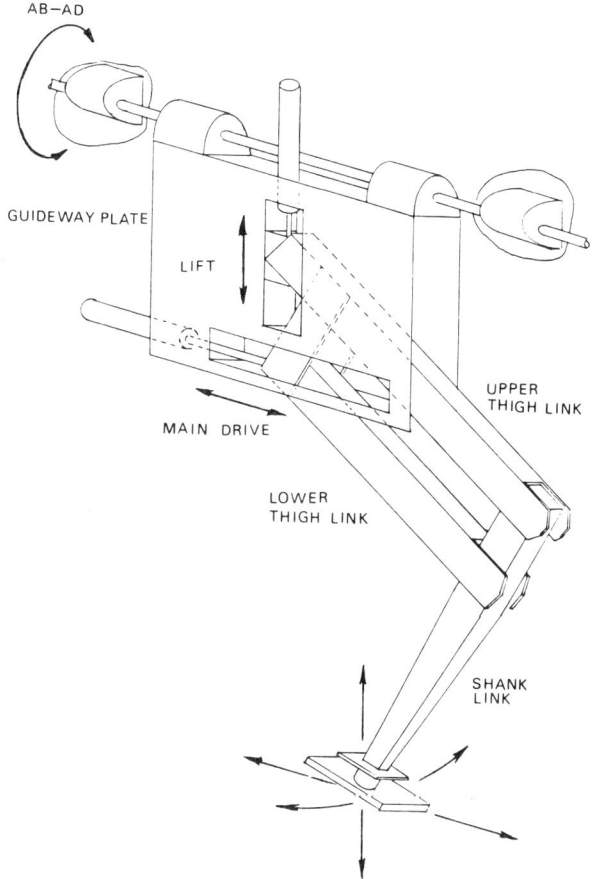

Figure 2 Schematic representation of pantograph leg arrangement

system is shown schematically in Figure 4. The master cylinder is actuated by rotation of the upper-leg members relative to the horizontal slide. The master and slave cylinders have the same diameter so the sum of their displacements is constant. The foot alignment is only approximate but varies by less than 3° over the working volume. An exact system is, of course, possible but entails a more complicated mechanical configuration. A controlled compliance is built into the system allowing some angulation of the foot under load. Excessive angulation will be prevented by mechanical stops. The compliance is provided by accumulators and may be adjusted by altering the pressure maintained in the system when unloaded.

Gradability

A major influence on the geometric configuration of the vehicle is the requirement for crossing large obstacles and for operation on steep gradients. Operation on

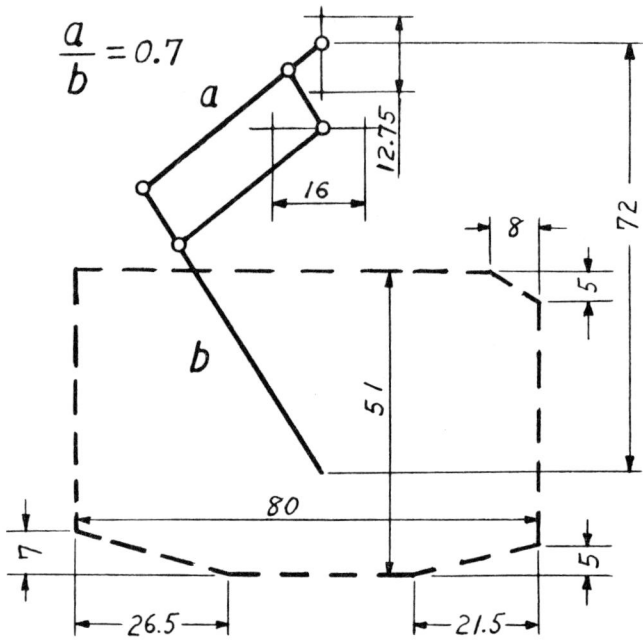

Figure 3 Working volume of leg

extreme gradients is potentially limited by three factors. The first of these is vehicle geometry. The second is capability of maintaining adequate traction. The third is the availability of sufficient driving power from the power train.

Vehicle geometry limits the gradient on which the vehicle can operate because of the necessity of maintaining static stability. As is shown in Figure 5 (a and b), the effect of climbing directly up a slope with the body attitude parallel to the slope is to move the centre of mass backward with respect to the support polygon. There are two basic strategies available to counteract this effect. The first of these is to lower the vehicle walking height while maintaining the same body attitude. This reduces the distance from the center of mass to the ground and hence reduces the displacement of the centre of mass (Figure 5c). Since the legs are capable of executing a full stroke even when raised to near the top of their working envelopes, this is an effective strategy.

The second strategy is to reduce the inclination of the body by extending the rear legs more than the front. This means that the legs must stroke along an inclined line relative to the body (Figure 5d). For the high ratio of vehicle length to vertical leg lift adopted for the ASV, this is not a very effective strategy. The maximum gradient, which can be handled without reducing the strokes of the front and rear legs, can be found from Figure 5d to be

$$G = \frac{H}{2p + L}$$

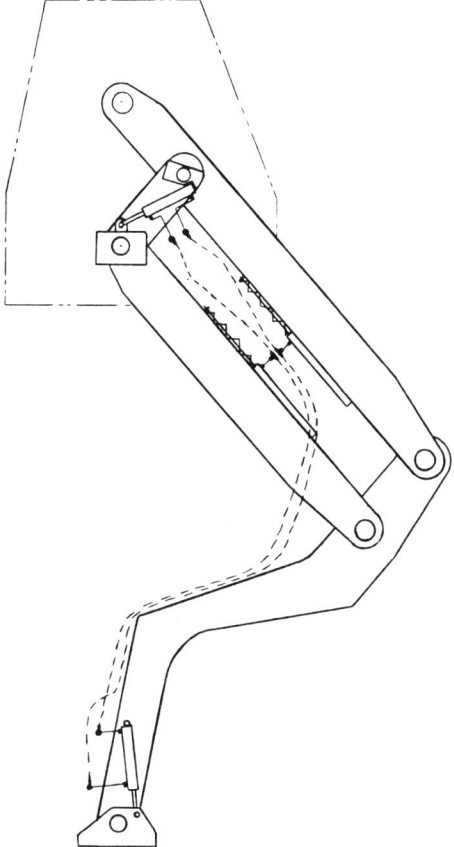

Figure 4 Schematic representation of foot attitude maintenance system

where H is the maximum leg lift height, p is the pitch of the legs and L the maximum leg stroke. The gradient G is related to the slope angle, α, shown in Figure 5a by the relation $G = \tan \alpha$. For the ASV this works out to 25 per cent. This strategy is not really compatible with the strategy of lowering walking height since reducing vehicle body height reduces the available portion of the leg working envelope in the vertical direction. One result of using this strategy is that the foot-attitude maintenance mechanism would cause the machine to try to stand on its toes. This might carry a traction advantage in some soil conditions. Otherwise, this strategy is less atractive than the first.

The stability margin can be increased for the lower duty cycle wave gaits[5] by reducing the leg stroke. This is most easily seen for a tripod gait (Figure 6). Considering, for the moment, level walking and referring to Figure 6b, the static stability margin, S, may be expressed as

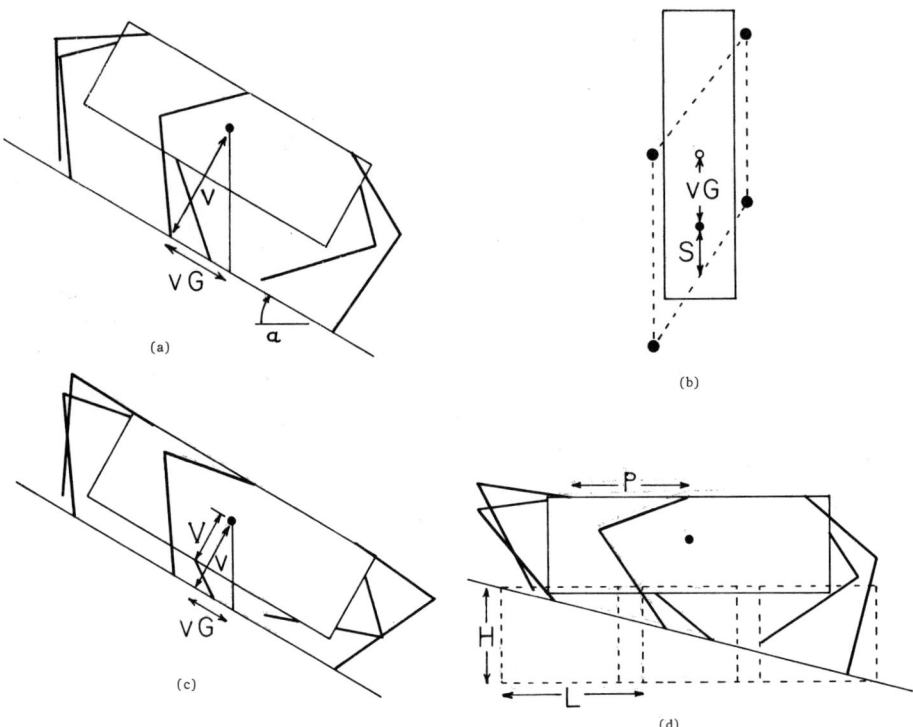

Figure 5 Maintenance of static stability on gradients

$$S = \frac{1}{2}(p - l)$$

where p is leg pitch, as before, and l is leg stroke. Further, when the leg stroke is shorter than its maximum (L), the centre of the stroke can be moved backwards relative to the vehicle body a distance

$$d = \frac{1}{2}(L - l)$$

This has the effect of moving the entire support polygon backward a distance d relative to the centre of mass. Therefore, referring again to Figure 5a and assuming that loss of static stability by tipping backward is the critical condition, the longitudinal static stability margin becomes

$$S = \frac{1}{2}(p - l) + \frac{1}{2}(L - l) = vG$$

or

$$S = \frac{1}{2}(L + p) - l - vG \tag{1}$$

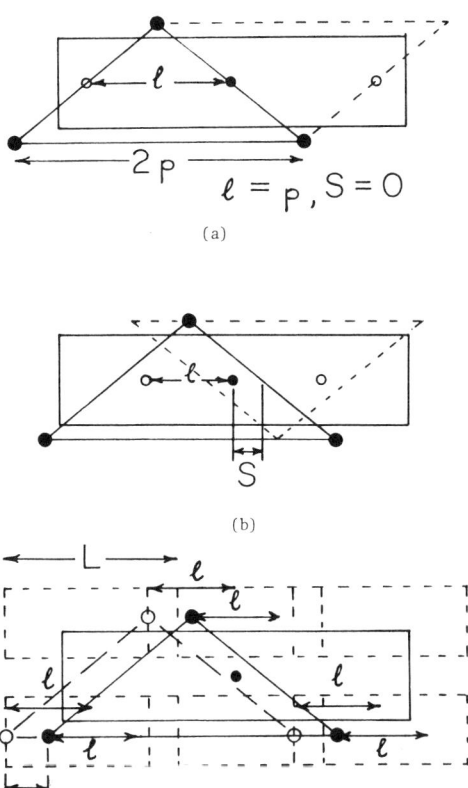

Figure 6 Effect on stability margin of shortening stroke

The limiting slope is obtained by letting S and l approach 0 and reducing v to its minimum value V.

$$G_{max} = \frac{L+p}{2V}$$

For the ASV, this works out to 240 per cent. Even if one takes $l = L/2$ as a working minimum stroke the gradient at which stability is lost is

$$G = \frac{p}{2V}$$

which is 110 per cent for the ASV.

As has been noted many times,[5] the stability margins of wave gaits increase with increasing duty factor. Considering only the simultaneous cases, the equation corresponding to equation (1) is

$$S = \frac{1}{2}(L+p) - \frac{5l}{8} - vG \qquad (2)$$

for a parallelogram gait and

$$S = \frac{1}{2}(L+p) - \frac{2l}{5} - vG \qquad (3)$$

for a pentapod gait. Note that the extreme slopes given by these expressions are the same as that given by equation (1). If one takes $l = L/2$ as the working minimum stroke one gets 160 and 190 per cent respectively for ASV dimensions.

Turning now to cross-slope locomotion one must consider both the lateral and longitudinal stability margin. Here it is assumed that the vehicle will move in the longitudinal rather than the lateral direction, although side-stepping might be a useful manoeuvre on a steep slope.

In these conditions, as shown in Figure 7, reduction of body inclination by extending the down-slope legs is the most effective strategy. The maximum gradient that can be handled with the legs vertical and the body horizontal is

$$G = \frac{H}{W}$$

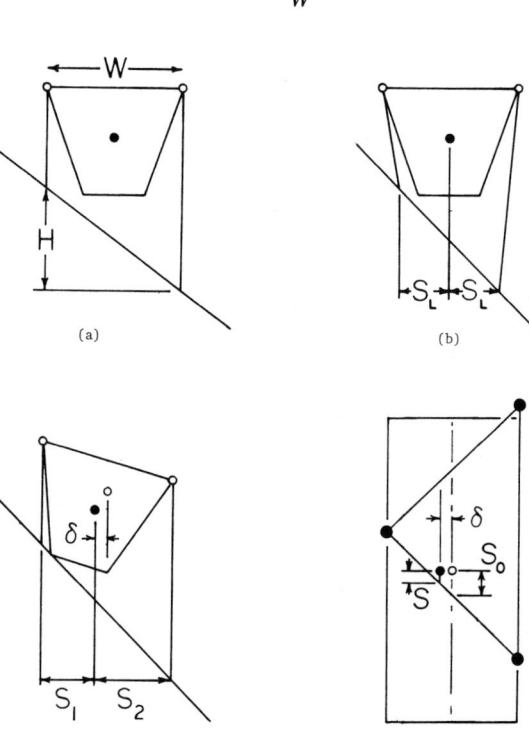

Figure 7 Maintenance of static stability on cross-gradients

where W is track width. This is 73 per cent for the ASV. Steeper slopes may be handled without loss of longitudinal stability margin by adducting the legs as shown in Figure 7b. This, of course, entails a loss of lateral stability margin. Alternatively, the body may be allowed to tilt as shown in Figure 7c. This increases the lateral stability margin on the down-slope side but reduces that on the up-slope side. It also reduces the longitudinal stability margin. This effect is illustrated for a tripod gait in Figure 7d.

The matter of traction is much less clear-cut and depends strongly on the nature of the soil over which the vehicle is moving. In principle, a foot that descends vertically, and which gains in traction with deformation of the soil, should enjoy an advantage over a wheel, which loses traction with soil deformation, over a considerable range of soil conditions.[8] Obviously, use of differently designed soles for different soils offers considerable advantages. Biological legged systems can maintain traction on loose-soil slopes quite close to the natural angle of repose which, of course, represents the upper limit for any traction system. It remains to be seen how much cross-slope traction will be affected by the lack of ankle accommodation to side slopes. It is probable that traction limitations will be the true determinant of manoeuvrability on extreme slopes.

As far as the availability of power is concerned, if a gross weight of 2650 kg is assumed, at the designed cruise speed of 2.25 m/s and the specified gradient of 60 per cent, a power of 30 kW is required to overcome gravity. Since it is projected that 18 kW will be needed to drive the vehicle on level ground at this speed, the total power needed to climb this grade is 48 kW. This is less than the rated peak power of the engine which is 67 kW. In fact it will be possible to draw even higher power for a limited period of time because of the use of an energy storage flywheel. Thus, grade climbing ability should not be limited by available power.

Obstacle crossing

The vehicle geometry is also strongly affected by the requirements of obstacle crossing. Figure 8 shows the critical positions for: (a) ditch crossing and (b) step climbing. The vehicle will be able to cross a 2.15 m ditch or a 1.65 m vertical step.

The sequencing of leg movements for crossing obstacles has been extensively investigated both by means of computer simulation, by using an Evans and Sutherland PS 300 display system, and by means of high-speed photographs of insects crossing obstacles of similar geometry.[9] The appropriate sequence of movements turns out to be remarkably similar regardless of the nature of the obstacle. It is illustrated in Figure 9 for ditch crossing. Starting with all legs in their mid-position and with the front feet at the edge of the obstacle, the rear legs are first brought as far forward as possible with the centre of mass of the body moving forward to a position between the middle and front legs. At the same time the centre of mass is brought forward. The middle legs are then brought forward in a paired movement and the feet are placed alongside the front feet. The front legs are then lifted and extended across the obstacle and placed on the far side while the centre of mass moves to a position just behind the middle feet. The centre of mass is moved forward of the middle feet and the rear legs are lifted and brought forward to place the rear feet alongside the middle feet. The middle legs are then lifted and the feet are placed across the obstacle. The front feet are then moved forward with the

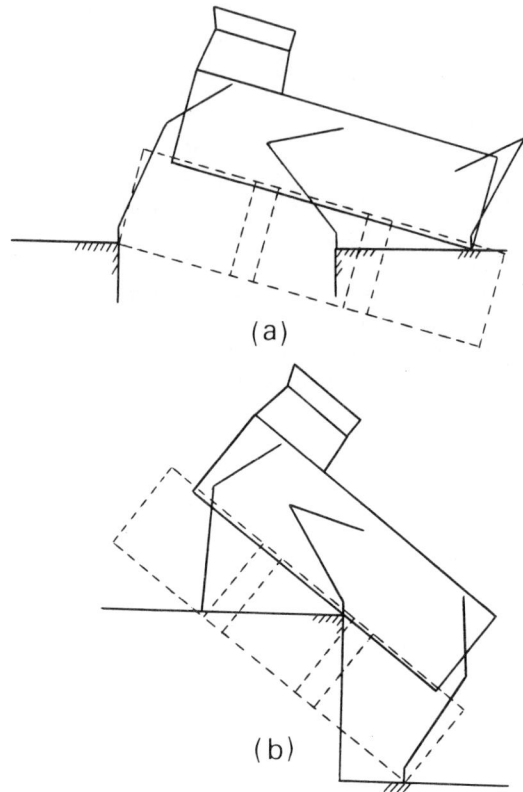

Figure 8 Critical positions in obstacle crossing: (a) ditch; (b) vertical step

centre of mass again moving to a position just behind the middle feet. The centre of mass is moved forward of the middle feet and the rear legs are lifted and moved across the obstacle. The middle and front legs are then moved forward to resume stance with the legs centred.

Notice that all leg movements are paired with the two legs on opposite sides of the machine moving together. Notice also that the movements can be characterized as three cycles of four similar movements: (i) movement of the body to bring the centre of mass forward of the middle feet, (ii) movement of the rear legs accompanied by further body movement, (iii) movement of the middle legs, (iv) movement of the front legs again with accompanying body movement. The paired movements allow the centre of mass to be placed as close as possible to the obstacle without losing stability. The rear to front cycle is similar to the rear to front cycles found in optimally stable wave gaits for walking on even terrain. Movements in the vertical direction and about the pitch axis are superimposed on those above for crossing obstacles such as vertical steps and walls. In fact, a slightly wider ditch can be crossed by adding pitch movements. The basic motion sequence remains the same in all cases.

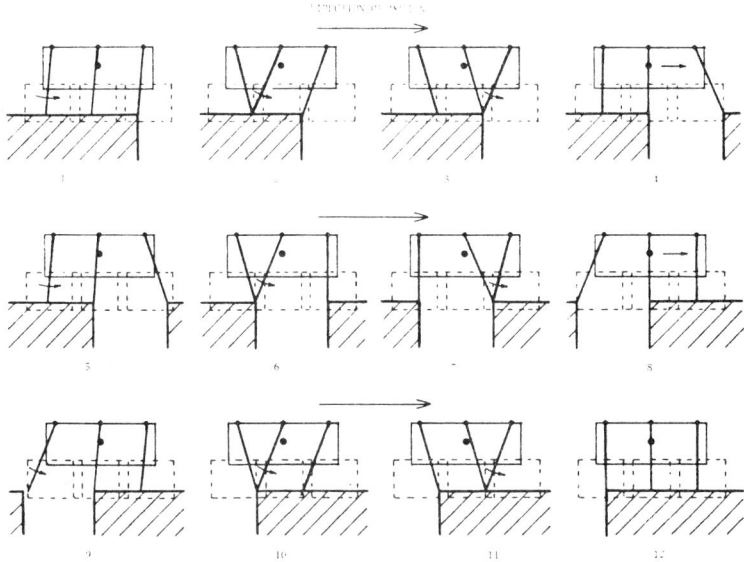

Figure 9 Movement cycles in crossing maximal width ditch

Conclusion

The adaptive suspension vehicle is now under construction. A full-scale leg prototype has been tested in the laboratory and has demonstrated the effectiveness of the hydrostatic drive concept.[4] The vehicle was tested in summer 1984. Apart from the aspects of the design discussed here, details of structural design may be found elsewhere.[10]

The work reported here was supported by the Defense Advanced Research Projects Agency under Contract MDA-903-82-K-0058.

References

[1] Anon *Logistical Vehicle Off-Road Mobility* Project TCCO 62-5, US Army Transportation Combat Developments Agency, Fort Eustis, VA, February, 1967
[2] Raibert M H and Sutherland I E (1983) Machines that walk. *Sci. Am.*, **248**(2), 44–53
[3] McGhee R B, Orin D E, Pugh D R and Patterson M R *A Hierarchically Structured System for Computer Control of a Hexapod Walking Vehicle* Fifth CISM-IFToMM Symposium on Theory and Practice of Robots and Manipulators, Udine, Italy, June, 1984
[4] Waldron K J, Vohnout V J, Pery A and McGhee R B (1984) Configuration Design of the Adaptive Suspension Vehicle. *Rob. Res.* in press.

[5] McGhee R B (1984) Vehicular legged locomotion In *Advances in Automation and Robotics*, ed. G N Saridis., Jai Press
[6] Song S M, Waldron K J and Kinzel G L *Computer-aided Geometric Design of Legs for a Walking Vehicle* Proc. of 8th Applied Mechanisms Conf., St Louis, Missouri, 19—21 September, 1983, pp 70—1 to 70—7
[7] Song S M, Vohnout V J, Waldron K H and Kinzel G L *Computer-aided Design of a Leg for an Energy Efficient Walking Machine* Proc. of 7th Applied Mechanisms Conf., Kansas City, Missouri, December, 1981, pp VII—1 to VII—7 (to appear in *J. Mech. Mach. Theory*)
[8] Bekker M G (1969) *Introduction to Terrain-Vehicle Systems* University of Michigan Press, Ann Arbor, Michigan
[9] Pearson K G (1982) *Cinematographic Analysis of Animal Walking* Final report on contract RF 714250-01, University of Alberta, Edmonton, Alberta, Canada
[10] Vohnout V J, Alexander K S and Kinzel G L *The Structural Design of the Legs for a Walking Vehicle* Proc. of 8th Applied Mechanisms Conf., St Louis, September, 1983, pp 50—1 to 50—8

Geometrical and Kinematical Qualitative Characteristics for Functional Capacities of Manipulation Systems

L Lilov and B Bekjarov

Institute of Mechanics and Biomechanics, Bulgarian Academy of Sciences, Sofia, Bulgaria

Summary: In this paper a method for introducing geometrical and kinematical qualitative characteristics is suggested. This method makes clear the genesis of all characteristics used at present. On the other hand, it can be used as a basis for the generation of new estimations, each of which represents a specific aspect of manipulation-systems operations. Also, the suggested method can be used to express formally and to estimate quantitatively, most important for the practical quality of manipulation systems, kinematics of their motions. This allows for the selection of optimal manipulation systems on the basis of properly chosen characteristics and for the determination of areas in three-dimensional space, in which an arbitrarily selected manipulation system has the largest functional capacities. The geometrical and kinematical qualitative characteristics used at present are interpreted as special cases. Moreover, a lot of new estimations are introduced to characterize some important aspects of the performance of manipulation systems. On the basis of this method a package of programs CAMS is suggested. The CAMS package consists of modules for calculating and visualizing in an interactive mode the changes most important for practical geometrical and kinematical qualitative characteristics in three-dimensional (working) space.

Introduction

One of the basic problems appearing at the preliminary stage of manipulation-systems projects is to establish qualitative criteria to be used as estimations for functional capacities and for the performance of manipulation systems. It is of great importance for the practice to establish qualitative characteristics which can estimate functional capacities of the system in geometric and kinematic terms and to create methods, numerical algorithms and programs for computer calculating of these characteristics for every concrete system. At the same time, of great importance is the problem for synthesis of systems with optimal geometrical and kinematical characteristics in the sense of chosen quality criteria. At present the following characteristics are used as such criteria: service coefficient, attainability, reach region, mobility coefficient, etc.[1-4] Each of these characteristics reflects a specific aspect of manipulation-systems functional capacities. However, up to now, there has been no general approach to introducing geometric and kinematic characteristics. Existing ones are isolated and not connected with each other. The problem of introducing new characteristics is not elucidated. So, many important and essential aspects of manipulation systems remain unexplored.

In this work a unified approach and method for introducing geometrical and kinematical qualitative characteristics is suggested.

Main notions and notations

Let M be an arbitrary manipulation system with n degrees of freedom and generalized co-ordinates $q_1, \ldots, q_n$. Suppose that certain constructive restrictions are imposed on the manipulation-system movements. Let these restrictions be of the form

$$q = (q_1, \ldots, q_n) \in Q = \left\{ q \in R^n : q'_j \leqq q_j \leqq q''_j, \quad j = 1, \ldots, n \right\},$$

$$\dot{q} = (\dot{q}_1, \ldots, \dot{q}_n) \in Q_1 = \left\{ \dot{q} \in R^n : \dot{q}'_{j1} \leqq \dot{q}_j \leqq \dot{q}''_{j2}, \quad j = 1, \ldots, n \right\}$$

Let $A = R^3 \times B$ be the Cartesian product of the set R^3 of all the vectors $\bar{r}_H = (r_{H1}, r_{H2}, r_{H3})$ defining the position of an arbitrary gripper point H in the three-dimensional space and the variety B, consisting of all orthogonal 3×3 matrices $\alpha = \left\{ \alpha_{ij} \right\}_{i=1}^{3} {}_{j=1}^{3}$ defining the angular position of the gripper with respect to an absolute co-ordinate system. The set A will be named a variety of gripper positions of the manipulation system. The distribution of gripper-points velocities is defined by the linear velocity $\bar{v}_H = (v_{H1}, v_{H2}, v_{H3})$ of the point H and the angular velocity $\bar{\omega} = (\omega_1, \omega_2, \omega_3)$ of the gripper. Evidently, the pair $(\bar{v}_H^T, \bar{\omega}^T)^T$ belongs to the variety $A_1 = R^3 \times R^3$ which will be named a variety of the gripper-points velocities. The Cartesian product $A \times A_1 = A \times R^3 \times R^3$ will be named a variety of the gripper-points positions and velocities. Each element of the variety $A \times A_1$ will be considered as an 18-dimensional vector $a = (a_1, \ldots, a_{18})$ with components

$$(a_1, a_2, a_3) = (r_{H1}, r_{H2}, r_{H3}); \quad \begin{Vmatrix} a_4 & a_5 & a_6 \\ a_7 & a_8 & a_9 \\ a_{10} & a_{11} & a_{12} \end{Vmatrix} = \begin{Vmatrix} \alpha_{11} & \alpha_{12} & \alpha_{13} \\ \alpha_{21} & \alpha_{22} & \alpha_{23} \\ \alpha_{31} & \alpha_{32} & \alpha_{33} \end{Vmatrix}$$

$$(a_{13}, a_{14}, a_{15}) = (v_{H1}, v_{H2}, v_{H3})$$

$$(a_{16}, a_{17}, a_{18}) = (\omega_1, \omega_2, \omega_3)$$

Let a mapping $F^* : Q \times Q_1 \to A \times A_1$ from the set $Q \times Q_1$ to the variety $A \times A_1$ is defined by

$$F^*(q, \dot{q}) = a \in A \times A_1$$

Evidently, this transformation defines the functional dependence of the gripper position, translational and angular velocities on generalized co-ordinates and velocities. Let F define the dependence of point H position on configuration.

Geometrical and kinematical characteristics of manipulation systems

Let μ_k be a functional specifying the volume measure in R^k, and C be a subset of the variety $A \times A_1$. As a characteristic for functional capacities of an arbitrary manipulation system in the space $R^n \times R^n$ of the generalized co-ordinates and velocities there will be used the quantity

$$\chi^*(C, b+L) = \frac{\mu_{\dim(L)}[(b+L) \cap (F^*)^{-1}(C)]}{\mu_{\dim(L)}[(b+L) \cap (Q \times Q_1)]} \quad (1)$$

where $b+L$ is a linear variety in $R^n \times R^n$ space. Let $\delta = (\delta_1, \ldots, \delta_{18})$ be an 18-dimensional vector with components 0 or 1 and let D be a closed subset of variety $A \times A_1$. Suppose that diag δ is an 18×18 diagonal matrix $\{d_{ij}\}_{i=1, j=1}^{18, 18}$, where $d_{ii} = \delta_i$.

We shall now introduce an equivalence relation $\mathcal{R}_\delta$ in variety $A \times A_1$ defined as follows:

$$a', a'' \epsilon A \times A_1, a' \mathcal{R}_\delta a'' \Leftrightarrow \text{diag } \delta . a' = \text{diag } \delta . a''$$

Vector δ will be denoted also with the symbol $\delta = \delta_{i_1, \ldots, i_k}$ $(i_1 <, \ldots, < i_k)$, where i_j are the numbers of components which are not zero.

As geometrical and kinematical characteristics for functional capacities of manipulation systems will be used the set

$$S^*(D, \delta, b+L) = \{F^*[(b+L) \cap (Q \times Q_1)] \cap D\}/\mathcal{R}_\delta \quad (2)$$

and the quantity

$$\lambda^*(D, \delta, b+L) = \frac{\mu_{\dim(D/\mathcal{R}_\delta)}[S^*(D, \delta, b+L)]}{\mu_{\dim(D/\mathcal{R}_\delta)}[D/\mathcal{R}_\delta]} \quad (3)$$

where $D/\mathcal{R}_\delta$ is quotient space obtained after partitioning of set D into classes of equivalence.

Examples of geometrical and kinematical characteristics

Let us consider now the sets $Z_r = F^*(Q \times Q_1)/\mathcal{R}_{\delta_{1,2,3}}$, $Z_v = F^*(Q \times Q_1)/\mathcal{R}_{\delta_{13,14,15}}$, $Z_\alpha = F^*(Q \times Q_1)/\mathcal{R}_{\delta_{4,\ldots,12}}$, $Z_\omega = F^*(Q \times Q_1)/\mathcal{R}_{\delta_{16,17,18}}$. Suppose that Π_r, Π_α, Π_v, Π_ω are arbitrary closed sets and $\Pi_r \supset Z_r$, $\Pi_\alpha \supset Z$, $\Pi_v \supset Z_v$, $\Pi_\omega \supset Z_\omega$. Suppose also that $\Lambda_r \subset Z_r$, $\Lambda_\alpha \subset Z_\alpha$, $\Lambda_v \subset Z_v$, $\Lambda_\omega \subset Z_\omega$. Now let $D^* = \Pi_r \times \Pi_\alpha \times \Pi_v \times \Pi_\omega$. Then $Z_r = S^*(D^*, \delta_{1,2,3}, R^{2n})$, $Z_\alpha = S^*(D^*, \delta_{4,\ldots,12}, R^{2n})$, $Z_v = S^*(D^*, \delta_{13,14,15}, R^{2n})$, $Z_\omega = S^*(D^*, \delta_{16,17,18}, R^{2n})$.

Evidently Z_r is the manipulation system reaching region, i.e. the set consisting of these and only these points of R^3 in which the gripper specific point H can be positioned. By analogy the sets Z_α, Z_v, Z_ω will be named respectively the angular reaching region, the reaching region of the translational velocities and the reaching region of the angular velocities of the gripper. For example, the reaching region of the translational velocities is the set consisting of these and only these vectors $\bar{v}$ for which exists such a pair $(q, \dot{q}) \epsilon Q \times Q_1$ that when manipulation system M has generalized co-ordinates and velocities equal to $(q, \dot{q})$, the point H has velocity $\bar{v}$.

Obviously the quantity $\lambda^*(D^*, \delta_{1,2,3}, R^{2n})$ is exactly the geometrical characteristic named the manipulation system attainability.[4]

If $C = \Lambda_r \times \Pi_\alpha \times \Pi_v \times \Pi_\omega$, $b = 0$, $L = R^{2n}$ then the quantity obtained by equation (1) will be named the approach coefficient. The approach coefficient characterizes the manipulation system M capabilities to position with different configurations the gripper point H in points of the set $\Lambda_r \subset R^3$.

Suppose that $\bar{r}$ is the radius—vector of arbitrarily fixed point in three-dimensional space. Let $b = 0$, $L = R^{2n}$, $\delta = \delta_{4,7,10}$ and $D_r = \bar{r} \times \Pi_\alpha \times \Pi_v \times \Pi_\omega$. If the axis x of the co-ordinate system connected with the gripper is selected as the gripper axis then the value $\lambda^*(D_r, \delta_{4,7,10}, R^{2n})$ is exactly the service coefficient in point $\bar{r}$.[4]

If we choose $\bar{r}_0 = F(q_0)$ where q_0 is an arbitrary configuration, $D = \bar{r}_0 \times \Pi_\alpha \times \Pi_v \times \Pi_\omega$, $\delta = \delta_{13,14,15}$, $b = (q_0, 0)$, $L = 0 \times R^n$, the quantity obtained by equation (3) will be named the gripper translational velocities attainability coefficient in the configuration q_0. That characteristic estimates manipulation-system capabilities to realize different translational velocities of the gripper when $q = q_0$. In an analogous way the quantity $\lambda^*[\bar{r}_0 \times \Pi_\alpha \times \Pi_v \times \Pi_\omega, \delta_{16,17,18}, (q_0, 0) + 0 \times R^n]$, will be named the gripper angular-velocities attainability coefficient. This characteristic is bearing information about manipulation-system capabilities to realize angular speeds of the gripper when $\bar{r}_0 = F(q_0)$.

Applications

On the basis of the desired method CAMS-1 and CAMS-2 software packages for automatic analysis and synthesis of manipulation systems in interactive mode are designed. The CAMS-1 package operates on minicomputers PDP 11-34, SM-4, etc.

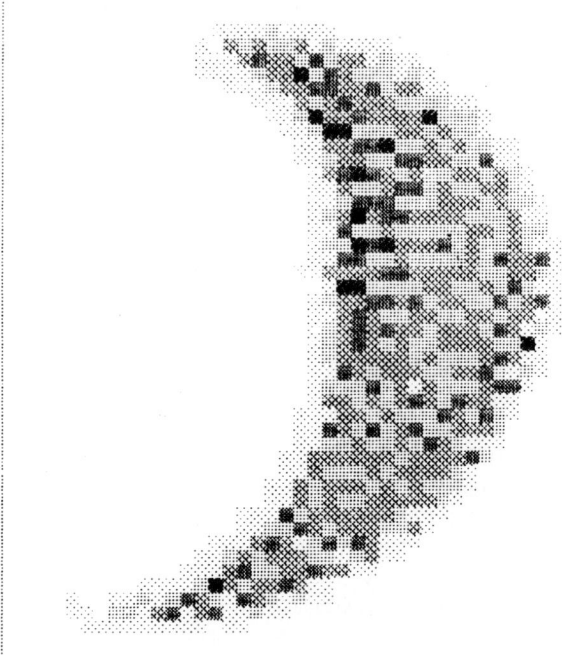

Figure 1 Visualization of changes in the working space of approach coefficient of RB-211 industrial robot

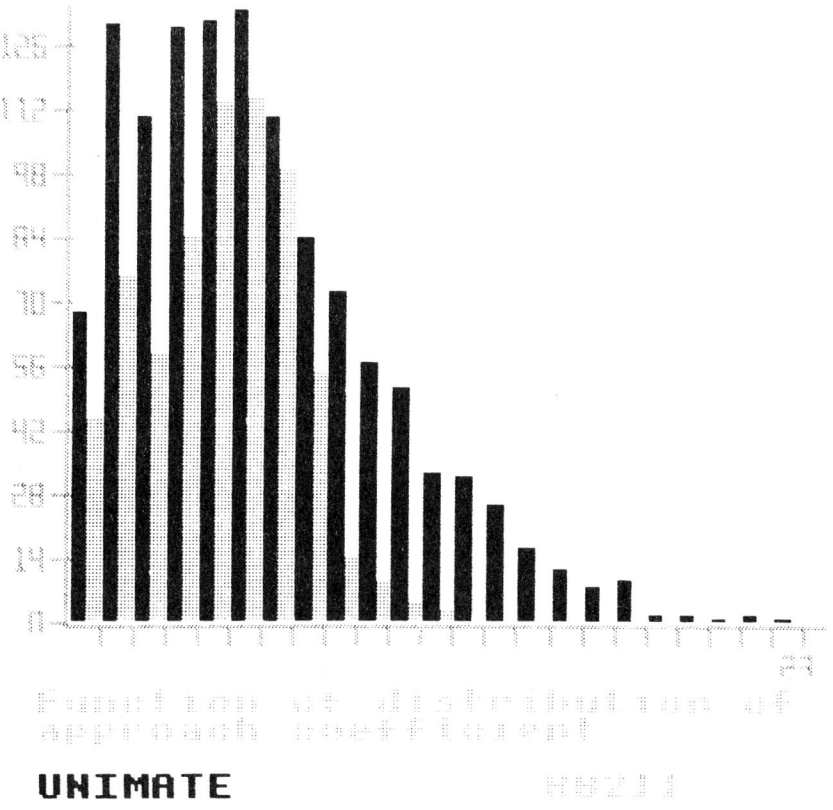

Figure 2 Density function of approach coefficient of industrial robots UNIMATE 2030 and RB-211

The CAMS-2 package operates on microcomputers BBC, PERQ, APPLE, IMCO etc. There is also a version of package operating in a batch mode. The CAMS-1 and CAMS-2 packages consist of modules for calculating, visualizing and statistical analysis of the changes within the working space of qualitative characteristics such as approach coefficient, service coefficient, gripper translational- and angular-velocities attainability coefficients, attainability, reaching region, etc. Several results of CAMS-1 and CAMS-2 software packages work are shown in Figures 1–3. The input data for CAMS package is the kinematical scheme of the considered manipulation system.

The CAMS package could be applied on the stage of preliminary projects or for evaluation of the kinematics of such complex mechanical systems as industrial robots, lifting devices of electric cars and motor cars, measurement devices etc.

Figure 3 Visualization of changes in the working space of service coefficient of UNIMATE 2030 industrial robot

References

[1] Roth B (1976) *Performance Evaluation of Manipulators from a Kinematic Viewpoint* NBS, Special publication 459
[2] Rovetta A (1981) *On the functional analysis of mechanical arms for robots* IV CISM-IFToMM Symposium, Warsaw
[3] Konstantinov M and Genova P (1981) *Workspace and manoeuvrability criteria for robots* IV CISM-IFToMM Symposium, Warsaw
[4] Kobrinsci A A (1978) On mechanical qualities of manipulation systems. *DAN*, **241** (4)

Manipulation Devices Based on High-class Mechanisms

U A Djoldasbekov, L I Slutskii and J J Baigunchekov

S M Kirov Kazakh State University, Alma-Ata, USSR

Summary: The fundamentals of high-class mechanisms (HCM) application in designing the executive devices for manipulative robots are presented in this paper. The examples of their use directly in the executive organs and gripping devices are given. The technique of HCM kinematic synthesis to realize a required movement of the manipulator's working point in the plane from one driving engine is shown. A number of problems for mechanics of robots, manipulators and some analogous devices, where the use of HCM is rather promising, are indicated.

The use of open kinematic chains in the executive organs of manipulative robots has already become traditional. However, it should be noted that closed kinematic chains can be very effective in these devices. So, one of the most important features of the closed kinematic chains is a higher accuracy of positioning due to a greater rigidity of construction. Also, the drive system between the driving links and the motor is simplified, the latter being, as a rule, mounted on the foundation leads to a smaller weight of the manipulator. Finally, closed mechanisms are capable of realizing complicated program trajectories only due to the mechanical properties of the system.

The above refers mostly to manipulators designed on the basis of high-class mechanisms (HCM). Owing to the presence of variable closed joint-level contour, HCM have wide kinematic and dynamic capabilities, which permits to regard HCM as a new technological basis for manipulators with original productive features. This consideration, well known to specialists in the mechanism and machine theory,[1] has recently attracted the attention of specialists in robot engineering,[2,3] the chief factor being recognized to be the possibility to realize the robot's complicated stereotyped movements only due to its mechanical part without complications in the control unit or program supply.

This paper presents the results of wide experience in HCM analysis and synthesis which allows to pass from stating the possibility of using these mechanisms in robots and manipulators to designing concrete kinematic schemes. Two main spheres of HCM application can be established by means of analysis: HCM application in the executive organs of manipulators; HCM application in the gripping organs of robots and manipulators.

An example of the construction of the manipulator executive organs with the use of HCM is a design where pantograph mechanisms, Assur group, class IV, are used as a transfer arm's links. This design as well as its advantages in performing different types of manipulating operations are described.[4]

Considerable possibilities are opened up with the use of HCM in designing automatic operators and other auxiliary transporting devices of automatic machines.

For example, here one can construct single drive mechanisms reproducing the required movements of two working organs.[5]

Apart from their application in the design of the executive organs of handling manipulators, rectilinear guiding mechanisms constructed on the HCM basis serve as a foundation for the construction of handling machines, pilers, etc. Here the mechanism's working point can travel linearly from one drive which, in comparison with the known devices, makes the machine easy to operate. Since most of the mentioned machines are man-operated, the simplifcation of the manual control, in this case, results in a higher productivity of labour.

The synthesis technique for the above guiding mechanisms can be made clear by the following example. To realize plane stereotyped trajectories robot engineering employs plane manipulators representing an open kinematic chain with two degrees of mobility. In automatic machines, handling and other devices a simplified control requires a manipulator design where the working organ travels along a given trajectory depending on one generalized co-ordinate. For designing such manipulators one chooses an open three-link kinematic chain O_1ABP (Figure 1) having three degrees of freedom where the working organ P has two degrees of freedom and the driving link O_1A has one degree. Consequently, the point P and the link O_1A have independent laws of motion $X_p = X_p(t)$, $Y_p = Y_p(t)$ and $\varphi = \varphi(t)$. Two extra degrees of freedom of the open three-link chain are successively excluded. First, the link BP is attached to the post by the rocker DC, which excludes one degree of freedom of the chain O_1ABP. For this it is necessary to define the round square point C and its centre D in the plane BP.[6] The parameters of the mobile plane BP are

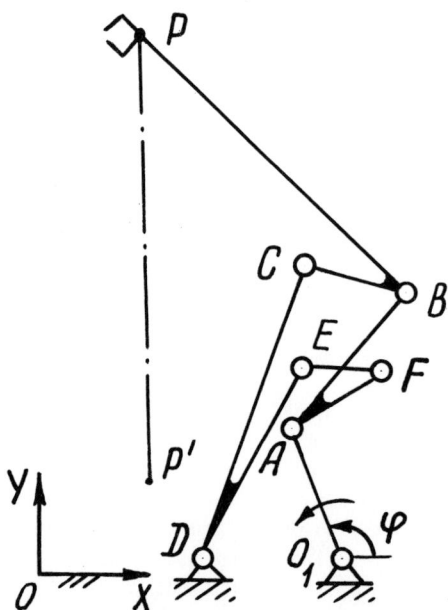

Figure 1 An open three-link kinematic chain O_1ABP

$$\begin{bmatrix} 1 \\ X_{B_i} \\ Y_{B_i} \end{bmatrix} = \begin{bmatrix} 1 \\ X_{A_i} \\ Y_{A_i} \end{bmatrix} + M_{AB} \begin{bmatrix} 1 \\ 0 \\ 0 \end{bmatrix} \tag{1}$$

$$(\varphi_{BP})_i = \operatorname{arctg} \frac{Y_{P_i} - Y_{B_i}}{X_{P_i} - X_{B_i}} \tag{2}$$

where

$$\begin{bmatrix} 1 \\ X_{A_i} \\ Y_{A_i} \end{bmatrix} = \begin{bmatrix} 1 \\ X_{O_1} \\ Y_{O_1} \end{bmatrix} + M_{O_1 A} \begin{bmatrix} 1 \\ 0 \\ 0 \end{bmatrix}$$

$$M_{O_1 A} = \begin{bmatrix} 1 & 0 & 0 \\ l_{O_1 A} \cos \varphi_i & \cos \varphi_i & -\sin \varphi_i \\ l_{O_1 A} \sin \varphi_i & \sin \varphi_i & \cos \varphi_i \end{bmatrix}$$

$$M_{AB} = \begin{bmatrix} 1 & 0 & 0 \\ l_{AB} \cos (\varphi_{AB})_i & \cos (\varphi_{AB})_i & -\sin (\varphi_{AB})_i \\ l_{AB} \sin (\varphi_{AB})_i & \sin (\varphi_{AB})_i & \cos (\varphi_{AB})_i \end{bmatrix}$$

The position A the link AB in the matrix M_{AB} is defined by solving the problem of the ABP link position

$$(\varphi_{AB})_i = (\varphi_{AP})_i \pm \arccos \frac{l_{AB}^2 + l_{BP}^2 - (X_{P_i} - X_{A_i})^2 - (Y_{P_i} - Y_{A_i})^2}{2 l_{AB} \cdot l_{BP}} \tag{3}$$

where $(\varphi_{AP})_i = \operatorname{arctg}(Y_{P_i} - Y_{A_i})/(X_{P_i} - X_{A_i})$

and $i = 1, 2, \ldots, n$ is the number of the assigned positions and the driving link $O_1 A$ of the point P along its trajectory.

An extra degree of freedom of the obtained five-link chain $O_1 ABCD$ is excluded by joining the links AB and DC with an additional connecting rod EF. This is required to define the round square point F and its centre in the plane AB in reverse motion (the plane DC being fixed). The AB plane parameters in reverse motion are

$$\begin{bmatrix} 1 \\ X_{A_i}^* \\ Y_{A_i}^* \end{bmatrix} = L_D^{-1} \begin{bmatrix} 1 \\ X_D - X_{A_i} \\ Y_D - Y_{A_i} \end{bmatrix} \tag{4}$$

$$(\varphi_{AB})_i^* = 2\pi - [(\varphi_{AB})_i - (\varphi_{DC})_i] \tag{5}$$

where

$$L_D^{-1} = \begin{bmatrix} 1 & 0 & 0 \\ 0 & \cos(\varphi_{DC}) & \sin(\varphi_{DC}) \\ 0 & -\sin(\varphi_{DC}) & \cos(\varphi_{DC}) \end{bmatrix}$$

The presence of the variable closed-circuit $EFBCE$ ensures a small size of the designed mechanism when folded, and the effort from the driving link O_1A to the grip is transmitted through the base link ABF to the connecting rods FE and BC simultaneously.

These features make it possible to use the designed IV class mechanism (Figure 2) in mobile handling manipulators. To prolong the rectilinear trajectory of the point P the IV class mechanism can be fitted with the link EJH, by observing the condition $EJ\|FH$ and $FE\|HJ$. The IV class mechanism with a critical trajectory of point B may be used as an artificial human arm (Figure 3). The driving link O_1A is actuated by the remaining part of the shoulder.

HCM may also be used for simulating the movements of a human foot.

Apart from the HCM kinematic properties their characteristic force features should be mentioned. The latter, being the force redistribution among the elements of a closed mobile chain, allow to increase the load-carrying capacity of a front-end tilting loader twice only due to the replacement of two two-drive groups by one Assur group of class IV, second order.

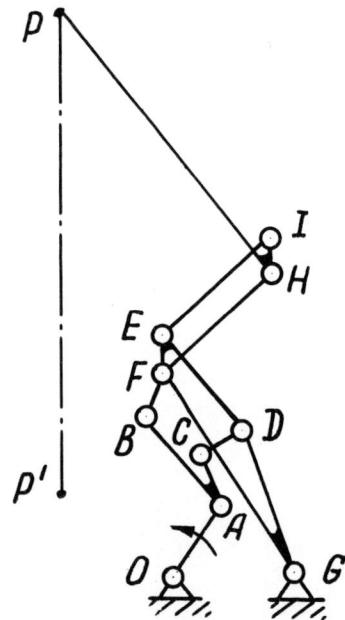

Figure 2 Designed IV class mechanism

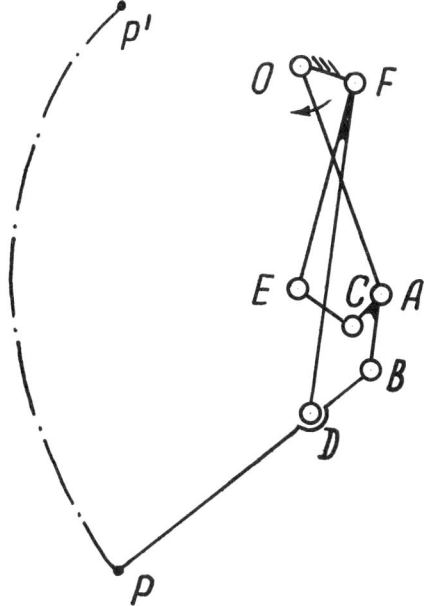

Figure 3 IV class mechanism used as an artificial human arm

The use of HCM in the gripping devices of robots and manipulators is based on considerable reconstructibility of the mechanism's mobile contour. In its turn this ensures the adaptation of the gripper to the shape of the object of manipulation. Here we note two main problems and ways to solve them using the mechanisms under consideration. The first problem concerns gripping three-dimensional objects of arbitrary shape. In this case Assur groups, say of class IV, may be mounted on the gripper's jaws normally to their surface (Figure 4). The links connecting the groups to the base jaw are fitted with springs. The group on one jaw enters the gap between the groups on the other jaw. So, in this case, HCM serves as finger elements, when in contact with different parts of the manipulated object each of them is, in its own way, deformed by the jaw's motion. The proper arrangement of HCM in a similar gripper ensures reliable gripping of three-dimensional objects of arbitrary shape.

Another version of grippers employs the properties of HCM as a planar mechanism. In this case the HCM mobile plane contour *ABCDEF*... (Figure 5) at points, say, *BDF*... is fitted with gripping elements (electromagnetic clutches or pneumatic suckers). The driving links connected with the driving device may be attached to the *ACE*... or other points, thus making it possible to arrange a required number of grippers at assigned points of the plane. This permitted the design a number of gripping devices for conveying sheet bars of various sizes and shapes by a robot. These are characterized by the possibility of quick readjustment of the gripper to different types of manipulated objects. Depending on the shape complexity of

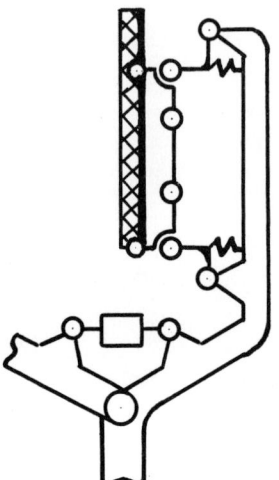

Figure 4 Assur groups (class IV) mounted on gripper's jaws surface

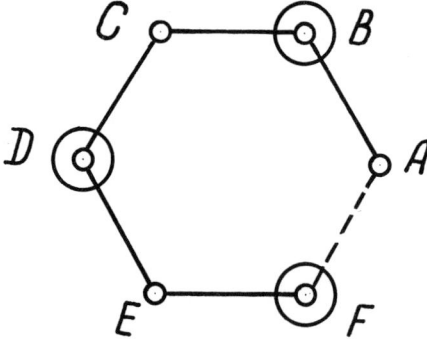

Figure 5 HCM mobile plane contour *ABCDEF*

conveyed objects and, accordingly, the total number of the advanced point of the clutch, similar constructions can successfully employ mechanisms of the V, VI and higher classes.

Earlier, high kinematic capabilities of HCM ensured by their greater complexity as compared with the second- and third-class mechanisms, did not, however, allow to use them in designing manipulating devices. This was due to some technical difficulties when solving problems of the analysis and, moreover, the synthesis of

HCM in accordance with assigned technological conditions. In this connection at the Kazakh State University the grapho-analytical and then analytical HCM theories have been developed to solve problems of analysis and synthesis.[7] Based on the universal vector–matrix calculus apparatus the developed methods enable one to solve not only kinematic, but also dynamic and kinetostatic problems. From the above-mentioned it may be concluded that HCM may find a wide and promising application in designing mechanical devices of manipulative robots.

References

[1] Djoldasbekov U A and Baigunchekov J J (1975) *Kinematics of Assur Groups of High Classes and Orders* IVth World Cong. on the TMM, Newcastle upon Tyne, vol 3
[2] Tsai Y C and Soni A H (1981) Accessible region and synthesis *Trans. ASME J. Design*, **103**(4)
[3] Klein (1982) Verfahren zum Entwerfen herkömmlicher Gelenkgetriebe für Handhabungsgeräte. *Maschinenmarkt*, **88**(49)
[4] Djoldasbekov U A and Slutskii L I (1983) Manipulators with variable link lengths: kinematics and possibilities. *J. Mech. Mach. Theory*, **18**(4)
[5] Djoldasbekov U A and Ivanov K S (1979) *The Synthesis of High Class Mechanisms for Reproducing Movements of Two Interacting Links* 5th World Cong. on the Theory of Machines and Mechanisms, Montreal, vol I
[6] Djoldasbekov U A and Baigunchekov J J (1981) Optimal synthesis of high class mechanisms. *Vestn. Akad. Nauk Kaz. SSR*, no 7 (in Russian)
[7] Djoldasbekov U A and Baigunchekov (1981) *The Dynamic Analysis and Structural Kinematic Synthesis of High Class Mechanisms* 5th All-Union Cong. on Theoretical and Applied Mechanics (Abstracts). Nauka Publishers, Alma-Ata (in Russian)

Synthesis and Design of Mechanical Hands for Robots with Application of Computer-aided Design

A Rovetta

Department of Mechanics, Politecnico di Milano, Milan, Italy

Summary: This work deals with the application of CAD methodology in the realization of mechanical design and of software of the control of a mechanical hand developed for robots. Using CAD methodology and continued co-ordination and comparison with the results of experimental tests, the same dynamic equations could be used for the synthesis and the mechanical hand project and consequently for the software of control of the hand. The software of the control program is applied on a microprocessor.

Introduction

This work deals with the application of CAD methodology in the realization of an articulated mechanical hand for robots. The grasping process takes place by means of a mechanical sequence, which depends on the morphology of the piece, on the characteristics of the grasping system, on the absolute and relative movement of the parts, on the external forces and internal actions of the different components of the system. Such a complexity can be analysed using mathematic models of the grasping process (mechanical of the multibody systems, dynamic equations with non-linear elements in the interaction between objects and fingers of the mechanical hand, etc.), which require a number of parameters relatively elevated.

Since the complexity of the holding system cannot be easily reproduced to develop the design phase nor can it be integrally adopted for the realization of the software of the control system, a model with a mathematic base was realized. By using CAD methodology and the continued arrangement and comparison with the experimental results, the same dynamic equations for the synthesis and the mechanical hand project, with the software and for the control of the robot hand, have been used.

The software of the control program is applied on a microprocessor. The prototype of the articulate mechanical hand developed is a consequence of the integration and harmonization between the CAD results used in the mechanical design and in the drawing up of the software of the control. The system is suitable for the holding of objects of generic shape.

This work is original because of the complexity of the mechanical structure and of the electronic control of the articulated hand can be increased through the use of CAD methodology.

Design of mechanical structure and of software of control of mechanical hand for robots

The original idea for the mechanical articulated hand, used for the grasping of objects of different shapes, came from the realization of the preindustrial prototype by means of defining a mathematic model for the simulation of the movement and of the dynamic process (Figure 1).

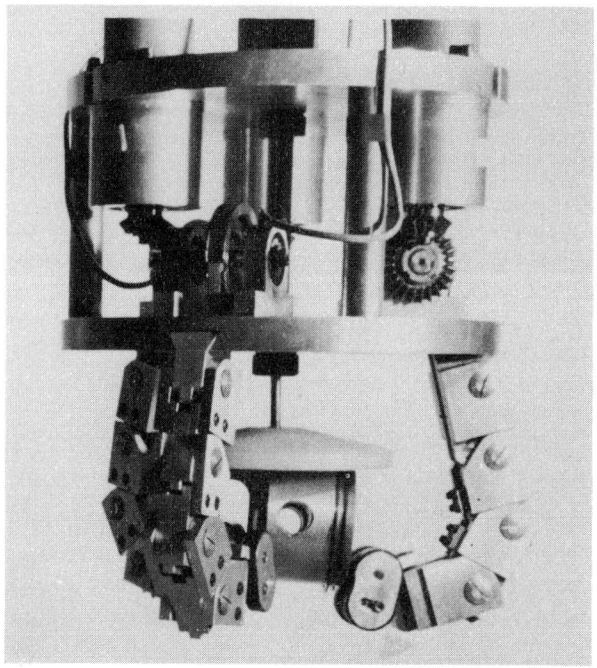

Figure 1   Preindustrial prototype model of mechanical articulated hand: prehension spatial

The simulation model was used both for the mechanical project of single elements of the structure; ie the rods, the pivots, the supports, the cables, the springs for preloading and restoring, and the project for the software control of the hand.

Modelling of prehension process

The grasping process between hand and object requires a morphologic adaptation between the finger and the external surface of the object with action and reaction of contact, influenced by friction, by the inertial forces, by the forces on the object. The forces transmitted from the mechanical fingers can be theoretically evaluated only in an approximate way.

The models of the prehension process consider single fingers moving with respect to the object independently of each other. In the first prototype model (Figure 2) prehension is bidimensional, in the preindustrial prototype (Figure 1) prehension is spatial. The fingers are actuated by three motors, controlled by a microprocessor by means of force-sensory signals which detect the traction on the cables actuating the

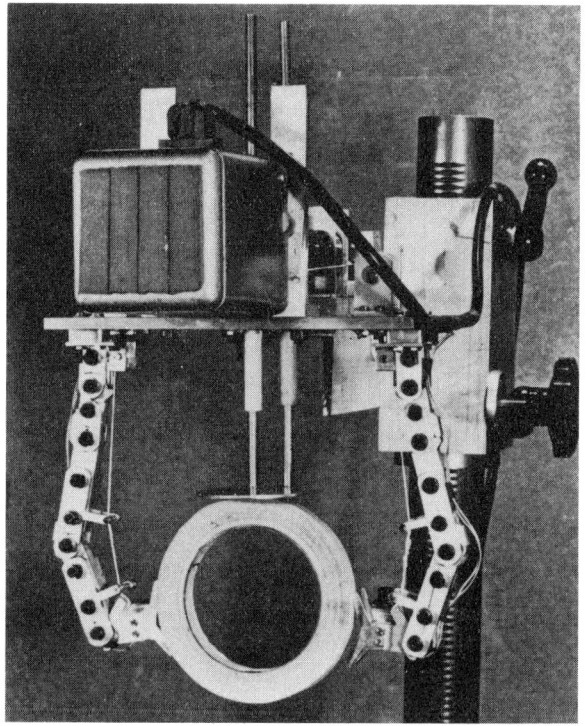

Figure 2 First prototype model of prehension process: prehension bidimensional

motion of the fingers (Figure 3). The mechanical grasping model is elementary and considers three fingers at $120°$, with a central palm that completes the prehension (Figure 4). The grasping of symmetrical objects, to reproduce the sequence of the finger movement and to develop modelling with CAD methodology, has been examined.

Geometrical model of the hand

The sequence of successive positions of the fingers defines the grasping procedure. Such a sequence can be described graphically, on the basis of the geometric structure of the hand (Figure 5). The geometric parameters of the mechanical hand project are: dimensions of the proximal, medial, distal phalanges, determined by the dimensions and force on the object to be grasped; initial and final angles of three phalanges with respect to the mechanical system (Figure 5) with stop blocks to limit the rotation; initial and final angles of the inverse joint; this assures the opposite opening of the fingers when the object tends to slide away from the hand, or when the dimension of the grasped object that requires a greater opening of the fingers; angle of the attachment of the fingers to the plate of the hand, which determines the field of work of the hand and the maximum volume of the object to be

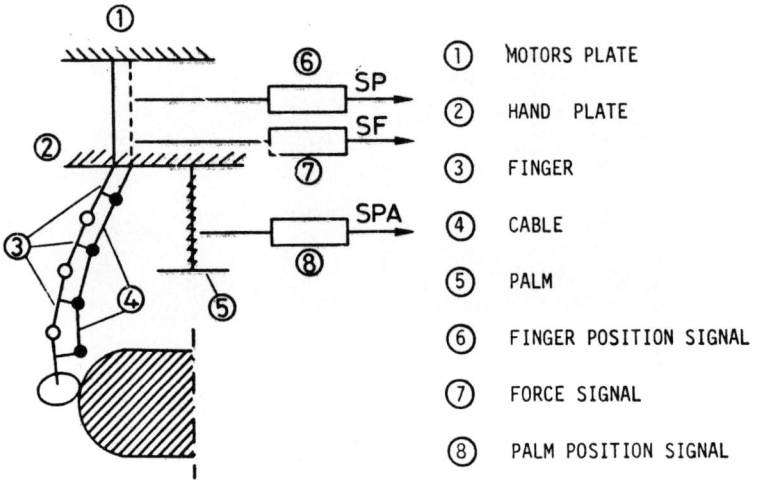

Figure 3 Prehension prototype model: force-sensory signals detect traction on cables actuating motion of fingers

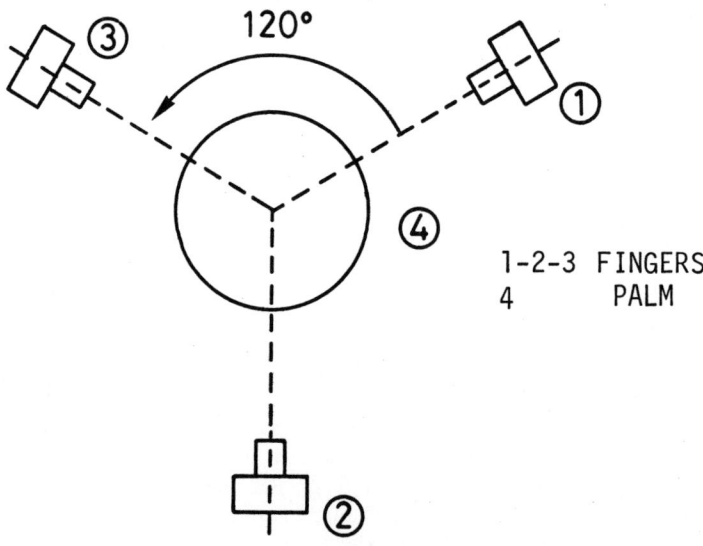

Figure 4 Mechanical grasping model of hand

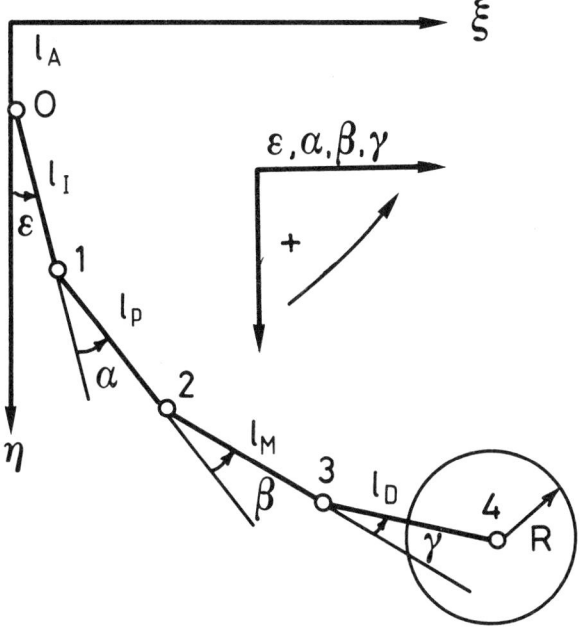

Figure 5 Grasping procedure sequence of hand described graphically

grasped; radius of the pulp; shape of the plate of the palm.

The CAD methodology permits the estimation of the influence of all these parameters through a graphic representation that supports the designer in the system-designing phase and for the choice of components (Figure 6 a, b).

Dynamic analysis of grasping process

The dynamic actions between object, hand and environment determine the geometric and dynamic aspect of the settlement of each finger of the hand. The mechanical project must possess hardware that provides the maximum operative flexibility to the hand. The dynamic analysis of the holding process has been developed determining, for every shape of the finger, the external and internal forces of the system.

The flowchart of the computer program is shown in Figure 7. Considering the force F exchanged between finger and object as applied on the pulp of the finger, according to a line action of the θ angle inclination, the tension component on the cable of every finger can be determined according to the following expressions (1). In the approaching phase

$$T_a t_a = M_{k_a} + M_w \tag{1a}$$

In the grasping phase, during the rotation of the last phalanx

$$T_\gamma t_\gamma = F_{b_\gamma} + M_{k_\gamma} + M_w \tag{1b}$$

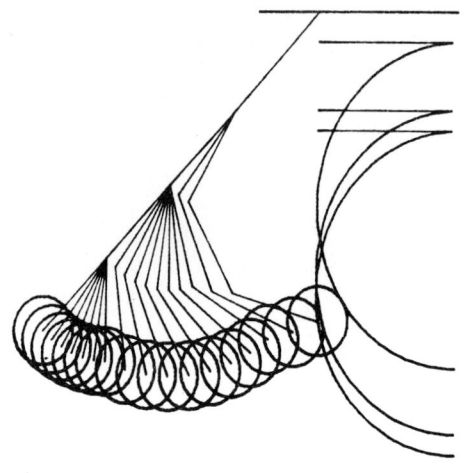

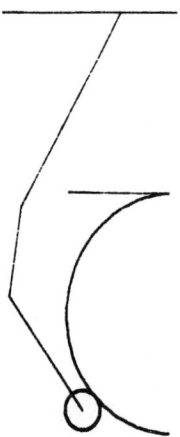

Figure 6 Graphic representation of influence of geometrical parameters of mechanical hand by CAD methodology. a, MANI program; b, PAUM program

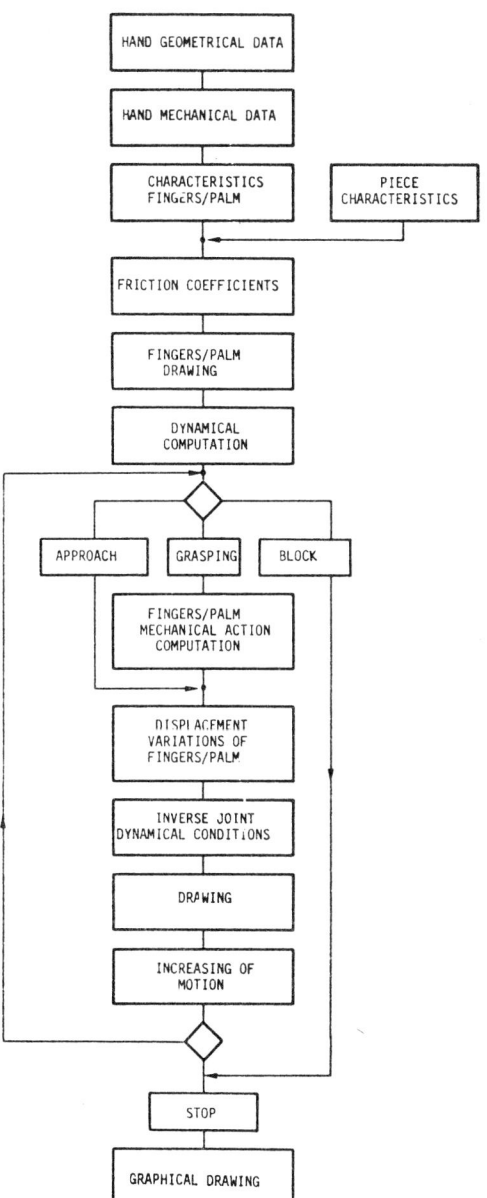

Figure 7 Flowchart of computer program

where

$$b_\gamma = l_d \cos[\epsilon + \alpha + \beta + \gamma - \psi - (\theta + \Phi_a)] + r \sin\phi_a \tag{1c}$$

$$M_{k_\gamma} = M_{o_3} + k_3(\gamma - \gamma_i) \tag{1d}$$

In the grasping phase, during the rotation β of the second phalanx

$$T_\beta t_\beta = F b_\beta + M_{k_\beta} + M_w \tag{1e}$$

where

$$b_\beta = b_\gamma + l_M \cos[\epsilon + \alpha + \beta - \psi - (\theta + \phi_a)] \tag{1f}$$

$$M_{k_\beta} = M_{k_\gamma} + M_{o_2} + k_2(\beta - \beta_i) \tag{1g}$$

In the grasping phase, during the rotation of the first phalanx

$$T_\alpha t_\alpha = F b_\alpha + M_k + M_w \tag{1h}$$

where

$$b_\alpha = b_\beta + l_p \cos[\epsilon + \alpha - \psi - (\theta + \phi_a)] \tag{1i}$$

$$M_{k_\alpha} = M_{k_\beta} + M_{o_1} + k_1(\alpha - \alpha_i) \tag{1j}$$

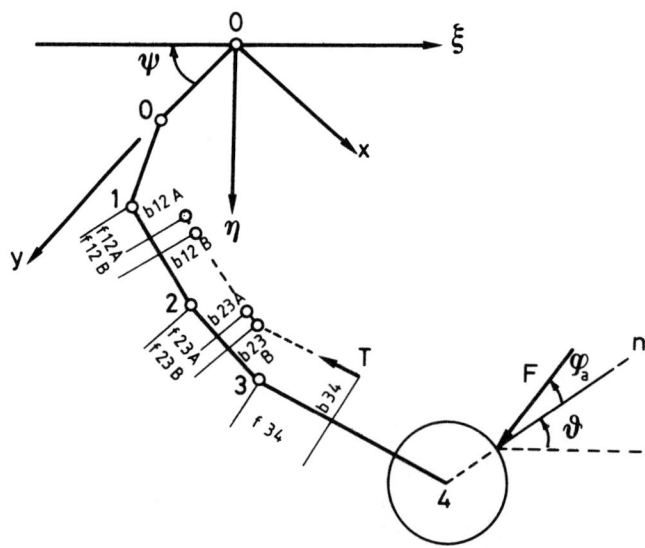

Figure 8

The meaning of the symbols is shown in the Appendix. The dynamic equations depend on the configuration of the fingers, defined from the angles $\alpha, \beta, \gamma, \epsilon$. The sequence of the fingers can be drawn on the basis of the geometric structure of the hand, and by the loads on the fingers, with the help of the CAD program denominated MANI. The torques of preloading M_{0_1}, M_{0_2}, M_{0_3} of the springs k_1, k_2, k_3 located in the joints of the phalanges are determined according to the relation (2)

$$M_{0_1} > M_{0_2} > M_{0_3} \tag{2}$$

Every inverse joint contains a restoring spring; the torques of preloading M_{os} are determined from the relation (3)

$$M_e < M_{os} + k_s (\epsilon_f - \epsilon_i) \tag{3}$$

The dynamic equations of equilibrium contain also the actions of active and reactive forces.

The inertial forces of the single phalanges are not considered because, in the calculus phase for the design, the determination of such forces, relatively reduced in the application of the hand until now realized, increased the weight of the mathematic model without offering an increase of precision in the calculus and in the control.

Significance of mathematic model

The mathematical (geometric and dynamic) model appears to be limited, but results can be adjusted to the purpose of harmonization between project and control of the mechanical hand. The results of the mathematic model are shown in Figure 9

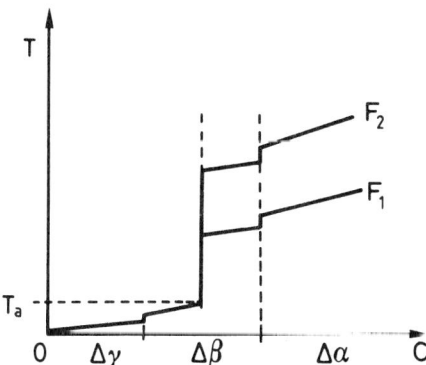

Figure 9 Results of mathematic model

where, for the sequence of different positions, is reported the value of the active force that exercises the traction action on the cable of each finger of the mechanical hand.

In this way it is revealed that during the approach phase, when the object is not yet grasped by the hand, the fingers of the hand close and the cable exercises the necessary force to surpass the dynamic resistance of the springs according to the dynamical equations. From the results obtained with the computer according to the CAD methodology, the software control designer can determine the theoretical course for the unloaded movement of the finger and determine the control function of the system on the basis of the results of the mathematical model and the comparison with the data on the experimental test on the prototypes.

If T_a indicates the traction force on the cable of the jth finger during the approaching phase, the mathematical relation that assures the control computer that it is in the approaching phase is that the sensory signals, performed by the sensorial system of the hand, according to the functional scheme shown in Figure 3, is

$$S_T < T_a \qquad (4)$$

Approximation hypothesis

The mathematical model contains some restrictive and approximate hypotheses. The main hypotheses are: the action of the pulp, in the plane tangent to the surface contact in a perpendicular direction to the finger plan, exercises a bending action on the mechanical finger (the reaction is presented from the joint of the plate attached to the hand); the coefficient of friction is presumed constant; unity of the mechanical efficiency in the mechanism of articulation and of contact between the pivot and the cable is presumed; we consider the relatively reduced values of inertial forces and torques of the phalanges of the palm and of the piece.

Such limiting hypotheses can be surpassed by more elaborate calculus methodology without altogether modifying the mechanical project and with some modification in software of control. The contact between the fingers, palm and object takes place on a contact line due to the morphology of the pulps. The settling phase in the prehension assures the software designer, because such a phenomenon offers an element of intrinsic stabilization in the grasping process.

Integration of CAD in the realization of software of control

The project obtained through CAD, which describes the movement of single fingers and determines the dynamic conditions of functioning, has helped develop the relations between the disposition of the hand and tension in the driving cable for the object being held.

Consequently, the control software can be developed by programming the sequence of finger movement on the basis of dynamic model results, even though simplified. The sequence of movement follows the same rules for which the hand has been designed.

Degrees of freedom

In the synthesis of the mechanical hand, the degrees of freedom of the single fingers, and consequently of the hand, allow the maximum functioning flexibility and adaptability in the grasping of objects of whatever form to be obtained. Because the articulated hand has three degrees of freedom in the fingers and a fourth degree of freedom for the rotation in the inverse joint, the system with N fingers can present $4N$ degrees of freedom.

The design of the spring in each joint has been developed in a way that every phalanx can move only consecutively to the adjacent one; therefore, each finger presents a single degree of freedom. The other degrees of freedom are either stopped at the end of the movement from the mechanical blocks or they have not been activated because the stiffness and the preloading of the springs, conveniently set, prohibit it.

The equations that assure such constraints conditions to the degrees of freedom are the following (5):

$$M_{kj} > M_{k(j-1)} + k(\Delta)_{(j-1)} \quad (5)$$

where the meaning of the symbols are given in the Appendix.

The presence of the inverse joint increases the degrees of freedom, because it intervenes in opening the hand and admits a rotation around the upper point of the finger. In such dynamic conditions, the grasping system can present up to six degrees of freedom. The system assumes a configuration that depends (see Figure 6) on the grasped object and from the force exchanged between object and single finger. To represent and describe, even analytically, the sequence of the movement of every finger, since the numerous variables of the system intervene in non-linear equations, and the dynamic interaction between hand and object contains elements variable according to the relative movement of the piece inside the fingers, the computer (CAD), used in an interactive way, was shown to be indispensable (Figure 6a,b).

Relation between realization of motion and finger movement

The hand carries out (see Figure 10) a movement of the phalanges controlled in three rotational degrees of freedom and controlled by the force for the inverse The trajectory of the extreme point of mechanical fingers, indicated in Figure 10, is made up of a series of circumferencial arcs. In the first stage of the movement the centre of the circumference is in point C and the radius is equal to the length of the phalanx. In the second phase the centre is in joint B and the radius is equal to the distance BD. In the third phase the centre is in the pivot A and the radius is equal to the AD distance, as represented in Figure 10.

The opening of the inverse joint superimposes a rigid rotation of the whole finger around the inverse joint. The relation between the movement of the extreme of the cable and the configuration undertaken by every finger is obtained using trigonometrical formulae, which are derived from the design of the configuration of each finger, where, at every length of the acting cable there corresponds a position of the finger.

In the case of motion without the intervention of the inverse joint, the relation is univocal, but when the inverse joint intervenes, to the configuration with one degree of finger freedom, the rigid rotation around the inverse joint is superimposed.

The functional relation assumes therefore in the absence of the inverse joint motion, the form (6)

$$[C(\alpha, \beta, \gamma)]_{\epsilon=0} = Z(T) \quad (6)$$

where C represents the configuration of the fingers and Z is a function of the movement of the traction cable.

In the presence of inverse joint action, assigned the movement of the cable, there remains to be defined ϵ and the angles of rotation α, β, γ according to relation (7)

$$Z(T) \rightarrow C'(\alpha, \beta, \gamma) \quad (7)$$

The configurations C' represent a set of possibilities conditioned by the reaction in the inverse joint, according to the relation (8)

$$M_e < M_{0_4} \quad (8)$$

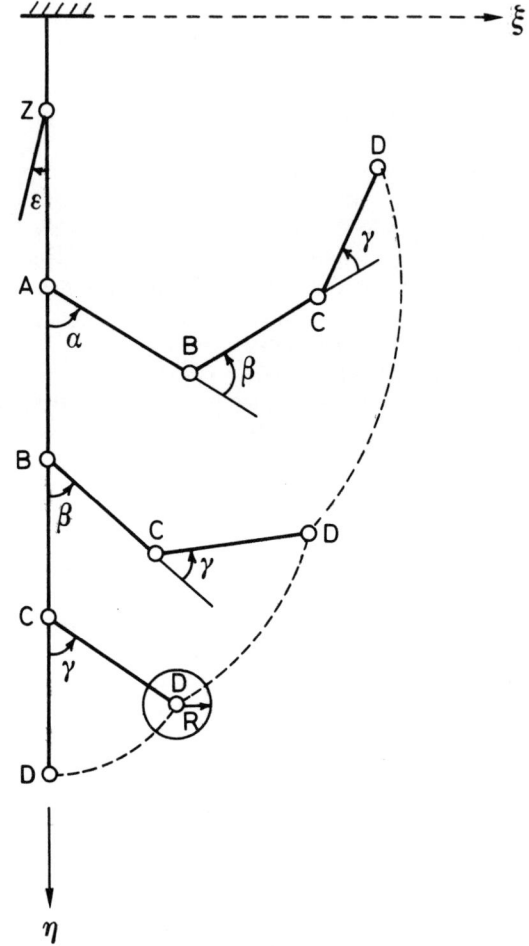

Figure 10 Trajectory of extreme point of mechanical fingers

where M_e is the torque, which is applied to the inverse joint, and M_{0_4} is the corresponding torque of preloading.

This non-linearity of behaviour is made evident by the CAD and from the experimental tests on the prototype and constitutes an element of complexity in the control of the mechanical hand.

Presence and action of pulp

The pulp is formed (see Figure 11) by two arcs of circumferences connected between them by a third arc. The centre of the two arcs are symmetrical with respect to the axis of the last phalanx; the radius of the two arcs is determined in the design phase on the basis of the functional necessity of exercising a continuous and regular contact between the piece and fingers of the hand. After defining the position of the

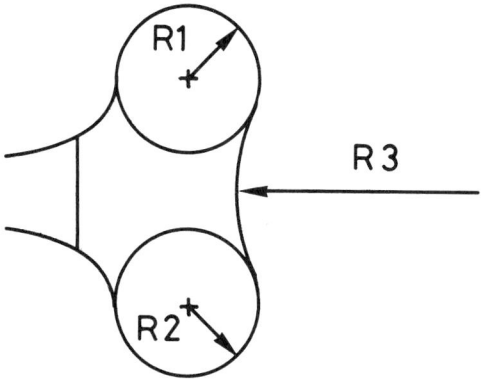

Figure 11 Pulp formed by two arcs of circumferences connected between a third arc

last phalanx, the co-ordinates of the centres of the three arcs on the pulp, R_1, R_2 and R_3 are also obtained. The position of the contact point between object and finger is defined by the form of the object with respect to the plane in which every finger lies. In a symbolic form, we have (9)

$$(\xi, \eta)_P = (\xi, \eta)_D + f(R, \theta) \tag{9}$$

where the meaning of the symbols are given in the Appendix.

Model with circular pulp

The contact between finger and object is performed on parts of the circular arcs. The basic analytical model is formed by a circle with radius R_o. The dynamic scheme of contact is shown in Figure 12, where the components F_n and F_t of the

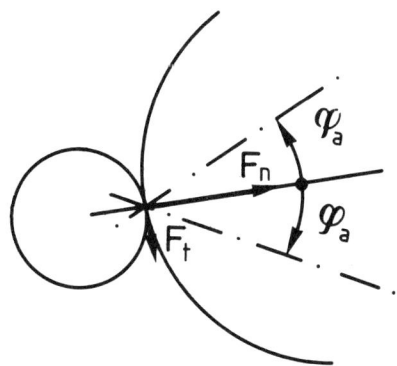

Figure 12 Dynamic scheme of contact

forces exchanged between finger and object in the plan of the same finger are represented.

In the absence of friction F_t is missing; in the presence of friction F_t assumes different values depending on the action of the phase of adhesion, without relative movement, or of dynamic friction, with relative movement.

In the case of adhesion it is $F_t < \mu_s \cdot F_n$; in the case of friction it is $F_t = \mu_d \cdot F_n$. The F force, in the absence of friction, passes through the centre of the pulp and therefore its direction is known. In the presence of friction, it is inclined according to the schemes shown in Figure 12, where the tangential reaction is directed toward the superior plate. In case the hand opens, such a reaction changes the direction and is directed in the sense of departing from the superior plate.

Analysis with CAD methodology of prehension process

The MANI program, realized in FORTRAN 77 language, describes the prehension process between the finger and a spherical object, by representing the position of the phalanges and of the piece in the following phases of approach; first contact, prehension, lifting, and stopping.

The MANI program presents (Figure 6a): the geometric design of a finger and of the spherical part concerned with contact; the determination of the actions and reactions that are dynamically exchanged between finger and object; the calculus of the forces on the rods, on the pivots, on the cables, etc.; the determination of the relation between configuration of the finger and of the palm of the system and the traction force in the cable.

The operator can vary the parameters of the project system, according to the scheme in Figure 7 and control the function of the cable traction of a finger, when the form and the weight of the piece, the structure of the hand, palm, fingers, the radius of the pulp, the friction coefficients between finger and object, the angles for the work of the phalanges are modified.

The PAUM program, realized in FORTRAN 77 language, represents a finger in the prehension phase, in contact with the object, when the pressure angle of the force, the basic dimensions of the phalanges, the angles between the phalanges, the weight and the form of the sphere grasped, the angle of attachment of the hand and the position of the palm are assigned. The PAUM program provides the designer with a geometric representation of the system, by using computer-aided design methodology, in an immediate and synthetic form (Figure 6b).

For the realization and the construction of the mechanical hand, represented in Figure 1, developed in collaboration with designers from Soc Alfa Romeo Auto SpA Research Section, the PAUM program was used to choose the series of mechanical data of the hand. The principal dimensions for the construction, carried out by utilizing the MANI program data were determined from geometric results obtained from CAD. Such a procedure can be repeated for the design of other hands, with different materials, morphology, dimensions, modifying the calculus fomulae in the structure of the software programs.

Software of hand control

The scheme for the dynamic control operating the hand is represented in the scheme of Figure 13. The program, called AMBR, is developed in BASIC language.

CAD and the Design of Mechanical Hands   335

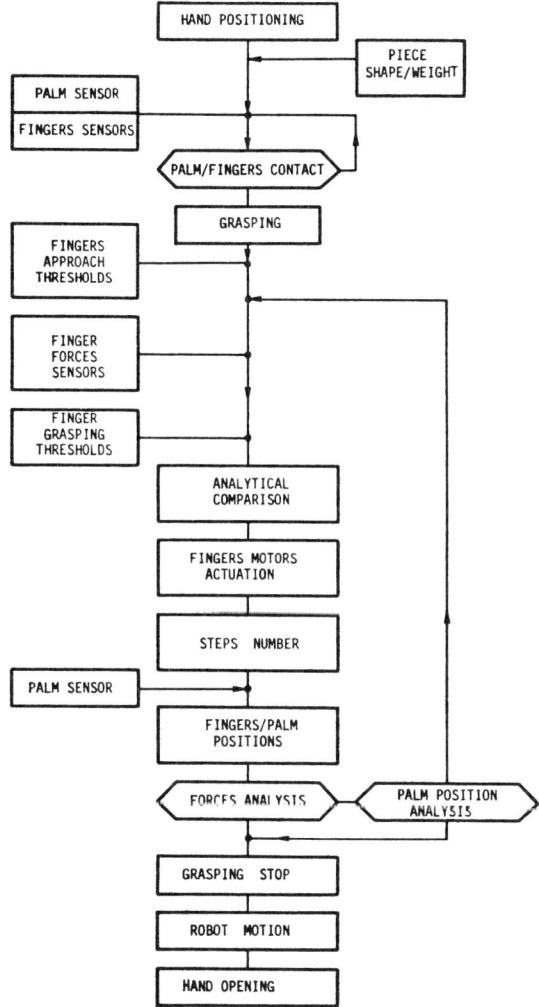

Figure 13   Scheme for dynamic control operating the hand: AMBR program

The control system acts on an eight-bit processor. The sensory signals are sent by three strain-gauge elements, arranged on a pulley, which exert the traction force on the cable, and from a potentiometer that measures the position of the palm. The three force signals of the fingers and the position signal of the palm are elaborated by the microprocessor, according to the same mathematical formulae that are used for the CAD planning.

On the basis of such data, from the value of the force T on the cable, the F force exchanged between the finger and object is foreseen and the operative sequence of the fingers is decided. The signal of the palm indicates three possible conditions: (1) presence of the piece between the fingers; (2) prehension of the piece between the fingers; (3) stop for the ending of the grasping process.

The force transmitted to the palm is

$$P = K_p(p - p_o) + P_o \qquad (10)$$

where the meaning of the symbols are given in the Appendix.

The sensory signals of the fingers can indicate a series of conditions that are foreseen internally by the software control. Among these are: (1) absence of contact between finger and object; (2) beginning of contact on a finger; (3) beginning of grasping; (4) development of holding process; (5) bad contact of a finger; (6) eventual falling of the piece; (7) stopping of a finger for overloading; (8) stopping of prehension sequence; (9) reopening of the hand.

The structure of the software of control can be simplified, even by using the results of dynamic computations, comparing the sensory signals with threshold values. The threshold values define, for every object, the minimum value of force below which there is contact between finger and object (approach phase), and the value for which begins the prehension (initial holding phase). Moreover, there are comparison values for regular holding, for maximum overloading and for stable prehension. The palm, as it occurred for the mechanical design, guarantees and assures, through its movement sensory signals, the regularity of prehension. The control software controls the movement of three step motors, according to the dynamic process utilized in the CAD analysis, even if such a model was elementary, with spherical object, considering the prehension in the plane of every single active finger.

Harmonization between mechanical design and software of control

Use of CAD methodology has permitted the geometric functional characteristics of the prehension process to be evident. The results, even though applied to an elementary model of the holding process, have been transferred in the design of the software of the mechanical hand. The software results arising from the mechanical hand project surpass complexity inborn in the dynamic prehension process through the data obtained with the computer used in an interactive form. The harmonization between mechanical design and realization of software of control has permitted an articulated complex structure of many degrees of freedom, with a microprocessor at eight bit, with 48 kbytes of memory, to be actuated.

This research was developed with a support from the Italian National Council of the Researches (CNR).

References

[1] Rovetta A (1979) On the prehension of the human hand. *J. Mech. Mach. Theory* (12)
[2] Kato I (1978) *Mechanical Hands*, Tokyo
[3] Salisbury J K & Roth B *Kinematic and Force Analysis of Articulated Mechanical Hands* ASME, 82-Det-13, Design and Production Engineering Technical Conf., Washington, DC, September, 1982

Appendix

Table of symbols

b_j	Arm for the force on the pulp with respect to the jth joint
k	Elastic constants of the springs in the joints
p	Movement of the palm
t_j	Arm of the traction force in the cable with respect to the jth joint
C	Function relative to the configuration of the finger
F_n	Normal force between the finger and object
F_t	Tangential force between the finger and object in the plan of the finger
M	Preloading torque of the spring in the joint
M_w	Torque due to the mass of phalanx
N	Numbers of fingers
P	Force transmitted by the palm
R	Radius of the pulp
S	Sensory signal
T	Force of traction in the cable
α,β,γ	Rotation angle relative to the phalanges
ϵ	Rotation angle relative to the counter joint
μ_d	Coefficient of dynamic friction between finger and object
μ_s	Coefficient of static friction between finger and object
ϕ_a	Angle of friction
Ψ	Angle of inclination in the attachment of the hand
Δ_j	Maximum angular variation of the jth joint

Index

i	Initial
f	Final
e	External
o	Of preloading

A New Design Method of Servo-actuators Based on the Shape Memory Effect

S Hirose, K Ikuta and Y Umetani

Department of Physical Engineering, Tokyo Institute of Technology, Tokyo, Japan

Summary: The possible realization of micro-actuators driven by the shape memory effect is discussed. The mechanism, specifications and requirements of the shape memory effect as applied to robot actuators are investigated. A theoretical model is developed that can simulate the thermoelastic and kinematic transformations associated with the shape memory effect. By using a new design configuration, a prototype SMA actuator has been realized.

Introduction

To fabricate a robot with multi-degrees of freedom that can realize versatile and dextrous motions, the development of a micro- and lightweight actuator for the muscle part is needed. Conventional electrical or hydraulic actuators do not satisfy these requirements.

Recently, it has become clear that alloys showing shape memory effect (SME) can generate substantial stress on heating, thus converting heat directly into mechanical work.[1] By using shape memory alloys (SMA), solid-state micro-actuators suitable for robot actuation have been developed.[2] In Japan several experimental manipulator models using SMA have been constructed and demonstrate their motions.[3] But to realize practical devices, a suitable design configuration is needed.

In this paper, after investigating the basic requirements of SMA when they are used in robot actuators, a new design array is proposed. The second section is a general description of the SME for a robot researcher. The third section discusses the possibility to realize SMA actuators. Anticipated advantages of the SMA actuator, drawbacks and countermeasures are considered in this section. The fourth section proposes a theoretical model for SME. Finally the last section introduces a new design configuration (the ζ-array) for SMA actuator. The construction of a prototype model of SMA actuator based on the new design principle is also presented in this section.

Shape memory effect

What is the shape memory effect? Before discussing the technical problems associated with SMA actuator, the shape memory effect should be explained. The SME is the phenomenon exhibited by some alloys (i.e. Ti-Ni or Cu-Zn-Al).[3] The SME is a two-phase transformation of the alloy. In a first stage the alloy is formed in heat-treatment at high temperature and is given the desired shape (parent phase). The Ti-Ni alloy is obtained at about 750 K. The alloy can be deformed from the parent shape by an external force at low temperature (intermediate phase). This temperature should be lower than the martensite finish temperature M_f of the alloy (see Table 1). When the alloy is heated over the austenite finish temperature A_f of

Table 1 Specifications of typical Ti-Ni alloy

Density	6.5×10^3 kg/m^3
Specific heat coefficient (Cp)	0.24×10^3 J/kg K^{-1}
Thermal conductivity	0.2×10^2 J/m s^{-1} K^{-1}
Specific resistance	$50 \sim 100 \times 10^{-8}$ Ω m
Transformation temperatures	M_f 270 M_s 305 A_s 327 A_f 345 k
Young's modulus martensite austenite	E_M 2.9×10^4 MPa E_A 6.2×10^4 MPa
Maximum recovery strain	$6 \sim 10$ %
Maximum recovery stress	$500 \sim 600$ MPa

the alloy, a reverse transformation process occurs and the parent phase is recovered. In the SME the recovery transformation from any intermediate shape to the parent shape or the reverse motion can be repeated millions of times without any harmful effect on the alloy. Moreover, the stress producing the deformation can be very high and the recovery strain large enough to bring the alloy to its parent phase. A typical Ti-Ni alloy wire, for instance, produces up to 6 per cent strain and about 500 MPa stress in its SME.[4,5] Crystallographically, the SME is caused by a thermoelastic martensite transformation. This is the same first-order phase transformation that occurs in ordinary metals [i.e. Fe-C (steel)].

However, the generation mechanism here is completely different. In the case of ordinary metals the transition of the crystal structure after the transformation is caused by the diffusion of atoms and therefore displacement of the atoms is irreversible and the velocity of the transformation, dominated by the diffusion process, is slow. In contrast, the SME is caused by a thermoelastic martensite transformation and a flip motion of the crystal lattice between different equilibria in terms of free energy. In the case of Ti-Ni alloy, the structure changes from CsCl(B2) at high temperature to a monoclinic crystal at low temperature.

In a thermoplastic martensite transformation, the variants in the martensite phase always have good coherency and are easily interchangeable. The stress which produces the twin deformation among the variants is less than the yield stress of the dislocation slip deformation. SME is thus reversible and occurs instantaneously.

The basic specifications of SME are shown in Figure 1. In Figure 1, line A and line B indicate the critical stress for a dislocational slippage in austenite and martensite phase respectively. Line C indicates the critical boundary to induce the martensite phase from the austenite phase. From this boundary, we can know that the transformations between austenite and martensite phases depend not only on temperature but also on stress. This phenomenon is similar to the phase transformation between water and steam at boiling point. When water is in pressurized vessel, the boiling point rises. Based on this consideration, line C can be well expressed by a Clausius-Clapeyron-like equation[6] as

$$\frac{dT}{d\sigma} = \frac{T_0 \cdot \triangle \epsilon}{\rho \cdot \triangle H} \quad (\cong c) \tag{1}$$

Where T_0 is the transformation temperature under no load condition, $\triangle \epsilon$ is the strain after the transformation, ρ is the density of the alloy and $\triangle H$ is the latent heat of the transformation.

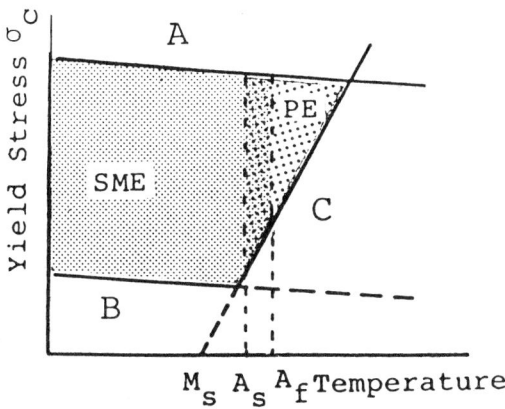

Figure 1 Basic specifications of the SME

It is worth noticing that the twin deformation in the martensite phase occurs just under line B. Just as additional pressure applied to steam generates more water, SMA in austenite phase also changes to martensite phase only by application of additional stresses. This kind of martensite is, on purpose, called stress-induced martensite (SIM).[7] The stress-induced martensite of an SMA gives rise to the interesting pseudoelasticity (PE) function. The pseudoelasticity function occurs when an SMA is kept at a temperature higher than A_f.

At this temperature, the SMA is in austenite phase, and transforms to martensite phase only by applying stress. Since the transformation is reversible, the SMA exhibits extremely large pseudoelastic deformations. Besides the pseudoelasticity, the existence of the Clausius Clapeyron-like effect induces specific problems to the shape-deformation process of the SMA. The characteristics of a typical SMA are summarized in Table 1.

SMA actuators

To demonstrate the specifications of SMA actuators, we first examine actuators presently used in robots, namely electric motors and hydraulic cylinders. From the standpoint of size and output/weight ratio, these are not satisfactory. An electric motor consists of a high-speed rotor, its bearing and magnet. So to acquire the low-speed high-power motion of a robot actuator, a reduction gear operation is needed, but the miniaturization of an electric motor is limited. Hydraulic or pneumatic devices are comparatively simple, but need sealing devices to resist the leakage of the highly pressurized liquid. It is also not feasible to miniaturize the mechanism of a hydraulic system. On the other hand, an SMA actuator makes use of the deformation of alloy and is simple. It is comprised of the alloy itself and the heating and cooling devices. The simplest method of heating and cooling the SMA is to supply electric current to the SMA wire itself and generate Joule heat and to cool it down by natural air ventilation respectively. In this case an SMA and a pair of lead wires are enough to make a complete actuator.

The extreme simplicity of an SMA actuator coupled with the solid-state phenomenon of the shape memory effect produces higher output force (order of 500 MPa in case of Ti-Ni). Therefore a micro-, lightweight and high-output power actuator can be expected in SMA actuator. Of course, the simplicity of SMA actuator ensures its reliability. Another important feature of the SMA as basic material for a servo-actuator is that its electric resistance varies with the transformation ratio. By monitoring its resistance change only, an SMA can be considered as a sensing device for the servo-actuator. Although SMA actuators have these desirable characteristics, many problems remain to be solved before these devices can be used in practice.

The low-energy efficiency is of prime consideration. The SME is, in principle, considered to be an engine which converts heat into work, and thus the efficiency cannot exceed that of a Carnot cycle. Since the efficiency of a Carnot cycle is very low in the low-temperature operation range, the efficiency of an SMA actuator is estimated to be very low. No exact value has yet been reported, but it does not exceed 10 per cent. The low efficiency of SMA actuators suggests that these devices should not be considered as a replacement for conventional actuators, but as their supplements.

Owing to their dependence on heat transfer, SMA actuators have very slow motion. But it is possible to realize a comparatively rapid response even in a heat-dominated SMA actuator. The basic idea is to improve the coefficient of heat transfer between the SMA and its surrounding heat sinks by an optimum design of heat-transfer parameters. It is obvious that if an SMA is used in water, its coefficient of heat transfer increases drastically.

Another problem with an SMA actuator is the difficulty to control the non-linearity and the complicated specifications of the SME. We think that the intense analysis of the SME and the progress in material design of the alloy will solve this problem so that a controllable and dextrous operation of SMA actuators will be attained in the near future. In the next section we report the results of our theoretical analysis of the SMA.

A SMA actuator should fit where a great number of compact actuators is needed and where energy efficiency or time response of the actuator are not the main requirements. A micro-actuator used to drive an active cord mechanism[10] of an active stem of gastroscope is one application where the energy is supplied from the base and it is not necessary that the bending motion should be too fast.

Model of shape memory effect

This section introduces the recent results of a research program we have been conducting on a model of the SME.[8,9] The model is derived in three steps; from an expression of the mechanism of the thermoelastic martensite transformation and models of the kinematic properties of martensite and austenite phases, the model of the SME is synthesized.

Model of thermoelastic transformation

The typical tendency of austenite and martensite transformations of an SMA is shown by broken lines in Figure 2. Since the effect is based on a first-order phase transformation, there exists hysteresis, though little compared with a normal martensite transformation. The transformation is modelled linearly as shown by the

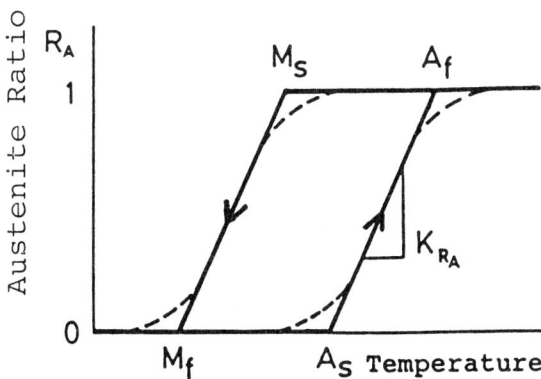

Figure 2 Temperature dependence of the austenite ratio R_A

solid lines of Figure 2. The magnitude of the transformation is expressed by a coefficient, the austenite ratio R_A, given by

$$R_A = \frac{\text{(volume in austenite phase)}}{\text{(total volume of SMA)}} \qquad (2)$$

Strictly speaking, a minor hysteresis must be considered in the transformation. But as a preliminary approximation, we consider only the major hysteresis. Further work on the point is in progress now. Because of the Clausius-Clapeyron-like effect of the thermoelastic transformation, the austenite ratio R_A is affected not only by temperature but by stress. This has already been explained (see Figure 1).

By taking into account the effects of stress and temperature, we modelled the austenite ratio R_A as follows:

$$R_A = [\![K_{R_A} \cdot (T - T_{low} - c \cdot \sigma)]\!] \qquad (3)$$

where, $K_{R_A} = 1/(T_{high} - T_{low})$

$$[\![x]\!] \equiv \begin{cases} 0, & x < 0 \\ x, & 0 \leqslant x \leqslant 1 \\ 1, & 1 < x \end{cases}$$

$$T_{low} = \begin{cases} T_{M_f} & \text{in case of cooling} \\ T_{A_s} & \text{in case of heating} \end{cases}$$

Model of kinematic characteristics

The kinematic property of the martensite phase is schematized as shown in Figure 3(a). It consists of an elastic range and a twin deformation range. It should be

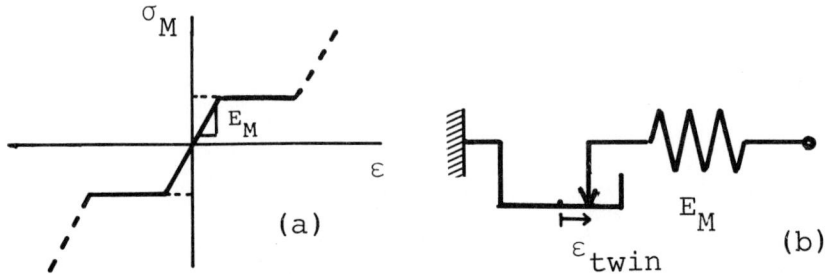

Figure 3 Basic model of a martensite phase

noticed that the twin deformation range is similar to a plastic deformation, but different in its mechanism. The kinematics are modelled by a sliding element and a spring part as shown in Figure 3(b). In the case of the polycrystalline Ti-Ni the limit strain of the twin deformation is about 6 per cent.

In the austenite phase the kinematics are simply modelled as shown in Figure 4(a). The model is valid because the SMA should always be operated within the elastic range of the austenite phase to guarantee the actuator a complete recovery

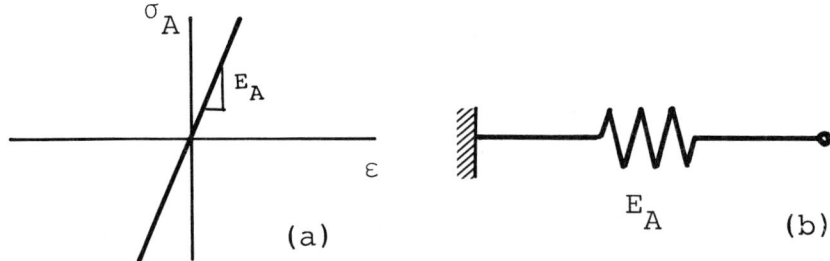

Figure 4 Basic model of an austenite phase

back to the memorized shape. This characteristic is expressed by a single spring as shown in Figure 4(b).

Synthesis of SME model

To express the SME occurring in an elemental polycrystalline SMA, the martensite and austenite factors are assumed to array in parallel as shown in Figure 5. The model is based on the sublayer model commonly used in the field of solid mechanics. The ratio of the martensite and austenite is assumed to change according to the austenite ratio R_A. To introduce the parallel model, the load subjected

Shape Memory Effect and Servo-actuator Design   345

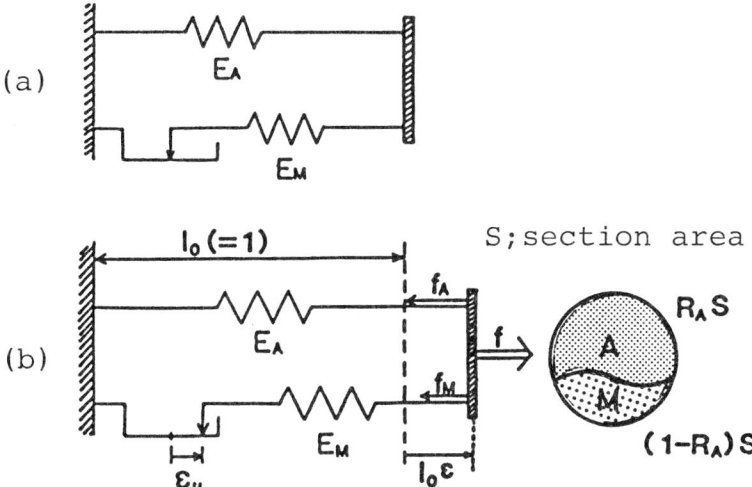

Figure 5 Composed model of SMA in both unloaded (a) and loaded (b) conditions

to the SMA element is formulated as follows:

$$\sigma = R_A |\sigma_A| + (1-R_A)|\sigma_M| \qquad (4)$$

where, σ_A and σ_M are the stress induced in austenite and martensite phases respectively.

The austenite ratio R_A of equation (3) is thus derived by using (4). As a result the fundamental expression relating the temperature T, stress σ and strain ϵ of the SME is formulated.

Experimental verification of model

To verify the feasibility of the theoretical model, a preliminary experiment on an SMA wire was executed. In the SME the temperature, stress and strain are not independent parameters. Therefore, the experiments were conducted by fixing one of these parameters and measuring the relation between the two others. Figure 6 shows the three experimental results and the corresponding theoretical results.

The experimental specimen was a Ti_{50}-Ni_{50} wire of 1.0 mm in diameter and with a gauge length of 50 mm. The specimen was confined in a thermostat and the Instron-type tensile machine was used. The sample was annealed at 623 K for 1 h and gradually cooled down. The transformation temperatures M_f, M_s, A_s and A_f were determined by the DSC method.

Although the modelling procedure was only approximate the obtained model agrees well with experiment.

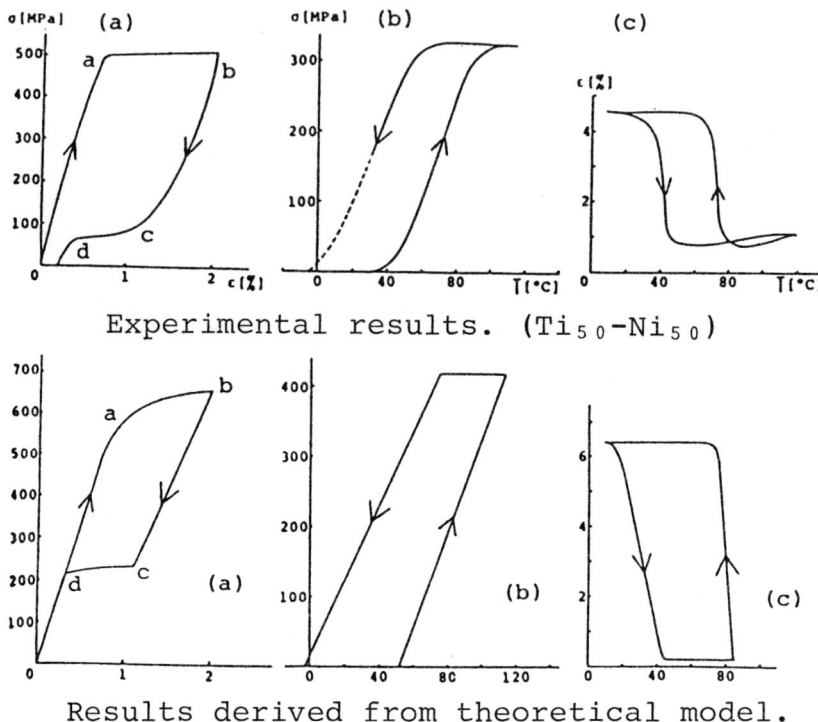

Figure 6 Comparison of the theory and experiments; (a) T=353K, (b) $\epsilon=0.7$ per cent, (c) $\sigma=125$ MPa

New design configuration for SMA actuators

To demonstrate the feasibility of realizing the SMA actuator, a prototype machine was constructed. The mechanical model is based on a newly developed design principle. The new design principle, hereafter called ξ-array, is explained first.

ξ-Array

The design principle which is proposed here suggests to array the SMA wire as shown in Figure 7(c). This layout produces a greater amount of traction forces by SMA wires arrayed in parallel when connected in series so as to produce serial electric resistances. Conventionally, this kind of mechanical structure has been used but the configuration produced SMA wires arrayed in parallel not connected in series as is the case in the present model.

As the newly developed configuration is reminiscent of the Greek letter ξ, we call the array, ξ-array. Unlike the single-wired array (Figure 7a) or a normal-parallel array method (Figure 7b), where a parallel electric resistance is formed, the ξ-array (Figure 7c) is made of a long and slender SMA wire spread on a relatively smaller

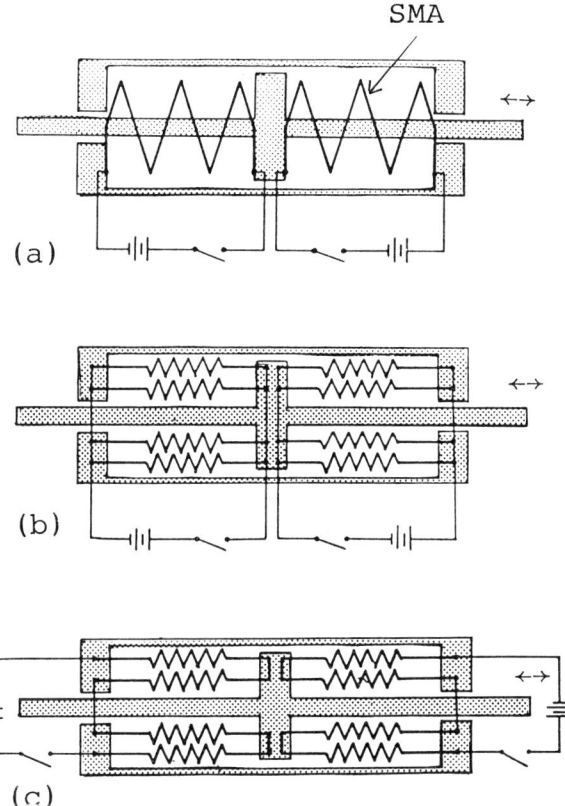

Figure 7 SMA configurations: (a) conventional single wire array, (b) conventional parallel array, (c) proposed ξ-array

space; this provides a higher electrical resistance.

The ξ-array therefore produces the following specifications. (1) The lead wire, which supplies electric current from the power source to the SMA actuator, can be made slender. Since in an SMA actuator system, the specific resistance of the SMA is only a few times that of the lead wire (i.e. the resistance of a Ti-Ni SMA is about 50 times that of the copper), the application of the ξ-array will improve the energy loss and heating along the lead wire. (2) Unlike conventional SMA actuators of the same mechanical structure which operate under a low-voltage high-current source, an SMA actuator of the ξ-array is driven with high-voltage low-current electric-power source. This is of great importance because, for example, even if the produced power is the same, a power source of 100 V, 1 A output is more accessible than the 1 V, 100 A output one. The peripheral device which drives the SMA can also be constructed easily for the same reason. (3) The electric resistance of the SMA, which varies with the austenite ratio R_A, can be measured easily. In conventional systems the electric resistance of SMA is said to be valuable as a monitoring parameter of the SMA condition, but the resistance change is very small and has hindered the usefulness of application. The ξ-array increases the absolute value of the electric resistance and thus makes it easier to measure its variation with R_A. (4) The time-respomse is improved. The ratio of heat transfer is large and the cooling velocity improved because a slender and long SMA wire is used in the ξ-array.

Experimental model

Figure 8 shows an experimental SMA actuator with the ξ-array design configuration. The specifications are shown in Table 2. Although some necessary adjustments (i.e.

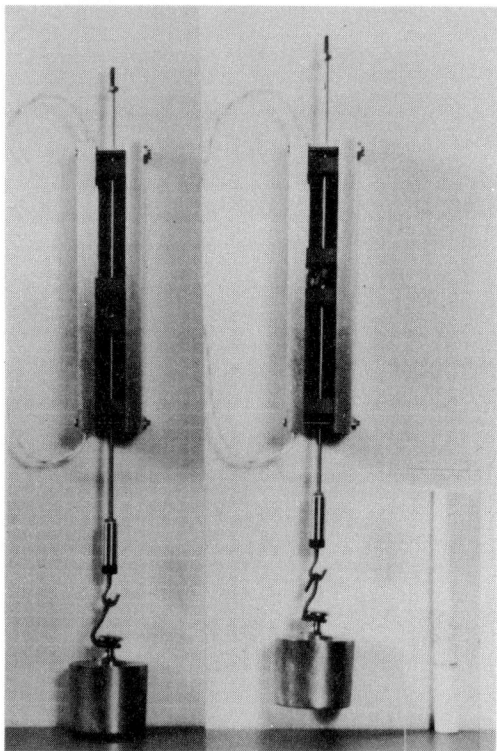

Figure 8 Experimental model of SMA actuator with ξ-array

design parameters of SMA wire, control system, etc.) are still to be optimized, the actuator exhibits satisfactory performances.

Based on the data from this mechanical model and the basic research on the SME aforementioned, further work is in progress to optimize the fabrication and control procedures to implement a more practical actuator.

Table 2 Specifications of the constructed SMA actuator

Dimension	96 × 22 × 20	mm
Total weight	46	g
Maximum produced force (without displacement)	400	gf
Maximum displacement (without load)	10	mm
Electrical resistance (for one ξ-array)	9.3	Ω

The authors are indebted to Dr Y Suzuki, Y Tamura (Furukawa Electric Co), Dr K Enami (Osaka University) and Dr S Miyazaki (University of Tsukuba) for their valuable advice and cooperation and Mr Masahiro Tsukamoto for his assistance.

References

[1] Perkins J (1975) *Shape Memory Effects in Alloys* Plenum Press, New York
[2] Honda D, Miwa Y & Iguchi N (1983) Application of SME to Digital Control Actuator. *Trans. JSME-C*, **49** (448), 2163-2169 (in Japanese)
[3] Hosoda Y *et al* (1983) *Three Fingered Robot Hand by Using SMA* Proc. of 1st Annual Conf. of Robotic Society of Japan (in Japanese)
[4] Miyazaki S, Ohmi Y, Otsuka K & Suzuki Y (1982) Proc. ICOMAT-82, Belgium
[5] Saburi T, Tatsumi T & Nenno S (1982) Proc. ICOMAT-82, Belgium
[6] Tong H C & Wayman C M (1974) *Scripta Met.*, **8**, 93-100
[7] Wollants P *et al* (1979) *Z. Metallkde*, **70**, 146-151
[8] Hirose S, Ikuta K & Umetani Y (1983) *Study of Servo-Actuator Based on SMA No. 1 and No. 2* Proc. of 22nd Annual Conf. of Society of Instrument and Control Engineers, pp 543-546 (in Japanese)
[9] Hirose S, Ikuta K & Umetani Y (1983) *Study of Servo-Actuator Based on SMA No. 4* Proc. of Robotic Society of Japan, pp 205 206 (in Japanese)
[10] Hirose S & Umetani Y (1981) *An Active Cord Mechanism with Oblique Swivel Joints and its Control* Proc. of 4th Romansy Symposium, Warsaw, Poland

Coverage Optimization of Articulated Manipulators

G Fraize, J Vertut and R Hugon

Commissariat a l'Energie Atomique CEN/SACLAY-DPT/STEP, 91191 Gif sur Yvette, France

Summary: In the most common architectures articulated manipulators have articulations perpendicular to the two main segments (upper and lower arm). This study does not deal with the architecture of the terminal device orientation. It is demonstrated that the limited angular field of both segments is necessary to keep far from angularities ending with infinite force and zero velocity capability, corresponding to infinite equivalent mass in the given direction. Keeping force and inertia in reasonable relative variation in the coverage results also in a reasonable isotropy of these properties in different directions. The paper presents a method of maximization of the area covered by the wrist in the plan of the two segments, which must be equal in length, consequently to a given elbow angular limit. Then according to the two possibilities of motion at the shoulder the total volume is also optimized as a function of the first pivot angular motion. The covered volume versus volume occupied by the manipulator is then calculated. This volume efficiency will be limited to the mass efficiency studied in another paper.

Introduction

Among various architectures of manipulators one most common is called class one,[1,2] with a planar articulated arm turning around a fixed axis of its plane (Figure 1). The coverage of such a manipulator was analysed in a paper by Vertut[3] in the first Ro Man Sy according to the classical wrist-joint arrangement, basically in

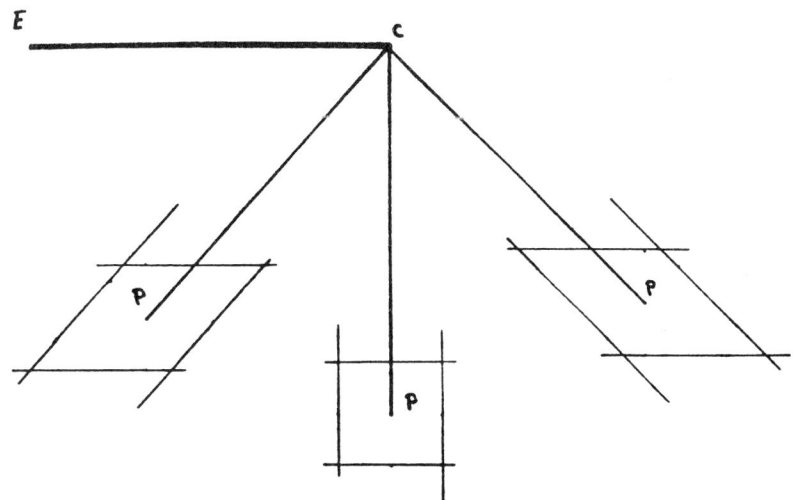

Figure 1   Class-one manipulator

an enclosure-like telemanipulator into its box. This study showed that successive semiconcentric zones of coverage have increasing geometrical dexterity (i.e. larger angular capability of the end effector around a given point) from limits of coverage up to the central zone.

Further work[4] showed that on a motorized manipulator, according to a given actuator architecture, force, velocity and inertia capability vary with the direction and position. The present work combines coverage maximization within a given isotropy of force velocity, inertia and acceleration.

Force velocity, inertia and acceleration of articulated manipulator

As shown in Figure 1 the articulated arm (without the last segment) has two actuators coupled by a parallelogram and the possible force f on each segment is the same.

$$C_{1\,max} = l_1 f \qquad C_{2\,max} = l_2 f$$

All possible combinations of C_1 C_2 result in forces at the wrist into the parallelogram shown in Figure 1 (here a diamond shape due to $l_1 = l_2$).

In maximal extension α, maximal force is

$$F = \frac{f}{\sin \alpha/2}$$

This leads to a work limit with $\alpha = \beta$ generally $\leqslant 45°$. In an average elbow position $F = f\sqrt{2}$ at 45° extension (or retraction) $F = 2,6f$ and with 30° $F = 3,9f$. When rotation of the whole arm is operated, if C_3 is the rated torque it can be shown that $C_3 = 2fl \cos \alpha/2$ to get f in E, with extended elbow, then retracted elbow gives also

$$F = \frac{f}{\sin \alpha/L} \ln R$$

This leads to limit θ_1 and θ_2 not to exceed that shortest distance from θ_3 axis, if we accept a factor 2,6 or 3,9 force anisotropy.[3] Velocity varies in the opposite as shown also in Figure 1. If we consider inertia, due to segments, counter weights and actuators, the matrix ends with an ellipse in the armplane.

This elliptic diagram gives the force $\vec{a}$ that indicates a given acceleration: $\vec{\gamma}$ (which is not colinear to $\vec{a}$) more the ellipse is eccentric and the higher this angle can be. With our MA 23 manipulator,[5] as illustrated in Figure 2, inertia eccentricity is about 1,5 in middle position and 3,25 at 45° with 5 kg load, with maximal apparent inertia 47 kg, and maximal force to acceleration angle of 11,3°. This is easily extended in space with θ_3.

Now if we calculate the maximal acceleration we find a parallelogram diagram shown in Figure 3. Here we see the double effect of a 20 kg mass that reduces overall acceleration and moves that diagram down 7,76 m s^{-2} at 14° from vertical, due to gravity.

All this illustrates that the 45° limit of extension retraction provides reasonable force, velocity, inertia and acceleration isotropy.

Coverage of Articulated Manipulators 353

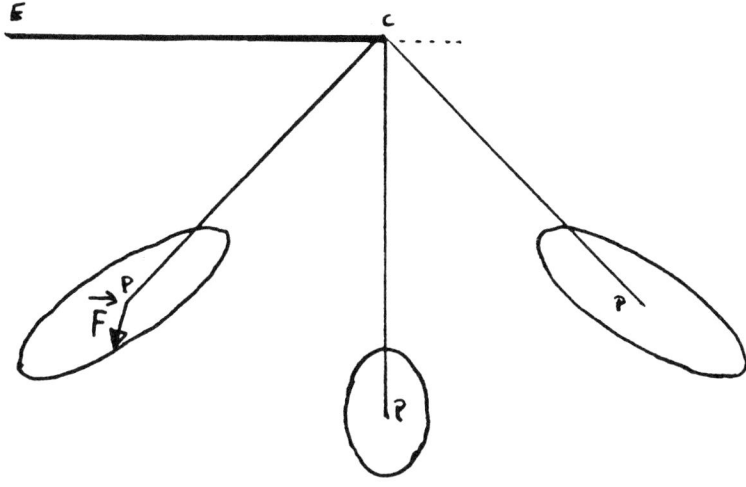

Figure 2 MA 23 manipulator

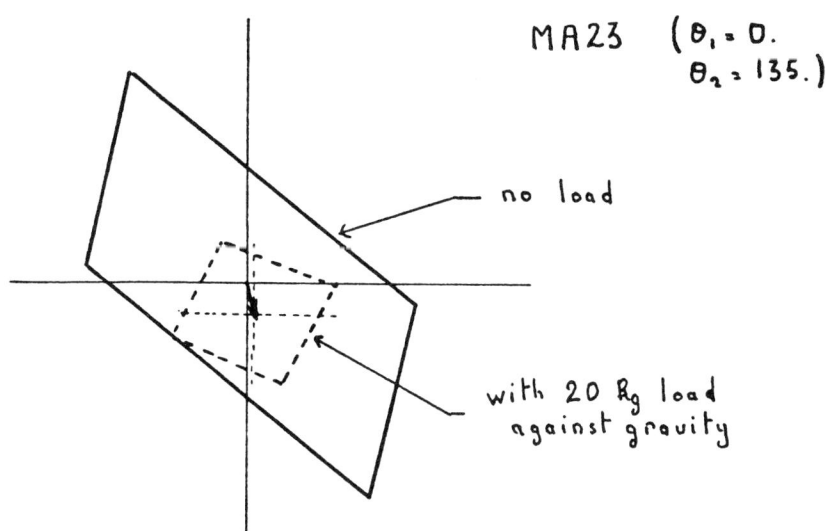

Figure 3 Parallelogram diagram from maximal acceleration

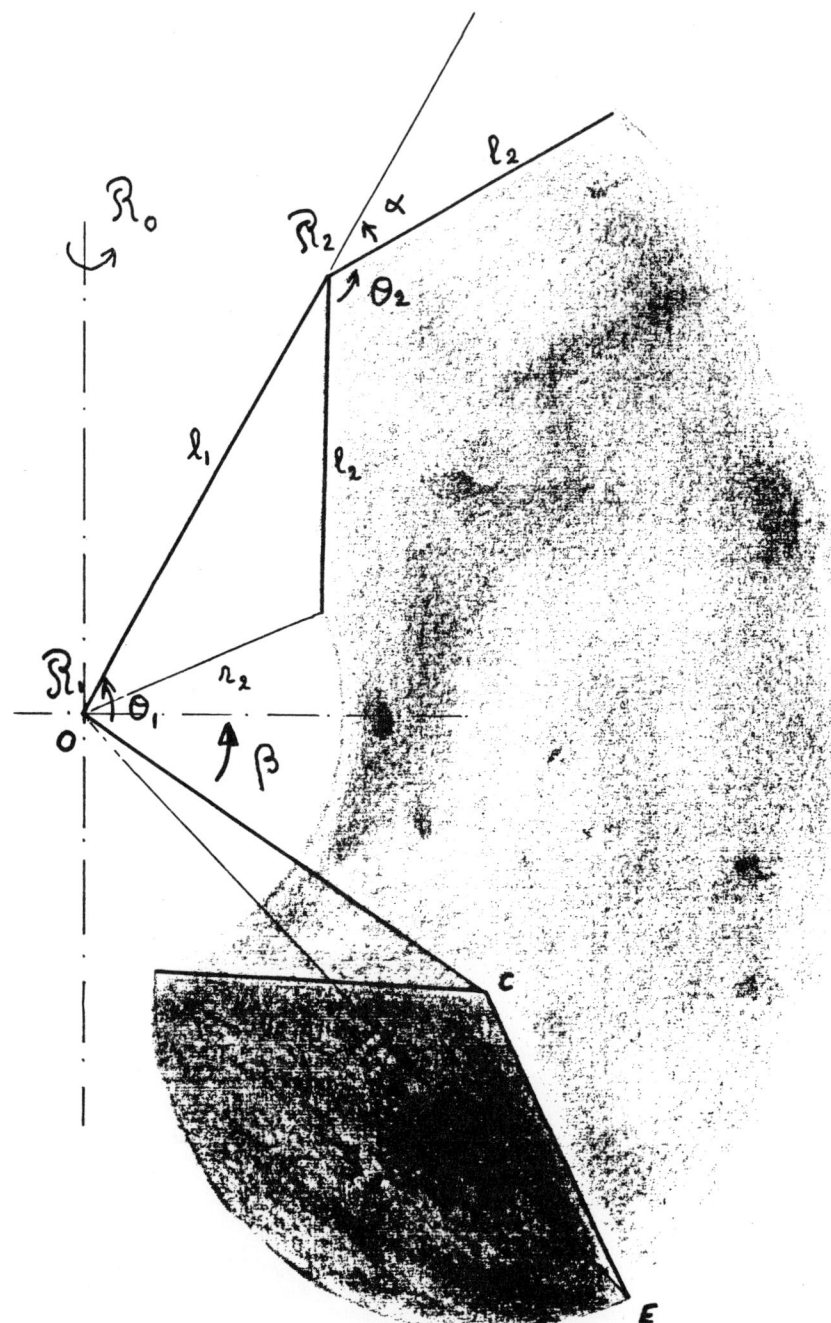

Figure 4 Variables and parameters allowing surface calculus

Optimization of coverage in manipulator plane

Calculus of surface

Figure 4 shows the variables and parameters defining the surface calculus. R_0 stands for the rotation of the whole arm. R_1 stands for the shoulder rotation and R_2 for the elbow rotation.

Surface S remains constant by rotation of θ around point O. Thus S_1 is easily given by

$$S = \frac{\theta_1}{2}(r_1^2 - r_2^2)\ \theta_1 \text{ into } rd$$

R_1 and R_2 are given in OCP in triangle by

$$R_1^2 = l_1^2 + l_2^2 + 2l_1 l_2 \cos \theta_2$$
$$R_2^2 = l_1^2 + l_2^2 + 2l_1 l_2 \cos (\alpha + \theta_2)$$

This results in

$$S = \frac{90\,\theta_1}{\pi}\ l_1 l_2 \left[\cos \alpha - \cos (\alpha + \theta_2)\right] \tag{1}$$

or

$$S = \frac{90\,\theta_1}{\pi}\ l_1 l_2 \sin \frac{\theta_2}{2} \cdot \sin \left[\alpha + \frac{\theta_2}{2}\right] \tag{2}$$

Figure 5 gives the variations of S for $\alpha = 0$.

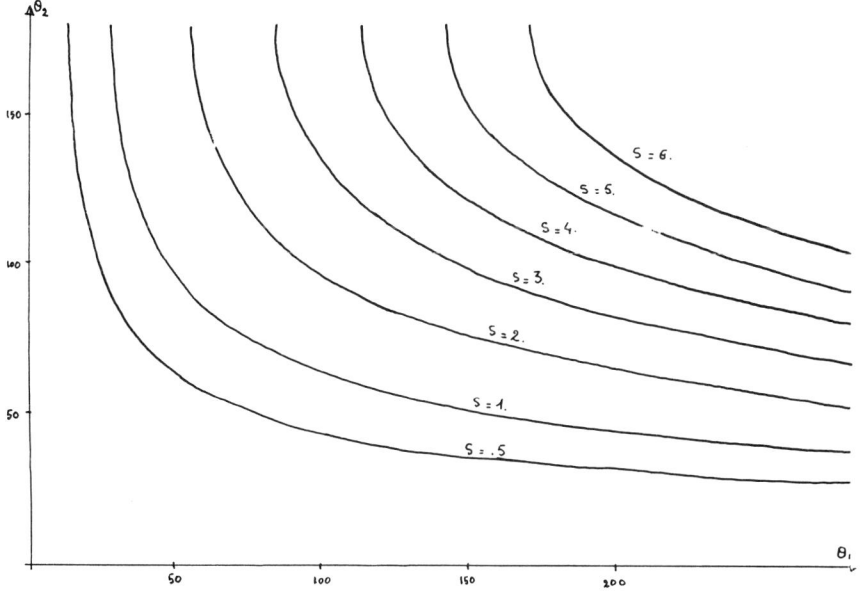

Figure 5 Variations of S for $\alpha = 0$
$l_1 = l_2 = 1$

Optimization of surface

Arm segments lengths
Equations (1) and (2) show that surface S will vary in ratio with the $l_1 l_2$ product. If the full extended arm radius ($l_1 + l_2$) is given, the greater S surface is obtained as $l_1 = l_2$.

Angular ranges
α results from force–inertia constraints. So S is an increasing function of θ_1 and θ_2. With the parallelogram configuration, we assume that the actuators are located on the supporting frame, as also required to reduce force, speed and inertia anisotropy in the average working position. Then the lower arm complete angular range is $\theta_M = \theta_1 + \theta_2$. The surface is an increasing function of θ_M. But if θ_M is a geometrical constraint, the equation (2) gives the optimal values of θ_1 and θ_2.

If α is considered as a parameter, Figure 6 allows one to determine this optimal range easily.

If α is considered as a variable, equation (2) gives the optimal value of α for $2\alpha + \theta_2 = \pi$. This means that the forearm should have a symmetrical angular range in regard to a perpendicular line to the arm. So if α has no technological constraint (buttressing) this optimization avoids the singular position in which arm and forearm are lined up, which would result in poor force or speed capability. Figure 6 points out this α value for several θ_M values. These curves can be used in two different ways. If α is fixed, the intersection of α curve with $\theta_1 + \theta_2 = Cte$ lines gives θ_1 and θ_2. If $\theta_M = \theta_1 + \theta_2$ is fixed, the intersection of $\theta_1 + \theta_2 = Cte$ lines with optimized α broken line gives α, θ_1 and θ_2.

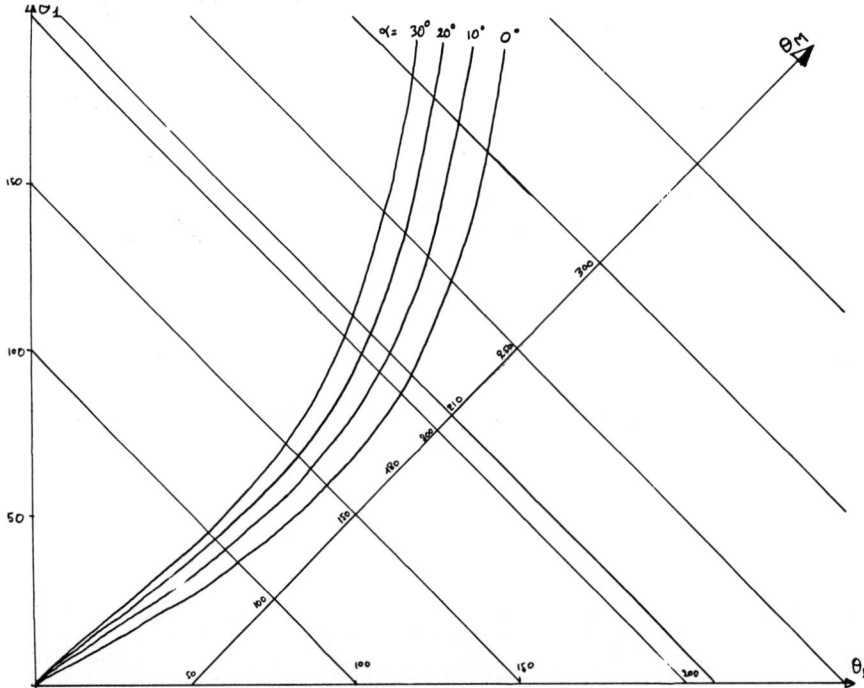

Figure 6 Parameter α allows for determination of optimal angular range

Definition of merit factor

Figure 4 points out several areas scanned when θ_1 and θ_2 are varied. The ρ geometrical merit factor is defined as the ratio between the work usable surface and the whole scanned surface by arm and forearm. This factor helps to characterize the arm ability to work in an encumbered environment.

In the same way, a global merit factor may be defined. This factor is the ratio between the effective working volume and the whole scanned volume by arm and forearm and depends on the frame geometry, the actuators technology, the architecture, etc. It is given, in the above assumption, by

$$g = \frac{[1 + K^2 + 2K\cos(\alpha + \theta_2)][(\theta_M - \theta_2) + K\sin(\alpha + \theta_2) + K^2\theta_2]}{2(\theta_M - \theta_2)K[\cos\alpha - \cos(\alpha + \theta_2)]}$$

where $K = \dfrac{l_2}{l_1}$ $\theta_M = \theta_1 + \theta_2$

Variations of geometrical merit factor

θ influence

For a fixed θ_m, and provided K is about 1 ($0.8 \leqslant K \leqslant 1.2$), the maximum value of ρ is reached for θ_1/θ_2 ratio close to the θ_1/θ_2 ratio that optimizes the S meridian plane surface.

K influence

It is shown by Figure 7; optimization of the ρ results in shortening of the forearm, while optimization of the S surface results in its lengthening. According to the small

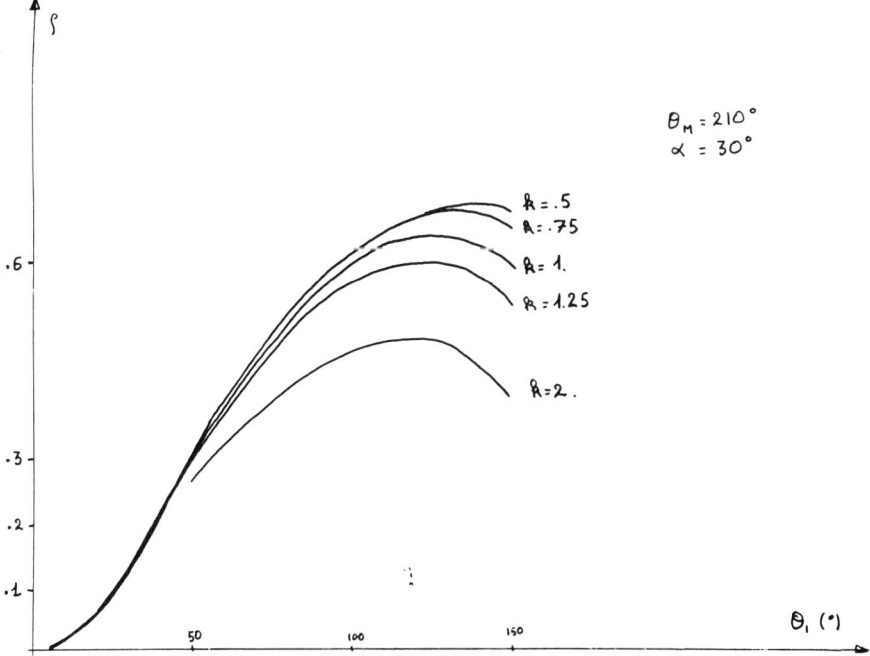

Figure 7 K influence

variation of ρ around $K=1$, K should be chosen between 0.8 and 1. In addition we notice that if lessening K leads to an increase in θ_2, it could result in a technologically impractical arm (forearm's stop 'under' the arm).

θ_M influence
Increasing θ_M improves simultaneously S surface and the geometrical merit factor.

Optimization of covered volume

The scanned volume is calculated from the S surface thanks to the Guldin theorem

$$v_t = \theta_0 r_G S$$

where r_G is the distance from S isobarycentre to R_0 axis.

From now on, it is assumed that $K=1$. Figure 8 shows that there is an optimal θ_1/θ_2 ratio for a fixed θ_M, α being a parameter. A $10°$ variation of θ_1 around its optimal value may increase by 10 per cent the working volume.

Figure 9 shows the α influence on the optimal θ_1/θ_2 ratio. This influence is weak unless θ_M is small (e.g. $\theta_M = 300°$). It is then pointed out that an $\alpha \neq 0$ allows for the increase in the working volume. For instance, for $\theta_M = 210°$, by varying α from 0 to $35°$ the working volume increases by 8 per cent. This is obtained without spoiling the isotropy. Let us notice that the α value that optimizes the working volume is lower than the α value that optimizes the S surface ($2\alpha + \theta_2 = \pi$).

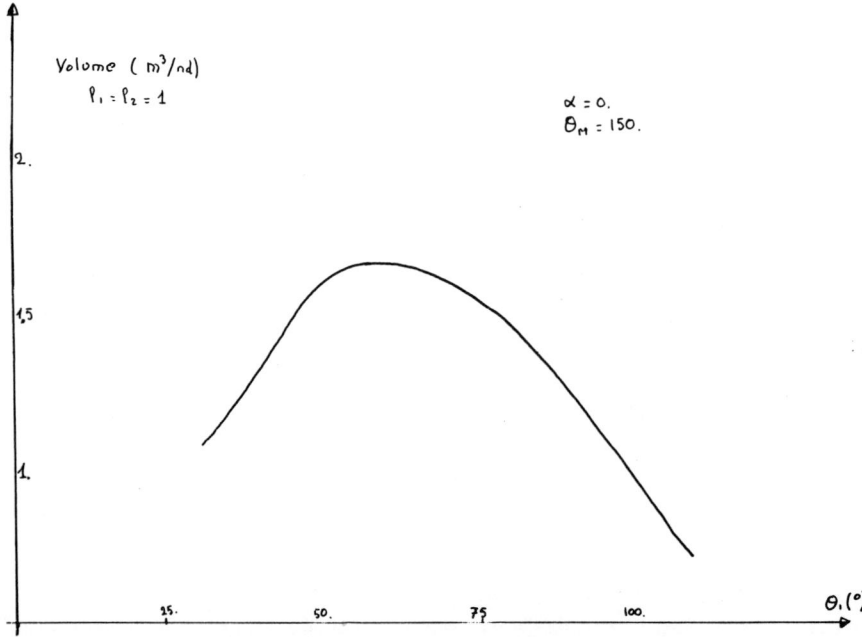

Figure 8 Optimal θ_1/θ_2 ratio for a fixed θ_M, α a parameter

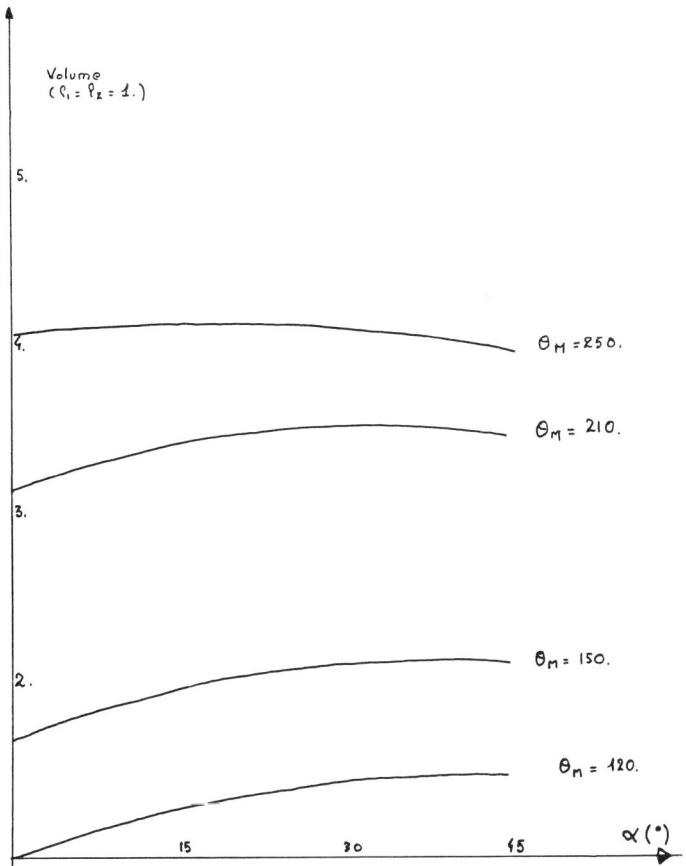

Figure 9 α influence on optimal θ_1/θ_2 ratio

Figure 10 shows the θ_1/θ_2 ratio for the maximized working volumes, at several α values. This graph should be read in the same way as that in Figure 5. The S surface isobarycentre calculus allows us to optimize the R_0 axis position, that should be perpendicular to OG (G isobarycentre). This results in the determination of the optimal β angle (β as defined in Figure 5 into the arm/forearm plane).

Figure 11 allows for the optimization of β for an average α value ($\alpha = 15°$). This may be performed only by knowing α, β_1 and β_2.

Conclusion

This work attempts to optimize the coverage within isotropic limits of force, velocity, inertia and acceleration and shows the real trade off that is particularly tight on force-reflecting servo manipulators[6] but is still very important for any robots with good dynamic characteristics.

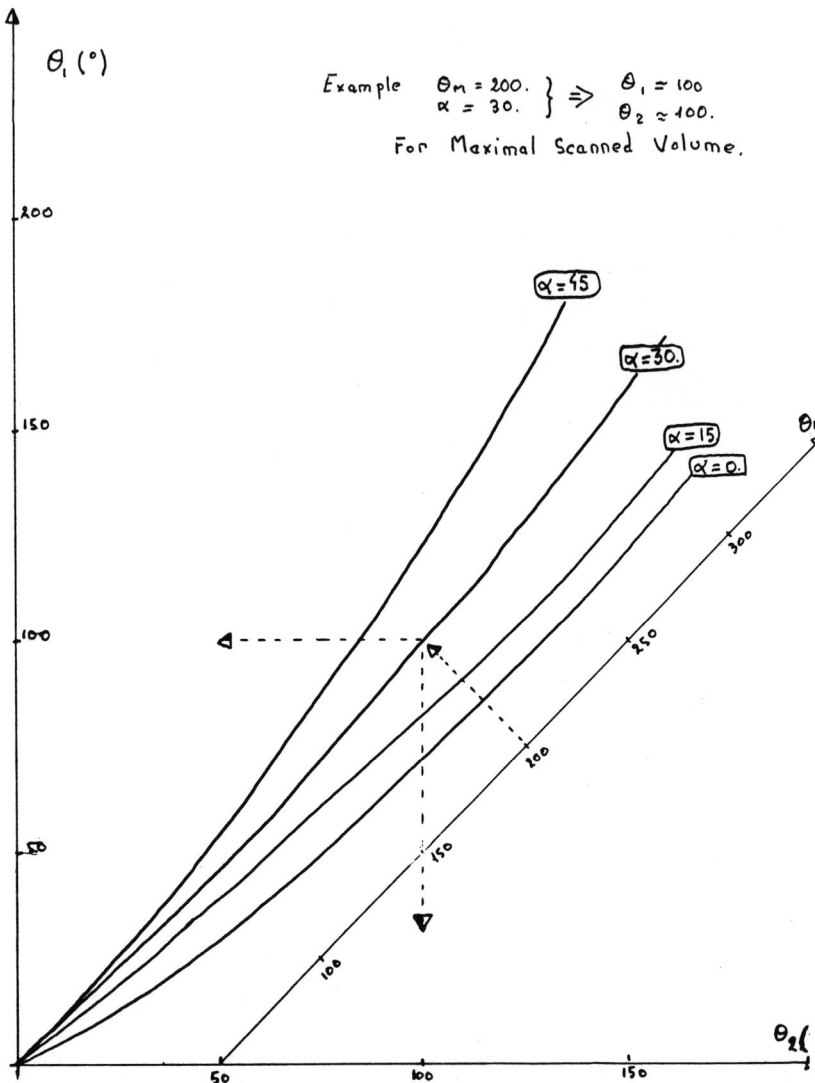

Figure 10 θ_1/θ_2 ratio for maximized working volumes at several α values

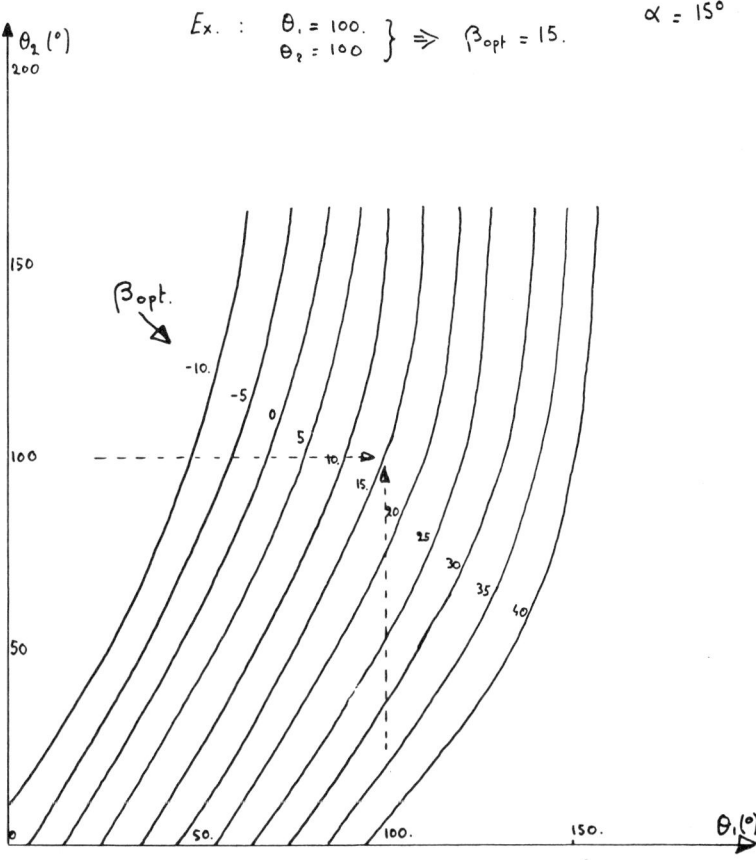

Figure 11 Optimization of β for $\alpha = 15°$

References

[1] Liegeois A and Dombre E (1979) *Analyse des Robots Industriels. Relations entre Structure, Performances et Fonctions* Rapport INRIA No. 79102 (projet SURF), Montpellier
[2] Coiffet P (1982) *Modelling and Control* Volume 1 of the *Robot Technology Series* Kogan Page, London.
[3] Vertut J (1974) *Contribution to Analyse Manipulator Morphology, Coverage and Dexterity* 1st Ro Man Sy, Udine, Italy
[4] Vertut J and Liegeois A (1981) General design criteria of manipulators. *J. Mech. MAch. Theory* 16(1), p 65
[5] Vertut J *et al.* (1976) *Advances in the New MA 23 Force Reflecting Manipulator System* 2nd Ro Man Sy, Warsaw, Poland, p 307
[6] Vertut J and Coiffet P (1984) *Téléopération* (in French) (1984) Hermes, Paris; (in English) Kogan Page, London; Prentice-Hall, New Jersey

Part 6
Biomechanics of Motion: Locomotion

Study of Propelling Agents Construction Features of Orthogonal Walking Robots by Using Plane Mechanisms

V S Balbarov, A P Bessonov and N V Umnov

Institute for the Study of Machines, USSR Academy of Sciences, Moscow, USSR

Summary: The existing methods of organizing the manoeuvring of walking machines with orthogonal (Cartesian) propelling agents do not permit in full measure the realization of the merits of propelling agents of these kinds: efficiency of the walking and simplicity in control. A readjustable guiding mechanism developed by Chebyshev in the form of a horizontal drive of orthogonal type of legs provides a new approach to the solution of the problem of manoeuvring. Necessary readjustments of the mechanism for obtaining segments of arcs of various curvatures and correct orientation of these arcs are fulfilled by the use of an additional mechanism such as a steering linkage. The possibility of using Watt mechanism as a vertical drive for orthogonal propelling agents is considered and also the example of combining the two kinds of mechanisms in one unit is considered in this paper.

Among possible kinematic schemes for legs of a walking vehicle those of orthogonal (Cartesian) types[1-3] take a special place. Division of a drive which is typical of these propelling agents into two independent drives[4] creating mutual perpendicular lines of motion of a supporting point of the leg provides positive qualities for the vehicle, two of which seem to be attractive: efficiency of displacement[2] and simplicity of control.[4] Past work[5] proves that one can obtain good efficiency by using special kinematics of a leg. However, the realization of these ideas with the aid of a guiding mechanism located in the vertical plane[6] has shown that theoretically the vehicle will have no wasted energy on displacement whilst walking at a certain height. In other words, efficiency of walking has come into conflict with adaptive possibilities.

The requirement of providing ideal efficiency in the whole area of adaptation can be realized only by use of an orthogonal propelling agent with simplicity of control, as with the 'cruiser' motion of the machine, i.e. all drives working in reverse regimen having constant speed in each phase of motion.

However, when manoeuvring this model is somewhat distorted. One fails to realize the required relative motion of the supporting points of all legs in the form of parts of concentric arcs.[7] None of the known turning systems can realize exactly the required relative movement with the aid of combination of simple drive movements. In all these cases it is necessary to realize variable speed of motion in the drives, thus needing the use of computers, functional drive, etc.

Let us consider another approach to the realization of an approximative turn. We shall consider only the plane motion supposing that motion on the third co-ordinate from separate drive will be realized in the ordinary way for orthogonal type of legs. The approach is based on the use of features of guiding mechanisms, specifically λ-mechanism by Chebyshev,[8] to change the path curvature of a generating point at the reorganization of parameters of the mechanism. In Figure 1 some

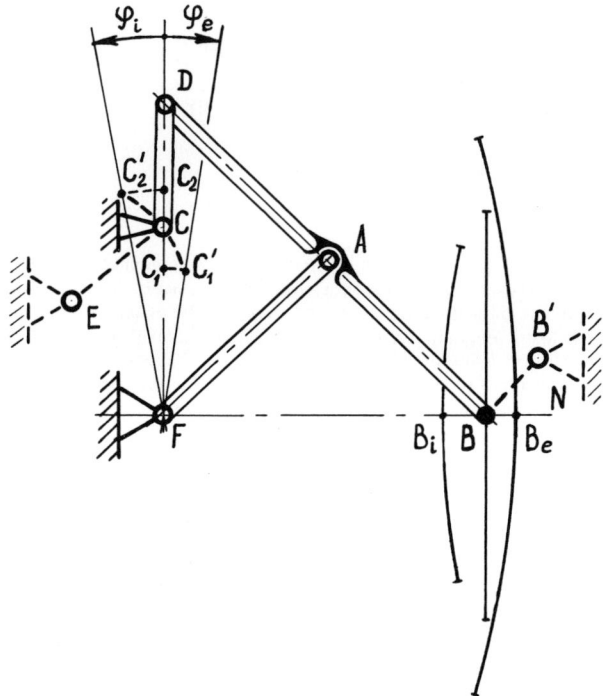

Figure 1 Paths depending on distance FC

paths taken up, depending on distance FC, are shown. Paths 1 and 2 have different signs of curvature and different velocity. If such a Chebyshev mechanism is located in the horizontal plane as a horizontal drive of the orthogonal leg and a vertical drive of this leg passes through point B then the obtained combination of these mechanisms can be used as a unit for the walking system permitting the realization of arbitrary manoeuvre in the horizontal plane. It should be emphasized that at any manoeuvres the speed of rotating cranks CD of all legs of both sides of the machine is kept equal constant.

Parameters of the necessary mechanism readjustment can be determined as follows. Let us introduce relative lengths of links $AB = FA = AD = 1$, $FC/FA = d$, $CD/FA = r$ and draw lines of equal curvature in the area of existence of Chebyshev mechanisms (Figure 2, line 1). For all this, the speed of the generating point for various mechanisms realizing equal curvature will be different. This is seen from the family of lines of equal speeds (Figure 2, line 2) the shapes of which do not coincide with that of line 1.

Let us consider the position of two legs of such a type belonging to one row of vehicle legs for a walking machine by realizing a turn relative to point O (Figure 3). In this case the curvature of the path of relative motion of supporting point B_e of an external mechanism, relative to the direction of mechanism turn, must be

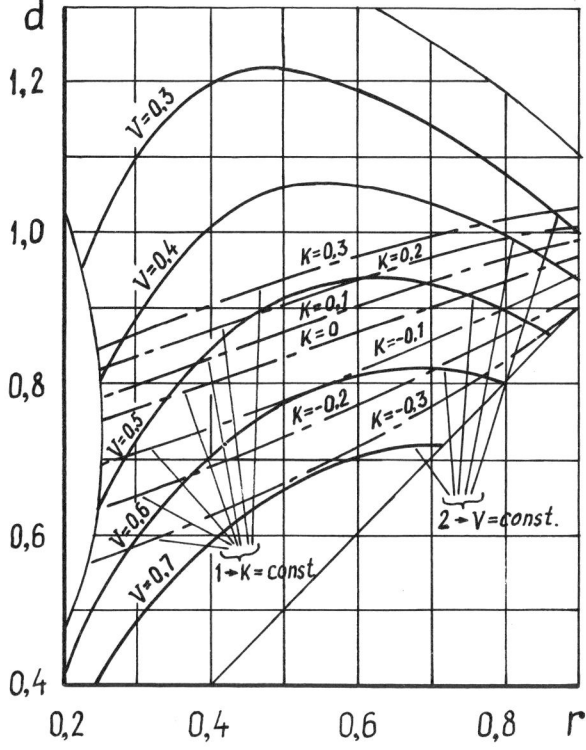

Figure 2 Determination of mechanism readjustment parameters

$$K_e = 1/(b_e + \sqrt{D^2 + (R + B)^2}) \qquad (1)$$

Accordingly, the curvature of the path of point B_i of the internal mechanism at the same moment will be

$$K_i = 1/(\sqrt{D^2 + (R - B)^2} - b_i) \qquad (2)$$

In (1) and (2) b_e and b_i will be determined as $b_{e,i} = \sqrt{4 - (d_{e,i} + r)^2}$ (Figure 1).

When turning in the opposite direction the external mechanism will become an internal one and the curvature of the path of its point B_e can be accounted for according to (2).

Since at the kinematically exact turn the centre of curvature of the path of body points and the instantaneous centre of velocity coincide,[7] then point O will be the centre of body velocities having both points B_e and B_i. The velocities of these points will be

$$V_e = \frac{V}{R}(\sqrt{D^2 + (R + B)^2} + b_e) \qquad (3)$$

$$V_i = \frac{V}{R}(\sqrt{D^2 + (R - B)^2} - b_i) \qquad (4)$$

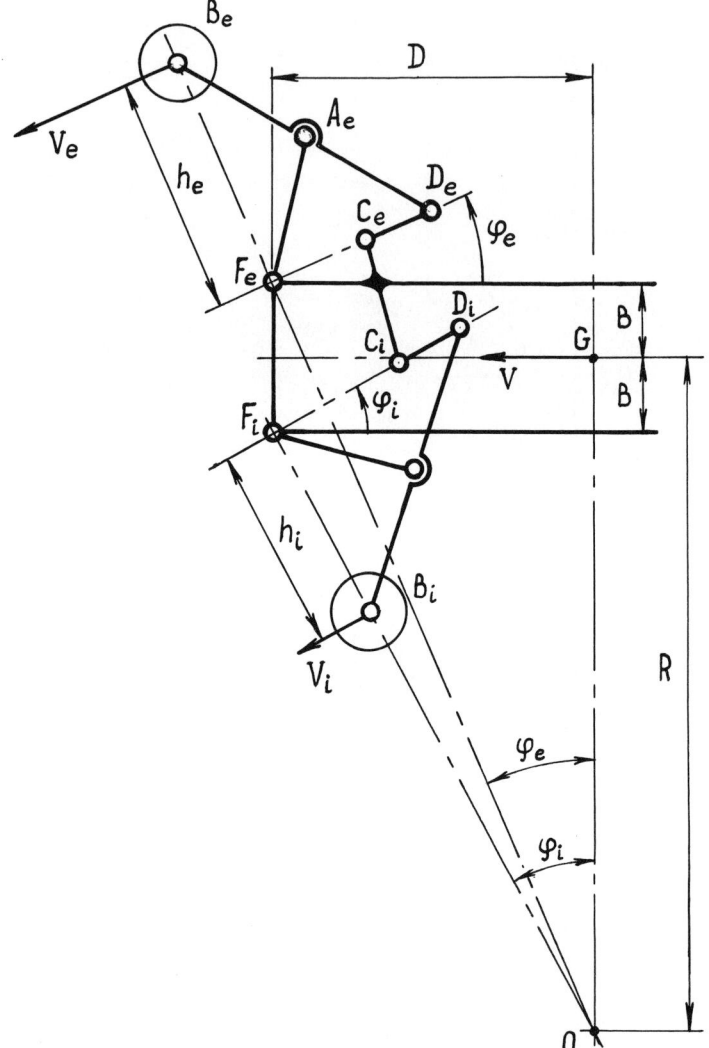

Figure 3 Position of two legs of walking machine, relative to point O

where V is velocity of point B of the mechanism in the generation of a straight line. This is a velocity of straight-line walking, the centre of vehicle G (Figure 3) will have the same velocity at the turn of any radius, $V = \omega_{CD} \cdot r \cdot b/(d+r)$.

Naturally, conditions (1)–(3) and (2)–(4) must be fulfilled simultaneously. This means that from all the mechanisms satisfying value K_e according to (1) at given R, i.e. from all mechanisms the parameters of which are located on one line $K = K_e$ (Figure 2), it is necessary to select only those in which the velocities equal V_e from (3) at the same R. This condition must be satisfied within the whole range of values of K, i.e. $-K^* < K < +K^*$, where K^* is maximum given value of trajectory curvature of the machine centre.

The combination of conditions (1) and (3) is realized, for instance, by superposition of the family of lines 1 and 2 in Figure 2. The new family of lines obtained (Figure 4) called regulation curves gives the necessary dependence of readjusting mechanism parameters providing simultaneous fulfilment of conditions (1) and (3), then (2) and (4) for the given dimensions B and D (Figure 3) of the vehicle. It is worth paying attention to the fact that the readjustment of mechanism parameters in accordance with the regulation curve (Figure 4) requires a simultaneous changing of two parameters of the mechanism.

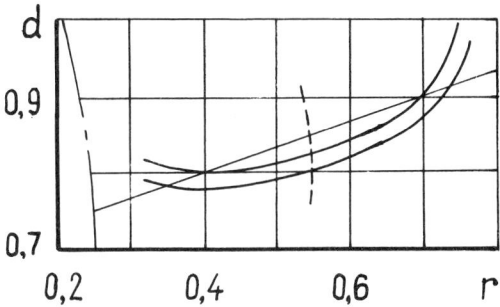

Figure 4 Regulation curves

In Figure 3 Chebyshev mechanisms are shown in turned position. This is connected with the path which is symmetrical to line FN (Figure 1). To ensure that the general centre of the path curvature of relative movement of all legs lays in point O (Figure 3) or exactly on line OG at changing R it is necessary that the external mechanism should be turned relative to the centre of rotating rocker F_e at angle

$$\varphi_e = \text{arctg}\,[D/(R+B)] \qquad (5)$$

or the internal mechanism relative to F_i at angle φ_i

$$\varphi_i = \text{arctg}\,[D/(R-B)] \qquad (6)$$

It is interesting to note that if, on readjustment the external mechanism point, C is shifted, not to point C_1 required for obtaining the curvature of the path of supporting point B according to (1) but to point C'_1 ($FC_1 = FC'_1$), then simultaneously with the readjustment of parameters the necessary turn of the path of the supporting point will occur at angle φ_e according to (5). As to the internal mechanism the required position of the centre of rotation of the crank will also be not C_2 but C'_2. Displacement of point C along curve $C'_1 C_2 C'_3$ can be realized by locating point C on the lever CE (Figure 1).

Moreover, placing point C of the internal mechanism of the same row also on such a lever, we can control the turn of the vehicle by turning the steering levers of each mechanism. This can be fulfilled if the steering levers of one row are connected by the symmetrical mechanism analogous to a steering linkage of the car (Figure 5).

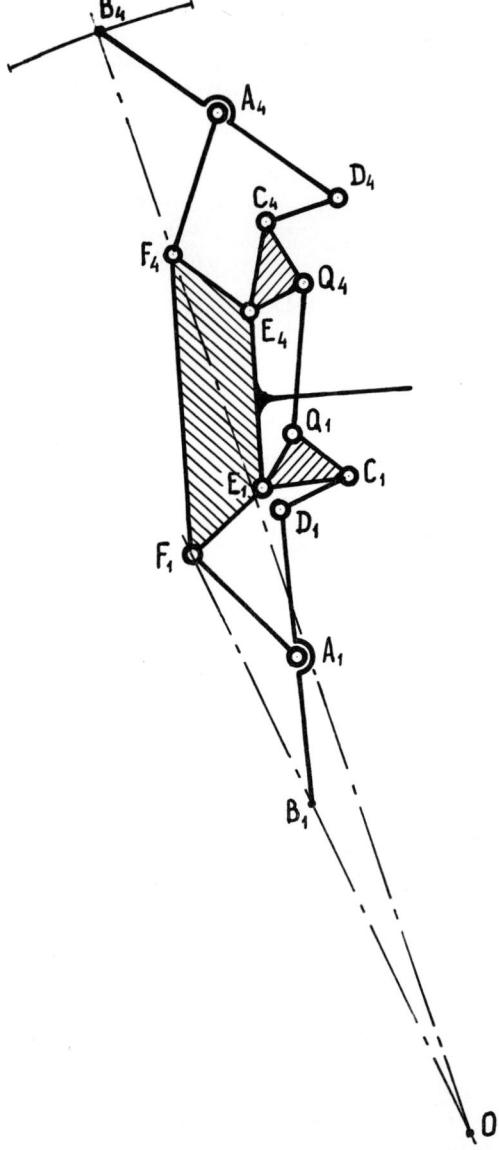

Figure 5 Steering levers connected by a symmetrical mechanism

The selection of parameters of the steering mechanisms is brought to common synthesis of linkage function generators. Thus the control of turning legs of one row was brought to the control of one angular parameter of the steering linkage.

The proposed system differs from a simple turn of the line of the propelling agent motion so that, simultaneously with the turn, a readjustment of the mechanism parameters will occur. This system realizes not kinematic exact turn[7] but a fine approximation to kinematic exact circulation. In other words, it is impossible to change the curvature of movement, by using the described mechanisms, without changing mutual state of legs on terrain within flexibility of supports or deformation of parts of body and legs. Besides the increase of wasted energy on walking, such a regimen is connected with the possibility of breaking the device by jamming the legs.

A natural way out is the involvement into the kinematic system of a group of additional links-compensators, for instance, link BB' (Figure 1) to increase the number of degrees of freedom and to permit readjustment of the radius of turn while moving. Of course, the involvement of compensators as an additional kinematic chain is mainly of conditional character. Practically, it is sufficient to involve pliability in certain points for excluding jamming.

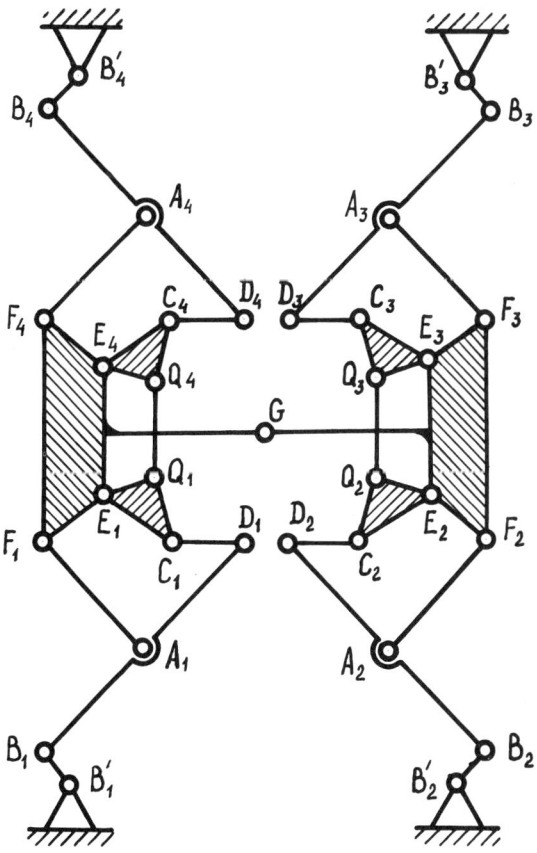

Figure 6 Four-legged system with compensators

The example of four-legged system with compensators is shown in Figure 6. Note that the availability of compensators in the system is favourable as they permit the additional compensation of all systematic errors connected with inaccuracy of synthesis and that the system of turn according to Figure 5 changes only one parameter of the mechanism but not two as the regulation curve requires (Figure 4).

However, when compensating links are used, it is necessary to take into account that at some special locations in the system there will possibly appear instantaneous mobilities. It can arise, for instance, in the case when compensators $B_1 B_1', B_2 B_2', B_3 B_3', B_4 B_4'$ (Figure 6) will be parallel.

The vertical drive of orthogonal propelling agent of the walking machine has no peculiarities. For this, it is convenient to use Watt mechanism mainly because the supporting point S (Figure 7) is far from joints, and the connecting rod SU moves practically in vertical deviating slightly from straight line WW. The fact that the velocity of vertical displacement is uneven in contrast to the mechanisms of horizontal displacement has no essential meaning.

To join λ-mechanism and Watt mechanism in one unit, it is necessary to place the point B (Figure 1) on line WW (Figure 7). A part of Chebyshev mechanism AB (Figure 1) is taken as link of Watt mechanism (Figure 7). The mechanism obtained such as a six-link one, is shown in Figure 8.

Crank CD is rotated with constant speed in this mechanism. Another independent drive turns link AT and, as a result, point S of the leg lowers on the terrain. At the signal of a supporting sensor the drive of link AT switches off and brakes. By this adaptation to the roughness of the terrain a lack of energy waste at the phase of support is obtained. Then the drive of link AT switches again but, this time, for lifting. At the extreme upper position of the leg during the whole phase of swing the vertical drive is braked again. The cycle is repeated with the beginning of lowering link AT.

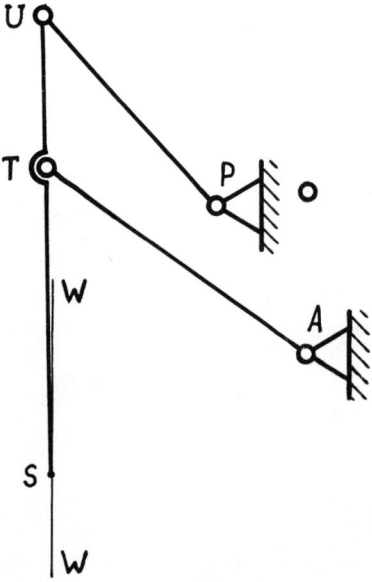

Figure 7 Watt mechanism

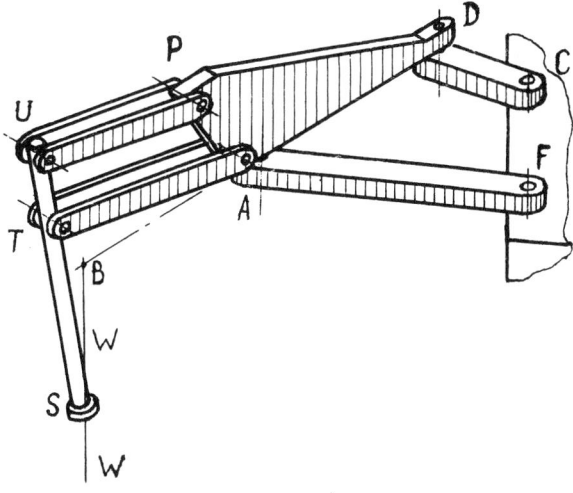

Figure 8 Six-link mechanism

Thus the proposed kinematic scheme of orthogonal type of leg of the walking machine permits the organization of the manoeuvring of the walking vehicle by retaining the principal merits of an orthogonal type of propelling agent: efficiency, adaptation and simplicity in control.

References

[1] Bessonov A P and Umnov N V (1983) Stabilization of the position of the body of walking machines. *J. Mech. Mach. Theory*, **18**(4), 261–265.
[2] Hirose S and Umetani Y (1978) *Some Considerations on a Feasible Walking Mechanism as a Terrain Vehicle* Proc. 3rd CISM-IFToMM Symposium on Theory and Practice of Robots and Manipulators Udine, Italy, pp 357–375
[3] Kessis J J, Rambaut J P and Penné J (1981) *Walking Robot Multi-level Architecture and Implementation* Proc. 4th CISM-IFToMM Symposium on Theory and Practice of Robots and Manipulators, Warsaw, Poland, pp 347–355
[4] Pogrebnja A Ya (1975) Investigation of motion of six-legged vehicle *Mashinovedenie* (3) 34–36 (in Russian)
[5] Waldron K J and Kinzel G L (1981) *The Relationship between Actuator Geometry and Mechanical Efficiency in Robots* Proc. 4th CISM-IFToMM Symposium on Theory and Practice of Robots and Manipulators, Warsaw, Poland, pp 366–374
[6] Orin D E and McGhee R B (1981) *Dynamic Computer Simulation of Robotic Mechanisms* Proc. 4th CISM-IFToMM Symposium on Theory and Practice of Robots and Manipulators, Warsaw, Poland, pp 337–346
[7] Bessonov A P and Umnov N V (1978) *Features of Kinematics of Turn of Walking Vehicle* Proc. 3rd CISM-IFToMM Symposium on Theory and Practice of Robots and Manipulators, Udine, Italy, pp 87–97
[8] Artobolevsky I I (1975) *Mechanisms in Modern Engineering Design* vol 1, no. 651, p 432. Mir, Moscow

A Hierarchically Structured System for Computer Control of a Hexapod Walking Machine

R B McGhee, D E Orin, D R Pugh and M R Patterson

Department of Electrical Engineering, Ohio State University, Columbus, OH 43210, USA

Summary: Control of walking machines involves a hierarchy of computational tasks which is naturally suited to a multicomputer implementation. This paper describes the hardware and software for one such system presently under construction. Particular attention is paid to problems of man-machine and intercomputer communication during vehicle operation and to integration of artificial sensory information into higher levels of control.

Introduction

Designers of off-road vehicles have long been aware that the performance of such machines is inferior to that of cursorial animals in rough-terrain locomotion. The advantages of natural systems arise from intrinsic characteristics of legged locomotion that include greater mobility, higher speed and reduced energy requirements in comparison with conventional wheeled or tracked automotive vehicles.[1] Research efforts over the past two decades have shown that it is possible to obtain animal-like behaviour in machines, provided that the relation of the supporting elements of the machine to the terrain is actively adjustable to permit effective accommodation of terrain irregularities. Such machines are called 'adaptive-suspension vehicles' or, sometimes, simply 'walking machines'.[1,2]

Early experiments with adaptive-suspension vehicles required direct co-ordination of individual joint motions by a human operator.[2,3] Although this technique was successful to the extent that excellent off-road mobility was demonstrated by a quadruped walking machine, both in dense obstacle fields and over very soft soil, it was found to be impractical due to the high demands placed on the operator's motion co-ordination skills, resulting in rapid fatigue and marginal stability. As a result, beginning in about 1970, research was initiated on the possibility of assigning low-level co-ordination tasks to a computer while requiring the operator to deal with only the more complex vehicle-control problems such as route selection and control of speed and heading. These research efforts resulted in successful demonstration of such 'supervisory' control in 1977 by two laboratory-scale hexapod walking machines. One of these machines, the OSU hexapod,[4,5] was controlled by a uniprocessor digital computer, while the other, the MGU hexapod,[6] was controlled by a hybrid analog-digital computer. Both were externally powered, and each was connected to its computer by a trailing umbilical cord.

With the advent of modern 16-bit microcomputers, it has become feasible to construct self-contained walking machines with supervisory control realized by an on-board computer. The first such machine walked in late 1982 at Carnegie-Mellon University.[7] and was controlled by a uniprocessor computer, the Motorola 68000.

Preliminary experiments indicate, however, that refined co-ordination of motion for rough-terrain locomotion is difficult for a computer of this size. Rather, at the present time, a hierarchical decomposition of the control task for multiprocessor implementation seems to be more appropriate.[8,9] Such an implementation has the further advantage that higher levels of sensing and control, such as the use of computer vision in motion planning and foothold selection, can be added in a modular fashion without significantly altering previous layers of control computer hardware and software.[10] An experiment of this sort is now under way at Ohio State University with respect to a large hydraulically powered hexapod walking machine called the 'ASV-84'. The mechanical design of this machine is described elsewhere in these proceedings.[11] The purpose of the present paper is to explain the organization of the hardware and software employed in the on-board multiprocessor computer used for control of this vehicle. In what follows, particular attention is paid to problems of man-machine and intercomputer communication, as well as to integration of artificial sensory information into higher levels of control.

Operational modes

The ASV-84 is being developed as a test-bed vehicle for the study of sensors, for the evaluation of alternative prime movers and energy distribution systems, and for the further development of control techniques for semi-autonomous or fully autonomous operation. Because the current state of control and sensing technology does not permit fully autonomous operation of walking machines under all terrain conditions, this vehicle is provided with a cab for a human operator who participates in vehicle control at various levels depending on task and terrain complexity.[12] The operator's cab contains aircraft-style controls and displays, including a three-axis joystick for vehicle steering and speed control. An optical radar mounted on top of the cab provides a dense-range map of the terrain immediately ahead of the vehicle which is used in some control modes for foothold selection and body orientation. The following paragraphs provide a brief description of each major control mode envisaged for this vehicle.

Utility

This mode is intended to perform a 'preflight' checkout to verify correct functioning of all major vehicle subsystems. Both visual observations and redundant transducer signals can be used for this purpose. Self-test software includes some capability to isolate faulty electronic or mechanical modules to facilitate field or shop repair. This mode is also used for reprogramming the control computer.

Precision footing

In this mode the operator is able to control individual legs by means of joystick, keyboard or other commands. Control of foot positions is in body-fixed Cartesian co-ordinates. A CRT display of vehicle-stability margin derived from a vertical gyroscope and foot-force and position transducers is provided to assist the operator. Feedback of swing-phase foot position relative to terrain is primarily through operator vision, although this function can be assisted by the use of proximity sensors mounted on the vehicle legs. Body-motion control can be either automatic[10] or manual in this mode. In the manual mode the operator can assign his joystick axes either to translational or rotational body velocity control.

Close manoeuvring

This is a three-axis control mode in which the turning centre for body rotation can be placed anywhere along the vehicle longitudinal axis. Once this has been done, arbitrary combinations of yaw rotational rate, forward velocity and lateral velocity can be commanded by a three-axis joystick. Stepping is regulated automatically with swing-phase foot elevation controlled primarily by proximity sensors to achieve an operator-specified ground clearance.[13] Body roll and pitch can be regulated either to a fixed set-point or adjusted automatically to conform to the terrain slope.[14] Force feedback is used to control foot loading and to prevent the development of unwanted antagonistic forces between supporting legs.[5] The optical radar is not used in this mode since its field of view is limited to $\pm 40°$ in azimuth from the vehicle centreline.

Terrain-following

All vehicle sensors are used in this mode. The optical radar provides terrain preview data for use by the on-board computer in the selection of foothold locations and the determination of average terrain slope and elevation for body attitude and altitude regulation.[15] During the swing phase of limb motion, proximity sensors on each leg are used in conjunction with optical radar data for local control of foot elevation and for collision avoidance. During support phase, force feedback is used to achieve active compliance to smooth-body motion and control leg loading.[5,16] Body-turn rate, forward velocity and lateral velocity are determined by operator inputs.[4] This mode makes use of algorithms for free (non-periodic) gaits to improve rough-terrain mobility at moderate speeds.[12,15,17] Both the maximum body crab angle[4] and the minimum turning radius are limited to values which ensure that all footholds used by the vehicle lie on terrain which has been mapped by the forward-looking optical radar.

Cruise

This is the most efficient mode of operation with respect to fuel economy. It is suitable for locomotion over reasonably smooth terrain. The design goal for vehicle speed in this mode is 8km/h. Body crab angle is limited to a relatively small value and minimum turning radius is of the order of several body lengths. The on-board computer uses optical radar data to determine a desired foot-lift height during the swing phase of leg motion. The proximity sensors assist in control of foot velocity at ground impact. It is expected that cruise mode will utilize an 'equiphase' tripod gait in which the footfalls of supporting legs are evenly spaced in time to minimize shock and vibration transmitted to the vehicle body by the cyclic action of the legs.[18]

Dash

This is a projected mode in which all aspects of vehicle performance will be sacrificed for speed. Specifically, manoeuvrability will be limited, ride characteristics are expected to be rough and fuel economy is likely to be poor. An alternating tripod gait[2] will probably be used for this purpose. The control computer will command body attitude and swing-phase foot-lift height. Top speed should be of the order of 12km/h in this mode.

Computer architecture

Experience to date with the OSU hexapod indicates that a network of microcomputers probably provides the most effective configuration for the ASV-84 on-board computer.[8] The following paragraphs describe one partitioning of computational tasks among such computers which is consistent with the above defined control modes and which tends to minimize intercomputer data communication rates. Figure 1 is a graphical representation of the computer architecture implied by this partitioning. All computers in this diagram are physically realized in terms of Intel iSBC 86/30 single-board computers. These computers make use of the 8086 microprocessor with an optional incorporation of the 8087 floating-point coprocessor as well as 16 channels of analog input and eight channels of analog output lines. A description of the function of each computer in this system follows.

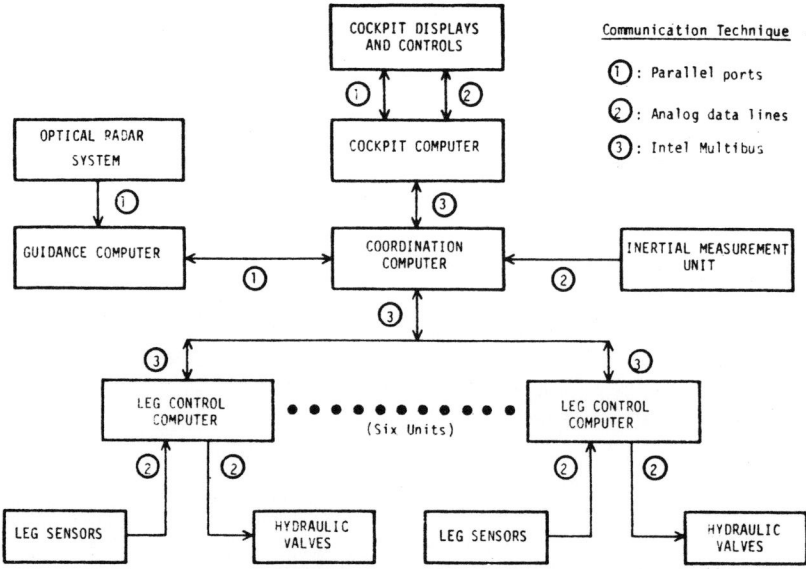

Figure 1 On-board computer architure for ASV-84 vehicle

Guidance computer

This computer receives range data from the optical radar and produces a stabilized terrain map in earth-fixed Cartesian co-ordinates at a 2Hz frame rate. As shown in Figure 1, it also receives information from a co-ordination computer. This information consists of body attitude, body altitude, all six body velocity components relative to the supporting terrain, foot-support states, individual foot positions expressed in body co-ordinates, and operator velocity and steering requests. The output of this computer consists of timing and trajectory commands for swing-phase legs and of commanded body positions and velocities. Eventually, the guidance computer should also control the scanning angles of the optical radar, although this is not contemplated for the initial phases of ASV-84 testing. The guidance computer contains four iSBC 86/30 boards.[15]

Co-ordination computer

This computer is the master computer in the sense that all intercomputer communications must pass through it. Specifically, the co-ordination computer receives designated footholds, swing-phase foot trajectories, and commanded body positions and velocities from the guidance computer. It also receives operator commands from a cockpit computer as well as body attitude information from an inertial-measurement unit. It then communicates with leg-control computers to provide appropriate foot-motion commands. These commands must be derived as a compromise between operator inputs and constraints imposed by the dynamic and kinematic limitations of individual legs. As complicated as this process sounds, it is well understood with respect to control of the OSU hexapod vehicle.[4,5,8,10] For legs in support phase, commands from the co-ordination computer consist of desired foot velocities and forces in body-fixed Cartesian co-ordinates. For swing-phase legs, either point-to-point control or continuous velocity control is used, depending on the particular operational mode. The co-ordination computer is composed of two iSBC 86/30 boards functioning in a partial duplex mode in which each computer monitors the other's function. Both of these computers are connected directly to primary-system sensors and either can automatically initiate emergency shut-down procedures in case of failure of a major vehicle subsystem.

Cockpit computer

This computer reads levers, dials and push buttons manipulated by the human operator. It also operates all cockpit instrumentation, including at least one CRT display. This display is used during normal operation as well as for system check-out and diagnostics.

Leg control computers

The actuator control valves for each leg are operated by a control computer associated with that leg. Each such computer receives commands from the co-ordination computer in body-fixed co-ordinates. It then translates these to joint co-ordinates and implements the resulting motions through closed-loop velocity control of each joint. Jacobian control, as used in the OSU hexapod, permits this to be done without explicitly solving for desired leg joint angles.[16] In certain operational modes leg computers use proximity sensor information to maintain foot clearance above the terrain during the swing phase of leg motion and also use this information to achieve a soft landing at the end of swing phase.

Computer communications

Two different approaches to intercomputer communications are used in the ASV-84 computing system. For the guidance computer, data rates are low enough to permit communication with the co-ordination computer by means of parallel data ports. Leg control computers involve higher data rates, and will therefore be connected with the co-ordination computer through a high-speed data bus (Intel Multibus), with a shared memory 'mailbox' type of communication. The same communication technique is used for the cockpit computer. Transmission of partial data blocks between asynchronous processes is prevented in all cases by a buffering scheme based on dynamic reassignment of input and output buffers for each communication channel.

Summary and conclusions

At the time of this writing, a breadboard version of the ASV-84 computer has been completed. The optical radar system has been delivered and laboratory testing with the guidance computer is under way. Software for the precision-footing mode of control has been completed and validated by using the OSU hexapod as a physical test-bed. Terrain-following software has been installed on the breadboard computer and is being evaluated by using a PDP-11/70 computer to simulate the optical radar, terrain and vehicle mechanical system. Outdoor testing of the completed ASV-84 vehicle was scheduled for late 1984. The authors hope that this testing will establish a new level of performance for walking machines and will facilitate the development of specialized adaptive-suspension vehicles designed for specific applications.

This research was supported by the Defense Advanced Research Projects Agency under Contract MDA 903-82-K-0058.

References

[1] Waldron K J et al. (1984) Configuration design of the adaptive-suspension vehicle. Int. J. Robotics Res., **3** (2), April
[2] McGhee R B (1984) Vehicular legged locomotion. In Advances in Robotics and Automation vol. 1, ed. G N Saridis. Jai Press, Connecticut
[3] Mosher R S (1969) Exploring the Potential of a Quadruped SAE Paper no. 690191, Int. Automotive Engineering Conf. Detroit, Michigan, January
[4] Orin D E (1982) Supervisory control of a multilegged robot. Int. J. Robotics Res., **1** (1), 79-91
[5] Klein C A, Olson K W & Pugh D R (1983) Use of force and attitude sensors for locomotion of a legged vehicle over irregular terrain. Int. J. Robotics Res., **2** (2), 3-17
[6] Gurfinkel V S et al. (1981) Walking robot with supervisory control. J. Mech. Mach. Theory, **16**, 31-36
[7] Raibert M H & Sutherland I E (1983) Machines that walk. Sci. Am., **248** (2), 44-53

[8] Klein C A & Wahawisan W (1982) Use of a multiprocessor for control of a robotic system *Int. J. Robotics Res.,* **1** (2), 45-59
[9] Russell M (1983) Odex I: the First Functionoid. *Robotics Age,* **5** (5), 12-18
[10] Ozguner F, Tsai S J & McGhee R B (1984) An approach to the use of terrain preview information in rough-terrain locomotion by a hexapod walking machine. *Int. J. Robotics Res.,* **3** (2), April
[11] Waldron K J et al. (1984) *Mechanical and Geometric Design of the Adaptive-suspension vehicle* Proc. of RO MAN SY-84 Symposium, Udine, Italy, June, 1984
[12] Klein C A & Patterson M R (1982) Computer coordination of limb motion for locomotion of a multiple-armed robot for space assembly. *IEEE Trans. Systems, Man and Cybernetics,* **SMC-12** (6), 913-919
[13] Broerman K R (1983) Development of a proximity sensor system for foot altitude control of a terrain-adaptive hexapod robot. MSc Thesis, Ohio State University, Columbus, OH 43210, August
[14] Lee W J (1984) A simulation study of interactive computer control for rough-terrain locomotion by a hexapod walking machine. PhD Dissertation, Ohio State University, Columbus, OH 43210, March
[15] Patterson M R, Reidy J J & Brownstein B J (1983) Guidance and actuation techniques for an adaptively controlled vehicle. Final Technical Report, Battelle Columbus Laboratories, Columbus, OH 43201, March
[16] Klein C A & Briggs R L (1980) Use of active compliance in the control of legged vehicles. *IEEE Trans. Systems, Man and Cybernetics,* **SMC-10** (7), 393-400
[17] McGhee R B & Iswandhi G I (1979) Adaptive locomotion of a multilegged robot over rough terrain. *IEEE Trans. Systems, Man and Cybernetics,* **SMC-9** (4), 176-182
[18] Wang S L (1983) Study of a hexapod walking vehicle's maneuverability over level ground and obstacles and its computer simulation. MSc Thesis, Ohio State University, Columbus, OH 43210, August

Realization of Plane Walking by the Biped Walking Robot WL-10R

A Takanishi, G Naito, M Ishida and I Kato

Department of Mechanical Engineering, Waseda University, Ookubo, Shinjuku-ku, Tokyo, Japan

Summary: The purpose of this study is to accomplish plane walking by a hydraulic-powered biped walking robot on a flat floor. Plane walking consists of three types of fundamental pattern walkings: straight walking, sideway walking and turning. The control method is a program control with a preset walking pattern. In forward walking the gait is a quasi-dynamic walking. We propose a new quasi-dynamic walking-control method as follows: change-over phase is divided into four phases according to the floor contact of soles, a walking pattern is designed by computer simulation and the output to a machine model is interpolated with a parabola function. In the other walkings the gaits are static walkings which are statically stable through all walking cycles. The model WL-10R is an anthropomorphic biped walking robot with 12 degrees of freedom driven by an electro-hydro servo mechanism. Additionally, WL-10R has a control device on its upper body. As a result of experiments, smooth and stable quasi-dynamic forward walking is achieved; the walking time is about 4.8s with 45cm stride. Stable static plane walkings are realized.

Introduction

This laboratory began studies on biped walking in 1969. In 1972 it developed the 11 DOF (degrees of freedom) hydraulic-powered biped walking robot WL(Waseda Leg)-5, a subsystem for the WABOT(WAseda roBOT)-1, accomplishing automatic biped walking by computer control for the first time in the world.[1-3] Its gait was static walking which was statically stable in each phase during a walking cycle. The speed of straight walking was 40s per step with 17cm per step stride and it was possible to change a direction with 40s per step to turn 15° per step. The action was seemingly intermittent in both walking styles.

Since 1973, the studies have been aimed at achieving dynamic straight walking, which should be as smooth and rapid as man's walking. In 1975, hydraulic-powered biped walking robot WL-8D(Dynamic), which had 10 DOF for legs and 2 DOF for the upper part of the body, was developed. As a control method for dynamic walking, ZMP(Zero Moment Point) control was introduced.[4] With this control, 2 DOF on the upper part of the body was utilized for compensation so that the ZMP, whose total moment generated due to gravity force and inertia force is zero, lay at each sole. Though the walking was not realized in this experiment, it was found that accurate biped walking requires some improvement of a preset walking pattern and precise control laws.

In 1980, a quasi-dynamic walking-control method was proposed. The quasi-dynamic walking was regarded as a transitional step from static to dynamic walking. With this control, the quasi-dynamic straight walking was achieved by the 10 DOF hydraulic-powered biped walking robot WL-9DR(Refine).[5] The walking speed was

10s per step with a 45cm per step stride. The control method was a program control with a preset walking pattern, which had been produced as angle data of each DOF according to the walking analysis and the repetition of experiments. The control laws were as follows: One walking cycle was divided into two phases, a single support phase and a change-over (to standing) phase. During single-support phase swing leg was moving forward statically and the position of a COG (centre of gravity) was within a stable region of a supporting leg's sole. During the change-over phase the supporting leg of COG was changing over from a hind leg to a fore-leg as follows: the machine model was regarded as an inverted pendulum and a movement of COG was analysed as a trajectory in a phase plane, the trajectory of COG which had been moving out from a stable region of the hind leg's sole was entering into a stable region of the foreleg's sole.

In 1983, by the 12 DOF hydraulic-powered biped walking robot WL-10R, in which were installed microcomputers as a control device on the upper body, more stable and smooth straight quasi-dynamic walking than before was achieved. Additionally, static turning, static sideway walking and the plane walking which was constructed by these walkings, were realized. In this paper we describe the concepts and the control methods of stable and smooth quasi-dynamic straight walking and plane walking.

Plane walking

As for biped walking robots, a control device and/or power source was not installed on the body, and its gait was almost all straight walking. But in the near future, when the practical walking robots should be widely used, it is necessary that these robots have independent hardware and are able to do plane walking. From this point of view, we made it the main target for our study to make plane walking on the level of static or quasi-dynamic walking, and to install the control device on the body as the first step to hardware independence.

Concept of Plane Walking

We set the Cartesian co-ordinate axes of x-y-z, as shown in Figure 1, for walking robot to be treated mathematically. Therefore, the x-z plane forms a sagittal plane, the y-z plane forms a lateral plane and the x-y plane forms a floor plane.

Plane walking is a form considered to be man's usual walking. He may walk straight as well as diagonally or from side-to-side. As space for walking is restricted to a floor, there are totally 3 DOF for walking adding 2 DOF of x-y plane and 1 DOF of rotation around z axis. In connection with these 3 DOF, we call the walking on x axis 'straight walking', the walking on y axis is called 'sideway walking' and the rotation around z axis 'turning'. Additionally, walking to a plus or minus direction on x axis is 'forward' or 'backward walking', similarly 'rightway' or 'leftway walking' on y axis and CCW (Counter Clockwise) or CW (Clockwise) turning around z axis. These are the fundamental patterns of plane walking and general plane walkings are formed by serial or parallel combinations of these fundamental walkings.

We have been treating one cycle of straight walking as something which is divided into a single support and a change-over phase. This is to say we deal with it

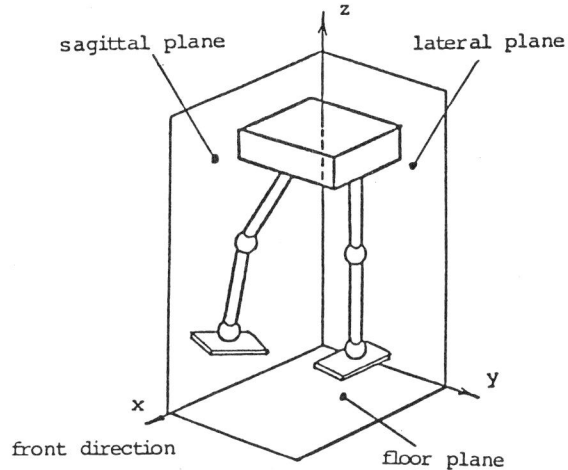

Figure 1 Co-ordination of walking system

abstractly that walking system should consist of two elements of COG and its supporting mechanism and walking is made up of interactive movement of each element. On the other two fundamental walkings, which are sideway walking and turning, the same concept should be applied. All of the fundamental walkings are considered to be made up of repetition of remarkable movement of COG and swing leg.

We designed a new machine model and control methods for biped walking based on these already defined concepts.

Control method

The control method is a program control with a preset walking pattern. It is pre-designed before walking as angle data of each DOF by computer simulation. Walking is achieved by the appropriate time interval output of interpolated preset walking pattern which is stored in a control computer on the machine model. Therefore, the way of walking pattern design is the essential point to realize walking.

Change-over phase control

We regard the machine model as an inverted pendulum, and analyse its movement on a phase plane shown in Figure 2. The change-over movement of last machine model WL-9DR started only by hind-leg's kick in the first stage, after that two legs were kept in a locked state, and finished as shown in Figure 3. This method has an advantage in simplifying a walking pattern design, but has the problems that walking becomes unstable by the occurrence of a strong impact at every floor contact of heels or toes and, still more, a machine model is damaged quickly. So

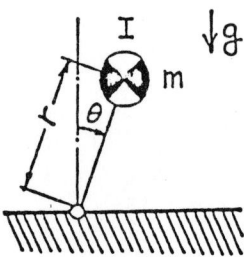

I : moment of inertia
m : mass
g : gravitational acceleration
θ : angle of center of gravity
r : pendulum length

Figure 2 Inverted pendulum model

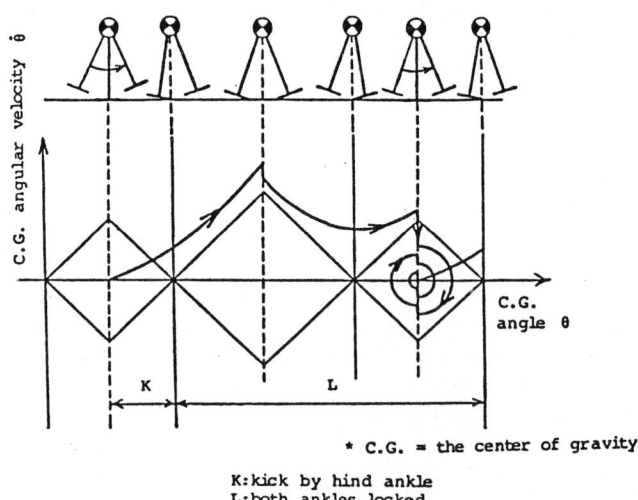

* C.G. = the center of gravity

K: kick by hind ankle
L: both ankles locked

Figure 3 Change-over phase of WL-9DR

we realize low impact and smooth walking with precise movement on two ankles in change-over phase as follows.

As shown in Figure 4, the change-over phase is divided into four phases A - D according to toe and heel contact of both soles. The strong impact is suppressed

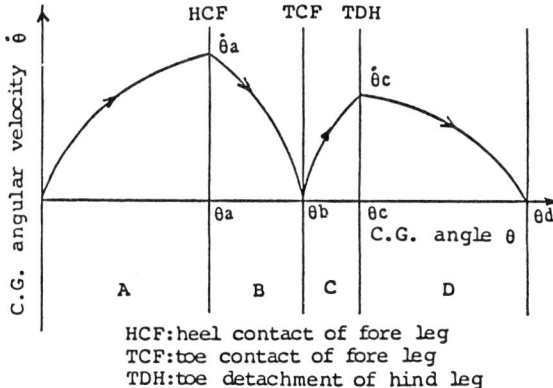

Figure 4 Change-over phase of WL-10R

because all the points of discontinuity on the trajectory are removed by the movements of ankles in the following way: (phase-A) accelerate with constant acceleration of the hind ankle, until foreheel contact occurs; (phase-B) decelerate from last velocity in phase A to velocity zero, with constant acceleration of the fore-ankle, until foretoe contact occurs; (phase-C) accelerate, with constant acceleration of the hind ankle, until hindtoe detachment occurs; (phase-D) decelerate from last velocity in phase C to velocity zero, with constant acceleration of the fore-ankle.

Control laws in straight walking

In straight walking the walking pattern is designed according to the control laws as follows: (a) Divide one walking cycle into a single support and change-over phase. (b) During a single-support phase, move forward the swing leg lest support sole should be detached by reaction torque. At the same time, adjust the difference of COG position caused by the movement of the swing leg with pitch axis's DOF in ankle. (c) During a change-over phase, divide it into four phases according to the contact condition of both soles, and design a walking pattern according to the control laws discussed in the last section. (d) The number of finite-state points for preset walking pattern in one cycle is six in single-support phase and four in change-over phase. During machine walking, a walking pattern is output interpolated with linear function in single-support phase and with parabola function (constant acceleration) in change-over phase.

Control laws in turning

Turning is controlled through all walking cycle by a static balance of COG as follows: (a) Divide one turning cycle into a COG movement phase and a turning phase. (b) During a COG movement phase, move a COG into the centre of stable area by supporting sole keeping two legs support state. (c) During turning phase, the turn of the yaw axis lest supporting sole should slip by reaction torque. At the same time, adjust a difference of COG caused by this movement by using pitch and roll axis's DOF in support ankle. (d) An output of walking pattern to the machine model in both phases is interpolated with linear function. As for turning, it has many variations according to the first state or turn angle.

Control laws in sideway walking

Sideway walking, as with turning, is controlled by static balance of COG. (a) Divide one walking cycle into a single-support phase and a COG-movement phase. (b) During single-support phase, move a swing leg sideway and contact to the floor lest support sole should be detached by reaction torque. At the same time, adjust a difference of COG caused by this movement by using roll axis's DOF in support ankle. (c) During COG-movement phase, move a COG into the centre of stable area by the other sole, keeping the two legs support state. (d) An output of walking pattern is interpolated with linear function in both phases.

System configuration of biped walking robot WL-10R

Machine model WL-10R

The machine model WL-10R is an anthropomorphic biped walking robot having 12 DOF, shown in Figure 5. Arrangement of DOF is 2 (pitch and roll) DOF for each ankle, 1 (pitch) DOF for each knee, 3 (pitch, roll and yaw) DOF for thigh, totalling 12 DOF. Electro-hydro servo system, by using RA (rotary actuator) with servo valve for DOF on yaw axis and RSA (rotary servo actuator) with DC motor for the other DOF, is employed for position control. The frame is made of CFRP (carbon fibre reinforced plastics) for making the structure lighter. A set of control computer is installed on the body; its total weight is about 80kg.

As far as sensors are concerned, a pulse encoder is provided for DC motor control and a potentiometer for yaw axis control. A potentiometer is installed at each output shaft of RSA for response data acquisition during machine walking. Each sole is equipped with four microswitches to detect the ground contact of the sole.

Control system

The WL-10R's control system can be shown as a block diagram in Figure 6. This system has a hierarchic structure, comprising a main control system with a 16-bit CPU Z8002 and six subcontrol systems with an 8-bit one-chip MCU Z8. The main control system edits and corrects walking patterns while stopping and selects specified walking patterns and outputs angle data to subcontrol systems while walking. The main control system has a 12-bit A/D converter with 16 channel inputs and has 256 Kbytes ROMs for storage of many kinds of walking patterns. Each subcontrol system controls two DC motors with one MCU according to angle data transmitted from main control system. Additionally, this system can communicate through a serial communication line to a host computer system SYSTEM-8000 (CPU:Z8001, RAM:1.5 Mbytes, Hard Disk: 48 Mbytes, MT:17 Mbytes, OS: UNIX System-III) which is used for walking-pattern design and control-program development.

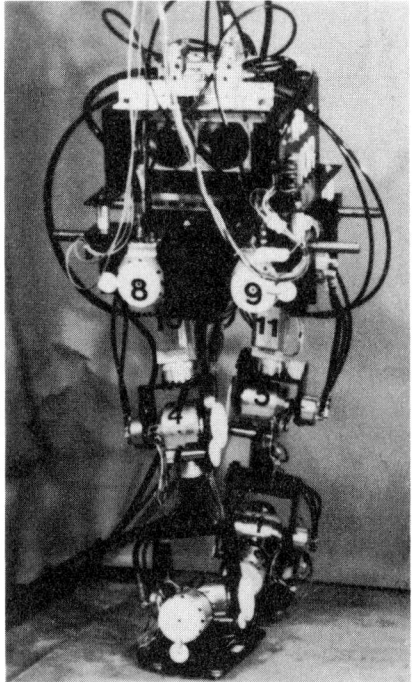

Figure 5 Machine model WL-10R

Walking experiment

Six types of preset walking patterns, forward, backward, rightway, leftway walking, CCW and CW turning, were designed according to the control laws aided by a simulation program named Walk Master having two-dimensional graphic output function. Forward walking, leftway walking and CW turning produced with Walk Master are shown in Figures 7 - 9. As a result of walking experiments with these patterns, smooth and stable quasi-dynamic forward walking is achieved, and stable static walkings are realized in other types of walking. Based on the experimental results, the response of machine model in forward walking is shown in Figure 10 by using graphical output function of Walk Master, and the trajectory in change-over phase is shown in Figure 11. The walking time in each walking is shown in Table 1.

Conclusion

Smooth and stable quasi-dynamic forward walking was achieved. The walking time was about 4.8s per step with a 45cm per step stride. Stable static backward, leftway, rightway walking, CCW and CW turning, which are fundamental patterns of

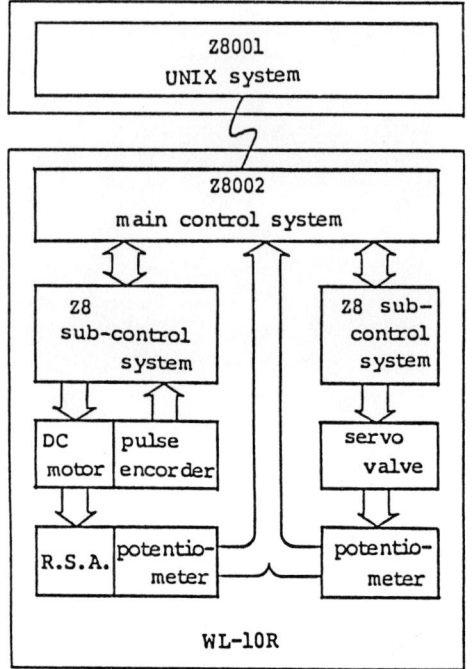

Figure 6 System block diagram of WL-10R

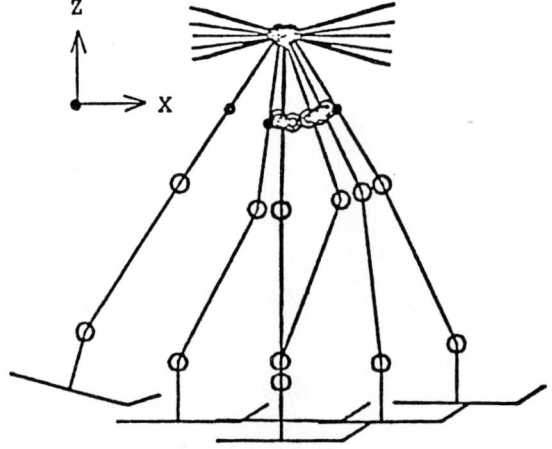

Figure 7 Producted forward walking pattern

Biped Walking Robot WL-10R   391

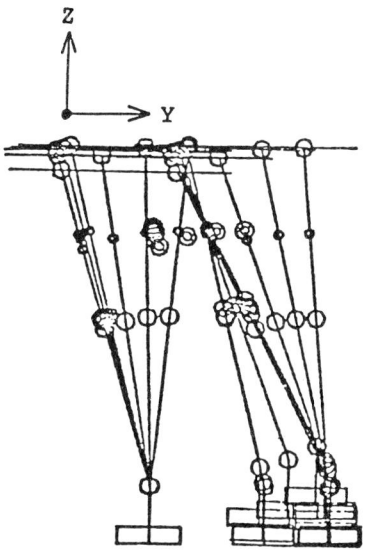

Figure 8 Producted leftway walking pattern

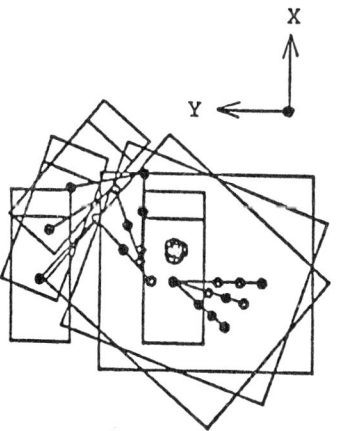

Figure 9 Producted CW turning pattern

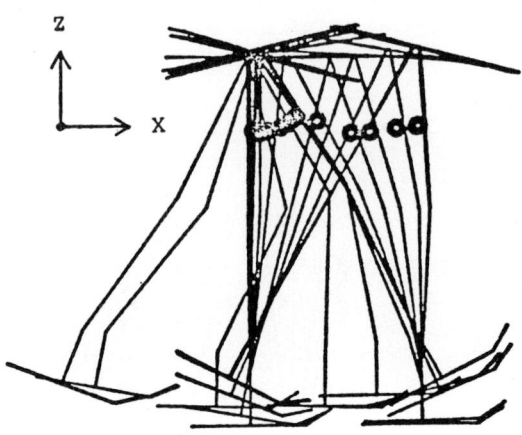

Figure 10 Response of WL-10R in forward walking

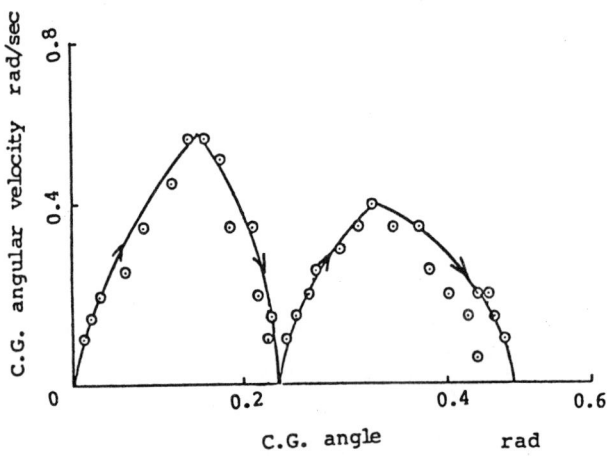

Figure 11 Response trajectory in change-over phase

Table 1 Walking time of WL-10R

Walking style	Stride (cm) (turning angle deg)	Time (s)
Forward walking	45	4.8
Sideway walking	15	15
Turning	90	20

plane walking, were realized. As a result, the validity of newly proposed quasi-dynamic walking and plane-walking control methods were experimentally supported.

References

[1] Kato I & Tsuiki H (1972) *The Hydraulically Powered Biped Walking Machine with a High Carrying Capacity* Proc. 4th Int. Symp. on External Control of Human Extremities, Dubrovnic.
[2] Kato I *et al* (1973) Bulletin of Science and Engineering Research Laboratory, Waseda University, No. 62 (special issue on WABOT)
[3] Kato I, Ohteru S, Kobayashi H, Shirai K & Uchiyama A *Information-Power Machine with Sense and Limbs* Ro Man Sy '73, pp. 12-24
[4] Ogo K, Ganse A & Kato I *Quasi Dynamic Walking of Biped Walking Machine* Ro Man Sy '78, 12-15 September
[5] Kato T, Takanishi A, Ishikawa H & Kato I *The Realization of the Quasi Dynamic Walking by the Biped Walking Machine* Ro Man Sy '81, 8-12 September, pp. 341-351

Hexapod Walking Robots with Artificial Intelligence Capabilities

J J Kessis, J P Rambaut, J Penné, R Wood and N Mattar

Laboratoire de Robotique et Intelligence Artificielle, University of Paris 7, 2 Place Jussieu, 75251 Paris, France

Summary: The potential usefulness of walking robots for work, maintenance and exploration in difficult environments is well acknowledged. For effective performing of these tasks, walkers have to become fully robotic, i.e. to be implemented with high-level software by using artificial intelligence concepts and techniques, concurrently with well-designed mechanics and intermediate software levels for control and sensing. The four-level control architecture we devised for our first six-legged prototype (see Ro Man Sy '81) was found to be efficient, easily modifiable and extensible. However, we find it useful to add to the existing structure (level, 1; leg, 2; gait generation, 3; plan interpreter, 4; intelligence and plan generation) a 1.5 'Tonus' level for effector tonicity and leg adjustment according to terrain constraints. The hardware is tending toward a full multi-microprocessor organization. A significant feature of our approach is the existence at level 3 of an interpreter for our socialized walking robot plan language LP 4.5, designed to be automatically generated by the upper level; gaits are among the primitives of LP 4.5, which makes it easy to program the robot. As implemented now, with a rotating ultrasonic telemeter, the robot is able to exhibit such autonomous behaviours as following edges, escaping, exploring an unknown universe, etc. Paddle driving is also possible under plan control. An equilibrium sensing organ allows the maintenance of the platform horizontal on uneven ground. Methods experimented for producing level-4 intelligent behaviours on a difficult terrain include heuristic graph-search procedures (e.g. A*) and multi-level expert system advanced techniques. A stronger prototype, which carries a payload of 40 kg, has been built. The mechanical design is similar with Cartesian two-motors planar legs exhibiting lateral compliances; however, the leg mechanism is directly Cartesian, without the original triangle-and-pantograph system of the first prototype. The computer systems are compatible. This heavier robot can bear complex sensing systems and perform quasi-real-scale terrain experiments, such as feasibility studies for plant maintenance.

Introduction

Robots, and specially mobile robots, because of their unknown universe,[1-3,7] give an experimental support to artificial intelligence research. Besides, implementing artificial intelligence capabilities is mandatory for building true robots, i.e. perceptive and adaptive ones, finding optimal paths and means and behaving according to the specified goals. In addition, walking robots [4-6,9,10] offer specific problems. First, their multi-articulated structure, similar to the one of manipulators', has to be well designed and controlled. Co-ordination problems involve the gait concept, which we had to improve and generalize. Difficult terrain adaptability, the main potential usefulness of walkers, implies the perception and modelization of a three-dimensional universe, a problem which is as yet physically and conceptually difficult.

Our contribution, at present, was to build two hexapod prototypes, H1 and H2, and to implement a logical architecture to satisfy the above-mentioned goals. H1 was described at Ro Man Sy '81.[9] It exhibits an original triangle-and-pantograph planar Cartesian leg system[8,9] with two degrees of freedom on a leg and built-in compliances (lateral, for turns; vertical reversible mechanism, for intricate terrain capability). The H2 hexapod offers a 40 kg payload. Mechanically the H2 leg is direct Cartesian, without pantographs.

In the present paper we describe the present status of the multilevel logical architecture which is common to the H1 and H2 robots. We then emphasize some original features, mainly the LP 4.5 language, and the fourth-level capabilities.

Multilevel logical architecture

From the beginning of this work we devised a four-level control architecture for our hexapod walking robot. Table 1 shows the four control levels in their present state of implementation. As experiments progressed on the robot, we developed the

Table 1 Multilevel architecture of the hexapod. + = operating; x = in development

Basic	Advanced
Level 1 Cartesian planar reversible mechanism intrinsic compliant terrain adaptability +	
Level 1.5 ('Tonus')	'Reflex' leg level terrain adaptability x
Level 2 (Gait) Basic 'straight-on' gait generator +	Generalized gaits (rear, turns, etc.) + Modified gaits (gait-level terrain adaptability) x
Level 3 Sequential plans with level 2 gaits as primitives +	Evolutive plans conditionals, basic perception +
Level 4 ('Intelligence') Universe and terrain perception/modellization path finding plan generation	 x + x

concepts involved at each level, as shown from left (basic) to right (advanced) in the table. Some additional sensing levels exist and they are outside of the (non-strict) above hierarchy. The hardware implementation is a multi-microprocessor system with bus and line data interchange.

Leg level

Each leg is a Cartesian planar reversible mechanism (see above) actuated by reversible servomotors. This allows an intrinsic limited terrain adaptability: the robot walks on small blocks without limping. It is interesting to point out that physical and timing considerations brought us to implement an intermediate 1.5 level.

'Tonus' level

This additional 1.5 level was not in our original design. It proved to be useful, while implemented on a dedicated processor, for continuous sending of orders to servomotors, thus improving tonicity of the H1 robot. Although not required for H2 motors, this level is conceptually useful for 'economic' implementation of 'reflex' adaptabilities first experimented at level 3.

Gait level

At present, the gait generator at this level produces what we call generalized gaits allowing rear walk, turns, etc., by varying gait parameters like amplitudes and sign of every degree of freedom to each leg. Details about our generalization of the gait concept may be found in Ro Man Sy '81.[9]

This level will contribute to terrain adaptability in two ways: the first one, gait changing (with the problem of transition's gaits) when encountering difficult terrain; the second one, generating modified gaits (i.e. gaits with new modifiable parameters, such as each-leg vertical neutral point setting).

Plan level

Our project being to obtain an autonomous behaviour by generating plans according to goals, world and terrain, the third level is a plan interpreter of a plan language LP 1.5 which has as fundamental statement a couple (gait, duration); gaits, as generated by level 2, are thus among the primitives of level 3. At its present state the language is enriched with conditionals, sensor tests, machine language calls, etc. Fitted with such various evolutive plans and by using a rotating ultrasonic telemeter to get a rough model of its environment, the hexapod exhibits adaptive behaviours.

Intelligent level

Although the plan level allows rather sophisticated behaviours, these have to be programmed specifically as evolutive plans. So we are developing a fourth level for automatic generating of such plans. This level has obviously to cope with complex universe perception and modelization, including three-dimensional vision, and also path choice and decision taking in such universes according to goal specifications. These works are in development, with the LISP language on a microcomputer, being connected to the robots.

LP 4.5 language

Manipulator robot language specialists often distinguish low-level and higher-level robot control languages. For instance, Latombe[11] describes motor, effector, object and goal languages. LP 4.5, to our knowledge the first walking robot dedicated language, is hard to characterize from this point of view ('pedipulation' being quite different of manipulation in spite of the many-degrees-of-freedom likeness) but assuredly high levelled enough for relieving the programmer of taking care of 'effector' leg control. This characterizes the object level for manipulators according to Latombe's classification. From a computer scientific point of view, however, LP 4.5 current is somewhat similar internally to an assembly language, including conditionals. The source code is 'assembled', generating a one-to-one mapped object code. Object code 'evolutive plans' are executed in an interpretive way.

LP 4.5 instruction set

Walking statements

This statement type is fundamental. It defines gaits as primitive functions of the language. Due to versatility of our generalized gaits, few statements types allow the generation of all types of movements.

ALLU n, t. The basic statement execution of the gait n during t elementary times. The n is the number (0-15) of a gait inside the current gait bank. ALLU and ALLC increment cyclical time without resetting it.

ALLC t. Execution of a previously selected gait whose number is contained in the gait register. It allows adaptive behaviour. Special machine-language routines, called for instance by EXAM, may select a gait according to external conditions. For instance, for manual joystick driving we experimented (although non-robotic!) because of possible use in certain vehicles (t is the same as above).

REPO n, t. Initialization statement. The robot 'sits' (retracts legs to lie on pedestal), sets cyclical time to zero, initializes leg horizontal pattern according to gait n, then rests during t elementary times.

DEBT. Stand-up statement. Normally this statement is executed after a REPO and before a ALLU or ALLC. This sequence is essential for preventing leg control conflicts, possibly damaging for the robot. This is why the initialization (REPO) is always proceeded in resting posture and must be made at every gait change. For during the walk gait change transition gaits (as occurring in animals) should be implemented. This is an open research subject.

TMPO n. Modifies speed by altering the value of the 'elementary time'.

CNTR p, v. This new statement changes the vertical centring of the leg p to a value v for equilibrium purposes.

Sequence control statements

BRAN 1. Branch to label 1.

BEVE c, 1. Branch on event. Jumps to label 1 if current conditions code equal to c.

BARI p, 1_1, 1_2, 1_3. Special arithmetic branch. p is a register number (usually containing some sensing information). The contents of register p are compared with a comparand register (1, d) set by CONS statement. Branching is as follows: to 1_1 if $(p) < (1) - (d)$; to 1_3 if $(p) > (1) + (d)$; to 1_2 otherwise.

CONS V1, Vd. Sets of the registered pairs are compared to values $V1$, Vd. A couple of statements CONS and BARI were designed to cope with sensing data. They allow to specify (CONS) a value $V1$ and a precision range Vd; then testing (BARI) a designated sensing datum for conformity to $V1$, under or overrun within precision Vd.

Sensor control statements
These are the most idiosyncratic statements of LP 4.5, fitted to control rotating telemeter angular position and move.

RADF p. Sets telemeter position to p.

RADM p. Set telemeter initial position to p, then start rotating it by fixed angular steps at each elementary time.

External call statements
These powerful statements branch to routines outside the language.

EXAM p, n. Branch to routine n passing parameter p. Various condition codes or registers may be set by the routine when returning. EXAM is mainly used to branch to specific sensing or actuation microprocessor-machine-language written subroutines. Condition codes and returned values may be tested by BEVE and BARI.

MONI n. Like EXAM, without return.

EXIT. Special exit to a plan menu.

(MONI and EXIT are used to terminate the current LP 4.5 plan)

Communication statements
For communicating with other levels.

EMSG n, 1. Send message number n to level 1. This statement is mainly designed for communication with the intelligence level.

Among the improvements we are developing, a gait compiler partly for increasing the generality of LP 4.5 implementation by adding declarative parts describing gaits by properties (symmetry, waviness, number of elementary times) or by conventional terms (trippled, turning, etc.).

This allows automatic language level production of the gait tables (for execution through the gait generator), each being linked to a gait number (the one mentioned in the LP 4.5 executable gait statements). This, in addition, is a step toward a total 'device independence' of the language.

Artificial intelligence level

The intelligence level is designed to control the overall behaviour of the robots by generating LP 4.5 programs for the plan level. Handwritten LP 4.5 plans already allow, with only level 3, complex adaptive behaviours such as following walls, avoiding obstacles, escaping from confinement, all taking into account a simple range-finding ultrasonic perception of the universe. The level 3, embarked on the battery-operated H2, thus allows local autonomy of the robot. However, complex situations, and initialization, require more analysis, as is implemented in the level 4 microcomputer.

At the moment, the communication with level 4 is being implemented. So the 'intelligence' capabilities are experimented in simulation. Mainly two approaches were implemented.

Heuristic approach

The problem is to find an optimal path in a complex environment. Algorithms, mainly A*, are known and used in the two-dimensional prismatic environment of wheeled mobile robots.[2,3,12] We experimented the adaptation of such algorithms to a model of a three-dimensional terrain. The optimization is more difficult, due to the multiplicity of criteria (speed, power consumption, etc.) and to the necessary modelization of the robot itself (size, maximum crossable threshold, allowable tilt, etc.).

Expert system approach

To solve the general problem of modellizing an unknown universe by using partial information from sensors like range finders (with possible 'noise') we tried a multi-level production system as an approach. Written in LISP, the system builds a multi-level world map using a multi-expert structure in a way similar to the Hearsay-II speech-recognizing system.[13] Instead of speech elements, the levels here are in the present state, sensor (point), segment, room, the last being the most abstract. As in Hearsay, the addition of a single lower-level description, a single point, may cause a change in the description at all higher levels. We shall not detail the software implementation, which uses rule production-systems techniques. The room-level experts build an abstract world map with connection of relations and passable spaces, in a form usable by strategy-selection experts, reacting to goal descriptions added to the general data base. If the robot lacks sufficient information to achieve the goal, a new exploration phase is entered. Otherwise, a set of 'prototype plans' (i.e. sequences of pseudo LP 4.5 instructions with variable references to be instantiated) is generated and transferred to the plan level for execution. The robot may thus behave autonomously, due to the conditional character of LP 4.5, until a problem unsolvable at level 3 occurs, producing a new call to level 4.

Conclusion

The present status of our system is the result of interaction of our primary design with experiments on our robots. We are planning the next generation, with an advanced walking robot language (WRL) exhibiting more versatility, homogeneity and device independence.

Concurrently, we shall pursue works on automatic generation of such languages, according to perception and decision robotic needs, and artificial intelligence plan-generation concepts; physically, the robots will be improved by adding better sensors and actuating (including possible manipulators) means.

References

[1] Giralt G, Sobek R & Chatila R (1979) *A Multi-level Planning and Navigation System for a Mobile Robot: a First Approach to Hilare* Proc. 6th IJCAI, Tokyo, p 335

[2] Marcé L, Jullière M, Place H & Périchot H (1980) A semiautonomous remote controlled mobile robot. *Indust. Robot*, 7(4), 232

[3] Chatila R (1981) Système de navigation pour un robot mobile autonome, Thesis, Toulouse

[4] Orin D E (1982) Supervisory control of a multilegged robot. *Int. J. Robotics Res.*, 1(1), 79-91

[5] Okhotsimsky D E, Gurfinkel V S, Devyanin E A & Platonov A K (1979) *Integrated Walking Robot. Machine Intelligence 9*, p 313. J Wiley and Sons, New York

[6] Hirose S & Umetani Y (1978) *Some Consideration on a Feasible Walking Mechanism* 3rd Int. Symp. on Robots and Manipulators, Udine, Italy, p 357

[7] Place H, Jullière M & Marcé: L (1983) Qu'en est-il des robots mobiles? *Nouv. Automatisme*, 35, 31-39

[8] Kessis J J & Rambaut J P *Mécanisme Cartésien* French patent no. 81-13843

[9] Kessis J J, Rambaut J P & Penné J (1983) *Walking Robot Multi-level Architecture and Implementation* 4th Symp. on Theory and Practice of Robots and Manipulators, Ro Man Sy '81, Warsaw, Poland, pp 297-304

[10] Raibert M H & Sutherland I E (1983) Machines that walk. *Sci. Am.*, 248, 44-53

[11] Latombe J C (1982) *Journées ARA Pole Robotique Générale* Poitiers, France

[12] Ghallab M (1982) *Optimisation des processus décisionnels pour la Robotique*, Thesis, Toulouse

[13] Erman L D, Hayes-Roth F, Lesser V R & Reddy D R (1980) The Hearsay-II speech understanding system: integrating knowledge to resolve uncertainty. *Comput. Surv.*, 12(2), 213

Legged Locomotion Machine Based on the Consideration of Degrees of Freedom

M Kaneko, M Abe, S Tachi, S Nishizawa, K Tanie and K Komoriya

Mechanical Engineering Laboratory, MITI Tsukuba Science City, Ibaraki 305 Japan

Summary: Minimum walking functions are defined for legged locomotion machines capable of proceeding on rough terrain. The necessary degrees of freedom are considered by using a four-legged machine which offers the minimum number of legs capable of keeping static stability and it is determined that only six are sufficient to realize the minimum functions. Although reduction of the number of active degrees of freedom generally leads to walking inflexibility, it also causes some desirable features, i.e. the simplicity of co-operational control of legs and the realization of fast locomotion, etc. From this point of view, the six-legged locomotion machine in this study is based on the idea of reducing the number of active degrees of freedom, while keeping the minimum functions. For this purpose, the approximate straight-line link mechanism is applied to the legs. It is shown that this mechanism is effective for the legs from the point of energy and in reducing the number of active degrees of freedom. This mechanism also has the possibility to realize the six-legged machine for rough terrain by only eight degrees of freedom. Although the flexibility is, of course, limited, the proposed machine can be controlled much easier than the conventional machines.

Legged locomotion machines and degrees of freedom

Table 1 shows the number of active degrees of freedom in typical legged machines[1-9] (*no steering function) which do not require any dynamic balance control. The machines which have the greatest number of active degrees of freedom possess three

Table 1 Number of active degrees of freedom in typical legged machines. *No steering function

4 legs	Tokyo Institute of Technology[1]	12
	Mechanical Engineering Laboratory[2]	8*
6 legs	Ohio State University[3]	18
	Moscow State University[4]	18
	Carnegie-Mellon University[5]	18
	Odetics Inc[6]	18
	Paris University[7]	12*
	Roma University[8]	12*
8 legs	Komatsu Ltd[9]	10

actuators for each leg and therefore totally such machines[1,3-6] possess with 3k active degrees of freedom (k=number of active degrees of freedom), since wheeled vehicles and crawlers can move freely with only two active degrees of freedom.

Generally, reducing the number of active degrees of freedom leads to the simplified control system and the fast locomotion within the limited walking functions. From this point of view, although the degrees of freedom seem to be the fundamental study in developing of the legged machine, this problem has not yet been studied thoroughly.

In this study the minimum walking functions on rough terrain are defined in the following way. It is possible: (i) to keep static stability; (ii) to move backward and forward and to steer; (iii) to keep the body horizontal; (iv) to keep the absolute height of the body constant as far as the leg length can permit.

Function (ii) means that the machine can be steered in the desired position and direction like a car. Function (iii) keeps the sufficient static stability margin and the machine from tipping over. Function (iv) is required for energy efficiency. It is also desirable to keep the absolute height of the body constant for practical actuators without energy-storing functions to save energy.

On the other hand, although it is possible for the machine with three active degrees of freedom per leg to select the suitable gait and to select the foot position freely, we can consider that these functions are related to the flexibility of locomotion but not absolutely required for the legged machine.

Necessary conditions for active degrees of freedom

Necessary conditions of active degrees of freedom have to be considered on the basis of static stability, body position and posture of support plane formed by the feet in loaded phase. It is assumed that static stability is ensured in this study. Since it is expected that fewer legs lead to reducing the number of active degrees of freedom, a generalized four-legged machine (Figure 1) is considered, where $\vec{G}$ is the

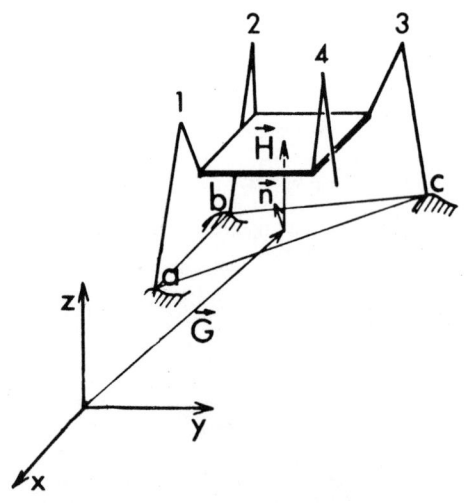

Figure 1 Generalized four-legged machine and its vector notation

vector to express the centre of gravity of the support triangle formed by the feet in loaded phase, $\vec{H}$ is the vector to express the height between the centre of gravity of the support triangle and the body and $\vec{n}$ is the unit vector and its direction is perpendicular to the support triangle. Eventually, function (ii) means that $\vec{G}$ can be determined in any position on the terrain and function (iii) means that $\vec{n}$ can be turned in any direction independent of the body posture and function (iv) means that $\vec{H}$ can be determined in any position within the legs' movable limit. Therefore, to realize functions (ii)-(iv), it is necessary that at least $\vec{G}, \vec{n}, \vec{H}$ could be determined freely. The components of $\vec{G}, \vec{n}, \vec{H}$ are expressed by

$$\vec{G} = (X_G, Y_G, Z_G) \tag{1}$$
$$\vec{n} = (\cos a, \cos \beta, \cos \gamma) \tag{2}$$
$$\vec{H} = (0, 0, h) \tag{3}$$

where a, β, γ is the angle between each axis fixed on the body and $\vec{n}$, respectively, and therefore the following relation exists:

$$\cos^2 a + \cos^2 \beta + \cos^2 \gamma = 1 \tag{4}$$

On the other hand, once the terrain is given, Z_G [in equation (1)] depends on the parameters X_G, Y_G and therefore can be written as

$$Z_G = Z_G(X_G, Y_G) \tag{5}$$

Actually, the number of independent parameters reduces in '5'. Since each independent parameter corresponds to the active degrees of freedom, five is the minimum necessary to realize functions (ii)-(iv).

Sufficient conditions for active degrees of freedom

Let us consider the four-legged model in Figure 2(a) to show the sufficiency of the necessary condition. This model is equipped with four legs and a body capable of sliding, and with a weight capable of rotating, and with one passive degree of freedom in the connecting point between its front-leg unit (or rear-leg unit) and body. The basic sequence of locomotion is shown in Figure 2(b). Since it is clear that this model has functions (i), (iii) and (iv), the problem as to whether this model can satisfy functions (i)-(iv) or not, leaves us with only having to examine the possibility of two-dimensional walking [function (ii)]. This point is demonstrated in Figure 3. The movement of $\overline{L_1 L_2}$ from the initial state to the final state can be understood as the combination with the rotation of $\overline{L_1 L_2}$ and the movement of P_1. The rotation of $\overline{L_1 L_2}$ can be accomplished easily and therefore the problem results in how point P_1 can be moved from $P_1(Xs, Ys)$ to $P_1(Xf, Yf)$. Figure 3(b and c) shows that point P_1 can be moved independently for X and Y. Therefore, theoretically it is possible for point P_1 to be moved in any position by mixing two directional movements. Since the same idea can be applied also to the rotation and movement of $\overline{L_3 L_4}$, it was proved that this model satisfies the functions (i)-(iv). Five of six active degrees of freedom in this model correspond to the number discussed in the necessary condition and the other one is required from the point of balance.

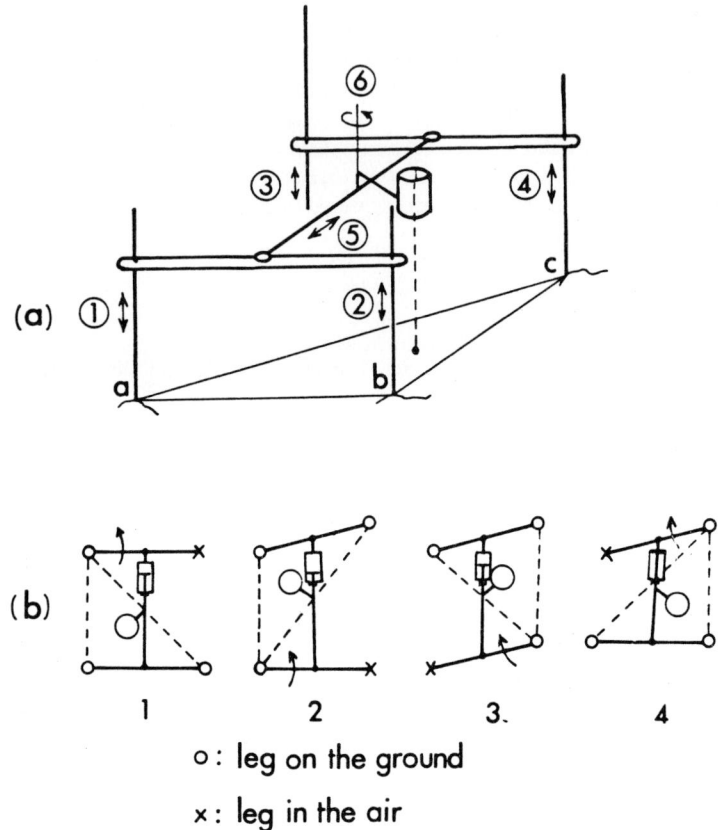

Figure 2 Four-legged machine with six active degrees of freedom and its basic sequence of locomotion

Six-legged locomotion machine based on a fixed gait

It was shown in the previous section that the four-legged machine with minimum walking functions can be realized only by six active degrees of freedom. Such a machine performs awkwardly, however, because its weight must be shifted with each step to keep its balance. Under these circumstances, we started to study the six-legged machine (MELWALK) without active balance control, and with the minimum functions and with a fewer number of active degrees of freedom. Our aim is for a more simplified machine in the same sense of controllability and a machine faster than the conventional machines[3-6]. The minimum functions can be realized by alternating a tripod gait and additional degrees of freedom. Such a gait is convenient to simplify the mechanism and to keep balance without control. An approximate straight-line link mechanism[10] is applied to the leg for this purpose. The basic link-unit construction is shown in Figure 4. Two remarkable features are

Legged Locomotion Machine 407

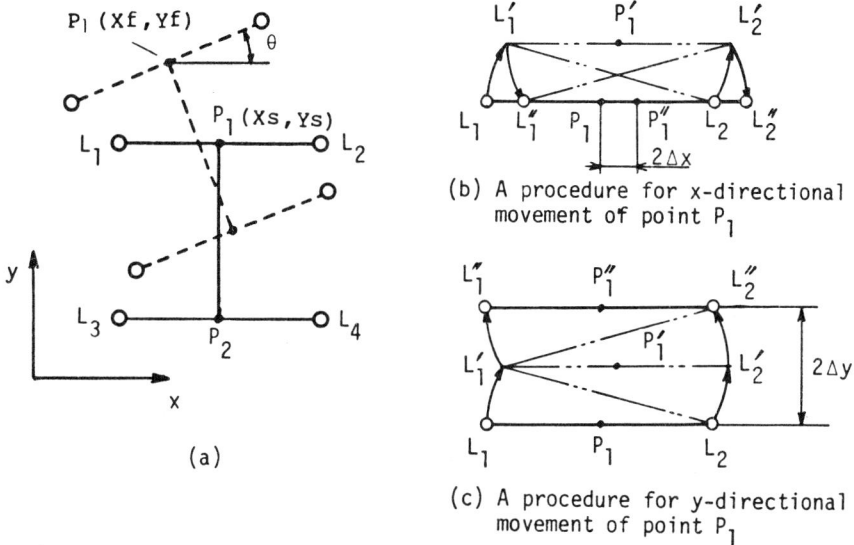

(b) A procedure for x-directional movement of point P_1

(c) A procedure for y-directional movement of point P_1

Figure 3 Two-dimensional walking of the four-legged machine

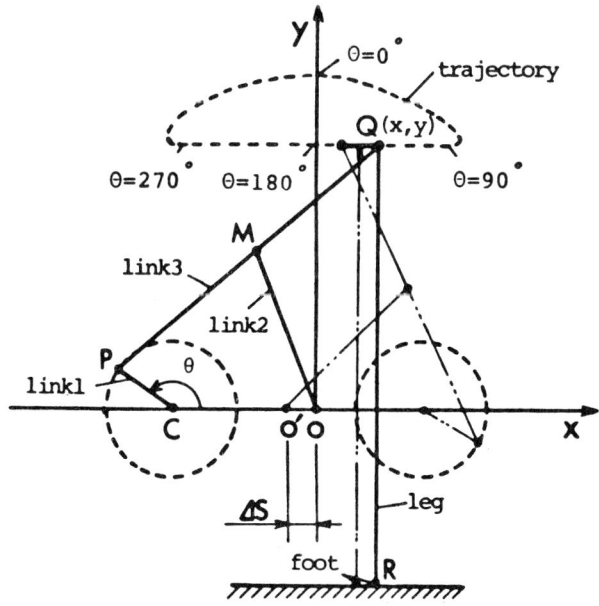

Figure 4 Approximate straight-line link mechanism and its application to leg unit

recognized in this mechanism: (1) if the approximate straight line is used as the loaded phase, the energy consumed by the reaction force of the support load is very small because the driving actuator receives extremely small feedback force caused by the reaction force; (2) since the body can be moved along the approximate horizontal surface, it also leads to reduced energy consumption because elimination of up-and-down movement of the body is essential in reducing energy consumption.

So far we have built two machines (MELWALK — mark I, II). Mark I has one active degree of freedom and therefore it can move only straight backward and forward. Mark II (Figure 5) is constructed by two bases with three legs and each base can rotate around its centre axis. Therefore mark II can move two-dimensionally on

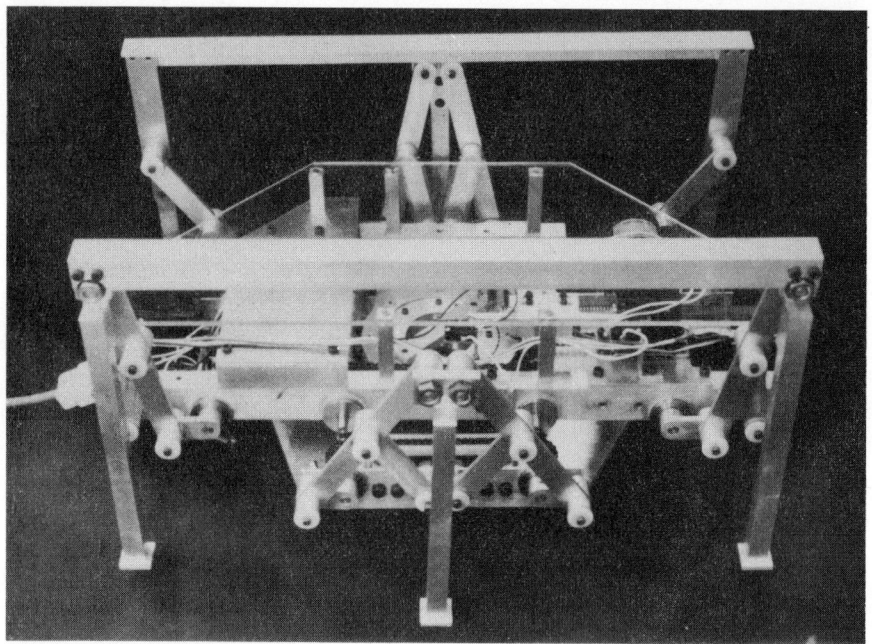

Figure 5 Six-legged machine with two active degrees of freedom (MELWALK mark II)

a flat plane.

The specific power proposed by Gabrielle et al.[11] is effective to evaluate the energetic efficiency while walking.

$$\epsilon = \frac{E}{W \cdot L} \qquad (6)$$

where E, W, L are energy consumption in walking, weight of the machine involving payload and distance of locomotion respectively. The specific power means the energy which the unit mass of the machine consumes during the locomotion of the unit length. The measured specific power with mark I is shown in Table 2 where $W = (M_1 + M_2)g$ and M_1, M_2 are mass of the machine and mass of payload. The specific power of the four-legged machine [1] is also shown in Table 2. Although the specific power depends on walking speed, etc., and therefore it is not a suitable way

Table 2 Specific power

M_2 = 0 kg	0.53
M_2 = 4 kg	0.35
M_2 = 8 kg	0.30
Four-legged machine[1]	25.50

to compare both machines simply, there is no doubt that in MELWALK very little energy is required for driving the actuator. It is also recognized from the fact that mark I is capable of easily carrying payloads three times its own weight.

Application on rough terrain

The definite advantage of legged locomotion machines against wheeled vehicles is that they can proceed even on rough terrain; however mark II cannot be adapted for this terrain.

Now we are developing mark III with legs capable of lengthening or shortening as well as the other functions of mark II. As it is shown in Figure 6, by keeping the minimum functions our machine has only eight active degrees of freedom, and

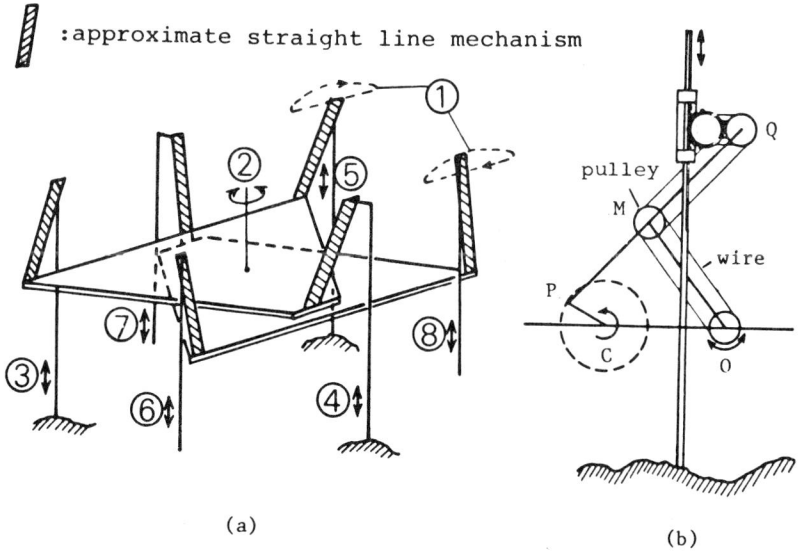

Figure 6 Application of the proposed machine to rough terrain

therefore 10 active degrees of freedom have been deleted from the conventional machines.[3-6] The control algorithm becomes surprisingly simple and a computer program which controls such a machine accomplishes three tasks. First, it regulates the leg length so that they adapt to the terrain just before one set of three legs changes from an unloaded phase to a loaded phase. When one of the three legs reaches its movable limit before touching the ground, the body must be shifted down. The second task is to control the actuator to propel the body along the approximate straight line or to change the body direction. This control is quite easy because each actuator can be operated independently. The third task is to avoid obstacles. When a leg in the air detects an obstacle which it cannot get over, the leg must be lifted. In the same way, when the front part of the body detects an obstacle, the three legs on the ground must lift the body synchronously.

As a result, drastic simplicity of control and fast locomotion can be expected for small sacrifices of flexibility in comparison with conventional machines.

Conclusion

The necessary and sufficient conditions on active degrees of freedom were examined under minimum walking functions defined for a legged locomotion machine capable of proceeding on rough terrain. As a result, it was revealed that at least five active degrees of freedom are required for such a machine without considering balance and six are sufficient even if the shift of the centre of gravity is considered.

To realize simplicity of control and fast locomotion, a six-legged machine based on a fixed gait was examined from the point of the specific power, degrees of freedom and controllability. It became evident that the proposed machine shows excellent values in the specific power and needs only eight active degrees of freedom even for application on rough terrain.

References

[1] Hirose S & Umetani Y (1980) The basic motion regulation system for a quadruped walking machine. *ASME* Paper no. 80-DET-34
[2] Taguchi K, Ikeda K et al. *Four-legged Walking Machine* Proc. Ro Man Sy Symp., Warsaw, Poland, 1976
[3] McGhee R B et al.(1979) Adaptive locomotion of a multi-legged robot over rough terrain. *IEEE Trans. Systems, Man and Cybernetics,* **SMC-9**
[4] Devjanin E A, Gurfinkel V S el al. *The Six-legged Walking Robot Capable of Terrain Adaptation* Proc. Ro Man Sy Symp., Warsaw, Poland, 1981
[5] Raibert M H & Sutherland I E (1983) Machines that walk. *Sci. Am.*, **13**
[6] Bartholet T G *The First Functionoid Developed by ODETICS INC* Proc. ICAR Symp., Tokyo, Japan, 1983
[7] Kessis J J, Rambaut J el al. *Walking Robot Multi-level Architecture and Implementation* Proc. Ro Man Sy Symp., Warsaw, Poland, 1981
[8] Patternella M et al. *Feasibility Study on Six-legged Walking Robots* Proc. 4th ISIR Symp., Tokyo, Japan, 1974
[9] Ishino Y et al. *Walking Robot for Underwater Construction* Proc. ICAR Symp., Tokyo, Japan, 1983
[10] Artabolevsky I I (1975) *Mechanisms in Modern Engineering Design* vol 1, Mir Publishers,
[11] Gabrielle G & von Karmen T (1950) *What price speed?* Mech. Eng. **72** (10)

Trotting and Bounding in a Planar Two-legged Model

K N Murphy and M H Raibert

Robotics Institute, Carnegie-Mellon University, Pittsburgh, PA 15213, USA

Summary: This paper describes algorithms for control and balance in a simple multi-legged model. The model has two springy legs that operate in a plane, representing the lateral half of a quadruped. We have decomposed control of the model into three separate parts. The first part controls vertical bouncing, the second part controls forward running and the third part controls body attitude. Results of simulating the model show that two variations of the control system result in two different running gaits, trotting and bounding. The algorithms used to control this model are closely related to those used earlier to control systems with just one leg.

Introduction

Most animals balance on supple springy legs when they walk and run. In an effort to model such behaviour, and to develop ideas that might lead to legged vehicles that can move with the grace and agility of animals, we are studying a simple multi-legged model that balances on two spring legs.

A number of workers have modelled multilegged systems that balance as they walk in the plane.[1-3,9,10] This work ranges from study of the behaviour of simple inverted pendulums to work on five-link bipeds, while focusing on systems with continuous support and without elastic energy storage in the legs.

Matsuoka[4,5] and Raibert et al.[6-8] have each studied systems that balance as they hop on one leg. Raibert found that a system with one leg could be controlled with a very simple three-part algorithm. A separate part of that algorithm controlled hopping height, body attitude and forward running velocity. Hopping height was controlled by delivering a thrust with the leg when the body reached its minimum vertical altitude during each hop. This thrusting resupplied the energy lost on each hop, due to friction and ground impact. The attitude of the body was controlled by torquing the hip during stance, when friction keeps the foot from moving. A linear servo drove the body level. The forward velocity controller moved the foot forward to a specific position in front of the hip. This foot position determined the forward acceleration of the system during the subsequent period of stance. This three-part controller worked successfully to control physical one-legged systems that balanced in two (2D)- and three (3D)-dimensions.

The success and simplicity of this three-part decomposition for the control of systems with one leg encouraged us to study a system with more than one leg. Since the problem of leg coupling and co-ordination was completely avoided with the one-legged hoppers, several questions arose. What is needed to co-ordinate the actions of many legs? Can we generalize the control of a one-legged machine to control of a multilegged machine? Is balance on several legs similar to balance on one leg?

To answer these questions we have devised a planer model with two legs. The model has a long body with hips at each end. By definition, the model is a biped since it only has two legs. However, our intent is to model the lateral half of a quadruped. With only two legs in a plane, the model is not so complicated as a quadruped in 3D space, but it still allowed us to explore some of the basic behaviour of a quadruped. We are exploring how ideas originally formulated in the context of a system with one leg can be generalized to the multilegged case. Our purpose is to understand how systems with a long body may run and how to co-ordinate the actions of several legs. We also want to learn how to control four-legged systems.

Model

The model, shown in Figure 1, has a rigid body os mass M_3 and moment of inertia I_3. The legs attach to the body a distance r_3 from the centre of gravity of the body.

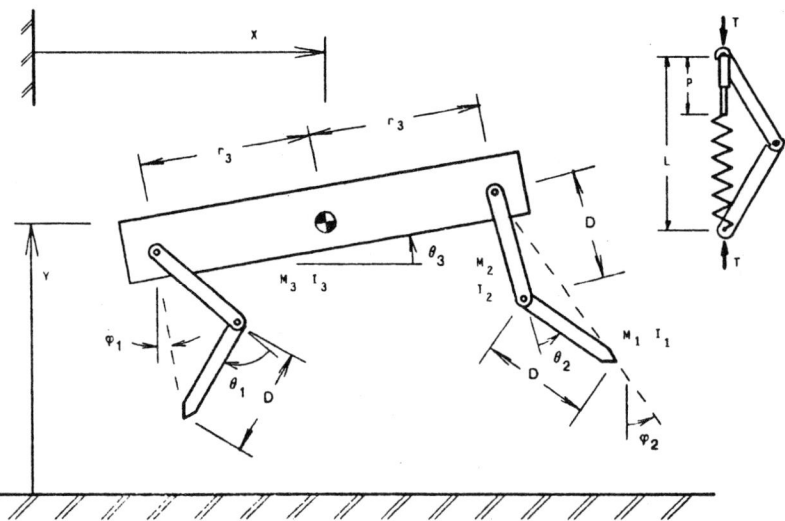

Figure 1 Planar multilegged model used for simulation and control. The body and the two links of both legs have mass and moment of inertia. All four joints are simple hinges. Control torque is generated at both hips. Each knee is driven by a position actuator in series with a spring. The model is restricted to motion in a plane

Each articulated leg has two links that are modelled as uniform rods of length D. The lower links have mass M_1 and moment of inertia I_1. The upper links have mass M_2 and moment of inertia I_2. The simulation parameters were chosen to match those we would obtain if we were to build such a machine.

Torque actuators drive the hip joints. While a foot is in the air, the hip actuator orientates the leg with respect to the body, driving the leg to a desired angle. While a foot is on the ground, the hip actuator sweeps the leg backward driving the body forward.

A position actuator in series with a spring drives each knee (see Figure 1). The position servos in the knees excite and maintain hopping. They can also be used to control the body attitude. For simplicity, the actuators are assumed to be perfect position servos that can act instantaneously. The static force required to compress the leg to a given length, L, is called the leg thrust, T.

$$T = K_S[L_0 - (L - P)] = K_S(L_0 - L) + K_S P \qquad (1)$$

where K_S is the spring constant, L_0 is the free length of the spring and P is the length of the position actuator. The thrust can be separated into two parts. The first part, $K_S(L_0 - L)$, is determined solely by the length of the leg. It is called passive leg thrust. The second part, $K_S P$, is determined by the length of the position actuator. This part is called active thrust. The total thrust is controlled by changing the length of the position actuator. The active thrust can be positive or negative, but the total thrust can never be negative since no 'glue' holds the foot to the ground.

There is a mechanical stop on the knee which is modelled as a stiff spring and damper. The stop restrains the leg from extending too far by preventing the knee angle, θ, from becoming too small.

We find that the model oscillates in two basic modes that correspond to different gaits. The first mode is a vertical oscillation. The body stays level as it bounces up and down. This is trotting. The other mode is an angular rocking oscillation. The centre of gravity moves very little as the system rotates back and forth, bouncing on one foot and then the other. This is bounding. As long as the legs sweep back and forth correctly, the forward motion has little effect on either of these two oscillations over a large range of forward running velocities.

Control

Control of the model has been decomposed into three separate parts, one for vertical motion, one for forward motion and one for angular motion. The three parts act independently, but are co-ordinated by a finite state sequencer. Two variations of the control system were explored. The first variation uses all three control parts, vertical, forward velocity and attitude control. This results in trotting. The second variation uses only the first two parts. It does not explicitly control the attitude of the body. This results in bounding. These gaits are explained in the Results section.

The timing of control actions is co-ordinated by a finite-state sequencer that relies on the state of the feet, hips and body. Each foot undergoes a period in the air followed by a period on the ground. These periods are known as flight and stance respectively, and the transitions between the periods are known as lift-off and touch-down. The centre of gravity of the body rises and reaches a maximum height known as top, falls, reaches a minimum height known as bottom and then rises again. There is a top and bottom associated with each of the two hips as well as with the centre of gravity of the body.

The relative timing of state transitions is not constant but varies from gait to gait.

For example, when bounding, one foot will touch-down and lift-off while the other foot remains in the air. Also, a transition may occur twice in each cycle. For example, when bounding, the centre of gravity of the body peaks and bottoms twice in each cycle.

Vertical control

Control of hopping height was found to be very simple for a one-legged hopping machine. Thrusting with the leg resupplied the energy lost on each hop due to friction and ground impact. The multilegged model uses a similar method. A leg thrusts a constant amount when its hip reaches bottom. Thrusting is accomplished by lengthening the leg-position actuator. The time when the thrust is delivered is determined independently for each leg.

Velocity control

The concept of the CG-print, the locus of points over which the centre of gravity passes while the foot is on the ground, has been introduced in control of the one-legged hopping machines. For a multilegged system, we extended the idea of a CG-print to the idea of hip-prints. The hip-print is the locus of points over which the hip passes while the corresponding foot is on the ground.

When the feet are placed in the centre of the hip-prints, the machine spends the first half of the stance period accelerating backward and the second half accelerating forward. In this case, a system slows down the first half ofstance and speeds up the second half. This leaves the velocity at take off about equal to the original velocity at touch-down (Figure 2).

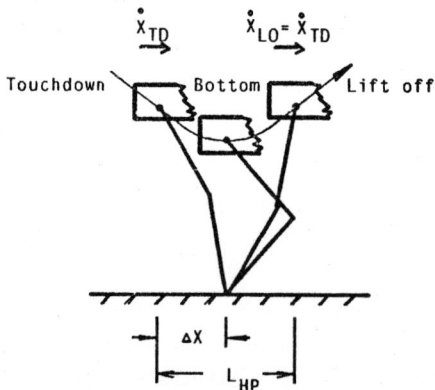

Figure 2 Time sequence of the rear hip shows the hip-print of length L_{HP}. While in the air, the foot swings in front of the hip a horizontal distance, Δx. By placing the foot in the centre of the hip-print, $\Delta x = L_{HP}/2$, the model spends the same amount of time accelerating backward as it does accelerating forward. Horizontal velocity, $\dot{x}$, is thus left almost unchanged

We estimate the length of the hip-print as

$$L_{HP} = \dot{x} t_s \tag{2}$$

where $\dot{x}$ is the forward velocity and t_s is time duration of stance. During flight, the foot should be positioned in front of the hip a distance equal to half the length of the hip-print. To accomplish this, the angle that the leg should make with the vertical, θ_d, is:

$$\theta_d = \sin^{-1} \frac{\dot{x} t_s}{2 L_0} \tag{3}$$

During flight, hip torques drive the leg to the desired angle, θ_d, by using a linear servo

$$\tau = K_p (\theta - \theta_d) + K_d \dot{\theta} \tag{4}$$

where K_p and K_v are position and velocity gains. This algorithm for placing the foot provides no velocity stability and actually slows the model down slightly on each step. The model must be able to change and maintain a desired velocity. Accelerations are accomplished by using hip torques while a foot is on the ground. Hip torques drive the legs backward and the body forward. This torque, τ, is set proportional to the error in forward velocity

$$\tau = K_6 (\dot{x} - \dot{x}_d) \tag{5}$$

where $\dot{x}_d$ is the desired horizontal velocity.

Attitude control

Attitude control attempts to keep the body level at all times by changing the difference in leg thrust. This method relies on the fact that vertical ground forces cause significant movements on the body. When the feet are positioned an equal horizontal distance from the centre of gravity, the sum of the vertical forces affects the vertical acceleration of the body while the difference in vertical forces affects the angular acceleration. Increasing the thrust of one leg while decreasing the thrust of the other leg produces a control moment on the body. If the magnitude of the increase in thrust and the decrease in thrust are equal, the vertical oscillations are unaffected.

The body is driven level by using a linear servo. The active thrust of each leg is modulated to produce a control moment on the body. The change in length of the position actuators, Δ_p, is

$$\Delta_p = \pm (K_1 \theta_3 + K_2 \dot{\theta}_3) \tag{6}$$

where K_1 and K_2 are position and velocity gains. These changes in the length of the position servo are added to the change required by the vertical control. Currently, differential thrust is applied only when both feet are on the ground because at that time an increase in thrust in one leg must be accompanied by a decrease in thrust in the other leg.

Results

To test these control algorithms and to evaluate their performance, we simulated the planar multilegged model. The equations of motion were developed and then integrated numerically.

Trotting

The first variation of control uses all three control parts, vertical, forward velocity and attitude control. The controller keeps the body level. The results are shown in Figure 3. An initial error in body attitude of 5° is corrected in one hop. When

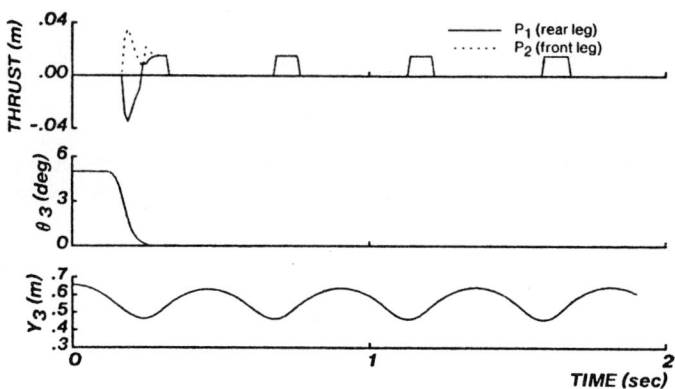

Figure 3 Hopping with attitude control. Differential leg thrust corrects errors in body attitude. A constant leg thrust maintains hopping height. During the first hop, the body angle is driven to zero. On the remaining hops, thrust only maintains hopping height. The graph of thrust shows the change in the length of the position actuator of each leg which is proportional to the active thrust

active attitude control is used, the model can accelerate quickly. As shown in Figure 4, the model starts with no forward velocity. In two hops, it accelerates to the desired velocity of 2 m/s and maintains this speed during stable running. The resulting gait can be equated with the trotting of a four-legged animal. Trotting is a gait where the system bounces alternately on diagonal pairs of legs. The two pairs operate 180° out of phase from each other. Each leg of the planar model represents one of the diagonally opposite pairs of legs on a four-legged animal.

Bounding

The second variation of control uses only two of the three control parts, vertical and forward velocity control. This variation does not actively control the body attitude. The result is bounding.

The behaviour of the system and the stability of bounding is shown in Figure 5. The model was dropped with a small initial body attitude. A random pattern of bouncing began. After 3 s the model stabilized in a pattern that alternated from one foot to the other. The legs operated 180° out of phase from each other. The centre of gravity remained nearly stationary as the body pitched back and forth.

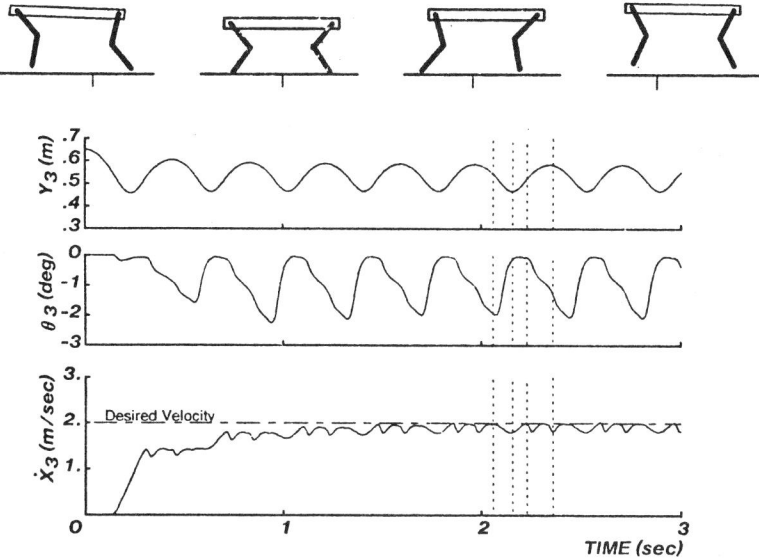

Figure 4 Trotting. The legs use a constant thrust for vertical control with differential thrust for attitude control. During flight, each foot swings forward to the estimated centre of its hip-print. During stance, a hip torques to correct the horizontal velocity. The errors in θ_3 occur when the feet leave the ground and are swept forward. This causes the body to pitch nose downward

We are not yet sure why the model stabilized in this manner. This sort of oscillation was stable for a wide range of values for the body moment of inertia, with the mass held constant.

Control of forward velocity while bounding is shown in Figure 6. With the model bouncing as described, we slowly increased the desired velocity. The model accelerated up to speeds of 5 m/s (10 mph). When acceleration was maintained at a low value, it did not affect the pattern of bouncing from foot to foot.

This pattern of running closely resembles the bounding of four-legged animals. Bounding is a gait where the front pair of legs move together and the rear pair move together. The two pairs operate 180° out of phase from each other, one pair touching down and lifting off while the other pair remains in the air. Each leg of our two-legged model represents a pair of legs of a bounding quadruped.

The model needed to stabilize in the bouncing mode before accelerating. When large accelerations were attempted, the pattern of hopping from foot to foot broke down. The front foot stayed on the ground and could not be swung forward. This caused the model to trip and fall. However, when the acceleration was small, the model stayed in the bounding pattern and large velocities were achieved. There was a limit on forward velocity. As the model bounded faster, the height of centre of gravity of the body decreased along with the magnitude of its angular oscillation.

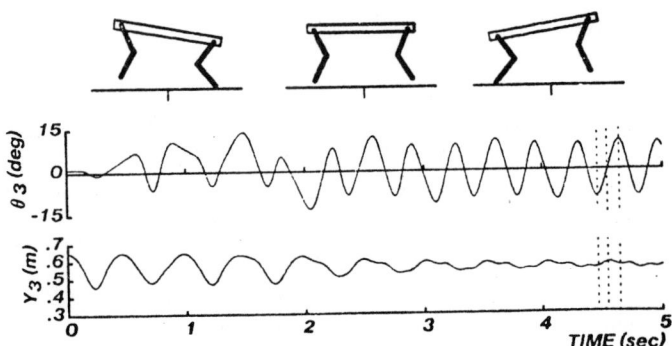

Figure 5 Hopping without active attitude control. Each leg thrusts independently when its hip reaches bottom. A constant thrust is used. The desired velocity is set to zero. At first there is a random hopping pattern, but it is soon replaced by a stable pattern of bouncing from one foot back onto the other. The centre of gravity remains nearly stationary while the body pitches back and forth

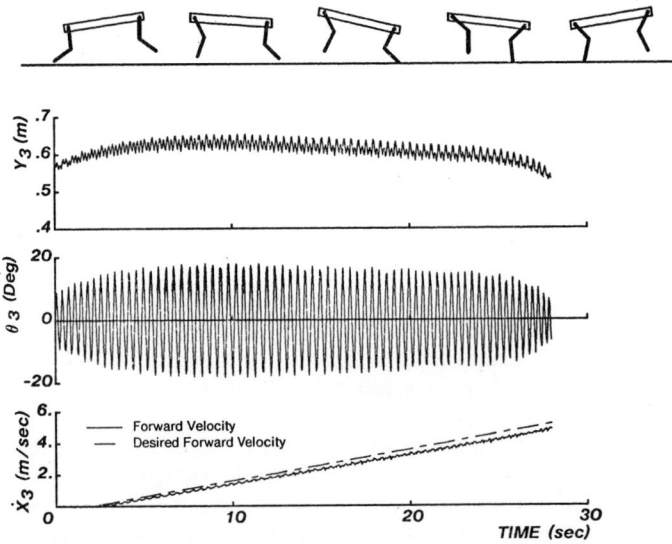

Figure 6 Bounding. The model stabilized in the bounding pattern and accelerated slowly to 5 m/s (10 mph). As the speed increased, hopping height decreased and the model eventually stubbed its toe and tripped

These two factors reduced the ground clearance of the foot as it swung forward.

Eventually, the model stubbed its toe, tripped and fell. This can be corrected by either stiffening the knee springs or by contracting the leg before swinging it forward.

Discussion

The two legs of the planar model operate separately while bounding. The control for one leg does not depend on the actions nor the state of the other leg. Each leg can be seen as controlling its own hip. This conjures the image of a pair of one-legged hoppers joined together. We do not know if this controller were extended to a quadruped whether all four legs could operate separately or if the two front legs and the two rear legs must be co-ordinated to achieve a bound.

Unlike bounding, the control for trotting does not totally separate the actions of the two legs. The attitude control requires synchronized action from both legs. Differential thrust is used only when both feet are on the ground. Although the controllers for the vertical motion and the forward velocity separate the actions of the legs, they need not. For example, since the body is nearly level at bottom, the body centre of gravity bottoms at about the same time as both hips. Thus the legs could thrust when the body bottoms without a noticeable effect.

Conclusions

We developed a planar model that represents one lateral half of a quadruped. Having only two legs reduces the problem of co-ordinating many legs, but still allows study of simple gaits. A long body allows the model to imitate the prominent motions of a quadruped.

Control of the model was decomposed into three separate parts, one each for vertical motion, forward motion and angular motion. Vertical motion is initiated and maintained by thrusting with both legs. Velocity control requires two separate actions. When a foot is in the air, the leg swings forward a distance determined by the forward velocity. When a foot is on the ground, hip torques that are proportional to the error in forward velocity act to stabilize velocity. Attitude control actively drives the body level by changing the difference in thrust between the two legs. This difference in thrust produces a control moment that drives the body level.

Two variations of the control system were explored, resulting in two different gaits, trotting and bounding. Trotting results when all three parts of the controller are used. The body stays level as it bounces. Bounding results when active attitude control is not used. The model stabilizes in a mode of bouncing from one foot to the other. Small accelerations can be accomplished without disturbing the bounding pattern. The model ran at speeds of 5 m/s. The fact that the model bounds with such a simple control surprised use. We are currently trying to understand why it is stable in this gait.

This research was sponsored by a grant from the System Development Foundation and by a contract with the Defense Advanced Research Projects Agency (DoD), Systems Sciences Office, ARPA order no. 4148.

References

[1] Hemami H, Cvetkovic V S (1976) *Postural Stability of Two Biped Models via Lyapunov Second Method* Proc. 1976 JACC, West Lafayette, Indiana
[2] Hemami H & Farnsworth R L (1977) Postural and gait stability of a planar five link biped by simulation. *IEEE Trans. Automatic Control* **AC-22**(3), 452-458
[3] Juricic D & Vukobratovic M (1972) Mathematical modelling of bipedal walking system. *ASME* Publication 72-WA BHF-13
[4] Matsuoka K (1979) *A model of Repetitive Hopping Movements in Man* Proc. 5th World Congress on Theory of Machines and Mechanisms, IFIP
[5] Matsuoka K (1980) A mechanical model of repetitive hopping movements. *Biomechanisms* **5**, 251-258 (in Japanese)
[6] Raibert M H (1984) Hopping in legged systems: modelling and simulation for the 2D one-legged case. *IEEE Trans. Systems, Man and Cybernetics*, **3**, in press
[7] Raibert M H & Brown H B Jr (1984) Experiments in balance with a 2D one-legged hopping machine. *Trans. ASME, J. Dynam. Sys., Meas. Control,* in press
[8] Raibert M H, Brown H B Jr & Chepponis M (1984) Experiments in balance with a 3D one-legged hopping machine. *Int. J. Robotics Res.*, **3**(2)
[9] Vukobratovic M & Okhotsimskii D E (1975) *Control of Legged Locomotion Robots* Proc. Int. Federation of Automatic Control Plenary Session
[10] Vukobratovic M & Stepaneko Y (1973) Mathematical models of general anthropomorphic systems. *Mathemat. Biosci.*, **17**, 191-242

Part 7
Application and Performance Evaluation

Determination of Important Design Parameters for Industrial Robots from the Application Point of View: Survey Paper

R D Schraft and M C Wanner

Fraunhofer-Institute for Manufacturing Engineering and Automation (IPA), Stuttgart, Federal Republic of Germany

Summary: In most cases the production technology has to be carefully considered for the overall robot design. A practical approach for setting up performance specifications with the help of worksite analysis will be presented with an overview of the most important design philosophies. The paper closes with important results achieved from worksite analysis.

Introduction

With the decision for certain performance specifications for industrial robots serious questions such as: Which type of handling tasks are anticipated and which market share can be realized?, Can the high costs for research and development be covered by a certain number of sales?, Is there any need for further development, e.g. sensors, peripheral units, etc?, are quire common.

The answer is a systematic approach to determine the performance specifications including a discussion of the potential of different design philosophies and solutions.

Determination of important design parameters by worksite analysis

Usually the foundation for an analysis is the present worksite.[1] The human worker performs operations within an already existing manufacturing system. Subject of the investigation is the kind and frequency of these operations.

The principal steps in this procedure are: (1) detailed worksite analysis of the present system; (2) formulation and evaluation of alternative system solutions; (3) analysis of requirements for the robot system.

The set up of performance specifications is the next logical step. They can be classified as follows: essential requirements which must be fulfilled in any case; minimum requirements (limiting values which must not be exceeded); desirable requests.

In the following chapters we try to concentrate our efforts to find the parameters for the kinematic chain.

Worksite analysis of the present system

All parameters listed below are related to a given worksite and volume of work. The information is collected with a checklist *in situ*.

Mobility structure
Presentation of the workpieces within the workspace; evaluation of possible alternative solutions; necessary movements for the handling process related to the different workpieces; whether CP-control is needed for any of the tasks; number and identification of identical movements; number and identification of identical workpieces.

Workspace
Workspace of the manual system (maximum); workspace of the workpiece on the workpiece carrier (minimum); possible workspace of an automatic system (estimation).

Workload
Workload of the different workpieces and estimation of gripper weight.

Volume of work
Number of different workpieces being assembled; total number of workpieces being assembled; cycle time.

Flexibility
Change-over frequency of the manual system.

It is useful to include a drawing of the present worksite and the operation sequence from the workplan.

Formulation and evaluation of alternative system solutions

In some cases the manual system has to be completely rejected or modified because of the following: (1) Some operations are not suited for automation. The degree of possible automation can be estimated by the so-called 'automatic-inhibition' factors caused by: parts presentation (workpieces packed, defined temperature, sensitiveness, etc.); assembly process (assembly with both hands, slack workpieces, etc,); complex control functions (function-, vision-control, etc.). (2) Sometimes the operation sequence can be modified to improve the degree of automation.

The data from the worksite analysis are modified to include the above-mentioned parameters.

Analysis of requirements

Experience has shown that more than 100 worksites should be investigated within one technology (e.g. assembly).[2] For this step the use of software packages such as SPSS are most useful. Important parameters for the kinematic chain can be selected with the following data: mobility, workspace, workload and volume of work as function of the industry (automotive, electronic, etc.) within one technology; workspace, workload, volume of work and flexibility as function of the mobility; automation inhibition factors as function of the mobility.

State of the art in robot design

With industrial robots we have three translatory (Z, Y, X) and three rotatory axes

(A, B, C) for combination with a kinematic chain. If we take for example six degrees of freedom, we can find 46,656 combinations.[3]

In practice only five different kinematic chains (as far as the arm is concerned) have entered the market with success (their principal characteristics and possible wrist construction are shown in Figure 1).

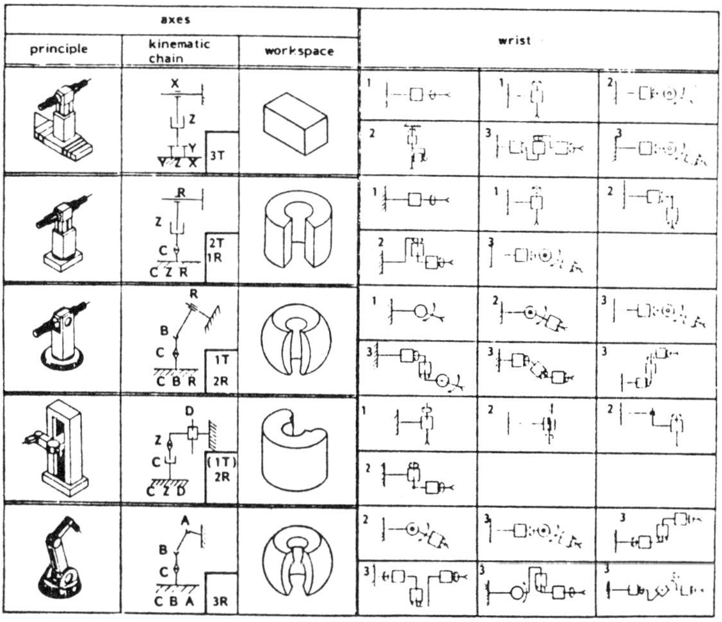

Figure 1 Most frequently used axes and wrist configurations of industrial robots

There are many reasons for this fact, such as:[4] kinematic considerations (e.g. series connection of the same DOF; controller design (e.g. singular configurations); costs; application demand (e.g. only a limited number of DOF are needed for the task); flexibility offered by the robot makes no sense if sensors and peripheral units are the bottleneck.

Before we start to analyse the results of the workplace analysis and their influence on robot design we should review existing design philosophies.

Modular design
For this design concept we should take the Bosch FMS (as shown in Figure 2) as an example. Such a system consists of various modules (axes, wrist, gripper, drive

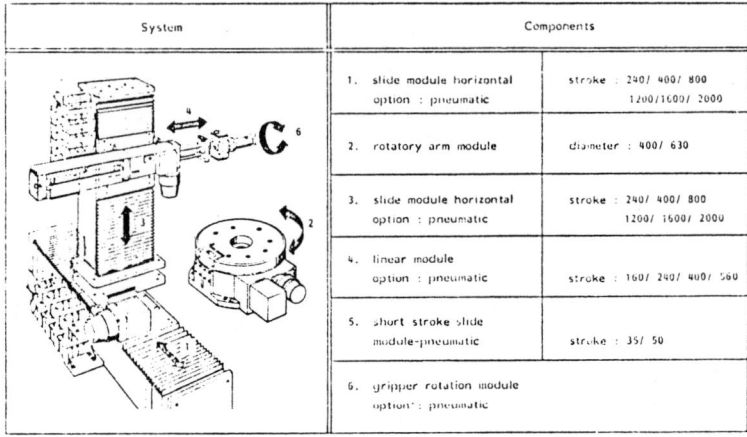

Figure 2 Bosch FMS as an example of the modular design technique

system, controller, etc.) which can be combined to a robot for a defined task. Such a system is, to a large extent, suitable only for translatory axes and becomes less attractive with increasing numbers of axes. On the positive side we should note that such a system can be tailored to many tasks without any modification of the design, so high batch numbers for the single modules are common.

Task-oriented design
A typical example is the SCARA assembly robot as shown in Figure 3 (Dainichi Kiko PT300H). The robot has a limited number of axes (in this case four) and is suited for specific tasks. In such a case worksite analysis is extremely important to achieve sufficient applications. The robot itself is cheap related to other designs if enough sales can be realized.

Universal design
This describes a philosophy leading to a robot and controller structure suited for various tasks. The example presented in Figure 4 is a KUKA IR 160 designed for tasks such as spot and arc welding, machining and assembly of heavy workpieces. These requirements are leading to an overall complex and sophisticated design. The idea is to cover the high costs of research and development by a high number of sales, possibly due to the universal design. It should be noted that even the universal-design robot needs clearly defined performance characteristics to keep the complexity of the system within controllable limits.

Results of worksite analysis

Numerous worksite analyses have been carried out at the IPA and the industry,

Design Parameters for Industrial Robots 427

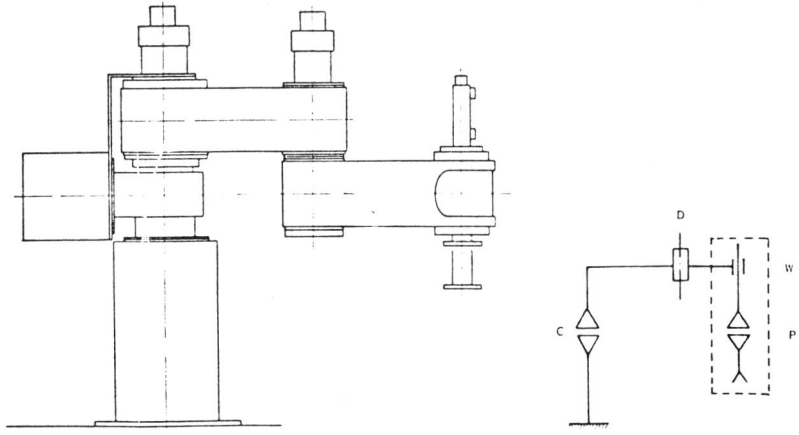

Figure 3 Task-oriented design
represented by a Dainichi KIKO PT 300 H robot

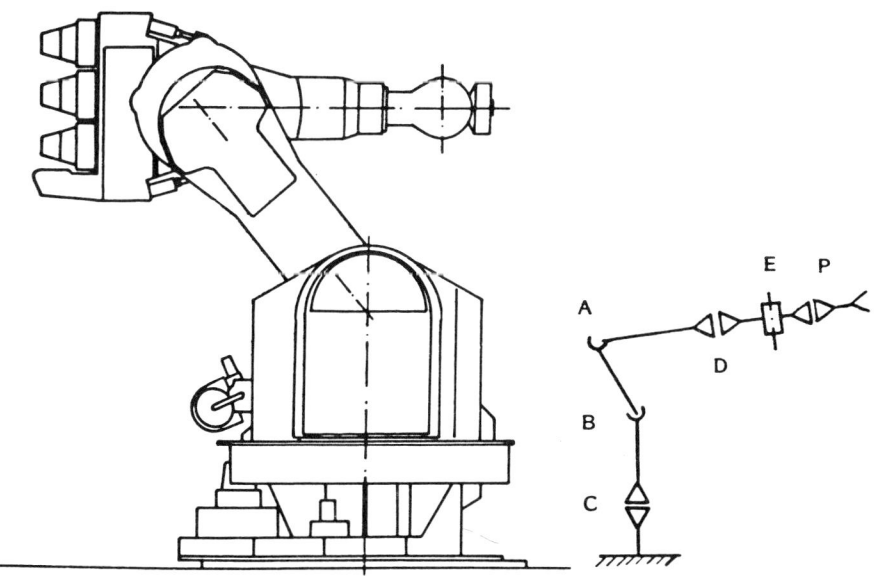

Figure 4 Universal robot design: KUKA IR 160/100 series

some of which have been published.[2,5] The most important facts related to the individual technologies are: spray painting (in most cases universal design with six axes or more, high acceleration and deceleration with limited accuracy); welding (five to six axes with high demand on sensor functions; highly mobile robots needed for the future); assembly (see example of the electronics industry[5]); small working area (see Figure 5), low weights (see Figure 6) and complex tasks (see Figure 7) are leading to modular designs or robots designed for specific tasks, in many cases only Cartesian movements; the value of the robot is only 20-30 per cent of the total system] ; handling (here robots with cylindrical and Cartesian co-ordinates have the highest share; the technology trend goes to integrated systems such as machining-centre, robot, transport, etc.).

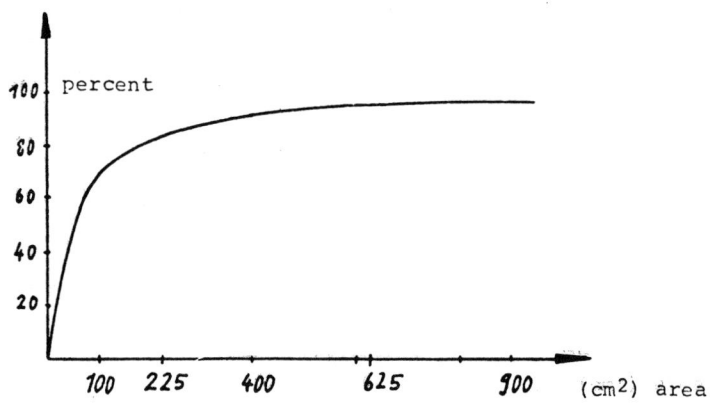

Figure 5 Distribution of the maximum working area per subassembly

Conclusions

The design parameters of industrial robots are closely related to the task. The principal goal is a balanced economic and technical overall solution including peripheral devices. The described approach for setting up realistic performance parameters is an important step in this direction. Applications indicate satisfactory results from the technical and economic point of view.

References

[1] Warnecke H J & Schraft R D (1982) *Industrial Robots* IFS Publications, Bedford
[2] Herrmann G (1976) Analyse von Handhabungsvorgängen im Hinblick auf deren Anforderungen an programmierbare Handhabungsgeräte in der Teilefertigung, Dr Ing Dissertation, Universität Stuttgart, Stuttgart, Germany

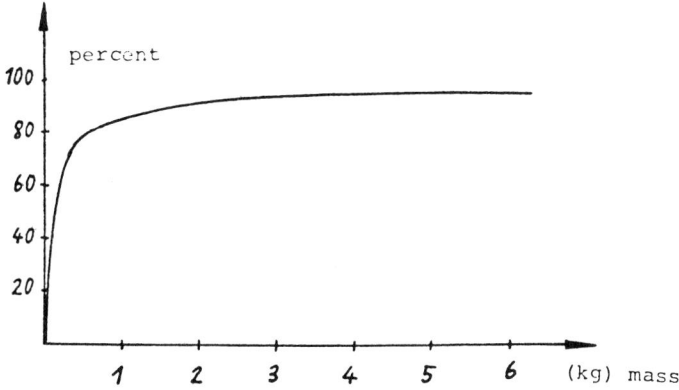

Figure 6 Distribution of the masses of workpieces in assembly

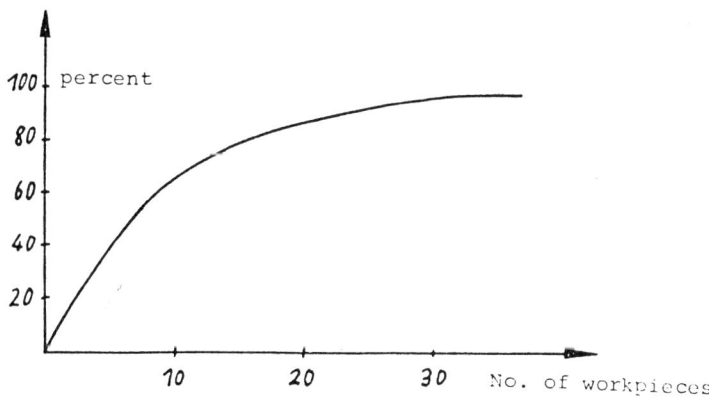

Figure 7 Distribution of the number of workpieces per subassembly

[3] Schraft R D (1977) *Systematisches Auswählen und Konzipieren von programmierbaren Handhabungsgeräten*, Dr Ing Dissertation, Universität Stuttgart, Stuttgart, Germany
[4] Schraft R D & Wanner M C (1984) Bestimmen der Achsanzahl von Industrierobotern nach vorgegebenen Aufgaben. *Maschinenmarkt*, **90** (4), 57-60
[5] Drexel P (1982) *Modulares, Flexibles Montagesystem im FMS von Bosch* 3rd Conf. on Assembly Automation, pp. 103-128

Automatic Assembly by Reference Searching and Position Adjustment before Insertion

F Artigue and C François

LIMRO-IUT de Cachan, University of Paris-Sud, 94230 Cachen, France

Summary: In automatic assembly operations, adaptability can be achieved first by searching the receiving-piece references, then by adjusting the workpiece position before the insertion phase. The efficiency of this method is shown in the case of the automatic fitting of a fork, including two bores between the flanges of a welded built-in frame, and inserting of the two corresponding studs. The described assembly machine involves workpiece grippers associated with an eight-channel displacement transducer for receiving-piece location measurement and geometrical control and a workpiece repositioning unit with five servo-controlled degrees of freedom. A system of similar building architecture involving a more general concept to reduce the technological specificity induced by each kind of assembly operation is being studied.

Introduction

Mechanical piece automatic assembly is possible only if certain requirements regarding the piece relative location are met before and during the insertion phase. Besides the uncertainties induced by the assembling robotized system itself, these requirements depend on the kind of pieces to be assembled, their geometrical characteristics, their building tolerances and the insertion clearance.

Industrial robot positioning errors make it usually difficult to meet with these requirements, particularly in the case of very independent carrying systems devoted respectively to the receiving piece and the workpiece (wire-guided robot/multi-armed robot for example).

Most studies on these problems have led to devices using the forces which appear during the insertion phase to correct the relative location of the pieces in contact. Such an accommodation can be passive, by using RCC-type devices,[1,3] or active, using force-sensing devices[4] or mixed.[5]

An original system using first a measurement of the relative location between the parts to be assembled and the robot, then a repositioning sequence before insertion has been developed at LIMRO Laboratory. This method has been successfully tested on an actual assembly operation.

Assembly sequence

The assembly sequence is described in Figure 1. It consists of the following operations: gripping of the workpiece; measurement of the receiving-piece location; realignment of the workpiece and geometrical control of the receiving piece; retraction of the transducer and final insertion. This assembly method has been

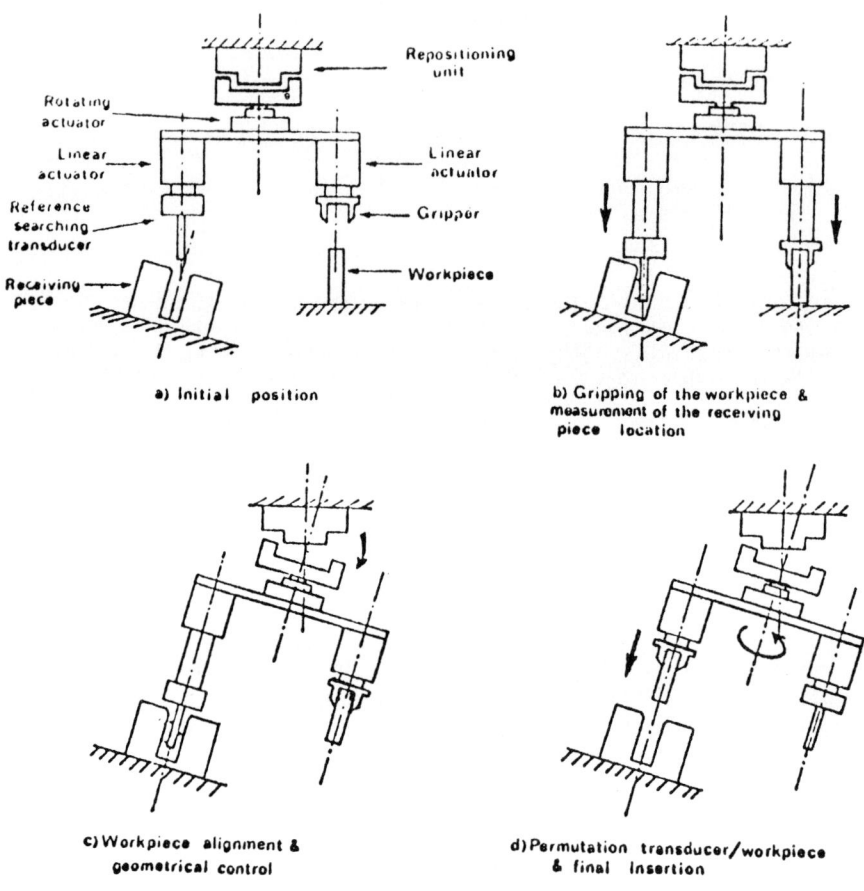

Figure 1 Assembly sequence

applied to the automatic fitting of a fork including two bores between the flanges of a welded built-in frame and inserting the two corresponding studs.

Application

A schematic view of the parts to be assembled is shown in Figure 2. The minimum fitting clearance is typically 0.1 mm. The frame is carried by a wire-guided robot, and located in front of the assembly station, resulting in an absolute uncertainty of the flange location of ±2 mm.

Figure 3 shows the main parts of the assembly machine which has been realized to perform this automatic assembly. The system involves workpiece grippers associated with a reference-searching transducer. These elements can be permutated

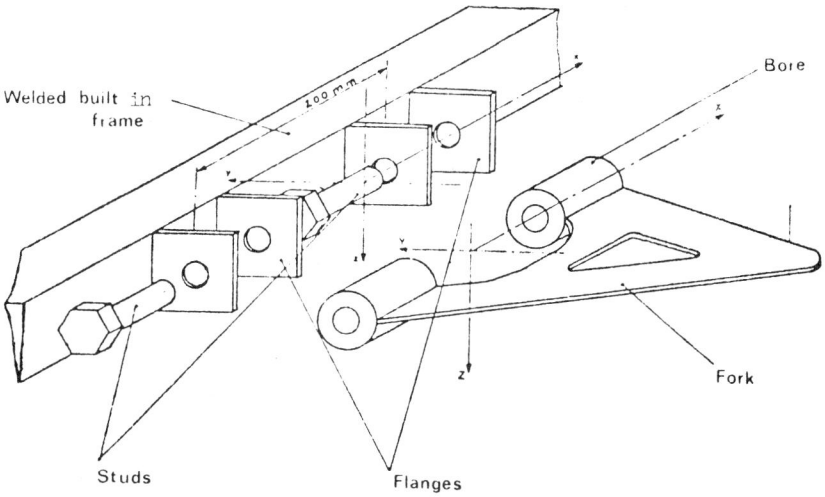

Figure 2 Schematic view of the pieces to be assembled

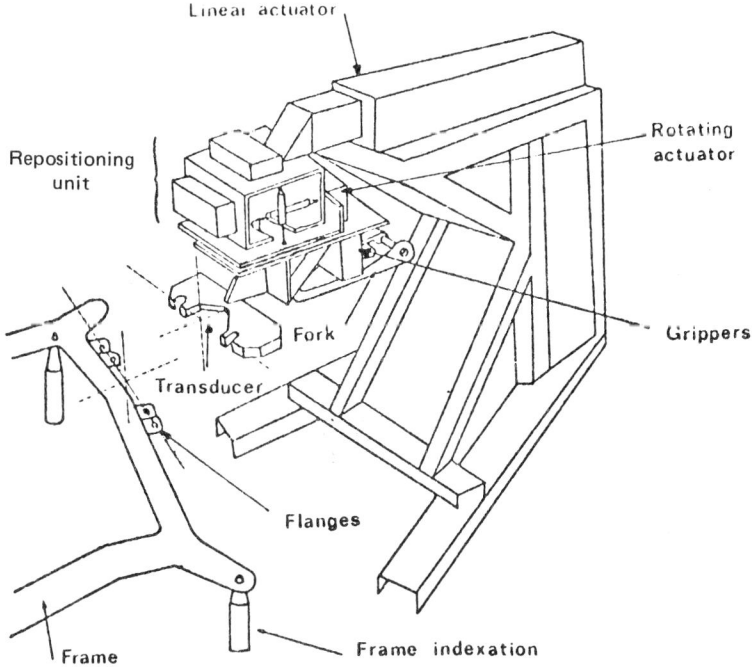

Figure 3 Schematic view of the assembly machine

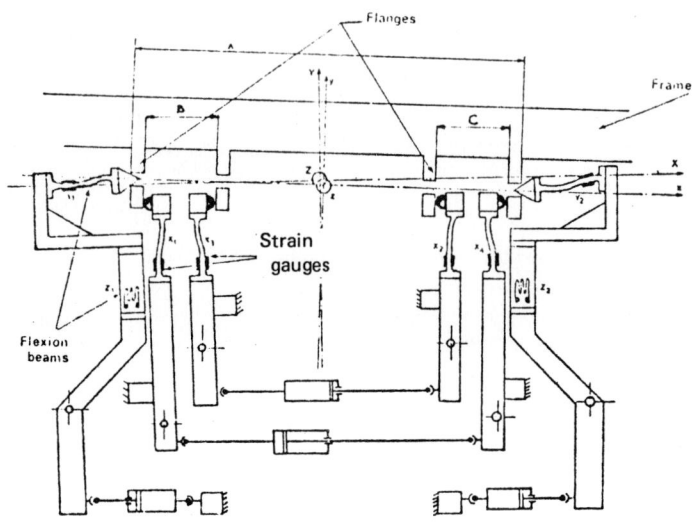

Figure 4 Schematic view of the reference searching transducer

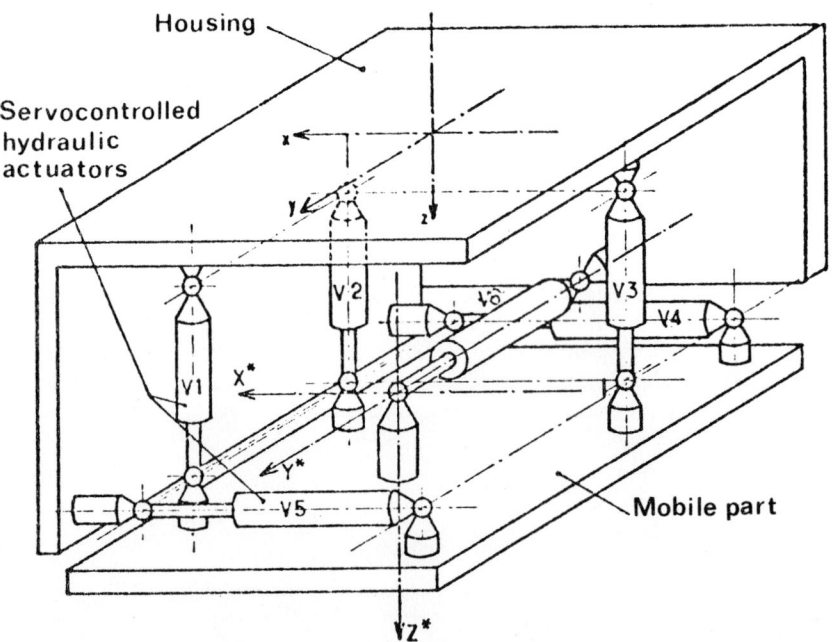

Figure 5 Five DOF servo-controlled repositioning unit

through a rotating actuator which is fastened to the mobile part of a repositioning unit. The whole device can be taken to the assembly area by a linear pneumatic actuator which performs a quick transport and ensures a precise stop position. The reference-searching transducer involves six fingers composed of strain-gauge-bearing flexion beams (Figure 4). During the transportation phase, fingers are retracted and mechanically protected by two iron cheeks. In the measuring area, fingers are actuated by small pneumatic cylinders so that the measurement of the actual location of the flanges relative to a reference position can take place. The corresponding data are computed and used for driving the repositioning unit. This device involves six servo-controlled hydraulic actuators (Figure 5) and can perform small displacements (typically 5 mm) with great accuracy (0.02 mm).

When a correct fitting position is reached, geometrical control of the flanges takes place, then the transducer is retracted, workpiece/transducer permutation is carried out and fork and stud insertion is achieved.

The described system securely performs the whole assembly sequence in a mean time of 10 s, which is about half the time usually devoted to the same kind of assembly operation achieved manually.

Generalization

The first prototype built at LIMRO involves a reference-searching transducer which is specific of the assembly to be carried out. To increase flexibility of the system, studies are being developed concerning a matrical displacement transducer whose only mechanical-sensing fingers would be relatively specific. In this case, the transducer operation is based on the measurement of the spatial orientation of a solid on which mechanical-sensing fingers are fixed and whose reference axis can be set with those of the receiving piece.

Principles and modelling

Figure 6 represents a solid whose position is defined relative to an absolute co-ordinate system $OXYZ$ and six push-rods Pi leaning against the solid surface. Each push-rod has a single degree of freedom in translation and the push-rod tip can freely glide on the solid surface. If push-rods are position-sensing transducers, the device may be used as a reference-searching transducer. If push-rods are linear actuators, the device may be used as a positioning unit. When the solid moves with small amplitude displacements, i.e. translation $\vec{T}$ and rotation $\vec{R}/o$, the displacement of a push-rod tip contact point Mi can be described by a $\vec{Di}$ vector

$$\vec{Di} = \vec{T} + \vec{R} \cdot \overrightarrow{OMi}$$

At Mi point, the solid surface translates along its normal vector $\vec{Ni}$ with an amplitude Di

$$Di = \vec{T} \cdot \vec{Ni} + (\vec{R}/o \cdot \overrightarrow{OMi}) \cdot \vec{Ni} \qquad (1)$$

By using standard linear approximations, equation (1) may be written as a matrix equation

$$[Di] = [M][T,R] \qquad (2)$$

where $[T,R]$ is the matrix of the $\vec{T}$ and $\vec{R}/o$ components relative to OX, OY, OZ;

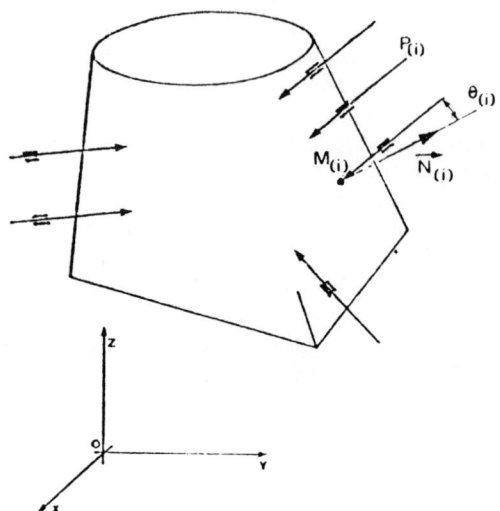

Figure 6 Solid position defined relative to absolute co-ordinate system $OXYZ$

$[M]$ is the direct matrix of the system. If $[M]^{-1}$ exists, thus

$$[T, R] = [M]^{-1} [Di] \qquad (3)$$

Equations (2) and (3) may be used respectively for driving a repositioning unit and a reference-searching transducer. In case of driving of the repositioning unit by the data arising from the transducer, the following equation may be written:

$$[Di]_{R \cdot U} = [M]_{R \cdot U} \times [M]^{-1}{}_T \times [Di]_T$$

where $[Di]_T$ is the matrix of the position-sensing transducers data, $[M]^{-1}{}_T$ is the matrix relative to the reference-searching transducer, $[M]_{R \cdot U}$ is the matrix relative to the repositioning unit and $[Di]_{R \cdot U}$ is the matrix useful for driving the linear actuators of the repositioning unit.

Optimization

Among the numerous ways to position the push-rods, some arrangements lead to a triangular matrix $[M]$ with few coefficients different from zero. A preferred arrangement is shown in Figure 7. In such a case

$$[M]_{R \cdot U} = \begin{bmatrix} 1 & 0 & 0 & 0 & 0 & 0 \\ 0 & 1 & 0 & 0 & 0 & 0 \\ 0 & 0 & 1 & 0 & 0 & 0 \\ 0 & 1 & 0 & a_1 & 0 & 0 \\ 0 & 0 & 1 & 0 & b_1 & 0 \\ 1 & 0 & 0 & 0 & 0 & c_1 \end{bmatrix} \text{ and } [M]^{-1}{}_T = \begin{bmatrix} 1 & 0 & 0 & 0 & 0 & 0 \\ 0 & 1 & 0 & 0 & 0 & 0 \\ 0 & 0 & 1 & 0 & 0 & 0 \\ 0 & -\frac{1}{a_2} & 0 & \frac{1}{a_2} & 0 & 0 \\ 0 & 0 & -\frac{1}{b_2} & 0 & \frac{1}{b_2} & 0 \\ -\frac{1}{c_2} & 0 & 0 & 0 & 0 & \frac{1}{c_2} \end{bmatrix}$$

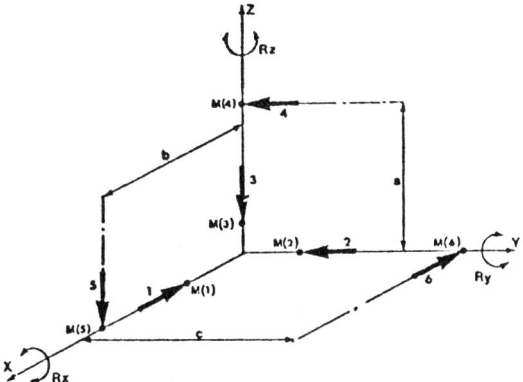

Figure 7 Optimization of position of push-rods

Thus

$$[M]_{R \cdot U} \times [M]^{-1}{}_T = \begin{bmatrix} 1 & 0 & 0 & 0 & 0 & 0 \\ 0 & 1 & 0 & 0 & 0 & 0 \\ 0 & 0 & 1 & 0 & 0 & 0 \\ 0 & 1-\frac{a_1}{a_2} & 0 & \frac{a_1}{a_2} & 0 & 0 \\ 0 & 0 & 1-\frac{b_1}{b_2} & 0 & \frac{b_1}{b_2} & 0 \\ 1 & \frac{c_1}{c_2} & 0 & 0 & 0 & \frac{c_1}{c_2} \end{bmatrix}$$

Then, driving a positioning unit by the data arising from a so-designed matrical transducer is simple and induces very small position errors.

Conclusion

The adaptative assembly method involving first receiving-piece reference searching then workpiece-position adjustment before insertion exhibited high efficiency in an actual case of automatic assembly. Further improvements are being studied and a new prototype capable of achieving screwing operations is being built.

The authors acknowledge the contribution of R Manuel in the construction of the prototypes. This work was partially funded by the Regie Nationale des Usines Renault.

References

[1] Whitney D E and Nevins J L *What is the Remote Center Compliance and What Can it Do?* Proc. 9th Int. Symp. on Industrial Robots, Washington, DC, March, 1979
[2] Lane J D *Evaluation of a Remote Center Compliance Device for Assembly Application* Proc. 1st Int. Conf. on Assembly Automation, Brighton, March, 1980

[3] Drake S, Watson P and Simunovic S *High Speed Robot Assembly of Precision Parts Using Compliance Instead of Sensory Feedback* Proc. 7th Int. Symp. on Industrial Robots, Tokyo, October, 1977
[4] Hill J W (1981) Force controlled assembler. In *Industrial Robots* vol 2, *Applications* ed. W R Tanner. ASME Publications
[5] Seltzer D S (1981) Use of sensory information for improved robot learning. In *Industrial Robots* vol 1, *Fundamentals* ed. W R Tanner. ASME Publications

Participants

Participants

Bulgaria

Christov V ITKP — Bulgarian Academy of Sciences, A Bonchev Street, bl 2, Sofia
Kiriazov P Institute of Mechanics and Biomechanics, A Bonchev Street, bl 8, 1113 Sofia
Konstantinov M Central Laboratory for Manipulators and Robots, VMEI, Darvenitza, Sofia

Canada

Lawrence P Department of Electrical Engineering, University of British Columbia, Vancouver, BC

Federal Republic of Germany

Bremer H Lehrstuhl für Mechanik B, Technische Universität München, Arcisstrasse 21, 8 München 2
Kreuzer E Institut B für Mechanik, Universitat Stuttgart, Pfaffenwaldring 9, 7000 Stuttgart 80
Schiehlen W O Institut für Mechanik, Universität Stuttgart, Pfaffenwaldring 9, 7000 Stuttgart 80
Schwertassek R DFVLR — Institut für Dynamik der Flagssysteme, 8031 Post Wessling
Truckenbrodt A TC Technologie Consulting, Westendstrasse 177-179, 8000 München 21
Wolz U Institut für Mechanik, Universität Karlsruhe, Kaiserstrasse 12, 7600 Karlsruhe 1

France

Andre G IRISA, Laboratory Automatique, Campus de Beaulieu, 35042 Rennes Cédex
Espiau B IRISA, Campus de Beaulieu, 35042 Rennes Cédex
Forestier J P Department of Automatic Control, Centre d'Etudes et de Recherches de Toulouse, 2, Av E Belin, 31055 Toulouse
François Ch LIMRO-IUT de Cachen, 9 Av de la Division Leclerc, 94230 Cachen
Fournier R CEA-CEN Saclay Bat 89, 91190 Gif sur Yvette
Kessis J J Laboratoire de Robotique et Intelligence Artificielle, University of Paris 7, 2 Pl Jussieu, 75251 Paris Cédex 05
Merlet J-P INRIA — Bat 24, Domaine de Voluceau, Rocquencourt, 78153 Le Chesnay Cédex
Micaelli A CEA Saclay, 91190 Gif sur Yvette
Vertut J Commissariat à l'Energie Atomique, DPT, BP 6, 92660 Fontenay aux Roses
Zapata R LAMM-USTL, Place E Bataillon, 34060 Montpellier

German Democratic Republic

Bögelsack G Sektion Gerätetechnik, Technische Hochschule Ilmenau, 6300 Ilmenau

Great Britain

Abel E B424 Engineering Projects Division, AERC Harwell, Didcot, Oxfordshire OX11 0RA

Hungary

Filemon E Technical University of Budapest, BME I, Budapest 1521

Italy

Bianchi G Dipartimento di Meccanica, Politecnico di Milano, Piazza L da Vinci 32, 20133 Milano
Dario P Centro 'E Piaggio', Facolta di Ingegneria, Universita di Pisa, Via Diotisalvi 2, 56100 Pisa
Rovetta A Dipartimento di Meccanica, Politecnico di Milano, Piazza L da Vinci 32, 20133 Milano
Siciliano B Dipartimento di Informatica e Sistemistica, Universita di Napoli, Via Claudio 21, 80125 Napoli

Japan

Hirose S Department of Physical Engineering, Tokyo Institute of Technology, 2-12-1 Ookayama, Meguro-ku, Tokyo
Ikuta K Department of Physical Engineering, Tokyo Institute of Technology, 2-21-1 Ookayama, Meguro-ku, Tokyo
Kaneko M Mechanical Engineering Laboratory, MITI, Tsukuba Science City, Ibaraki 305
Kato I Waseda University, Faculty of Science and Engineering, 3-4-1 Shinjuku, Tokyo 160
Kawase T 3-4-1 Okubo, Shinjuku, Waseda University, Tokyo 160
Sato Y First Engineering Department – Robotics Division, NEC Corporation, 17-5 Minami Naruse, 40 Chome Machida City, Tokyo 198
Sugano S 3-4-1 Ohkubo Shinjuku-ku, Tokyo
Tachi S Mechanical Engineering Laboratory, Tsukuba Science City, 1-2 Namiki, Sakura-mura, Ibaraki 305
Takanishi A 3-4-1 Ohkubo, Shinjuku-ku, Tokyo

Poland

Kędzior K Technical University of Warsaw, Al Niepodległości 222 r 206, 00-663 Warsaw
Macukow B Institute of Mathematics, Warsaw Technical University, Plac Jedności Robotniczej 1, 00-590 Warsaw
Morecki A Technical University of Warsaw, Al Niepodległości 222 r 206, 00-663 Warsaw

Switzerland

Faessler H Institut für Mechanik, ETH-Zentrum, 8092 Zürich

USA

Bejczy A 4800 Oak Grove Drive, Pasadena, CA 91109
Book W J School of Mechanical Engineering, Georgia Institute of Technology, Atlanta, GA 30332
Brady M 769 Artificial Intelligence Laboratory – MIT, 545 Technology Square, Cambridge, MA 02139
Corker K Jet Propulsion Laboratory (T 1201) 4800 Oak Grove Drive, Pasadena, CA 91109
Dubowsky S Department of Mechanical Engineering, Massachusetts Institute of Technology, Cambridge, MA 02139

Duffy J University of Florida, Center for Intelligent Machines and Robotics, Gainesville, FL 32611
Jacobsen S C Department of Mechanical Engineering, University of Utah, Salt Lake City, UT 84112
Kane T Division of Applied Mechanics, Stanford University, Stanford, CA 94305
Khatib O Robotics, Cedal Hall, Stanford University, Stanford, CA 94305
Lipkin H Department of Mechanical Engineering, University of Florida, Gainesville, FL 32611
Paul R School of Electrical Engineering, Purdue University, West Lafayette, IN 47906
Raibert M Computer Science, Carnegie Mellon University, Pittsburgh, PA 15213
Roth B Department of Mechanical Engineering, Stanford University, Stanford, CA 94305
Salisbury K MIT-AI Laboratory NE43-832, 545 Technology Square, Cambridge, MA 02139
Shiller Z Department of Mechanical Engineering, Massachusetts Institute of Technology, 77 Massachusetts Avenue, Cambridge, MA 02139
Smith Ch S System Development Foundation, 181 Lytton Avenue, Suite 210, Palo Alto, CA
Waldron K Department of Mechanical Engineering, Ohio State University, Columbus, OH 43210

USSR

Frolov K Mechanical Engineering Research Institute, Griboedova Street 4, Moscow Centre 101000

Yugoslavia

Karan B 'Mihailo Pupin' Institute, Volgina 15, 11000 Beograd
Katic D Institute 'Mihailo Pupin', Volgina 15, Beograd
Kirčanski M Institute 'Mihailo Pupin', PO Box 15, 11000 Beograd
Kirčanski N Institute 'Mihailo Pupin', Volgina 15, 11000 Beograd
Lenarcic J Institute J Stepan, Jamova 29, 61000 Ljubljana
Stokić D Institute 'Mihailo Pupin', Volgina 15, Beograd
Vukobratović M Institute 'Mihailo Pupin', Volgina 15, Beograd

RAYMOND H. FOGLER LIBRARY
DATE DUE

BOOKS ARE SUBJECT TO
RECALL AFTER TWO WEEKS